The World of Ancient Israel

Sociological, Anthropological and Political Perspectives

Encapsulating as it does research that has been undertaken on the sociological, anthropological and political aspects of the history of ancient Israel, this important book is designed to follow in the tradition of works in the series sponsored by The Society for Old Testament Study which began with the publication of *The People and the Book* in 1925.

The World of Ancient Israel is especially concerned to explore in greater depth than in comparable studies the areas and degrees of overlap between approaches to the subject of Old Testament research adopted by scholars and students of theology and the social sciences. Increasing numbers of scholars have recognised the valuable insights that can be gained from a cross-disciplinary approach, and it is becoming clear that the nature of the early biblical traditions about the formation of the Israelite state must be examined in the light of comparative anthropology if useful historical conclusions are to be drawn from them.

While summarising the current state of study, this book at the same time poses major questions for scholars of ancient Israel's history.

The World of
Ancient Israel

Sociological, Anthropological and Political Perspectives

Essays by Members of the Society for Old Testament Study

edited by

R. E. CLEMENTS

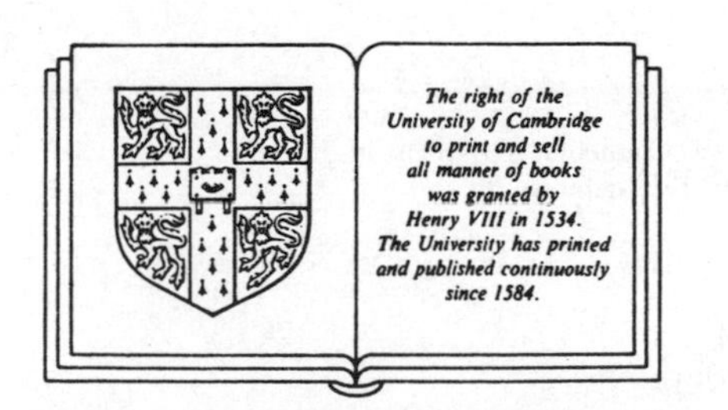

CAMBRIDGE UNIVERSITY PRESS

Cambridge

New York *Port Chester*

Melbourne *Sydney*

Published by the Press Syndicate of the University of Cambridge
The Pitt Building, Trumpington Street, Cambridge CB2 1RP
40 West 20th Street, New York, NY 10011–4211, USA
10 Stamford Road, Oakleigh, Melbourne 3166, Australia

First published 1989
Reprinted 1991
First paperback edition 1991

Printed in Great Britain at the University Press, Cambridge

British Library cataloguing in publication data

The World of Ancient Israel.
1. Biblio O.T. Special subjects: Israel. Social aspects
I. Clements, R.E. (Ronald Ernest), *1929–*
II. Society for Old Testament study
221.8′933

Library of Congress cataloguing in publication data

The world of ancient Israel: sociological, anthropological, and political perspectives : essays by members of the Society for Old Testament Study / edited by R.E. Clements.
p. cm.
Includes index.
ISBN 0 521 34243 0
1. Jews—Civilization—To 70 A.D. 2. Sociology, Biblical.
3. Bible. O.T.—Theology. I. Clements, R.E. (Ronald Ernest).
1929– . II. Society for Old Testament Study.
DS112.W66 1989
909′.04929—dc19 88-37707 CIP

ISBN 0 521 34243 0 hardback
ISBN 0 521 42392 2 paperback

VN

Contents

Preface

The present volume is designed to follow in the series sponsored by The Society for Old Testament Study which began in 1925 with the publication of *The People and the Book* (Clarendon Press) edited by A. S. Peake. Since then further volumes have appeared dealing with contemporary issues and researches in the field of the Old Testament (*Record and Revelation*, edited by H. Wheeler Robinson, 1938; *The Old Testament and Modern Study,* edited by H. H. Rowley, 1951; *Tradition and Interpretation*, edited by G. W. Anderson, 1979). Other volumes have been concerned with the historical background to the world from which the Old Testament emerged, notably the two volumes edited by D. Winton Thomas, *Documents from Old Testament Times* (1958) and *Archaeology and Old Testament Study* (1967). Alongside these books may be placed the collection of essays edited for the Society by D. J. Wiseman with the title *Peoples of Old Testament Times* (1973).

The present volume may appear to be rather different in scope and more varied in character than these predecessors, but it is hoped that it will fit worthily beside them and serve as a complement to them.

A primary reason for attempting to deal with the broader issues of a sociological, anthropological or political nature relating to the Old Testament is to be found in the increasing number of scholars who have recognised the valuable insights that are to be gained from doing so. So far as the early history of the period covered by the Old Testament is concerned, it is increasingly evident that the nature of the early biblical traditions concerning the formation of the Israelite state must be examined in the light of comparative anthropology if useful historical conclusions are to be drawn from them.

Beyond such specific questions, however, there is a growing band of scholars who have come to recognise many significant areas of overlap between the scientific study of an ancient people and their religion and broader issues concerning the role of religion in societies, both ancient and modern. It is greatly to be hoped that they will find in the essays contained here some encouraging signs of a sharing of that interest by members of the Society.

I am greatly indebted to all those members of the Society who have contributed to the present volume, and for their promptness and co-operation in acceding to my requests. A significant debt is also owed to the editorial advisers of the Cambridge University Press, initially Mr Robert Williams and latterly Mr Alex Wright, who have throughout been most positive and helpful in support of the volume now presented.

R. E. Clements

Contributors

DR. P. J. BUDD, *Lecturer, Westminster College, North Hinksey, Oxford.*

DR ROBERT P. CARROLL, *Reader in the Department of Biblical Studies and Head of Department, The University, Glasgow, Scotland.*

PROFESSOR R. E. CLEMENTS, *Samuel Davidson Professor of Old Testament Studies, King's College, London.*

THE REV. R. J. COGGINS, *Senior Lecturer, Department of Biblical Studies, King's College, London.*

PROFESSOR ROBERT DAVIDSON, *Professor of Hebrew and Old Testament, Department of Biblical Studies, The University, Glasgow, Scotland.*

DR E. W. DAVIES, *Lecturer, Department of Religious Studies, University College of North Wales, Bangor.*

DR PHILIP R. DAVIES, *Senior Lecturer, Department of Biblical Studies, The University of Sheffield, Sheffield.*

DR GRACE I. EMMERSON, *Lecturer, The Department of Theology, The University of Birmingham, Birmingham.*

PROFESSOR FRANK S. FRICK, *Albion College, Albion, Michigan, USA.*

PROFESSOR BERNARD S. JACKSON, *Professor of Law, Keynes College, The University of Kent, Canterbury.*

PROFESSOR GWILYM H. JONES, *Professor of Religious Studies, University College of North Wales, Bangor.*

PROFESSOR MICHAEL A. KNIBB, *Professor of Old Testament, King's College, London.*

DR J. D. MARTIN, *Senior Lecturer, Department of Biblical Criticism and Hebrew, St Mary's College, St Andrews, Scotland.*

PROFESSOR A. D. H. MAYES, *School of Hebrew, Biblical and Theological Studies, Trinity College, Dublin, Eire.*

PROFESSOR J. W. ROGERSON, *Professor of Biblical Studies, The University of Sheffield, Yorks.*

DR K. W. WHITELAM, *Department of Religious Studies, University of Stirling, Scotland.*

PROFESSOR R. N. WHYBRAY, *Professor Emeritus, Faculty of Theology, University of Hull, Humberside.*

DR H. G. M. WILLIAMSON, *Lecturer, Faculty of Oriental Studies, University of Cambridge.*

Abbreviations

AES	*Archives européennes de sociologie*
ANET	*Ancient Near Eastern Texts Relating to the Old Testament*, ed. J. B. Pritchard, 3rd Princeton, 1969
AOAT	*Altorientalische Texte zum Alten Testaments*, ed. H. Gressmann, 2nd ed Göttingen, 1926.
ASTI	*Annual of the Swedish Theological Institute*, Jerusalem.
ATANT	Abhandlungen zur Theologie des Alten und Neuen Testaments
ATD	Das Alte Testament Deutsch
BA	The Biblical Archaeologist
BAL	Berichte über die Verhandlungen der (Königlich) Sächsischen Akademie der Wissenschaften zu Leipzig.
BASOR	*Bulletin of the American Schools of Oriental Research*
BBB	Bonner Biblische Beiträge
BIES	*Bulletin of the Israel Exploration Society*
BJRL	*Bulletin of the John Rylands Library*
BKAT	Biblischer Kommentar. Alten Testament
BWANT	Beiträge zur Wissenschaft vom Alten und Neuen Testament
BZ	*Biblische Zeitschrift*
BZAW	Beihefte zur Zeitschrift für die Altesstamentliche Wissenschaft
CBOTS	Coniectanea Biblica. Old Testament Series
CBQ	*Catholic Biblical Quarterly*
DBS	*Dictionnaire de la Bible, Supplement*
ET	*Expository Times*
ETL	Ephemerides Theologicae Lovanienses
Ev Th	*Evangelische Theologie*
FRLANT	Forschungen zur Religion und Literatur des Alten und Neuen Testaments
HAT	*Handbuch zum Alten Testament*
HSM	Harvard Semitic Monographs
HTR	*Harvard Theological Review*
HUCA	*Hebrew Union College Annual*
ICC	International Critical Commentary
IDB	*The Interpreter's Dictionary of the Bible,* 4 vols.
IEJ	*Israel Exploration Journal*
JAAR	*Journal of the American Academy of Religion*
JBL	*Journal of Biblical Literature*

JJS	*Journal of Jewish Studies*
JNES	*Journal of Near Eastern Studies*
JQR	*Jewish Quarterly Review*
JSOT	*Journal for the Study of the Old Testament*
JSOTSS	Journal for the Study of the Old Testament. Supplement Series
JSS	*Journal of Semitic Studies*
JTS	*Journal of Theological Studies*
KAT	Kommentar zum Alten Testament
KHC	Kurzer Hand-Commentar zum Alten Testament
KuD	*Kergyma und Dogma*
NCB	New Century Bible
NICOT	New International Commentary on the Old Testament
NTS	New Testament Studies, Cambridge
OBO	Orbis Biblicus et Orientalis. Fribourg-Göttingen
OTL	Old Testament Library
OrAnt	*Oriens Antiquus*
OTS	Oudtestamentiesche Studien, Leiden
PEQ	*Palestine Exploration Quarterly*
RB	*Revue biblique*
RGG	*Die Religion in Geschichte und Gegenwart*, 3rd ed.
RIDA	*Revue Internationale des Droits de l'Antiquité*, Brussels
RVV	Religionsgeschichtliche Versuche und Vorarbeiten
SBLDS	Society of Biblical Literature. Dissertation Series
SBS	Stuttgarter Bibel-Studien
SBT	Studies in Biblical Theology
SJT	*Scottish Journal of Theology*
SNVAO	Skrifter uitgitt av det Norske Videnskaps-Akademi i Oslo
StTh	*Studia Theologica*
SThK	Studien für Theologie und Kirche
SVT	Supplements to Vetus Testamentum
ThB	Theologische Bücherei
ThLZ	*Theologische Literatur Zeitung*
TDOT	*Theological Dictionary of the Old Testament*
THAT	*Theologische Handwörterbuch zum Alten Testament*
TSK	Theologische Studien und Kritiken
ThWAT	*Theologische Wörterbuch Zum Alten Testament*
ThZ	*Theologische Zeitschrift*
UF	*Ugarit-Forschungen*
VT	*Vetus Testamentum*
WMANT	Wissenschaftliche Monographien zum Alten und Neuen Testament
ZAW	*Zeitschrift für die Alttestamentliche Wissenschafft*
ZDPV	*Zeitschrift des Deutschen Palästina-Vereins*
ZMR	*Zeitschrift für Misionskunde und Religionswissenschaft*
ZThK	*Zeitschrift für Theologie und Kirche*
ZwTh	*Zeitschrift für wissenschaftliche Theologie*

PART I

Introductory perspectives

CHAPTER ONE

Israel in its historical and cultural setting

RONALD E. CLEMENTS

The study of the Old Testament through a reconstruction of the history of the rise of the nation of ancient Israel, its growth to maturity under the monarchy, followed by the beginnings of the Jewish dispersion, has been a major goal of scholarship since the early part of the nineteenth century. So far as Great Britain was concerned its first significant expression was the publication in 1829 of H. H. Milman's *History of the Jews*, Vol. 1, followed in Germany by the more critical works of H. G. A. Ewald (3rd ed. 1864–7; Eng. Tr. 4th ed. in 8 vols. 1884) and J. Wellhausen (1878; Eng. Tr. 1885; cf. D. A. Knight: 1983). Very prominently the model chosen for such a scholarly task was that of the writing of a 'national' history, tracing the events and evaluating the personalities which led to the establishment of a national identity (cf. Clements: 1985, 122ff.: Iggers; 1968). This in turn called for an examination of the rise of those institutions of government which imposed and affirmed this national existence. The major problems which beset such an undertaking were recognised to be those of reaching an effective critical evaluation of the extant narrative source materials, followed in the twentieth century by the conjoining of this evaluation with the results of archaeological researches.

It has consequently been regarded as a prime requisite for serious critical study of the Hebrew Bible that careful literary evaluation of the texts should be supplemented by a knowledge of the results of archaeological researches in the territories of ancient Egypt, Syria and Mesopotamia.

The model of a national history of ancient Israel was largely based upon comparable efforts in a similar direction for the classical empires of Greece and Rome. It would, in retrospect, be hard to overestimate the extent to which researches into the history of ancient Israel were influenced by comparable researches into the history of ancient Greece and Rome during the nineteenth century. This, however, is simply to point out how extensively a particular kind of scholarly undertaking acquired methods, aims and credentials of a distinctive kind which became internationally regarded as standard (A. Momigliano: 1950). The requirements of *Altertumswissenschaft* – the science of the study of antiquity – took on a self-authenticating momentum, irrespective of the extent to which such a scientific task could be regarded as providing the best way of communicating a sense of the riches of these ancient civilisations to the modern world. Particularly was this so in regard to the writings of the Hebrew Bible where the wider interests of religious education have quite properly remained a major factor.

1. Social anthropology and biblical history

It is apposite to an awareness of the achievements and consequences of more than a century of serious scholarly engagement with the subject of the history of ancient Israel that a significant number of factors have aroused a call for extensive re-evaluation of the task (Whitelam: 1986). These factors have not all been of one kind, nor have they all pointed in the same direction. Certainly at the top of such a list we may place the contention that the attempts so far made at historical reconstruction have failed to implement with anything like the rigour that is necessary the proper demands of historical method (cf. especially van Seters: 1983). The extent to which the biblical narratives, which were constructed for other purposes than simply to provide a collection of historical data, can be used to yield up sufficient information for a rounded historical reconstruction to be achieved, remains strongly contested. However, even among writers who do not share such a degree of dissatisfaction with the reconstructions that have so far been made, other considerations remain very significant.

Prominent among these must be the awareness that the model of a 'national' history has never been very satisfactory so far as the treatment of ancient Israel is concerned. Israel constituted a single nation for only a very small part of the period covered by the Hebrew Bible, and, although a certain 'national ideal' is strongly evident in the Old Testament, nationhood did not provide the predominant form of the biblical community. Subsequent to the completion of the biblical canon, the religious communities of Church and Synagogue for which the Bible remained the centre of tradition, no longer regarded the national form of ancient Israel as anything other than one element to be taken account of in a very complex future hope.

Much recent work in the study of the biblical history has, accordingly, been devoted to an analysis and evaluation of the nature and significance of the Israelite community, reaching far beyond the period of its existence as a nation, or the sister nations of Israel and Judah (cf. especially P. D. Hanson: 1986; N. A. Dahl: 1941; 2nd ed. 1963).

It is, however, a matter of importance to biblical scholarship that, ever since the publication of the *Scienza nuova* of Giambattista Vico (3rd ed. 1744), the very study of history has embraced concerns of evaluation and social analysis which relate significantly to ideas of culture and social existence of particular relevance to the Bible (Berlin: 1976). Certainly this has been true of the study of ancient history, with all that this has offered by way of insight into the human condition. The study of anthropology and sociology as independent disciplines has, accordingly, continued to exercise a repeated, if often fitful, influence upon biblical scholarship (Rogerson: 1978). As an increasing volume of material has come to light relating to the rise and development of law and legal administration, the organisation and administration of city life, the power and authority of kingship, so the importance of these institutions to ancient Israel has increasingly been recognised. From a situation in which it appeared, prior to the late eighteenth century, that their emergence within Israel was without precedent, it is now abundantly clear that their growth was part of a very prolonged process which began far earlier in the ancient Near East. The use of the comparative method for understanding, and gaining fuller insight, into the way in which these developments took place in ancient Israel must now be regarded as wholly justified.

There is yet a further reason why an attempt to bring together a range of studies dealing with the anthropological, sociological and political aspects of Israel's life should be attempted at the present time. A quite central feature of the biblical history concerns a body of traditions relating to the origins of Israel as a nation. Such a tradition of origins provides the historical core of the entire Pentateuch and reaches beyond this to embrace also the books of Joshua and Judges. Significantly, it was the desire to gain a clearer grasp of the meaning and value of this historical core which constituted the most novel and controversial of all the achievements of Old Testament scholarship during the nineteenth century. The source analysis of the so-called Hexateuch (Genesis–Joshua) became a key foundation for a radically fresh reconstruction of the biblical history, hitherto scarcely anticipated by scholars (R. J. Thompson: 1970).

When this came to be augmented by the results of researches in the field of Egyptology (cf. H. Hengel: 1979), and subsequently by conclusions drawn from the archaeological investigations of many biblical sites, it appeared that a relatively secure picture could be reconstructed showing how Israel became a nation (cf. H. H. Rowley: 1950). Already in 1930, however, A. Alt (Alt: 1966[=1930]) had drawn into the discussion of such a historical reconstruction, questions about the comparative model to be applied for understanding how the Israelite state came to be formed. Since then, and with an increasing momentum, this has become the central issue concerning the study of the entire period of Israel's origins (cf. Lemche: 1985; Herrmann: 1988). The entire contents of the first five books of the Bible (The Pentateuch) constitute a kind of 'charter', or 'constitution', for Israel as the 'people' of God. What social and political form this people should assume as a historical entity is not consistently defined, since national, cultic and ethnic factors are all included in varying degrees. Moreover a miscellany of historical, and quasi-historical, traditions are incorporated into these writings as a major part of the concern to present a picture of Israel's identity and destiny. To attempt to single out only the more reliably historical elements of this extensive compendium of tradition must be regarded as a very partial approach to its interpretation.

It has become increasingly clear, the wider the field of researches into the origins of Israel, that its experience of nationhood was closely paralleled by that of other neighbouring nations (Buccellati: 1967). Israel was not alone in undergoing the transition from being a cluster of tribes, in which kinship was a primary bond of unity, to becoming a nation. In making this transition two features were of paramount importance. First among these was that of territory, so that the definition of the extent of Israel's land-holding and the claim to entitlement to it, were of central importance. Quite clearly the concern to provide this, both explains the primary purpose of the historical traditions preserved in the books of Joshua–Judges and also the religious theme of divine promise which pervades the Pentateuch (cf. Westermann: 1980[1976]). The second of these features was that of central government which, for ancient Israel, inevitably meant the institution of kingship. So far as most of the peoples and communities which constituted Israel's neighbours were concerned, the kingship embodied the principle and identity of the nation. It could be claimed that the person of the king was the indispensable link between the divine and human worlds which gave to the nation a form of eternal validity. It is no surprise therefore to discover that the books of 1 & 2 Samuel, which overtly present the story of Israel's first two kings, are wholly dominated by a complex interweaving of reflections upon this major institution.

These considerations alone, that concern for establishing Israel's entitlement to the land it came to occupy and to justify the introduction of monarchy thereby creating a national community, have been primary factors in shaping a major element of the biblical tradition, explain the need for examining them more closely. Moreover, as the Hebrew Bible is itself very conscious of the extent to which Israel's experiment in nationhood was closely matched by that of surrounding peoples (as witness the 'foreign nation' oracles of the prophets), so the value of comparative data provided by other communities is given added relevance. How do tribes become nations? No very uniform and complete picture can be provided, although it is evident that a great deal of valuable light can be shed upon so complex a process by an examination of comparative data from areas other than that of the ancient Near East (Claessen & Skalnik: 1978).

In summing up the relevance of sociological and anthropological studies to the concern with the historical aspects of the Old Testament, it may be claimed that they have increasingly demonstrated their ability to shed a remarkable amount of light upon the way in which the biblical tradition has taken shape.

2. Social context and theological meaning

It is a matter of historical importance that those developments of the Enlightenment which gave rise to a greatly intensified and critical concern with religious history also engendered a significant shift in the role played by the Bible in theology. The outcome of this was a desire to maintain a clear distinction between biblical and dogmatic theology (Kraus: 1970; Hornig: 1961). From the perspective of scientific biblical study, it becomes very evident in retrospect that the concern to define the scope and method of biblical theology, and more particularly of an Old Testament theology Kraus: 1982, 209ff.), has found itself consistently beset by problems and difficulties which lack firm resolution. The very insights and aims of historical research have necessarily lent themselves more favourably to the task of reconstructing the context in which the Old Testament originated than they have to evaluating its theological and ethical ideas. A review of some of the salient issues may serve to show how a deepened sense of scholarly engagement with features pertaining to the social and political aspects of the biblical literature may contribute towards a better grasp of its theological richness.

In the forefront of such issues we may place the fact that the Old Testament sets the concept of Israel as a community in the very centre of its claim to speak meaningfully about divine truths. To understand the Old Testament literature as offering a witness to the existence and purpose of God one must take fully into account that it understands and defines the being of God in terms of actions towards, and on behalf of, Israel as a people. It is this recognition that led W. Eichrodt to utilise the concept of a covenant between God and Israel as a structural point of unity for interpreting the theological meaning of the Old Testament in a systematic fashion (Eichrodt: 1961/1967).

This proceeding has proved a starting point for a far-reaching debate, both about the extent to which the idea of 'covenant' pervades the biblical literature and about its suitability for use as a co-ordinating principle. The range and significance of the former contention is examined below very fully by R. Davidson (cf. also Nicholson: 1986). On the latter issue, however, it is noteworthy that an equally wide-ranging discussion has ensued in the wake of Eichrodt's work. This in itself is a matter of importance if the critical study of the Old Testament is to remain a substantive part of any theological and educational concern with its contents.

Valuable and stimulating as Eichrodt's claim has proved to be, it becomes apparent that it represents an unduly narrow and idealistic presentation of a prominent characteristic of the biblical writings. Consistently throughout the Hebrew Bible there is a consciousness, often very central and profound and sometimes more peripheral, that divine activity is understood in relation to the life of the people Israel. How Israel is understood, as tribal community, nation-state, or a rather amorphous diffusion of scattered religious communities, varies in different areas of this literature, as it varied at different periods of history. Some recent approaches to the study of the Old Testament (notably Mendenhall: 1973; Gottwald: 1979) have attempted to use one model, or phase, of this biblical presentation of a human social order to demonstrate how the divine purpose is manifested. It is highly questionable whether one historical mode of Israel's socio-political existence can be used as the norm for demonstrating a divine 'order', any more than the one term 'covenant' could enshrine its ideological content. Such diverse writings as those by Eichrodt and Gottwald serve to show, however, that such broad abstractions as 'covenant' and 'nation' require to be given much fuller elaboration and content in the light of the contemporary political setting in which they arose, if they are to prove theologically meaningful.

It is certainly clear that the literature of the Hebrew Bible has expressed its major theological ideas in relation to a variety of concepts and models of human communities. What a socio-political approach to this literature may hope to contribute is a fuller awareness of the forces which served to give shape to the biblical community, and to shed light on the cultural context in which it emerged and developed.

There is a further aspect of this attempt to see the literature of the Old Testament in relation to its social and anthropological context which cannot be ignored, but which ultimately raises issues far beyond the range of the present essays. It is, however, a feature that all attempts to interpret this literature theologically must be aware of. So far as all these writings are concerned the idea of God, and at times of a number of different gods, remains an indispensable presupposition. Ideas of creation, natural order, social order, of time and the spatial realm, are all established in relation to such a belief in God. The notion of a 'secular' society in anything like the way in which such a term can be understood in the modern world, simply did not arise. This may be held as true, even though some modern scholars have felt able to detect traces of a 'secularising' tendency in the Old Testament through a process of rationalising and the deconsecrating of the sacred realm. Thereby the ultimate world-view of the Old Testament is seen to mark a significant step in theological advancement. Nevertheless ancient Israel's cosmology was fundamentally religious in its character so that the most fundamental institutes of society – kingship, law, cultus and education – were all founded upon religious assumptions. To this extent the 'religious' quality of Old Testament ideas and affirmations are frequently very unlike modern religious ideas, which necessarily relate to a much sharper differentiation between the sacred and the secular. In consequence of this, particular interest attaches to ancient Israel's ideas of the holy and the profane, and not least to ideas of life and death itself, where two distinct realms in conflict with each other could be envisaged. Among Israel's neighbours, and certainly at one time within the Israelite community itself, the tensions between life and death could be viewed as consequences and counterparts on earth to conflicts that repeatedly took place in the divine sphere.

All of this suggests strongly to the modern reader of the Old Testament that the consciousness of religion impinged upon the life and thought of the men and women of ancient Israel in a very different manner from what it does today. To attempt to convey to the modern reader the range of values that were summed up by the idea of God, as this was understood in ancient Israel, can only convincingly be undertaken by giving full attention to the social and human context in which such an idea was originally expressed.

There is a further reason why a deepened concern to uncover a better understanding of the social structures and environment in which the Old Testament emerged may be of particular interest to students of theology. Much of the special impact which this literature has enjoyed has arisen because of the distinctive ethical concern of many of its pronouncements. Old Testament law codes, most especially that of the Ten Commandments, but extending to a far wider range of its contents, have provided for many a primary body of legal formulations outlining fundamental principles of virtue and justice. In the Judaeo-Christian tradition this has consistently been a major aspect of the way in which a continuing relevance of the Old Testament has been felt. It is justified to go so far as to claim that it has been this expression of ideas of law and justice which has given to the Christian Church a basic reason for the continued retention and study of the Old Testament. Such a concept of an 'Old' Testament has thereby been distinguished in its religious authority from the 'New', a situation which has led to an ambiguity in the attachment of the Christian Church to this literature.

With the recovery in the late nineteenth century of other law codes from the ancient Near East, most especially the celebrated Code of Hammurabi, a far wider picture of the rise and development of law and systems of justice in the ancient world has come to light. Understandably, but not always helpfully, the initial reaction of biblical scholarship to this has been defensive, and has initially encouraged the setting of the Old Testament apart from this wider tradition. This has arisen in response to the desire to defend the claim of the biblical laws to offer a unique system of divinely revealed justice. It is recognisable, however, that the development of law in ancient Israel formed one part, and represented one branch, of a far wider movement in the ancient world (cf. Epsztein: 1986). This certainly needs to be taken fully into account in any serious study of what such concepts as justice and righteousness conveyed in their biblical contexts. Moreover, how law was perceived and how it was seen to operate, and not least the inevitable experience of its limitations and defects, were all part of a very intricate process of promoting a healthy and acceptable social order.

Closely related to this necessity for relating fundamental ethical concepts to the institutions which were empowered to uphold and defend them, is the strong moral legacy left by the prophets. At one time critical approaches to the Old Testament during the nineteenth century lent strong support to a picture of the prophets as ethical reformers and innovators. Yet only in more recent decades has sufficient attention been given to uncovering the economic, political and institutional framework in which the prophets worked, for a satisfactory picture of their ethical significance to be obtained. What was at one time taken as originality and innovation, can often be seen more adequately to mark reaction and reiteration of traditional ideas.

3. The Bible as literature

It is self-evident that the Bible is a collection of writings, and that among its contents are compositions of very diverse kinds. The desire to understand the literary character of these writings has led to a considerably varied series of scholarly approaches. In the first phase of critical re-evaluation during the nineteenth century the concern to identify, and where possible date, sources appeared to represent a paramount scholarly task. During the twentieth century the study of the shorter 'forms', or 'types', of composition which lay embedded in the longer writings has acquired far greater importance, most especially through the work of Hermann Gunkel (Klatt: 1969). Clearly the Old Testament was composed as the product of a very prolonged literary activity in which few wholly separate and self-contained independent works can be identified. The distinction between 'authors' and 'editors' has become increasingly blurred, and in some cases almost meaningless. The prophetic books for example, were clearly not written by prophets, but represent distilled collections of prophetic material, often from diverse ages. History writing, too, shows every sign of having been a complex work of composition, addition and reinterpretation which, in most cases, cannot now be traced back with anything more than a reasonable probability as to its main phases.

It is significant, however, that the Hebrew Bible, as a collection of books however loosely defined in their scope, marks a major phenomenon of the way in which literacy has changed human society. By late antiquity the very existence of the canonical writings of the Hebrew Bible was itself proving a not inconsiderable factor in stimulating and promoting the importance of literacy. Jews, and later Christians also, learned to read in order to study the sacred books. This aspect of the impact of the Hebrew Bible upon the spread of literacy cannot be overlooked and it is noteworthy that the world out of which its writings emerged was one in which orality and literacy were rapidly changing their respective places as major determinants of human social organisation. Just as writing changed profoundly the manner of human thought and social organisation, so also did it change with equal profundity the nature of religion. It is sufficient to point to only a few of the ways in which this is evident from the pages of the Old Testament. It may also be further pointed out that one of the major weaknesses of the earlier intense preoccupation with the so-called 'form criticism' of the biblical writings has been the over-attention that it has engendered to the stage of oral formation and composition. Once written, many oral forms quickly withered away or were subsumed and substantially modified in larger literary formulations. The manner in which this has affected the development and shaping of narrative has begun to receive more substantial attention (cf. Long: 1968; Sternberg: 1985), but it is clear that all the literary forms to be found in the Old Testament display such developmental changes to some degree. Recent studies of the forms of literature in such books as Genesis and Exodus (Coats: 1983; McKane: 1979; T. L. Thompson: 1987) show the vital importance of relating the short anecdotal tale, as well as in the larger collections of such tales, to the communities from which they originated. The role of narrative in a community becomes an inseparable part of the self-understanding of that community and interpretation of the narrative becomes interlocked in an awareness of its cultural and social values.

If this is true in respect of the formulation and preservation of narratives which display an overtly historical form, then equally can it be seen to be so in regard to the development of written codes and collections of laws. There can be few areas of social order in antiquity which underwent more far-reaching changes as a result of the shift from orality to literacy than that of law and legal administration. Of special interest to the student of the biblical literature therefore is the fact that its legal collections reveal most instructive and significant changes as written law took precedence over *ad hoc* legal judgements made by respected leaders. The trend towards greater rationalisation of legal principle, the desire for closer and more circumscribed definition of offences and their punishment, combined with a concern to bring about greater effectiveness in extending the rule of law, are all discernible in the Old Testament. The valuable study by M. Fishbane (Fishbane: 1985) of the underlying shifts and elaborations of law in the biblical collections points dramatically to the way in which written law brought fundamental changes in the concepts of justice and order to ancient Israel.

Just as literacy made a deep impact upon legal administration, so also can we recognise that it also brought great changes to the practice of prophecy and the pursuit of wisdom. Once again it may be argued that the original oral forms of utterance, both oracular and didactic, from which written preservation took place, were greatly changed once written collections came to be made. In few areas is this more marked than in the case of prophecy (cf. Clements: 1986; Carroll: 1979, 1981) where it provided an opportunity for forming chains of prophecies and for extending dramatically the time-scale over which the prophecy could be regarded as fulfilled. The composition of books of prophecies, a process still only very inadequately understood, was not simply a process of collection and preservation, but also one of reinterpretation and appropriation into the life of the community. The extent to which the work of writing down and editing a prophet's sayings represented a process of 'routinisation' and of accommodating and harmonising the insights of the prophet into the institutional structure of Israelite society still awaits fuller exploration. The belief in the existence of prophetic 'schools', a view which the present writer has consistently opposed, has masked the extent to which the written form of prophecy can be seen frequently to have altered, and at times markedly transformed, the import of the prophet's original words, even at times reversing their warnings or assurances!

In this regard, even where the present writer has diverged considerably from the views of others over the formation of such extensive literary compositions as the books of Isaiah (cf. Clements: 1982; C. R. Seitz: 1988) and Jeremiah (Clements: 1988), it is striking that a significant consensus is beginning to emerge. The complexity of the transition from orality to literacy is everywhere evident in the prophetic writings of the Old Testament, and it is vitally important to reflect that such a collection of written prophecy is a unique legacy from the ancient world. Even among other peoples where prophets and oracular utterance were everyday features of the religious life, literary examples of their sayings have only haphazardly been preserved. Yet in fact it is clear that in Israel written preservation made possible the harmonising of apparently divergent prophecies with each other, and led to the use of such prophecies to authorise major changes in cult and political administration. Major shifts in cultic practice, particularly over the offering of sacrifices, came to be authorised by the word of prophecy preserved in writing.

It may similarly be urged that the pursuit of wisdom was also subjected to significant shifts and developments as a result of making the transition from oral to written preservation. Undoubtedly the original oral aspects of wisdom teaching in short injunctions and admonitions are clearly apparent in the book of Proverbs. Yet wisdom encouraged the composition of written lists and its literary development made possible the production of elaborate artistic works by wisdom teachers, among them the books of Job and Ecclesiasticus. These reveal all the consequences of the impact of literacy upon processes of thought and the use of language. The very understanding of what constitutes wisdom, leading to the notion that the wise man must also be a 'scribe', underwent a profound change because writing had provided a new tool by which the pursuit of wisdom through comparison and reflection could be effected. In the study of biblical wisdom too, therefore, it may be urged that the use of comparative data drawn from a wide field of human experience relating to the spread of literacy can be of great help in clarifying the presuppositions and social significance of the biblical text.

Bibliography

Alt, A., 1966 [1930]. 'The Formation of the Israelite State in Palestine', *Essays on Old Testament History and Religion*, Eng Tr. R. A. Wilson, Oxford: B. H. Blackwell, 171–237. =*Die Staatenbildung der Israeliten in Palästina*, Reformationsprogramm der Universität Leipzig, 1930.

Berlin, I., 1976. *Vico and Herder. Two Studies in the History of Ideas*. London: Chatto & Windus.

Buccellati, G., 1967. *Cities and Nations of Ancient Syria*, Rome: Istituto di Studi del Vicino Oriente.

Carroll, R. P., 1979. *When Prophecy Failed*, London: SCM Press.

1981. *From Chaos to Covenant. Uses of Prophecy in the Book of Jeremiah*, London: SCM Press.

Claessen, H. J. M. and Skalnik, P. (eds.), 1978. *The Early State*, Studies in the Social Sciences 32, The Hague: Mouton Publishers.

Clements, R. E., 1982. 'The Unity of the Book of Isaiah', *Interpretation*, 1982, 117–29.

1985. 'The Study of the Old Testament', *Nineteenth Century Religious Thought in the West*, Vol. 3, eds. N. Smart, J. Clayton, P. Sherry and S. Katz, Cambridge: CUP, 109–41.

Clements, R. E., 1986. 'Prophecy as Literature. A Re-appraisal', *The Hermeneutical Quest. Essays in Honor of J. L. Mays*, Princeton Theological Monographs 4, Allison Park, PA, 59–76.

Clements, R. E., 1988. *Jeremiah*. Interpretation. A Bible Commentary for Teaching and Preaching, Atlanta: John Knox Press.

Coats, G. W., 1983. *Genesis, with an Introduction to Narrative Literature*, The Forms of OT Literature 1, Grand Rapids: Wm. B. Eerdmans.

Coote, R. B. and Whitelam, K. W., 1987. *The Emergence of Israel in Historical Perspective*, Sheffield: Almond Press.

Dahl, N. A., 1941 [1963]. *Das Volk Gottes. Eine Untersuchung zum Kirchenbewusstsein des Urchristentums*, Oslo: Det Norske Videnskaps-Akademi; 2nd ed. Darmstad: Wissenschaftliche Buchgesellschaft, 1963.

Eichrodt, W., 1961. *Theology of the Old Testament*, Vols. 1 & 2, Eng tr. J. A. Baker, London: SCM Press, 1961, 1967. =*Theologie des Alten Testaments*, Stuttgart: E. Klotz, 1959/1964.

Epsztein, L., 1986 [1983]. *Social Justice in the Ancient Near East and the People of the Bible*, Eng. Tr. J. Bowden, London: SCM Press. =*La Justice sociale dans le Proche-Orient ancien et le Peuple de la Bible*, Paris: Editions du Cerf, 1983.

Fishbane, M., 1985. *Biblical Interpretation in Ancient Israel*, Oxford: Clarendon Press.

Goody, J., 1977. *The Domestication of the Savage Mind*, Cambridge: CUP.

Gottwald, N. K., 1979. *The Tribes of Yahweh: A Sociology of the Religion of Liberated Israel 1250–1050 BCE*, London: SCM Press.

Hanson, P. D., 1986. *The People Called. The Growth of Community in the Bible*, New York & San Francisco: Harper & Row.

Hengel, H., 1979. *Die Vorfahren Israels in Agypten. Forschunggeschichtlicher Überblick uber die Darstellungen seit Richard Lepsius* (1849), Frankfurter Theologische Studien 27, Frankfurt am Main: Josef Knecht.

Herion, G., 1986. 'The Impact of Modern and Social Science Assumptions on the Reconstruction of Israelite History', *JSOT* 34, 1986, 3–33.

Herrmann, S., 1988. 'Studien zur Ethnogenese', Bd. 2, *Rheinisch-Westfälische Akademie der Wissenschaften*, Abh. 78, Westdeutscher Verlag.

Hornig, G., 1961. *Die Anfänge der historisch-kritischen Theologie. Johann Salomo Semler Schriftverständnis und seine Stellung zu Luther*, Forschungen zur systematischen Theologie und Religionsphilosophie Bd. 8, Lund–Göttingen: CWK Gleerup.

Iggers, G. G., 1968. *The German Conception of History: The National Tradition of Historical Thought from Herder to the Present*, Middleton, Ct.: Wesleyan Univ. Press.

Klatt, W., 1969. *Hermann Gunkel. Zu seiner Theologie der Religionsgeschichte und zur Entstehung der formgeschichtlichen Methode*, FRLANT 100, Göttingen: Vandenhoeck & Rupprecht.

Knight, D. A. (ed.), 1983. *Julius Wellhausen and His Prolegomena to the History of Israel*, Semeia 25.

Kraus, H.-J., 1970. *Die Biblische-Theologie. Ihre Geschichte und Problematik*, Neukirchen-Vluyn: Neukirchener Verlag.

1982. *Geschichte der historisch-kritischen Erforschung des Alten Testaments*, 3rd ed., Neukirchen-Vluyn: Neukirchener Verlag.

Lemche, N. P., 1985. *Early Israel. Anthropological and Historical Studies on the Israelite Society Before the Monarchy*, SVT. 37.

Long, B. O., 1968. *The Problem of Etiological Narrative in the Old Testament*, BZAW 108, Berlin: Alfred Töpelmann.

McKane, W., 1979. *Studies in the Patriarchal Narratives*, Edinburgh: The Handsel Press.

Mendenhall, G. E., 1973. *The Tenth Generation. The Origins of the Biblical Tradition*, Baltimore: Johns Hopkins U.P.

Mendenhall, G. E., 1976. 'Social Organization in Early Israel', *Magnalia Dei. The Mighty Acts of God*, eds. F. M. Cross, W. E. Lemke and P. D. Miller, Garden City NY: Doubleday, 132–51.

Momigliano, A., 1950. 'Ancient History and the Antiquarian', *Journal of the Warburg and Courtauld Institutes*, 13, 1950, 285–315.

1977. *Essays in Ancient and Modern Historiography*, Oxford: B. H. Blackwell.

Nicholson, E. W., 1986. *God and His People. Covenant and Theology in the Old Testament*, Oxford: Clarendon Press.

Ong, W. J., 1982. *Orality and Literacy. The Technologizing of the Word*, London & New York: Methuen.

Reventlow, H. Graf, 1985 [1982]. *Problems of Old Testament Theology in the Twentieth Century*, Eng. Tr. J. Bowden, London: SCM Press. =*Hauptproblems der alttestamentlichen Theologie im 20 Jahrhundert*, Erträge der Forschung 173, Darmstadt: Wissenschaftliche Buchgesellschaft, 1982.

1986 [1983]. *Problems of Biblical Theology in the Twentieth Century*, Eng. Tr. J. Bowden, London: SCM Press. =*Hauptprobleme der Biblischen Theologie im 20. Jahrhundert*, Erträge der Forschung 203, Darmstadt: Wissenschaftliche Buchgesellschaft, 1983.

Rogerson, J., 1978. *Anthropology and the Old Testament*, Oxford: B. H. Blackwell.

1984. *Old Testament Criticism in the Nineteenth Century. England and Germany*, London: SPCK.

Rowley, H. H., 1950. *From Joseph to Joshua. Biblical Traditions in the Light of Archaeology*, Schweich Lectures 1948, London: Oxford U.P.

Seitz, C. R., 1988. 'Isaiah 1–66. Making Sense of the Whole', *Reading and Preaching the Book of Isaiah*, ed. C. R. Seitz, Philadelphia: Fortress Press, 105–26.

Seitz, C. R. (ed.), 1988. *Reading and Preaching the Book of Isaiah*, Philadelphia: Fortress Press.

Sternberg, M., 1985. *The Poetics of Biblical Narrative. Ideological Literature and the Drama of Reading*, Bloomington: Indiana University Press.

Thompson, R. J., 1970. *Moses and the Law in a Century of Criticism since Graf*, VTSupp 19, Leiden: E. J. Brill.

Thompson, T. L., 1987. *The Origin Tradition of Ancient Israel, 1. The Literary Formation of Genesis and Exodus 1–23* (JSOTSS 55, Sheffield).

Van Seters, J., 1983. *In Search of History: Historiography in the Ancient World and the Origins of Biblical History*, New Haven: Yale U.P.

Vico, G., 1968 [1744]. *The New Science of Giambattista Vico*. Eng. Tr. T. G. Bergin and M. H. Fisch, Ithaca and London: Cornell UP rev. ed.

Westermann, C., 1980 [1976]. *The Promises to the Fathers. Studies in the Patriarchal Narratives*, Eng. Tr. D. E. Green, Philadelphia: Fortress Press. =*Die Verheissungen an die Väter*, Göttingen: Vandenhoeck & Rupprecht, 1976.

Whitelam, K. W., 1986. 'Recreating the History of Israel', *JSOT* 35, 45–70.

CHAPTER TWO

Anthropology and The Old Testament

JOHN W. ROGERSON

Twenty years ago Old Testament scholars were broadly in agreement on a number of topics that overlapped with anthropology. The Israelites, prior to the establishment of the monarchy, were semi-nomads, who had either forcefully or peacefully entered Canaan, and had become sedentary (Weippert: 1967). At this early period of their history, and indeed for some centuries thereafter, they experienced the world in a way different from that of western industrialised socicties. Pioneering work by scholars such as H. Wheeler Robinson, S. H. Hooke, Sigmund Mowinckel and Johannes Pedersen, work based upon anthropological studies, suggested that the Israelites had a somewhat mystical, if not semi-magical, relationship to the world around them (Robinson: 1936, Hooke: 1933, Mowinckel: 1922, Pedersen: 1963–4).

In Israelite social organisation the group was more important than the individual, with the result that a group could be held responsible and punished for a misdeed of one of its members, as when Achan's family was put to death because Achan had kept for himself some spoil from Jericho (Joshua 7:24–6, Robinson: 1906, 266). But this seemingly crude method of carrying out justice was itself only an example of the fundamentally different way in which Israelites classified and encountered the world around them.

Magical practices, for example, although forbidden in the Old Testament, were widely engaged in; and this meant, according to J. G. Frazer's influential account of magic, that Israelites believed in the powers of imitation and contact (Frazer: 1957, Rogerson: 1978). If something that was desired could be imitated, then it could be influenced. Thus the fertility of the land could be influenced by a type of sacred prostitution whose intention was to imitate, at the human level, the fecundity of the land. Belief in the power of contact meant that if something such as hair or nail clippings that had once been part of a person or object, continued to be a part of that person or object after separation, then harm done to what was separated would cause harm to the person or object of which it had been part. However, the dividing line between magic and religion was not clear cut. In their worship, the Israelites enacted sacred dramas, in which the king played a central role, possibly undergoing symbolic humiliation and enthronement, in order to ensure God's blessing upon the nation during the coming year (Hooke: 1933, Mowinckel: 1922). Further, Israelites believed in the power of words, and especially that blessings and curses, once uttered, set in motion a train of events that could not be reversed.

Israelites also did not recognise the limits of their personality in the way that we do today, but believed that the personality of an individual could become completely merged with that of a group, as when the language of a Psalm oscillates between 'I' and 'We' (Psalm 44.4–7). A personality could also extend into another person, so that no difference was perceived by a prophet between himself and God, or by a messenger between himself and the king who sent him (Johnson: 1961). Finally, the Israelite lived in a world which knew no difference between the ordinary and the miraculous. Any object or event was potentially alive with mysterious forces, and could become the occasion for a manifestation of divine power (Rogerson: 1977).

A consensus, even an incomplete one such as is outlined here, invites, of course, contradiction; and it would not be difficult to cite positions opposed to the consensus view. As long ago as 1947 for example, Walther Eichrodt stressed the importance of individual responsibility in Israel's early lawcodes, a point that has to be placed alongside the corporate idea of responsibility apparently implied in Joshua 7:24–6 (Eichrodt: 1947). Further, it was popular twenty years ago to argue that the Canaanites among whom the Israelites lived were indeed governed by magical thought processes, but that Israel had distanced itself from these. Whereas Canaanite religion was closely tied to the cycles of the agricultural year, and thus remained indebted to magical practices, Israelite religion was based upon history and upon ethical monotheism. Prosperity depended upon loyalty to God who had revealed himself in the events of Israel's history, and there was no place for magical thought (Fohrer: 1969).

In spite of these, and other exceptions, that could be cited, I believe that what I have outlined as a consensus view is basically fair; and I have outlined it at some length in order to be able to indicate how much things have changed in a comparatively short period. The greatest amount of activity has been concentrated on the view that the premonarchic Israelites were semi-nomads who settled down following their entry into Canaan, and this view has been strongly challenged if not totally disproved. The idea that the Israelites lived in a sort of mystical world where everything was in contact with everything else, and where the limits of personality were blurred, has also been strongly challenged. Further, new items of interest have emerged, especially the study of prophecy from an anthropological standpoint. Twenty years ago anthropology no longer had the importance for Old Testament study that it had had in the days of Wheeler Robinson and Hooke. Today, the situation is quite different. While not being at or near the top of the agenda, anthropology is certainly not at or near the bottom of the agenda of concerns in Old Testament study.

The change has come from various directions, a factor that will need to be considered later. In Britain, the impulse came from anthropologists themselves. As long ago as 1961 E. R. Leach published a paper entitled 'Lévi-Strauss in the Garden of Eden' in which he applied to Genesis 2–3 the structural interpretation of myths then being pioneered by the French anthropologist Claude Lévi-Strauss (Leach: 1961, Rogerson: 1970). However, it was not until 1966, when Leach published a major paper 'The Legitimacy of Solomon', that British Old Testament scholars began to realise that the world of anthropology had changed considerably since the days when what I have outlined above as the consensus was established (Leach: 1966, Rogerson: 1970). Had Leach remained the only British anthropologist writing about the Old Testament, however, the matter might well have been soon forgotten. Leach took an extremely sceptical view of the historical value of the Old Testament, and he later summed up his view of the contribution of anthropology to Old Testament study in the following words:

> I hold that anthropologists first need to make a case for saying that no part of the Bible is a record of history as it actually happened. Then, on the positive side, they can show that the whole of the Bible has the characteristics of mytho-history of the sort that anthropologists regularly encounter when they engage in present-day field research. (Leach: 1980)

In fact, what Old Testament scholars have wanted, rightly or wrongly, from anthropology, is help with understanding aspects of Israel's history, not a demonstration that 'no part of the Bible is a record of history as it actually happened'. Consequently, it was a book by another anthropologist, Mary Douglas, also published in 1966, that caused some British Old Testament scholars not only to take notice of anthropology, but to realise that it had much to contribute to Old Testament study (Douglas: 1966). The chapter of Mary Douglas's *Purity and Danger* that has become most famous is that on the rationale for some creatures being designated as unclean in the Old Testament. But the whole book was an attack on the idea of 'primitive mentality'. By implication it undermined the idea of 'primitives' living in a sort of mystical communion with the world, an idea central to what I have called the consensus; and while not suggesting for a moment that there was no difference between 'primitives' and modern industrialised peoples, it indicated that such differences as there were could best be explained in terms of how peoples classified the objects of the natural world, and how their social organisation and beliefs combined with the classification of the natural world to form an integrated system. This will be more fully explained later.

In the United States the renewal of interest in anthropology came from Old Testament scholars, not anthropologists. It had always been a particular strength of American scholarship that it was involved in archaeology, and in discovering as much as possible about the ancient Near East, especially in the period preceding and up to the founding of the Israelite monarchy. The mention of warlike nomadic groups in the Mari texts, of *sasu* nomads and *sutu* nomads in Egyptian and Akkadian texts respectively, together with the perennial problem of the *habiru* of the Amarna letters, made it necessary for scholars to turn to anthropology to try to understand the precise nature of these groups. This led in turn to a re-examination of the ideas of nomadism, semi-nomadism and sedentarisation, ideas that were part of the consensus with which this essay began.

In an essay published in 1962, G. E. Mendenhall challenged on anthropological grounds the consensus view that the Israelites had been semi-nomads who sedentarised (Mendenhall: 1962). Among the points that he made was that semi-nomadism was not part of a natural process of social evolution whereby groups moved from nomadism, through semi-nomadism to settled life. In fact semi-nomadism developed out of settled agricultural life. Further, Mendenhall argued that settled farmers and nomadic groups usually lived together in harmony, and this fact put a question mark against the idea that the Israelite conquest was an incursion of warlike nomads into the land of Canaan. Mendenhall saw the primary opposition as that between farmers and cities, and, with the aid of archaeology, argued that Israel came into being when farmers withdrew their allegiance from the city-states in Canaan and founded an alternative society whose ideology was that of a group of former slaves who had been liberated by God from bondage in Egypt. However, Mendenhall's article does not seem to have aroused much interest until the publication, in 1973, of his book *The Tenth Generation*, in which his position was argued more fully (Mendenhall: 1973).

With anthropology having become an important part of the agenda in American Old Testament study, many studies began to be published. In 1977 Robert Wilson's *Genealogy and History in the Biblical World* took a preliminary look at biblical and ancient Near Eastern genealogy in the light of studies of African people (Wilson: 1977). He followed this up in 1980 with *Prophecy and Society in Ancient Israel* which addresses the question of the relation of prophets, or intermediaries as he called them, to their support groups and society as a whole (Wilson: 1980). In 1981 an entire issue of *Semeia* was devoted to 'Anthropological Perspectives on Old Testament Prophecy', of which two of the contributors, Overholt and Long had published papers in this field in 1974 and 1977 respectively (Overholt: 1974; Long: 1977). In a different area a group of scholars including Frank Frick and James Flanagan were working on the origins of the Israelite state, the result being works such as Frick's book *The City in Ancient Israel* and Flanagan's article 'Chiefs in Israel' (Frick: 1977; Flanagan: 1981).

Special mention must be reserved for the work of Norman Gottwald. He entered the field in 1974 with an essay 'Were the early Israelites Pastoral Nomads?', and then began to develop the thesis that was fully presented in his monumental *The Tribes of Yahweh. A Sociology of the Religion of Liberated Israel 1250–1050 B.C.E.* (Gottwald: 1979). This work not only contained the most thorough discussion of Israelite social organisation to have appeared by 1979, but it also raised a fundamental question of method. This will be considered later in greater detail, but in short, Gottwald espoused a position in anthropology known as cultural materialism, a view which regards religion as a product of economic and material factors. Although on the face of it Gottwald's account of Israel's origins in terms of a peasants' revolt against Canaanite city-states was almost identical to that of Mendenhall, there was a fundamental difference. Mendenhall believed that the revolt had been caused by a new religious ideology, that of the liberated slaves from Egypt. Gottwald believed that texts are the products of society, and that Israel's religious ideology was a *result* of the formation of an egalitarian and liberated society and not its cause.

On the continent of Europe interest had also been centred upon the contribution of anthropology to Israel's origins. C. H. J. de Geus's *The Tribes of Israel* contains thorough attempts to discover the nature of Israel's social organisation (de Geus: 1976), while Niels Peter Lemche's *Early Israel. Anthropological and Historical Studies on the Israelite Society before the Monarchy* is probably the most comprehensive discussion of the contribution of anthropology to understanding Israel's origins to have appeared in any language (Lemche: 1985). Mention should also be made, however, of Bernhard Lang's work on prophecy and on the economic background to the prophecies of Amos (Lang: 1980, 1983, 1985) and of Frank Crüsemann's *Der Widerstand gegen das Königtum*, that explains opposition to monarchy in terms of the continuing existence, in Israel, of a type of social organisation that was based upon the ideology of the diffusion rather than the concentration of power (Crüsemann: 1978).

This has necessarily been a long introduction to the subject of this essay. In what follows, there will be four sections dealing respectively with Israelite self-awareness, the social dimension of Israelite prophecy, Israel's origins and social structure, and emics verses etics in anthropological study of the Old Testament.

1. Israelite self-awareness

According to the consensus view outlined above, Israelites were similar to 'primitives' in the way they understood the world and themselves. Being pre-scientific, they knew little about what actually causes events; thus they could readily ascribe to supernatural powers happenings that we today know to have natural causes. They had no words in their language for 'miracle' or 'supernatural' and thus had no conceptions of these ideas. They did not recognise individuality as we do.

These ideas were based upon studies of primitives carried out in the nineteenth and early twentieth centuries, before the rise of the structural-functionalist school of anthropology in Britain. The earlier studies were often based upon random observations by untrained observers, who imposed their own categories of understanding upon what they saw. In particular, this earlier type of anthropology was concerned with the mental processes of the primitives. 'What can it be like to live in a society which believes in the power of magic?' was a typical question, and the answer was given in terms of modern Western scientific understanding: life in such a society must be an irrational chaos in which anything and everything is potentially possible (Rogerson: 1977).

With the advent of studies of 'primitives' based upon careful and prolonged fieldwork among them, it was apparent that their lives were by no means irrational and chaotic, and that the portrait of them living in a mystical sort of world full of potential for divine revelation was a caricature. Between 1926 and 1930 the British anthropologist E. E. Evans-Pritchard lived for some 20 months with the Azande, a people of the southern Sudan. His classic monograph, *Witchcraft, Oracles and Magic among the Azande* investigated Zande magic not from an intellectualist point of view, that is to say, not with the question in mind, 'how does the understanding of the world by the Azande compare with that of modern science?', but by seeing how Zande magic functioned in the life of the people (Evans-Pritchard: 1937). He discovered that witchcraft, oracles and magic were important social mechanisms that enabled the Azande to cope with uncertainty and with distressing practical issues such as illness and death. In many areas of their lives, however, the Azande were not all that different from modern westerners; and if they had been radically different, it would not have been possible for a Western observer to learn their language and live among them. Two points may be briefly noted. First, when using the poison oracle that involved giving a small dose of poison to a chicken, and then seeing whether or not it lived, the results of the first test would usually be checked. Thus, if, in the first test, the death of the chicken would indicate a particular answer, and the chicken in fact died, the process would then be repeated, with the survival of the chicken required to confirm the answer that the first test had seemed to give. This is certainly not evidence for chaotic or irrational thought. A second point concerns the distinction between the natural and the supernatural. Evans-Pritchard pointed out that although there were no Zande words for these concepts, the Azande were certainly aware of the distinctions (Evans-Pritchard: 1937, 80–1).

Studies such as those by Evans-Pritchard were behind Mary Douglas's attempt to account for the Old Testament prohibitions of certain creatures in terms of their place in a comprehensive system of classification and social organisation. Her solution was to see the prohibitions in the light of Genesis 1, where the world is classified into the three areas of heavens, earth and waters, each with its appropriate inhabitants (Douglas: 1968, pp. 41–57). According to Douglas, inhabitants of the heavens should have wings and two legs, inhabitants of the earth should either have two legs and walk upright or four legs and go on all fours, while inhabitants of the waters should have fins. Creatures that violate these classifications, for example, creatures with four legs that fly, or creatures with no legs that slither along the ground, are anomalous, and therefore prohibited.

Of course, it is not as simple as this in fact in the Old Testament. There is a distinction between four-legged animals that both chew the cud and divide the hoof, and those that lack one of these characteristics. Only the former are 'clean'. However, whatever the criticism of Douglas's explanation of the reason for the prohibition of certain creatures (Carroll: 1978), she drew attention to the possibility of trying to reconstruct the complex system of symbols that constituted the Israelite understanding of the world.

An important contribution in this area is Douglas Davies's interpretation of Old Testament sacrifice, itself a response to Mary Douglas's work (Davies: 1977). Starting from the view that Mary Douglas had explained the prohibitions of animals in terms of an intelligible set of rules that could also be linked to Israel's general understanding of the world, Davies sought to do the same for Israelite sacrifice. He argued that offences were not only wrongdoing in the sight of God, but they had social consequences, and that it was necessary for these to be dealt with if society was to be an ordered and harmonious whole. However, the efficacy of sacrifices could not be understood, as by earlier Old Testament scholarship, in purely psychological terms, with the implied question 'how did Israelites think that sacrifices worked?' Further, sacrifices were to be seen as part of a code which, when read off, indicated something of the network of symbols that constituted the Israelite understanding of the world.

In Leviticus 14 the ritual for the rehabilitation of a healed 'leper' is recorded. After a ceremony involving two birds, one of which is released and the other is killed, the leper has to wash his clothes, shave all his hair, bathe, and then spend seven days in the camp but outside his own tent. On the seventh day he must again shave off all his hair, wash his clothes and bathe. On the eighth day his full restoration to the community is marked by a series of sacrifices. This ritual of rehabilitation resembles the ritual for consecrating priests, described in Leviticus 8 and 9. Here, the candidates spend seven days outside the Tent of Meeting before being consecrated on the eighth day.

It is clear that a sort of rite of passage is taking place on both occasions, and the seven-day limbo helps to mark the transition – in the case of the leper from outside the community to within it, and in the case of priests from within the community to within the sphere of the holy.

Douglas Davies points out that in the ritual of the day of Atonement in Leviticus 16 space and symbolism are again part of the code of the ceremony. The high priest must bathe before he robes. As in the case of the leper's restoration where two birds are used, of which one is released, so here there are two goats, one of which is sacrificed, the other of which is released in the wilderness. After the priest has made a sacrifice on his own behalf, he cleanses every part of the sanctuary by sprinkling blood, thus cleansing the sanctuary of all the impurities and wrongdoings of the Israelites. Then, laying his hands on the head of the scapegoat, he confesses over it all the sins of the Israelites, after which it is taken away from the community into the wilderness, that is, a place outside the realm of ordered social reality.

These examples will serve to indicate that, whatever else they may have been, sacrificial rituals were a social mechanism which enabled society to make adjustments, such as in the rehabilitation of a leper, and to cope with the corporate effects of wrongdoing, as in the day of Atonement ritual. Above all, these examples indicate not the presence of chaos but of order. Indeed, one of the main purposes of these sets of rules is to exclude chaos in the first place by classifying as far as possible the world into ordered spheres, and then to deal with anomalies as they arise. There may have been good medical grounds for excluding 'lepers' from Israelite society; but they were excluded because their ailment made them anomalous, and their restoration involved a complex social code. Anomalous animals were identified, and were dealt with by being prohibited for food and sacrifice. Above all, the breaking of ritual and moral prescriptions introduced anomalies which could threaten the stability of society, and to deal with these there was an elaborate system of ritual.

If we begin to approach Israelite self-awareness from this point of view, a quite different picture begins to emerge from that of the quasi-primitive in a sort of mystical communion with nature and society. Reality is carefully ordered and structured, and the holy is very clearly marked off from the everyday; access to it is strictly regulated (Douglas: 1975). This is not to say that everything that twenty years ago formed the consensus has now to be rejected. It remains likely that Israelites saw society as an aggregate of groups rather than as a collection of individuals, that in worship the king could embody the aspirations of the whole community, and that individuals in worship or prayer could feel that their experiences were those of the whole group. These ideas from the consensus view now need to be divorced, however, from a view of 'primitive mentality' that is seen to have been a caricature of 'primitives' themselves, and not at all appropriate to the Old Testament.

Yet there are fundamental problems about this picture of an ordered Israelite society with its coherent set of symbols. When did this society exist, and was it so uniform that the order and symbols were accepted by all? E. R. Leach solved this problem by denying any historicity at all to the Old Testament, and by treating it as though it were a collection of texts made on one occasion by an anthropological field worker (Leach: 1980). Davies, too, was aware of the problem, and protected himself by viewing Leviticus as 'a post-exilic compilation expressing the world view of the nation's religious leaders and incorporating their understanding of the nature and identity of Israel and the gentile world' (Davies: 1977, 389–90). Yet it is clear from the Old Testament itself that Israelite society was not homogeneous, and that differing ideologies were in competition. The prophetic denunciation of popular and official religion, for example, indicates that before the exile, the situation was not as envisaged by Davies after the exile. The significance of magic and sacred prostitution, not to mention the many methods of trying to gain access to supernatural information prohibited in Deut. 18:9–14, are indications not of a chaotic intellectual understanding of the world, but of the existence of competing sets of symbols in terms of which life was ordered and understood.

Although much has been learnt from structural-functionalist anthropology in the past twenty years, it obviously has its limitations when it is applied not to a society that can actually be observed, but to a society known only to us through very incomplete historical records.

2. Social dimensions of Israelite prophecy

This is a deliberately short section, included at this point because it enables the discussion in the previous section to be amplified. Recent work on Israelite prophecy in the light of anthropology has exhibited the same sort of move away from speculating about the psychology of Israelites that was noticed in the previous section. Whereas earlier scholarship was interested in the mental states of individual prophets, recent work has asked questions such as 'how did society recognise or accept that a person was a prophet?', 'how did society's expectations of what a prophet should be like affect the prophets themselves?', 'what place did prophets and their support groups occupy in society?' Wilson has put the matter well by writing 'anthropological studies have shown that societies themselves play an important role in the process by which some of their members become intermediaries. People do not normally become intermediaries in isolation from the rest of society, but the society is intimately involved in the process' (Wilson: 1980, 43).

Probably the clearest attempt to answer these questions has come from David Petersen in his *The Roles of Israel's Prophets* (Petersen: 1981). Dependent upon role theory, and on anthropologist Ieuan Lewis's *Ecstatic Religion. An Anthropological Study of Spirit Possession and Shamanism* (Lewis: 1971), Petersen has divided Israelite prophecy into two main types: peripheral possession prophecy and central morality prophecy. The former type arises among socially oppressed or underprivileged members of society, and involves the formation of a group led by a prophetic-type figure. Its god is amoral (Petersen: 1981, 43–50). The central morality prophets arise when society as a whole is under pressure, they may well be individuals without support groups, and they legitimate or sanction public morality (Petersen: 1981, 66–9).

This distinction certainly makes sense of some of the Old Testament data. The prophetic groups led by Elijah and Elisha certainly look like peripheral possession prophets, living at the margins of society and with an amoral god destroying by fire the men sent to arrest Elijah (2 Kings 1.9–12). On the other hand, Isaiah and Jeremiah seem to be more individual figures, both operating in times of national crisis in the centre of things in Jerusalem. They seem to be good candidates for central morality prophets.

Whether this typology explains all Israelite prophecy is, of course, another matter, and Wilson prefers to survey a large body of anthropological literature and to eschew any neat typology. The result is that his work is rather more generalised, but with an interesting treatment of Jeremiah at times in conflict with his support group, a group that had considerable power in Jerusalem (Wilson: 1980, 245–8, Long: 1981, 43–8).

These and similar studies introduce into the discussion what is missing in section 1 above – the element of diversity and conflict in society. Long, indeed, argues that rivalries between prophets such as that between Jeremiah and Hananiah are, on the basis of anthropological literature, to be regarded as the norm, and Wilson points to the importance of a prophet's support group in such instances, with the likelihood that in cases of conflict, the prophet with the stronger support group will prevail (Long: 1981, 39). It is clear that the whole question of conflict and its resolution, not just in the area of prophecy, is a major area for further investigation for Old Testament interpretation.

3. Israel's origins and social structure

If, twenty years ago, there was a consensus that Israel's origins were to be sought in semi-nomads who settled down in Canaan around 1200 BC, by the late 1970s a different consensus was emerging, particularly in America, according to which the Israelites had been peasant farmers in Canaan who withdrew or revolted from the influence of the city states and formed a new society with a tribal structure and an egalitarian ideology. This position, advocated most powerfully by Norman Gottwald, drew upon several anthropological strands. One strand was that Israelite society was segmentary and therefore egalitarian in ideology, since it was assumed that in a segmented society power was shared by complementary and equally-ranked segments, with no group or persons having permanent authority over the rest of the society (Gottwald: 1979, 298). Another strand was that Israelite tribes were not 'true' tribes, but were of a secondary type believed to come into existence in opposition, or response, to oppressive power exercised by a central body (Gottwald: 1979, 298). These opinions were applied to the Old Testament by Gottwald in a thorough and careful manner, in the course of which it was argued that the basic social unit (Hebrew *bēṯ āḇ*) was the nuclear, or extended, family. The next social unit, consisting of a number of households, was the clan (Hebrew *mišpāḥāh*) which in Israel was endogamous (i.e. marrying within the group) (Gottwald: 1979, 257–92). It was the last factor, the endogamous nature of the clans, that led Gottwald to the conclusion that Israelite tribes were not 'true' tribes, since anthropological evidence indicated that clans were normally exogamous (i.e. marrying outside the group).

In 1985, Gottwald's thesis was subjected to a most rigorous appraisal by Niels Peter Lemche in what can only be called a model of how anthropology should be studied in regard to the Old Testament. Since Lemche supersedes everything previously written on the subject, his work must be examined in some detail. Basically, Lemche offers a step-by-step critique of Gottwald, drawing upon a most extensive knowledge of the anthropological literature, which knowledge is also applied to what is known of ancient Near Eastern societies. It would be a pity, however, simply to regard Lemche's book as a critique of Gottwald. It is in fact a resource book of the greatest value, which students of Israel's origins cannot afford to overlook, even if they are tempted to skip the long anthropological sections.

A key statement in Lemche is that 'a broad general knowledge of anthropology will limit the number of more or less arbitrary common-sense explanations of those social conditions which may have served as the presuppositions for concrete historical events' (Lemche: 1985, 83). Lemche is right to stress the limitations of common-sense explanations, especially where societies are concerned, and he is rightly cautious about using anthropological works which are a sort of armchair theorising on the basis of first-hand studies. It is the first-hand studies that scholars need to know.

On the basis of first-hand sources, Lemche proceeds to examine types of nomadism, the reasons for sedentarisation, farmers and urban dwellers and egalitarianism and segmentation. In each case, although he is not frightened to generalise, he shows that each area of discussion yields complex and varied results. Among nomads, there is an example of a people with a segmentary lineage system but with a monopoly of power traditionally exercised by three princely families (Lemche: 1985, 97). As against this is a people with no chiefs or leaders, newcomers to the area which they inhabit, but living in close relationship with the settled populace of the area (Lemche: 1985, 106 ff). Lemche sees as basic features of pastoral nomads a common basic unit of 5 to 8 people making up a household, no primogeniture, and with the camp as the basic co-operative unit (Lemche: 1985, 112 ff). He also notes that nomads can have an egalitarian ideology without necessarily having an egalitarian system of rulership. However, Lemche prefers to see nomadism as essentially a *multi-resource* phenomenon. Nomads do not prefer to live in marginal territory, and there are no special zones that are especially suited to nomadic life. Rather, they adjust their social and economic organisation to the political realities of areas where they are (Lemche: 1985, 130). An interesting point that is made is that nomads do have the ability to gain military superiority over settlements, by being able to mobilise and concentrate superior numbers of fighters at a given point (Lemche: 1985, 133).

Why do nomads sedentarise? There are various and complex reasons. In some cases, it may be that nomads get into debt, are forced to become day labourers, and consequently settle down (Lemche: 1985, 102). Alternatively they may generate surplus wealth which they invest by purchasing land and eventually settling on it (Lemche: 1985, 101). In any case, it must not be assumed that sedentarisation is an advance on nomadism. It may well not be. The nomad has mobility, and is thus harder to control by central authority. To settle down is to forfeit this freedom. Lemche notes that it is rare for a whole nomad group to sedentarise, and that if this happens, it is because of the intervention of a central powerful authority. It is more usual for some of the nomads to settle, producing a situation in which nomads and settled peoples in an area are actually related (Lemche: 1985, 144).

Under the heading of farmers and urban dwellers, Lemche is critical of Gottwald's view that cities and peasant cultures are anti-morphemes, or in opposition to each other. He cites examples of where cities and villages are part of a continuum, with mutual interaction (Lemche: 1985, 170ff). He also notes a case where the society has some features in common with those upon which Gottwald bases his revolt theory. However, in this instance there is no indication of a likely revolt (Lemche: 1985, 183). In this section, Lemche concludes that there is no instance in the anthropological literature of the existence of the type of opposition between peasants and city presumed by Gottwald.

The section on egalitarianism and segmentation centres on Gottwald's contention that Israelite clans were endogamous, and that therefore Israelite tribes were not 'true' tribes. Lemche argues that this is a mistake, which does not account for the fact that while African societies are mostly exogamous, Near Eastern societies as a whole are generally endogamous (Lemche: 1985, 224). Lemche also argues that it would be better to speak of acephalous rather than segmentary societies, and of societies with an egalitarian ideology rather than egalitarian societies. This avoids any presumption that segmentary societies are necessarily egalitarian in ideology and praxis, a presumption for which there is little support in the anthropological literature.

In a section that discusses early Israelite social organisation, Lemche challenges, surely correctly, the assumption that there were three main social divisions, represented by the Hebrew terms *bēṯ āb* (extended family or household), *mišpāḥāh* (clan) *šēbet* (tribe) (Lemche: 1985, 248–70). He argues, convincingly in my view, that *bēṯ āḇ* is used of lineages as well as of families. The difference between these terms is that a family is a residential group while a lineage is a descent group which may be made up of a number of residential groups. The term *mišpāḥāh,* Lemche argues, overlaps with *bēṯ āḇ* and probably means 'lineage' *and* 'maximal lineage'. In fact, this term is much less common than *bēṯ āḇ*, even though some scholars have tried to make it the most important social unit in early Israel. Lemche is of the opinion, again surely correctly, that the principal social unit in Israel was the lineage, and that this existed independently of tribal organisation, and survived the establishment of the monarchy, being the social unit within which fell, for example, the obligation to redeem land (cf. Jeremiah 32). Lemche is much less certain about what Israelite tribes were, and he refers at one point to Evans-Pritchard's remark that it was difficult to define and isolate a Nuer tribe (Lemche: 1985, 241).

At the end of Lemche's massively detailed discussion, the following points seem to emerge. First, the peasant revolt theory is unlikely on anthropological grounds since it rests upon an incorrect view of the relation between peasants and cities, and the false assumption that Israelite tribes consisted of endogamous clans and were therefore secondary tribes formed by a re-tribalisation process. Also, it could not be shown that a tribal or segmentary society is necessarily egalitarian in ideology and praxis. Second, on anthropological grounds it is not possible to rule out the immigration theory of Israel's origin or even for that matter some form of conquest theory (Lemche: 1985, 290). It must be said at once that Lemche himself does not espouse either of these views; but he certainly does not rule out the immigration theory, and certainly some form of conquest theory could be defended from his section on nomads.

What Lemche's study makes clear is that when the anthropological literature has been comprehensively studied, many questions remain unanswered, or unanswerable, because of our lack of historical information. This is particularly true in the case of the origin of Israelite tribes. Lemche outlines the problem clearly. Even if we accept that Israelite tribes were territorial units with potential for common action under the leadership of particular individuals, this still does not explain the origin of the tribes, those tribal names that are clearly personal names, and the evidence that some tribes disappeared or were absorbed into other tribes (Lemche: 1985, 282ff). There is also a problem concerning the origin and significance of the twelve-tribe system. If, as seems to be the case, there is no evidence in the book of Judges for a twelve-tribe system prior to the monarchy, where did the system come from? Perhaps the answer depends upon what view is taken of the political importance of the tribes. Lemche, again helpfully, challenges the view that the establishment of the monarchy brought to an end the process of expansion, absorption and readjustment of the tribes. Provided that tribal affiliation was a matter of internal loyalties for the peoples concerned and constituted no political threat to the state, these processes of readjustment could have occurred throughout the monarchy (Lemche: 1985, 184–5). The possibility cannot be ruled out that the twelve-tribe ideology was the creation of the Davidic and Solomonic monarchy, designed to legitimate rule over groups that had not previously come under a central authority. To say this is not to deny that, prior to the monarchy, some Israelite tribes were prepared to unite on occasions in the face of common enemies (e.g. Judges 4–5).

At the end of the day, the conclusions of scholars about Israel's origins will depend upon such things as their view of the date and manner of composition of the Pentateuch. Anthropology can indicate the complexities of social organisation and indicate broadly what is possible and what is not. It cannot be a substitute for historical research. Thus it is likely that anthropology will continue to be used to support positions that are derived from historical and textual studies. For example, a recent work on Abraham by Udo Worschech takes a relatively conservative view of the historical reliability of the Abraham traditions in applying to them the result of anthropological study (Worschech: 1983). At the other end of the scale, Lemche sides with those who would give an exilic date to the composition of the patriarchal narratives, and would make the Deuteronomist precede the Yahwist. This leads to the conclusion that the concept of a united Israel which results in history writing in which all-Israel was dealt with was not possible before the exile (Lemche: 1985, 384). It is clear from this that the primary forum for the discussion of Israel's origins has become the study of the date and composition of the Pentateuch and Deuteronomistic History. Anthropology can only play a supporting and not a central role in this matter.

4. Emics versus etics in anthropological study of the Old Testament

It is now necessary to consider the implications of Norman Gottwald's view that Israel's religious ideology was created by its social conditions rather than *vice versa*. In making this claim he has put emics and etics on the agenda of Old Testament study (Harris: 1976). Emic approaches to anthropology centre on what peoples think about themselves, whereas etic approaches seek to frame quasi-scientific theories about culture which are open to general discussion and falsification. Examples of emic interpretation would be Evans-Pritchard's studies of the Nuer and the

Azande. Although these are, of course, far more than merely reports of what Zande and Nuer think about themselves, the aim of these studies is not to formulate general theories about culture but to give an account of Zande and Nuer beliefs in relation to the social mechanisms that regulate their lives.

An advocate of the etic approach is the American anthropologist Marvin Harris, a scholar to whom Norman Gottwald's *The Tribes of Yahweh* owes a good deal, and whose own position is impressively set out in his *Cultural Materialism. The Struggle for a Science of Culture* (Harris: 1979). Harris sees anthropology as a *science*, and his heroes are the Victorian scientists of culture such as Spencer, Tylor and Frazer, while his villains include Evans-Pritchard and Mary Douglas. Harris's dissatisfaction with emic anthropology is that it cannot be proved or disproved and in any case adds nothing significant to the sum of knowledge. For example, Evans-Pritchard's account of Zande magic is Evans-Pritchard's account, and a different observer might interpret Zande magic in a different way. Further, nobody in Western society will accept the Zande belief that illness is caused by witchcraft, however accurate Evans-Pritchard's observations may be.

While not denying altogether the value of emic anthropology, Harris wants to devise a research strategy based upon the statement of Marx that

> The mode of production in material life determines the general character of the social, political and spiritual processes of life. It is not the consciousness of men that determines their existence, but on the contrary, their social existence determines their consciousness. (Marx: 1970, 21)

As applied to anthropology, this means that culture is divided into three levels, Infrastructure, Structure and Superstructure. Infrastructure will include the production of food in relation to the environment of a people, their population size, their work patterns, etc. Structure will include kinship systems, political organisation, family life, the enforcement of law. Superstructure will include myths, symbols, magic and religion.

Following Marx, Harris affirms that the Infrastructure affects the Structure and the Superstructure and not *vice versa*. For example, a predominantly hunting society may hunt an animal virtually to extinction. It may then have to hunt another animal, and this may entail different social organisation. The almost extinct animal may also become 'taboo', and myths may be invented in order to justify the 'taboo'. Emic anthropology would simply correlate the non-hunting of the animal with the beliefs that justified the prohibition. Etic anthropology, however, would start from an environmental basis, and would look for an explanation in material terms.

It is interesting to note at this point that Harris sharply attacks Mary

Douglas's account of the reason why certain creatures are prohibited in the Old Testament. His chosen point of attack is Douglas's claim that pigs were prohibited because they defied the classification of ungulates, because they ate carrion, and because they were kept by non-Israelites (Douglas: 1975, 272). Harris replies that if pigs eat corpses, so do goats, which were not unclean in Israel. Further, Israel was not alone in restricting pigs; so did the Egyptians and Sumerians. Finally, Israel's neighbours kept cows, sheep and goats, so why were these not banned to Israelites? Harris's own explanation for the prohibition of pigs deserves to be quoted in part:

> The pig's utility resides primarily in its flesh. It can't be milked, it doesn't catch mice, it can't herd other animals, it can't be ridden, it can't pull a plow, and it can't carry a cargo. On the other hand, as a supplier of meat the pig is unrivalled.
> (Harris: 1979, 192)

Harris goes on to say that as the pig's natural environment – forests, river banks and the edges of swamps – became more restricted, they had to be fed on grains as supplements, and thus became competitive with human beings. 'Pastoral nomads . . . [and] . . . seminomadic groups . . . would find it tempting to rear the pig for short-time benefits, but the practice would become extremely costly and maladaptive as it intensified' (Harris: 1979, 192).

It has to be said that Harris seems to have made a good case against Douglas, who takes no account of environmental factors in her explanation. Whether, on the other hand, the Old Testament prohibitions of the rock badger, the hare, the seagull, the waterhen, the pelican and the stork can be similarly explained in environmental terms, seems unlikely (Leviticus 11). It also has to be asked whether Evans-Pritchard's account of Zande magic and witchcraft can best be understood in environmental terms, or as attempted answers to the ultimate questions of illness, death and misfortune.

There can be no doubt, however, that etic anthropology is on the agenda for Old Testament study, and must be taken seriously. The study of the environment in Israel, agricultural practices, population growth and population control will become increasingly important. One can mention already a contribution such as David Hopkins's *The Highlands of Central Canaan* (Hopkins: 1985). On the other hand, it is important that etic approaches should not be allowed to exclude emic approaches altogether, which is what Norman Gottwald seems to be advocating. Gottwald wishes to free Old Testament study from the idealistic and supernaturalistic categories that have up to now been dominant (Gottwald: 1979, 700–9). He favours a biblical sociology. This would investigate the Infrastructure of ancient Israel at every stage of its development, trying to establish how changes in Infrastructure led to changes in social organisation and beliefs. There is also a hermeneutical side to this programme. Biblical sociology would investigate the fortunes and transformations of what, to Gottwald, is the pristine manifestation of Yahwism, namely the religious ideology of liberated egalitarian groups. It would trace the falling away from pristine Yahwism in the course of Israel's history, as the egalitarian society became a monarchy, power was centralised, and oppression replaced freedom. Viewed in this light, the Old Testament is a challenge to modern readers to replicate the original achievement of Israel by creating a liberated egalitarian society appropriate to the circumstances of our world.

Without accepting that Israel ever was an egalitarian society, it is possible to endorse Gottwald's call for Old Testament study to become less idealistic, in the sense of concentrating on the Superstructure at the expense of the other levels; and indeed the past twenty years have seen a marked shift in the desired direction. The consensus outlined at the beginning of this essay, as far as it concerned Israelite self-awareness, was largely concerned with Israelite psychology. Structural-functional anthropology has indicated how Israelite psychology (the Superstructure) can be better understood in terms of social mechanisms (the Structure). Similarly, it has been noted above that studies of Israelite prophecy have begun to take account of the social factors in prophetic activity.

On the other hand, to concentrate purely on the etic approach will be to run the danger of reading the Old Testament purely in terms of a cultural determinism. There are many studies in anthropological literature of the role played by individuals in radically changing social conditions. Of course, such changes do not happen in a social vacuum. Certain social and ecological conditions have to be present as the necessary causes. But the sufficient cause may be an individual or group without whose intervention nothing would happen, and whose individuality may influence the course that events take.

A good example of what I have in mind is the rise of the kingship. In a recent article C. Hauer has argued that the emergence of the state in Israel was the result of at least two factors (Hauer: 1986). One was environmental, in that Israelite society had reached the limits of what the environment could bear. The other was personal agency in the form of the Philistines. 'Philistine power had impacted a circumscribed environment. Those who fled did not face the best prospects of survival. But given the limitations of the Israelite subsistence strategy, submission was hardly more tolerable, or adaptive. The situation of the highland villages was genuinely desperate . . . They could give up, submit or flee . . . or they could organise to resist. Social circumscription resulting from Philistine activity engendered the process of state formation in Israel as a circumscribed . . . not fully compacted environment had not' (Hauer: 1986, 10).

Whether or not this statement is correct can only depend on whether it is borne out by research into agricultural strategies in Israel in the eleventh century BC. Methodologically, however, the approach is surely correct. The suggested environmental situation was the necessary cause, the Philistine pressure was the sufficient cause. Without the latter the Israelites could have developed alternative agricultural strategies or population control. Had Philistine pressure been applied in different environmental circumstances, Israel's military response would not have involved moving towards a state.

What is called for, then, is a proper balance between different types of anthropology; a blend, if you like, of the strategies described under the four headings above. Although Old Testament studies have moved a long way from the consensus described at the outset, it would be wrong to suppose that anything like a new consensus has emerged. British and American scholars in particular have been influenced by the respective and differing anthropological traditions in their own countries, and a significant role is played by the assumptions that scholars make about matters such as the date and mode of composition of the Pentateuch. On the other hand, scholars now have available to them a vast amount of anthropological theory and literature that was hardly known about in Old Testament circles twenty years ago. The next twenty years has the potential to establish a new consensus firmly based upon a thorough knowledge and judicious use of anthropology.

Bibliography

Borowski, O., 1987. *Agriculture in Iron Age Israel*, Winona Lake: Eisenbrauns.

Carroll, M. P., 1978. 'One More Time. Leviticus Revisited', *Archives européennes de Sociologie*, 19, pp. 339–46, reprinted in Lang, *Anthropological Approaches*, pp. 117–26.

Crüsemann, F., 1978. *Der Widerstand gegen das Königtum*, WMANT 49, Neukirchen: Neukirchener Verlag.

Davies, D., 1977. 'An Interpretation of Sacrifice in Leviticus', *ZAW* 89, pp. 388–98; reprinted in Lang, *Anthropological Approaches*, pp. 151–62.

Douglas, Mary, 1966. *Purity and Danger*, London.

1975. *Implicit Meanings. Essays in Anthropology*, London.

Eichrodt, W., 1947. *Das Menschenverständnis im Alten Testament*, Zürich.

Evans-Pritchard, E. E., 1937. *Witchcraft, Oracles and Magic among the Azande*, Oxford: OUP.

Flanagan, J., 1981. 'Chiefs in Israel', *JSOT* 20, pp. 47–53.

Fohrer, G., 1969. *Geschichte der israelitischen Religion*, Berlin, Eng. Tr. *History of Israelite Religion*, London 1973.

Frazer, J. G., 1957. *The Golden Bough*, abridged edition, London.

Frick, F. S., 1977. *The City in Ancient Israel*, SBL Dissertation Series 36, Missoula: Scholars Press.

1985. *The Formation of the State in Ancient Israel. A Survey of Models and Theories*, Social World of Biblical Antiquity Series 4, Sheffield: Almond Press.

Geus, C. H. J de, 1976. *The Tribes of Israel, An Investigation into some of the presuppositions of Martin Noth's Amphictony Hypothesis*, Studia Semitica Neerlandica 18, Assen.

Gottwald, N. K., 1974. 'Were the Early Israelites Pastoral Nomads?', J. J. Jackson and M. Kessler (eds.), *Rhetorical Criticism. Essays in Honor of James Muilenburg*, Pittsburg Theological Monograph Series I, pp. 223–55.

1979. *The Tribes of Yahweh. A Sociology of the Religion of Liberated Israel 1250–1050 B.C.E.*, New York.

Harris, M., 1976. 'History and Significance of the Emic/Etic distinction', *Annual Review of Anthropology*, vol. 5, Palo Alto, California, pp. 329–50.

1979. *Cultural Materialism. The Struggle for a Science of Culture*, New York.

Hauer, C., 1986. 'From Alt to Anthropology. The Rise of the Israelite State' in *JSOT* 36, pp. 1–16.

Hooke, S. H. 1933. *Myth and Ritual. Essays on the Myth and Ritual of the Hebrews in Relation to the Culture Pattern of the Ancient East*, London.

Hopkins, D. C., 1985. *The Highlands of Central Canaan. Agricultural Life in the Early Iron Age*, Social World of Biblical Antiquity Series 3, Sheffield: Almond Press.

Johnson, A. R., 1961. *The One and the Many in the Israelite Conception of God*, Cardiff: Univ. of Wales.

Lang, B., 1980. *Wie wird man Prophet in Israel? Aufsätze zum Alten Testament*, Düsseldorf.

1983. 'The Social Organisation of Peasant Poverty in biblical Israel', *Monotheism and the Prophetic Minority*, Sheffield, pp. 114–27, reprinted in B. Lang (ed.), *Anthropological Approaches to the Old Testament*, London: SPCK.

1985. *Anthropological Approaches to the Old Testament*, London: SPCK.

Leach, E. R., 1961. 'Lévi-Strauss in the Garden of Eden: an examination of some recent developments in the analysis of myth', *Transactions of the New York Academy of Sciences*, II, 23, 4, pp. 368–96.

1966. 'The Legitimacy of Solomon: some structural aspects of Old Testament history', *Archives européenes de Sociologie*, 7, pp. 58–101.

1980. 'Anthropological Approaches to the Study of the Bible during the Twentieth Century', G. M. Tucker, D. A. Knight (eds.), *Humanizing America's Iconic Book*, California.

Lemche, N. P., 1985. *Early Israel. Anthropological and Historical Studies on the Israelite Society before the Monarchy*, SVT 37, Leiden.

Lewis, I., 1971. *Ecstatic Religion. An Anthropological Study of Spirit Possession and Shamanism*, Harmondsworth: Penguin.

Long, B. O., 1977. 'Prophetic Authority as Social Reality', eds. G. W. Coats and B. O. Long, *Canon And Authority*, Philadelphia: Westminster, 3–20.

1981. 'Social Dimensions of Prophetic Conflict', *Semeia* 21, *Anthropological Perspective on Old Testament Prophecy*.

Marx, K., 1970. *A Contribution of the Critique of Political Economy* (1859), New York.
Mendenhall, G. E., 1962. 'The Hebrew Conquest of Palestine', *Biblical Archaeologist* 25, pp. 66–87.
1973. *The Tenth Generation*, Baltimore: Johns Hopkins Univ.
Mowinckel, S., 1922. *Psalmenstudien*, II, Oslo: Dybwad.
Overholt, T. W., 1974. 'The Ghost Dance of 1890 and the nature of the Prophetic Process', *Ethnohistory*, 21, pp. 37–63.
Pedersen, J., 1963. *Israel*, Oxford: OUP.
Petersen, D. L., 1981. *The Roles of Israel's Prophets*, JSOTSS, 17, Sheffield.
Robinson, H. Wheeler, 1906. *Deuteronomy and Joshua*, Century Bible, Edinburgh.
1936. 'The Hebrew Conception of "Corporate Personality"', *Werden und Wesen des Alten Testaments, BZAW*, 66, Berlin, pp. 49–62. Reprinted in H. W. Robinson, *Corporate Personality in Ancient Israel*, Philadelphia: Westminster, 1980, pp. 25–44.
Rogerson, J. W., 1970. 'Structural Anthropology', *BSOAS* 33, pp. 490–500.
Rogerson, J. W., 1977. 'The Old Testament View of Nature: Some Preliminary Questions', *Oudtestamentische Studien*, 20, pp. 74ff.
1978. *Anthropology and the Old Testament*, Oxford: Blackwell, p. 48.
Weippert, M., 1967. *Die Landnahme der Israelitischen Stämme in der neueren wissenschaflichen Diskussion*, FRLANT, 92, Göttingen: Vandenhoeck & Ruprecht.
Wilson, R. R., 1977. *Genealogy and History in the Biblical World*, New Haven.
1980. *Prophecy and Society in Ancient Israel*, Philadelphia: Westminster.
Worschech, U., 1983. *Abraham. Eine sozialgeschichtliche Studie*, Europäische Hochschulschriften, 23, Frankfurt am Main: Lang.

CHAPTER THREE

Sociology and the Old Testament

ANDREW D. H. MAYES

The aim of this essay is to trace the influence of sociological thought on Old Testament study. This is here understood to imply not in the first instance a concern with the social history of Israel, but rather a concern with the theoretical foundations on which such studies rest. The essay begins, therefore, with a brief consideration of major trends in sociological thought, and then turns to the influence of these trends on the study of the Old Testament and ancient Israel.[1]

I Early sociological thought

The 'Golden Age' of sociological thinking was marked by the works of Marx, Weber and Durkheim in the second half of the nineteenth century and the first two decades of the twentieth century. It was then, largely as a result of the disruptive effects of the industrial revolution and the French revolution, that the basic questions concerning the nature of society received their classic formulation and provoked responses which continue to influence sociological theory (Nisbet: 1967). Two major sociological traditions emerged: one, the conflict tradition, goes back to Marx and Weber, and, given his direct contribution to Old Testament study, may here be referred to also as the Weber tradition; the other, which has come to be referred to as the functionalist tradition, looks to Durkheim as its founding father.[2] The nature of, and the difference between, the two traditions may be briefly characterised as follows: for Weber society is a mode of organisation of individuals, and sociology is the study of the understandable and purposive actions of such individuals; for Durkheim society is the prior reality, and social phenomena are *sui generis* realities to be understood only in relation to other social phenomena rather than by reference to the psychology of the individual. The implications of this for the perception of the nature of society and the relationship between religion and society should be clarified.

(i) The conflict tradition

The conflict tradition is so called because it sees society as consisting of 'groups and individuals trying to advance their own interests over others, whether or not overt outbreaks take place in this struggle for advantage' (Collins: 1985, 47). While Marx was concerned with the economic basis of capitalism and with its future breakdown, within the framework of a deterministic view of history, Weber sought the background of capitalism, its origin and development, within the framework of an analysis of society on the one hand and government on the other.

In his study of society Weber adopted much of Marx's analysis but while Marx used the term 'class' in a broad and comprehensive economic, political and cultural sense, Weber used it in a purely economic sense. Other forms of social grouping also existed, among which the most significant was what Weber defined as the 'status group' (Weber: 1948, 186ff.). Status groups are communities characterised by a specific life style, and restrictions on social intercourse; they may evolve into closed castes, a condition which is found with pariah peoples the world over, the Jews being the most impressive historical example.

In his study of government, Weber (1947, 324ff.) distinguished three types of legitimate domination: legal authority, traditional authority and charismatic authority. Legal authority is exercised by an individual within a rationalised system characterised by a hierarchical organisation of offices, in which the person who exercises authority is himself subject to law; traditional authority is based on personal loyalty and is exercised within the framework of tradition without any rational hierarchy of offices, or clearly defined spheres of competence subject to impersonal rules; charismatic authority, exercised by an individual who exhibits superhuman or at least exceptional powers or qualities, is sharply opposed to both rational and traditional authority, and is bound by no rules or precedents. These are ideal types of authority, none of which is usually found historically in pure form: characteristics of one type are often found in another, while it may also happen that, through a process of 'routinization', charismatic authority may develop into traditional or legal authority (Weber: 1948, 295ff.).

Weber provided no systematic definition of religion comparable to that of Durkheim, though he clearly understood it in very different terms (Weber: 1963). It is that by which meaning is brought to experience. There are two major types of religion, characterised by radically different attitudes to the world: on the one hand, there is the 'inner-worldly attitude', and, on the other, the 'world-rejecting attitude'. This distinction almost coincides with the distinction between asceticism and mysticism, and that between occidental religion and oriental religion. Inner-worldly asceticism includes especially ascetic Protestantism, and teaches the principle of the loyal fulfilment of obligations in the world as the sole method of proving religious merit; world-rejecting mysticism, on the other hand, is concerned primarily with achieving mystical union with the divine (Weber: 1963, 168f.).

Nor did Weber provide any description, comparable to that of Durkheim, of the relationship between religion and society. This, in fact, is the subject of intense debate in Weber studies, particularly because it is on this point that Weber is generally understood to have radically distanced himself from Marx. It has frequently been supposed that his book, *Protestant Ethic*, was intended as a refutation of the Marxist historical materialist thesis that religion is the ideological superstructure to given social conditions; but, apart from the fact that Marxism itself cannot be dismissed in such crudely materialistic terms, this rejection of materialism is by no means an adequate account of Weber's view. Weber noted in that book (1930, 183): 'it is, of course, not my aim to substitute for a one-sided materialistic an equally one-sided spiritualistic causal interpretation of culture and of history'. He did not, however, go on to develop a systematic explanation of the relationship between religion and society, and, apart from noting (1952, 206ff.) that new religious conceptions presuppose an attitude which asks questions of the world and so a marginalised social and historical situation, he left the matter unresolved. His occasional use of the term 'elective affinity' (1948, 62f., 284f.) to describe the relationship between social strata and their religious conceptions provided no solution. This is a paradoxical term (Thomas: 1985, 39ff.), which in part ('elective') implies free choice, but otherwise ('affinity') implies a determined, non-elective relationship. At best, it can be said that Weber's use of the term, which he adopted from Goethe, was an attempt to overcome the dualism of chance and necessity, mind and matter, and, in the religious context, 'to demonstrate the limitations of the materialist and idealist interpretations . . . without denying the relative justification for both' (Thomas: 1985, 51).

(ii) The functionalist tradition

Durkheim's approach amounts to a reification of society. Pre-social, individual nature consists only of vague and confused dispositions; society is the prior reality which determines the individual, materially, mentally and spiritually. The collective consciousness which imposes itself on the individual comprises those beliefs and sentiments common to the members of a given society. Depending on the nature of the society, this collective consciousness may be strong and pervasive or weak and limited. At the early stage of development, society is characterised by mechanical solidarity and the collective consciousness is strong: individuals scarcely differ from one another, they are members of the same collectivity, and resemble one another because they feel the same emotions, cherish the same values and hold the same things sacred. Such societies have a segmental structure, consisting of similar, juxtaposed clan groups. In its developed form, society is characterised by organic solidarity: the collective consciousness becomes less pervasive, more abstract and focused on the individual; there is a general loosening of social bonds and traditional restraints of kinship, class and locality. The transition from mechanical to organic solidarity is marked by a growth in differentiation among members of society resulting from an increase in density of the society. Density increases not mainly through growth in population but through the concentration of populations in cities. This leads to a struggle for survival, for which social differentiation is the peaceful solution enabling the greater number of individuals to survive: the individual performs his own function as a complement to, rather than in competition with, his fellows. So social and historical change is by a process internal to society rather than the result of the volitional act of the individual (Durkheim: 1933).

For his account of religion, Durkheim (1915) was particularly indebted to W. Robertson Smith.[3] For the latter, totemism was a phase of religious belief through which all societies passed, and communion sacrifice was the central and basic rite in all religions. In the killing and eating of the totemic animal, which was the material representation of the clan, the clan celebrated and revitalised its unity. Religion was thus a social fact and a function of society: 'A man did not choose his religion or frame it for himself; it came to him as part of the general scheme of social obligations and ordinances laid upon him, as a matter of course, by his position in the family and in the nation . . . Religion did not exist for the saving of souls but for the preservation and welfare of society' (Smith: 1927, 28f.).

Under the influence of Hubert and Mauss, Durkheim held against Smith that expiation and oblation could not be excluded from the primitive function and significance of sacrifice, but he firmly maintained the totemic and ritualistic understanding of primitive society and its unity which Smith expounded. For Durkheim (1915, 43) 'religious beliefs are always common to a determined group, which makes profession of adhering to them and of practising the rites connected with them. They are not merely received individually by all the members of this group; they are something belonging to the group, and they make its unity. The individuals which compose it feel themselves united to each other by the simple fact that they have a common faith.' This understanding of religion clearly identifies it with the content of the collective consciousness of society; it binds society together and provides indispensable integrative symbols.

Totemism is, for Durkheim, the most primitive type of religion known, and to discover its origins is to discover that which gives rise to the religious sentiment in humanity. Totemism recognises three objects as sacred: the totem, the representation of the totem, and the members of the clan which venerates the totem. Since the totem frequently has no intrinsic significance, its sacredness must stem from its symbolic nature, and since it is a symbol of the whole clan group, it must be concluded that totemism in fact involves the veneration of the social group itself. So the conclusion may be drawn (Durkheim: 1915, 206): 'In a general way, it is unquestionable that a society has all that is necessary to arouse the sensation of the divine in minds, merely by the power that it has over them; for to its members it is what a god is to his worshippers. In fact, a god is, first of all, a being whom men think of as superior to themselves, and upon whom they feel that they depend . . . Now society also gives us the sensation of a perpetual dependence'.

II The Weber tradition in Old Testament study

(i) Weber

Weber's *Ancient Judaism*, written towards the end of his life, is a largely descriptive account of the origin and rise of Judaism; it reflects, however, typically Weberian sociological concepts and ideas. Weber's general sociology is a historical sociology, and his approach is to define a situation and then seek its origins. So, in *Ancient Judaism*, he first defines the nature of the post-exilic Jewish community and then seeks its origins in the history of ancient Israel. The Jewish community is described as a status group and pariah community; it is not an economic class or a political party. It is, therefore, a group which has a consciousness of unity not primarily based on economic considerations. The group is bound together positively by certain common beliefs and customary practices, and negatively by restrictions in the spheres of marriage and dietary habits. The pariah community is a status group, and, with definite limitations, Weber finds that to be the most appropriate classification for the post-exilic Jewish community.[4] For the origins of this community Weber goes back to the formative period of Israel in Palestine.

After a discussion of the social structures of nomadic bedouin, cities in Palestine, the peasant farmer and the semi-nomadic herdsman, Weber turns to the laws of the Book of the Covenant and Deuteronomy, and then to the question of the covenant. The relationship between these topics and their relevance to 'Israel' is not immediately clear, especially insofar as the cities, the peasantry and semi-nomadism (nomadism being seen as irrelevant to the situation of Israel) are treated as mutually hostile social forms. What Weber is in fact doing here is constructing ideal types, making theoretical constructions which have a heuristic function (Giddens: 1971, 141f,; Schäfer-Lichtenberger: 1983, 24ff.). These are social types, and the question of their possible historical and ethnic identity is secondary. None of them is to be isolated historically and immediately identified as Israel; they are, rather, types of life in Palestine within the overall context of which Israel is to be historically located. The transition from the ideal type to the historical situation of Israel is made through the study of Old Testament law, for it is this which reflects historical Israel in its ongoing development (Weber: 1952, 61). The primary concern of the law is with the village and town dwelling peasant on his own land, but it has in mind also the peasant in his relations with the urban patrician and the semi-nomad: Israel is to be found across this social spectrum as a gradually developing urban society. What held it together as a single people, despite the social and economic antagonisms which divided its constituent elements and which the law sought to regulate, is revealed by the nature of the law as law of Yahweh. Israel's unity is founded on a union of different groups in covenant with Yahweh.

How Weber understands this union to have been first established is far from clear. He is emphatic that it was not the life conditions of a social group which produced the idea of a covenant with Yahweh: 'This form of historical materialistic construction is here, as elsewhere, inadequate' (1952, 80). The only positive answer offered, however, is that the origins of the covenant union were 'determined by quite concrete religious-historical and often highly personal circumstances and vicissitudes' (*ibid.*). In the light of Weber's general sociology, he apparently means by this, in the first place, that it was on the basis of the understandings and interpretations of their situation held by individuals that the belief in a common covenant with Yahweh emerged, and, secondly, that the laws of the Book of the Covenant and Deuteronomy represent the progressive 'rationalisations' of the original charismatic breakthrough achieved at the beginning by Moses and the exodus group. This breakthrough to a basic insight from which new social and historical situations could be confronted, was realised historically in the creation of the covenant community of Israel.

The development of Yahwism in a rational and ethical direction was largely the work of the Levites: the technical means available to them for discerning the will of Yahweh, the casting of lots yielding a 'yes' or 'no' answer to specific questions, had the effect of promoting rational questions concerning specific issues and of minimizing emotional and mystic irrationalism. It is this levitical teaching of the laws and commandments of the covenant, culminating in the ethical decalogue and the development of a rational 'workaday ethic of the masses' (1952, 249), which formed the source of the teaching of the classical prophets; they 'preached the levitic ethic, the existence and knowledge of which they treated as self-evident' (1952, 277f.).[5]

The prophet was defined by Weber (1963, 46) as 'a purely individual bearer of charisma, who by virtue of his mission proclaims a religious doctrine or divine commandment'. He distinguished, however, between two types of prophet, corresponding to the distinction between mystical and ascetic forms of religion: the one is represented by the Buddha, the other by Muhammed. In the former case, he is 'an exemplary man who, by his personal example, demonstrates to others the way to religious salvation'; in the latter case he is 'an instrument for the proclamation of a god and his will' (1963, 55) demanding obedience as an ethical duty. Israelite prophecy is of the ethical type: 'Nowhere [in Israel] do we find the tranquil, blissful euphoria of the god-possessed, rarely the expression of a devotional communion with God . . . the presence of Yahweh [is never experienced] as a blissful incumbency of the godhead, but rather always as a duty and command, mostly as a hectic stormy demand' (Weber: 1952, 312f.). Mystical possession of other-worldly godliness and speculation concerning the meaning of the universe were rejected by the Israelite prophets in favour of plain devotion to the divine demand.

On two issues Weber made a specifically sociological contribution to the study of prophecy. In the first place, he resisted any temptation to identify the prophets with particular political or social groups. Political realities certainly conditioned the emergence of prophecy, and, in Weber's view, constituted the message of the most impressive prophetic oracles. Yet the prophets are not to be identified as political figures: their preaching was always religiously oriented. No more can they be identified as deriving from an underprivileged social stratum. Not only does the Old Testament itself indicate the generally high social standing of most of the prophets (1952, 277ff.), but it may also be confirmed from the specifically sociological point of view (1963, 80ff.) that neither the peasantry nor the nobility appear as the carriers of rational, ethical movements such as Israelite prophecy. The peasantry are primarily involved with weather magic and ritualism, while the life pattern of the nobility requires of its religion rather a legitimising function to justify its social status. For Weber it is the middle class which 'by virtue of its distinctive pattern of economic life, inclines in the direction of a rational ethical religion' (1963, 97). This may be taken as generally applicable to the situation of ancient Israel also, and it fits with Weber's close association of the prophetic ethic with the preaching and pastoral activity of the Levites.

Secondly, Weber argued that prophecy belongs to the ongoing process of 'rationalisation', in which religion gives meaning to existence. In this process the prophetic proclamation marks a breakthrough or sudden leap forward, and is followed by a period in which the new insight is absorbed and systematised in the religious following which succeeded the prophet. This 'routinisation' of prophecy denotes the process by which 'the doctrine of the prophets enters into everyday life, as the function of a permanent institution' (1963, 62). It represents the transformation of revealed religion into a priestly enterprise characterised by pastoral care and the religious cultivation of the individual. This is the process and the relationship in which Moses stands with the levitical preachers who succeeded him; it is also the process and the relationship in which the priesthood and the post-exilic Jewish community stand with pre-exilic prophecy. The teaching of the prophets made clear the latent monotheism and universality of the Israelite idea of God; it also expressed the idea of humility and absolute obedience as the only mode of relationship with God. These are the distinctive characteristics of the post-exilic pariah community which may thus be seen to be directly rooted in pre-exilic prophecy.

(ii) Alt and Noth

Weber's work proved extraordinarily productive and influential, particularly in the thinking of Alt and Noth. Three topics in particular illustrate this: the charismatic, the ideal type city state, and Israel as an oath community. The first two were treated especially by Alt (1966, 173ff., 241ff.), and the third by Noth (1930).

Alt used the term charisma with reference both to the deliverers of Israel in the pre-monarchic period and to forms of kingship in Israel. In each case, leadership was personal and individual and quite distinct from the traditional leadership of the tribal elders and from the dynastic form which kingship also adopted. The pre-monarchic deliverers occupied no institutional office and surrounded themselves with no administrative machinery; their authority was vested in themselves alone. Saul differed from them only in that he was given permanent leadership to meet an enduring crisis; like his predecessors, however, he exercised a personal and individual authority which rested on divine designation and popular acclamation. This form of kingship was found also later in the northern kingdom after the death of Solomon. Only with Omri was the pattern broken, for he founded a dynasty in which both his son and his grandsons succeeded him. This change was closely associated with a particular feature of Omri's kingship, his establishment of a new capital city; this paralleled an earlier action of David who was also the founder of a dynasty. In both cases dynastic kingship was linked to the foundation of a capital city. At this point the second area of Weber's influence on Alt is to be traced.

Weber described the type of the city very much in terms of the Mediterranean *polis*: it was an independent social structure, the seat of the monarchic and military authorities, and also of the local deity and priesthood. This understanding of the city was adopted by Alt with particular reference to Jerusalem and Samaria. When David captured Jerusalem from the Jebusites, he did so with his own men who owed loyalty to him alone; so the city became his property and was not incorporated into the tribal territories. Since it was legally his city and the city of his descendants after him, his kingship was necessarily, in Jerusalem first and then in Judah which accepted the situation, a dynastic kingship. In a parallel move, Omri bought the hill of Samaria and built there his capital city. It too became his private property and that of his descendants after him, and so his kingship also had a dynastic form.

Noth's indebtedness to Weber was perhaps even more significant. His persuasive presentation of the theory that Israel in the pre-monarchic period had an amphictyonic organisation reflects the strong influence of Weber's sociological perspective. The immediately obvious point of contact is that just as Weber saw pre-monarchic Israel as an 'oath community', deliberately created out of a variety of socio-economic types, so also Noth saw Israel as a covenant community deliberately established out of formerly independent clans and tribes. In both cases Israel is a new religious community, constituted by its covenant relationship with Yahweh. Both Weber and Noth think in terms of existing raw material which is used to create new institutions; both are vague about how and by whom that raw material is used; both imply the irruption into history of new, charismatically founded institutions; for both Israel originates in the land of Palestine; and for both this covenant community represents the true Israel which survived the imposition on it of an essentially foreign monarchic structure.

Alt and Noth became the dominant influence in the historical understanding of Israel, and have remained so until the present. Although all three of the topics referred to have been the focus of more recent critical discussion, which has seriously undermined the reconstructions which they offered, it was through their work that the sociological perspective of Weber became established and that the possibilities which that sociological perspective offered for understanding Israel became clear.

III The Durkheim tradition in Old Testament study

(i) Causse

Causse was chiefly concerned with the transition in Israelite religion and society from the pre-logical mentality, for which religion is scarcely distinct from magic, to the rational individualism of later Israelite ethical thinking (1937; see Kimbrough: 1978). Early Israel carried over from its nomadic past a family and clan social structure which practised a primitive collectivism. The elders represented the living soul of the group which realised its unity in them. The group was characterised by 'organic solidarity':[6] there was no individual differentiation; there was collective responsibility before the law; the relationship of the individual to the group was a mystical communion coming to expression in certain rituals and strengthened by the group's common worship of Yahweh. The sacrificial cult, which was simple and spontaneous, both established a mystic kinship relationship with Yahweh and was the most powerful binding influence founding the solidarity of the group.

With the rise of the monarchy, the authority of the state interposed itself in the lives of Israelites and the authority of the family father declined. Moreover, the monarchy had its own mystical base, and Yahweh became the God of the state and Universal God rather than God of the tribes. So the cult became separated from the life of the primitive group, and the simple joyful, natural worship of the family grouped around its patron God declined. The prophets represented a conservative reaction against the state, which aimed to restore the old culture and patriarchal organisation of the simple peasantry. In practice, however, their preaching undermined the old tribal clan ways, for they condemned the local sanctuaries where the clans and families realised their social unity in cultic song and festival. In place of the mystical, cultic foundation to Israel's solidarity with Yahweh the prophets put an ethical foundation: moral behaviour is the indispensable condition of right relations with God. In thus moralising and rationalising the cult the prophets opened the way to an individualistic conception of religious and social organisation; the institutions of collective life and national religion had only a secondary importance.

The Deuteronomic reform attempted to put a brake on the decline of ancient social organisation by restating old laws, rites and institutions. Ancient law, however, could no longer be imposed and accepted simply because it was old, and so the lawgiver had to persuade his hearers with exhortations, explanations and rational motives. The old mystical authority and unity of the social group no longer existed; it had been replaced by rational authority, and commands based on a moral order which individuals had to be persuaded to obey. Thus, the Deuteronomic reform effected the transition from primitive collectivism to individualism and the interior religion that the prophets had proclaimed; it thus paved the way for the Jewish community in which, through obedience to the torah, the individual could lead a holy and perfect life.

Causse was heavily influenced by the sociological tradition represented by Fustel de Coulanges, Robertson Smith and Durkheim, particularly for his view of the family as a cultic community, the gradual emergence of individualism out of a primitive collectivism, the basically ritualistic nature of primitive religion and the expression of social unity in primitive ritual. This supplied the sociological framework within which he then set the broad evolutionary approach, with its emphasis on the prophets as those who introduced morality into religion, which derived from Reuss, Graf and Wellhausen.[7] The other major influence on Causse, and the one which was responsible for the major weakness of his work, was Lévy-Bruhl, for it was on the basis of the latter's early writings that Causse tried to penetrate the mentality of primitive and civilised communities in order to uncover the inner development of the transition from primitive collectivism to individualism. His use of the categories of pre-logical and logical thinking went beyond what Durkheim considered the proper task of sociology, and in any case reflected an understanding of the nature of human thinking which was quickly shown to be faulty (Evans-Pritchard: 1965, 78ff.; Rogerson: 1978, 53ff.).[8]

(ii) Gottwald

Gottwald's dismissal (1980, 625) of Durkheim as an idealist and his espousal (1980, 631ff.) of the Marxist approach to the understanding of the relationship of religion to society, may make his inclusion at this point somewhat surprising. There are, however, good reasons for seeing Gottwald in this context rather than in the conflict tradition to which Marx belongs. The distinctive characteristics of conflict theory, which understands society within the framework of the interaction of different classes and status groups, are wholly absent from Gottwald's study: here Israel appears as a harmonious, undifferentiated unity. Gottwald adopts a functionalist approach to Israelite society, which certainly has its roots in Durkheimian social theory, and emphasises its synchronic, structural dimension, rather than its diachronic and historical. On the other hand, while Gottwald quotes Marx in order to establish that religion is an epiphenomenon of material processes, his reading of Marx is rather selective, and tends to ignore the latter's view that religion originated in a class structured society as an ideological weapon of dominance. The form of Marxism which Gottwald has adopted is perfectly adaptable to the structural-functionalist approach he otherwise uses. Marx is introduced in order to break out of the spiral of structural-functionalism to reach a decision on which is in the end determinative: religion or material circumstances.

Gottwald's study is a classic statement of the sociological understanding of pre-monarchic Israel within the framework of the Durkheim tradition.[9] The work is divided into two parts: the first is concerned with basic literary and historical questions and culminates in a full and comprehensive analysis of Israel's pre-monarchic social structure; the second compares Israelite and non-Israelite social structures and culminates in a discussion of the religion of Israel and its relationship to its social context.

The literary discussion of the first part covers the sources available and sees the cult as the setting within which the process of tradition formation took place and where the unity of Israel was brought to real and to literary expression; the historical discussion describes the various models which have been used to understand Israelite origins; the analysis of Israel's social structure is intended to confirm the revolt model of her origins by presenting 'tribal' Israel as a family based society whose tribalism was a deliberately chosen instrument of resistance to centralisation. Israel's social structure was a radical alternative to the social structures of the environment, by means of which there was established an egalitarian mode of agricultural and pastoral life; her tribalism was 'politically conscious and deliberate social revolution and, more loosely, a civil war in that it divided and counterposed peoples who had previously been organized within Canaanite city states' (1980, 325).

The second part of Gottwald's work begins with an examination of existing social structures in Palestine, in order to reinforce the conclusion that Israel was a tribal society originating in Palestine in the context of internal revolt. The Amarna texts are taken to show a country in turmoil, divided between the ruling urban élite and the subject peasantry. It is here that the real tension existed, rather than between the semi-nomad and the settled, for semi-nomadism is in fact a late, marginal development, a specialised offshoot of the agricultural-pastoral village community. Israelite origins lie within the latter socio-economic sector, and so Israelites had a strong indigenous rootage in the land. Their opponents in their 'conquest' of the land were not Canaanites as such but the city state rulers.

Israel's origin and social structure were unique and it is this which is fundamental to her religious uniqueness. In a thorough critique of Bright's separation of Israel's religion from her history and society, of Mendenhall's idealism in making Israel's faith the prior reality which determined her form of society, and of Fohrer's reservation of an essential core of Israelite faith immune from historical and sociological analysis, Gottwald argues that religion is a function of society and a comprehensive symbol system which articulates its totality. The social egalitarian structure of Israelite society brought the Yahwist religious innovation into existence. In turn the Yahwist religion then acted back upon society in order to sustain the fundamental egalitarian social relations. Indeed, 'the Yahwistic cult and ideology validated and motivated egalitarian social relations to so great an extent that it proved to be the single most significant servomechanism for society' (1980, 646).

The relationship between religion and society can thus far be understood within the framework of a structural functionalist approach, but this is not in the end satisfactory, for it does not explain which is finally determinative: Israel's religion or her society. The approaches of both Durkheim and Weber are rejected as inadequate, idealist solutions to this question. So Gottwald turns to Marxist historical materialism, and the view ascribed to Marx that 'at the root of all social organisation and mental ideation, including religion, is the way human beings within nature act upon nature to produce their means of subsistence and thereby fashion their own social nature' (631) is accepted as being 'the most coherent and promising understanding for developing research strategies in the social sciences' (633). So the conclusion is drawn that '"Yahweh" is the historically concretized, primordial power to establish and sustain social equality in the face of counter-oppression from without and against provincial and nonegalitarian tendencies from within the society. "The Chosen People" is the distinctive self-consciousness of a society of equals created in the intertribal order and demarcated from a primarily centralised and stratified surrounding world. "Covenant" is the bonding of decentralised social groups in a larger society of equals committed to cooperation without authoritarian leadership.' (692). Israel was a cult community whose unity and egalitarian social structure found ideological expression and validation in devotion to Yahweh, within which context she produced a national tradition identifying herself as the people of Yahweh. Her religion was a concrete form of expression for concrete social relations anchored in the forms and relations of production; it is to that last context that future research should, in Gottwald's view, be directed, in order to strengthen the base of the cultural materialist approach.

IV Recent sociological study of the Old Testament

Within the last decade or so there have appeared numerous studies which directly or indirectly relate to the sociological study of the Old Testament and ancient Israel. In most cases these are studies of the social history of Israel and have little in the way of explicit sociological theory. In all cases they do, however, presuppose such a theory and may usually be fairly clearly fitted within one or other of the two sociological traditions described in this essay. It is impossible to cover all relevant discussion, especially within a limited space; it is possible, however, to review briefly a representative selection of contributions to the two chief sociological concerns: the nature of Israelite society, and Israelite religion in Israelite society. It is with regard to the sociological theory presupposed by these contributions that they are approached, and so they will be divided between those that reflect the Weber tradition and those which belong to the Durkheim tradition.

A. The Weber tradition in recent Old Testament study

(i) Israel

Thiel (1980) stands fully in line with the Alt–Noth school though he brings to that approach, which otherwise has such a strong literary orientation, a broad and comprehensive sociological support. There is little in the way of sociological theory in Thiel's closely documented study, but his general approach to his topic and many detailed comments and observations indicate his adherence to the Weber tradition; in fact, his work thoroughly updates Weber's own understanding of pre-monarchic Israel in the light of more recent study. He gives a detailed account of the nature of bedouin society, semi-nomadism and urban society, seeing Israel's origins mainly within the semi-nomadic context and her settlement as a long and largely peaceful process leading from semi-nomadic pastoralism with subsidiary agriculture through a more equally distributed economic practice to a full agrarian economy with subsidiary pastoralism. From earliest time Israel was of heterogeneous composition; her community consciousness over against the Canaanites was based on common faith in

Yahweh. Although the amphictyony analogy has become doubtful, one must, in Thiel's view, understand some institutional form for her religious unity.

The problem of how Israelite identity received institutional expression is particularly acute within the Weber tradition, especially in the light of the demise of the amphictyony analogy. Many of the arguments involved here are not in general of a sociological nature, but rather very much concerned with the dating and reference of Old Testament texts; they need not, therefore, be reviewed at this point.[10] An exception is Gottwald's point (1980, 345ff.) that whereas in the classical world the amphictyony was a cultic institution adopted by a people already united in military and other leagues, in Israel it has been made to serve a much more comprehensive role, being the very framework within which Israel's political, social and ethnic consciousness was formed. This in itself probably implies an illegitimate use of the analogy, and so the question of how Israelite identity and self-understanding in the pre-monarchic period were expressed is still very much an open question.

Dietrich (1979) has described a contrast between Canaanite and Israelite in terms of two very different cultures: an urban society marked by strict social classification, concentrated wealth, division of labour; and a rural tribal society marked by social equality, little specialisation in labour and property held in common. This contrast he has traced into the monarchic period, seeing it as the framework within which royal policies should be understood. This is a common paradigm within which to place Canaanite and Israelite, but the contrast should not be seen in too simplistic terms. Frick's study (1977) of the Israelite city has shown that many urban–rural contrasts are typical of industrialised society, and should not be read into the pre-industrial situation; before industrialisation cities retained a strong tie with agriculture and the rural community; they depended on the hinterland for food while the hinterland depended on the city for a market. The city, moreover, was small, covering an area of between five and ten acres with a population ranging between one and three thousand, many of whom led an agricultural life. Israel's early social development he describes as a movement from a pastoral and agricultural patriarchalism to a loosely structured society of city states, into which the monarchy introduced a centralised bureaucracy. A difference between Canaanite and Israelite understood in terms of a distinction between urban and rural is scarcely realistic, at any rate for the monarchic period.[11] Moreover, even if a cultural dualism of this nature is partially applicable to the pre-monarchic period, it is unlikely that this of itself can supply a sufficient basis for Israelite ethnic self-consciousness.

(ii) Israelite religion

Some recent study of Israelite religion is by no means incompatible with this complexity in the study of Israelite society. Not only is it now most unlikely that early Israel considered herself to stand in a covenant relationship with Yahweh (Nicholson: 1986), but it is also becoming clear (Lang: 1983) that the presentation of Yahweh as the only God of Israel from the pre-monarchic period onwards is a late construction which runs up against great historical difficulties. The worship of Yahweh alone was the programme of an active pressure group within Israel which came to dominance particularly in times of crisis, and the breakthrough to monotheism was achieved only in the setting of that final catastrophe when the prophetic demand for Yahweh's exclusive worship, with its threat of punishment for disobedience, was vindicated. This was a movement promoted by prophets throughout Israel's history, figures whom Weber called 'charismatic' in order to express their creativeness as individual sources of innovation and indeed revolution against both rational bureaucracy and traditionalism.

Discussion of charisma has tended to concentrate on pre-monarchic leadership and the monarchy. Malamat (1976; also Weisman: 1977) has given it a full sociological treatment, closely following Weber and emphasising that it can be isolated only as an ideal type rather than historically. This is perhaps the resolution to some of the problems posed by Alt's application of the type to kings in Israel, for it is quite clear, *contra* Alt, that a distinction cannot be drawn between charismatic and dynastic kingship (Thornton: 1963; Buccellati: 1967, 195ff.): kingship was by nature dynastic, though that does not exclude, and indeed it might even require, that it should exhibit charismatic traits. This is, in fact, more faithful to Weber's own view (1947, 382) that the nature of authority is historically never simple, and that, for example, the legal authority of a government cannot be purely legal but requires a charismatic element if its prestige is not to be undermined.

More problematic, however, is Weber's own use of the term charisma for the prophets: the prophets in Weber's view were solitary and independent individuals (1952, 286ff.), but he analyzed charisma as a type of relationship between a leader and his followers (1947: 358ff.). It is possible that the type of the prophet should be distinguished from the type of the charismatic (Petersen: 1979, 132ff.), but it is probably more satisfactory to modify Weber's understanding of the prophets, to see them less as solitary outsiders than as powers for radicalisation from within (Berger: 1963, 940ff.), who were recognised and followed either by defined groups of disciples or by less closely bonded elements scattered throughout Israelite society.

Finally, in this context, reference should be made to the study of apocalyptic by Hanson (1979; also Plöger: 1968), which, using Troeltsch, Weber and Mannheim, argues that apocalyptic movements, alienated from central religious and political institutions, constructed an alternative symbolic universe, characterised by visionary expectation of the intervention of God into history to effect their deliverance, salvation and vindication. The conflict was between a church, regarded as being compromised with the world, co-extensive with society, rationalised and formalised, and a sect, a primary social group, rejecting the values of the dominant society and maintaining the original pure faith; and its expression in literature reflects the contrast between ideology, which justifies and maintains the status quo, and utopia, which is the vision of transformation.[12]

B. The Durkheim tradition in recent Old Testament study

(i) Israel

Gottwald has been strongly criticised by Brandfon (1981) for using the same idealist approach which in others he rejected: for Gottwald, Marxism plays the role that in other reconstructions is played by Yahwism. Brandfon's further point, that Gottwald ignores the possibility that Israelite social egalitarianism in Canaan may have been an unintended consequence of a variety of events, expresses a primarily materialist approach which has serious consequences. It leads to a devaluation of reconstructions based on the Old Testament (for which the rise of Israel was certainly not accidental or unintended), and encourages the attribution of a primary role to non-biblical sources which allow a better understanding of Israel's environment and may provide sociological models within the framework of which Israel might be understood. So Whitelam (1986) and Chaney (1986) criticise current history-writing for its concern with the unique event or individual, which proceeds from the belief that great men make history, and argue that dependence on the written sources which reflect this bias must be given up in favour of developing long-term perspectives based on archaeology. History-writing concentrated on the individual is rejected as idealist, as a failure to recognise that the individual is simply part of a totally integrated system which is ultimately dependably related to an agricultural and environmental foundation.

In recent years Durkheim's description of Israel as a segmentary society

(1933, 177) has been revived, and it has been argued, especially by Crüsemann (1978, 201ff.) and Schäfer-Lichtenberger (1983, 333ff.), that pre-monarchic Israel was a genealogically ordered segmentary society comprising equal unilinear descent groups. Certain problems have been perceived in this analogy, however, and it has been noted (Lemche: 1985, 219ff.) that segmentary division is characteristic also, if not mainly, of non-egalitarian societies or chiefdoms. The model of the chiefdom has been considered as an analogy, either for Israel under Saul and the early part of David's reign (Flanagan: 1981; Frick: 1985, 71ff., 191ff.), or, as an association of chiefdoms, for Israel in the time of the judges (Rogerson: 1986, 22ff.). It is characteristic of chiefdoms that theocratic claims are made on behalf of the chief; such claims give a religious focus to power and help to overcome and transcend the structural weaknesses of stateless societies.

In the search for the foundation of the Israelite system (whatever model may be used to describe it), a search for the 'why' rather than the 'what' of Israelite history and society, Coote and Whitelam (1986; 1987) propose to see Israel's emergence in the context of agrarian relations and processes extending over millenia. Israel emerged during an imperial power vacuum associated with a decline in trade which destroyed the economic base of urban society and promoted agriculture and pastoralism in the highlands of Palestine as a means of risk reduction. The Israelite monarchy was the result of numerous internal and external social and environmental forces best understood by use of Carneiro's theory of circumscription (so also Hauer: 1986), according to which, an increasingly limited geographical area leads to a struggle for limited resources, which in turn results in a hierarchical social system. Similarly, Frick (1985), having reviewed some general theories which see history as evolutionary process, argues for a synthetic approach which sees the state developing from a chiefdom as a result of a number of factors relating to variation in agricultural risk, diversity and productivity, as well as to the size and character of the environment, the two most important environmental determinants being water and soil. The state arose in a process of adaptive transformations in which the role of agriculture is of first importance.

(ii) Israelite religion

Israelite religion understood as the expression of social identity or as dependably related to society is presupposed in Brueggemann's description (1979) of two trajectories to be traced through the religious history of Israel, each reflecting the theology/ideology of different social groups: the Moses covenant trajectory, rooted in the Israelite tribal community, and the Davidic covenant trajectory, with its universalist ideology of social stability rather than of social transformation and liberation.

The work of Douglas (1966) and Soler (1979) also belongs in this context, though the straightforward sociological determinism of Durkheim does not appear. Rather, with a closer dependence on Lévi-Strauss, they argue that the classificatory systems which appear in the dietary laws of the Hebrews derive not directly from the social world but rather are part of that social world which as a whole reflects the activity of the mind in ordering and classifying in a 'binary' way (Hamnett: 1984, 211ff.). Clean animals are those which conform to the classificatory system by which reality is perceived, while the unclean are those which do not conform. The distinction thus becomes symbolic of the Hebrew understanding of the nature of divine order in creation.

The studies of prophecy by Wilson (1980) and Petersen (1981) do not offer an analysis of the social structure within which the prophets functioned, but they do presuppose a concept of society as a pre-existent reality which in time of stress and rapid social change produces prophets. Prophets are seen as 'intermediaries' who function as spokesmen for support groups. With the help of the work of Lewis especially, intermediaries are divided into two groups: peripheral intermediaries appear in minority groups, and their activities may maintain social stability by providing a dynamic way of alleviating tensions between minorities and the majority; central intermediaries belong to the central social and religious institutions and their concern for the maintenance of society is expressed in preaching strongly infused with politics and morality. Wilson has applied the paradigm to the extra-biblical context as well as to Israel, and argues for the possibility of movement between the different settings: the central intermediary may be forced out of his position to the periphery, while the peripheral intermediary may enlarge his support group to the point that it becomes the majority in society.

Petersen's study also has a narrower theoretical interest in the analysis of prophetic ecstasy by means of role theory. The theory presupposes (Berger: 1966, 110ff.) that society's determination of individuals takes place through given social roles which individuals enact and which shape their being. Role theory is not just a description of various social activities; it supplies a social anthropology. Men play dramatic parts in the great play of society, and the individual is the masks that he must wear to do so. The self is not simply a given entity but a process continuously created and recreated in each social situation that one enters. Petersen notes that role theory is also concerned with the intensity with which a person enacts a role, and that the level of involvement may be plotted on a spectrum marked off in stages ranging from effective non-involvement through routine involvement, ritual acting, engrossed acting, classical hypnotic role taking, histrionic neurosis, ecstasy and bewitchment. Prophetic behaviour, he believes, was probably never so intense as the stage of ecstasy.

v Conclusion

Much, if not most, of the recent explicitly sociological study of the Old Testament and ancient Israel stands in the Durkheim tradition. As Herion (1986) has noted, it is marked by positivism (the only valid form of knowledge is objective knowledge of the kind accepted by the natural sciences), reductionism (the tendency to explain the complex in terms of the simple, as through the use of models), relativism (issues of morality and religion are never wholly right or wrong in any absolute sense), and determinism (the tendency to think that human values, choices and action are determined by certain variables in the social and cultural environment).[13] The situation would be little changed by the adoption of Runciman's sociological methodology advocated by Rogerson (1985), for this approach, which distinguishes particularly between the explanatory level (which may exhibit the characteristics noted above) and the descriptive level (which is concerned with what it was like to be in a particular society or situation), does not allow the beliefs and actions of individuals to be real causes of events and situations, but treats the actions of individuals as determined by social and economic forces, and their beliefs as epiphenomena of material circumstances.

In following this approach, sociological study of the Old Testament and ancient Israel may be falling behind recent advances in sociological theory, for, if Giddens (1987, 6ff., 52ff.; and also Gouldner: 1970) is right, there is coming into existence a fresh understanding of the nature of human action which, with certain significant qualifications, works with the idea of human freedom. These qualifications concern, firstly, the relationship between cultural convention and individual action, a relationship to be understood on the analogy of Saussure's linguistic model of relationship between *langue* and *parole*, and, secondly, the intertwining of what is intended with what is not intended in the consequences of human action. This latter point is of particular significance, since it allows not only for the unforeseen consequences which arise from the fact that individual action takes place in the context of a social and cultural system, but also for the fact that individuals have both conscious and unconscious motives for their actions, and the latter as well as the former have social consequences.[14]

The restoration of the individual to society, in the qualified form that Giddens describes, implies the recognition that great men do make history, even though in doing so they not only shape but are shaped by the conventions of their age. Moreover, it opens the way to an expansion of studies, such as that of Carroll (1979), which make the fullest possible use of social psychology in the understanding of Israelite religion and society. As far as the religion of Israel is concerned, if it is true that society is to be understood in terms of men creatively acting in response to their cultural and material environment, then their thinking, including their religious thinking, is part of that ordering activity. Israel's religion is not then simply an objectification of primary social realities, but rather a part of that process of culture formation through which men order their worlds.

Notes

Much of the work on this essay was done during a period of research in Tübingen generously supported by the Alexander von Humboldt-Stiftung.

1 For other, and differently organised, accounts of the influence of sociological thinking on Old Testament study, cf. Hahn: 1966, 157ff.; Kraus: 1972; Schottroff: 1974; Frick and Gottwald: 1983.

2 The label 'functionalist' implies a view of society as an interlocking system to be analysed in a holistic way. For a discussion tracing the nature and history of the approach, cf. Swingewood: 1984, 227ff.

3 Robertson Smith was himself influenced by *The Ancient City* by Fustel de Coulanges, one of Durkheim's teachers; cf. Lukes: 1975, 61ff., and especially Beidelman: 1974.

4 This 'teleological' approach has been criticised as possibly justifying its explanations in terms of the *telos* rather than in relation to the successive sets of circumstances which make up the whole historical sequence (Rogerson: 1985, 253). This objection has a certain force, though it should be noted that Weber's intention was not to write a history of Israel; cf. also Fahey: 1982, 63, who notes that the decisive questions for Weber are 'wherein the indubitable peculiarity of Israelite religious development lies' and 'how that peculiarity is historically conditioned' (Weber: 1952, 428). Weber's use of the term 'pariah people' has also been criticised as both a value-loaded term and as lacking a sufficient basis in history (Guttmann: 1925, 219f.; Schmueli: 1968, 182ff.). However, given the qualifications which Weber himself attached to its use (1952, 3f.; 1963, 108ff.), it may still be accepted (as an ideal type) as a useful perspective from which to approach ancient Judaism.

5 The role which Weber assigned to the Levites came under early criticism from Guttmann (1925, 215ff.), but even he acknowledged that if the Levites did not provide such religious leadership in pre-prophetic times some such leadership must be found.

6 The description of organic solidarity which Causse gives, however, corresponds rather to what Durkheim termed mechanical solidarity.

7 Reuss was a predecessor of Causse in Strasbourg; he had studied in Germany and introduced evolutionary historical criticism into French biblical scholarship.

8 Lévy-Bruhl's views form a large part of the background of the theory of 'corporate personality', associated especially with H. Wheeler Robinson and A. R. Johnson, which has likewise come under recent criticism; cf. Rogerson: 1970.

9 See reviews by Lenski (1980) and Brueggemann (1983). Much of Gottwald's social analysis finds earlier presentation in de Geus (1976); the latter's definition of the totality of Israel in terms of *connubium* and *forum* is preferable to Gottwald's much vaguer Israelite federation. Gottwald, however, is treated here rather than de Geus because of the much more explicitly sociological nature of his work.

10 For a survey, with bibliography, cf. my study (1985, 56ff.).

11 Alt's separation of Jerusalem and Samaria as independent city states has been strongly criticised by Buccellati (1967, 181ff.) and Schäfer-Lichtenberger (1983, 369ff.). Alt's theory may represent a too hasty application to a particular historical situation of what for Weber was an ideal type.

12 A critical response to Hanson has been given by Kovacs (1976) who suggests alternative ways of interpreting apocalyptic using sociological models different from those adopted by Hanson.

13 Herion has, however, introduced some confusion into an otherwise valuable analysis by accusing Wilson and Gottwald of attributing the same kind of relativistic thinking to the ancient Israelites themselves.

14 For a discussion of the relationship between psychoanalytic theory and sociology cf. Bocock (1976); and for a vigorous argument for the use of psychoanalytic theory in the understanding of history, cf. Gay (1985).

Bibliography

Alt, A., 1966 (a). 'The Formation of the Israelite State in Palestine', *Essays on Old Testament History and Religion*, Oxford: Blackwell, 173–237 (translated by R. A. Wilson from *Die Staatenbildung der Israeliten in Palästina*, Reformationsprogramm der Universität Leipzig 1930; later published in *Kleine Schriften zur Geschichte des Volkes Israel* II, München: C. H. Beck 1953, 1–65).

1966 (b). 'The Monarchy in the Kingdoms of Israel and Judah', *Essays on Old Testament History and Religion*, Oxford Blackwell, 241–59 (translated by R. A. Wilson from 'Das Königtum in den Reichen Israel und Juda', *VT* 1, 1951, 2–22; later published in *Kleine Schriften zur Geschichte des Volkes Israel* II, München: C. H. Beck 1953, 116–34).

Beidelman, T. O., 1974. *W. Robertson Smith and the Sociological Study of Religion*, Chicago: Univ. of Chicago Press.

Berger, P., 1963. 'Charisma and Religious Innovation: the social location of Israelite prophecy', *American Sociological Review*, 28, 940–50.

1966. *Invitation to Sociology*, Harmondsworth: Penguin.

Bocock, R., 1976. *Freud and Modern Society*, Walton-on-Thames: Nelson.

Brandfon, F. R. 1981. 'Norman Gottwald on the Tribes of Yahweh', *JSOT* 21, 101–10.

Brueggemann, W., 1979. 'Trajectories in Old Testament Literature and the Sociology of Ancient Israel', *JBL* 98, 161–85.

1983. 'Review of N. K. Gottwald, *The Tribes of Yahweh*', *The Bible and Liberation: Political and Social Hermeneutics*, edited by N. K. Gottwald, New York: Orbis, 173–81.

Buccellati, G., 1967. *Cities and Nations of Ancient Syria: An Essay on Political Institutions with Special Reference to the Israelite Kingdoms*, Studii Semitic: 26, Rome Università di Roma.
Carroll, R. P., 1979. *When Prophecy Failed: Reactions and Responses to Failure in the Old Testament Prophetic Traditions*, London: SCM.
Causse, A., 1937. *Du groupe ethnique à la communauté religieuse. Le problème sociologique de la religion d'Israel*, Études d'histoire et de philosophie religieuses publiées par le faculté de theologie protestante de l'université de Strasbourg No. 33, Paris: Felix Alcan.
Chaney, M. L., 1986. 'Systemic Study of the Israelite Monarchy', *Semeia* 37, 53–76.
Collins, R., 1985. *Three Sociological Traditions*, Oxford: OUP.
Coote, R. B. & Whitelam, K., 1986. 'The Emergence of Israel: Social Transformation and State Formation following the Decline in Late Bronze Age Trade', *Semeia* 37, 107–47.
1987. *The Emergence of Early Israel in Historical Perspective*, Sheffield: Almond Press.
Crüsemann, F., 1978. *Der Widerstand gegen das Königtum: Die antiköniglichen Texte des Alten Testamentes und der Kampf um den frühen israelitischen Staat*, WMANT 49, Neukirchen: Neukirchener Verlag.
Dietrich, W., 1979. *Israel und Kanaan: vom Ringen zweier Gesellschaftssysteme*, Stuttgarter Bibelstudien 94, Stuttgart: Katholisches Bibelwerk.
Douglas, M., 1966. *Purity and Danger: an analysis of the concepts of pollution and taboo*. London: Routledge & Kegan Paul.
Durkheim, E., 1915. *The Elementary Forms of the Religious Life*, London: Allen & Unwin (translated by J. W. Swain from *Les formes élémentaires de la vie religieuse: le système totémique en Australie*, Paris, 1912).
1933. *The Division of Labour in Society*, New York: Free Press (translated by G. Simpson from the 1st [1893] and 5th [1926] editions of *De la division du travail social*).
Evans Pritchard, E. E., 1965. *Theories of Primitive Religion*, Oxford: OUP.
Fahey, T., 1982. 'Max Weber's Ancient Judaism', *American Journal of Sociology* 88, 62–87.
Flanagan, J. W., 1981. 'Chiefs in Israel', *JSOT* 20: 47–73.
Frick, S., 1977. *The City in Ancient Israel*, SBL Dissertation Series 36, Missoula: Scholars Press.
1985. *The Formation of the State in Ancient Israel: a Survey of Models and Theories*, Sheffield: JSOT Press.
Frick, F. S. & Gottwald, N. K., 1983. 'The Social World of Ancient Israel', *The Bible and Liberation: Political and Social Hermeneutics*, edited by N. K. Gottwald, New York: Orbis, 149–165.
Gay, P., 1985. *Freud for Historians*, Oxford: OUP.
de Geus, C. H. J., 1976. *The Tribes of Israel: an investigation into some of the presuppositions of Martin Noth's amphictyony hypothesis*, Assen: Van Gorcum.
Giddens, A., 1971. *Capitalism and Modern Social Theory: an analysis of the writings of Marx, Durkheim and Max Weber*, Cambridge: CUP.
1987. *Social Theory and Modern Sociology*, Oxford: Blackwell.
Gottwald, N. K., 1980. *The Tribes of Yahweh: a sociology of the religion of liberated Israel, 1250–1050 B.C.E.*, London: SCM.
Gouldner, A. W., 1971. *The Coming Crisis of Western Sociology*, London: Heinemann.
Guttmann, J., 1925. 'Max Webers Soziologie des antiken Judentums', *Monatsschrift für Geschichte und Wissenschaft des Judentums* 69, 195–223.

Hahn, H. F., 1954. *The Old Testament in Modern Research,* London: SCM.

Hamnett, J., 1984. 'Durkheim and the Study of Religion', *Durkheim and Modern Sociology*, edited by S. Fenton, Cambridge: CUP, 202–18.

Hanson, P. D., 1979. *The Dawn of Apocalyptic: The Historical and Sociological Roots of Jewish Apocalyptic Eschatology*, Philadelphia: Fortress Press.

Hauer, C., 1986. 'From Alt to Anthropology: The Rise of the Israelite State', *JSOT* 36, 3–15.

Herion, G. A., 1986. 'The Impact of Modern and Social Scientific Assumptions on the Reconstruction of Israelite History', *JSOT* 34, 3–33.

Kimbrough, S. T., 1978. *Israelite Religion in Sociological Perspective: the work of Antonin Causse*, Studies in Oriental Religions, vol. 4, Wiesbaden: Otto Harrassowitz.

Kovacs, B. W., 1976. 'Contributions of Sociology to the Study of the Development of Apocalypticism: a theoretical survey', Consultation on the Social World of Ancient Israel SBL: St. Louis (32pp).

Kraus, H. J., 1972. 'Die Anfänge der religionssoziologische Forschungen in der alttestamentlichen Wissenschaft', *Biblisch-theologische Aufsätze*, Neukirchen: Neukirchener Verlag, 296–310.

Lang, B., 1983. *Monotheism and the Prophetic Minority: an essay in biblical history and sociology*, Sheffield: JSOT Press.

Lemche, N. P., 1985. *Early Israel,* SVT 37, Leiden: Brill.

Lenski, G., 1980. 'Review of N. K. Gottwald, *The Tribes of Yahweh*', *Religious Studies Review* 6/4, 275–8.

Lukes, S., 1975. *Émile Durkheim: His Life and Work, a Historical and Critical Study*, Harmondsworth: Penguin.

Malamat, A., 1976. 'Charismatic Leadership in the Book of Judges', *Magnalia Dei. The Mighty Acts of God: Essays on the Bible and Archaeology in Memory of G. Ernest Wright*, edited by F. M. Cross, W. E. Lemke, P. D. Miller, Garden City, New York: Doubleday, 152–68.

Mayes, A. D. H., 1985. *Judges*, Sheffield: JSOT Press.

Nicholson, E. W., 1986. *God and His People. Covenant and Theology in the Old Testament*, Oxford: OUP.

Nisbet, R., 1967. *The Sociological Tradition*, London: Heinemann.

Noth, M., 1930. *Das System der Zwölf Stämme Israels*, BWANT IV/I, Stuttgart: Kohlhammer.

Petersen, D. L., 1979. 'Max Weber and the Sociological Study of Ancient Israel', *Sociological Inquiry* 49, 117–49.

1981. *The Roles of Israel's Prophets,* JSOT Suppl. 17, Sheffield: JSOT Press.

Plöger, O., 1968. *Theocracy and Eschatology*, Oxford: Blackwell (translated by S. Rudman from *Theokratie und Eschatologie*, WMANT 2, Neukirchen-Vluyn: Neukirchener Verlag, 1959,[2] 1962).

Rogerson , J., 1970. 'The Hebrew Conception of Corporate Personality', *JTS* 21, 1–16.

1978. *Anthropology and the Old Testament*, Oxford: Blackwell.

1985. 'The Use of Sociology in Old Testament Studies', SVT 36, 245–56.

1986. 'Was Early Israel a Segmentary Society?', *JSOT* 36, 17–26.

Schäfer-Lichtenberger, C., 1983. *Stadt und Eidgenossenschaft im Alten Testament: Eine Auseinandersetzung mit Max Webers Studie 'Das antike Judentum'*, BZAW 156, Berlin: de Gruyter.

Schmueli, E., 1968. 'The "Pariah People" and its "Charismatic Leadership". A Revaluation of Max Weber's "Ancient Judaism"', *Proceedings of the American Academy for Jewish Research* 36, 167–247.

Schottroff, W., 1974. 'Soziologie und Altes Testament', *Verkündigung und Forschung* 19, 46–66.

Smith, W. R., 1927 [1890]. *Lectures on the Religion of the Semites*,[3] London: A & C Black.

Soler, J., 1979. 'The Dietary Prohibitions of the Hebrews', *New York Review of Books* 26/10, 24–30.

Swingewood, A., 1984. *A Short History of Sociological Thought*, London: Macmillan.

Thiel, W., 1980. *Die soziale Entwicklung Israels in vorstaatlichen Zeit*, Berlin: Evangelisches Verlagsanstalt.

Thomas, J. J. R., 1985. 'Ideology and Elective Affinity', *Sociology* 19, 39–54.

Thornton, T. C. G., 1963. 'Charismatic Kingship in Israel and Judah', *JTS* 14, 1–11.

Weber, M., 1930. *The Protestant Ethic and the Spirit of Capitalism*, London: Allen & Unwin (translated by Talcott Parsons from 'Die protestantische Ethik und der Geist des Kapitalismus', *Archiv für Sozialwissenschaft und sozialpolitik*, vols. 20 and 21, 1904–5, reprinted in *Gesammelte Aufsätze zur Religionssoziologie*, I, Tübingen 1920, 17–206).

1947. *The Theory of Social and Economic Organization*, New York: Free Press (translated by A. M. Henderson and Talcott Parsons from *Wirtschaft und Gesellschaft*, Part I, 1925).

1948. *From Max Weber in Sociology*, London: Routledge & Kegan Paul (translated and edited by H. H. Gerth and C. Wright Mills).

1952. *Ancient Judaism*, New York: Free Press (translated and edited by H. H. Gerth and D. Martindale from 'Das antike Judentum', *Archiv für Sozialwissenschaft und Sozialforschung*, 1917–19, reprinted in *Gesammelte Aufsätze zur Religionssoziologie* III, Tübingen 1921).

1963. *Sociology of Religion*, London: Methuen 1963 (translated by Ephraim Fischoff from 'Religionssoziologie' in *Wirtschaft und Gesellschaft*,[4] Tübingen 1956).

Weisman, S., 1977. 'Charismatic Leaders in the Era of the Judges', *ZAW* 89, 399–411.

Whitelam, K., 1986. 'Recreating the History of Israel', *JSOL* 35, 45–70.

Wilson, R. R., 1980. *Prophecy and Society in Ancient Israel*, Philadelphia: Fortress Press.

PART II

Israel

CHAPTER FOUR

Ecology, agriculture and patterns of settlement

FRANK S. FRICK

A significant gap separates anthropologists from biblical scholars with respect to historical explanation. Histories of ancient Israel, especially when treating Israel's origins on the LB–Iron I horizon, are written either from a viewpoint which views history as the story of deliberate actions of discrete persons or groups, usually in the political sphere, or from one which focuses upon tools and techniques, abstracting technological advances from environmental demographic configurations of the agricultural system in which they developed.

Such approaches, however, are ill-suited for explaining the cultural change which occurs in the emergence of ancient Israel. In an attempt to plug the explanatory gap the fiction of incursions of new ethnic groups has been employed. New 'types' in the archaeological record are attributed to newly arrived peoples, with little consideration given to explanations which assume a systemic view of ancient society in which the processes of societal change are seen as responses to risks stemming from environmental constraints and as attempts to develop subsistence strategies to minimise such risks.

Anthropologists, by contrast, typically approach historical explanation by regarding societies as problem-solving systems, the constituent parts of which are linked by a series of feedback mechanisms, whereby alterations in one part of the system effect system-wide change. The path to an understanding of social history is generalisation, the formulation of general relationships between events and sociocultural processes, of which specific individual occurrences and phenomena are concrete expressions or manifestations.

An area in which such generalisations have been of interest to anthropological archaeologists, and one applicable here, is that of the evolution of complex societies. One approach to sociocultural evolution takes as its starting point the idea of ecological succession, succession being a descriptive term referring to the classification of ecological systems in terms of increasing complexity over time. Taxonomy, however, is not substituted for analysis of sociocultural processes, but provides a framework for assessing what is present in a system at a given point in time and what changes take place in the relationships between the variables as it develops. Ecological succession thus introduces the concepts of energy, information and structure in a systemic matrix, and opens the way for the notion of 'predatory expansion' (Sahlins, 1962), in which one sociocultural form is better adapted than, and thus prevails over, alternative adjustments within a particular ecological niche or niches.

This approach views cultural evolution as the 'output' or effect of any one or more of a number of factors. It recognizes that there is no single causal nexus.

Two systemic models of cultural evolution are of interest here. One, proposed by Barbara Price (1978), assumes a hierarchy of function in which some cultural traits bear more explanatory weight than others. In Price's model, traits topping the hierarchy are ones linked to the harnessing, distribution and control of energy. The more energy encapsulated in a piece of data, the more reliable is its use as evidence. How can such a hierarchy be discerned from archaeological and ethnographic data? Price maintains that many archaeological criteria used in attempts to explain culture change, usually based overwhelmingly upon ceramic evidence, as well as much of the ethnographic evidence, are of little use. They are largely secondary features representing little energy expenditure. Stronger confirmation of social, political, and economic processes stems from other evidence, such as the scale or mass of architectural features. Construction projects represent a transformation of energy into matter, energy produced and circulated in a human community.

Another reliable class of data which can be used in sociocultural explanation is settlement patterns, which represent the material isomorph of the entire mode of production. Thus in Price's model it is primarily architectural and settlement data that provide reliable evidence of sociocultural integration and processes of sociocultural change.

Following Price's lead, in considering cultural change in ancient Israel, attention should be given both to architectural and settlement pattern data, especially to the intrasite aggregation and intersite patterning of agricultural-pastoral settlements as they reflect a combination of environmental and sociocultural factors.

While Price's model does not treat agriculture explicitly, that of Sanders and Webster does (1978). Their model proposes a modified multilineal paradigm in which different evolutionary trajectories can be seen as relating to variations in agricultural risk, diversity, and productivity, as well as to the nature of the environment. They propose a hierarchy with the degree of agricultural risk and diversity as first-order factors, and second-order factors being those related to the properties of the environmental niche.

Risk, a first order factor, involves: 'Any environmental parameters essential to production of energy (e.g., moisture, temperature) with wide, relatively frequent, and unpredictable variations' (Sanders and Webster, 1978: 253). Since this factor affects different ecological niches in different ways, corresponding productive diversity is expected.

Diversity, another first order factor, entails 'The closeness and pattern of spacing of contrasting environmental conditions significant in terms of human exploitation' (Sanders and Webster, 1978:253). Diversity concerns the extent to which a society embraces different ecological zones and the relationship of those zones to one another.

Productivity, a second order factor, is 'The potential of the landscape to produce energy in the form of subsistence products for the support of human populations' (Sanders and Webster, 1978:261). While there are ecological constraints to the level of production, what is pertinent here is the role of such cultural factors as levels of technology, social organisation and information flow.

The geographical area of early Israel constitutes, according to Sanders and Webster, an example of 'type A' productivity. This means that agricultural intensification increases the input–output ratio and the demographic capacity of the land. This kind of productivity typically occurs in arid or semi-arid areas like Palestine, where agricultural intensification involves technological innovations that have a measurable effect both upon agricultural yields and crop security.

Considering the two factors of risk and diversity, early Israel can be characterised as including medium- and high-risk environments and medium-diversity environments with 'type A' productivity. Combining these factors, the model predicts that within a circumscribed area, high-risk environments should be settled by agricultural societies later than low-risk regions, assuming that choices are available. Stimulus for intensive cultivation is high and it should appear early. Assuming that the relationship between population growth and agricultural productivity is mutual-causal rather than linear, population growth should be rapid once the area is settled. Population distribution should be uneven, reflecting adaptation to lower-risk zones and zones available for intensification (Sanders and Webster, 1978:298).

This model, combining control of ecological variables and multilineal trajectories of change with an overtly systemic evolutionary approach, is one which in our estimation lends itself well to the situation in ancient Israel, its agricultural base, ecological setting, and settlement patterns.

Agriculture and social organisation in early Israel

What is agriculture and what does it do? Agriculture is 'the deliberate caring for, manipulation of, or cultivation of plants so as to enhance their utility for human consumption or use' (Athens, 1977:362). Agriculture concentrates usable productivity, increasing consumable yield per unit area of land. It involves human intervention in the ecosystem process, seeking to maintain an artificial ecosystem.

Agriculture thus encompasses both techno-environmental and societal concerns, so what is called for is an analysis of the way in which differential constraints imposed by the internal functioning of varying levels of agricultural intensification, together with the extent of agricultural risk and diversity, provide the setting for social mechanisms and processes to operate as the strategies for dealing with the particular problems that arise in a given environment.

A. The ecology of the Palestinian Hill Country

It is now established fact, whatever historical reconstruction one may endorse, whether of the 'conquest', 'settlement', or 'revolt' variety, that ancient Israel initially became established as a recognisable sociopolitical entity in the Palestinian Hill Country.

Events surrounding Israel's formative stages in the time of Samuel, Saul, and David, all focused on the Central Highlands, with subsequent movement into the lowlands, into the plains of Jezreel and Esdraelon, to the Huleh basin, onto the coastal plain of Philistia and the western Shephelah, into the Transjordan, and finally into the Negev, as secondary expansion following upon the success of Israel's having become established in the Central Highlands.

What are the ecological parameters of this region (geomorphology, climate, natural vegetation and soils) and how are they related to the key variables of agricultural risk and diversity?

1. *Meteorological variables in the Central Highlands*

In order to utilise meteorological data which derive from modern meteorological observations, the question of whether or not there have been significant changes in climate since the LB-Iron I period must be addressed. It seems clear that general climatic patterns in Palestine have not changed significantly since around 6,000 or 7,000 BC (Baly, 1974). With respect to agricultural risk, however, there is the crucial factor of variations within general climatic patterns. Considering these, Baly says: 'That climate is not static but rather in a state of constant fluctuation is now beyond doubt, and it would be a great mistake to take any set of climatic figures as "normal"' (1974:65).

When a map delineating the regions of early Israelite settlement in the Highlands (cf. Aharoni, 1967:196) is superimposed on one depicting average annual rainfall (cf. *Atlas of Israel*: IV/2), it appears that while the entire area falls within the 200 + mm./year range in a 'rainy year' (e.g. 1944/45), in a 'dry year' (e.g. 1946/47) a good portion of the area falls to the 100–200 mm. range.

Such observations emphasise the worthlessness of simple mean annual rainfall amounts when assessing agricultural risk and diversity. A dry year within a series of normal or wet years rarely has serious consequences for agriculture. But Palestine, like other semi-arid regions suffers from occurrences of series of sub-normal years. Amiran observes that three consecutive dry years, each with negative deviations of thirty per cent or more from average values are too often part of the experience of farmers: 'Whereas a farmer can weather a single dry year, a series of such years spells want' (1964:104). Coincidentally, Amiran's three-year figure is used to describe the disastrous drought in the time of Elijah (1 Kgs. 18.1) and becomes a biblical yardstick for measuring agricultural disaster. Baly confirms the tenacity of this yardstick in the lament of modern farmers, 'We have had no rain for three years', meaning not that there literally had been no rain, but that the rain had been insufficient to produce adequate harvests (1974:74). Thus special importance attaches to the variability of annual rainfall.

In assessing rainfall in the central highland chain, Jerusalem is chosen as a site representative of the Highlands. This represents a maximal choice, in that no areas in the region exceed Jerusalem in mean annual rainfall. This choice is also recommended by the fact that there exists for Jerusalem the longest series of recorded rainfall data in the eastern Mediterranean area. Such data are available for Jersusalem for 106 of the 108 years from 1846/47 to 1953/54 (Rosenan, 1955). Amiran (1964:104), in testing for series of years with a negative deviation of 30 per cent or more, constructs two statistical summaries, one covering a dry cycle and the other a rainy one.

It is significant that even in the 18-year *rainy* cycle (1944/45–1961/62) five years had negative deviations of 30 per cent or more. Even more critical is the spacing of these dry years.

	Total amount of deviation	No. of years of occurrence
Dry cycle (1920/21–1937/38)		
Number of years		18
Positive deviations	26	4
Negative deviations	365	14
Positive deviations of 30% or more	0	0
Negative deviations of 30% or more	283	7
Negative deviations of 50% or more	106	2
Rainy cycle (1944/45–1961/62)		
Number of years		18
Positive deviations	85.4	4
Negative deviations	369	14
Positive deviations of 30% or more	79	2
Negative deviations of 30% or more	243	5
Negative deviations of 50% or more	117	2

The Jerusalem rainfall data for the period 1920/21 to 1960/61 can also be represented in a histogram, in which each asterisk represents a 4 per cent deviation from the mean average rainfall, which is represented by the center line (with a minimum of one asterisk shown if there is any deviation from the mean at all). The top line represents 1920/21, with subsequent lines representing succeeding years.

On the basis of this histogram it appears that two cycles of three or more consecutive years with 30 per cent or more negative deviation occur in 40 years, a figure suggesting a considerable degree of agricultural risk.

Using similar data, Neumann (1956), with the figure of 560 mm. as Jerusalem's mean annual rainfall (=M), expresses variation in precipitation in terms of a standard deviation of 142 mm. (standard deviation [=s.d.] is a measure of dispersion in a frequency distribution equal to the square root of the mean of the squares of the deviations from the arithmetic mean of the distribution). Neumann observes 34 years which would fall into what could be called a dry series, represented by the range of M minus 0.50 s.d. (= < 489 mm.) to M minus 1.50 s.d. (= < 347 mm.) and correspondingly, 34 years comprising a wet series in which the range was M plus 0.50 s.d. (> = 631 mm.) to M plus 1.50 s.d. (> = 773 mm.) (Neumann, 1956:60). Again, this indicates a high degree of variability in precipitation, pointing to a considerable degree of agricultural risk, certainly with respect to any medium- to long-term agricultural strategy.

Jerusalem Rainfall (1920/21–1960/61)

Positive deviation	Negative deviation
	*
*******	
**	
*************	
*	
***	
********	
*	
*****	
******	
**********	
**************	
*********	
***	
**********	
	****
	**
	*****
**	
***	
	********
	*******
*****	
	********
************	
	*********
*************	
*****	
*	
**********	
	***
**********	
******	
************	
****	
*****	

Perhaps the most meaningful statistical method for measuring the variability of rainfall for the purpose of assessing agricultural risk is one developed by D. Sharon, whose study is based on the calculation of the standard deviation (in per cent) of the annual amount of rain, plotting standard deviation isopleths on a map which is reproduced opposite 1965:172).

In Sharon's map, Jerusalem, together with about half of the area settled by pre-state Israel falls within the 30–40 per cent range in the measure of standard deviation, with most of the northern part of the area falling in the 20–30 per cent range. Beersheba, the Negev, and the Jordan Valley south of Beth-shean fall in the 40 per cent range. Sharon translated standard deviation figures of 20 and 40 per cent (the low and high figures in the range) into the following table (171):

s.d.	probable %age of years with deviation of		
	< =20%	< =40%	< =60%
20%	68	96	99.7
40%	38	68	87

The conclusion following from this table is that wherever there is a standard deviation of 40 per cent, deviations of less than 20 per cent from the annual mean rainfall can be expected in only 38 per cent of the years, whereas in 32 per cent of the years, deviations that exceed 40 per cent will occur. Furthermore, in 13 per cent of the years, deviations exceeding 60 per cent might be encountered. Sharon concludes: 'The data . . . presented in our map, supply information on the variability of rainfall which might be expected at each specified probability level. The latter could also be interpreted in terms of the risk associated with the relative or absolute deviation of each size, at each station' (171).

On the basis of Sharon's data, together with the other data on rainfall variability, the following can be said with respect to agricultural risk. The bulk of the early Israelite territory is in a medium-risk agricultural environment, when rainfall variability alone is taken into consideration. Rainfall variability in areas which were under Canaanite-Philistine control in the Shephelah and the Plain of Philistia was greater and thus agricultural risk was higher, for the most part, than in most of the early Israelite territory. Similarly all of the Negev, which saw extensive agricultural development only under state sponsorship is in a higher risk area.

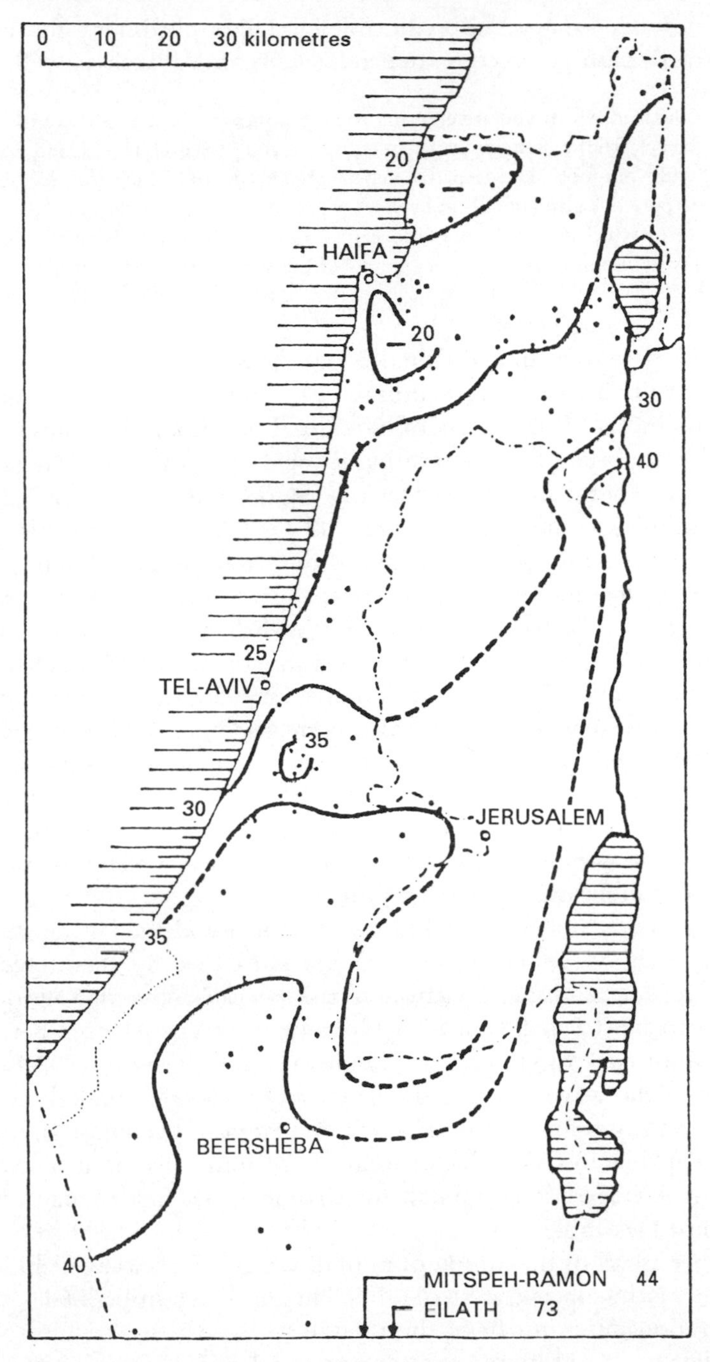

1. Rainfall map showing standard deviation.

This dependence upon unpredictable rainfall implied not only risk but, from Israel's faith perspective, dependence upon Yahweh as well:

> The land which you are entering to take possession of it is not like the land of Egypt, from which you have come, where you sowed your seed, and watered it with your foot, like a garden of vegetables; but the land which you are going over to possess is a land of hills and valleys which drinks water by the rain from heaven, a land which the Lord, your God, cares for; for the eyes of the Lord, your God, are always upon it, from the beginning of the year to the end of the year.
> (Deut. 11.10–12)

Variability in total annual rainfall is not, however, the only factor to be considered in assessing agricultural risk. Equally significant are the variations in the distribution of rainfall throughout the rainy season. Especially important for dry farming is the date of the initial rainfall that marks the end of the summer dry season (the 'autumn rain' of Jer. 5.24) and the date of the last rains (the 'spring rain' of Jer. 5.24). The former is needed to prepare the soil for ploughing and seeding and the latter has important effects on the maturation of crops. The critical nature of these two rainfall dates is again reflected religiously in the belief that they are one of Yahweh's rewards to his people in return for covenant faithfulness: 'I will give the rain for your land in its season, the early rain and the later rain, that you may gather in your grain and your wine and your oil' (Deut. 11.14; cf. Jer. 5.24; Hos. 6.3; Joel 2.23). Rain at the end of the season, if the timing is right and not too late, brings cereal crops to successful maturation, especially wheat which was the preferred cereal. Such rains near the end of the growing season may, however, devastate barley, which is particularly susceptible to rain during harvest time.

The first rains 'normally' fall in mid-October and the last rains in late April or early May; but again such normal dates, by themselves, are insufficient for assessing agricultural risk, because the first significant rainfall can be delayed well into November or even December. Baly (1974:49–50) cites figures from Transjordan for the year 1937–8 as an example of the way in which the date of first effective rainfall must be considered in assessing agricultural risk. In that year, even though the area around Kufrinje in Gilead had a total of 765 mm. of rain, a figure well above the average annual rainfall for that area, the first rainfall did not come until December.

Another aspect of the timing of rainfall which affects its availability for agriculture is the concentration of rainfall in a limited number of days. Such concentration causes much of the rainfall to be lost to agriculture since before the rain can infiltrate and saturate the soil, much of it is lost to runoff.

In addition to runoff losses, the area also suffers moisture losses from solar radiation which evaporates as much as 50–60 per cent of rainfall as soon as it falls (Orni and Efrat, 1973:148). Solar radiation also removes the moisture remaining in the soil throughout the dry season.

A final meteorological variable in the appraisal of agricultural risk and diversity, is temperature variation. The temperature range in the Highlands is greater than in the plains (cf. *Atlas of Israel*; IV/2, maps G and H) and the highland winters are both longer and colder. The average minimum temperature in winter at Jerusalem, for example, is 44° F., but night frosts are not uncommon. Olives, a principal Highland crop, suffer from such cold temperatures, for while they can endure long periods of drought and will grow where there is even less than 200 mm. of rain annually, they can be killed by prolonged frost, and even when they are not killed, cold winter temperatures significantly reduce yields.

These meteorological variables, accompanied by limited availability of water for agricultural purposes from other sources (springs and streams), add up to a considerable degree of agricultural risk and necessitate the development of technological means of water conservation and control in the form of terrace systems and other techniques, as well as the accompanying development of sociopolitical strategies which can buffer such threats to subsistence.

2. *Soil fertility in the Highlands*

Variability in soil fertility may be of little significance for one specific crop while being of considerable significance for another. Cereals, for example, are much more demanding of soil fertility than are root crops, and since Israel's subsistence was basically dependent upon cereals (Borowski, 1979:207), soil fertility is of considerable importance when considering agricultural diversity in the area of early Israel. In the following descriptions of soil types, it is necessary to exercise caution in accepting modern soil profiles as true indicators of their LB-Iron I predecessors. Under the climax vegetation of the region, much of which had already disappeared by Iron I, soils would have had better-developed profiles and greater depths than our descriptions indicate (Hopkins, 1985:111–23).

Four basic soil types occur in the Highlands: (1) *terra rossa*, (2) *brown forest*, (3) *rendzina*, and (4) *basaltic* (Baly, 1974:79).

Terra rossa soils are very productive, supporting a wide range of crops when situated on topographies permitting the accumulation of humus. They derive from the decomposition of hard limestones and dolomite, yet have low lime contents of 0–10 per cent. They are, however, usually shallow (< 50 cm. deep), and are clayey in texture when the accumulation of humus is lacking, under which conditions their cultivation is difficult and they are rather easily washed off the sides of hills (*Atlas of Israel* IV/2; introduction to soil map). The rocky areas in which such soils occur, when coupled with their shallowness and erosiveness means that such soils can only be productively farmed by means of the construction of terraces. As a shorthand device, this potentially very productive soil type will be labelled class I below.

The second type is the *Mediterranean brown forest* soil, which results from the breakdown of soft limestone (nari). These soils are generally 40–60 cm. deep and are found in areas of varying rockiness. Their lime content is usually 0–20 per cent. Their organic content is similar to that of the terra rossa (*Atlas of Israel* IV/2). These soils are called class II soils below.

Rendzina soils result from the weathering of chalk and marl. They are usually 40–75 cm. deep, have a high lime content of 30–80 per cent, and are poor in organic matter. They have a considerably higher pH than the previous two soil types and are productive only at the lower range of lime content (*Atlas of Israel* IV/2). They are more permeable and less susceptible to erosion, a characteristic which their topographical positions on rounded synclinal structures enhances. These will be labelled class III soils below.

The fourth basic soil type of the highlands is the *basaltic*, which occurs primarily in the eastern parts of Upper and Lower Galilee, having developed from the deposit of extinct volcanic activity. Soils of this type are ordinarily quite shallow (30–50 cm.), have a lime content of 0–25 per cent, contain minimal organic matter (only 1–2 per cent), and have a clayey texture (*Atlas of Israel* IV/2). They are relatively unproductive because of their physical properties and also because they occur with large basalt boulders, which are difficult to clear. They are accordingly designated below, in terms of their productive potential, as class IV soils.

Bearing in mind that such macro assessments of soil fertility do not take into account such things as land gradients or the extent of rockiness on the micro scale, what can be said about the early Israelite territory in terms of soil fertility? The detailed soil map which appears in the *Atlas of Israel* (IV/2) provides the best available data for answering this question. In making general statements about soil fertility the difficulties associated with biblical border descriptions are recognized (Cf. Aharoni, 1967: 227–45; especially Map 18 on 229). It is assumed here that the boundary descriptions in Jos. 13–19, while reflecting administrative divisions under the monarchy, derive from a source representing tribal claims during the late pre-monarchical period (Alt, 1927; Bright, 1981; de Vaux, 1878: 727–30; Noth, 1935; Cross and Wright, 1956).

The technical terms in these boundary descriptions, as opposed to the city lists in the same passages, are composed of a unique set of connecting verbs that belong to a vocabulary delineating territory in a manner relevant to land usage and not simply convenient geophysical land marks (Aharoni, 1967:228). 'Their obscure technicality reflects a primary and topologically sensitive delineation of territory whereby natural resources (i.e., land) are allotted to human groups sharing similar productivity schemes' (Meyers, 1983:52).

Benjamin's area includes class I soils as the dominant type in about 40 per cent of its area, with class II soils as the secondary soil type interspersed in the western part of the area. Those areas of Benjamin falling in the rain shadow consist mostly of unproductive brown desert skeletal soils and desert stony land, with some pockets of alluvium in the Jordan valley.

Judah's area is more extensive than Benjamin's and has a more complicated soil map. The borders of Judah are missing in the boundary lists in Joshua. There are neither internal boundaries for the groups that were incorporated into Judah (Simeon, Caleb, Kenaz, etc.), nor are there any external ones. Thus we infer that the southern, eastern and western boundaries of Judah are identical with those of the land of Canaan, and that the northern boundary corresponds to Benjamin's southern border. Judah's territory incorporates an area of class I soils. This area, lying roughly between Jerusalem and Hebron, runs along the top of the Central Highland ridge. Surrounding this central area are soils having lower productivity. To the west and south, and adjoining the border with Philistia, there is a sizable area of class II soils only slightly smaller than the area of class I soils. In the south, in an area having approximately a 16 km. radius around Beersheba, upland soils give way to desert soils, the primary soil types being brown desert skeletal soils and loess raw soils, the latter of which, if moisture conditions are favourable, is the most fertile of the desert soils; but one which inclines to sâlinisation under poor drainage. The rain shadow area of Judah's territory encompasses mostly infertile desert soils and desert stony land, with some fertile alluvial soils in the wadi beds that descend to the Dead Sea. Significant farming in this high-risk area, which took advantage of the accumulations of fertile alluvium washed down from the Highlands began only under state sponsorship (Stager: 1972; 1975; 1976). The soils of this area are more affected by salinity than any other in the early Israelite territory.

In the northern part of the Western Highlands, the territory of Ephraim has almost all class I soils with some small pockets of class II soils, colluvial-alluvial soils in wadi beds, and some areas where there is a complex of soils, generally with class I soils as the dominant type and either class II or III as the secondary type.

The area of Manasseh and Issachar in the Highlands, bordered on the north by the Jezreel Valley, has a complex soil map. While class I soils comprise about a third of the area, these are intermixed with areas where there is a complex of soils of classes I, II, and III. There is also a number of large pockets of alluvial and colluvial-alluvial soils in intermontane basins and wadi beds. These alluvial soils are deep and generally have a clayey texture. Shrinking and cracking phenomena are often quite pronounced in such soils. The lime content of these soils varies from 10–50 per cent, they have little organic matter content, and their pH ranges from 7.4–8.0 (*Atlas of Israel*; IV/2, introduction to soil map). The colluvial-alluvial soils were formed from the alluvium of mountain soils of all four classes. They are generally gravelly and are comparatively deep. The chemical composition of these soils is quite similar to that of the parent soil and their pH falls within the range 7.4–8.2.

The area of Zebulun, Asher and Naphtali in Lower and Upper Galilee is again a complicated one in terms of soil types. Lower Galilee has a maximum of only about one-fourth of its area comprised of class I soils, with an equivalent area of class IV soils. The remaining half has mostly class II soils with some alluvial soils in valleys. Upper Galilee has a greater portion of class I soils, perhaps one half of its area. The other half includes a complex of soils, mostly of classes I and II, with some class III and alluvial soils.

With this summary of soil fertility in the Western Highlands it should be noted that such generalisations based on soil maps illustrate gross patterns of diversity over rather large areas and do not take into account the significant microdiversity that exists. The patterning of the larger units of analysis, however, almost certainly reflects differences in the microdiversity within respective units as well.

A study which considers microdiversity is that of D. Webley (1972). Webley maintains that the distribution of sites in an agrarian society is related to the distribution of soil types, with emphasis placed on the controlling role that soils play in the exploitation of an area. In order to correlate various factors of land capability, Webley assesses each soil type for its ability to support both pasture and arable crops. The results of his assessment appear in the following land capability classification (Webley, 1972: 170).

Webley simplifies this classification in a table displaying soil types with their agricultural potential within the catchments of 22 archaeological sites. The table opposite modifies Webley's (Cf. Webley: 170).

One can deduce from this table that, terra rossa, Mediterranean brown, and colluvial-alluvial soils are the most productive agriculturally, while the

Land capability classification

Arable

Class 1
Gradient under 15%; soil over 20 cm. deep; well-drained;
1a – plant foods replenished;
1b – plant foods not replaced

Class 2
Gradient as 1; arable limited; inbuilt deficiencies;
2a – impeded drainage;
2b – salt excess;
2c – impoverished

Class 3
Gradient over 20%; no arable possible; erosion possible

Pasture

Class 1
Good grazing for: sheep, goats, cattle, pigs

Class 2
Limited grazing for: some animals – cattle, pigs, goats, camels

Class 1/2
Good grazing (1); soil; rainfall 600 mm.; sheep and goat
Limited (2); rock; rainfall 300 mm.; goat and gazelle

Distribution of archaeological sites with soil types and their agricultural potential

Soil type	Drainage	Arable	Pasture	No. of sites
Terra rossa	Good	1b	1	22
Mediterranean brown	Good	1b	1	15
Rendzina	Good	2	2	29
Basaltic	Poor	2	2	6
Alluvial	Poor	2	2	37
Colluvial-alluvial	Good	1a	1a	9
Brown skeletal desert	Good	2c	[1]*	10
Stony desert land	Excess	2c	[1]	7
Loess raw	Good	[2]	[2]	7

[*Brackets denote seasonal use]

presence of rendzina and basaltic soils permit pastoralism as well. While two different soils per site is the normal minimum, a characteristic distributional feature of sites with a long settlement history is that they have greater diversity of soil types within their catchment area. In most cases a similar pattern prevails: sites are located on freely drained land with at least two soil types nearby and, in some cases, three or more. Successful sites thus maximise agricultural diversity and spread risk by being able to exploit alternative resources. This analysis does not discount politico-strategic reasons for site location; it rather accentuates the fact that a site will emerge as an important centre precisely because it is economically viable given the kind of agricultural risks that are characteristic of its area.

Agricultural technology in early Israel

Technology represents a means by which people solve problems of production and distribution. Since tools and equipment channel and transmit energy, their effects on the energy budget of a society can be profound and direct. They are important in the archaeological record as indicators of a society's investment of energy. Through technological increase in the scope, intensity, effectiveness and accuracy of directed effort, the productivity of land and the reliability of procurement can be expanded.

In specific situations the complex of tools and implements reflects solutions to problems peculiar to particular contexts (Jochim, 1981: 114). Moreover, every technological variant carries with it a number of constraints and secondary ramifications that can affect all other components of a social system. We now turn our attention to the specific situations in which the agriculture of early Israel was carried on, to the ways in which technological means were employed to deal with the problems presented by her situation, and to the ways in which technological variants affected and were affected by other sociocultural components.

The occupation of the Hill Country at the beginning of the Iron Age was the result of a number of historical factors. Our primary interest here is in the technology accompanying the intensification of settlement in an area in which there were numerous obstacles to productive agriculture, including those risk factors directly related to environmental constraints which we have already reviewed, as well as a number of other factors such as the erosion of soil on the steep hillside gradients resulting in the loss of an already meagre layer of topsoil, the extreme rockiness of many of the soil types represented in the Highlands, and the problems associated with the maintenance of soil fertility in different kinds of contexts.

Of all the technologies and techniques utilised by Highland farmers, the construction of hillside agricultural terracing, which began in earnest by 1,200 BC was one of the principal means employed to enable the development of a reliable agricultural subsistence under such conditions.

A. Agricultural terracing in the Highlands

The place of agricultural terracing in early Israel has recently received increasing attention (Davis, 1981, Stager, 1982, Edelstein and Gibson, 1982, Hopkins, 1983, 1985). Hopkins provides a necessary cautionary note for our consideration of terracing in his observation that the appeal to terraces as the material explanation for the (initial) expansion of settlement in the Highlands rests on very restricted evidence as to the date of the initial appearance of terraces and on an unsubstantiated view of terraces as the absolute prior condition for such expanded agricultural settlement. An analysis of the aims, costs, and social correlates of terrace-culture suggests that it is found in the context of developing agricultural communities rather than as the *sine qua non* for the creation of a community. What is needed is a consideration of the fit of terrace-culture within village agriculture as a whole (1985: 180–6).

Hopkins is correct in arguing against the place of terraces in explanations in which advances in technology upstage other, systemic considerations. Terraces are part of the process of agricultural intensification in developing agrarian communities, and terraces are associated with intensive, short-term fallowing, in which a year of cultivation was followed by a year of fallow, a system designed, among other things, to maintain the fertility of the soil in the particular ecological niche of the Highlands (Turkowski, 1969:21).

The contexts of agricultural intensification have been much discussed (Boserup, 1965; Harris, 1977; Netting, 1974). Since techniques, such as terracing, which are associated with intensification require additional labour and time, they may, despite increased gross productivity, lead to a decreased time and labour efficiency in some cases. As a result, it is generally agreed that intensification is often adopted only when productivity per land unit must be raised, even at the expense of more work and potentially lowered productivity per unit of time or labour. Agricultural intensification was thus reinforced in a situation such as prevailed in early Israel, where there was a scarcity of productive land relative to the demands upon it.

The construction of agricultural terraces in the Highlands served three main functions: (1) the transformation of a slope into a series of level surfaces suitable for farming; (2) the prevention of runoff erosion and the enhancement of soil and water accumulation: and (3) the removal of stones to increase arability of the soil by forming a layer of cultivable soil (Ron, 1966:34). These functions were facilitated by construction methods. Retaining walls on the forward edge of the horizontal surface of the terrace were made of unhewn stones taken from the surface, accomplishing both the purpose of land clearance and drainage, since terrace walls were constructed without mortar, allowing water seepage, providing for the drainage of the soil and preventing the wall's collapse from water pressure. Terrace construction could thus render rocky soils with poor drainage characteristics, such as the basaltic soils in Galilee, more arable, and enhance the arability of other soils. The drainage of the terrace itself was also enhanced by construction methods. Inside its wall, the terrace was built up with different material: first a gravel layer, then a soil layer, then a layer of stones or gravel, and finally a layer of organic soil. A fill of gravel was usually placed immediately behind the terrace wall. In this way, the rainwater would be soaked up in the soil in which the plants were growing and the surplus would flow to the terrace below (Edelstein and Gibson, 1982:53).

While farming communities could do nothing to change either the amount or timing of precipitation which their crops received, terracing provided a way of significantly reducing the amount of water lost from runoff. Terracing facilitated increased infiltration and caused terraced hill slopes to experience a faster replenishment of groundwater supplies, rendering them less vulnerable to the vagaries of the rainfall regime (Hopkins, 1985:175).

The soil within terraces was not always indigenous, but was sometimes transported to the terraces. The fact that soil was brought to some terraces has been established by observing the soil in sections of collapsed terraces (Edelstein, 1983). This accumulation of soil is unlike water-laid soil: its components being different in size, shape and position. On this artificial base other soil accumulated over time since terracing provided a shelf where organic matter and minerals could accumulate, thus replenishing the soil, and preventing the loss of the soil base to erosion. The latter is an indispensable tool from the standpoint of long-term land utilisation and village stability, a point which emerges again and again from studies of terracing communities (Hopkins, 1983:187).

Three different perspectives on terraces are represented by Ron (1966), Hopkins (1985), and de Geus (1975). Ron, a geographer is mainly concerned with geomorphological aspects, and gives little attention to the role which terracing plays in the development of agricultural intensification and the accompanying sociopolitical changes, which are areas of primary concern for Hopkins. De Geus emphasises the need for field studies of ancient agriculture and suggests some of the social implications of terracing. All three, however, are in agreement in viewing terracing as a complex operation requiring large investments of time and labour, both in construction and maintenance. Because of such high labour costs, terrace systems are usually found in cultivating communities characterised by a particular set of conditions. In a study of land use in Israel, Amiran links the establishment of terrace systems to economic and demographic factors: '. . . The amount of labour invested in these ancient terraces and their maintenance was tremendous, an investment possible only when labour was a cheap commodity and when the crops grown on these terraces commanded a good price in a stable market' (1964: 102). Beaumont envisions a correlation between terracing and high population density in the history of east Mediterranean farming (1976: 133–5). These suggestions raise vital questions about the correlations between terracing, sociopolitical, socioeconomic, and demographic conditions in early Israel.

Further suggestions about the sociopolitical aspects of the development of terracing have come from the excavation of terraces by Edelstein and Kislev at Mevasseret Yerushalayim. They stress the unitary nature of terracing systems and suggest that they were not the work of individual farmers (Edelstein and Kislev, 1981). They also cite the agronomist Yosef Klatzman who comments that in modern times strong incentives are necessary to encourage governments to support terrace farming, since it produces relatively low yields in return for intensive labour input. Edelstein and Kislev ask: 'If this situation were applicable in antiquity, as well, what could the incentive have been then?' (56).

In an attempt to answer this question, the reconstruction which follows draws upon the work of Leon Marfoe (1979) who, in studying modern Lebanon deals with ecological relationships that pattern sociopolitical behaviour in the highlands of the Lebanon and Anti-Lebanon ranges, as well as with resulting lines of cleavage between social groups that serve either to limit or to facilitate the extension of centralised power.

Agriculture in the Lebanese highlands, as in early Israel is basically dependent on terrace agriculture and intensive orchard cultivation, both of which are quite labour-intensive and require long-term capital investments with the promise of slow, but eventually satisfactory, returns. The close relationship between long-term investment in terraces and orchard crops, household self-sufficiency, and highland agriculture tended to produce a system less susceptible to land concentration than in the lowlands. Land concentration, when it took place, preferred the form of 'lineage capture', in which the lineage which had the most sons and which practiced endogamy could increase its holdings by converting useless land into working terrace farms with each successive generation.

> In other words, social stability in the highlands meant not the ability to fragment into smaller units and recoalesce into large segments but involved instead the formation of large generationally tiered social pyramids, with each successive generation providing a rapidly broadening base of small residentially stable household units. (Marfoe, 1979:21)

The residential immobility of each village and its terraced fields and the restrictions imposed by terraceable lands upon village populations resulted in a series of fixed socioeconomic relations within and between villages. The social landscape that emerged from these relations consisted of a number of overlapping lineage-pyramids, tied to each other by cross-kinship bonds, with the head of the most important lineages – the chiefs – at the peak.

Here, then, is a partial explanation for the way in which the fissioning which was an endemic characteristic of early Israel as a segmentary society could have been buffered and checked, given the subsistence parameters of Highland terrace agriculture. It also offers an explanation for Israel's subsequent transformation into the conical clan chiefdoms of Saul and David, as described by Flanagan (1983). The patterns of Highland agriculture also help account for the relatively long period of stability that early Israel knew as a segmentary society before moving to a chiefdom, for as Marfoe observes, both terrace farming and lineage endogamy were self-reinforcing factors that led to demographic stability unknown in the Lowlands. Social groups, because of their physical immobility, were defined as much by their villages as by their lineages and their fixed socio-economic relations with one another.

If terrace systems were, as seems likely, the impulse of forces internal to the village, then it is unlikely that the primary productive unit, the *bêt 'āb*, could have supplied the necessary labour. The construction of terrace systems may well be one of the regular functions of the *mišpāḥāh*, here constituting the source and direction for a collective labour group (Hopkins, 1985:255–61). Organised agricultural activities beyond the *bêt' āb* were also necessitated by the variability of the precipitation regime and the existence of numerous micro-environments. The variability of the precipitation regime was decisive for decisions regarding the basic field work of ploughing and sowing operations for the all-important cereals. One can picture the intersection of the climatic year and the production cycles of particular crops as creating an optimal window during which the ploughing and sowing would be most propitious. Because of the variability of the seasonal distribution of rainfall, it benefits the farming household to stagger sowing over the length of this window, so as not to be dependent on the occurrence of any particular rainfall pattern (Hopkins, 1983:188).

Normally a staggered pattern of sowing could have been accomplished by an individual household. But if the size of the window was reduced by the pattern of rainfall or some other factor, the risk of crop failure would mount, there would be greater difficulty in gaining access to draft animals, and the necessity of going beyond the labour supply of the *bêt 'āb* would arise.

Harvesting with its sequential set of operations made it the most intensive operation of the agricultural year. It is likely that some form of collective work groups provided relief at this time of peak labour demand, as is evidenced by the biblical references to the village threshing floor, the *gōren* (2 Sam. 6.6; 1 Sam. 23.1; Ruth 3.2; 1 Kgs. 22.10).

Also contributing to the facility of inter-household co-operation and to the levelling of harvest labour demand in general were the environmental circumstances which produced differing ripening times in the various micro-environments. This phenomenon is not confined to the contrast between the Coastal Plain and the Central Highlands, but is also experienced within the Highlands themselves. The particular mix of cereals grown in different areas also spread harvesting and labour demands, most notably the different maturation rates of wheat and barley (Hopkins, 1983:189).

These conditions of Highland agriculture led to the structuring of social institutions to realise risk spreading and the optimisation of labour in an environment which set limits on village autonomy and fostered inter-village co-operation.

B. Agricultural productivity and settlement patterns

When speaking of settlement patterns, our main interest is the definition of the social arrangements for the exploitation of economic resources. Above all, the basic issue is the relationship which exists between population, social structures and agricultural productivity.

While the Hill Country was not, relatively speaking, an environment which was naturally conducive to agriculture, the beginning of the Iron Age saw an increase in population in this area. Ahlstrom has observed that it is noteworthy that new cities were not established to accommodate this population increase (1982:133). The central Hill Country had always included some urban centres, but there is no evidence of new cities having been built in the Hill Country following the upheavals of the thirteenth century BC. The absence of new cities implies that the majority of the new population lived in small rural agricultural settlements, and archaeological surveys now facilitate the understanding of settlement patterns. Such surveys have yielded the following summary:

Summary of Hill Country survey for LB and Iron I sites

Altitude	LB	Iron I	Iron I (new foundations)
600–900 m.	5	36	31
300–600 m.	14	54	44
below 300 m.	4	24	22
Site Total	23	114	97
Site Density	1/183 km.^{2}	1/37 km.^{2}	

(Stager 1985: 4)

From this summary it is obvious that both the number and density of settlements in the Hill Country showed a dramatic increase from LB to Iron I. LB settlements were larger (mean size, ca. 3 ha.; median size, ca. 5 ha.) than Iron I settlements (mean size, ca. 1.7 ha.; median, ca. 1.0 ha.; 70 per cent under 3 ha.), but the total settled area was only 69 ha. in LB compared with 192 ha. in Iron 1. This translates into about a 2 per cent annual increase in population between 1200 BC and 1150 BC (Stager, 1985:3).

These new settlements were established by settlers who came to the Highlands with fixed cultural patterns of village life and founded settlements in medium- and high-risk agricultural areas, but ones with potentially productive soil maps (cf. the accompanying distribution map from Stager, 1985:2). Small hilltop villages sustained by terrace farming, such as ʻAi and Raddana, are typical of the many new settlements founded in the hills at this time. Such villages have common intrasite patterns, including house forms and village plans reflecting a social structure which was adapted to subsistence strategies in the Hill Country environment.

The standard pillared house-type in the newly-established Iron I villages was a small rectilinear building of two to four rooms entered from an exterior courtyard. The movable artifacts found in such houses make it clear that they were the dwellings of farmers and herders (Stager, 1985:12). Architectural features of these homes indicate that the side rooms on the ground floor served as stables. These rooms, in contrast to the central room,

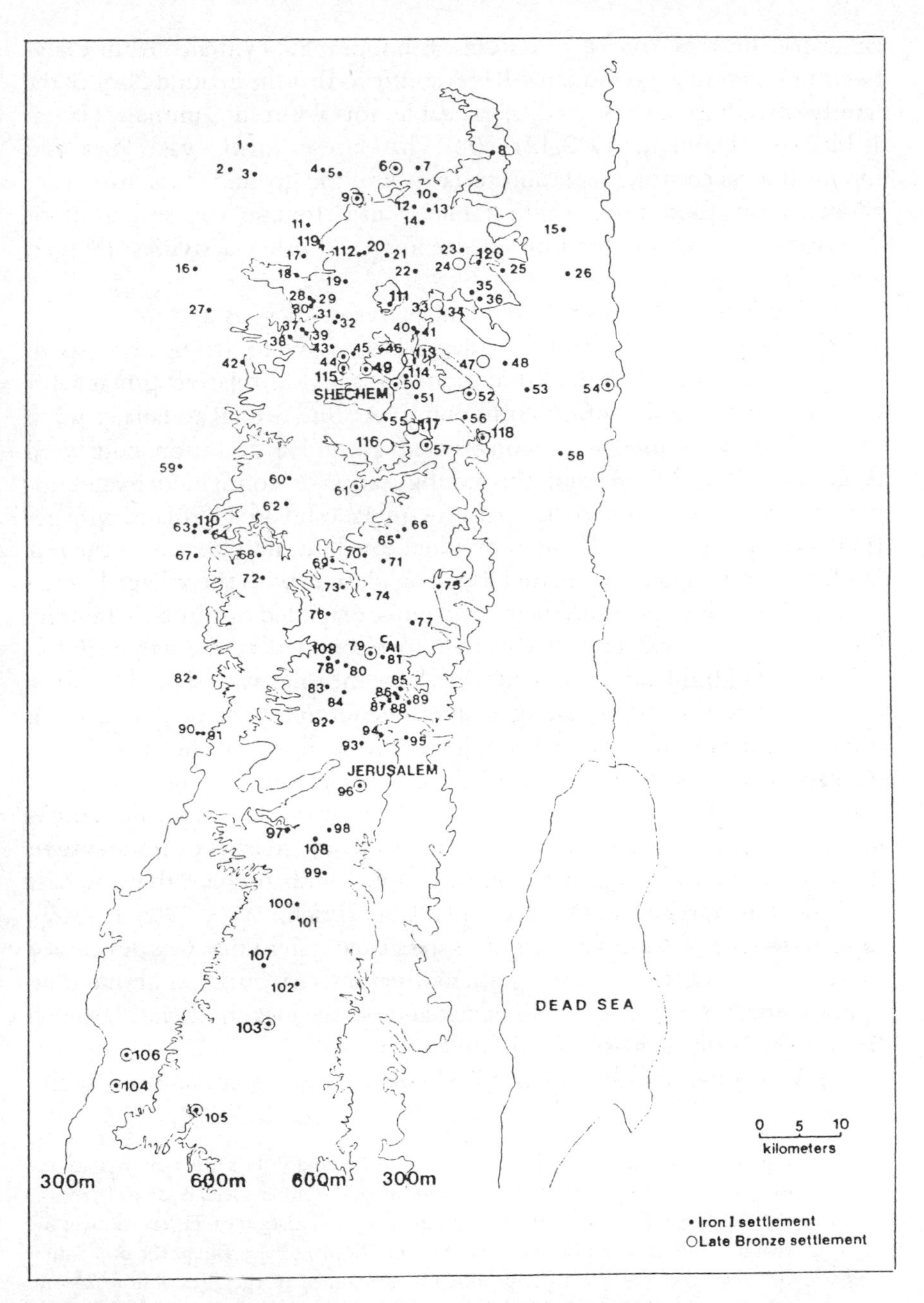

2. Distribution map of Iron I (dots) and Late Bronze (circles) settlements in the Central Highlands of Palestine.

never had hearths, ovens, or cisterns. Ethnographic evidence from early-twentieth-century Palestinian villages confirms that the ground floor of the family dwelling also served as a stable for domestic animals (Jäger, 1912:24–6; Dalman, 1942:121–30). This house form was 'First and foremost a successful adaptation to farm life: the ground floor had space allocated for food processing, stabling, and storage; the second floor (*ʿăliyyāh*) was suitable for dining, sleeping, and other activities' (Stager, 1985:17).

On the level of intrasite settlement patterns, there is a consistency of village planning in the Iron 1 village. Houses were arranged so as to maximise the use of agricultural land yet provide relative privacy for extended or multiple family compounds. At Site S in Raddana, e.g., as many as three houses were constructed around a common courtyard (Callaway, 1985:38). Again, this configuration is confirmed by ethnographic evidence about social patterns in Palestinian Highland villages (Lutfiyya, 1966:142–3). If the individual dwelling unit housed a nuclear family, then the spatially isolated dwelling clusters with the village housed the *bêt ʾāb*, i.e. 'lineages' and their subgroups, extended or multiple families (Stager, 1985:22) and the village itself corresponded to the *mišpāḥāh*.

The Iron I Highland settlements thus have the following shared features: (1) pillar-type houses; (2) an agricultural economic basis of dry farming with a significant, if not equal supplement from flocks of sheep and goats (Callaway, 1985:42) which provided for risk spreading in high-risk areas; (3) social 'isolation' in which the village was an economic entity, independent of other villages and not subject to any market or trade system (cf. Nieuwenhuijze, 1962:300). This, coupled with the fact that intersite settlement hierarchies developed only later (Frick, 1979; 1985:157–69), suggests that the village was part of a subsistence system that was developed more in response to the environmental parameters outlined above than upon political or economic influences; and (4) the local household, the *bêt ʾāb* was the basic socio-economic unit.

Hopkins' observations (1985:271–2) offer a fitting conclusion to this study:

> It may be possible to understand the transformation of the settlement map of the early Iron Age Highlands and the evolution of the larger social body of Israel as a process propelled by the attempt of a growing population of settlers to meet the challenges of agricultural subsistence in the Highlands . . . But as the population . . . increased . . . the total production demanded of the agricultural-pastoral system multiplied. At the same time an increased number of hands provided the potential for movement up the scale of agricultural intensity, and the number of villages where agriculture constituted the primary means of subsistence began to grow.

Bibliography

Aharoni, Y., 1967. *The Land of the Bible: A Historical Geography*. Trans. A. F. Rainey from the Hebrew, 1962, 1967. Philadelphia: Westminster.

Ahlstrom, G. W., 1982. 'Where Did the Israelites Live?', *Journal of Near Eastern Studies*, 41:133–38.

Alt, A., 1927. 'Das System der Stammesgrenzen im Buche Josua', pp. 13–24 in *Beiträge zur Religionsgeschichte und Archäologie Palästinas [Festschrift Ernst Sellin]*. Leipzig: A. Deichert.

Amiran, D. H. K., 1964. 'Land Use in Israel', pp. 101–12 in *Land Use in Semi-Arid Mediterranean Climates*, UNESCO/International Geographic Union. Paris: UNESCO.

Athens, S. J., 1977. 'Theory Building and the Study of Evolutionary Process in Complex Societies', pp. 353–84 in *For Theory Building in Arichaeology*, ed. L. R. Binford, NY: Academic.

Atlas of Israel, 1970. *Atlas of Israel*, 2nd edition, Jerusalem: Survey of Israel, Minister of Labour.

Baly, D., 1974. *The Geography of the Bible, New and Revised Edition*. NY: Harper and Row.

Beaumont, P., Blake, G. H. and Wagstaff, J. M., 1976. *The Middle East: A Geographical Study*. London: Wiley.

Borowski, O., 1979. *Agriculture in Iron Age Israel*, Ph.D. dissertation, University of Michigan.

Boserup, E., 1965. *The Conditions of Agricultural Growth: The Economics of Agrarian Change under Population Pressure*, Chicago: Aldine.

Bright, J., 1981. *History of Israel, 3rd Edition*. Philadelphia: Westminster.

Callaway, J. A., 1985. 'A New Perspective on the Hill Country Settlement of Canaan in Iron Age I'. pp. 31–49 in *Palestine in the Bronze and Iron Ages: Papers in Honour of Olga Tufnell*, ed. J. N. Tubb. London: Institute of Archaeology.

Cross, F. M. and Wright, G. E., 1956. 'The Boundary and Province Lists of the Kingdom of Judah', *Journal of Biblical Literature*, 75:202–26.

Dalman, G., 1942. *Das Haus. Arbeit und Sitte in Palästina, Das Haus*. Vol. 7. *Arbeit und Sitte*. Gütersloh: C. Bertelsmann.

Davis, J. B., 1981. 'Hill Country Dry Farming: A Revolutionary Development of Iron Age I', paper presented at the Southeastern Regional Meeting of the Society of Biblical Literature, March 14.

De Geus, C. H. J., 1975. 'The Importance of Agricultural Research into the Palestinian Agricultural Terraces, with an Excursus on the Hebrew word gbi', *Palestine Exploration Quarterly*, 107:65–74.

De Vaux, R., 1978. *Early History of Israel*. Eng. tr. Philadelphia: Westminster.

Edelstein, G., 1983. Personal communication.

Edelstein, G. and Gibson, S., 1982. 'Ancient Jerusalem's Rural Food Basket', *Biblical Archaeology Review*, 8:46–54.

Edelstein, G. and Kislev, M., 1981. 'Mevasseret Yerushalayim: Ancient Terrace Farming', *Biblical Archaeologist*, 44/1:53–6.

Flanagan, J. W., 1983. 'Succession and Genealogy in the Davidic Dynasty', pp. 35–55 in *The Quest for the Kingdom of God: Studies in Honor of George E. Mendenhall*, eds. H. B. Hufffmon, F. A. Spina, and A. R. W. Green. Winona Lake, IN: Eisenbraun's.

Frick, F. S., 1979. 'Religion and Sociopolitical Structure in Early Israel: An Ethno-Archaeological Approach', pp. 233–53 in *SBL 1979 Seminar Papers*, ed. P. J. Achtemeier. Vol. 2. Missoula: Scholars.

1985. *The Formation of the State in Ancient Israel: A Survey of Models and Theories*, The Social World of Biblical Antiquity Series, 4. Sheffield: JSOT.

Harris, M., 1977. *Cannibals and Kings*, NY: Random House.

Hopkins, D. C., 1983. 'The Dynamics of Agriculture in Monarchical Israel', *SBL Seminar Papers*, 22: 177–202.

1985. *The Highlands of Canaan: Agricultural Life in the Early Iron Age*, The Social World of Biblical Antiquity Series, 3. Sheffield: JSOT.

Jochim, M., 1981. *Strategies for Survival: Cultural Behaviour in an Ecological Context*, NY: Academic.

Lutfiyya, A. M., 1966. *Baytin. A Jordanian Village: A Study of Social Institutions and Social Change in a Folk Community*, The Hague: Mouton.

Marfoe, L., 1979. 'The Integrative Transformation: Patterns of Sociopolitical Organization in Southern Syria', *Bulletin of the American Schools of Oriental Research*, 234: 1–42.

Meyers, C., 1983. 'Of Seasons and Soldiers: A Topological Appraisal of the Premonarchic Tribes of Galilee', *Bulletin of the American Schools of Oriental Research*, 252: 47–59.

Netting, R. M., 1974. 'Sacred Power and Centralization: Aspects of Political Adaptation in Africa', pp. 219–44 in *Population Growth: Anthropological Implications*, ed. B. Spooner. Cambridge, MA: Massachusetts Institute of Technology.

Neumann, J., 1956. 'On the Incidence of Dry and Wet Years', *Israel Exploration Journal*, 6: 58–63.

Nieuwenhuijze, C. A. O. van, 1962. 'The Near Eastern Village: A Profile', *Middle East Journal*, 16: 295–308.

Noth, M., 1935. *Studien zu den historisch-geographischen Dokumenten des Josua buches.* Zeitschrift für das Deutsches Palästinas Vereins, 58: 185–225.

Orni, E. and Efrat, E., 1973. *Geography of Israel, 3rd edition,* Philadelphia: Jewish Publication Society.

Price, B. J., 1978. 'Secondary State Formation: an Explanatory Model', pp. 161–86, in *Origins of the State*, eds. R. Cohen and E. R. Service. Philadelphia: Institute for the Study of Human Issues.

Ron, Z., 1966. 'Agricultural Terraces in the Judean Mountains', *Israel Exploration Journal*, 16: 33–49; 111–22.

Rosenan, N., 1955. '100 Years of Rainfall in Jerusalem: A Homotopic Series of Annual Amounts', *Israel Exploration Journal*, 5: 137–53.

Sahlins, M. D., 1962. 'The Segmentary Lineage: an Organization of predatory Expansion', pp. 89–119 in *Comparative Political Systems*, eds. R. Cohen and J. Middleton. Garden City, NY: American Museum of Natural History.

Sanders, W. T. and Webster, D., 1978. 'Unilineality, Multilineality, and the Evolution of Complex Societies', pp. 249–302 in *Social Archaeology*, eds. C. L. Redman *et al.*, NY: Academic.

Sharon, D., 1965. 'Variability of Rainfall in Israel: A Map of the Relative Standard Deviation of the Annual Amounts', *Israel Exploration Journal*, 15: 169–76.

Stager, L. E., 1972. 'Ancient Irrigation Agriculture in the Buqeiʾah Valley', *American Schools of Oriental Research 1972–73 Newsletter*, 2: 1–4.

1975. *Ancient Agriculture in the Judean Desert: A Case Study of the Buqēah Valley*, Ph.D. dissertation, Harvard University.

1976. 'Farming in the Judean Desert in the Iron Age', *Bulletin of the American Schools of Oriental Research*, 221:145–58.

1982. 'The Archaeology of the East Slope of Jerusalem and the Terraces of the Kidron', *Journal of Near Eastern Studies*, 41:111–21.

1985. 'The Archaeology of the Family in Ancient Israel', *Bulletin of the American Schools of Oriental Research*, 260:1–35.

Turkowski, L., 1969. 'Peasant Agriculture in the Judean Hills', *Palestine Exploration Quarterly*, 101:21–33; 101–12.

Webley, D., 1972. 'Soils and Site Location in Prehistoric Palestine', pp. 169–211 in *Papers in Economic Prehistory*, ed. E. S. Higgs. Cambridge: Cambridge University Press.

Wolf, E. R., 1966. *Peasants*, Foundation of Modern Anthropology Series. Englewood Cliffs, NJ: Prentice-Hall.

CHAPTER FIVE

Israel as a tribal society

JAMES D. MARTIN

The title of this chapter fairly obviously focusses our attention on that period of Israelite history which lies between the 'appearance' of 'Israel' in Palestine and the eventual formation of an 'Israelite state' in the form of a monarchy under David and Solomon. It is in relationship to that particular period that writers have for so long happily talked about 'the Israelite tribes', but such a mode of reference has for the most part been largely unquestioning and has simply assumed that, since the biblical sources have spoken about 'tribes' and have depicted these tribes as being organised in a 'system' of twelve tribes all descended from a single eponymous ancestor, Israel/Jacob, tribes, thus organised, there must have been. However, in recent years – say, the last fifteen – there has been a great increase in the application of socio-scientific models to the study of this period of Israelite history. Those who have been zealous in this new area of study have not confined their interest to a static Israel of the premonarchic period but have pushed their area of enquiry both backwards and forwards. In the former sphere, they have posed the question of the origins of this 'tribal Israel' and have asked, again from a socio-scientific perspective, where 'Israel' came from and how this ethnic entity emerged as a force in Palestine. In pushing the area of enquiry forwards, such a method of investigation has looked at the premonarchic period with a view to the nature of the society from which an Israelite state emerged and has asked whether 'monarchy' is, as has so often been supposed, something completely new which is of a fundamentally different nature from the society which immediately preceded it or whether it is to be understood as having emerged by a process of natural and continuous development from that society.

These three areas of study are all inter-related, though not all who have written on this period have focussed on all three areas. Most have, in fact, concentrated on only one of them, so it will be not inappropriate for us to deal with them singly and to begin in the middle, namely with the social and political structure of Israelite society in the immediately premonarchic period.

One of the first writers to direct Old Testament scholars to the socio-anthropological approach was John Rogerson in a book published in a Blackwell's series called 'Growing Points in Theology'. In one of the chapters in that book, Rogerson dealt in a comprehensive way with 'Tribes, Clans and Groups' (1978, 86–101), pointing out as a first step not only the fact that social anthropologists themselves have found it extremely difficult, if not in fact impossible, to come to any consensus definition of the word 'tribe', but also the fact that so much biblical scholarship has operated on the basis of a complete failure to realise the need for an extremely careful analysis of socio-political concepts such as 'tribe'. But Rogerson goes on from there to wonder whether, in any case, anything would be gained by attempting to define, within the context of the Hebrew Bible, terms such as *šēḇeṭ* and *mišpāḥāh*, since the Israelites were unlikely to be aware of their own social structure and make use of kinship terminology in ways which would be acceptable to modern anthropologists. Whether we need be quite so negative in our attitude to trying to define these terms in Hebrew is a question to which we shall return, but Rogerson outlines three possible directions in which research in this area of Israelite history might be advanced on the anthropological front.

In the first instance he suggests an anthropological/structural analysis of the extensive genealogical material found in the Hebrew Bible and emphasises here, as he does elsewhere in this chapter, his firm conviction that such investigation can not satisfactorily be done either by Old Testament scholars alone or by anthropologists alone but that what is required, in view of the enormous problems on each side of this investigation, is a co-operative approach. Secondly, Rogerson points to a number of what were then recent studies throwing light on the social background and organisation of the ancient Near East (for a list see Rogerson 1978, 97 n. 29), but while he thinks that these might in turn be useful in throwing light on the social structure of ancient Israel, he sounds a note of caution that such studies must be based on real scientific analysis if their terminology and interpretation are not to prove so ambiguous and imprecise as to be useless in the ancient Israelite context. Thirdly, Rogerson advocates a cautious use of anthropological models from other societies in an endeavour to throw light on the political organisation of Israelite society in the premonarchic period. Here he points to the possible value of the detailed study of the Nuer people of the southern Sudan by the British anthropologist E. E. Evans-Pritchard, who lived with the Nuer on several occasions in the 1930s. The Nuer model, Rogerson believes, with its stress on the concept that groups may come together for united action but may, in a very short space of time and in changed circumstances, find themselves at odds with each other, may be of some assistance in helping us to understand Israel's political structures in the period of the Judges. We shall see this in more detail in the work of de Geus, but it may be useful to point, even at this stage, to the dangers inherent in the over-enthusiastic adoption of ethnological models from a discipline in which the average Old Testament scholar is essentially an amateur, and often a not very skilled amateur at that.

Rogerson ends his chapter by pointing to the work of two Old Testament scholars who had already made a contribution to the study of Israelite tribes from an anthropological point of view, G. E. Mendenhall in a chapter entitled 'Tribe and State in the Ancient World: The Nature of the Biblical Community' (in 1973, 174–97) and C. H. J. de Geus 'The Unity of Israel' (in 1976, 120–92).

Mendenhall's point of departure from the anthropological point of view seems to be in the work of only one anthropologist, the American E. R. Service. Although Mendenhall strikes an independent note in his study of ancient Israelite tribes, his dependence on a single anthropologist does represent another danger for the biblical scholar *qua* amateur anthropologist, namely the reliance on a single authority (or narrow range of authorities), without either being cognisant of or taking serious account of the rich diversity of views prevailing among social anthropologists themselves. Much of Mendenhall's discussion is related to a greater or lesser degree to his 'peasants' revolt model' for the emergence of Israel (1962), and he does tend to assume the existence of a 'federation of tribes' in ancient Israel. He assumes the existence of such a 'federation' but considers that its *nature* needs to be examined anew, at which point he turns to ask the question as to what precisely we 'mean by a tribe' (1973, 183). For his answer he makes use of two ethnological models, the modern Bedouin tribe and, more importantly for him, the Roman *tribus*. Both of these he regards as political organisations, and he believes that the Israelite *šēḇeṭ*, the etymological origin of which is the staff of office held by the one who is sent with delegated authority (as in Judg. 5:14), reflects the same kind of historical situation as does the Roman *tribus*. And so, for Mendenhall, the Israelite tribe is an administrative unit within the federation whose existence he assumes, though he regards it as probable that such social groupings entered the tribal federation as already corporate bodies (1973, 184–5). In early historical societies – and alongside ancient Israel he cites Rome, Athens and Byblos – tribes were typologically early forms of political structure about whose real nature and functions we know very little. Beyond this statement about the nature of an ancient Israelite 'tribe', Mendenhall otherwise has little to say about the *actual* structure of Israelite society.

Rogerson (1978, 100) regards Mendenhall as anthropologically creative, his main significance perhaps being to have acted as the springboard for the work of Gottwald, to which we shall come shortly. Rogerson certainly regards this anthropological creativity as a bonus point for Mendenhall whom he describes as having 'allowed for a much more dynamic social situation in ancient Israel' (1978, 100). This last, however, is probably as much connected with his revolt model as with the social structure of the Judges period. Rogerson does criticise Mendenhall (as he does also de Geus) for his negative attitude towards Israelite genealogies and believes that these, along with other kinship information, should be examined from an anthropological point of view. However, apart from the work of R. R. Wilson (1977), of which Rogerson was already aware, only Flanagan (1981) has made much of a contribution in this area (see further below p. 112).

Let us turn now to the work of de Geus (1976) who makes use of a broader anthropological base than does Mendenhall and who is also probably more directly involved with the historical biblical material than is Mendenhall. The sub-title of de Geus's book makes it clear that his main subject of discussion is 'the presuppositions of Martin Noth's amphictyony hypothesis', but in a central chapter on 'The Unity of Israel' (1976, 120–92), he begins by asking what he considers to be the basic question, namely, 'What are we to understand by the concept "an Israelite tribe"?' (1976, 124). De Geus goes on to the further question as to whether there are any indications that these tribes functioned as politically independent units and proceeds from there to an examination of the original social and economic structure of premonarchic Israel. In that context he makes the following points:

1. The Israelites did *not* have a pre-Palestinian existence as flock-herding nomads. Pastoral nomadism is in reality a specialised offshoot of agriculture and not a way of life that always or usually preceded an agrarian, sedentary life-style.
2. Tribal organisation can no longer be regarded as a necessary preliminary stage along the road to the formation of a state. On the contrary, it is a considerable obstacle along such a road, and de Geus quotes the anthropologist M. H. Fried to the effect that 'tribalism is an evolutionary cul-de-sac' (1976, 131).
3. Genealogies have only a slight historical value and serve simply to express the living continuity inherent in a unilateral and/or

unilineal kinship system. On this count he, too, is subject to the same criticism as Rogerson directed against Mendenhall (see above p. 98).

De Geus then goes on to analyse the sociological terms *bēṯ ʾāḇ, mišpāḥāh* and *šēḇeṭ* and concludes that the *bēṯʾāḇ* is an 'extended family' of more than three generations which practises exogamy (i.e. marries *outside* the family). This, says de Geus, assumes that it forms part of a larger social unit which practises endogamy (i.e. marries *inside* itself), and this he identifies as the next-size social unit, the *mišpāḥāh* which, for want of a better term, he translates as 'clan'. He regards the 'clan' as the most important social unit in ancient Israel, a unit which, for practical purposes, coincided with the town, though he does admit that sometimes clans are rather larger units. The political organisation of ancient Israel found its focal point in the clan/town. 'Tribe' was a much vaguer term and tended to be a grouping of related clans which had few functions of its own. Such groupings might form within a geographical or territorial area in order to resist pressure from outside, but such solidarity tended to be incidental, specific to a particular problem or problems and was not necessarily lasting. In fact, for de Geus, it is difficult to differentiate clearly between 'tribe' and 'people'. The ancient Israelite tribe was a 'branch' of the people as a whole and had no meaning without that whole. Rogerson criticises him for not being aware that 'family' and 'clan' may also be rather ill-defined terms, but de Geus does admit that the distinction between 'family' and 'clan' is 'sometimes wavering' and that this indefiniteness may be 'due to rather inexact terminology' (1976, 137). And elsewhere he concedes that the vagueness discernible in the 'contours' of the concept 'tribe' is increased by the way in which the terms 'clan' and 'tribe' are used in a fashion that strikes us as careless (1976, 150). This is an important cautionary observation to make with regard to the examination of ancient Israel's social structure on the basis of the terminology used of it in the biblical texts, though it is doubtful whether one should strike such a negative note as does Rogerson, who describes the attempt to define such Hebrew terms with a view to understanding Israel's social structure as 'a serious methodological mistake' (1978, 95). Rogerson might be correct if one thought that such definitions were all that were required for such an understanding, but they are surely part of the final picture.

Mendenhall's work, especially his use of the 'peasants' revolt' model for the appearance of the Israelites in Palestine (1962), has been taken up by Gottwald in a number of publications, but most extensively in his *The Tribes of Yahweh* (1979). Gottwald's concern in that book is explicated to some extent by its subtitle: 'A Sociology of the Religion of Liberated Israel

1250–1050 B.C.E.'. In other words, he aims to present a sociological analysis of the 'peasants' revolt' model, and he regards the religious factor as the main catalyst for such a revolt. He does, however, have a section of that book which deals with social structure in particular, namely Part VI, which is entitled 'Models of the Social Structure (1): All Israel; Tribes; Protective Associations; Extended Families' (1979, 235–341).

Gottwald believes that he can construct an elaborate and detailed structural organisation for ancient Israelite tribal society. At the highest organisational level stands Israel itself, which Gottwald describes as 'a Confederacy or League of Tribes' and 'the widest societal and culture-bearing unit of associated egalitarian Yahwistic tribes' (1979, 338). The basic characteristics of this confederacy are a concern for the Yahwistic cult, laws and ideology, a commitment to economic egalitarianism as reflected in the socio-economic laws and a readiness to organise military opposition to external, threatening forces such as those of the Canaanites and the Philistines. This confederacy is subdivided into the autonomous, segmentary divisions described by the terms 'tribes', '*mišpāḥōṯ*' and 'families'. The next layer, therefore, in Gottwald's reconstructed social organisation is that of the 'tribe', the 'primary organizational segment'. The tribe in Gottwald's view is 'an autonomous association of segmented extended families grouped in village/neighbourhood "protective associations" [Gottwald's term for *mišpāḥōṯ*], averaging about 50 per tribe, functionally interlocking through inter-marriage, practices of mutual aid, common worship, and a levy of troops' (1979, 339). What shapes these 'tribes' into such units is their common experience of oppression and rebellion, as well as their territorial grouping in areas which are determined by factors such as terrain, climate or enclaves of Canaanite city-states. The 'secondary organizational segment' is the *mišpāḥāh*, which Gottwald 'translates' as 'protective association' and defines as 'a cluster of extended families living in the same or nearby villages . . . providing socio-economic mutual aid for its constituent families, contributing troop quotas to the tribal levy, and indirectly serving alone or in concert to provide a local jural community' (1979, 340). Finally (or perhaps firstly?), there is the tertiary segment of the 'extended family' or 'household' which is 'a primary residential and productive socio-economic unit of two or more generations' and included 'wives, sons, and unmarried daughters of some or all male descendants of the family head' (1979, 341).

It is clear that Gottwald is describing a very detailed and elaborate scheme, but one is forced to ask whether we have any real evidence that such an elaborate structure actually existed in ancient Israel in pre-monarchic times. We have already had occasion to refer to the ambiguity and lack of definition inherent in these sociological terms in Hebrew, and while Gottwald goes some way towards acknowledging that in some passages in the Old Testament these terms do not always bear their 'normative' significance, he usually feels able to explain these deviations in one way or another (text-critically or contextually) and does not allow these uncertainties and ambiguities to deflect him from his overall scheme. But Gottwald's structure is obviously built not on Old Testament evidence alone, since the latter is clearly inadequate as a basis for such elaboration; it is determined partly by two other factors: first, a contrast, within the context of the determining 'peasants' revolt' model, with the structures of the Canaanite society against which 'Israel' was rebelling and, second, the kinds of models which social anthropologists are able to construct from their observations of societies which may broadly be described as 'tribal', the latter usually dating from the nineteenth or early twentieth centuries and from the sub-Saharan areas of Africa, though the Near East, either ancient or (roughly) contemporary, has also sometimes furnished the basis for such models. In both of these areas the work of Gottwald has been heavily criticised, primarily in a recent book by the Danish scholar N. P. Lemche (1985), a book which not only has a fair share of infelicities of English style (in spite of its having been translated by an Englishman) but is also so bestrewn by a multiplicity of typographical errors that one cannot conceive of its ever having been proof-read.

In the context of Canaanite social structure, there is no direct evidence which would enable us either to corroborate or to disprove the postulates which Gottwald produces as that against which Israelite social structure was a reaction. Our closest evidence would be from Ugarit, which is distanced not only in time but also in geographical location, but where there is, in any case, very little evidence either. From what we *can* tell about Ugaritic society, it would seem as if the families there were small and nuclear (i.e. *not* extended, as is generally believed to have been the case in the Israelite context), the genealogical depth is poor, and it is probably impossible to draw any very firm conclusions about the structure of Canaanite society from such scanty material (Lemche, 1985, 206–7).

When it comes to the anthropological base of Gottwald's conclusions about Israelite society, Lemche levels much the same criticism against it as did Rogerson against Mendenhall's base (see above p. 97), namely that it is much too narrow or even potentially erroneous. On the question of 'lack of breadth', Lemche points out that when Gottwald speaks of 'current theory about tribalism', he is drawing on the work of a very limited circle of American social anthropologists, mainly that of Fried, Sahlins and Service, primarily the latter who is, of course, also the one to whom Mendenhall also refers, and fails to take any serious account of any other views on the nature of 'tribe' (Lemche, 1985, 209ff.). When it comes to a definition of 'clan', a social unit which, Gottwald is at pains to point out, though for no very obvious reason, does *not* exist in its normally accepted form in ancient Israel, Gottwald actually utilises one which appeared in a social anthropology textbook which first saw the light of day in 1877 (Lemche, 1985, 232)! So, in Lemche's view, not only is Gottwald's anthropological base far too narrow, it is also outdated.

Another of the linch-pins of Gottwald's argument is that ancient Israel was what anthropologists call a 'segmented society'. In such societies, sometimes referred to, perhaps more accurately, as 'segmentary lineage systems', there is no centralised power, rather a *distribution* of power throughout a number of groups or 'segments', all of which have equal status (Rogerson, 1986, 17). This view of ancient Israelite society is not, of course, unique to Gottwald. As Rogerson (1986) has pointed out, 'it is rapidly becoming received opinion in Old Testament studies that premonarchic Israel was indeed a segmentary society' (1986, 17). But in Gottwald's structure this is a significant point, since for him segmentary systems are by definition egalitarian ones, and egalitarianism is one of the key characteristics of a social structure which has emerged from a 'peasants' revolt' model. In Gottwald's case in particular, Lemche subjects this assertion, that 'segmentary' equals 'egalitarian', to logical analysis and again concludes that, precisely because Gotwald bases his discussion on such a narrow range of definitions and fails to take into account other possible definitions of the relevant terminology, the basis for his idea of an egalitarian, segmentary society is uncertain. 'In short, as defined by Service and others, and as utilized by Gottwald, the expression "segmentary societies are egalitarian ones" has little to recommend it' (Lemche, 1985, 223).

Rogerson (1986) also looks at the question of whether 'segmentary society' is a useful designation for ancient Israel and, having examined the work of more recent anthropologists (especially that of C. Sigrist in *Regulierte Anarchie* [1967], also utilised by Lemche), he concludes that, although many parallels between segmentary societies and premonarchic Israel may be found, there are at least two characteristics of segmentary societies which do not find a parallel in ancient Israelite society. In the first place, there is no rule of primogeniture or of ultimogeniture in true segmentary societies. The eldest son may indeed take over the role of 'head of household' when a parent dies, but in order to preserve 'segmentation' he is obliged to treat his brothers equally. Secondly, segmentary societies display a lack of parental authority and legal power. In the light of these two elements, which are the opposite of what is found in Israel, Rogerson warns us 'against an over-hasty and superficial equation of pre-monarchic Israel with segmentary lineage societies' and points out that 'the analogy with the Old Testament is hardly persuasive' (1986, 24).

The anthropological basis for the description of ancient Israel as a segmentary society is, once again (see above pp. 96 and 101), the studies of African tribal societies of the nineteenth and twentieth centuries (see, e.g., the works cited by Rogerson, 1986, 24 n. 6), with the study of the Nuer tribe of the Sudan by the British anthropologist E. E. Evans-Pritchard perhaps the best known and certainly the most influential. Gottwald makes no direct reference to this last since, as we have already noted, his anthropological base is comparatively restricted, but Sahlins, one of the anthropologists whom Gottwald does cite, has relied substantially on the work of Evans-Pritchard.

In a recent article, David Fiensy has subjected the 'Nuer model' to re-evaluation and has pointed to its enormous influence on the anthropological approach to the study of ancient Israelite society. However, Fiensy goes on to indicate a number of areas where Evans-Pritchard's analysis of Nuer society and culture has recently been subject to criticism and concludes that 'recent anthropological studies have seriously questioned the model of an acephalous [i.e. without a central leader-figure], segmented Nuer society' (Fiensy, 1987, 78) and quotes one contemporary anthropologist (A. Kuper) as saying, 'I see no reason to salvage any part of the Nuer model' (Fiensy, 1987, 79). Fiensy is not entirely negative in his conclusion – not so negative, at any rate, as is Rogerson (1986), for example – but concludes that 'more study on this problem needs to be done' (1987, 80). Perhaps more significant, however, are these words from his penultimate paragraph: 'The Old Testament specialist must follow the current debate in anthropology to ensure that biblical research is not based on discredited ethnological theories' (1987, 80). This brings us back to the plea made by Rogerson in his earlier publication for 'some form of inter-disciplinary co-operation' as the basis for adequate research in this whole area (1978, 101). This plea seems largely to have gone unheeded. While a number of scholars make more or less overt reference to advice or counsel given by anthropology colleagues in the course of their work, no publication has appeared over the joint names of an anthropologist and an Old Testament scholar.

Let us look, finally, within the context of the nature of Israelite society in the premonarchic period, at the contribution of Lemche (1985), to whose work we have already had occasion to refer. Much of Lemche's book is taken up with criticism of de Geus and (Mendenhall-)Gottwald, but he also has a contribution of his own to make.

In a chapter entitled 'Social Structure in Israel in the pre-National Period' 1985, 245–90) Lemche, in his turn, subjects to analysis the three sociological terms used in Hebrew to describe Israelite society: *bēṯ ʾāḇ*, *mišpāḥāh* and *šēḇeṭ* (or *maṭṭeh*). He begins with the lowest level, the *bēṯ ʾāḇ*, a term often rendered in English by 'family' and generally believed in the ancient Israelite context to have referred to an 'extended family'. By 'extended family' scholars have usually understood several generations living together as a residential unit; in Gottwald's view, for example, this comprised up to five generations, and he considered that 'a thriving *bēth-ʾāv* might easily comprise from fifty to one hundred persons'. Lemche reacts to these statements in a number of ways. In the first instance, in view of the short life-span which was prevalent at the time, he considers it unlikely that an 'extended family' would include any more than three generations at most. Secondly, it is clear from archaeological evidence that no structures in ancient Israel were large enough to contain a group of people of the size envisaged by Gottwald. It is unclear, therefore, what precisely the latter means when he speaks of a 'residential unit'. It is obvious that the Old Testament contains references to families which contain only a very small number of members, and these are 'nuclear families'. We have already noted that what little evidence there is about social structure in Ugaritic society suggests that the nuclear family was the norm there (above p.101). Anthropologists use the term 'lineage' to refer to a social group of fifty or more people who live as separate family groups. Gottwald, then, has confused the terms 'lineage' and 'family', nor has he clearly distinguished between 'nuclear families' and 'extended families'. Lemche goes on to analyse the passages where *bēṯʾāḇ* is used in the Old Testament and to determine, if possible, the precise societal level or levels to which the expression refers in any given passage (1985, 251–9). The conclusion which he reaches is that *bēt ʾāḇ* is used to refer both to extended families and to lineages and that it is therefore necessary, in individual cases of the occurrence of the term, to undertake an analysis in order to determine in which sense it is being used. It is clear, from a number of passages, that 'nuclear families' did exist in ancient Israel, though since most of the figures encountered in the Old Testament are great men, the emphasis does tend to be on extended rather than on nuclear families. In Judg. 14:19, however, the expression *bēṯ ʾāḇ* is used to refer to the nuclear family which comprises Samson, his father and his mother (cf. vv. 2, 9). The main point which becomes clear from Lemche's analysis is that this lowest term in the Israelite context is used to refer to a variety of social groupings ranging from the nuclear family up to and including the lineage.

Lemche then goes on to analyse the next kinship concept, the *mišpāḥāh* (1985, 260–74). On the basis of Josh. 7:17, *mišpāḥāh* is regarded as the level between 'family' and 'tribe', a level which, in accordance with standard sociological descriptions, is usually held to be the 'clan'. *Mišpāḥāh* occurs most frequently in the Old Testament in genealogical contexts which are for the most part of Priestly provenance. Such occurrences in lists may well be due to Priestly systematising and may therefore tell us very little about the original 'sociological' significance of the term. It is the relatively infrequent occurrences of *mišpāḥāh* in narrative contexts which must be analysed to see what such a sociological significance may have been. As a result of such an analysis, Lemche comes to several conclusions. On the one hand, it appears that it was possible to refer to any of several levels within Israelite social structure as a *mišpāḥāh*; most probably what is intended is the lineage, which, as we have seen, is a level for which the term *bēṯ ʾāḇ* is also used, and the 'maximal lineage', the level which comes between the lineage and the tribe. The terms *mišpāḥāh* and *bēṯ ʾāḇ*, then, overlap to some extent, and the boundaries between them are fluid. The former refers to the higher rather than to the lower levels of Israelite society, while the reverse is the case with the latter. The overlap between them occurs at the midway point. It is also, Lemche argues, incorrect to suggest, as has so often been done, that the *mišpāḥāh* represents the most important social or political factor in Israelite society. One outstanding argument against such a suggestion is the astonishing fact that none of the three commonest leadership titles (*zāqēn*, *rōʾš*, *nāśīʾ*) is in fact used alongside *mišpāḥāh*. For the ancient Israelite, the 'family', of whatever size, must have been of decisive importance. Several 'families' no doubt combined to form a 'lineage', and these 'lineages' would, either severally or in combination, form the population of a village or a small town. 'Lineages' in such situations were no doubt the important political units in ancient Israel, and Lemche's main conclusion from this part of his chapter is that the *mišpāḥāh* was not a social unit with any significant political role. At the end of this section there is an excursus on 'Marriage in Israel', the conclusion of which is that *en*dogamous marriages were the norm in ancient Israel, but that *ex*ogamous ones were not unheard of.

Finally Lemche comes to his analysis of the two terms which are usually translated as 'tribe', namely *šēḇeṭ* and *maṭṭeh* (1985, 274–90). Here he is less easy to pin down. Israelite tribes, he says, are constructed on the basis of a number of segmentation levels ranging from sub-tribes down to nuclear families. If the sources do not permit us to conclude that such was the case, we cannot either assume or conclude that these tribes were governed by some kind of egalitarian ideology such as Gottwald argues for. The Priestly information about tribes is late and again probably betrays scant knowledge of circumstances in the pre-national period. Only Judges and possibly Samuel contain material that can be used for an examination of leadership in Israelite tribal society, and since almost every tradition in these sources tells us something about a chieftain-type figure, we could probably deduce that such a figure was a commonly acceptable one in ancient Israelite tribal society. This was not, then, an egalitarian society but one out of which specific leaders emerged to cope with specific historical situations such as attack or oppression on the part of hostile neighbours. Such chieftainships were probably of fairly short-term duration, but there was no apparent resentment in ancient Israel to such centralised leadership, and this, as we shall see, is an important element in recent studies of the emergence of monarchy. The main point which Lemche wishes to make is that Israelite tribes had only an ephemeral political organisation; even if chieftainships existed, they probably made very little difference to the daily political life of the tribe, where, as we have already seen, Lemche believes the family/lineage played the more dominant role.

Lemche does appear to *assume* the existence of 'tribes' in ancient Israel, and his analysis of this term seems less rigorous than that to which he subjects the other two terms. On the question of what the nature of an Israelite tribe actually was, he admits that our sources do not provide us with a definitive answer, since all of the traditions which speak of the origins of Israel – and only a historical answer, he believes, can break what he considers to be the circular nature of the definitions proposed hitherto – speak of *all* the Israelite tribes. Thus Lemche links the question of 'nature' with the question of 'origins', but his connecting thread between these two concepts is not made very obvious. In this question of origins, however, he is already setting off on the road that leads backwards from the *nature* of Israelite society in the pre-monarchic period to that earlier question which is addressed by a number of the writers who deal with pre-monarchic (or pre-national) Israel.

For many years the controversy which raged concerning Israel's origins was whether the Israelites arrived in Palestine by a process of 'conquest' or by one of (comparatively peaceful) 'settlement'. The latter approach tended to assume that Israel's pre-settlement origins were 'nomadic', but both the 'conquest' approach and the 'settlement' approach could be classified broadly as an 'immigration' hypothesis. In other words, however one conceives precisely of Israel's arrival in Palestine, both schools of thought were united in regarding 'Israel' as having come from outside

Palestine. Lemche, to remain with him for the time being, is of the opinion that the biblical traditions normally drawn upon for the study of this question have to be treated with extreme caution. Traditions about the pre-national period no doubt existed prior to the exile, but their written formation, he believes, cannot be dated any earlier than the exilic period (1985, 384). They are, therefore, removed by more than half a millenium from the events which they purport to describe. Even if we were to adhere to an early monarchical date for the Yahwist, the written fixation would still be removed from the pre-national period by something like 300 years (1985, 377–8). In view of the nature of the biblical traditions, Lemche would insist that archaeological support would be necessary for any hypothesis about Israel's origins, and while he admits that archaeology provides evidence of dramatic events in the region in this period (that of the transition from the Late Bronze Age to the Early Iron Age), there is no reason to believe that this evidence has anything to do with a specifically *Israelite* immigration. It cannot be denied that population movements took place both inside and into Palestine, but there is very little in the way of hard evidence which would force us to make an assumption about *Israelite* population movements, and there is certainly nothing in the archaeological material which would tell us anything about a *political* entity known as 'Israel' (1985, 405–6). What Lemche is saying is twofold: he is stressing the genuine limitations of archaeological evidence, but he is also saying that, since such evidence is the *only* evidence which can be relatively securely dated to the period in question, it is the *only* evidence which can be relied upon for a reconstruction of the broad outlines of Israel's origins. Archaeology, then, does not confirm an immigration model for Israel's origins. We have, of course, already seen that de Geus denies a nomadic phase as a prelude to a settled phase for ancient Israel and has pointed out that nomadism is actually an offshoot of settled agrarianism rather than a prelude to it (above, p. 98).

More recently, of course, another model has been added to the range of theories, that of the peasants' revolt. This was first elaborated by Mendenhall as long ago as 1962, but its main proponent has, of course, been Gottwald in his 1979 monograph. To such an extent have both of these scholars been associated in people's minds with the 'revolt' model that they tend to be bracketed together and held jointly responsible for it, even by as recent a writer as Lemche in 1985. Yet Mendenhall himself has strongly dissociated himself from Gottwald and in fact denounced Gottwald and Gottwald's interpretation in no uncertain terms (Mendenhall, 1983). Mendenhall makes the point (1983, 92) that in his earlier article (1962) he used the term 'peasants' revolt' only once and states that Gottwald's work is an attempt 'to force the ancient historical data into the Procrustes' Bed of nineteenth-century Marxist ideology' (1983, 91). He goes on: 'In the process, of course, anything that doesn't fit the system is either explained away, or more often quietly ignored. Gottwald's "scientific" account of the "liberated" tribes of Yahweh consists largely of an endless series of hyphenated [the title of Mendenhall's article is 'Ancient Israel's Hyphenated History'] pseudo-social science terms foisted with limitless faith upon the hapless ancient tribesmen who unfortunately were too benighted to know that they were conforming to the canons of a nineteenth-century ideology' (1983, 92). Mendenhall's view of the events which actually happened may be summed up as follows: From the collapse of the city-states many fled to thinly populated regions where they led less stressful if more economically insecure lives. As a result, these thinly populated regions show considerable and sudden growth in occupation. In the power vacuum created by the collapse of the larger social organisations, control over what is left of the 'cities' is taken by professional military bands, pirates by sea and by land. In reaction against the prospect of again being dominated by urban political forces, the non-urban population comes together in a covenant of peace under a God whose demands meet the needs of all. This coming together is what Mendenhall describes as 'the intense solidarity of the Yahwist federation' (1983, 98–9). This 'working hypothesis', as he calls it, is supported not only by the archaeological evidence available but also by cautiously used sociological models, and it is certainly not disproved by anything in the biblical traditions (1983, 99–102).

The other essays that appeared in the same volume as did that of Mendenhall all expound the 'revolt' model in one way or another, and indeed the article by M. L. Chaney is a much more approachable exposition than is that of Gottwald (1979). Although that volume (ed. by Freedman and Graf) was first published in 1983, most of the essays in it had been written much earlier. Gottwald's 1979 book is mentioned only in a footnote in Chaney's article and does not appear in his bibliography, and Mendenhall's article is in fact a review of Gottwald's book. Already in 1978 a number of the *Journal for the Study of the Old Testament* had appeared which was largely devoted (*JSOT* 7, 1–52; see also *JSOT* 8, 46–9) to a discussion of the 'peasants' revolt' model. But these discussions have now largely been overtaken by events, since the debate took on a different aspect after the appearance of Gottwald's 1979 monograph.

We have already seen, in earlier pages, something of Lemche's criticisms of Gottwald (Lemche, 1985; above *passim*), and we have also seen Mendenhall's violent reaction against Gottwald's approach (Mendenhall,

1983). In this last essay of Mendenhall's, he rather carefully avoids amplification of the 'revolt' aspect of his original model but speaks, rather, of an 'escape' from the stresses inherent in a disintegrating urban social system. Although he does not himself use the term, what he is describing is neither 'immigration' nor 'revolt' but 'emergence', and indeed the subtitle of the volume in which his essay appeared is 'The Emergence of Ancient Israel'. It is towards a concept of 'emergence' that most recent scholarship about Israel's origins has been moving. In the same year as the Freedman–Graf collection of essays, there appeared also a book by B. Halpern with 'emergence' in its title (Halpern, 1983). Halpern's book is only partly about the process that is indicated by the older 'settlement-conquest' terminology, and at the end of the day it becomes clear that the book is really about the establishment of an Israelite state and about the 'emergence' of monarchy. We shall return to that topic shortly and simply observe here what Halpern has to say about the origins of Israel. It is, in fact, not entirely clear what Halpern's view of Israelite origins really is. At one point he states that 'close examination of the Amarna materials, therefore, does not sustain Mendenhall's and Gottwald's hypotheses' (1983:63), but he appears to believe that the peasants' revolt model does have some merit. In spite of the fact that one chapter of Part II of his book is called 'The Israelite Conquest' and might lead one to suppose that he is championing that particular model, he concludes that section of his book which deals with the 'origins' question (1983:45–106) by stating that 'Israel was a strident "No!" to the lowlands and centralized domination of Canaan' (1983, 106). So, in spite of the 'emergence' of his title, Halpern still seems to be an adherent, in some sense at least, of the 'revolt' model.

Lemche proves to be bolder in his approach, and while, in his chapter on the archaeological evidence (1985, 386–406), he states that 'nothing in the archaeological evidence *contradicts* the revolution hypothesis', he goes on to say that, on the other hand, the same evidence does not '*prove* that the revolution hypothesis is the only conceivable explanation of Israel's origins' (1985, 406). In his 'Conclusion', which is entitled 'Evolutionary Israel: An Alternative Explanation of Israel's Origins', he moves more in the direction of an 'emergence' or, in his word, 'evolution' model. Lemche speaks very tentatively of 'the emergence of tribal societies in the Near East at the close of the Bronze Age and the beginnings of the Iron Age' and of 'the emergence of the Israelite tribes, or rather, of a number of Palestinian tribes whose various populations became unified in the kingdom of Israel after the formation of the state' (1985, 430). In this last we can see that for Lemche, as indeed for others working in this field, one cannot begin to speak of 'Israel' as a historical entity until the establishment of the monarchy. It is in this sense that the word 'Israel' must be being used in the title of Halpern's book referred to above.

But where did this tribal society emerge from? It was, says Lemche, 'the result of a movement which owed its origins to the choices made by individual persons, families and lineages with respect to their way of life. In other words, the parties involved had said goodbye to their previous existence, which had been made miserable by the poor social conditions which were all the Canaanite states had to offer in the Late Bronze Age' (1985:431). Here, then, is no 'peasants' revolt' but a movement of individuals and families from the wretchedness of existence under the city-state system to a new life of necessarily greater self-reliance in less fertile terrain than the plains where the city-states were, in the isolated mountainous regions of Palestine. The great need was to transform this less productive terrain into something that was productive, and it is this aspect of Israel's 'evolution' which is dealt with in greater detail in Hopkins's book *The Highlands of Canaan* (1985).

Hopkins's detailed study of what is subtitled 'Agricultural Life in the Early Iron Age' is framed by an introduction, part of which is called 'Agriculture and the Emergence of Israel' (1985, 21–4), and by a conclusion entitled 'Subsistence Challenges and the Emergence of Israel' (1985, 265–75). Here Hopkins considers the *mišpāḥāh* to be a 'supra-household social grouping', the main purpose of which was to provide 'a context for the sharing of risks', a judgment which he feels is adequately supported not only by the biblical data but also by 'ethnographic analogy' (1985, 269). It was the challenges of agricultural life in this harsh setting which led to the 'emergence' of Israel in Hopkins' view, challenges which 'permitted no social isolation for household or village, but impelled these into larger circles of social relationships' (1985, 271). It was in this way, he argues, that Israel as a society 'evolved' with its social groupings evolving in their turn as 'support groups'. This idea is undoubtedly reminiscent of Gottwald's understanding of *mišpāḥōṯ* as 'protective associations' (see above p. 100).

One of the mainstays both of Mendenhall's and of Gottwald's reconstructions was the significant role played in the formation of the people by the religion of Yahweh. This is particularly prominent in Gottwald's work, as can be seen from the subtitle of his major monograph (1979). 'A Sociology of the *Religion* of Liberated Israel'. Even in Mendenhall's harsh rejection of Gottwald's views, a religious factor still plays a dynamic role in Israel's origins. This aspect, too, is criticised by Lemche who, in a careful analysis of the Old Testament traditions, has shown that the covenant concept seems to have played no significant role in Israel's religious life before the sixth century BC (1985:306–85). He considers it a fundamental mistake simply to assume that, because Israelite religion itself claims to have been unique from its very beginnings, it must have been so, and he goes on to suggest that in fact 'its special characteristics were the results of a long historical development, rather than its point of departure' (1985:435). Just as he had suggested earlier that Israel's historical traditions arose in an age which is much later than the age to which they purport to refer, so, too, her religious traditions reflect the thinking of the end of a process rather than its origins.

Let us turn now briefly to the area of enquiry which pushes forward to ask the question about the nature of the society from which the Israelite *state*, and especially the introduction of monarchy, emerged. The usual view, and this is the view which is fostered by the biblical tradition itself, is that monarchy was an alien institution *vis-à-vis* the social structure of the Israel of the Judges period and that, in wishing it upon itself, Israel was somehow destroying its ancient, inherited tribal traditions. But recent work in this field, again, to some extent at least, from an anthropological point of view, has reached the conclusion that 'the emergence of Israel and . . . the transition to statehood must be seen as a continuum . . . and not as a dialectical conflict'. The monarchy is not an alien institution imposed upon Israel but is 'an outgrowth of the particular configuration of circumstances surrounding the emergence of Israel in Palestine' (Coote and Whitelam, 1986, 115). This view emerges from a broader perspective of Palestinian history than is usual in Old Testament scholarly circles, a perspective against which alone Israel's emergence and transition to statehood are to be seen as part of a whole complex of processes which span many centuries. This *longue durée* view of history – as opposed to the kind of history which endeavours to reconstruct the minutiae of separate events – is indebted to the approach of Fernand Braudel, the French historian of the Mediterranean world in the age of Philip II, and it is Braudel who has been a major influence on Coote and Whitelam both in their 1986 essay and in their more developed monograph of 1987. In the latter, in the title of which the term 'emergence' appears again, they begin by surveying 'aspects of Palestinian history in the very broadest terms' (1987, 8) in order to enable 'the emergence of Israel and the rise of the state . . . to be set firmly in the context of the recurrent patterns' (1987, 9). Broadly speaking, their view of Israel's 'emergence' is similar to that of Hopkins; in other words, 'Israel' emerges from a background of 'rural instability' in order to provide the economic stability necessary for subsistence agriculture. But this loose confederation of various groups is held in equilibrium by a particular configuration of circumstances. This was their view in 1986 (1986, 123);

their 1987 view does not seem to have changed very much beyond perhaps giving expression to their 'increasing doubts about the unity of early Israel' (1987, 10), a unity which they find difficult to locate any earlier than the reign of David, if even then (1987, 7).

Another contribution to the idea of a continuum between pre-monarchic and monarchic Israel was made in an important article by Flanagan (1981). He built his hypothesis on the anthropological foundation of Colin Renfrew (an article in a collection of essays called *Reconstructing Complex Societies*, 1974). Flanagan cites the twenty traits listed by Renfrew which distinguish chiefdoms from egalitarian societies (1981, 51–2) and considers that most of these features can be documented in Israel (1981, 69). Flanagan is here referring primarily to literary traditions; Frick (1985:94–5), referring to archaeological evidence and citing the views of Ruth Tringham, believes that about half of Renfrew's features cannot be discerned in the archaeological remains of a non-literate society. But both Flanagan and Frick would agree that the concept of Israel as a chiefdom, that evolutionary stage in societies between tribalism and kingship, when individual chiefly figures emerged as leaders of varied non-egalitarian social groups (Flanagan: 1981, 47; for a neat definition of a 'chiefdom' see Hauer: 1986, 7 in the course of an article in which a view broadly similar to this is expounded), provides the continuum between pre-monarchic and monarchic Israel which is lacking in most earlier studies. Viewed from this point of view, there is a natural development from Israel as a tribal society through chiefdoms under the leadership of Saul and David to full-blown statehood and monarchy as embodied in Solomon. This is what Flanagan (1981, 47) refers to as a 'cultural evolutionary hypothesis', and it provides additional support for the 'historical continuum' view of statehood in ancient Israel which has been proposed by others, notably most recently by Coote and Whitelam (1986 and 1987).

It is perhaps worth noting that, in the course of his article (see especially 1981, 58–65), Flanagan has made a study of genealogies and that here we have a response, consciously based on the work of Wilson, to Rogerson's early plea for serious note to be taken of this material (1978, 100–1). Whether one can be quite so definite about a preceding 'egalitarian, segmental phase among the Yahwists' (1981, 55) as Flanagan supposes, we have already had occasion to doubt, in that the concept of Israel as a 'segmentary society' has been questioned, as has not only the concept of Israelite society as 'egalitarian' but also the role of Yahwistic religion as either a cohesive or a cathartic force at this early stage. Lemche (see above p.106) has already spoken about 'chieftainships' in pre-monarchic Israel, but in that context he was referring to the 'judges' figures in that period.

Flanagan, on the other hand, would regard Saul as the first of the 'chiefs', with David standing 'on the boundary line between chiefdom and kingdom' (1981, 67). It may, however, be that Israel as a chiefdom can be pushed further back as Lemche suggests, without destroying the overall concept of 'continuity' between pre-monarchic and monarchic Israel which recent work has suggested.

Is it possible to see an overall pattern in these recent 'anthropological' approaches to the study of early Israel, and is it feasible to suggest directions in which such work might profitably move? The broad trends are reasonably clear. Studies on Israel's origins tend to suggest 'emergence' or 'evolution' as the descriptions of the process whereby Israel made its appearance on Palestinian soil. The 'immigration' model has been largely abandoned, though the 'revolt' model still has its adherents. Those who advocate the 'emergence/evolution' model regard it perhaps as a less abrasive version of the 'revolt' model, with which it has certain affinities. With regard to the question of the nature of Israelite society in the pre-monarchic period, there is no clear consensus. Some scholars, Gottwald for example, describe it from the top downwards, and the pattern that emerges is clear and detailed. Others, Lemche for example, describe it from the bottom upwards, and this leads to an analysis which sees the lower to middle levels of society as more concisely definable and where the higher levels are more amorphous. This lack of precision at the top end of the social perspective is in line with the view expressed by such scholars that Israelite 'unity' can scarcely be spoken of before the time of David. There is, again, a fairly obvious trend at the upper end of the pre-monarchic period towards seeing the advent of statehood and monarchy in ancient Israel as a natural development, a historical continuum from the preceding period, as opposed to the widely accepted view of discontinuity in the nature of these two stages of social development.

These three areas – origins, social structure, advent of monarchy – have not, however, been very cohesively welded together as yet. Those who have dealt with 'origins' usually have little to say about the structure of the society which thus emerges, while those who deal with 'social structure' usually have little to say about 'origins'. A greater feeling of comprehensiveness can be felt in those who are dealing with the 'emergence' of statehood, and this is no doubt to a great extent conditioned by their *longue durée* approach to Palestinian history generally. This is a welcome approach to the history of ancient Israel, and it is greatly to be hoped that the comprehensiveness inherent in it can be extended to encompass, in a more balanced way, origins and social structure as well as advent of statehood. What is required is a *plus longue vue* of this whole period and not simply a book which has a particular axe to grind or which is concerned with one of these aspects to the virtual exclusion of the others. The three areas of study are interconnected, and we need a perspective on the Israel of this period which includes them all.

There are, in addition, three aspects of the studies surveyed here where either caution or ongoing concern is required. The first of them is perhaps already implicit in the *longue durée* approach to history, in that Coote and Whitelam's 'minimal recourse to biblical texts' (Gottwald, 1986:5) is a deliberate policy. Where caution is needed, then, is with regard to the nature and therefore the value of the biblical traditions. This sounds like an old chestnut, one which was vexing Martin Noth, for example, over fifty years ago. A position of extreme scepticism is, as we have already observed (above, p.107) adopted by Lemche. Rogerson (1986) is perhaps also tending in the same direction with his parenthetic 'assumption' that Judges and 1 Samuel 'can be used as evidence for pre-monarchic social organization' (1986, 20; see also 1986, 23 where he makes the point that pre-monarchic attitudes may not have been totally eradicated by the advent of monarchy). Norman Whybray's *The Making of the Pentateuch* (1987) is but the latest in a whole series of studies from many different quarters which have made us think twice about the historical reliability of the biblical traditions which purport to deal with Israel's early history. This is one question which needs to be taken seriously in future studies in this area.

If the biblical texts contain little, if any, historically reliable information, where is solid ground to be found? The answer lies in the realm of archaeology. We have already seen the archaeological context explained in the work of Lemche (1985, 386–406, see above p.107), and it also features prominently in the work of Hopkins (1985). More recently, Brandfon has underlined the importance of archaeology's role in reconstructing Israel's history. No longer are the issues the old ones of whether or not archaeology confirms or denies a biblical 'conquest' narrative. Scholars have now moved away from regarding the biblical traditions as providing us with an account of 'events' in Israel's history to regarding archaeology as not just 'the "mere" background of history' but as providing 'the structural basis which influences, to some extent, the events'. Brandfon continues: 'The relationship between archaeological data and the historical events in early Israel's history is, accordingly, redefined, allowing the archaeological evidence to be seen not as unsatisfactorily limited but as an entrée to a new and broad field of historical inquiry' (Brandfon, 1987, 31–34, the quotations from p. 34). Since archaeological excavation and investigation is an ongoing scholarly activity, so this aspect of the study of Israel's early history must be an ongoing one which, since it alone is datable with a degree of precision to the period under review, must be allowed a major control element in the picture which is drawn.

Lastly, we come to the use of sociological models in the study of pre-monarchic Israel. Although this is generally thought to be a recent contribution to biblical scholarship, it is not perhaps as new as some might think. Pedersen, for example, as early as 1940, had introduced the concept of 'chieftainship' in his understanding of pre-monarchic Israel (1940, 33–106). We have seen throughout this chapter how fraught with danger is the sociological approach for the unwary. Models which have been seized upon with enthusiasm by some scholars and have even become 'common currency' in Old Testament scholarship have subsequently been found to be flawed or have come to be regarded with suspicion in anthropological circles. As a result, Old Testament scholars have sometimes found themselves wedded to outmoded anthropological ideas and concepts. It is here that the greatest controversy rages and here that the greatest amount of work has still to be done, and that in spite of all the advances of recent years, Rogerson's plea for co-operative activity (1978, 97 and 101), already referred to several times above, still stands as an as yet largely unfulfilled ideal. The attitudes of biblical scholars to socio-anthropological approaches to ancient Israel's history range from extreme scepticism to hope and enthusiasm. At the one end of the scale stands Mendenhall: 'Only a couple of months ago I asked one of our most eminent sociologists whether modern sociology could be used as the basis for reconstructing an ancient society. The response was a vigorous negative' (1983, 91). Not too far distanced from him is Lemche: 'Sociological methods are useful only to a limited extent in connection with the interpretation of phenomena which are poorly illuminated by the available sources . . . It is simply out of the question to superimpose one or another conception of the nature of tribal societies upon the data concerning Israel and then to conclude that its structure was so and so, its ideology had this and that contents, and that its historical origins and development must have taken such and such turns' (1986, 291).

The opposite extreme is represented by Frick (1985). We have made only a passing reference to Frick's book (see above, p.112) which is 'A Survey of Models and Theories' and deals with various areas which have been discussed above, such as 'segmentary societies', 'chiefdoms', 'agriculture and social organisation' and 'the path to statehood' (to cite the titles of chs 2–5). But this book is an example of a tendency which is in danger of becoming prevalent in the context of biblical scholarship, namely the use of socio-anthropological theory and jargon with a bare minimum of reference to the Old Testament ('only light documented'!; 1985, 196), so much so that the book becomes almost unreadable without an Honours Degree in Social Sciences. This is a path to be avoided at all costs, if those who are enthusiastic about this approach are not to lose in advance those whom they would wish to convince and in turn enthuse. Such studies must be expressed in terms which are comprehensible to those without in-depth knowledge of social anthropology, even though they are – and must be – written by those who have such knowledge. Those who are as yet resistant to such an approach must be met at the place where they are, and their resistance is not going to be overcome by an onslaught of social scientific terminology.

A more hopeful attitude is perhaps found expressed in Hauer (1987, 17), where he suggests that 'we are really in the early stages of the application of anthropology in the history of Israel'. If this is indeed the situation and if the pace of the way forward can be kept steady, then perhaps real advances can be made and the sceptics can be convinced and carried along. A more moderate and more realistic view of the *status quo* is expressed by Miller: 'The whole discipline of sociology is still searching for bearings. I think the dust will have to settle a great deal more before we can speak of any assured results in the area of sociology and biblical history' (1987, 56).

Bibliography

This represents only a selection of recent works dealing with this period. Other references may be found in the Bibliographies of the works cited below.

Brandfon, F. R., 1978. 'Kinship, Culture and "Longue Durée"', *JSOT* 39, 30–8.

Chaney, M. L., 1983. 'Ancient Palestinian Peasant Movements and the Formation of Premonarchic Israel', in Freedman and Graf, 39–90.

Coote, R. B. and Whitelam, K. W., 1986. 'The Emergence of Israel: Social Transformation and State Formation Following the Decline in Late Bronze Age Trade', *Semeia* 37 (=Gottwald, 1986), 107–47.

1987. *The Emergence of Early Israel in Historical Perspective* (The Social World of Biblical Antiquity Series: 5), Sheffield, Almond Press.

Fiensy, D., 1987. 'Using the Nuer Culture of Africa in Understanding the Old Testament: An Evaluation', *JSOT* 38, 73–83.

Flanagan, J. W., 1981. 'Chiefs in Israel', *JSOT* 20, 47–73.

Freedman, D. N. and Graf, D. F. (eds.), 1983. *Palestine in Transition. The Emergence of Ancient Israel* (The Social World of Biblical Antiquity Series: 2), Sheffield, Almond Press.

Frick, F. S., 1985. *The Formation of the State in Ancient Israel. A Survey of Models and Theories* (The Social World of Biblical Antiquity Series: 4), Sheffield, Almond Press.

Geus, C. H. J. de, 1976. *The Tribes of Israel* (Studia Semitica Neerlandica: 18), Amsterdam, Van Gorcum.

Gottwald, N. K., 1978. 'The Hypothesis of the Revolutionary Origins of Ancient Israel: A Response to Hauser and Thompson', *JSOT* 7, 37–52.

1979. *The Tribes of Yahweh. A Sociology of the Religion of Liberated Israel 1250–1050 B.C.E.*, Maryknoll, Orbis (British Edition, SCM, 1980)

1983. 'Early Israel and the Canaanite Socio-Economic System', in Freedman and Graf, 25–37.

1985. 'The Israelite Settlement as a Social Revolutionary Movement', in *Biclical Archaeology Today*, ed. A. Biran etc., Jerusalem, Israel Exploration Society, 34–46.

1986. ed., *Social Scientific Criticism of the Hebrew Bible and Its Social World: The Israelite Monarchy* (= *Semeia*, 37).

Halpern, B., 1983. *The Emergence of Israel in Canaan* (SBL Monograph Series: 29), Chico, Scholars Press.

Hauer, C. Jr., 1986. 'From Alt to Anthropology: The Rise of the Israelite State', *JSOT* 36, 3–15.

1987. 'Anthropology in Historiography', *JSOT* 39, 15–21.

Hauser, A. J., 1978. 'Israel's Conquest of Palestine: A Peasants' Rebellion?', *JSOT*, 2–19.

1978. 'The Revolutionary Origins of Ancient Israel: A Response to Gottwald', *JSOT* 8, 46–9.

Hayes, J. H., 1987. 'On Reconstructing Israelite History', *JSOT* 39, 5–9.

Herion, G. A., 1986. 'The Impact of Modern and Social Science Assumptions on the Reconstruction of Israelite History', *JSOT* 34, 3–33.

Hopkins, D. C., 1985. *The Highlands of Canaan. Agricultural Life in the Early Iron Age* (The Social World of Biblical Antiquity Series: 3), Sheffield, Almond Press.

Lemche, N. P., 1985. *Early Israel. Anthropological and Historical Studies on the Israelite Society before the Monarchy*, Leiden, E. J. Brill.

Mendenhall, G. E., 1962. 'The Hebrew Conquest of Palestine', *BA* 25, 66–87.

1973. *The Tenth Generation. The Origins of the Biblical Tradition*, Baltimore, The Johns Hopkins University Press.

1978. 'Between Theology and Archaeology', *JSOT* 7, 28–34.

1983. 'Ancient Israel's Hyphenated History', in Freedman and Graf, 90–103.

Miller, J. M., 1987. 'In Defense of Writing a History of Israel', *JSOT* 39, 53–57.

Miller, J. M. and Hayes, J. H., 1986. *A History of Ancient Israel and Judah*, Philadelphia, Westminster Press.

Pedersen, J., 1940. *Israel: Its Life and Culture*, III–IV, Oxford and Copenhagen.

Renfrew, C., 1974. 'Beyond subsistence and economy: the evolution of social organisation in prehistoric Europe', in C. B. Moore (ed.), *Reconstructing Complex Societies*, (Supplement to the *Bulletin of the American Schools of Oriental Research* 20), 69–96.

Rogerson, J. W., 1978. *Anthropology and the Old Testament*, Oxford, Blackwell.

1986. 'Was Early Israel a Segmentary Society?', *JSOT* 36, 17–26.

Thompson, T. L., 1978. 'Historical Notes on "Israel's Conquest of Palestine: A Peasants' Rebellion"', *JSOT* 7, 20–27.

Whybray, R. N., 1987. *The Making of the Pentateuch. A Methodological Study*, (*JSOT* Supplement Series: 53) Sheffield, JSOT Press.

Wilson, R. R., 1979. *Genealogy and History in the Biblical World*, New Haven, Yale University Press.

CHAPTER SIX

Israelite Kingship. The royal ideology and its opponents

KEITH W. WHITELAM

The small states of Ammon, Edom, Moab and Israel appeared as near contemporaneous state formations in the Levant during the Early Iron Age. Yet it is the small kingdom of Israel which emerged in the central highlands of Palestine sometime around 1000 BCE which has, until recently, been the focus of the bulk of scholarly attention by biblical specialists. The reasons for this are not difficult to discover. The kingdom of Israel is both the subject of, and responsible for, the formation and development of many of the traditions in the canon of the Hebrew Bible. The Israelite monarchy was able to take advantage of the temporary decline of the great riverine powers of Egypt and Mesopotamia to exploit its position astride the strategic overland trade and military routes of the Levant. It was able to extend its territorial control over the area at the expense of its immediate neighbours to reach a modest size and influence in the region. However the growing internal pressures from the heterogenous socio-political groups of which it was composed and increasing external pressures from the re-emerging powers to the north and south led to the fragmentation of the kingdom within less than a century of its formation. What political autonomy the subsequent kingdoms of Israel and Judah enjoyed were short-lived and often merely illusory as the territorially, demographically and militarily superior riverine civilisations of Egypt and Mesopotamia reasserted their long-standing interests in this strategic area. The Israelite and Judaean monarchies were brought to an end by the Assyrians and Babylonians little more than four hundred years after the formation of an Israelite state in the highlands of Palestine. The focus of scholarly attention, however, has derived from the fact that this relatively short-lived state has left such a profound effect upon world religious traditions through the preservation of various aspects of Israelite royal ideology in the Hebrew Bible and its effects in shaping the messianic beliefs of later Jewish and Christian communities.

The formation of the state and its ideology

The study of the formation of the Israelite state and its attendant royal ideology forms part of the wider historical and anthropological study into the formation of early state societies and the dynamics of royal ideology, ritual and power. State level organisations have, in recent years, become of particular concern to historians, anthropologists and social scientists. It now seems clear that despite the complex interaction of multiple factors involved in the stimulus of a society to statehood, there are remarkable similarities between early states no matter where they occur.[1] The comparative study of the Israelite monarchy with evidence from other state-level societies allows the historian to discover what is typical, or what is atypical, about its organisation and development. It also allows the historian to break free from the confines and constraints of twentieth-century experience of social organisation and not impose these on the society being studied.

Israelite society is often presented as a static, monolithic entity while the inauguration of the monarchy is portrayed as a historical 'accident' that was a departure or denial of the true nature of Israel but which it was powerless to prevent. All societies are dynamic and complex collections of overlapping and intersecting groups (see Mann: 1986, 1). Significant changes in the socio-political realm, such as the introduction of kingship and the move to statehood, are bound to have profound reverberations throughout the whole of society producing major structural transformations. The centralisation of military, economic, political and religious power entailed in the introduction of kingship produces shifts and strains in the relationships between the various groups throughout society. A definition of the state is notoriously difficult, but generally it is accepted that it represents a centralised government which has the power to enforce laws, collect taxes and conscript labour from the many different communities within a defined territorial unit.[2] The royal bureaucracy, with its political and religious specialists, was responsible for maintaining or enforcing the relationship between the centre, a ruling royal elite, and the peripheries of society. The transition from segmented egalitarian structures to a defined stratified society with the king at the centre drawing upon the wealth of regional and inter-regional trade and the resources of village communities produced structural transformations which were bound to lead to opposition and conflict. Chaney (1986) has already drawn attention to the failure of much previous research to understand monarchic society in systemic terms and to look for inter-social conflict or investigate the underlying changes in institutional integration.

The heavy investment of early state societies in the ideological justification of kingship through written, graphic and ceremonial means indicates the importance of understanding the nature of royal ideology and the way that it functioned or was addressed to different audiences to overcome opposition and thus maintain royal power. The use of force was too costly and on the whole inefficient in maintaining royal power, giving rise to the heavy investment in means to propagate the royal symbolic universe (see Whitelam, 1984, 1986). States could only survive if they attained legitimacy, often through the manipulation of religious symbols, since reliance upon coercion and force would destroy the very relationships upon which the ruling elite depended for their wealth and power. Royal ideology provided a justification for the control of power and strategic resources; it proclaimed that the king's right to rule was guaranteed by the deities of the state. A heavy emphasis was placed upon the benefits of peace, security and wealth for the population of the state which flowed from the king's position in the cosmic scheme of things.

A study of the nature of Israelite kingship and ideology needs to distinguish between the two main forms of opposition to which it gave rise. The process of centralisation set in train during the transition from pre-state to state level society produced considerable inter-tribal and intra-social conflict. One form of opposition to kingship stemmed from groups and individuals who had the most to lose from the structural transformations. The formation of the state meant in reality the transfer of sovereignty over arable land to the king. It gave rise to a complex situation in which there were competing chiefdoms, local notables and various rural groups and village communities attempting to protect their arable land and its produce from the claims of the ruling urban elite.[3] The strength of resistance to the social and political transformations which kingship entails may appear to decrease over time but often continues in peripheral areas or underground movements to erupt in periodic popular protests against the exploitation and oppression of monarchic rule. The second form of conflict in relation to kingship which must be distinguished from the first is the endemic struggle for power among the urban elite. These struggles for power, which draw upon popular unrest for their support, are not attempts to reform or replace kingship with some other form of socio-political organisation, but attempts to usurp royal power. This form of struggle and conflict appears to be endemic to early states and the development of much royal ideology needs to be understood against this background.

The state develops graphic, ceremonial and written means of emphasising and legitimating class differences while establishing the king's right to rule over the competing claims of other urban or rural groups. As the king's power increases so does the ability to invest greater resources in enhancing power and propagating this symbolic universe to internal and external audiences. The study of Israelite royal ideology by biblical specialists which has concentrated upon largely descriptive accounts, or broad comparisons with ancient Near Eastern monarchies, needs to be set in the context of these wider issues.

Opposition to the establishment of kingship

Traditional studies of the rise of the monarchy in Israel have concentrated, naturally enough, on the analysis of the narratives within the Deuteronomistic History, especially 1 Sam. 7–15. The ruling assumption has long been that if these narratives are placed within their socio-political settings they will reveal valuable information with which the historian can reconstruct how kingship originated in Israel. This has been the traditional way of understanding and interpreting the complexities and ambiguities of the narratives in 1 Sam. 8–12, and elsewhere, which refer to the rise of kingship.

Historical reconstructions of the inauguration and development of the Israelite monarchy have been shaped and dominated by Wellhausen's classic source-critical treatment of 1 Sam. 7–12. His identification of an early, authentic, pro-monarchic source (1 Sam. 9.1–10.16; 11) and a late, exilic, fictional, anti-monarchic source (7.2–8.22; 10.17–27; 12) has provided the benchmark for all subsequent discussions. The historical conclusions, however, which he drew from this literary analysis are questionable. He believed the monarchy to be the high point of Israelite development prior to the Exile, 'the greatest blessing of Jehovah' (Wellhausen: 1885, 253), bringing order to the anarchic period of the Judges. However, what is less explicit is the profound influence of conceptions of the nation-state current in nineteenth-century Germany on his own view of the significance of the Israelite monarchy. Wellhausen's views, like those of many of his contemporaries in German biblical scholarship, were shaped by the belief that Bismarck's unification of Germany represented the pinnacle of historical development. This underlying assumption of much nineteenth-century German historiography has had a profound effect upon conceptions of the nature and importance of the state in biblical studies from Wellhausen to Alt and Noth. The far-reaching effects of this on modern biblical studies are only just beginning to be realised and appreciated (Clements: 1983, 173; Coote and Whitelam: 1987, 174–5). Crüsemann (1978, 6–8) has pointed out that many of Wellhausen's ideas were presented in tributes to commemorate the Kaiser's birthday. Furthermore, the conclusion that the anti-monarchic material could not possibly have arisen during the monarchic period but must have been a retrojection of some theocratic ideal from the exilic or post-exilic period is at odds with an understanding of the systemic strains and conflicts involved in major socio-political transformations.

The notion of an early pro-monarchic source and a later anti-monarchic source has affected historical investigations and the type of questions raised concerning Israelite kingship ever since. A crucial endorsement of Wellhausen's position came from M. Noth (1957) who equated the later anti-monarchic source with the stance of the Deuteronomistic Historian to kingship. For Noth, the Deuteronomistic History was a sustained and negative appraisal of Israelite history and its monarchy up to its collapse in 587 BCE. Although Wellhausen believed that the anti-monarchic material could not have been contemporary with the period of the rise of the monarchy, Noth (1960, 164–5) adopted a somewhat ambivalent position in his own classic treatment of Israelite history in which he presented the rise of kingship as a denial of early Israel's true theocratic ideal. He accepted Wellhausen's literary analysis, but nevertheless believed that the anti-monarchic sentiments probably reflected an attitude that was current at the time of the inauguration of the monarchy. This was no longer a late exilic retrojection but stemmed from Israel's tribal religious organisation, the so-called amphictyony, based on the theocratic rule of its god Yahweh who inspired charismatic individuals, 'judges', in times of crisis. For Noth, kingship was an alien institution forced upon Israel by the historical accident of the Philistine military threat with which the amphictyonic organisation was unable to cope. Standard histories of Israel (Noth: 1960; Bright: 1981; Herrmann: 1981) which represent the monarchy in this way fail to account for, or explain, the nature of significant social change embodied in the move to statehood.

There has been widespread support for the attempt to place Wellhausen's anti-monarchic source in a much earlier historical context. One of the most influential treatments in this area has been Mendelsohn's analysis (1956) of Samuel's critique of kingship (1 Sam. 8) in the light of Ugaritic evidence for the nature of Canaanite kingship. He concludes that such negative sentiments might well reflect contemporary concerns about the nature of kingship based on the experience of neighbouring models. It need not stem originally from experiences of the abuse of royal power whether from the Solomonic period, as is often argued, or from the exilic period. Soggin's earlier work (1967) is representative of this position in that he acknowledges that the anti-monarchic material, including Judg. 8.22–3 and 9.7–20, may be later, but nonetheless accepts that they contain authentic traditions which indicate opposition to the inauguration of kingship. However, more recently (1985), Soggin has adopted a position much more in line with that of Wellhausen in that he attributes the material to an exilic redactor who was concerned to demonstrate the failings of the monarchy that contributed to the defeat of 587 BCE. In a detailed study of the nature of Israelite kingship, Ishida (1977) interprets the contradictions and tensions in this narrative complex as reflections of the factional viewpoints engendered in the formation of the monarchy. He is convinced that despite the later shaping of the narratives it is possible to extract valuable historical data on the conflicts which arose from this change. The continuing influence of this line of approach is demonstrated in Halpern's study (1981) of the constitution and ideology of the Israelite monarchy. He concludes that much of the material in 1 Sam. 8; 10.17–27; 11; 12 and Deut. 17.14–20 authentically reflects the limitations placed upon the Israelite monarchy from its inception.

The most extensive and anthropologically informed treatment of biblical traditions which reflect opposition to the inauguration of kingship has been carried out by F. Crüsemann (1978). This study is especially noteworthy since he draws explicitly on the work of the anthropologist C. Sigrist on African segmentary societies in order to construct a social and political context for the opposition to kingship. Although he believes that the traditions have their background in opposition to centralisation which is a common feature of the transition to state societies, he does not accept that they are contemporary with the origins of kingship. He concludes that Judg. 6–9 and 1 Sam. 8.11–17 are not late Deuteronomistic redactions but the products of groups during the reigns of David and Solomon who were faced with the oppressive burdens of taxation and conscription. This is true also of such passages as Num. 23.21 and Deut. 33.5, which emphasise the kingship of Yahweh, while Hosea 8.4 and 13.9–11, which are often dated late, are believed to have drawn upon the traditions in 1 Sam. 8–12. The popular unrest from the period of the united monarchy, which these passages reflect, manifested itself in the rebellions of Absalom and Sheba. This reaction to the oppressive nature of monarchy as it developed in Israel provided the spawning ground for the growth of anti-monarchic literature. The social location of this opposition was not some exilic theocratic community, but rather rural groups who resented the loss of sovereignty over their land. Such opposition only manifested itself at this later date in response to the encroachment of royal power since in origin the monarchy had been forced upon Israel by the scale of the Philistine threat. Thus this part of Crüsemann's conclusions stands in the broad tradition of the standard view that the monarchy was alien to the true or original nature of pre-monarchic Israel.

Crüsemann has advanced the discussion of the processes involved in the transition to monarchy by the way in which he has been able to present the tensions and differentiations of monarchic society in more realistic terms by reference to C. Sigrist's study of segmentary societies.[4] It can be questioned whether or not the rebellions of Absalom and Sheba reflect opposition to the centralisation of power derived from pre-state egalitarian groups, rather than the attempt by elite groups to usurp royal power. Crüsemann acknowledges that they were rebellions against the Davidic dynasty but nevertheless believes that they would have been perceived by many as attempts to restore pre-state forms of organisation. He has anticipated to some extent more recent attempts to understand the inauguration of the Israelite monarchy by appeal to studies on state formation. However, the most serious question concerning this innovative study concerns its dependence upon traditional literary assumptions that different strata can be identified and interpreted by reference to well-defined historical contexts. Crüsemann's conclusions need to be read in the light of recent work on the nature of the text which will be referred to below.

A further influential domain assumption which forms part of the standard view on the nature of the inauguration of the monarchy and the force of opposition to it in Israel derives from A. Alt (1966). He argued that following the division of the kingdom at the death of Solomon, northern Israel inherited and preserved a different understanding of the nature of kingship to Judah in the south. In a sense the north became the repository for the theocratic, charismatic ideal of pre-monarchic Israel. Alt drew a sharp contrast between the stability of the Davidic southern kingdom, which he attributed to an acceptance of dynastic kingship, and the political instability in the north prior to the reign of Omri, which was the result of the belief that the king was a charismatic figure chosen by Yahweh and did not have the right to rule simply by appeal to descent and primogeniture. A consequence of the influence of Alt's view on earlier scholarship is that it has become common to state that many of the anti-monarchic passages in the Hebrew Bible (Deut. 17.14–20; Judg. 8.22–3; 9; 1 Sam. 8; 12; Hos.) were of northern origin. However recent critiques of Alt's hypothesis by Thornton (1967), Buccellati (1967) and, particularly, Ishida (1977) have convincingly shown it to be seriously flawed.

The collapse of Noth's amphictyonic hypothesis which has had such a profound effect upon conceptions and presuppositions of biblical studies in general and the nature of early Israel in particular is one of the consequences of the tremendous upheaval experienced by the discipline in the last couple of decades. This has been part of the shift in emphasis away from the dominance of historical critical studies and presuppositions to a concern for literary evaluations and studies of the final form of the text. This shift has coincided with an increasing openness to the insights of other disciplines such as history, anthropology and the social sciences in general, although biblical specialists have always drawn upon these areas as the innovative work of Alt, Noth, Albright and many others clearly testifies. However the implications of these shifts and their far-reaching implications are only just beginning to be assessed. Clearly, many of the basic assumptions and findings of early and mid-twentieth century biblical scholarship concerning the inauguration of kingship and the nature of opposition to it need to be re-assessed.

The source-critical analysis of Wellhausen, and subsequent modifications of his views, which have been the basis for understanding the rise of the monarchy have come under increasing attack in recent years. It can no longer be assumed that attempts to identify particular literary strata and interpret them by reference to a particular social context, whether it be early monarchic or later exilic, necessarily leads to sound historical conclusions. The growing concern with literary artistry in the Hebrew Bible and the acceptance that narratives, such as 1 Sam. 8–12, are extremely artful constructions raises important questions about traditional attempts to mine these and other passages for 'authentic' historical recollections (see Barr, 1980; Alter, 1981). Eslinger (1985), for instance, has read 1 Sam. 1–12 as a unified narrative in which the different ideological conflicts of the historical-critical approach are understood as an essential part of the voice structure of the narrative. He calls into question attempts to identify different literary strata, pro- and anti-monarchical sources, that can then be placed in specific socio-historical settings. This issue of the relationship and relevance of literary evaluations to historical reconstruction is likely to remain a central area of debate within the discipline in the next few years.

Furthermore, traditional presentations of the monarchy as an alien institution depend upon questionable assumptions about the nature of early Israel. Noth's amphictyonic hypothesis, a notable casualty of the shifts in biblical studies in recent years, still exerts a tremendous implicit influence over underlying assumptions about the nature of early Israel. Even though it has become accepted that the analogy of Greek and Italian amphictyonic organisation cannot be applied to Israel, there remains the assumption that early Israel was a unified society, some form of religious tribal confederation devoted to the worship of Yahweh. A glance at the standard treatments of Noth (1960), Bright (1981) and Herrmann (1981), among others, will illustrate this. While it was thought that Israel originated as nomads or semi-nomads from outside Palestine in search of land and pasturage, as part of a protracted peaceful process of infiltration or in a swift and violent conquest, it was natural to believe that the Israelite monarchy was alien to an ideal pre-monarchic Israel in the form of a religious tribal league or confederation. G. Mendenhall (1975), who undermined many of the domain assumptions concerning the external origins of Israel with his theory of an internal peasants' revolt, drew an equally sharp dichotomy between pre-monarchic and monarchic Israel. He viewed the inauguration of the monarchy, particularly the kingdoms of David and Solomon, as a betrayal of what he termed 'the biblical revolution' of Mosaic Israel and characterised the monarchy as a 'rapid reversion to Late Bronze Age paganism'. However, such contrasts need to be called into question both from the point of view of questionable literary analyses and also questionable views about the nature of significant socio-political change.[5] Evaluations of archaeological data from recent surveys and excavations have led a number of scholars to question the long standing assumption that early Israel was an identifiable unity (Lemche: 1985; Coote and Whitelam: 1987). Advances in archaeological techniques and increased information about early states provide a valuable perspective from which to ask new questions about the nature of the transition to an Israelite highland state in the Early Iron Age.

Work by biblical scholars has used the expanding literature on the formation of such early states in order to shed further light on the societal processes which contributed to the development of an Israelite state. In particular, these studies have brought into question the long held notion that the Philistine threat was the primary cause in the transition to statehood. Rather, they suggest that a complex interaction of internal and external factors, in which the Philistine threat was at most a catalyst, took place. Frick (1985), Coote and Whitelam (1987), and Hauer (1986) all favour Carneiro's theory (1970) of state formation as most relevant to understanding the rise of Israelite kingship. He argues that states arise where the social and geographical constraints prevent the natural tendency of pre-state societies to fragment (see also Mann: 1986, 73–4). There is considerable agreement here that the environmental constraints imposed by the central hill country combined with the pressure exerted by the Canaanite city-states of the lowlands, the Philistines on the Mediterranean littoral, and the Amalekites and Midianites from the steppes produced conditions which encouraged centralisation rather than fragmentation. In particular, the degree of residential stability demanded by highland farming techniques, such as terracing and tree cultivation, is cited as an important factor in combination with environmental and social constraints in preventing fragmentation and encouraging centralisation (Marfoe, 1979; Frick, 1985; Coote and Whitelam, 1987). The demographic pressures on the circumscribed area of the central hill country of Palestine during the Early Iron Age provided the right combination of conditions which eventually resulted in an Israelite highland state.

The contribution of anthropology and archaeology to this debate therefore provides a different perspective from the traditional representation by biblical scholars of the monarchy as a denial of the essential premonarchic theocratic Israel. It helps to explain why pre-state societies cross the threshold to statehood and offers a new perspective from which to view opposition to such socio-political transformations. It is not a question of the denial of some essential nature of society which has been betrayed nor is it a question of the inevitable 'progress' (contra Mayes, 1977) of society to kingship. It is rather a question of trying to understand the complex interaction of many different factors which react with, and upon, one another in the move to statehood. It is only from this perspective that it is possible then to proceed to a discussion of the biblical traditions and of the extent to which they might reflect the opposition to monarchy at different points in its history. Such approaches lay the basis for a more realistic assessment of the ways in which a complex society like monarchic Israel functions (Chaney, 1986; Gottwald, 1986). Crüsemann has provided the groundwork for understanding some aspects of important social conflicts involved in the transition to monarchy. However, it remains to be seen how Israelite royal ideology functioned to address the challenges to the authority of the king from those who opposed the institution of monarchy and those who wished to usurp the king's power.

The centrality of royal ideology

It is a commonplace of anthropology that the establishment of monarchic power in early agrarian states was based upon religious legitimation of the role of the king. There is ample evidence from many different areas of the world that a heavy investment was made by the state in specialists who were primarily responsible for propagating a view of the world which emphasised the king's central role in the cosmic order. Royal rituals and ideology and the massive investment in monumental architecture were all designed to maintain and defend the established order. These interrelated elements of the royal world-view were multi-functional in that they addressed different audiences and the many different social conflicts and strains that were part of state level societies. A central feature of the royal world-view was that the cosmos was divinely ordered and that monarchic government and society were the mundane counterparts of this heavenly ideal. The earthly reality might well be one of political upheaval through factional disputes over the throne, but the ideological picture, the world-view propagated by the royal bureaucracy on behalf of the occupant of the throne, was one of delicate cosmic harmony in which the king played the central earthly role. Royal ideology and rituals were designed to stress the complex and dependent cosmological and earthly relationships.

The ground-breaking studies of Gunkel (1933) and Mowinckel (1922, 1962) in particular, and later Johnson (1967), among others, on the identification and interpretation of the Enthronement and Royal Psalms are necessarily the starting point of any discussion of Israelite royal ideology. The vast bulk of our information on various aspects of royal ideology is provided by these collections of Psalms, scattered material in the prophetic literature, and traditions within the books of Samuel and Kings. Many of the issues which concerned scholars earlier in the century, such as the debates on the nature of the New Year Festival or the definition of Royal and Enthronement Psalms, have not figured nearly so prominently in recent discussions. It is an important task of future research to utilise the results of previous scholarship in the light of more recent anthropological, historical and sociological treatments of ideology, ritual and symbolism based on many different and diverse agrarian states.[6] The major studies by the biblical scholars of the pre- and post-war periods are on the whole descriptive accounts of royal ideology as preserved in the biblical traditions; the overriding concern has been with the interpretation of collections of psalms in a cultic setting. They do not, on the whole, address the important questions of how such ideology functioned or how it was aimed at specific audiences in order to overcome threats to royal power without resorting to physical force.

It was clearly essential to justify the social differentiations of state society by appeal to a heavenly ideal. The king's place in the cosmic and social order was reflected in the way in which his functions mirror those of Yahweh in his heavenly role. The portrayal of Yahweh's kingship in the Enthronement and other Psalms (Pss. 47.6–8; 93.1; 96.10; 97.1; 98.6; 99.1) places great stress on the concept of cosmic order which is guaranteed by his rule. Cosmic order is continually subject to the threat of disorder and chaos from primeval forces, the threat of flood, famine, pestilence, or enemy attack, which Yahweh repels in his role as king (Pss. 93.3–4; 74.12–14; 89.10–11; 47.3–4, 8–9; 48.3–4; 68.30; 97.3, 7, 9; 98.2; 99.1–2). The same picture of Yahweh struggling with, and defeating, primeval forces of chaos and destruction can be found in much prophetic literature (Isa. 24.21–3; 41.21–4; 44.6–7; 52.7; Jer. 10.7, 10; Zech. 14.9, 16–17; Zeph. 1.7; 2.11; 3.14–19). The hierarchical relationships are depicted in Yahweh's central role in relation to the other divine beings in the heavenly council (Ps. 82). The delicate order in the cosmos based upon justice is reflected in the consequences of its disruption when the divine beings fail to fulfil their duties (Ps. 82) so that the very foundations of the earth are shaken. This is in contrast to the divine king's own fulfilment of this vital task (Ps. 89.14; 24.1; 74.15–17; 89.11–12; 29; 68.9).

The representation of the Israelite king's ideal roles incorporates many features which are frequently associated with kingship throughout the ancient Near East. The king's role and functions are the same as those of his deity, Yahweh, in the cosmic hierarchy. The king fulfils these functions on earth and occupies the same position within the hierarchical ordering of society as part of the complex interrelationships of cosmic order. It is an hierarchical ordering of society that can only be challenged with the gravest of consequences for the whole of Israelite society. It is this portrayal of the king's fundamental position as the central symbolic figure in a well defined social and political order that allows royal ideology and ritual to address the twin problems of the justification for monarchy against opposition to its development as well as addressing the problem of any threats from urban factions who might try to usurp the king's position and claim the throne for themselves.

It is made explicitly clear that society cannot function, or even continue to exist, without the rule of the king. The king's role in the protection of society as warrior, the guarantor of justice as judge and the right ordering of worship as priest are the fundamental roles which cover all aspects of the well-being of society. It is well known that this triple function of kingship, with particular emphasis on the roles of the king as judge and warrior, is common throughout the ancient Near East and is expressed in a great deal of royal literature from Mesopotamia through the Levant to Egypt. This is a picture which is common to many agrarian states throughout history. The significance of this royal world-view is that it provides religious sanction for the obedience of the state population to its king on the basis of the appeal to the rule of law. However, it is also explicitly clear that if various elements of the population ignore that appeal to law then the king has divine sanction for resorting to physical coercion to protect the kingdom and the cosmos. The stress placed on such claims by royal specialists who perform a variety of functions designed to legitimise the role of the king indicates the importance of these elements in holding together the complex social interrelationships that make up state level societies.

A major problem in understanding Israelite ideology is the fact that it is difficult, if not impossible, to grasp the history of development of material such as the psalms. This means that our view of royal ideology is essentially a static view of a well developed thought-system without any appreciation of the ways in which ideology or rituals may have changed over time. In fact it is difficult to draw a clear distinction between differences in Israelite and Judaean royal ideologies as the critiques of Alt's hypothesis of northern charismatic versus southern dynastic concepts of kingship have illustrated. A related problem is that it is not easy to differentiate between the ideal of royal ideology and historical reality, but it is a reasonable assumption based on comparative evidence, that the need for the investment of state resources in ritual, ceremonial and monumental architecture points to the ever-present threat of rebellion or usurpation.

It is interesting to note that the king's central roles of warrior and judge have not received the same amount of attention as sacral kingship which held the attention of scholars earlier in the century. In fact there is, as far as I am aware, no single treatment devoted to the ideological aspects of the king's role as warrior. The most recent considerations of this aspect of kingship form part of the wider treatments of Mettinger (1976) and Halpern (1981) on the relationship between theoretical and practical understandings of the Israelite monarchy. The judicial functions of kingship have received considerably more attention, particularly in recent years (Macholz, 1972a; 1972b; Whitelam, 1979). The ideal aspects of the king as judge, which are formally similar throughout the ancient Near East, are contrasted with historical reconstructions of the royal administration of justice based on the interpretations of textual material in Samuel, Kings and Chronicles. There is some disagreement over the extent to which the monarchy altered or interfered with judicial systems of pre-monarchic Israel. Clearly any such discussion is now dependent upon the changed perceptions of some scholars concerning the extent of our understanding of the nature and organisation of early Israel in the wake of the collapse of Noth's amphictyonic paradigm. The other area of contention is whether or not the king was able to make law, or inherited some divinely sanctioned legal code. Comparative evidence from other agrarian state societies would suggest that the latter alternative is part of a royal ideology which rested on claims to legitimation of the king's actions by the god or gods of the state.

The maintenance of law and order was a fundamental problem for state level societies given the great inequalities inherent in stratification. The centrality of the judicial responsibilities of the king throughout extant ancient Near Eastern literature from the various state archives points to its importance in the control and management of social and political tensions endemic to such societies. For Israel, the king's role as judge finds its counterpart in Yahweh's performance of this task in the divine realm. Psalm 72 is a classic statement of the dependence of cosmic order on the king's ability and duty to guarantee justice in his realm. The request at the beginning of the Psalm is for the gift of judicial ability (cf. 1 Kgs. 3). It then becomes clear that the provision and use of this gift determines the wellbeing of the nation as a whole since it is intricately tied to the fertility, prosperity and security of the nation (Ps. 72.3, 5–7, 15–17). The interrelationship between justice, order, fertility and prosperity is found throughout the royal psalms and other material within the Hebrew Bible (Pss. 45.2, 4, 6, 8–9; 89.21–3; 101; 110.1–2; 2 Sam. 23.3, 4, 6–7). If the king fails to provide justice, just like the divine beings of Ps. 82, then the social, political and ecological structure is thrown open to the ever-present powers of chaos. A feature of this psalm in the context of the functioning of royal ideology needs to stress clearly that it provides an extremely powerful justification for the role of the state embodied in the king. If there is no king then chaos will triumph. It is interesting to note that it has been customary to point out that Judg. 17–21 provides a similar justification for the existence of the monarchy as a guarantee against the excesses of a social system that is not ordered and structured as the state, but is ruled by the powers of chaos. The promise of the defeat of the king's enemies, represented as the powers of chaos, and the establishment of universal dominion (Ps. 72.8–11) provides a powerful warning to those who would usurp the throne.

The Babylonian text *Enuma Elish* expresses a similar justification for the institution and functions of monarchy in Babylonian society. Marduk as the divine warrior expels chaos and orders the cosmos. The epic concludes with the foundation of Babylon at the centre of the cosmos, with the temple to Marduk at its centre, and kingship as the only form of government that can prevent the triumph of the primeval powers of chaos. A comparable interrelationship of functions as part of the structure of a well ordered cosmos can be found in the great law codes of Lipit-Ishtar from Sumer or Hammurabi from Babylon. This cosmic concept of justice, *maʾat* in Egypt or *mēšarum* in Mesopotamia, in relation to the king clearly plays a pivotal role in the establishment and maintenance of royal power (Frankfort, 1948).

Although the vast literary deposits from the royal archives of the ancient Near East provide the most explicit statements of royal ideology, they were not the only means, or the most direct, by which the royal world-view was made manifest to different audiences. The great monumental buildings, palace-temple complexes, fortifications and public buildings, which characterised early states, were an important means of reinforcing and manifesting the social differentiations upon which royal power depended. These structures, which required a massive investment of state resources, displayed the authority, security, and permanence of royal rule. Dever (1982) has provided a comprehensive review of the basic archaeological data pertaining to the development of monumental architecture during the reigns of David and Solomon. The political significance of such royal building projects in relation to state religion has been emphasised by Ahlström (1982). The Solomonic fortifications at Megiddo, Hazor and Gezer with their impressive gates not only symbolised the authority and military power of the monarchy, but also signified the politically significant urban centre and its hierarchical relationship with the rural hinterland. The direct and more subtle symbolic aspects of these structures addressed the same issues of royal power and its maintenance in the face of opposition that are made more explicit in the literary deposits which have been the traditional focus of biblical and Near Eastern specialists (Whitelam, 1986).

The importance of the temple to the state and its importance in the royal symbolic universe is well known and hardly needs reiteration. The conclusion of the *Enuma Elish* provides a classic statement of the king's responsibility for providing a temple for the god or gods of the state and illustrates one of the main aspects of royal ideology in justifying monarchic rule. The temple, as the symbolic representation of the centre of the cosmos and the king's special relationship with the deity of the state, was the physical manifestation of claims asserted in the royal psalms. The deity, who guaranteed the state and dynasty, had his dwelling-place beside the king in the temple-palace complex. The king's special relationship with, and responsibility for providing, the temple for the state god finds its clearest expression in the Israelite traditions in 2 Sam. 7.1–17.[7] Busink (1970) and Gutman (1976) provide extensive discussions of various aspects of the Solomonic temple, particularly the influence of Near Eastern prototypes. The ways in which the temple and its royal rituals played a central role in the ideological justification of the state have recently been outlined by Lundquist (1982; 1983; Ahlström, 1982). C. Meyers (1983) has investigated the reconstruction and function of the temple and its iconography in the political economy of the Israelite state. The state temple and cult placed a particularly heavy drain upon labour and other resources of an agrarian economy. This siphoning off of valuable resources was presented in the royal rites of the temple, as expressed in the royal psalms, as necessary for the guarantee of peace, prosperity, wealth and fertility throughout the whole of society. The temple and its cult, repeated in the various shrines of the major urban centres of the kingdom, legitimated the king's role in the political and economic ordering of the state. The comparative study of Israelite monumental architecture and the economic significance of the royal cult is only in its infancy and hopefully will provide further insights into the dynamics of monarchic society.

Many of the most immediate images of state buildings were accessible to the widest possible audiences in that they stressed the permanency and authority of the royal order. However, as in other agrarian societies, literacy and access to the private rites of the temple and palace would have been restricted to the urban elite. It is this demographically small section of the population that had access to, and control of, the means of power. They posed, therefore, the greatest threat to the dynasty. Although many of the aspects of royal ideology which we have already described, such as the king's special relationship with Yahweh, are relevant, there are a number of noteworthy features of the presentation of kingship which address this threat more directly. In particular, the sacral nature of the king and his claim to be the anointed of Yahweh need to be understood in this context. Once again these topics have enjoyed considerable scholarly attention, but the major concern has been with their relevance to understanding Jewish and Christian messianic expectations and claims.

The king as the anointed of Yahweh was sacrosanct and inviolable. Such a claim was a powerful ideological tool since any attempts to usurp the throne meant rebellion against Yahweh. The fact that the phrase *māšîaḥ yhwh* in the Hebrew Bible is primarily applied to David and southern kings should not be taken as an indication that this was an exclusive claim of Judaean ideology. The use of this title in reference to Saul (1 Sam. 24.6, 10; 26.9, 11, 16, 23; 2 Sam. 1.14, 16) indicates that it was also probably an important feature of northern presentations of the status of the king. The claims about the king's inviolability are the reason why usurpers needed to demonstrate legitimacy for their actions in overthrowing the occupant of the throne. A fine example of propaganda designed to legitimise the overthrow of the previous regime can be found in the Hittite 'apology of Hattusilis III'. The apologetic and polemical nature of the representation of David's replacement of Saul on the throne in the books of Samuel has often been pointed out (Lemche, 1979; McCarter, 1981). The relevance of the 'apology of Hattusilis III' for understanding the traditions of David's rise to power and the struggle for succession has been examined by McCarter

(1980). It has also been suggested that these traditions explicitly addressed the problem of legitimising the Davidic claim to the throne and countered threats from the urban elite by stressing the sacrosanct nature of the king (Whitelam, 1984).

The precise nature of the king's person has long been a topic of fierce debate. It is generally accepted that the king was 'sacred' and, as we have seen, occupied a unique relationship with Yahweh. This fact alone is not surprising since Frazer's monumental study (1900), *The Golden Bough*, provides widespread examples of sacred kingship (see also Hocart, 1927; 1970). The question remains, however, in what sense the Israelite king was thought to be sacred. Israelite kings were presented as possessing qualities and characteristics that set them apart from ordinary mortals (2 Sam. 14.17, 20; 1 Kgs. 3.4–15, 16–28; 4.29–34; 10.1–9, 24; cf. Isa. 11.2–4). The fundamental question which occupied biblical scholars earlier in the century was whether or not the king was thought to be divine.

The history of this debate has been extensively reviewed (recently Miller, 1985). The myth and ritual school's contention that the king was divine was based on an understanding of what was thought to be a well defined pattern of ritual and cultic practices throughout the ancient Near East (Hooke, 1958; Engnell, 1943; Widengren, 1955). Their claims are understandable in the light of the many formal similarities throughout Near Eastern cultures and against the background of Frazer's work on divine kingship. Their claims were seriously weakened by a failure to appreciate or define the considerable differences between Near Eastern societies over a considerable period of time. They presented a static view of many different cultures and societies that did not adequately take account of important distinguishing characteristics. The critiques of Frankfort (1948), Bernhardt (1961), and Gray (1969), among others, have led to a more moderate position which prefers to speak of 'sacral' rather than divine kingship.

The explicit references to the king as the 'son' or 'first-born' of Yahweh are now generally understood as references to the special status which the king assumed at the time of his accession. The crucial passages in 2 Sam. 14.7, Ps. 2.7 and Ps. 89.27–8 have been interpreted, since the influential study of von Rad (1947), as references to a notion of divine or legal adoption during the enthronement ceremony. Johnson (1967) provides a detailed study of the royal psalms from this viewpoint. Mettinger (1976), who provides an excellent review and critique of the many problems involved in the history of this debate, also adopts a moderate position. A similar line is followed by Eaton (1976) who argues, unconvincingly, for an extension of the number of psalms which relate to the kingship and thereby broadens the discussion of various aspects of the king's person and functions.

However the debate is resolved, it is clear that the king's person was unique which meant that rebellions or usurpations could be treated as transgressions against Yahweh. It is questionable whether the extensive scholarly literature has adequately explained the significance of references to the king as 'god' in Ps. 45.6 and Isa. 9.6. Widely expressed attempts to explain away such explicit language as due to textual corruption, ellipsis, or grammatical niceties have not proved wholly convincing. It needs to be asked to what extent the audience or audiences of royal rituals would have drawn such careful distinctions in the use of language. It is also the case that the discussion has been conducted against a background of concerns with Jewish and Christian messianic expectations in which claims to the divinity of the king could be regarded as entirely ruled out. Since one of the basic functions of such language was to suggest the unique and inviolable nature of the king, it may well have been chosen for its ambiguities in order to protect and legitimise the king's role in society.

Conclusion

The preceding discussion of various aspects of Israelite kingship and its ideology has attempted to set a representative sample of widely explored work in the context of fuller comparative studies. The values of methodologies and research drawn from other disciplines, such as history, anthropology and the social sciences, should not be underestimated. There is a vast wealth of material from such disciplines which pertains to an understanding of the possibilities of Israelite social organisation. The problem has been to try to control and represent adequately such an array of data and opinions while at the same time giving adequate weight to the particularities of Israelite society. The emphasis of much previous biblical scholarship has been upon the uniqueness of Israelite kingship and its leading representatives. There is now a need for a comparative study of the dynamics and processes of monarchic society as a whole which can only come from the risks and, hopefully, rewards of interdisciplinary research.

Notes

1 There are a number of recent collections of essays and studies on the formation of early states which are relevant to understanding the emergence of an Israelite state. See Claessen and Skalnik (1978, 1981), Cohen and Service (1978), Haas (1982), and Carneiro (1970).

2 For definitions of the state see in particular Claessen and Skalnik (1978; 1981) and Cohen and Service (1978).
3 There is increasing archaeological evidence for growing social conflict at the end of the eleventh century BCE in Palestine, around the time of the emergence of an Israelite state. A number of sites were destroyed or abandoned around this time: Ai, Khirbet Raddana, Shiloh, Tel el-Ful, Tel Masos, Tel Esdar, Megiddo and Tel Abu Hawam.
4 Lemche (1985) has criticised Crüsemann's analysis particularly because of his over-reliance upon the analyses of Sigrist. Nevertheless, it still should be recognised as an important step in the utilisation of anthropological research in the analysis of monarchic society.
5 Gottwald (1986), interestingly in view of his elaboration of the revolt hypothesis, has investigated the social dynamics involved in the introduction of monarchy. He suggests that 'free agrarians' may well have played a role in the introduction of kingship in order to counteract Philistine domination and internal corruption.
6 Anthropological studies of royal power and ritual are a potentially fruitful area of research for understanding important elements of Israelite kingship. See Cannadine and Price (1987) and Larsen (1979).
7 The complex history of research into 2 Sam. 7 is well reviewed by Mettinger (1976).

Bibliography

Ahlström, G. W., 1982. *Royal Administration and National Religion in Ancient Palestine*. Leiden: Brill.

Alt, A., 1966. 'The Monarchy in the Kingdoms of Israel and Judah', *Essays on Old Testament History and Religion*, Oxford: Blackwell: 239–59. Tr. from 'Das Königtum in der Reichen Israel und Juda', *VT* 1 (1951):2–22.

Alter, R., 1982. *The Art of Biblical Narrative*. London: Allen and Unwin.

Barr, J., 1980. 'Story and History in Biblical Theology' in *Explorations in Theology* 7. London: SCN:1–17.

Bernhardt, K.-H., 1961. *Das Problem der altorientalischen Königsideologie in Alten Testament*. Leiden: Brill.

Bright, J., 1981. *A History of Israel*. Third Edition. London: SCM.

Buccellati, G., 1967. *Cities and Nations of Ancient Syria. An Essay on Political Institutions with Special Reference in the Israelite Kingdoms*. Rome: U. of Rome.

Busink, T. A., 1970. *Der tempel von Jerusalem*, I. Band: *Der Tempel Salomos*. Leiden: Brill.

Cannadine, D. and Price, S., 1987. *Rituals and Royalty. Power and Ceremonial in Traditional Societies*. Cambridge: CUP.

Carneiro, R. L., 1970. 'A Theory of the Origins of the State', *Science*, 169:733–8.

Chaney, M., 1986. 'Systemic Study of the Israelite Monarchy', *Semeia*, 37:53–76.

Claessen, H. J. M. and Skalnik, P., 1978. *The Early State*. The Hague: Mouton.

1981. *The Study of the State*. The Hague: Mouton.

Clements, R., 1983. *A Century of Old Testament Study*. Guildford: Lutterworth.

Cohen, R. and Service, E. R., 1978. *Origins of the State*. Philadelphia: Institute for the Study of Human Issues: 1–20.

Coote, R. B. and Whitelam, K. W., 1987. *The Emergence of Early Israel in Historical Perspective*, Sheffield: Almond.

Crüsemann, F., 1978. *Der Widerstand gegen das Königtum. Die antikönigliche Texte des Alten Testamentes und der Kampf um den frühe israelitischen Staat*. Neukirchen-Vluyn: Neukirchener Verlag.
Dever, W. G., 1982. 'Monumental Architecture in Ancient Israel in the Period of the United Monarchy' in *Studies in the Period of David and Solomon*, ed. T. Ishida. Winona Lake: Eisenbrauns:269–306.
Eaton, J. H., 1976. *Kingship and the Psalms*. London: SCM.
Engnell, M., 1943. *Studies in Divine Kingship in the Ancient Near East*, Uppsala: Almquist and Wiksell.
Eslinger, K., 1985. *Kingship of God in Crisis. A Close Reading of 1 Samuel 1–12*. Sheffield: Almond.
Frankfort, H., 1948. *Kingship and the Gods*. Chicago: University of Chicago Press.
Frazer, J. G., 1900. *The Golden Bough: A Study in Magic and Religion*, 3 vol., 2nd ed. London: MacMillan.
Frick, F., 1985. *The Formation of the State in Ancient Israel*, Sheffield: Almond.
Gottwald, N. K., 1986. 'The Participation of Free Agrarians in the Introduction of the Monarchy to Ancient Israel: An Application of H. A. Landsberger's Framework for the Analysis of Peasant Movements', *Semeia*, 37:77–106.
Gray, J., 1969. 'Sacral Kingship in Ugarit', *Ugaritica*, 6:289–302.
Gunkel, H. and Begrich, J., 1933. *Einleitung in die Psalmen*. Gottingen.
Gutman, J., 1976. *The Temple of Solomon*, Missoula: Scholars.
Haas, J., 1982. *The Evolution of the Prehistoric State*, New York: Columbia University Press.
Halpern, B., 1981. *The Constitution of the Monarchy*, Chico: Scholars.
Hauer, C., 1986. 'From Alt to Anthropology: The Rise of the Israelite State', *JSOT*, 36:3–15.
Herrmann, S., 1981. *A History of Israel in Old Testament Times* (Revised and Enlarged Edition). London: SCM.
Hocart, A. M., 1927. *Kingship*, Oxford: Clarendon.
1970. *Kings and Councillors: An Essay in the Comparative Anthropology of Human Society*, Chicago: University of Chicago Press.
Hooke, S. H., 1958. *Myth, Ritual and Kingship*, London: OUP.
Ishida, T., 1977. *The Royal Dynasties in Ancient Israel: A Study on the Formation and Development of Royal-Dynastic Ideology*, Berlin: De Gruyter.
Johnson, A. R., 1967. *Sacral Kingship in Ancient Israel*, Cardiff: University of Wales.
Larsen, M. T., 1979. *Power and Propaganda. A Symposium on Ancient Empires*, Copenhagen: Akademisk Forlag.
Lemche, N., 1979. 'David's Rise', *JSOT*, 10:2–25.
1985. *Early Israel. Anthropological and Historical Studies on Israelite Society Before the Monarchy*, Leiden: Brill.
Lundquist, J., 1982. 'The Legitimizing Role of the Temple in the Origin of the State', *SBL Seminar Papers*, Missoula: Scholars.
1983. 'What is a Temple? A Preliminary Typology', in *The Quest for the Kingdom of God. Studies in Honor of G. E. Mendenhall*, ed. H. B. Huffmon, F. Spina and A. Green, Winona Lake: Eisenbrauns:205–19.
McCarter, P. K., 1980. 'The Apology of David', *JBL*, 90:489–504.
1981. '"Plots True and False." The Succession Narrative as Court Apologetic', *Interpretation*, 35:355–67.

Macholz, G. C., 1972a. 'Die Stellung des Königs in der israelitische Gerichtsverfassung', *ZAW*, 84:157–82.

1972b. 'Zur Geschichte der Justizorganisation in Juda', *ZAW* 84:314–40.

Mann, M., 1986. *The Sources of Social Power*, vol. I, *A History of Power from the Beginning to AD 1760*. Cambridge: CUP.

Marfoe, L., 1979. 'The Integrative Transformation: Patterns of Socio-Economic Organization in Southern Syria', *BASOR*, 234:1–42.

Mayes, A. D. H., 1977. 'The Period of the Judges and the Rise of the Monarchy in *Israelite and Judaean History*, ed. J. Hayes and Miller, J. M., London: SCM:285–331.

Mendelssohn, I., 1956. 'Samuel's Denunciation of Kingship in the Light of Akkadian Documents from Ugarit', *BASOR*, 143:17–32.

Mendenhall, G. E., 1975. 'The Monarchy', *Interpretation*, 29:155–70.

Mettinger, T. N. D., 1976. *King and Messiah. The Civil and Sacral Legitimation of the Israelite Kingship*, Lund: CWK Gleerup.

Meyers, C., 1983. 'Jachin and Boaz in Religious and Political Perspective', *CBQ*, 45:167–78.

Miller, P. D., 1985. 'Israelite Religion' in *The Hebrew Bible and its Modern Interpreters*, ed. Knight, D. A., and Tucker, G. M., Philadelphia/Chico: Fortress/Scholars:201–37.

Mowinckel, S., 1922. *Psalmstudien* II, Oslo: Dybwad.

1962. *The Psalms in Israel's Worship*, 2 Vol., Oxford: Blackwell.

Noth, M., 1957. *Überlieferungsgeschichtliche Studien*, 3rd ed. Tubingen: Nieymeyer.

1960. *The History of Israel*, London: Black.

Rad, G. von, 1947. 'Das judaische Königsritual', *TLZ*, 72:206–16.

Soggin, J. A., 1967. *Das Königtum in Israel. Ursprünge, Spannungen, Entwicklung*, Berlin: Topelmann.

1984. *A History of Israel. From the Beginnings to the Bar Kochba Revolt, A. D. 135*, London: SCM.

Thornton, T. C. G., 1967. 'Studies in Samuel', *CQR*, 168:413–23.

Wellhausen, J., 1885. *Prolegomena to the History of Israel*, Edinburgh: Black.

Whitelam, K. W., 1979. *The Just King: Monarchical Judicial Authority in Ancient Israel*, Sheffield: JSOT.

1984. 'The Defence of David', *JSOT*, 29:61–87.

1986. 'The Symbols of Power: Aspects of Royal Propaganda in the United Monarchy', *BA*, 49:166–73.

Widengren, G., 1955. *Sakrales Königtum im Alten testament und im Judentum*, Stuttgart: Kohlhammer.

CHAPTER SEVEN

The concept of Israel in transition

H. G. M. WILLIAMSON

Until comparatively recent times, two main approaches have been taken in scholarly literature to the question of Israel's origins. One follows the biblical outline more or less closely in upholding the theory of a conquest of Palestine while the other thinks more in terms of a prolonged process of initially peaceful settlement by various nomadic groups. In recent years, however, a powerful alternative view has been developed and seems rapidly to be gaining popularity. Reference here is not intended to the so-called 'peasants' revolt' theory as pioneered by Mendenhall (1962) and elaborated in a very different manner by Gottwald (1979), for despite the fact that many of their criticisms of earlier views have found favour, their positive proposals show few signs of gaining acceptance. Rather, what characterises such recent writers as Lemche (1985), Thompson (1987), 11–40, and Coote and Whitelam (1987) is their agreement that 'Israel' emerged peacefully within the land as an inevitable consequence of the economic and social decline of late bronze age Canaan coinciding with the development of new agricultural techniques which enabled increasing numbers to withdraw from the city states, located principally in the valleys, and to start settling in the hitherto sparsely populated hill country of Judaea and Samaria.

A consequence of this new approach (which it is not our intention here to evaluate), to which only Lemche has addressed himself in any considered way, is that it becomes increasingly problematical to talk meaningfully of 'the origins of Israel' as though that could be dated even approximately. Indeed, Lemche sees the development of the familiar Pentateuchal outline of saving history becoming definitive only just before the Babylonian exile. For our present purposes, however, we may perhaps agree that by the year 587 BC, when the Babylonians finally overran Judah and Jerusalem, destroyed the temple, and led away many of the leading members of society into exile, the concept of 'Israel' had become generally agreed: there was an accepted pre-history of 'Israel' as a nation which, with the establishment of the monarchy, had become 'like all the nations' (1 Sam. 8.5). True, the kingdom had been divided into two following the death of

Solomon, and further that nation which continued to bear the name 'Israel' had ceased independent existence following the Assyrian conquest of 721 BC, but the ideals of 'Israel' will have been held to have continued in the southern kingdom of Judah. Thus on the eve of the exile it would probably have been broadly agreed that Israel was a people and nation with a specific history, admittedly decimated in numbers and reduced in territorial and political influence, but still standing in identifiable continuity with earlier days and thus potentially the seed-bed for a possible restoration to former glory.

With the exile and the vastly different circumstances of the post-exilic return and restoration, however, it was inevitable that continuity could be maintained only at the cost of extensive change. The loss of political sovereignty but the survival of a people and its religion meant that all manner of adaptation had to be made at a superficial level to law and religious practice. Beyond that, however, and at a much more fundamental level, there remained the question of self-identity: what now *is* Israel, and what does it mean to say that 'we' are Israel?

It is engagement with this issue that has largely determined the selection of material for consideration in the following pages. Although our survey concentrates on the prophetic and historical literature, it would be wrong to infer that the Law (and the Priestly writing in particular) is of no significance. Indeed, Blenkinsopp (1981) has well analysed some of the interplay between rival definitions of Israel and the formation of P itself. However, it cannot be said that P grapples with our issue in any serious fashion; it assumes Israel's existence in legislating for what Israel ought to be.

Another much favoured approach to our topic has been the attempt to trace the development of 'parties' within Israel and to link these with some of the factions which we know had developed by a much later period. Influential in this regard have been the 'eschatological' and 'theocratic' groups of Plöger (1959), and the 'visionary' and 'hierocratic' groups of Hanson (1975). Illuminating as such studies can undoubtedly be, they tend to study the issues as though they were totally independent of wider political considerations. It will be our contention in what follows that in fact it was these, and not so much internal religious disputes, which affected the most important shift in the concept of Israel. That will come in particular with our examination of the work of Ezra. But in order to appreciate the extent and nature of this shift, it is necessary also to survey some of the other major writers who grappled with our topic both before and after Ezra. Inevitably, therefore, we begin with the prophet who worked most immediately under the impact of the fall of Jerusalem.

The major study of Ezekiel's understanding of Israel is that of Zimmerli (1958; for a brief summary in English, see 1983, 563–5), which marks an advance over the less satisfactory survey of Danell (1946, 237–61), who concluded that 'the name Israel has no uniform sense there'; it could refer equally to the community in exile, those left behind in Palestine, the old northern kingdom or the people as a whole. By contrast, Zimmerli approached the problem from several different angles to conclude more convincingly that for Ezekiel 'Israel' was a single people related to an undivided land.

At the statistical level, Israel is mentioned 185 times, but Judah only 15; since several of these latter refer explicitly to Judah as a tribe rather than a nation, and others are widely held to be secondary, it is apparent that only very rarely is Judah set over against Israel as a separate entity (e.g. at 8.1 by comparison with 14.1). Frequently these references to Israel are in construct relationships, some of which are peculiar to Ezekiel. Noteworthy among the latter are *ʾaḏmaṯ yiśrāʾēl*, 'the land of Israel', (contrast the common *ʾereṣ yiśrāʾēl*), and *hārê yiśrāʾēl*, 'the mountains of Israel', sixteen times each and both referring to the land as a whole. Similarly, Ezekiel's favourite way of addressing the people is as *bêṯ yiśrāʾēl*, 'the house of Israel' (which contrasts with the infrequent use of the more individualising 'children of Israel'); indeed, it was to this 'house of Israel' that Ezekiel was called to serve as a watchman (3.17; 33.7).

Along with such positive arguments, Zimmerli also observes the absence of references to Israel in the context of the divisions among the people. Most noteworthy here, of course, was the division between north and south after the death of Solomon. In the historical allegories in chapters 16 and 23, 'Israel' does not occur once as a designation for the northern kingdom. Rather, in chapter 16 Jerusalem is contrasted with her 'sisters' Samaria and Sodom (cf. v. 46) – a device which at once retains the distinction at a purely political level by referring to the capital cities and yet at the same time avoids the old polarities by bringing in Sodom alongside Jerusalem and Samaria. Similarly, in chapter 23, the dual aspect of the people's unity is traced back not just to Solomon but to the sojourn in Egypt, where 'there were two women, the daughters of one mother' (v. 2).

Particularly significant, in Zimmerli's view, is the wording of parts of 37.15ff., the allegory of the two sticks, for these two sticks are not named 'the stick of Israel' and 'the stick of Judah', but rather 'For Judah and the Israelites associated with him' and 'For Joseph and (the whole) house of Israel associated with him'. Thus, even in this passage, which by speaking of the reunion of the people emphasises their division most strongly, both Judah and Joseph are equally included within Israel.

Finally, we should note that in Ezekiel's view the people are united by their common history which can be traced back to Egypt (chapter 20). It may be a union in constant rebellion and consequent exile, but it carries over nonetheless into the hopes for future return and restoration (20.40ff; 34; 36).

Zimmerli is undoubtedly justified in contrasting the situation in Ezekiel with that in his slightly older contemporary Jeremiah, for recent work has tended to underline the stringency with which Jeremiah observed the distinctions between the separate nations of Israel and Judah, especially in the early chapters (cf. Albertz: 1982) which otherwise bear comparison with aspects of Ezekiel's historical allegories. He too had hopes of the people's reunion, but he expressed it in terms of Ephraim/Israel's return from exile and reunion with Zion/Judah (cf. Jer. 30–1).

It is thus apparent that at the very watershed of the exile itself Ezekiel's response was far from political. Whether the distance of exile affected his outlook or not, he broke completely with prevailing reality in order to initiate (or return to) an idealistic, even utopian, view of Israel as the single people of God. There are certainly antecedents for his view in the Deuteronomic literature both in terms of phraseology (Zimmerli: 1958, 78) and in the dual history of the books of Kings; in view of what followed, it is also possible that we should allow for priestly influence. But it may be argued that none of this fully accounts for the fact that 'the concrete sociological components and the concrete politico-geographical aspects fade into the background in the face of the desire to give expression to theological content' (Zimmerli: 1983, 565). Similarly, it is clear from even a superficial knowledge of the subsequent history that Ezekiel found few wholehearted successors. We shall therefore need to be alert to his apparently idiosyncratic stance as we survey the later literature lest echoes of its contribution to the new definition be not heard.

Whatever points of contact there may be between Ezekiel and the anonymous prophet of Isaiah 40–55 (Baltzer: 1971), their attitude towards the concept of Israel is not among them. Once again a survey of usage of the word Israel itself furnishes as clear a guide as is possible in an area which has been fraught with disagreement amongst scholars. For presentation of the raw data on which this analysis is built, cf. Danell: 1946, 261–3; Orlinsky: 1967, 81–3; Elliger: 1978, 95–6, though the first two both contain minor inaccuracies.

Of the forty-two occurrences of the name Israel in Isaiah 40–55, nineteen are as part of a compound expression describing God, such as 'the Holy One of Israel'; these are unlikely to be of particular significance for our purposes.

Of the remaining occurrences, the overwhelming majority (seventeen) are used in parallel with 'Jacob' (all except one with Jacob standing first, before Israel). The description of Jacob/Israel in these passages can leave little doubt that the dejected exiles in Babylon are being addressed, either because they are described as such (e.g. 40.27; 42.24; 43.22, 28) or because they are being addressed as the recipients of an oracle of salvation and therefore currently stand in need and despair (e.g. 41.8, 14; 43.1; 44.1). Similarly, the bulk of the remaining examples look forward to future restoration, thus contrasting with the bleak present (e.g. 44.5, 21, 23).

This leaves only five passages for consideration, of which it is usually said that they refer to Israel by itself. This, however, is misleading. (i) At 44.21b Israel can scarcely be separated from Israel in the previous line (v. 21a), where it is parallel with Jacob. (ii) In the last verse of the paragraph 45.18–25 we have the only example in Deutero-Isaiah of 'the seed of Israel'; it can hardly be a coincidence, therefore, that near the start of the same paragraph (v. 19) there is an equally unparalleled reference to 'the seed of Jacob'. Evidently the two designations are interchangeable in the prophet's mind. (iii) The sense of 46.13 is not entirely secure, but here Israel is most probably used in parallel with Zion. Snaith (1967) sought to draw a sharp distinction in the prophet's thought between the exiles and the community that remained in Palestine, referred to as Jerusalem or Zion. In fact, however, the latter community does not come within the prophet's purview. Snaith's forced exegesis of 40.1–2 (pp. 177–8) is sufficient to show the difficulties into which his view runs, for it is unsatisfactory to seek to distinguish between 'my people' (= the exiles) and 'Jerusalem' (= the community in Palestine). However, there are occasions when the prophet, looking forward to the return and restoration of those in exile, can speak of the people proleptically under the figure of Zion or Jerusalem (e.g. 40.9–10; 44.26; 49.14–21; 52.7–10). This seems appropriate also in the case of 46.13. (iv) Apart from 49.1–6, which will be discussed more fully below, this leaves only 45.17 as a use of Israel standing alone, just as in the comparable 48.20 Jacob stands alone.

Two points require emphasis from this survey so far. The first is that it has emerged even more strongly than in previous studies that Israel and Jacob are interchangeable terms for this prophet and that both refer to the community in exile in Babylon. 48.1 is emphatically clear on this point (*pace* Snaith: 1967, 174), as Danell (1946, 262) has rightly observed. Secondly, however, it is not normally noticed that *all* these references occur in chapters 40–8 with the exception of those in 49.1–6, which may thus be regarded as something of a bridge passage. Since it is precisely the occurrence of 'Israel' in 49.3, 5 and 6 which has posed the chief difficulty in the exegesis of this passage, it may be that our observation furnishes a clue to its better understanding.

Isa. 49.1–6 is the second of the so-called 'servant songs', though it would generally be agreed today that they are not to be treated in total isolation from their context. (For a full survey of research, cf. Haag: 1985). In this passage, the servant explains to the 'isles' and 'peoples' (v. 1) how it has come about that he has a mission to them (v. 6). 'Exposition of the song has always to remember that everything it says has reference to the nations' (Westermann: 1969, 207). He was prepared for this task by God from the start (vv. 1b–2) and then presented publicly (v. 3). Despite frustrations (v. 4), he is now told that his ministry is no longer just to Jacob/Israel (vv. 5–6a) but that it is being extended to include the nations. (For a balanced and convincing critique of the ultra-nationalistic interpretations of Deutero-Isaiah which propose, for instance, that a 'light to the nations' means no more than a light to guide home the Jews of the dispersion, cf. Van Winkle: 1985).

These are the last two references to Jacob/Israel in Deutero-Isaiah, and they fit well into the pattern already observed; it is thus difficult to see how any identification of the servant in this paragraph with the Babylonian exiles as a whole can stand. Following immediately after chapters 46, 47 and 48 in particular, which deal so explicitly with the imminent fall of Babylon, this passage would present an intolerably harsh and totally unheralded change of referent if Jacob/Israel were now suddenly to refer to some other group, such as the dispersion as a whole.

The reason why such a possibility has even been entertained is, of course, because of the occurrence of 'Israel' in v. 3; if the servant is Israel in v. 3, scholars endlessly ask, how can he have a mission *to* Israel in vv. 5–6? The devices to which resort has often been made to circumvent this apparent difficulty are not convincing, in my opinion. In particular this must be emphasised in the face of those who still seek to argue that 'Israel' should be deleted from v. 3 (e.g. in recent decades Orlinsky: 1967, 79–89; Westermann: 1969, 209; Whybray: 1975, 137–8, all following in the footsteps of such earlier scholars as Michaelis: 1779, 249 and Duhm: 1914), a view emphatically rejected by Lohfink (1972). Rather, I believe, the solution lies in observing that v. 3 is not a *description* of Israel as the servant but rather a *designation* of the servant as Israel. To paraphrase prosaically the terse parallelism of the verse, 'He [God] said to me, "I now designate you as my servant; I now designate you 'Israel', in whom I will be glorified".' If this understanding of v. 3 is justified, then, of course, the apparent clash with vv. 5–6 disappears. The servant's designation as Israel in no way confuses him with Jacob/Israel to whom he has a ministry of restoration. He is here given a new identity with a new name – or rather, an old name redefined.

A few supporting observations and consequences are in order. First, since everything about 49.1–6 bespeaks a situation in transition, there is no need to deny that in Isaiah 40–8 the servant and Jacob/Israel appear to be identified and the possibility remains open that 42.1–4 reflects the prophet's ideal for his people in this regard. But the lack of response with which he was met led to a crisis of confidence (49.4) before he was taken forward to a new phase of ministry. Second, to read 49.1–6 in this sense as a transitional passage in the context of the work as a whole adequately explains the concentration of the word 'Israel' in 40–8 (after 49.1–6 it occurs only rarely, on each occasion as parts of the title of God: 49.7 [twice]; 52.12; 54.5; 55.5). Third, the striking use of 'Israel' on its own in 49.3, which has caused some scholars to doubt its authenticity, is now intelligible, and therefore should be allowed to stand. And finally, it should be stressed that this approach does not settle the issue of the identification of the servant, nor even whether an individual or collective interpretation is more appropriate. Despite the apparently individualistic language of 49.1, for instance, the same imagery is used collectively at 44.2. It would be fully compatible with the suggestion advanced here to identify the servant with (for instance) a righteous remnant amongst the people; in principle there is no difference between this new Israel as an individual or a group smaller than Jacob/Israel. That issue needs to be decided on other grounds which go beyond the confines of the present chapter.

To sum up, Isa. 49.1–6 presents us indeed with a portrayal of 'the concept of Israel in transition'. Unlike Ezekiel, the author of Isaiah 40–55 was initially concerned to address only the Babylonian exiles; despite his often exalted language, he was far less of a visionary than Ezekiel, addressing himself directly to the situation of his own community, whom he calls Jacob/Israel. Their lack of response, however, led to a shift in his aspirations and he seems to have experienced the need to narrow the meaning of Israel quite sharply (and here it becomes difficult to avoid otherwise unsatisfactory terms like 'the true Israel'), restricting it now to a faithful individual or group within the community. Thus already in the exile two major responses to Israel's loss of sovereignty were outlined, the one to restrict the term to the faithful, the other to ignore political and partisan realities in the maintenance of an age-old ideal. The danger with the former approach, of course, was fragmentation, for subsequent centuries revealed a variety of opinions as to what constituted 'the faithful', whereas the latter approach was equally endangered by tolerating so blurred a definition as to end up with the disintegration of Israel as a separate entity altogether.

The so-called prophets of the restoration give us few clues about attitudes to our topic in the immediately post-exilic period. Although Haggai never refers to 'Israel', there are still some commentators who follow Rothstein (1908, 5–41) in interpreting 2.10–14 in the light of Ezra 4.1–5: 'this people' and 'this nation' are Samaritans of some sort, and they should have no part in the restoration (cf. Rudolph: 1976; Wolff: 1986). If this were true, it would point to the very early development of a ghetto-like mentality in post-exilic Judah for which other evidence is lacking. (Deutero-Isaiah's narrowing of the concept of Israel, already discussed, was far from exclusive; its purpose was a purified Israel which should lead to the restoration not only of empirical Israel but in some sense of the nations too.) The dischronologised narrative of Ezra 4.6–24 suggests that it was only in the light of much later opposition that the northerners of 4.1–5 came to be regarded as 'the adversaries of Judah and Benjamin'. It is therefore preferable to follow the increasing number of those who understand the 'this people' of Hag. 2.14 to be the same as the 'this people' in 1.2, namely the Judaean community itself (e.g. Koch: 1967; May: 1968; Coggins: 1975, 50–2; Blenkinsopp: 1984, 232; Verhoef: 1987), and then tempting to go one step further with Petersen (1984, 81–2), who observes that 'Haggai's use of the term *gôy*, referring to the Judahites, is especially apt. By using this particular noun, Haggai is able to suggest that Judah, properly understood, will again possess land and be a political structure'; and again, 'The term *gôy* has a certain proleptic, even descriptive, quality in this text. Its use represents a very real hope by Haggai that Israel will be something more than a nondescript outpost of the Persian empire.' While Petersen's view is inevitably speculative, being based on so narrow a foundation, it seems more in keeping with what we should expect of Haggai in his historico-political setting than does Rothstein's.

Zechariah 1–8 too furnishes little evidence, but such as there is appears to be in keeping with what we have already noted. Of the two overt references to 'Israel', the first (2.2 [ET 1.19]) is textually doubtful (cf. Rudolph: 1976), but even if Petersen (1984) is right to defend it, it is backward looking, emphasising the completeness of the exilic dispersion. The focus for the future, so far as this prophet is concerned, clearly lies with Judah and Jerusalem as the place where God's presence will be known and to which, in consequence, even the gentile nations will come (2.15 [ET 2.11]; 8.22–3). Thus it is appropriate that the only other reference to 'Israel' (8.13) should come in a passage reapplying the promise to Abraham that 'as you were a curse among the nations, O house of Judah and house of Israel, so will I save you, and you shall be a blessing'. Once again, Zechariah's understanding of Israel would seem to be that of an outward-looking nucleus (without the need for city walls! – 2.8–9 [ET 2.4–5]) rather than an inward-looking enclave.

It is in the light of these remarks that we should examine the collection of prophetic material in Isaiah 56–66, generally known as 'Trito-Isaiah'. The basic critical issues relating to these chapters are no less formidable and unresolved for being familiar: are they the work of one man, and if so are they early post-exilic (see Elliger: 1928) or later (i.e. *c.* 450 BC; so Duhm: 1914, xx and 389)? If they are the work of more than one writer, are they to be dated over several centuries (e.g. Volz: 1932, 200) or a relatively short space of time (e.g. Whybray: 1975, 42)? In this confusing situation, warnings against the dangers of circular argument (from situation to date to setting) are well taken (Ackroyd: 1968, 119) and may be reinforced by the striking observation that the same verse (60.13) can be used to 'prove' both that the temple has not yet been built (Kaufmann: 1977, 57) and that it has been (Soggin: 1976, 335)!

An attempt to break this impasse in a way which has a decisive bearing on our theme has been made by Hanson (1975). Making use of what he calls 'the contextual-typological method' (supported by an intricate prosodic analysis), Hanson seeks both to arrange the oracles into chronological order, and to find within them evidence that the post-exilic community was already becoming sharply divided into two parties, both of which were struggling for control of the cult which was about to be, and then just had been, restored (i.e. 520–515 BC). The 'winners' in this struggle were the hierocratic party, represented in the literature by Ezekiel (especially as finally edited), Haggai, Zechariah 1–8 and the Chronicler. They were opposed unsuccessfully by the prophetic or visionary group, represented primarily in Trito-Isaiah and, later, Deutero-Zechariah. They took their inspiration from Deutero-Isaiah, 'though their circle probably came to encompass various dissident elements, including disenfranchised Levites' (p. 209). Hanson seeks to expound much of the polemic in Trito-Isaiah as being quite specifically the increasingly acrimonious charges of this marginalised group against the establishment. And particularly because of 63.16 ('Abraham does not know us, and Israel does not acknowledge us'), there is the strong implication that even as early as the sixth century BC the name 'Israel' was already being sucked into sectarian divisions. (Note how of a later period Hanson can say, 'a bitter conflict had torn a deep rift between hierocratic and visionary factions, implying for the latter that there were henceforth *two* Israels', p. 373.)

Hanson's thesis has been criticised from a number of angles (e.g. Carroll: 1979; Knibb: 1982, 169–76; Mason: 1982; Coggins: 1987, 52–9), though it has to be admitted that it remains as a most invigorating and creative reading of these oracles as of the other prophets which he discusses. Our concern here, however, must be limited to the question whether antagonisms within the post-exilic community had become so polarised as to say that 'Israel' was no longer a unifying concept for a de-politicised but nonetheless cohesive people, and had become instead merely a slogan by which each faction sought to claim legitimacy for itself. A study of the word 'Israel' will again provide a point of entry into the material.

It may at first seem surprising that the name occurs only six times in these chapters. The distribution of these occurrences is even more striking. Twice it is used in the divine title 'The Holy One of Israel' in a passage which is widely acknowledged to stand very close to the thought world of Deutero-Isaiah (60.9, 14; cf. Zimmerli: 1963, 222–3; Westermann: 1969. Snaith, 1967, indeed, believed that Isaiah 60–2 were by Deutero-Isaiah himself). These two references are thus not of great significance for our purposes.

More interestingly, Israel is used once in the prologue (56.1–8) and once in the epilogue (66.18–24) of Trito-Isaiah. In 56.8, at the conclusion of a passage which speaks of the restored cult in almost shockingly liberal terms (e.g. contrast vv. 4–5 with Deut. 23:2[1]), we are told of the Lord who 'gathers the outcasts of Israel' bringing others (hence presumably gentiles) to share in the worship of the temple which is to be 'a house of prayer for all peoples' (v. 7). Here, then, Israel is clearly being used in a wide sense for the diaspora as well as the Palestinian community, regarded quite evidently as a focus for the ingathering of the nations (cf. Polan: 1986, 76–9). The case is not dissimilar at the close of the book, where 'the children of Israel' (v. 20) are mentioned in a context which also speaks of the bringing in of the scattered Israelites as well as the gentile nations in order that 'all flesh may come to worship before' the Lord. Commentators generally agree that these two passages share the same outlook and have been consciously used (indeed, probably written to serve) as a framework for this whole section of the book. There is less agreement about their date, however. Hanson, comparing the similar outlook which he finds in Zechariah 14, would place them in the mid fifth-century BC (1975, 388–9). However, there seems to be a fundamental distinction between our passages and Zechariah 14, namely that in the latter the universalistic sentiment of v. 16 comes only after God's apocalyptic intervention (with full cosmic accoutrements) against the enemies of Jerusalem, a development which by Hanson's own typological method ought to set Zechariah 14 considerably later than passages which do not envision such a radical inbreaking. Furthermore, the inclusion of the diaspora as 'Israel' in Isa. 56.8 and of the cult community in 66.20 as 'the children of Israel' is suggestive of an inclusive rather than sectarian definition of the community. For such reasons it does not seem impossible that our passages still reflect the hopes that centred round the initial restoration of the cult, closer in sentiment to Zechariah 1–8 than to 14.

The only other two references to Israel in Trito-Isaiah come in 63.7 and 16, both, therefore, in the lengthy section 63.7–64.12 which many commentators (I believe rightly) understand as a lament of the Palestinian community which remained in the land during the exilic period. Indeed, there are a number of previously unobserved but striking parallels with the prayer in Nehemiah 9, for which I have suggested a comparable setting (Williamson: 1988). If this is correct, we should learn little from these occurrences for our purpose.

Hanson, however, argues that the passage was written later than Deutero-Isaiah, Isa. 60–2 and 57.14–19, and that it is dependent on the tradition of Deutero-Isaiah. As the writer appeals to God to act, he also betrays 'ominous signs that a fatal rift is threatening to divide the community' (p. 92). 'Abraham' and 'Israel' in 63.15 are taken to be the central Israelite community – the group recently returned from exile under the leadership of the Zadokites – and they are understood to be rejecting the writer and his group, whom Hanson sees as comprising, 'perhaps among various other dissident elements', the ousted Levitical priests who had not been in exile.

This bold hypothesis can hardly be accepted, however. In addition to the arguments normally advanced to favour an exilic setting for this passage, we should note specifically in reply to Hanson that (i) there are no substantial links between Isa. 63.7–64.12 and Deutero-Isaiah. It is striking that in his careful study of these links Zimmerli (1963) includes no reference to this passage under his main categories (citations and freer imitations) and only three fleeting references under his third category (more remote reminiscences), each of which might just as easily have been inspired by material other than Deutero-Isaiah (e.g. for the Lord's 'arm' in 63.12, cf. Deut. 4.34; 5.15, etc.). This lack of association with Deutero-Isaiah marks the passage out as distinctive in Trito-Isaiah. (ii) 'Israel' in 63.16 is most naturally understood as a reference to the patriarch Jacob and not to some contemporary group or party. The emphasis in the context on God as father led the writer to make a contrast with the 'fathers' of the nation; appropriately, as in the books of Chronicles, Jacob is called Israel in order to emphasise the link between the people and their ancestor. The corollary of Hanson's view, that the returning exiles also styled themselves 'Abraham' (or at least were so styled by their opponents) is without foundation. (iii) There seems to be considerable confusion over the identity of this hypothetical group, for Hanson wants to link it both with the Palestinian Levites and with the heirs of Deutero-Isaiah. These two factions can hardly be expected to have made good partners, however; the latter must initially have been enthusiastic supporters of the return, but in Hanson's view this would have made them unacceptable to the former. We must conclude, therefore, that Isa. 63.7–64.12 cannot play the major role in tracing the concept of Israel in transition that Hanson proposes.

Without this central plank in the two-party hypothesis, it becomes simpler to read much of the polemic in Trito-Isaiah at face value and in non-sectarian terms. The concerns for social justice and for cultic purity are certainly illuminated by sociological analysis, but that does not demand that they be necessarily taken as partisan, any more than in the case of Amos or Ezekiel. Even the sharp tone of Isa. 66.1–2 need not indicate absolute rejection of a temple any more than 1.15 does of prayer (to take a well-known example). There are, it is true, indications of tension, no more so than at 66.5, but it is not at all clear what the point at issue is here, especially if Whybray (1975) and others are right in treating it as an isolated oracle. What we should observe, however, is that those favoured in this verse are styled *haḥ^{a}rēdîm ʾel-d^{e}ḇārô*, '(you) who tremble at his [God's] word' (see also 66.2), a designation which, as Blenkinsopp (1984, 250) correctly points out, only recurs in a description of the support group of Ezra (cf. Ezra 9.4; 10.3). This, of course, would be an impossibility on Hanson's view, since Ezra belonged to his 'hierocratic party', but it becomes fully intelligible if here again the lines are not yet drawn in party terms.

These few remarks cannot, of course, do justice to the full range of relevant material in Trito-Isaiah, but they may suffice to enable us to draw a few conclusions regarding the concept of Israel in the restoration period. If we disregard the later polemic of passages such as Ezra 4, we have the distinct impression from the contemporary sources that there may not have been so many immediate points of tension between the exilic and Palestinian communities as is often supposed. Haggai is so silent on the issue that there continues to be uncertainty over which group he belonged to and who he was addressing! Zechariah is clearer, but not polemical, while we have argued that even the disputes in Trito-Isaiah may be understood along different lines. The incorporation of some of the Palestinian community's liturgy in Isa. 63.7–64.12 and in Nehemiah 9 points to a period of accommodation, as does the list in Ezra 2, which in all probability reflects the nature of the temple community in 520 BC (Williamson: 1985) as combining equally those who returned (listed by family association) and those who had remained in the land (listed by domicile; cf. Japhet: 1983). Though no longer a sovereign state, 'Israel' may still have been kept sufficiently alive in the memory and in literature to embrace the communities which had been geographically divided. The aspirations of Deutero-Isaiah may not have been realised, but at least until the temple was rebuilt it was possible to maintain that the restoration was not yet complete and that therefore the vision could be upheld of Israel as a nucleus in God's plans both for the return of the remaining exiles and for the consequent change of heart by the nations.

But it did not happen! So we must allow that time itself may have played an important part in the changing of attitudes. Certainly, when we come to our third and final group of texts we find ourselves entering a different world in which for some writers a decisive shift has at last taken place in the meaning and understanding of 'Israel'.

The relative dates of the composition of the various elements which go to make up the books of Chronicles, Ezra and Nehemiah are again a matter for dispute, and I can here only reiterate what I have argued for more fully elsewhere (cf. Williamson: 1982, 1983 and 1985). First in order come the accounts of the careers of Ezra and Nehemiah themselves (i.e. approximately Ezra 7–Nehemiah 13); based on earlier, first-hand accounts, this combined source may be dated *c.* 400 BC. Second, we may date the author of Chronicles in the middle of the fourth century BC (his work being lightly revised a generation later), while third and last comes the author of Ezra 1–6, *c.* 300 BC. It will be suggested in what follows that as regards our particular topic this arrangement of the literary sources also makes good historical sense.

Viewed against the background of the restoration period already discussed, the mission of Ezra to Jerusalem (probably in 458 BC) should be regarded as the decisive turning point in the development of the idea of Israel at this time. According to Koch's hypothesis (1974), 'Ezra's march from Babylon to Jerusalem was a cultic procession which Ezra understood as a second Exodus and a partial fulfilment of prophetic expectations' (p. 184), and in this connection he 'was sent "to all his 'people beyond the river'", including the Samaritans. His aim was to establish one Israel out of all 12 tribes' (p. 193). If this is so, Ezra should be seen as standing firmly in the tradition of Ezekiel. Unfortunately, however, Koch's analysis makes no distinction between what may reasonably be attributed to Ezra's first-person account and the manner in which this has been written up by his later editor, for even the most simple distinction on this ground (especially in Ezra 7.1–10) makes clear that much of Koch's evaluation must be editorial. The historical reality, by contrast, is likely to have been quite different.

There is a widespread measure of agreement that a proper understanding of Ezra's role must begin with the edict of Artaxerxes in Ezra 7.12–26 (cf. Noth: 1943; Kellermann: 1968; In der Smitten: 1973). Written in Aramaic, this edict entrusts Ezra with a fourfold task. The first two – to lead back to Judah any Jews who wished to leave Babylon and to transport various gifts and grants for the temple – are relatively straightforward, and the 'Ezra memoir' recounts in some detail how they were accomplished. They alert us, however, to the fact that Ezra's journey was not undertaken as a private affair, but as an official mission from the Achaemenid court.

This observation becomes important when we consider Ezra's third task, 'to conduct an inquiry into the situation in Judah and Jerusalem on the basis of the law of your God' (7.14). The scope and purpose of this inquiry are not spelt out at this point, but the subsequent narrative gives us certain clues. First, because the continuation of the edict shows great concern for the detail of the worship in the Jerusalem temple, it seems not unlikely that part of Ezra's inquiry should have concerned the degree to which there was conformity with the Mosaic law. We have the impression that the renewal of the recurrent grants and concessions of 7.17 and 21–24 may have depended on the outcome. If so, we may deduce that the Persian authorities gave official recognition to Ezra's lawbook (which seems to have been similar to, if not identical with, the Pentateuch) as the constitutional basis of the community, focussed on the temple. In his support of the cult, the Persian king required some formally agreed basis for his patronage, not least because it touched on (though was not coincidental with) the question of imperial taxation (cf. 7.21–4). The extent to which this was expected also to become the civil law of the province may be doubted (though for a possible parallel from Egypt, cf. Widengren: 1977, 515; Gottwald: 1985, 437). We may assume that, as a leader of the diaspora community in Babylon, Ezra had managed to work out a *modus vivendi* in regard to the delicate balance between loyalty to 'the law of your God' and 'the law of the king' (7.26), and it seems that this was what, as his fourth task, he was expected to teach to Jews in the Levant living outside the province of Judah (7.25–26). There is no historical possibility here of any expectation that the whole population of 'Beyond the River' should come under Jewish law; rather, as a new development the Persians gave official sanction to the notion that religious allegiance should be allowed some recognition alongside civil responsibility. 'There was a dual system of laws in the empire, the "king's law" applicable everywhere, and local laws which were codified by order of the king' (Frye: 1984, 119). Evidence that this was true of religious communities as much as of political authorities comes from the 'Passover Papyrus' from Elephantine (Cowley: 1923, 60–5).

A second observation regarding Ezra's 'inquiry' is that it apparently led almost immediately to an investigation of the issue of mixed marriages; indeed, Gunneweg (1981, and cf. 1985, 131) regards it as significant that in 10.16 a commission sat specifically to 'inquire' into the matter. In the light of our previous observation, this need no longer be considered unrelated; rather, it gives a clear indication of the lines along which Ezra, at any rate, understood legitimate participation in this newly privileged society might be enjoyed: it was to be primarily ethnic.

The rationale for this position is given in Ezra 9.1–2 (on which see more fully Fishbane: 1985, 114–23; Williamson: 1985, 129–32). Verse 1 sets the scene with a not unreasonable reapplication of Deuteronomic law which warned the invading Israelites against marrying the indigenous population of Canaan because of the danger that they would be led astray in their religion. In verse 2, however, this is taken a step further than Deuteronomy explicitly warranted by drawing into the exegesis the laws of holiness which forbade the mixing of unlike animals, crops or material (Lev. 19.19.). The new description of the community thus becomes that of 'the holy seed' who should not 'mingle themselves with the peoples of the land'.

Finally, two indications make clear that this is intended as a definition of Israel. First, the text is explicit in relating the offence to 'the people of Israel' (v. 1). Second, and perhaps more significantly, the community evidently sees itself standing in a typological relationship with the generation of the conquest. Israel enters the land from outside, and all those now in the land, regardless of their actual identity, are lumped together as 'Canaanites', with whom no close contact can be tolerated.

We may conclude this brief examination of Ezra's mission, therefore, by observing that to whatever extent Ezra and his fellow-exiles may have already privately espoused the policy of rigorous separation, it was to a large extent the dictates of the 'enlightened' Achaemenid policy towards the temple cult which drew the issue out into the open and gave the policy official sanction. The requirement of an external power to be able to define who it was dealing with administratively has had more effect on the history of Judaism than has perhaps been previously appreciated. To summarise our discussion bluntly, the transition in the concept of Israel may have owed more to the Persian administration in its treatment of an officially recognised local cult than to any internally motivated change of ideology or aspiration.

There is every indication that Ezra's policy caused deep divisions within Palestine and Jerusalem. If the biblical order of events is correct, Nehemiah for one will have been an enthusiastic supporter of his approach (cf. Neh. 13.23–8), and he clearly did not lack for collaborators. Equally clearly, however, many others took a directly contrary stance. It is likely that a lead was given in this by the more aristocratic classes, whether priestly or lay, since they stood to lose most both economically and socially if Judah became too isolated, especially from Samaria. Tobiah's family and business connections in Jerusalem should not be regarded as wholly untypical (cf. Neh. 6.17–19; 13.4–8).

Before attitudes polarised to breaking point, one last major writer attempted to steer a middle path of reconciliation. For much of this century, the Chronicler has been held to reflect closely the policies of Ezra (indeed, Albright: 1921 even revived the old Jewish opinion that Ezra *was* the Chronicler), and in part to have written his history as anti-Samaritan propaganda (cf. Torrey: 1910; von Rad: 1930; Noth: 1943; Rudolph: 1955). More recently, however, many writers have agreed both that the books of Chronicles should not be joined to Ezra and Nehemiah, and that the Chronicler's attitude towards the definition of Israel is markedly different from Ezra's (cf. Willi: 1972; Japhet: 1977; Braun: 1986). The conclusions of a detailed study of the use of the word 'Israel' in Chronicles and of the Chronicler's narrative structure as a whole (Williamson: 1977) justify this reappraisal.

The Chronicler opens his account with a genealogical portrayal of Israel in its ideal extent of twelve tribes. The line of God's election is traced directly from Adam to Jacob (significantly, always called 'Israel' in Chronicles) in chapter 1, while in chapter 9, following the tribal lists, it focusses on the post-exilic Jerusalem community. In the central section (chapters 2–8), however, the primary tribes of that community (Judah, Benjamin and Levi) are used to provide a framework for the other tribes rather than being grouped separately.

The reigns of David and Solomon, it is agreed by all, are portrayed as a 'united monarchy' indeed. The Chronicler here passes over adumbrations of the later divisions, and he emphasises in a fresh way the participation of 'all Israel' in the major events of the time (see most recently Im: 1985).

The Chronicler's contemporaries could have been forgiven for thinking, however, that this unity was irretrievably lost with the division of the monarchy after Solomon's death. To this, he responds in two ways. First, he shows that the division did not put either group hopelessly beyond the boundary of Israel. That title continues to be used as a symbol of continuity for both nations, and in particular he carefully shows that the northern tribes did not forfeit their position. They were to be regarded rather as those who had 'forsaken' the Lord – a position into which the southern tribes also fell sometimes and from which return by way of repentance was possible (cf. 2 Chron. 13.4–12).

Secondly, the Chronicler shapes his narrative in such a way as to show that, in theory at least, the position which was lost with the division of the monarchy was restored under Hezekiah (see most recently Throntveit: 1987, 109–25). In principle, therefore, the whole population was reunited in worship at that time at the Jerusalem temple, and nothing in the subsequent narrative reverses that position.

In all this (and more besides), the Chronicler may be making a final appeal to the spirit of the early restoration period, if not of Ezekiel himself. In deference to the exclusively inclined, he insists on the supremacy of the Jerusalem cult and on the necessity for purity in its service, but equally he reminds them that strength (as of a Hezekiah or Josiah) is a position from which to reach out rather than round which to close in. Likewise, he concedes to the 'assimilationists' of his day that they too had a legitimate place in Israel, that continuity ran through the community in the land, and that their faithfulness played no small part in the return of the exiles (e.g. 2 Chron. 30.6–9). At the same time, however, he demonstrates – again especially in the reforms of Hezekiah and Josiah – that Israel must be focussed on Jerusalem; any thought of separation would echo the northern kingdom's earlier 'forsaking' of God.

Although very little information is available for a reconstruction of the history of Judah and Samaria in the fourth century BC (for the present writer's attempt at a synthesis, cf. Williamson: forthcoming), it is highly probable that it was in the second half of this century that a rival religious community, later to be known as the Samaritans, was established on the previously deserted but venerable site of Shechem. This will have comprised a breakaway group of Jerusalem priests who joined with traditional lay elements from Samaria and possibly Judah (cf. Kippenberg: 1971). It would appear that the Chronicler's programme of reconciliation failed and that those who, for whatever motives, had attempted to sustain his ideals were forced out by the stricter party of Ezra's and Nehemiah's successors. The construction of a sanctuary on Mount Gerizim somewhere near the turn of the century gave tangible expression to this division, even if the final and irreversible schism did not follow for another century or so (Purvis: 1968).

The response to these events in Jerusalem may readily be detected in the final version of Ezra 1–6. Two points (justified in detail in Williamson: 1983 and 1985) deserve emphasis in the present context. First, many aspects of the account of the first return from Babylon and of the building of the second temple emphasise the Jerusalem community's continuity with pre-exilic Israel and the consequent legitimacy of the new temple. At a number of points Ezra 1 presents the return as a second Exodus, encouraging its first readers to regard themselves as the sole and direct heirs of the nation which had been born in Egypt. Furthermore, their temple stood explicitly on the site of Solomon's, its personnel and furnishing were the same, and progress towards its building was described in Ezra 3 in terms which pointedly recalled the account of Solomon's activity. In other words, the writer labours the point that Israel is now focussed in the Jerusalem cult community which others may join only on its own specific terms of separation (Ezra 6.21).

Secondly, the negative counterpart to this claim is given sharp expression in Ezra 4. In verses 1–5, those who had not shared in the experience of exile but who nevertheless regarded themselves as faithful Yahwists were refused participation in the temple building. Historically, there may have been sound legal and diplomatic reasons for this (Schultz: 1980); with hindsight, however, the author saw a deeper significance to which he gave expression by the insertion of the material in verses 6–23. The exchange of letters here recorded is chronologically out of place, but he saw in it the vindication of his description of the unwelcome applicants as 'the adversaries of Judah and Benjamin' (v. 1). Events nearer his own time had revealed, he argued, the true colours of those who endeavoured to gain entry to the community on grounds of equality, and history showed that the community was justified in maintaining a stance of isolation.

All this, of course, is a far cry from the aspirations of the exilic and early restoration writers. Our survey has suggested that initially the concept of Israel had been maintained either as an inclusive term that derived its ideals from the earliest period of the nation's history (Ezekiel, whose vision was most nearly maintained in later times by the Chronicler) or as a purified nucleus which should act as a light and magnet for others, including even the gentile nations (primarily Deutero-Isaiah). But the reality of life as a small colony in the vast Achaemenid empire which ironically sought to encourage the aspirations of local but loyal cults meant that political accommodation had to take precedence over an idealism which could not be understood at the centre of power as other than nationalist and hence potentially dangerous. Whether Ezra's extreme interpretation was inevitable as the only practical possibility may be debated, but once his programme had been introduced it proved well-nigh impossible to reverse. Not without trauma, Israel had been transformed from a national and political to a cultural and religious concept. Henceforth, the future of its cohesion had inevitably to focus on the temple and the law.

There has been considerable debate in recent years over the extent to which the history of the post-exilic period represents a loss of prophetic nerve and a decline into introverted legalism (for a passionate introduction with bibliography, cf. Levenson: 1987). The parameters of this discussion have been frequently set by theological concerns quite alien to the period in question, so that the ground rules for the debate now look antiquated and fundamentally flawed. It is unrealistic to expect that the Israel of, say, the united monarchy, could be recreated unchanged in the Persian province of Judah. The miracle of survival could only be achieved through transition, but the emerging community preserved not only the accounts of earlier voices but also those of an Ezekiel, a Deutero-Isaiah and a Chronicler within the corpus of its Scriptures. Vision and pragmatism were maintained side-by-side in a remarkable union which enabled a transformed Israel to survive against all the odds in the present without surrendering its unique contribution to the future.

Bibliography

Ackroyd, P. R., 1968. *Exile and Restoration. A Study of Hebrew Thought of the Sixth Century B.C.* (OTL, London).

Albertz, R., 1982. 'Jer 2–6 und die Frühzeitverkündigung Jeremias', *ZAW* 94, 20–47.

Albright, W. F., 1921. 'The Date and Personality of the Chronicler', *JBL* 40, 104–24.

Baltzer, D., 1971. *Ezechiel und Deuterojesaja. Berührungen in der Heilserwarthung der beiden grossen Exilspropheten* (BZAW 121, Berlin).

Blenkinsopp, J., 1981. 'Interpretation and the Tendency to Sectarianism. An Aspect of Second Temple History', in E. P. Sanders (ed.), *Jewish and Christian Self-Definition*, vol. 2, *Aspects of Judaism in the Graeco-Roman Period* (Philadelphia), pp. 1–26.

1984. *A History of Prophecy in Israel* (London).

Braun, R., 1986. *1 Chronicles* (Word Biblical Commentary 14, Waco).

Carroll, R. P., 1979. 'Twilight of Prophecy or Dawn of Apocalyptic?', *JSOT* 14, 3–35.

Coggins, R. J., 1975. *Samaritans and Jews. The Origins of Samaritanism Reconsidered* (Oxford).

1987. *Haggai, Zechariah, Malachi* (Old Testament Guides, Sheffield).

Coote, R. B. and Whitelam, K. W., 1987. *The Emergence of Early Israel in Historical Perspective* (Sheffield).

Cowley, A., 1923. *Aramaic Papyri of the Fifth Century B.C.* (Oxford).

Danell, G. A., 1946. *Studies in the Name Israel in the Old Testament* (Uppsala).

Duhm, B., 1914. *Das Buch Jesaja* (HKAT iii/1. 3rd edition, Göttingen).

Elliger, K., 1928. *Die Einheit des Tritojesajas* (BWANT 45, Stuttgart).

1978. *Deuterojesaja. 1. Teilband, Jesaja 40.1–45.7* (BKAT xi/1, Neukirchen).

Fishbane, M., 1985. *Biblical Interpretation in Ancient Israel* (Oxford).

Frye, R. N., 1984. *The History of Ancient Iran* (Munich).

Gottwald, N. K., 1979. *The Tribes of Yahweh. A Sociology of the Religion of Liberated Israel, 1250–1050 B.C.E.* (Maryknoll, N.Y. and London).

1985. *The Hebrew Bible – a socio-literary introduction* (Philadelphia).

Gunneweg, A. H. J., 1981. 'Zur Interpretation der Bücher Esra-Nehemia', *SVT* 32, 146–61.

1985. *Esra* (KAT xix/1, Gütersloh).

Haag, H., 1985. *Der Gottesknecht bei Deuterojesaja* (Erträge der Forschung 233, Darmstadt).

Hanson, P. D., 1975. *The Dawn of Apocalyptic* (Philadelphia).

Im, T.-S., 1985. *Das Davidbild in den Chronikbüchern. David als Idealbild des theokratischen Messianismus für den Chronisten* (Europäische Hochschulschriften xxiii/263, Frankfurt am Main).

In der Smitten, W. Th., 1973. *Esra: Quellen, Überlieferung und Geschichte* (Studia Semitica Neerlandica 15, Assen).

Japhet, S., 1977. *The Ideology of the Book of Chronicles and its Place in Biblical Thought* (Hebrew, Jerusalem).

1983. 'People and Land in the Restoration Period', in G. Strecker (ed.), *Das Land Israel in biblischer Zeit* (Göttingen), pp. 103–25.

Kaufmann, Y., 1977. *History of the Religion of Israel*, vol. IV, *From the Babylonian Captivity to the End of Prophecy* (New York).

Kellermann, U., 1968. 'Erwägungen zum Problem der Esradatierung', *ZAW* 80, 55–87.

Kippenberg, H. G., 1971. *Garizim und Synagoge* (RVV 30, Berlin).

Knibb, M. A., 1982. 'Prophecy and the emergence of the Jewish apocalypses', in R. Coggins, A. Phillips and M. Knibb (eds), *Israel's Prophetic Tradition. Essays in Honour of Peter R. Ackroyd* (Cambridge), pp. 155–80.

Koch, K., 1967. 'Haggais unreines Volk', *ZAW* 79, 52–66.

1974. 'Ezra and the Origins of Judaism', *JSS* 19, 173–97.

Lemche, N. P., 1985. *Early Israel. Anthropological and Historical Studies on the Israelite Society Before the Monarchy* (*SVT* 37, Leiden).

Levenson, J. D., 1987. 'The Hebrew Bible, the Old Testament, and Historical Criticism', in Friedman, R. E. and Williamson, H. G. M. (eds.), *The Future of Biblical Studies. The Hebrew Scriptures* (Semeia Studies, Atlanta), pp. 19–59.

Lohfink, N., 1972. '"Israel" in Jes. 49, 3', in J. Schreiner (ed.), *Wort, Lied und Gottesspruch. Beiträge zu Psalmen und Propheten. Festschrift für Joseph Ziegler* (Würzburg), pp. 217–29.

Mason, R., 1982. 'The Prophets of the Restoration', in R. Coggins, A. Phillips and M. Knibb (eds), *Israel's Prophetic Tradition. Essays in Honour of Peter R. Ackroyd* (Cambridge), pp. 137–54.

May, H. G., 1968. '"This People" and "This Nation" in Haggai', *VT* 18, 190–7.

Mendenhall, G. E., 1962. 'The Hebrew Conquest of Palestine', *BA* 25, 66–87.

Michaelis, J. D., 1779. *Deutsche Übersetzung des Alten Testaments*, VIII (Göttingen).

Noth, M., 1943. *Überlieferungsgeschichtliche Studien* (Halle) (Eng. Tr. of the second part, *The Chronicler's History* (JSOTSS 50, Sheffield, 1987).

Orlinsky, H. M., 1967. 'The So-Called "Servant of the Lord" and "Suffering Servant" in Second Isaiah', in H. M. Orlinsky and N. H. Snaith, *Studies on the Second Part of the Book of Isaiah* (*SVT* 14, Leiden), pp. 1–133.

Petersen, D. L., 1984. *Haggai and Zechariah 1–8* (OTL, London).

Plöger, O., 1959. *Theokratie und Eschatologie* (WMANT 2, Neukirchen) (Eng, Tr. *Theocracy Eschatology* (Oxford, 1968)).

Polan, G. J., 1986. *In the Ways of Justice Toward Salvation. A Rhetorical Analysis of Isaiah 56–59* (American University Studies VII/13, New York).

Purvis, J. D., 1968. *The Samaritan Pentateuch and the Origin of the Samaritan Sect* (HSM 2, Cambridge, Mass.).

Rad, G. von, 1930. *Das Geschichtsbild des chronistischen Werkes* (BWANT 54, Stuttgart).

Rothstein, J. W., 1908. *Juden und Samaritaner. Die grundlegende Scheidung von Judentum und Heidentum* (BWANT 3, Leipzig).
Rudolph, W., 1955. *Chronikbücher* (HAT 21, Tübingen).
1976. *Haggai – Sacharja 1–8 – Sacharja 9–14 – Maleachi* (KAT xiii/4, Gütersloh).
Schultz, C., 1980. 'The Political Tensions Reflected in Ezra-Nehemiah', in Evans, C. D. Hallo, W. W. and White, J. B. (eds), *Scripture in Context. Essays on the Comparative Method* (Pittsburgh), pp. 221–44.
Snaith, N. H., 1967. 'Isaiah 40–66. A Study of the Teaching of the Second Isaiah and its Consequences', in Orlinsky, H. M. and Snaith, N. H., *Studies on the Second Part of the Book of Isaiah* (*SVT* 14, Leiden), pp. 135–264.
Soggin, J. A., 1976. *Introduction to the Old Testament* (OTL, London).
Thompson, T. L., 1987. *The Origin Tradition of Ancient Israel*, 1. *The Literary Formation of Genesis and Exodus 1–23* (JSOTSS 55, Sheffield).
Throntveit, M. A., 1987. *When Kings Speak. Royal Speech and Royal Prayer in Chronicles* (SBLDS 93, Atlanta).
Torrey, C. C., 1910. *Ezra Studies* (Chicago).
Van Winkle, D. W., 1985. 'The Relationship of the Nations to Yahweh and to Israel in Isaiah xl–lv', *VT* 35, 446–58.
Verhoef, P. A., 1987. *The Books of Haggai and Malachi* (NICOT, Grand Rapids).
Volz, P., 1932. *Jesaja II* (KAT ix, Leipzig).
Westermann, C., 1969. *Isaiah 40–66* (OTL, London) (=Eng. Tr. of *Das Buch Jesaja 40–66* (ATD 19, Göttingen, 1966)).
Whybray, R. N., 1975. *Isaiah 40–66* (NCB, London).
Widengren, G., 1977. 'The Persian Period', in J. H. Hayes and J. M. Miller (eds), *Israelite and Judaean History* (OTL, London), pp. 489–538.
Willi, T., 1972. *Die Chronik als Auslegung* (FRLANT 106, Göttingen).
Williamson, H. G. M., 1977. *Israel in the Books of Chronicles* (Cambridge).
1982. *1 and 2 Chronicles* (NCB. Grand Rapids and London).
1983. 'The Composition of Ezra i–vi', *JTS* ns 34, 1–30.
1985. *Ezra, Nehemiah* (Word Biblical Commentary 16, Waco).
1988 'Structure and Historiography in Nehemiah 9', *Proceedings of the Ninth World Congress of Jewish Studies* (Jerusalem), pp.117–31.
Forthcoming 'Early Post-Exilic Judaean History', in J. A. Hackett *et al.* (eds), *The Bible and the Ancient Near East* (Atlanta).
Wolff, H. W., 1986. *Dodekapropheten 6. Haggai* (BKAT xiv/6, Neukirchen).
Zimmerli, W., 1958. 'Israel im Buche Ezechiel', *VT* 8, 75–90.
1963. 'Zur Sprache Tritojesajas', in *Gottes Offenbarung. Gesammelte Aufsätze zum Alten Testament* (Munich), pp. 217–33 (=*Festschrift für Ludwig Köhler* (Bern, 1950), pp. 62–74).
1983. *Ezekiel 2* (Philadelphia) (=Eng. Tr. of *Ezechiel 2, II Teilband* (BKAT xiii/2, Neukirchen, 1969)).

CHAPTER EIGHT

The origins of the Jewish diaspora

RICHARD J. COGGINS

Who were the diaspora?

The very idea implicit in the word 'diaspora' indicates that an important change had taken place in the character of Israel. From approximately the tenth century BC until 722 in the case of the northern kingdom, until 597 for Judah, these were two nation-states, situated among the other small states of Syria and Palestine. By contrast, toward the end of the Second Temple period the diaspora was a major social and religious phenomenon, fresh evidence relating to which is constantly being discovered. To a remarkable extent it was by that time the case that 'in private and in public Jews in Palestine and in the diaspora often adopted Gentile culture with enthusiasm' (Meyers and Kraabel, in Kraft and Nickelsburg: 1986, 201). Such a development implies very considerable changes in the community's self-perception in the intervening period of half a millennium.

When we consider the 'pre-exilic period', as it is conventionally described, we need have no doubt that some citizens of the two states travelled abroad from time to time; we hear of ambassadors to and from Egypt in Isaiah's time (Isa. 18.2; 31.1), or, earlier, of Solomon's and Jehoshaphat's attempts to establish overseas trade, but it would be misleading to speak of these as 'diaspora'. A closer approximation to that idea can perhaps be found in 1 Kings 20.34, where the agreement between Benhadad and Ahab provides for the establishment of Israelite *ḥuṣōṯ* (RSV: 'bazaars'; NEB 'a trading quarter') in Damascus, but this is an isolated reference of whose consequences we know nothing (Malamat: 1979, 184–6).

It would in any case be unusual to find passages of this kind being used in discussion of the diaspora, because literary convention has come to give that term a more limited reference, not so much to the expatriates of a nation-state as to the adherents of a religion who have been driven away by external forces from the usual centre of that religion. For that reason the beginning of our consideration must be the time of Judah's loss of independence as a result of the Babylonian attacks of 597 and 587.

Is it also appropriate to speak of a 'diaspora' of former inhabitants of the northern kingdom following the Assyrian attacks in the eighth century? Much that has been written about the supposed 'ten lost tribes' can be dismissed to the realm of fantasy, and we may certainly suppose that in both Israel and Judah the majority of the inhabitants continued to lead their lives in their native places; the means for mass deportation which have formed an appalling part of the technical apparatus of twentieth-century dictatorships were not available in the ancient world. It remains true that considerable numbers of citizens from both Israel and Judah were deported; ironically, we have more detailed information at this stage from Israel, where Sargon's 'Display Inscription' claims the removal of 27,290 prisoners (ANET, 284f).[1] (The claim of Sennacherib recorded on the 'Taylor Prism' to have 'made to come out from [Judah] 200,150 people, young and old, male and female' is scarcely to be considered as a claim to have carried out deportations on such a scale). 2 Kings 17.6 gives a general account of the places of deportation, but of the subsequent fate of the deportees nothing is known. It is perhaps significant that some prophetic oracles relating to the hoped-for restoration of former conditions retain an awareness of distinct northern and southern origins and envisage that that difference will continue (Jer. 31.16–22; Nahum 2.3 [EVV 2.2]; later the assumption is that those who return will be united as one community (Ezek. 37.15–28, and the 'restoration' passages in Haggai and Zechariah 1–8) (Greenwood: 1976, 376–85). It is obviously possible that one of the reasons for the difference in expectation between northern and southern deportees lay in the differences between Assyrian and Babylonian policy, and the suggestion has been made that the Judaean deportees were in effect a group of hostages (Zimmerli: 1979, 13). It is doubtful whether we have sufficient independent evidence to establish this point, but it raises important methodological questions concerning the treatment of the theme of exile from the two kingdoms. Some will maintain that the appropriate means of clarifying our overall picture is by fuller attention to external factors such as the policy pursued by successive Assyrian and Babylonian rulers; others will hold that the different treatment of the two exiles is essentially a literary matter, due much more to the fact that the traditions were mediated through the later Jerusalem community, for whom the experience of exile was an important part of its own self-understanding. For that community exile was an important purifying experience; for the northerners, by contrast, it was the final indication of divine displeasure.

Relevant also to our definition of the diaspora is the appropriate use of the word 'Jewish'. Long-established convention has led to the custom of confining the terms 'Jew', 'Jewish', to adherents of the religion commonly called Judaism, rather than simply applying it to citizens of the kingdom of Judah.

Even when it is accepted that the change from a nation-state to a religious community can most appropriately be linked with the Babylonian conquest there are two complications in evaluating the biblical evidence which should be noted before we proceed any further. For the Bible itself the *b^e^ne Yisrael*, the 'children of Israel', had always been the religious community, the people of Yahweh. The religious requirements had been set out at the very beginning of its story, before ever it had entered the promised land. In its subsequent history there had been, so the tradition held, many occasions of disobedience, when the people had fallen away from their former loyalty, but a basic religious awareness had, according to the biblical testimony itself, always been present. From its beginnings Israel had been different.

This is one of the points at which much modern scholarly opinion is most sharply at odds with the internal testimony of the biblical text. To an increasing extent the scholarly emphasis has been on the similarities between Israel and Judah and the surrounding states, in matters political, economic and religious (Smith: 1952, for an early adumbration of this view). This is perhaps the most basic level at which the 'sociological, anthropological and political perspectives' referred to in the title of this volume have been operative. On such a view the distinctiveness of Israel really only emerged when it became identifiable as a religious community, at the time of the Babylonian conquest or thereabouts, and an important role is envisaged for the Deuteronomists in this development of a distinctive self-awareness. It is strikingly different from the contention, very prevalent in the days of the 'biblical theology' movement, that Israel was in some sense always to be pictured 'against its environment'; the title of G. E. Wright's monograph (1950) very accurately reflected its chief concern.

The second complication arises when the fact of exile is considered. Even in common English usage the word normally denotes something more than the sheer physical fact of the removal of a group of people from their homeland to an alien environment. There is an emotional or spiritual factor involved. This is certainly true with the Old Testament accounts of the exile of the people of Jerusalem. Though some passages clearly imply that only a relatively small proportion of the total population was deported (Jer. 52.28–30 gives a total of 4,600), little interest is shown anywhere in the fate of those left behind. (The book of Lamentations forms a partial exception, but its poetic form scarcely allows precise judgements as to its setting). Such lack of interest may partly be due to the fact that the prevailing orthodoxy came to emphasise that all the inhabitants of the land had been exiled, that the land was left desolate for a complete lifetime of seventy years to 'enjoy its Sabbaths' (2 Chron. 36.20f.).[2] In short, when we are trying to understand the origins of the Jewish diaspora we shall almost certainly find that problems will continually arise from the tension between the self-understanding of the community as handed down to us in the Hebrew Bible and the type of reconstruction of the social and political developments that took place as understood by modern scholars.

Before we look at any of the causes or consequences of this development in detail, it is right to recall how extraordinary is the ideological victory that has been achieved by those who have presented the Babylonian exile as the true context of Israel's community. Whereas the descendants of those deported by the Assyrians in the eighth century presumably became absorbed into the communities where they were deported, those exiled by the Babylonians from Judah (a much smaller number, if the Jeremiah figures are to be accepted as a reliable indication) soon had specific claims being made on their behalf, that this group were the true inheritors of the tradition of the whole community. Jer. 24, with its contemptuous dismissal of those left in Jerusalem as 'very bad figs, so bad that they could not be eaten' (verse 2), and Ezek. 33.23–9, with its sweeping denunciations of those left in the land, can both be regarded as remarkably effective propaganda; much subsequent study, even at the most rigorously academic level, has accepted the claim that the real continuity lay with the exiles. The conspiracy of silence relating to those who remained in the land (the great majority of the population, one must assume: even in Ezekiel [33.24] they are pictured as grounding their hope for the future on the fact that they are many) has been astonishingly successful. The judgement of Noth (1958, 291) that 'the tribes left behind in the old country continued to be the centre of Israelite history and Israelite life' was rejected by Bright (1960, 325) and by many historians since; but it surely represents the more unbiassed assessment of the situation.

In this connection the development of words from the root *g-l-h* is revealing. The semantic field of the related terms extends well beyond the idea of exile (TDOT: II, 476–88), but in the account in Jer. 52 the causative form of the verb is used in that sense (RSV 'carried away captive'), in just the same way as it had been of the Assyrian deportation of the northerners (2 Kings 17.6). The noun is frequently found with a similar sense (2 Kings 24.15f; Jer. 29; Ezek. 1.1; and freq. in chs. 11–12). But in Ezra a remarkable shift of meaning takes place. Whereas at 1.11 and 2.1 the established sense is found, a significant change can be traced at 6.19–21. In the last of three references (verse 21) it is made clear that those being referred to are those who had returned from exile (*haššābîm mēhaggôlāh*), in the two preceding verses those keeping the festival at the restored Jerusalem temple are described as the *b^e nê-haggôlāh* (RSV 'returned exiles', but no word in the Hebrew corresponds to 'returned'). Then, in the ceremony relating to the repudiation of mixed marriages in ch. 10 the community is regularly described as the *gôlāh* (vv. 6–8, 16), in a way that can best be understood as a claim in regard to true membership of the Jerusalem community; it can be granted only to those who have the experience of having passed through exile. The link between being a member of the *gôlāh* and being oneself in exile has now been completely broken; presumably claims could have been made that one's forebears had been among those exiled, but claims of this kind become very difficult to establish beyond dispute. Gunneweg has described this development as a 'semantic revolution' comparable with that which took place in the development of the term *ʿam hāʾāreṣ*, so that the idea of deportation is no longer integral; instead the *gôlāh* comes to be perceived as the true community (Gunneweg: 1983, 439f.). It is clear that in this essay it will not be possible to assume any identification of the diaspora by the use of the term *golah*. Given that much modern scholarship would cast doubt on the whole idea of a mass return from exile, as described in Ezra 2, it is clear that the viewpoint of the book of Ezra represents a remarkably successful take-over bid for the 'true' interpretation of the community's history and sacred traditions. It is worth recalling of C. C. Torrey, who wrote as long ago as 1910, that though he may have been excessively sceptical in his doubts as to the reality of the exile, much of what he said about the ideological issues involved has proved to be remarkably farsighted, and despite its age his work is still worthy of study.

One other point with regard to the use of the term *gôlāh* should be noted. Hausmann in her study of the various words denoting 'remnant' has shown that this terminology is never used in the prophets of the exile or later to refer to the *gôlāh*; the range of reference of the terms is always quite separate (Hausmann: 1987, 101). It may also be relevant to note at this point that the use of the term 'diaspora' in the LXX does not appear to have any immediate bearing on our assessment; none of the passages in which it is used appear either to envisage it as a technical term to describe a specific group of people, or to regard it as the appropriate translation of '*golah*'.

The contribution of sociology

The application of modern sociological insights to biblical study has taken a variety of forms, but two are of immediate concern for the consideration of the emergence of the Jewish diaspora; a third will occupy our attention at a later stage. The first is the increased awareness that religious practice and religious laws did not exist in a vacuum; they were part of a larger social environment, which will have had an important role in shaping the form of that religious practice. Thus, to take an example from an earlier period, if Israel's ancestors had been nomads or semi-nomads that social environment should have left its traces in the religious material deriving from such a period, and its apparent absence has led some modern scholars to question such an origin for Israel (Gottwald, 1980). To this type of consideration we shall return particularly when considering the shaping of the law-codes in the Pentateuch.

But there is a different sense in which sociological awareness can be relevant. This concerns the understanding of themes which are expressed in the biblical text itself in a purely idealistic form but may have found some expression as a social institution in the life of the community. Thus, a classic example would be that of *b^erît*, conventionally translated 'covenant'. In the Old Testament itself it is presented as a basic theological idea, a means of expressing the relation between God and his people; despite the frequency of references, we are given little indication in the biblical text how this relation was to be implemented in the community's life, and reconstructions of covenant festivals and the like are purely modern scholarly proposals. (Deut. 31.9–13 refers to a reading of the law every seven years, and this requirement has been interpreted by Holladay [1986] as an important clue to the interpretation of Jeremiah; but no specific reference is made to 'covenant' in that passage, and there is indeed no indication from the biblical text whether such a ceremony ever took place). Proposals relating more specifically to covenant-renewal have in fact played a prominent part in modern discussion, with the suggestion that a pre-monarchical amphictyony with its central sanctuary provided the locus of covenant maintenance (Noth: 1930), or the attempt to place many psalms in the context of a covenant-renewal festival (Weiser: 1962).

When we come to consider the theme of exile, both of these applications of sociological insights have found their place. A good deal of recent study has been directed toward the understanding of the social structure of the community of Israel after the loss of its identity as a nation-state, and though our picture is inevitably a fragmentary one for lack of a coherent body of evidence, it is undoubtedly the case that a more credible picture of the Judaism of the sixth and following centuries BCE has emerged in recent years. That aspect of sociological study, which may be regarded as social history rather than sociology in the more precise sense, is fully covered by the relevant chapters of the Cambridge History of Judaism, Vol. 1, and will not be our direct concern here.

The second type of insight has not received such detailed study and invites further reflection. It would certainly not be true to say that it has been neglected; an important pioneer in this field was Antonin Causse, for many years Professor of Old Testament at Strasbourg, who actually wrote an article as long ago as 1927 with a title equivalent to that of the present essay: 'Les origines de la diaspora juive'. This was, however, essentially a preliminary sketch for his two major studies, *Les Dispersés d'Israël: les origines de la diaspora et son rôle dans la formation du Judaïsme*, first published in 1929, and *Du Groupe ethnique à la communauté religieuse* (1937). The work of Causse has recently been the subject of renewed interest after a long period of neglect. (Kimbrough: 1978, is a study of Causse's achievement which contains some revealing comments about the ignorance of Causse and his work; French-speaking Old Testament scholars have often claimed, with some justice, that their contribution has not been given proper attention by their colleagues in Germany and Britain.) One of Causse's basic concerns is related to the topic which gives this essay its title: when can one legitimately first speak of a diaspora? The opening paragraph of his earlier book claims that 'the majority of historians regard the development of the diaspora and its effective influence as dating only from the Hellenistic period' (Causse: 1929, 7, my translation; a footnote makes it clear that he had the work of Schürer particularly in mind).

The conclusion of this work by Causse, in many ways still a preliminary study, is in some ways even more striking. After devoting the body of the book to the importance of the change brought about by the events of the sixth century, he reaches the conclusion that by the Persian period it was proper to speak of Judaism as having inherited 'a new conception of the world, a new theology, a new piety, by which the ancient tradition was gradually overlaid' (Causse: 1929, 161). The copy of Causse's book which I have been using was that given by the author to Prof. W. O. E. Oesterley, who has underlined this section, and written in the margin the one word 'overstated'. 'Overstated' the conclusions may be, but they formed an important corrective to older views, and have to a considerable extent been vindicated by the widespread tendency within contemporary Old Testament scholarship to regard the exilic period as one of the most formative in the development of Judaism.

But in many ways, as has been noted, this work of Causse was only a preliminary study, and his major application of sociological insights to the world of the Old Testament was to find expression in his *Du groupe ethnique à la communauté religieuse*, whose sub-title, 'Le problème sociologique de la religion d'Israël' shows its relevance to our present theme. The work is dedicated to L. Lévy-Bruhl, described as 'the master of studies of "the primitive mentality"', and it is clear that Lévy-Bruhl's classification of different types of human thought influenced Causse greatly (Kimbrough: 1978, 101–23). The first two parts of the book are devoted to an exploration of the sociological development of Israel from the settlement down to the time of the Deuteronomistic reform, and are not our immediate concern; it is the third and longest part, 'Le problème sociologique de Judaïsme', which deals with the period of development from a nation-state into a religious community. It was in this section of his work that Causse explored such issues as the effect of the exile on the family and the particular roles of individual members of the family, with an increasingly important role for women (this is in sharp contrast to some other more recent studies which have seen this as a time of increased patriarchalisation: Terrien: 1985, 71–86); increasing concern for the individual, which he held to be discernible in the book of Ezekiel and elsewhere; new emphases within community life which played a crucial part in enabling the community to retain its identity. It was the recognition that developments of this kind took their origin from the changing social circumstances imposed by the breakdown of the nation state and the former ethnic basis of identity which led to a new awareness of the reasons underlying the changes in Israel's self-perception.

In a number of the points just noted the emphases of Causse differed strikingly from the better known sociological study of Max Weber. For Weber the exile meant that the Jews had become a 'pariah people'. He defined this expression as being appropriate for 'a distinctive hereditary social group lacking autonomous political organization and characterized by prohibitions against commensality and intermarriage originally founded upon magical, tabooistic and ritual injunctions' (Weber: 1963 [=1922], 108f.); in his work devoted more specifically to Judaism a whole section of 120 pages is concerned with the establishment of the Jewish pariah people (Weber: 1923, 281–400). In his discussion of its institutions and structure from the exile onwards he laid great weight on the role of the priests and the way in which their concerns shaped the perceptions of the community: rejection of mixed marriages, precise laws relating to preparation and sharing of food, strict Sabbath-observance, and the like, together with a subordination of the charismatic aspects of religion, represented by the prophets, to the requirements of due order. Causse accepted the designation as 'pariah people' in the sense that the nation no longer had its own home and the basis for a political structure, but, though he paid tribute to Weber's achievement, he regarded it as an 'improvisation singulièrement intuitive' (Causse: 1937, 9); Weber's reliance on others for his knowledge of current developments in Old Testament study meant that there were crucial flaws in his reconstruction, not least in the way in which he drew rather far-fetched parallels between the Jewish situation and that of other 'pariah peoples' from widely different circumstances. Certainly Causse was able to cover a broader and probably more representative range of material, and to bring out the creative way in which the group in exile was able to evaluate its past traditions without specific ethnic or geographical determinants.

An interesting comparison between the work of Weber and Causse is offered by F.-L. Hossfeld, who notes that underlying the obvious differences are some important similarities, such as the importance attributed by each to the place of the family, to the evaluation of the land, and to the handling of past traditions; he sees value in the characteristic emphases of each (Hossfeld: 1987, 125–8). Hossfeld also draws out the way in which in both the later strata of Deuteronomy and the P material in the Pentateuch 'models of the church' in a sense analogous to later Christian writings can be discerned, with important implications for the presentation of Israel as a community centred upon Torah and cult. These issues go beyond our immediate concern, for which it is the insights achieved by Causse, neglected though his work has been in detail, which can help in our better understanding of the institutions of Israel.

The institutions of the covenant community

A convenient starting-point in the consideration of such institutions will be the theme of covenant, already alluded to above. In his recent survey of different understandings of this topic, Nicholson makes much of the point that covenant was essentially a theological idea, and that the attempt to give it a specifically sociological function had proved to be a blind alley for scholarship. What he describes as 'the religio-sociological understanding of the origin and nature of the Sinai covenant' (Nicholson: 1986, 84), based upon the theory of an amphictyony and reinforced by analogies with treaty-models (be they Hittite or Assyrian) has given way to an understanding of *bᵉrît* as a theological idea without any discernible sociological function. (Nicholson gives general support to the proposals along these lines of Perlitt: 1969, especially, and Kutsch, in a variety of studies, without endorsing all their details; as against Kutsch, for example, he retains the conventional translation 'covenant'.) In this sense it will be seen that the more recent understanding is, as it were, 'anti-sociological';

what had formerly been placed within a specific sociological interpretation is now removed from that type of context and placed in the realm of the history of ideas. How far is this a characteristic, or indeed a legitimate development?

We can surely suggest that it is unlikely that a theological idea would have taken root so deeply as did that of *b^e^rît* had there not been some identifiable context within which it was given expression. As has been seen already the suggestion of covenant festivals and the like can only be a matter of speculation; what we do know is that the importance of *b^e^rît* was embodied in written form in traditions which came to have authority. In short, the emergence of the diaspora coincided with the emergence of Judaism as the religion of a book. The importance of the written word is already emphasised in the two prophets of the period when the exile was actually taking place: Jeremiah and Ezekiel.

In the case of Jeremiah there is the obvious example of his letter to the exiles, which was clearly to be regarded as an authoritative transmission of God's word, to be more highly regarded than the words of the prophets among the exiles, who also no doubt spoke in the name of the Lord (Jer. 29.8f.); presumably Ezekiel was not among those so contemptuously dismissed. The story in Jer. 36 is in some ways even more revealing. It is dated to 605, but is clearly intended to be of lasting significance in its emphasis on the indestructibility of true words from God through his servants. In this connection Brett has made the interesting suggestion, with reference to Deut. 31.24–9 in particular, that 'the Book of the Law was to function as a "witness" against all those who were in authority, including the Levites, since these authorities were sure to become corrupt. The written word has become a critical "check" to be set against later beliefs and practices' (Brett: 1987, 29).

This is an important insight to bear in mind when considering that development of Pentateuchal traditions which is widely held to have taken place at the time of the exile. It has come almost to be taken for granted that the P material in the Pentateuch took its final form among the Babylonian exiles in the 6th or 5th centuries BC; what has less often been discussed is the motivation lying behind the gathering of ancient material into its present form, or the social matrix from which it is likely to have emerged. Causse maintained that it was possible to see the intention of the Priestly code as being an idealisation both of the people's past, spelt out in terms of a wide-ranging philosophy of history within which all the ancient myths of human origins could be embodied, and of its aspirations for the future in utopian terms (Causse: 1937, 218). More recent study of the P strand in the Pentateuch has to a large extent pursued similar types of approach. Thus

Patrick, while recognising that the 'classical formulation' of P as dating from an exilic setting has been challenged in recent years, still regards as the most likely understanding the view that 'P's retrospect was simultaneously a prospectus . . . a programme for reconstruction, incorporating new ideas and rituals that had arisen from the experience of the exile and reflection on its causes'. It envisaged a future for the community 'not as a political kingdom but as a religious community centred round the temple and ruled by a religious hierarchy' (Patrick: 1986, all quotations from p. 146). (This viewpoint is very close to that of Causse, though no direct reference is made).

These comments are followed by a helpful commentary on detailed aspects of the P material, but there remain many unanswered (and perhaps unanswerable) questions: what were the circumstances which led to this compilation taking place? were the old traditions which were embodied already in written form (and if so how accessible were they to a community in exile?) or were these oral traditions handed down within priestly milieux, perhaps as part of the necessary indoctrination for the exercise of the priesthood? Similarly, a whole range of questions is raised by social anthropologists from the fact that these precise regulations were laid down at a time when there was no hope or immediate expectation of any of them being observed; how are we to understand the detailed requirements in Leviticus for the offering of the *ʿōlāh* if there was no temple in which to carry out the ceremony? Or what is the significance of rules relating to uncleanness when they are promulgated in a foreign land which is itself unclean? Just as, at a later date, study of the Mishnah and Talmud needs always to keep in mind the fact that the Torah of which they were an elaboration and commentary could to a large extent no longer be applied to the circumstances of the community, the same can be said of the Priestly material in the Pentateuch. Three of the six orders of the Mishnah relate to matters applicable only within the holy land, yet they were compiled at a time when access to the holy land was not possible; in a similar way, if the P material was put into its final form in exile it represents a utopianism whose motivation deserves as careful study as do the detailed requirements it embodies.

Though most of the questions just raised cannot be answered with any confidence there is one point which this activity among the diaspora does illustrate very clearly. The basic Torah by which the community was to be guided was associated with Sinai, that is to say, with a time and a place before the entry into the promised land. Only by taking upon itself the laws promulgated at Sinai could the community once more look forward to entry into that promised land. This point has been made by many writers discussing the final formation of the Pentateuch. Less clear, and less often discussed, is the issue whether the community in any meaningful sense expected to return to the land. Put another way, how soon and how deeply did the experience of diaspora come to be regarded as a continuing state of affairs? Many a Jewish family must have used the ritual prayer 'Next year in Jerusalem' at the celebration of its festivals without any expectation that the wish would be literally borne out; were the promises of a dramatic return found in Isaiah 40–55 similarly understood in a sense other than the literal? How exactly was it envisaged that the Torah might be put into effect? (Continuing disputes within present-day Judaism relating to Zionism are a reminder that the status of the diaspora is still a live issue).

The role of prophets

In the early years of exile, however, at least among those taken to Babylon, another tradition continued of the means of God's communication with his people: the prophets. (Whether there were also prophets among those in Egypt, other than the fugitive Uriah who was extradited back to Judah and his death [Jer. 26.20–3] and the unwilling Jeremiah [Jer. 43–4] we have no means of knowing). But for the early period of exile the importance of the prophetic office cannot, however, simply be written off. In the subsequent history of the diaspora there is little evidence of activity by named prophets,[3] and on most understandings of the prophetic role the particular function of the prophet had come to an end. Weber, as we have seen, explained this in terms of increasing priestly dominance, but other approaches are possible. Thus, in religious terms the warnings directed against the community had now been fulfilled; in sociological terms the appropriateness of such descriptions as 'central' or 'peripheral' prophet was now a thing of the past in view of the break-up of the established pattern of society. But in the early days following the downfall of Jerusalem those already established in the prophetic office were understood as carrying out important functions. In this connection it is noteworthy that all three of the major collections among the Latter Prophets in our present Hebrew Bible received extensive elaboration and editorial shaping during the exilic period; it is most likely, furthermore, that that elaboration took place in the diaspora. For Ezekiel the point is clearly made by the opening verse of the book which places the prophet 'among the exiles by the River Chebar'; for Isaiah it is almost unanimously agreed that chs. 40–55 have a Babylonian background, however their relation to other parts of the book be understood. For Jeremiah the place of composition is much more disputed; Carroll, 1986, 65–82, unlike some scholars, gives full recognition to the difficulties involving in establishing the place in which the Jeremiah tradition reached its final form, and though he seems to favour a Palestinian setting (69) readily acknowledges the extent of our uncertainty on this matter. (Nicholson, 1970, 116–35, is much more confident that a Babylonian background can be established).

Is it possible to establish the intentions underlying such editorial work in the changed circumstances of the community? To some extent, no doubt, veneration for past traditions will have played its part. There is no need to postulate formal 'schools' of prophetic disciples to suppose that there were those in the community who revered the memory of the words spoken in God's name by notable messengers in the past; who were convinced that the judgements incorporated in those words had now come to pass; and who wanted to ensure the continuing availability of those words.

But it is also likely that we can discern a somewhat different understanding of prophetic traditions in the diaspora situation. Westermann (1987, 186f.) has drawn attention to the way in which a strongly parenetic element enters the prophetic material from this period. In Jeremiah in particular the conditional words of salvation offered to some part of the community are linked with the plea to repent and turn from former disobedience which had been the cause of the community's present plight (cf. again the letter to the exiles, ch. 29); whether or not it is appropriate to speak of the pre-exilic prophets as preachers calling for repentance, it is clear that for the prophets of our period this was an important part of the way their role was perceived in the new situation of the community.

If the words of prophets provided some kind of explanation of the present situation of the community, might they not also be the appropriate means of legitimation of the way in which it should develop in its changed circumstances? Such an understanding, if justified, would provide a ready explanation for the shaping of prophetic traditions in the diaspora rather than in Palestine. Such a legitimation might be harshly condemnatory of the community's faults which had brought about the current state of affairs; this is most obviously so in the re-presentations of past history found in Ezek. 16, 20 and 23, where in each case what may be a later addition has used the past story as the basis for claims about the future of the community. Elsewhere the legitimation might be expressed in more consolatory terms, as in Isa. 40, where past sins are pardoned and that very fact provides the opportunity for further prophetic words.

Reference was made at an earlier point in this article (see above, p.168) to a third type of sociological consideration which is relevant to the understanding of the community at the time of the exile. This is described by Nicholson in the following terms. 'The sociology of religion has been interested [. . .] in the social function of religion and religious ideas in the sense of legitimating the structures and institutions of a society [. . .] Religion is part of a society's endeavour to impose meaning upon its experience of the world' (Nicholson: 1986, 192f.; he acknowledges his debt at this point to the work of P. Berger, in particular his *Social Reality of Religion*). In his discussion of the implications of this perception for our understanding of the place of religion in ancient Israel Nicholson regards the role of the pre-exilic prophets as decisive in mapping out a distinctive understanding within Israel, and we need not dispute the significance of the way in which their achievement was understood. But it may be necessary to distinguish more precisely than Nicholson does between the role of the prophets themselves in their immediate setting and the way in which their role was perceived by those who gathered their words together and set them down in writing.

An example may illustrate the point. It is a characteristic feature of the eighth-century prophets, especially Amos and Isaiah, that they condemn the exploitation of the poor, and this no doubt reflects in some sense the social conditions of their time. But it is also noteworthy that a significant change took place in the perception of the poor; in such a passage as Amos 2.6, for example, 'poor' and 'righteous' have come to be identified, a development with considerable consequences for later biblical tradition. While we cannot be certain of the circumstances in which this development of perception took place, the most likely context would seem to be that of the diaspora, where the older distinctions based on social standing within the community were no longer so directly applicable. (An adumbration of some of the implications of such a development can be found in Lohfink: 1987, 136–8; though his concern is theological rather than sociological, the overlap at this point is a significant one.) Thus here we find ourselves once again confronted with the importance of the exile and the way in which Israel's self-perception as people of God could survive and indeed flourish in a diaspora context.

Legitimation of the present really only provides the occasion for the expression of hopes concerning the future. Here the prophetic role continued to be important, both in terms of what are to the best of our knowledge totally new oracles (as in Isa. 40–55) and in those which are more obviously reinterpretations of an older tradition. The nature of this future hope has been explored by Gross (1987), who devotes much of his attention to the P material in the Pentateuch but also discusses a number of relevant texts in Jeremiah and Ezekiel. It may indeed be the case, as we have already seen, that the P material reached its final form in an exilic context and in the sixth century, but the fact of its use of earlier traditions and the way in which its presentation is deliberately in terms of a re-creation of the people's past makes it hazardous to do more than refer to it here; the recreation of the past may indeed provide a blueprint for the future, as has often been proposed, but we have no clear evidence that it was in fact read in that sense by the community in exile.

With the prophets of the sixth century the situation is different. Even if passages such as Jer. 23.5f.; 33.14–26; Ezek. 34. 23f.; 37.22–5 (those with which Gross deals) are secondary additions in their present context, there is surely some significance in the fact that they have been incorporated in the two prophetic collections which are attributed to the prophets of the time of the fall of Jerusalem. All of them share promises of an unconditional character; the call to particular forms of behaviour as the necessary condition for entering into the blessing, characteristic of the Deuteronomistic literature in particular, is here absent.

More important for our present context is the way in which the terms *ʿam* and *gôy* are used. Jer. 33.24 poses problems because of the apparent inconsistency in the use of *ʿam* in the two parts of the verse. Literally translated, the verse runs: 'Have you not seen what this people [*ʿam*] [sing.] are saying [plur], "The two clans which the Lord chose he has rejected"? and they have despised my people [*ʿam*] from being a nation [*gôy*] before them.' There will be dispute as to the identity of those being referred to as 'this people', the latter part of the verse is much less ambiguous: though no longer a nation (*gôy*) the community is and will continue to be 'my people'. This is an important element in the developing self-perception of the community, and it is paralleled, and perhaps taken further, in Ezekiel. There may be traceable here early stages of those ideological disputes which were to become so important in the later history of the community (Carroll: 1986, 638f.), but the immediate issue is the change in self-perception: Israel is to be both the people of Yahweh and at some date in the future a restored member of the community of nations.

In other prophetic passages, a more clearly eschatological element seems to be present. Thus in Isa. 11.10–16 Clements has identified a primary nucleus whose concern is the remnant of Israel, identifiable as the diaspora (Clements: 1980, 125). But it is likely that such developments only took shape as it became apparent that improvements in the community's lot could not be expected in the course of day-to-day political life, and may well have been a product of a later stage in the community's history. (Clements himself notes that such hopes presuppose a stage at which the diaspora had become conscious of itself as a 'dispersion', and suggests a fourth-century date for the final form of this passage). In a sense, that is to say, such hopes are beyond our present concern, but they are relevant in that they illustrate the way in which the community came to terms with its changed political and sociological context.

The contribution of structural anthropology

There are various other ways in which the fact of the diaspora had important implications for Israel's self-awareness as a society. Van Seters, for example, has argued very strongly that it was in this context that the story-making capacity of the community reached its peak, and he attributes both the Abraham traditions and the court history of David to this setting (van Seters: 1975, 309f.); in a later work he notes the similarity between Ezekiel's account of the glory of the Lord leaving the temple and the depiction in 1 Sam. 4.21 of the 'exile' (*gālāh*) of the glory from Israel at the time of the defeat of its army and the capture of the ark by the Philistines (van Seters: 1983, 352). But van Seters' views remain very controversial and no more can be done here than to draw attention to his proposals which could be very significant for our understanding of the diaspora.

Equally controversial is the approach from anthropological studies of quite a different kind. The work of Lévi-Strauss (who did not himself discuss biblical texts) has been applied to the biblical material by Leach (Leach & Aycock: 1983), and the change in the life of the community brought about by the destruction of Jerusalem and the beginnings of the diaspora can very naturally be understood along lines similar to those proposed for the reading of other biblical traditions. Leach himself did not pursue this point, but there are adumbrations of such a method in the work of Brueggemann. Though he is not himself a structural anthropologist, he shows how in Jeremiah in particular the tension between the claims of possession of the land and the inevitability of exile produce such oppositions, which are better understood as a literary assertion than as a description of the prophet's personal feelings. 'Land loss means the end of history', yet in exile a new history begins (Brueggemann: 1977, 110f).

An important aspect of structuralism is the way in which it defines terms in relation to one another rather than by calling in external referents. Thus 'exile' can only be defined in terms of the place from which one is exiled. The texts relating to the diaspora lend themselves particularly readily to an interpretation in terms of such binary oppositions; promised land/exile is only the most obvious of such contrasts.

One of the basic themes running through much of the Old Testament is that of possession of/dispossession from the land. The prophetic call to repentance, with its frequent use of the verb *šûb*, 'turn', 'repent', is framed in terms of a contrast between the old sinfulness which has led to the present disaster and the hoped-for new patterns which will assure the people of future divine favour. Even more crucial is the way in which these two pairs are to be seen in relation to one another: the prophetic oracles, in the way in which they have been handed down, make it clear that they regard the appropriate conjunction to be the unexpected one, that dispossession is to be the condition of repentance, and that possession is not to be regarded as a hopeful portent for the future but rather as a continuation of old sinfulness (Jer. 24; Ezek. 33). In Isa. 40–55 it appears as if the binary opposites envisaged are on the one hand the faithful community in exile and on the other those who turned to the worship of the ineffective Babylonian gods, but elsewhere the tensions are more commonly those between different understandings of the true community of Israel.

Oppositions of this kind are perhaps especially characteristic of religious communities and religious writing, where the tension between those who are inside and accepted and those who are outside and must be rejected is a particularly marked one; again the symbolism underlying the two kinds of figs described in Jer. 24 provides an obvious example. Such oppositions may come to affect every aspect of a community's life, for example the language which may properly be used (Neh. 13.23f.) as well as the food which may legitimately be eaten. The food-laws in Leviticus have been discussed in these terms by anthropologists, and as Douglas points out, they are set within the context of the holiness of the community (Douglas: 1966, 41–57). It would be widely maintained among those who approach the Old Testament from a historical-critical standpoint that much of the material in Leviticus was edited at this time of exile; it remains a matter of dispute among anthropologists whether historical considerations are relevant, or indeed legitimate, in the study of literature of this kind.

Conclusions

In one sense the change of understanding brought about by the application of sociological and anthropological perspectives to the Old Testament material is greater in our understanding of exile and diaspora than almost anywhere else. As we have seen, theological justifications and explanations were being sought at a very early stage for the fate of the community, and the nature of such explanations differed sharply from modern sociological or political appraisals. (Those aspects of the literature are fully and sympathetically treated by Ackroyd: 1968, chs. 1–6, and Klein: 1979.) The exile as divine punishment; the complete abandonment of the promised land; the picturing of dispersion as a purging experience through which the true community must have passed: these and comparable points of view are the expression of a theological commitment which seems to be far removed from the academic study of the modern social scientist.

And yet at another level the difference is less great than it might at first sight appear. One of the characteristic concerns of much sociological study is to explore the reactions of particular communities and societies to the stresses under which they find themselves, and in that sense the emergence of the diaspora, and the justifications and explanations given to that development are themselves important sociological material. In that sense at least, it may be that, like Molière's M. Jourdain who found to his surprise that he had been speaking prose all his life, students of the Old Testament have been concerned with sociological issues to a greater extent than they had realised.

Notes

1 The problems relating to the different forms of Sargon's inscriptions have been widely discussed; see J. Gray, I and II Kings, OTL, 2nd edn., 1970, 644f.

2 The article in this volume by Williamson shows that it is likely that in fact the supposed tensions between exilic and Palestinian communities may not have been anything like as acute as is assumed both from one reading of the biblical material itself and from many modern discussions. (See pp.141–61 above).

3 The discussion in Aune, 1983, ch. 5, appears to be confined to Palestinian evidence for this period.

Bibliography

Ackroyd, P. R., 1968. *Exile and Restoration*, Old Testament Library, SCM Press, London.

Aune, D. E., 1983. *Prophecy in Early Christianity and the Ancient Mediterranean World*, Eerdmans, Grand Rapids.

Brett, M. G., 1987. 'Literacy and Domination', *JSOT* 37, 15–40.

Bright, J., 1960. *A History of Israel*, Old Testament Library, SCM Press, London.

Brueggemann, W., 1977. *The Land*, Overtures to Biblical Theology, Fortress, Philadelphia.

Carroll, R. P., 1986. *Jeremiah*, Old Testament Library, SCM Press, London.

Causse, A., 1927. 'Les origines de la diaspora juive', *RHPR* 7, 1927, 97–128.

1929. *Les Dispersés d'Israël: les origines de la Diaspora et son rôle dans la formation de Judaïsme*, Alcan, Paris.

1937. *Du groupe ethnique à la communauté religieuse; le problème sociologique de la religion d'Israël*, Alcan, Paris.

Clements, R. E., 1980. *Isaiah 1–39* (New Century Bible), Marshall, London.

Douglas, M., 1966. *Purity and Danger*, Penguin, Harmondsworth. (The most immediately relevant chapter, 'The Abominations of Leviticus', has been reprinted in B. Lang (ed.). *Anthropological Approaches to the Old Testament* (Issues in Religion and Theology, 8), SPCK, London, 1985).

Gottwald, N., 1980. *The Tribes of Yahweh*, SCM Press, London.

Greenwood, D. C., 1976. 'On the Jewish Hope for a restored Northern Kingdom', *ZAW* 88, 1976, 376–85.

Gross, W., 1987. 'Israels Hoffnung auf die Erneuerung des Staates' in Schreiner, J. (ed.), *Unterwegs zur Kirche: Alttestamentliche Konzeptionen*, Quaestiones Disputatae 110, Herder, Freiburg.

Gunneweg, A. H. J., 1983. ''am hа'arets: a semantic Revolution', *ZAW* 95, 437–40.

Hausmann, J., 1987. *Israels Rest. Studien zum Selbstverständnis der nachexilischen Gemeinde*, BWANT 124, Kohlhammer, Stuttgart.

Holladay, W. L., 1986. *Jeremiah 1: a Commentary on the Book of Jeremiah 1–25*, Hermeneia, Fortress, Philadelphia/SCM Press, London.

Hossfeld, F.-L., 1987. 'Volk Gottes als "Versammlung"', in Schreiner, J. (ed.), *Unterwegs zur Kirche: Alttestamentliche Konzeptionen*, Quaestiones Disputatae 110, Herder, Freiburg.

Kimbrough, S. T. Jr., 1978. *Israelite Religion in Sociological Perspective*, Studies in Oriental Religions, 4, Harrassowitz, Wiesbaden.

Klein, R. W., 1979. *Israel in Exile: a theological Interpretation*, Overtures to Biblical Theology, Fortress, Philadelphia.

Kraft, R. A. and Nickelsburg, G. W. E. (eds), 1986. *Early Judaism and its Modern Interpreters*, Fortress, Philadephia.

Leach, E. and Aycock, D. A., 1983. *Structuralist Interpretations of Biblical Myth*, Cambridge University Press.

Lohfink, N., 1987. *Das Jüdische am Christentum*, Herder, Freiburg.

Malamat, A. (ed.), 1979. *The World History of the Jewish People*, 1st Series, 4, ii, Jewish History Publications, Jerusalem.

Nicholson, E. W., 1970. *Preaching to the Exiles*, Blackwell, Oxford.
1986. *God and his People*, Clarendon Press, Oxford.

Noth, M., 1930. *Das System der zwölf Stämme Israels*, BWANT III, 10, Stuttgart.
1958. *The History of Israel*, A. & C. Black, London.

Patrick, D., 1986. *Old Testament Law*, SCM Press, London.

Perlitt, L., 1969. *Bundestheologie im Alten Testament*, WMANT 36, Neukirchen-Vluyn.

van Seters, J., 1975. *Abraham in History and Tradition*, Yale University Press, New Haven.
1983. *In search of History*, Yale University Press, New Haven.

Smith, Morton. 1952. 'The Common Theology of the Ancient Near East', *JBL* 71, 1952, 135ff.

Terrien, S., 1985. *Till the Heart Sings*, Fortress, Philadelphia.

Torrey, C. C., 1910. *Ezra Studies*, in particular ch. 9, 'The Exile and the Restoration'; reissued Ktav, New York, 1970.

Weber, M., 1963 [=1922]. *The Sociology of religion*, Beacon, Boston. (Translation of *Religionssoziologie*, 1922).
1923. *Das Antike Judentum*, Tübingen. ET: *Ancient Judaism*, Collier-Macmillan, London/New York, 1967.

Weiser, A., 1962. *The Psalms*, OTL, SCM Press, London.

Westermann, C., 1987. *Prophetische Heilsworte im Alten Testament*, FRLANT 145, Vandenhoeck & Ruprecht, Göttingen.

Wright, G. E., 1950. *The Old Testament against its Environment*, SBT 2, SCM Press, London.

Zimmerli, W., 1979. *Ezekiel 1*, Hermeneia, Fortress, Philadelphia.

PART III

Fundamental institutions

CHAPTER NINE

*Ideas of law and legal administration: a semiotic approach**

BERNARD S. JACKSON

1. Introduction

Archaeology has not served well the study of the legal institutions of biblical society. We lack 'court' records – using that term in both its legal and politico-administrative senses. What we possess is a rich literature, into which it is *possible* – to put the matter at its highest – that some original sources from the real legal and administrative milieux may have been incorporated.[1] Certainly, we cannot assume without careful argument that the biblical codes come from any such milieu. And if they do, they have assuredly not survived in their original forms. But this situation should not be regarded as entirely negative. Irrespective of the origins of their materials, the biblical authors have provided us with a wealth of material which informs us of their views about law and legal administration. It is those ideas which this article seeks to explore, aided in this endeavour by asking questions and using methods drawn from contemporary semiotics.[2]

2. The problem

The study of biblical law has been influenced to some extent by debates regarding the character of the ancient Near Eastern 'codes'. There, we encounter two distinct genres of 'legislative' documents: the *mesharum* acts and the 'codes'. The former are immediate measures of debt-relief, normally intended to have only temporary force; the latter, on the other hand, state rules whose effect is to be enduring. Finkelstein (1961) has

* This is a revised version of a paper delivered in the Istituto di Teoria e Storia del Diritto, Facoltà di Giurisprudenza, Università degli Studi di Salerno, 15 May 1987, under the title 'Il carattere del diritto biblico: alcuni approcci semiotici'. It is part of a wider project on the relationship between law and religion in the early Judaeo-Christian tradition, supported by a grant from the Leverhulme Trust. Biblical quotations follow the New English Bible, except where otherwise indicated.

commented upon the pattern of enactment of these two forms of law: the *mesharum* act is found normally at the very beginning of a reign, while the 'code' occurs some years later. The ideal character of the codes may be inferred, *inter alia*, from the fact that they contain provisions which, if made effective, would render the *mesharum* acts unnecessary. Moreover, we have a large corpus of records of decided cases from the courts of Old Babylonia, and they fail to bear out any expectation that the codes were applied in the courts like modern statutes. Sometimes the rulings of the courts conform to the code, but frequently they do not; and the court records contain no quotations or even citations of the rules contained in the codes.[3] The conclusion seems to be that our modern model of law, based upon the 'application' of statutes in court, is not applicable to the ancient Near East.[4] The 'codes' have a different purpose – didactic, sapiential, monumental.

Although our data for comparison with the ancient Near East is relatively sparse, it is possible to discern a similar pattern in the Bible.

The story of the *deror* of King Zedekiah in Jeremiah 34 is very important in this respect. It tells us of a legislative act of the king, freeing debt-slaves, comparable to the ancient Near Eastern *mesharum* or *andurarum*; moreover, the narrative itself states that the necessity for this *deror* (legitimated by a covenant) derived from the fact that the previous 'code' provision (the law of the liberation of the debt-slave of Exod. 21.1) had not been observed. We do not possess a corpus of records of the Judaean or Israelite courts to compare with the provisions of the 'codes', and it would be unwise to treat the narratives of royal judicial activity as typical in this respect. However, the form in which the biblical 'codes' have been transmitted is such as to distance them even further than the ancient Near Eastern codes from the model of modern legislation. The biblical codes are found within a complex literary and narrative framework. To a large extent their character is best understood in terms of the literary and narrative relationships they bear with the surrounding material.

3. A semiotic methodology

If we reject the legislative model, we have to look for something to put in its place. To do so, I propose the adoption of a methodology derived from communication studies and semiotics. If we view what the Bible tells us about the communication of law in ancient Israel in this light, and if we take into account an internal semiotic analysis of the content of the biblical 'codes', we may make progress in understanding their true nature.

The classical model of communication involves the following elements. We have the people between whom messages are exchanged – the sender and receiver; we have a choice of the medium or channel of communication (writing, inscription on stone, and now electronic data) and the 'code' in which the message is expressed (a particular natural language, a particular register of that language, or a non-linguistic code, such as the colour code of traffic lights). Viewed in this light, modern legislation has the following characteristics. The 'sender' is the 'legislator', the 'receiver' the judge. The medium is the written word (finite, enduring, clearly identifiable). But a particular 'code' is used to decipher the meaning of those words. Modern legislation has a peculiar form of force: every single word in it is regarded as of 'binding' character; the judge must take into account all of the canonical words, and cannot substitute as his primary source of authority words from any other source. He cannot extrapolate from the words some 'main point'. It is this which generates the technical rules of statutory interpretation, and it is in this sense that the words of a statute constitute a message in a particular (communicational) 'code'.

Once the character of modern legislation is made explicit in this way, we can ask whether it is applicable to the Bible. I maintain that it is not so applicable, at least until we reach the period of Ezra. The modern legislative model breaks down for the following reasons. When communication takes place between the legislator (whether the king or the divinity) and the judges, there is no suggestion that the medium of a written text is used; conversely, when we do have the communication of a written text of laws, the judges are not the receivers. Moreover, there is no evidence that the texts of biblical law enjoy that form of force here described in relation to modern statutes, certainly before the time of Ezra.

The evidence for these claims can be summarised quite briefly. The norms of Deuteronomy and the account of Jehoshaphat's reform in 2 Chronicles present a very significant parallel on one central point, despite other differences in detail. Both of them record that the instructions given to the judges are of an entirely general character – to do justice and avoid corruption.

The charge given to the judges in the fortified cities of Judah by king Jehoshaphat is simply this:

> Be careful what you do; you are there as judges, to please not man but the Lord, who is with you when you pass sentence. Let the dread of the Lord be upon you, then; take care what you do, for the Lord our God will not tolerate injustice, partiality, or bribery. (19.5–7)

Very similar in tone is the instruction in Deuteronomy:

> You shall appoint for yourselves judges and officers tribe by tribe, in every settlement which the Lord your God is giving you, and they shall dispense true

> justice to the people. You shall not pervert the course of justice or show favour, nor shall you accept a bribe; for bribery makes the wise man blind and the just man give a crooked answer. Justice, and justice alone, you shall pursue, so that you may live and occupy the land which the Lord your God is giving you.[5]

The narrative of Jehoshaphat does indicate a two-tier judicial system. Members of the educated élite are appointed to be judges in Jerusalem, 'to administer the law of the Lord and to arbitrate in law suits among the inhabitants of the city' (2 Chron. 19.8). But even here, no mention of a written source of law is found, and the charge to the judges, once again, is predominantly general:

> You must always act in the fear of the Lord, faithfully and with singleness of mind. In every suit which comes before you from your kinsmen, in whatever city they live, whether cases of bloodshed or offences against the law or the commandments, against statutes or regulations, you shall warn them to commit no offence against the Lord; otherwise you and your kinsmen will suffer for it. If you act thus, you will be free of all offence. Your authority in all matters which concern the Lord is Amariah the chief priest, and in those which concern the king it is Zebediah son of Ishmael, the prince of the house of Judah; the Levites are your officers. Be strong and resolute, and may the Lord be on the side of the good!

There is, indeed, a tension in this passage, which – according to the NEB translation at least – appears to speak of sources of law ('statutes or regulations'), while at the same time insisting upon the authority of specified officials. In fact, the phrase *leḥukim ulemishpatim* can hardly refer to 'sources of law' in the modern sense; the whole context, commencing with *dam ledam*, indicates that the meaning to be assigned to these words is in terms of the type of subject matter, rather than the source of rules for adjudication. It is in just this sense that *mishpat* is used in the introduction to the 'Covenant Code' (Exod. 21.1).

On the other hand, both Deuteronomy and 2 Chronicles also tell us about a written text of law. In Deuteronomy, this is a book (*sefer*) which is to be prepared for the use of the king himself, and through the study of which the king shall become wise. In 2 Chronicles the king orders his officers to take copies of the book around the country, and to teach it to the people. In both sources,[6] written law has a didactic function; it is not the basis of adjudication.

As for the force of the words of biblical law – the 'code' in which they are expressed – we may infer from the evidence of the internal revision of a number of laws within the biblical period (notably the laws of slavery) that their words were not sacrosanct (even though they could be used as the basis of a ritual reading). It is only when we reach Ezra that the notions of 'text' and 'interpretation' are separated.

4. The use of inscriptions

If biblical law fails to conform to the communicational model of modern legislation, we have to look for alternatives. A good starting point is to consider the functions of different media which the Bible records as having been used to communicate rules of law, and to consider for what purposes they were used. Two such media are found: inscriptions and the '*sefer*'. In both cases, we find them used for a variety of functions. Nevertheless, these two media are distinguishable one from the other in terms of two general characteristics. The inscription provides the opportunity for greater permanence of a record than does the *sefer*, and the inscription also has a spatial dimension which the *sefer* lacks: the inscription must be placed at some particular site, while the *sefer* is, of its character, moveable. However, both of these differences are reduced once we contemplate the deposit of a *sefer* in an archive.

Sometimes, stone monuments were erected in an *uninscribed* form, relying upon folk memory to identify the event whose place they marked or the significance of their erection. For example, in Gen. 31.43–54 a pillar is erected to witness the covenant (*berit*, v. 44) between Jacob and Laban, and its significance is marked by giving the site a name which recalls that function; the monument also serves a function, according to the text as transmitted, analogous to that of a boundary stone:

> (v. 46) Then he (Jacob) told his kinsmen to gather stones (*avanim*), and they took them and built a cairn (*gal*) . . . Laban said, 'This cairn is witness [*ed*] today between you and me.' For this reason it was called Gal-ed . . . (v. 51) Laban said further to Jacob, 'Here is this cairn, and here the pillar [*matsevah*] which I have set up between us. This cairn is witness and the pillar is witness: I for my part will not pass beyond this cairn to your side, and you for your part shall not pass beyond this cairn and this pillar to my side to do an injury, otherwise the God of Abraham and the God of Nahor will judge between us.'[7]

But there is no suggestion in the narrative that the stone was inscribed. The covenant solemnities accompanying its erection – the mutual declarations, the sacrifice and the joint feast – were sufficient to fix its significance.

This feature of the covenantal model, the use of uninscribed stones to mark the place and serve as a monument to the event, occurs also in the Sinaitic narrative, in close proximity to – but distinct from – the writing down of the Decalogue:

> Moses wrote down all the words of the Lord. He rose early in the morning and built an altar at the foot of the mountain, and put up twelve sacred pillars [*matsevah*], one for each of the twelve Tribes of Israel. He then sent the young men of Israel and they sacrificed bulls to the Lord . . . Then he (Moses) took the book of the covenant (*sefer haberit*) and read it aloud for all the people to hear.
>
> (Ex. 24.4–8)

Any possibility of interpreting this passage as indicating that the divine message was written *on* the *matsevot* is excluded by the use later in the passage of the verb *lakaḥ* (to take), which implies that the message was written on something moveable – here, indeed, described as a *sefer*. Moreover, *matsevah* is one of the terms used for the stone monument in the account of the Covenant between Jacob and Laban, where there is no suggestion that the terms were reduced to writing.

It is not unreasonable to suggest that, historically, the use of the uninscribed stone as a monument preceded the use of the inscribed form. As for the latter, the most obvious function of inscribed stone is to mark the boundary of a territory (private or public), and to seek to deter potential violators of that boundary through the use of curses, as in the *kudurru* inscriptions of the ancient Near East.[8] It was but one step beyond this to add the record of an historical event which provided the source of title to that property. The victory stela has this dual function. On the one hand, it celebrates the prowess of the victor, or of the god who sponsored him. On the other hand, it marks the place of victory, thus of conquest and acquisition. But both the boundary function and the memorial function could be served by *uninscribed* stones. We have seen an example of the former in the story of Jacob and Laban. Joshua's monument at Gilgal exhibits the latter function too:

> When the whole nation had finished crossing the Jordan, the Lord said to Joshua, 'Take twelve men from the people . . . and order them to lift twelve stones from this place, out of the middle of the Jordan, where the feet of the priests stood firm. They are to carry across and set them down in the camp where you spend the night.' Joshua summoned the twelve men and said to them, '. . . These stones are to stand as a memorial among you; and in days to come, when your children ask you what these stones mean, you shall tell them how the waters of the Jordan were cut off before the Ark of the Covenant of the Lord when it crossed the Jordan. Thus these stones will always be a reminder to the Israelites.'[9]

But folk memory was not always relied upon in order to fix the meaning of a monument. Both the boundary stone and the victory stela (genres which overlap on some occasions) came to be inscribed. The famous Moabite stone, erected by Mesha around 840 BC to record his victory over Omri, king of Israel,[10] provides archaeological confirmation of a genre which we find mentioned also in the Bible. Immediately after the victory over the Amalekites, God instructs Moses to record in writing (*ketov zot zikaron basefer*) that 'I will blot out the memory of Amalek' (Ex. 17.14). This was designed to signify the permanence of the victory, just as Mesha proclaimed that 'Israel hath perished for ever.'

These functions of the inscription seem to precede the recording of law on stone. However, it is easy to understand the development. There is a tradition of the victorious lawgiver, which extends from Hammurabi through Justinian to Napoleon. This is not merely an observed historical parallel; the idea of the victorious lawgiver appears quite explicitly in the official documentation.[11] Culturally and psychologically, the connection is easy to understand: the military victor, who has shed blood (albeit in what he may claim to be a good cause) nevertheless has a need to redress the balance by promoting peace, and the ideological form of the promotion of peace is the establishment of law and order. I suggest that this, as much as any purely literary connection, explains the form of the Decalogue, which commences with an allusion to a victory: 'I am the Lord your God, who brought you out of the land of Egypt' (Ex. 20.2) and then continues with prescriptions.

I do not use the term 'ideological' loosely. The inscription of laws on stone cannot serve a primarily pragmatic function. This is not a form for easy reference, certainly when we conceive of substantial monuments in large and busy places. Imagine being a judge and having to rely upon the Code of Hammurabi as recorded on the monument now preserved in the Louvre. One might almost as well try to 'apply' the text of the Egyptian obelisk in the middle of the Place de la Concorde.

The inscription of laws on stone serves a primarily monumental purpose, as has been recognised in the case of the Laws of Hammurabi. Within the Bible, there are indications that the length of legal texts so inscribed came to increase. The original 'tablets of stone' inscribed by God for Moses (carrying a text, incidentally, which is quite incapable of being applied as law by judges)[12] was of relatively short compass, and Deuteronomy seems to go out of its way to stress that it was only this text that was so inscribed (Deut. 5.22). But by the time we reach Moses' last instructions, and their fulfilment after the crossing of the Jordan, we find that the length and scope of the text inscribed on stone monuments appears to have increased very considerably. Moses commands that when the people have crossed the Jordan, they shall set up 'great stones' (*avanim gedolot*) and 'inscribe on them all the words of this law' (*et kol divrei hatorah hazot*), placing them as a monument on Mount Ebal (Deut. 27.2–4). The performance of this obligation is recorded in Josh. 8: 'There in the presence of the Israelites he [Joshua] engraved on blocks of stone (*al ha'avanim*) a copy of the law of Moses (*mishneh torat mosheh*).' By this stage, the Israelite tradition appears to have been influenced by the model of the Mesopotamian legal codes, as exemplified by the Code of Hammurabi (which itself was widely copied). It is noticeable, however, that in the linked narratives of Moses' last days and of Joshua's fulfilment of Moses' instructions, we hear not only of inscribed stones but also of the writing of the law in a *sefer*. Moses wrote down 'these laws in a book' (Deut. 31.24) for deposit in the Ark of the Covenant (cf. Deut. 31.9), and commanded that there be a septennial reading at the Feast of Tabernacles 'of this law publicly in the hearing of all Israel' (Deut. 31.11).[13] The clear implication is that it is the text written by Moses in the *sefer* that is to be read out, not the text to be inscribed on the stones. When we reach Joshua's ceremonial at Ebal, the inscribing of the law on stone is followed by a public reading, but the latter refers to the *sefer hatorah*, and the text seems anxious to emphasise its extent (perhaps in contrast to the *mishneh torat moshe* which had been inscribed on the stones):

> Then Joshua recited the whole of the [the law][14] the blessing and the cursing word by word, as they are written in the book of the law. There was not a single word of all that Moses commanded which he did not read aloud before the whole congregation of Israel . . . (Josh. 8.34–5)

The narrative thus combines the monumental function of law inscribed on stone with the ritual function of reading from a holy book – holy in that it had been written by Moses, at the command (perhaps, dictation) of God.

5. The uses of the sefer

There has been debate as to whether the *sefer* uses the medium of hide or papyrus (see Haran 1982), but this distinction is relatively unimportant for present purposes. In either case, the medium is less permanent than stone, but more portable. As a result, it proved a more flexible medium, serving a wider variety of purposes. Most of those purposes, however, proved to have associations with the royal court. Here, too, the historical record seems to suggest a growth in the length of the text which might be committed to this medium. We start with the *mishpat hamelukhah* of Samuel, which – from the analogy of the corresponding material in Deuteronomy – seems not to have exceeded a few verses. Ultimately, we come to the text in the book of Ezra, which took from dawn until midday to read out – albeit, with a (contemporaneous?) interpretation.

We can classify the uses of the *sefer* under three headings: archival, didactic, and ritual.

5.1. Archival uses

The earliest period, outside the pentateuchal history, of which mention is made of the writing of law in a *sefer*, is that of Samuel (*1 Sam.*

10.25), where he writes a *mishpat hamelukhah*, and – significantly – deposits it in a sanctuary. That pattern, of a prophet depositing a particular text in the sanctuary, later the Temple, is repeated in Jer. 36, which deserves more detailed attention.

In the fourth year of Jehoiakim's reign, Jeremiah is commended by God to 'take a scroll' – *megillat sefer* – and write down all his earlier prophecies. Jeremiah cannot do so himself; he seeks the assistance of a court-scribe Baruch. Baruch is also asked to read the scroll publicly at the Temple. He does so, apparently with the cooperation of the Temple officials, since he reads it 'from the room of Gemariah son of Shaphan the *sofer*.' Gemariah's son Micaiah hears the prophecy, and communicates it to the other officials; he is said to repeat all of its words from memory of what was read out (v. 12). The officials – the *sarim* – thereupon call for Baruch and have him read the scroll to them. They are impressed and decide to inform the king. At the same time, they advise both Jeremiah and Baruch to go into hiding; the scroll is dangerous, the king's reactions may be unpredictable. Nevertheless, they deposit the scroll in the room of the scribe Elishama. Jeremiah's scroll has thus been 'planted' – we might say – in the Temple, with the connivance of the Temple officials. I put the matter in this provocative manner by way of allusion to Blenkinsopp's suggestion (1983:96) that the scroll found in the time of Josiah, just a few years earlier, may have been a 'plant'. In fact, Jeremiah has given us a vivid description of how this might be done. The king then agrees to hear the scroll, but after listening to 'three or four columns' (*delatot*), he cuts the proceedings short,[15] and throws the whole scroll onto the fire.

We may leave the story there. It is, however, worth noting that here, just as in the case of Samuel's deposit of a scroll in the sanctuary, the content of the document is very much concerned with affairs of State: the future of the kingdom and the fate of the king, in the light of God's anger. A point which the inscription and the *sefer* have in common is the fact that both are closely associated with supreme political power.

5.2 Didactic uses

Even when we turn to the didactic uses of the *sefer*, this association with the king retains its prominence. In Deut. 17.14–20, we find (a version of) the law of the king. It concludes (vv. 18–20):

> When he has ascended the throne of the kingdom, he shall make a copy of this law in a book at the dictation of the levitical priests. He shall keep it by him and read from it all his life, so that he may learn to fear the Lord his God and keep all the words of this law and observe these statutes. In this way he shall not become

> prouder than his fellow-countrymen, nor shall he turn from these commandments to right or to left; then he and his sons will reign long over his kingdom in Israel.

Clearly associated with this passage is the instruction given by king Jehoshaphat (2 Chron. 17.7–9):

> In the third year of his reign he sent his officers . . . to teach in the cities of Judah, together with the Levites . . ., accompanied by the priests Elishama and Jehoram. They taught in Judah, having with them the book of the law of the Lord [*ve ʿimahem sefer torat adonai*]; they went round the cities of Judah, teaching the people.

As noted earlier, these passages are kept separate from those relating to the instruction of judges, which contain no reference to a *sefer*, but require the judges only to act justly and avoid corruption.

5.3 Ritual uses

The archival uses of the *sefer* were specific enough. Though the communication of the message might be deferred, it was addressed to a particular individual, and was designed to have political effect. The didactic functions are similarly specific. It is the king who is to read the book, for his own moral improvement. Similarly, Jehoshaphat has his officers 'teach' (*lamad*) the people.

We can, however, identify a third type of use of the *sefer*, which I call 'ritual'. This is a public reading, associated with a festival or some special sacred event, the object of which is fulfilled by the act of public reading itself. It is, of course, the origins of the 'reading' of the Law in the synagogue today – a quite separate function from the teaching of Bible, or the adjudication of cases on the basis of Jewish law.

Such a ritual reading is first mentioned in the biblical narrative at the end of the book of Deuteronomy, when Moses gives his final commands[16] to his successor, Joshua:

> Moses wrote down this law and gave it to the priests, the sons of Levi, who carried The Ark of the Covenant of the Lord, and to all the elders of Israel. Moses gave them this command: 'At the end of every seven years, at the appointed time for the year of remission, at the pilgrim-feast of Tabernacles, when all Israel comes to enter the presence of the Lord your God in the place which he will choose, you shall read this law publicly in the hearing of all Israel. Assemble the people, men, women, and dependants, together with the aliens who live in your settlements, so that they may listen, and learn to fear the Lord your God and observe all these laws with care. Their children, too, who do not know them, shall hear them, and learn to fear the Lord your God all their lives in the land which you will occupy after crossing the Jordan.[17]

The motive of the reading is that of reinforcement of the religious force of the laws. By implication, the adults are taken already to know the rules; it is only the children who are said not to know them. We should not underestimate the importance of such an act of affirmation, or of the ritual time and setting of the reading. Nevertheless, we are still far distant from the modern use of the law book, as a permanent record of the authoritative wording of the rules, to be consulted whenever needed by both the subjects of the law and by those charged with its administration.

Such a ritual reading is also attributed to the occasion of the original giving of the law at Sinai (if, indeed, the vital words are original). After the theophany which accompanied the giving of the Decalogue, followed by the communication by God to Moses alone of the '*mishpatim*', Moses ultimately descends from the mountain, and we read of a covenantal affirmation of the law, accompanied by a sacrificial ritual. The literary-historical relations between the elements in this passage are notoriously difficult to disentangle. But for present purposes, it is sufficient to note that a ritual reading from a *sefer* came to be included in it (Exod. 24.3–9):

> Moses came and told the people all the words of the Lord, all his laws. The whole people answered with one voice and said, 'We will do all that the Lord has told us.' Moses wrote down all the words of the Lord.[18] He rose early in the morning and built an altar at the foot of the mountain, and put up twelve sacred pillars, one for each of the twelve tribes of Israel.[19] He then sent the young men of Israel and they sacrificed bulls to the Lord as whole-offerings and shared-offerings. Moses took half the blood and put it in basins and the other half he flung against the altar. Then he took the book of the covenant (*sefer haberit*) and read it aloud for all the people to hear. They said, 'We will obey, and do all that the Lord has said.' Moses then took the blood and flung it over the people, saying, 'This is the blood of the covenant which the Lord has made with you on the terms of this book.'

The central phrase of the above passage, *vayikaḥ sefer haberit vayikra b'eoznei ha'am* (Exod. 24.7), is echoed in the account of the ceremony organised by king Josiah on the occasion of his discovery of the law-book in the Temple (2 Kings 23.1–3):

> Then the king sent and called all the elders of Judah and Jerusalem together, and went up to the house of the Lord; he took with him the men of Judah and the inhabitants of Jerusalem, the priests and the prophets, the whole population, high and low. There he read out to them all the book of the covenant discovered in the house of the Lord (*vayikra be'ozneyhem et kol divrei sefer haberit hanimtsa bebeit adonai*); and then, standing on the dais, the king made a covenant before the Lord to obey him and keep his commandments, his testimony, and his statutes, with all his heart and soul, and so fulfil the terms of the covenant written in this book. And all the people pledged themselves to the covenant.

This passage combines the ritual reading, accompanied by covenantal affirmation, which we find in Exodus, with Deuteronomy's stress upon the presence of all sections of the population at the public reading. In none of the sources considered so far do we hear of any interpretation or discussion of the text accompanying its public reading.

6. The Ezra tradition

It is in the story of Ezra that we find the coalescence of these different communicational functions. Ezra comes not only as a religious reformer, but also as a royal administrator, familiar with the practice of Persian decrees. He wants the words of the law to be put permanently into the public domain, but not merely to fulfil a monumental function (as on the stones inscribed at Mount Ebal by Joshua); rather he wishes to combine the traditional ritual reading of the religious reform with a didactic function: the words should not only be read out, they should also be explained. Thus, the famous passage in which Ezra and his assistants (the Levites):

> expounded [*mevinim*] the law to the people while they remained in their places. They read from the book of the law of God clearly [*meforash*], made its sense plain [*vesom sekhel*] and gave instruction [*vayavinu*] in what had been explained to them. (Neh. 8.7–8)

This in itself combines the functions of Jehoshaphat's officers with the ritual of Josiah's reform. But Ezra was not finished. The next day, he summoned a smaller group to return, comprising the heads of the families, the priests and the Levites, to study the text further (*nehaskil el divrei hatorah*, v. 13). The process of specialisation had begun. Within the one text, there was room for both popular and more specialised audiences.[20]

7. The Biblical 'codes'

At the very least, the above analysis of the range of uses of the different means of recording the law provides hypotheses for our understanding of the character of the biblical codes. Unfortunately, none of the sources we have available presents a complete version of the communicational model. The narrative sources we have considered, which tell us about the senders and receivers of written law, the types of medium used for this purpose, and the different functions of both writing and reading, do not at the same time provide the texts of the documents they describe. We cannot, therefore, analyse the 'code' used to communicate these particular messages. Conversely, the biblical 'law-codes' present us with ample opportunities to study their communicational codes, but we have no direct access to the history of their pragmatics: the identities of their senders and receivers, the media used to transmit them, and the functions for which they were actually used. We do, of course, have narrative accounts of those pragmatics, and these narrative accounts must be treated very seriously, in combination with the content of the laws, in order to understand the message of the final authors (the editors) of the Pentateuch. But as far as historical questions are concerned, the best we can do is to compare the results of internal analysis of the law-codes with the communicational settings whose existence we have identified from other sources.[21] We have to look at each biblical 'law-code' separately, in this respect; they may not all have fulfilled the same communicational function.

In a forthcoming work,[22] I attempt such an internal analysis of the provisions of the 'Covenant Code' (Exod. 21–3). From this, I derive two principal conclusions. First, a remarkable number of the individual rules of the 'Covenant Code' may be described as 'self-executing laws' – rules so formulated (through the use of evidentiary tests and dispute-resolving mechanisms which are easy to administer, sometimes because of their somewhat arbitrary character) that the need to have recourse to third-party adjudication seems to be avoided altogether. Secondly, when we look at the overall literary character of these documents, we can identify features of the communicational code which go beyond the meanings of individual sentences, and depend upon discursive relationships between sentences and whole groups of provisions. A few brief examples must here suffice.

The self-executing laws include the following: release *ex lege* of the Hebrew male debt-slave, without the intervention of legal institutions, such as was often required in other ancient systems (Exod. 21.2); the evidentiary tests for kidnapping and theft (Exod. 21.37, 22.3, MT);[23] responsibility for the death of one's own slave (Exod. 21.20–1); division of the loss where one ox kills another (Exod. 21.35),[24] the legitimacy of self-help against an intruder (Exod. 22.1–2),[25] etc. At one time, there was a tendency to see such rules as manifestations of a 'primitive' stage of legal development, one where 'objective' tests were preferred to those focussing upon the moral responsibility of the accused. But this is hardly a credible picture, when we take account of the totality of biblical literature, even that ascribed to an early period. Subjective guilt was hardly beyond the cognitive competence of the ancient Hebrews. Rather, the rules we have in the Covenant Code represent a choice which we may describe in contemporary economic language as a wish to avoid the transaction costs of adjudication. By means of these rules, those who had disputes could solve them more or less on the spot, without involving themselves in the time and trouble of dispute-processing.

Yet the document also possesses literary characteristics which go far beyond the functional import of the individual rules. We find the phenomena of chiasmus, thematic reiteration through a sequence of interlocking double-series, and various allusions to the immediate narrative context.[26] To ask what is the significance of these phenomena is to pose questions about meaning, as well as of meaning. At the very least, we may conclude that such features presuppose a different, more literary audience than that presupposed by the individual laws. They make statements about law, as well as of law.

A good example is found in the relationship between the two slave paragraphs at the beginning of the Covenant Code.[27] The first paragraph deals with the male Hebrew debt-slave (Exod. 21.2–6); the second with the special status of the female *amah* – transferred permanently from the house of the debtor to that of the creditor, in order to become a wife (or concubine) to a member of the family (Exod. 21.7–11). The period of enslavement of the male Hebrew debt-slave is temporary – a maximum of six years (unless the slave himself opts to make the relationship permanent), while that of the *amah* is of its nature permanent, unless she is rejected from the family. There is, however, a *casus omissus* – the female debt-slave who is not to become an *amah*, but is to perform non-sexual (domestic and agricultural) duties. We have good evidence to suggest that this, in practice, was the most common case of debt-slavery of all. So why should it have been excluded?

The answer is that the editor, in this way, is able to emphasise what is seen as a fundamental difference between the legal positions of men and women. The first paragraph includes a rule that the creditor may give a woman to the male debt-slave, but that at the termination of the period of service he must leave her (and any children she has borne to him) in the house of the creditor. In effect, therefore, the master may use the temporary male debt-slave for breeding purposes without altering his status. There is no suggestion anywhere that he may do the same to the temporary female debt-slave. The second paragraph of the Covenant Code tells us under what circumstances a female debt-slave may be used for breeding purposes: it is only if she enters into the special status of *amah*, which at the same time gives her a permanent status within the family. In other words, by juxtaposing these two paragraphs, and by omitting any mention of the case which was the most common in practice, the message is conveyed that the status of a man is not affected by sexual services, whereas sexual services may not be demanded of a woman without altering her status.

It is not, I think, unreasonable to see the narrative of Ezra and the internal analysis of the Covenant Code as mutually corroborative on one important point: the same text may be directed at two different audiences, and may communicate different messages, conveyed by different codes, in relation to those audiences. The literary characteristics of the Covenant Code are not conveyed by a single 'reading' (certainly not, one of a ritual character). Interpretation and discussion are presupposed. This in itself is not sufficient to determine the dating of the literary structure of the Covenant Code. At the same time, we cannot simply discount the fact that the kind of communicational context presupposed by this literary structure is not attributed to any period earlier than Ezra.

It might not be unreasonable to hypothesise a customary origin for the content of the individual rules, and a scribal, court origin for the literary structure. The content of the rules certainly speaks to the concerns of ordinary people, rather than those of the administrators of the law. Moreover the kind of 'practical wisdom' we have observed in the form of self-executing laws is hardly likely to have been a product of the law-courts.[28] In fact, the idea that it was desirable to *avoid* litigation entered the canon of official wisdom, as seen from the Book of Proverbs (25.7–9):

> What your eyes have seen
> do not hastily bring into court.
> For what will you do in the end
> when your neighbour puts you to shame?
> Argue your case with your neighbour himself
> and do not disclose another's secret.[29]

Notes

1 The biblical record may serve us better as an historical source in respect of administrative matters and the (related) legal functions of the king. See the bibliography entries under Frick, Mettinger and Whitelam.

2 'Semiotics' is the study of systems of signification (how meaning is constructed) and communication (how meaning is transmitted). Under the label of semiotics is to be found work which draws upon approaches as diverse as linguistics, the philosophy of language, literary structuralism, cognitive psychology, systems theory, rhetoric and deconstruction. Several of these are already well represented in biblical studies. For my own earlier preliminary attempts to apply them to biblical law, see Jackson 1982, 1984, 1987; for a survey of semiotics, see Hervey 1982; on the relationship between semiotics and general legal theory, see Jackson 1985.

3 See, e.g., Figulla 1951.

4 But this is not a unanimous view. Contrary to the general trend of opinion, an argument in favour of something like a modern statutory function for the ancient Near Eastern law codes has recently been advanced by Westbrook 1985.

5 Note the use of the proverb regarding the effects of bribery – here an expression of popular wisdom.
6 Both quoted below, pp. 193–4.
7 There may well be some conflation here of traditions using the terminology of *gal* and *matsevah* respectively. But this does not affect the present argument.
8 See King 1912, Steinmetzer 1922.
9 Josh. 4.1–7. The chapter continues with what may well originally have been independent accounts of the same incident. But in all of them the *avanim* are uninscribed, even though their function is that of commemoration of the event.
10 ANET 320f.
11 E.g. the prologue to the Code of Hammurabi: 'Hammurabi . . . am I . . . the hero king who has restored Eridu to its original state . . . Invader of the Four Quarters . . . Avenging warrior of Larsa . . . the impetuous bull that overthrows the enemy . . . The promulgator of justice . . . When Merodach had instituted me governor of men, to conduct and to direct, Law and Justice I established in the land, for the good of the people' (Prologue, translation of C. Edwards, *The World's Earliest Laws*, London, Watt & Co., 1934, pp. 13–16; cf. also the Epilogue).

The Prooemium to the Institutes of Justinian commences with the words: *Imperatoriam maiestatem non solum armis decoratum, sed etiam legibus oportet esse armatam, ut utrumque tempus et bellorum et pacis recte possit gubernari et princeps Romanus victor existat non solum in hostilibus proeliis, sed etiam per legitimos tramites calumniantium iniquitates expellens, et fiat tam iuris religiosissimus quam victis hostibus triumphator.* ('Imperial majesty should be not only embellished with arms but also fortified by laws so that the times of both war and peace can be rightly regulated and the Roman Emperor not only emerge victorious in war with the enemy but also, extirpating the iniquities of wrongdoers through the machinery of justice, prove as solicitous of the law as he is triumphant over defeated foes', translation of J. A. C. Thomas, *The Institutes of Justinian*, Amsterdam, North Holland Publishing Company, 1975, p. 1).

Cf. various constitutional documents of the Napoleonic era, e.g. *Sénatus-consulte du 14 thermidor an II*, 1 August 1802, 'reconnaissance nationale envers le héros vainqueur et pacificateur' (nominating Napoleon as *Consul à vie*), and see the Chartre constitutionnelle du 4 juin 1814: 'La divine Providence, en nous rappelant dans nos Etats après une longe absence, nous a imposé de grandes obligations. La paix était le premier besoin de nos sujets: . . .' (M. Duverger, ed., *Constitutions et Documents politiques*, Paris, P.U.F., 6th ed., 1971, pp. 119, 121).
12 Not even Phillips 1970 claims this. For him, the Decalogue was the basis of Israel's criminal law in the sense that it inspired the promulgation of specific criminal offences.
13 On this tradition, see further *infra*, p.194.
14 For reasons not readily apparent on text-critical grounds, the NEB omits these words from its translation.
15 Quite literally: he 'cut them off with a penknife' (NEB), v. 23.
16 Interestingly, these are not commands relayed by Moses from God; Moses himself is portrayed as their author.
17 Deut. 31:9–13. See further Piattelli 1986.
18 At this stage, we are not told on what.
19 See the earlier discussion of this passage, *supra* p.189.

20 There is room here for speculation as to the historical origin of the 'statute' as we presently know it – a text whose very words, as opposed to whose meaning, are conceived to be authoritative, transmitted to the judges for application in the process of dispute-settlement. This phenomenon seems to have emerged around the same time in classical Greece and ancient Israel, in the former associated with a democratic ideology, in the latter with the affirmation of a sacred text. For further discussion, see Jackson 1975.

21 That is not to say, however, that we should accept the historical accounts which reveal different communicational contexts as themselves unimpeachable historical evidence; they, too, have their own narrative functions.

22 *Wisdom-Laws*, being a revised text of my Speaker's Lectures in Biblical Studies, University of Oxford, 1985 and 1986.

23 See Daube 1947:89–96; Jackson 1972:41ff.

24 See Jackson 1975a:130–41.

25 See further Jackson 1972:203–9.

26 See my forthcoming *Wisdom Laws*. For some examples, see Jackson 1988a.

27 For a more detailed analysis see Jackson 1988, 1988a.

28 A view often taken of the rules of the Covenant Code of Exodus. But neither the title of the collection – *mishpatim* – nor the form(s) of the laws provides good evidence of this.

29 RSV. In preferring *larov* to the MT *lariv*, the NEB overlooks the parallelism between verse 6 (context of the king's court) and verse 8 (context of judicial proceedings).

References and bibliography

Blenkinsopp, J. 1983. *Wisdom and Law in the Old Testament*, Oxford University Press.

Boecker, H. J. 1980. *Law and the Administration of Justice in the Old Testament and Ancient East*, London: SPCK.

Bovati, Pietro S.J., 1986. *Ristabilire la Giustizia*, Roma: Editrice Pontificio Instituto Biblico.

Carmichael, Calum M., 1985. *Law and Narrative in the Bible*, Ithaca and London: Cornell University Press.

Daube, David. 1947. *Studies in Biblical Law*, Cambridge University Press, reprinted New York: Ktav, 1969.

Epsztein, Léon. 1983. *Social Justice in the Ancient Near East and the People of the Bible*, London: SCM Press Ltd.

Falk, Ze'ev. 1964. *Hebrew Law in Biblical Times*, Jerusalem: Wahrmann Books.

Figulla, H. H. 1951. 'Lawsuit concerning a Sacriligeous Theft at Erech', *Iraq* 13:95–101.

Finkelstein, J.J., 1961. 'Ammisaduqa's Edict and the Babylonian "Law Codes"', *JCS* 15:91–104.

Fishbane, Michael. 1985. *Biblical Interpretation in Ancient Israel*, Oxford: The Clarendon Press.

Frick, Frank S., 1985. *The Formation of the State in Ancient Israel*, Sheffield: Almond Press (*The Social World of Biblical Antiquity Series*, 4).

Greenberg, Moshe. 1960. 'Some Postulates of Biblical Criminal Law', in *Yehezkel Kaufmann Jubilee Volume*, ed. M. Haran, pp. 5–28. Jerusalem: Magnes Press.

1986. 'More Reflections on Biblical Criminal Law', in Japhet 1986:1–18.

Haran, Menachem. 1982. 'Book Scrolls in Israel in Pre-Exilic Times', *JJS* 33:161–73.
Hervey, Sandor. 1982. *Semiotic Perspectives*, London: George Allen & Unwin.
Jackson, Bernard S., 1972. *Theft in Early Jewish Law*, Oxford: The Clarendon Press.
1975. 'From Dharma to Law', *American Journal of Comparative Law* 23:490=512.
1975a. *Essays in Jewish and Comparative Legal History*, Leiden: E. J. Brill (*Studies in Judaism in Late Antiquity*, X).
1982. 'Legal Drafting in the Ancient Near East in the Light of Modern Theories of Cognitive Development', In *Mélanges à la mémoire de Marcel-Henri Prévost*, pp. 49–66. Paris: PUF.
1984. 'The Ceremonial and the Judicial: Biblical Law as Sign and Symbol'. *JSOT* 30:25–50.
1986. 'Some Literary Features of the Mishpatim', In "*Wünschet Jerusalem Frieden*" Collected Communications of the XIIth IOSOT Conference, Jerusalem 1986, ed. M. August and K.-D. Schunck, pp. 235–42, Frankfurt: Peter Lang (*Beihefte zur Erforschung des Alten Testaments und des Antiken Judentums*, 13).
1987. 'Some Semiotic Questions for Biblical Law', *The Oxford Conference Volume*, ed. A. M. Fuss (Atlanta: Scholars Press), 1–25 (*Jewish Law Association Studies* III).
1988. 'Biblical Laws of Slavery: A Comparative Approach', in *Slavery and Other Forms of Unfree Labour*, ed. L. Archer, pp. 86–101, London: Routledge (History Workshop Series).
Japhet, Sara (ed.), 1986. *Studies in Bible*, Jerusalem: The Magnes Press (*Scripta Hierosolymitana*, XXXI).
1986a. 'The Relationship between the Legal Corpora in the Pentateuch in Light of Manumission Laws', in Japhet 1986:63–89.
King, L. W., 1912. *Babylonian Boundary Stones and Memorial Tablets in the British Museum*, London: The British Museum.
Mettinger, Tryggve. 1971. *Solomonic State Officials*, Lund: CWK Gleerup.
Patrick, Dale. 1985. *Old Testament Law*, London: SCM Press Ltd.
Phillips, Anthony. 1970. *Ancient Israel's Criminal Law*, Oxford: Blackwell.
Piattelli, Daniela. 1986. 'Riflessi Giuridici sulla Celebrazione della Feste d'Israele: Sukkot e la Lettura della Legge', *Apollinaris* LIX. 701–19.
Rofé, Alexander. 1986. 'Methodological Aspects of the Study of Biblical Law', *The Jerusalem Conference Volume*, ed. B. S. Jackson (Atlanta, Scholars Press), 1–16 (*Jewish Law Association Studies* II).
Steinmetzer, F. H., 1922. *Die babylonischen Kudurru (Grenzsteine) als Urkundenform*, Paderborn: Schöningh (*Studien zur Geschichte und Kultur des Altertums*, Bd. 11, Hft. 4–5).
Weinfeld, Moshe. 1972. *Deuteronomy and the Deuteronomic School*, Oxford: The Clarendon Press.
1985. *Justice and Righteousness in Israel and the Nations*, Jerusalem: The Magnes Press (Hebrew).
Wenham, Gordon. 1978. 'Law and the Legal System in the Old Testament', in *Law, Morality and the Bible*, ed. B. N. Kaye and G. J. Wenham, pp. 24–52. Leicester: Inter-Varsity Press.
Westbrook, Raymond. 1985. 'Biblical and Cuneiform Law Codes', *RB* 92:247–64.
Whitelam, Keith. 1979. *The Just King*, Sheffield: JSOT Press.

CHAPTER TEN

Prophecy and society

ROBERT P. CARROLL

βλέπομεν γὰρ ἄρτι δι' ἐσόπτρου ἐν αἰνίγματι – Paul

. . . etwas mehr Nichtwissen – Wellhausen

The analysis of prophecy in relation to society, especially the social location of prophecy in ancient Israel, recently has become one of the dominant features of current biblical scholarship's interest in biblical prophecy. Before Peter Berger's important position paper of 1963 the form that interest took was a more oblique part of the form-critical insistence on the *Sitz im Leben* analysis of the literature and the work of major scholars, including Max Weber, on the relation of prophecy to the cultus (cf. Hahn: 1956, 157–84; Weber: 1952, 267–335; 1966, 46–59). Since Berger's modification of Weber's analysis of the prophet as charismatic authority versus established authority, which itself received little immediate response among biblical scholars except for a weak reassertion of Weber's charismatic analysis (Williams: 1969), there has emerged a considerable body of more formal sociological analysis of biblical prophecy (Wilson: 1980). This work constitutes a serious comparative study of biblical texts and ethnographical materials bearing on the subject of prophecy and affords scholars a sound basis for serious work on a difficult aspect of the phenomenology of prophecy. Now towards the end of the twentieth century it is possible to see the horizons of the subject as a specification of the problematics of prophecy and its social location in relation to the biblical data and in conjunction with the comparative materials made available by archaeology and social anthropology. Each element constitutive of these horizons is itself a highly interpretive matter and thus the subject of prophecy and society may be regarded as an important aspect of the hermeneutical enterprise in biblical studies.

1. Delimiting the subject

Prophecy is a social phenomenon. That is, it is an activity carried on among and between people within a specific society and conforming to the social norms operative among such people. The social status of prophets would therefore be determined by the institutions and social values of their communities and a proper social analysis of prophecy would be an enquiry into the structures and values of ancient Israelite society. Such an enquiry would of necessity be book-length and in combination with a comprehensive account of prophecy would inevitably outrun the space available here for the treatment of prophecy and society. In order to delimit the subject in relation to the space available for its consideration it is necessary to restrict severely those aspects of prophecy which have a bearing on the topic and to provide a broad introduction to a complex amount of primary and secondary information. Excellent accounts already exist of biblical prophecy in general (e.g. Blenkinsopp: 1983; Lindblom: 1962; McKane: 1979; Sawyer: 1987; Tucker: 1985), its social aspects in particular (Culley and Overholt: 1982; Kselman: 1985; Petersen: 1981; Wilson: 1980), and various issues in the interpretation of prophecy (Barton: 1986; Carroll: 1979, 6–84; Coggins, Phillips and Knibb: 1982; Mays and Achtemeier: 1987). There is also a growing awareness among biblical scholars of a need to develop sociological analyses of the Bible and to provide relevant bibliographical materials for such study (Gottwald: 1983; Rogerson: 1985; Wilson: 1984). With so much secondary literature available on the subject it is unnecessary to retrace the same ground in this chapter. I will therefore attempt a rather different approach to prophecy and society by considering a number of theoretical issues which bear directly on the subject and which determine its boundaries and what may be said about it.

The central focus of this essay will be on the problematics of interpreting prophecy itself from the data available in the Bible conjoined with the equal difficulties of discerning 'social reality' behind the text as predicated by sociological theories. There are, of course, fundamental problems connected with doing the sociology of *ancient* texts because the past is not amenable to the scrutiny of sociologists (cf. Rodd: 1979; 1981). The use of modern social patterns and parallels as well as comparative materials from anthropological theory raises serious questions about method and equivalences between different societies (cf. Overholt: 1986; Smith: 1982). These problems cannot be resolved here but an awareness of them is absolutely fundamental for any serious research into the social understanding of prophecy. Given the limitations of space here I will confine my treatment to the problems of data, definition and analysis.

2. Problems of data

The primary data for prophecy in the Bible are to be found in the Deuteronomistic History (esp. the books of Samuel and Kings) and the collection of books associated with named prophets (Isaiah, Jeremiah, Ezekiel, and the Book of the Twelve). In rabbinic categories these two groups of books were known as the 'former prophets' and the 'latter prophets', thus recognising the essential similarities of the values governing both sets of books. Further material about prophets is to be found scattered throughout the Pentateuch, in particular the story and oracles of Balaam (Num. 22–4). All these data are complicated by matters of editorial developments which have distanced the *written* texts from their original settings and *oral* stages. Also the extent to which the editors have invented information or allowed later transformations of the material to be incorporated into the texts is a much debated one among scrutineers of the texts. Deuteronomistic editing of the 'latter prophets' is widely recognised by scholars (e.g. Schmidt: 1965; Seeligmann: 1977), as is the secondary nature of the colophons introducing the individual prophetic books (Gevaryahu: 1975). The precise relationship between these colophons and the works to which they are affixed is unknown and therefore it is not possible to say whether they reflect reliable historical information or represent editorial inventions of biographies of the prophets (Carroll: 1988). Such a lack of definitive information renders any and every account of prophecy open to serious objections as to matters of fact and subsequently any theory based on such defective data is itself rendered questionable.

Most scholars do not regard the primary data as problematic and so produce accounts of prophecy which seldom differ from their presentation in the texts of the Hebrew Bible (e.g. van der Toorn: 1987; Wilson: 1980), though all scholars are agreed about the difficulty of some of the interpretive elements within individual prophetic traditions. Yet even this feature of the difficulty of handling certain concepts and terms within the literature itself contributes to the overall problem of understanding the data in the first place. Given the wide range of differing opinions among scholars on the meaning of any text in the prophetic collection (a test case might be the recent commentaries on the book of Jeremiah) it should be axiomatic that primary data which themselves require interpretive sophistication are not easily amenable to simplistic cross-disciplinary theoretical treatments. Problems of such theoretical analyses will be considered in part 4 but they cannot be separated entirely from the problems of data because even theoretical sophistication cannot overcome defective information or data resistant to such theories. Similar caveats may be made against the use of material remains unearthed by archaeology to explain difficult texts or to illuminate texts without demonstrating that such artefacts are *directly* related to the relevant texts. Uncertainty of meaning and multiplicity of meaning are essential parts of the biblical texts and they undermine straightforward applications of archaeology and sociological theory to the Bible.

Illegitimate transfer of meaning. In his seminal book on semantics (1961:218) James Barr argues at one point against a semantic confusion which he variously calls 'illegitimate identity transfer' or 'illegitimate totality transfer'. Something similar to this procedure can be found in many approaches to the social interpretation of prophecy. It involves arguing from statements in the text to the social background they are said to represent and drawing normative conclusions about the nature of social behaviour in ancient Israel. Examples of the erroneous transfer of meaning from text to supposedly social background might be drawn from 2 Sam. 11.2 or 2 Kings 4.18–25 or from the stories of Judith and Holofernes or Susanna and the elders. The social realism of all these stories is quite limited, though there is nothing magical or unrealistic in them. But can we on the basis of these tales deduce that women were in the habit of taking baths on rooftops near the king's palace or of making sabbath journeys to prophets or of dressing themselves up in order to seduce foreign generals? Can we really insist that kings and judges were prone to spy on and seduce, or attempt to seduce, very beautiful women? What social customs can reliably be argued for from all these biblical stories? Surely this is the wrong way to read texts and involves too many unjustified hermeneutical moves to warrant a one-to-one correspondence between text and hypothesised social reality. To suppose a realism to these stories beyond the conventions of such storytelling is an illegitimate transfer of meaning from story to social background. Equally it is impermissible to argue from all the stories and legends of prophets in the Hebrew Bible to some type of literal and historical portrayal of the lives and activities of prophets. Such a mistaken conception of biblical literature appears in many secondary works on the prophets, none more so than in the tendency to read Jer. 36 as if it were an historical account of how prophetic books are composed rather than a fabricated story designed to convey an important theological point about the destruction of Jerusalem. There is no necessity to read such stories as recorded history or to infer from them the social practices of a particular period.

Peter Laslett (1976) offers a very good critique of this mistake of using texts to *recreate* their social world. There is, according to his arguments, simply too much we do not know about what the writer was doing when writing a particular document. We do not know what the author chose to leave out or imagined to be the case or even how normative the practice described (or imagined) may have been. 'Literary evidence cannot be supposed to have a temporally specific context' (1976:323) and, as Laslett insists, 'no excavation or analysis will ever authenticate the manner of the election of Saul to the kingship of Israel' (1976:322). Laslett calls this way of using literary evidence for doing historical sociology 'looking the wrong way through the telescope'. I prefer a variation on Barr's notion of the illegitimate transfer of meaning from one thing to another to describe a mistaken way of reading texts. Either description is appropriate. Both serve the purpose of underlining a procedural error in interpretation and insist on *the literariness of texts*. Texts are not photographs of social reality but are imaginative creations of their writers and it is a matter for intense debate and rigorous investigation what might be the conditions under which we could move from text to society with any confidence. But social reality cannot just be read off texts without considerable justification being offered for such warrants of implied social behaviour being detected behind the texts.

Similar remarks should be made about the application of archaeological findings to the Bible. The things found are themselves open to considerable interpretive debate and when used to interpret biblical texts double the amount of hermeneutic activity. Furthermore, the texts are not so securely dated that the application of discovered artefacts or prevailing material conditions, as *interpreted* by various archaeologists, to specific texts is unproblematic. What are called material culture texts may be easier to decipher than written texts due to the complexity of ideas expressed linguistically (Hodder: 1986, 123), but when they are read in conjunction with ancient written texts, as some biblical scholars insist on reading them, there tends to be an exponential increase in the interpretive difficulties generated. *If* the prophetic texts could be dated accurately and *if* the archaeological evidence was unambiguous in its import, then perhaps connections between the two could be made in some general terms. But the literariness of these texts removes them from specific social backgrounds and thus archaeology sheds less light on them than is often thought to be the case. The anthological nature of the collections of prophetic material also militates against the use of such texts for specific sociological purposes.

Transformations. The emphasis on the literariness of the texts about prophets is important because it introduces into the discussion reflection on the nature of the data to hand. It is generally agreed among scholars that prophecy was an oral phenomenon. The prophet was a *speaker* of the divine word. Oral utterance is the essence of prophecy. So the written forms in which the prophetic words have been transmitted to other generations represents a shift from the spoken word to the written word. We know prophecy now as literature rather than as spoken word. Such a shift from orality to literacy has removed prophecy from its original social setting to a decontextualised, timeless setting and any search for the *Sitz im Leben* of specific prophecies is irrelevant. The transformation of oral speech into literary text (cf. Goody: 1986; Ong: 1982; 1985) displaces the words in such ways that any analysis of them cannot also and at the same time be an account of the original word and situation. Changing situations have changed the import of the words. The time-conditioned nature of the original speaker's utterance has given way to the timeless reference of the written word addressed to future generations. The word is now context-free! Writing is a very powerful transformer of words (cf. Baumann: 1986) and enables them to change beyond their immediate context and to apply to circumstances far removed from their original setting. All the prophetic words that we have in the Hebrew Bible are written ones *now* and, with the few exceptions of words said originally to have been written (e.g. Isa. 8.1; 30.8; Hab. 2.2; Jer. 29.1; 30.2; 36.2; 51.60; 2 Chron. 21.12), must be regarded as coming under the influence of the transformer effects of the shift from speech to writing. Such a decontextualising process assists in the creation of prophecy *as* literature (cf. Clements: 1986).

If writing transforms prophecy there is also a further transformation of it within the books in which it appears. This is caused by the editing processes which have put together the anthologies of prophetic material or have inserted prophetic narratives into the Deuteronomistic History. The selection of material, its written forms edited in places to extend its meaning and reference, the juxtaposing of discrete and disparate pieces, and the provision of introductory colophons for each book all contributed to the further removal of prophecy from its original setting in the life of ancient Israel. These editorial transformations of material already transformed by writing must be regarded as the original creations of the prophetic traditions and it is now simply not possible to get back behind such editing to whatever may have constituted the 'original' prophecies! Hence the quest for sociological analysis and knowledge of biblical prophecy is short-circuited by the literariness of the traditions. The double decontextualisation of prophecy by writing and editing added to the nescience of modern scholarship about the ancient world of Israel confounds our attempts to use the biblical texts as prima facie evidence for the social location of prophecy.

Some scholars would try to break out of this encirclement of ignorance and displacement by using sociological theories and comparative ethnographical material to rectify what is defective in the texts (see part 4), but it is doubtful whether such rescue ploys can be successful. At best the theoretical component tends to produce ideal-typical reconstructions which lack that sharp particularity of the real and also mask from the reader the high degree of reconstruction of the texts entailed by such arguments. Archaeology and ethnography can hardly make good a fundamentally defective text. By defective here I simply mean that the text is fine as text, as literary object, but as a testimony to, or a palimpsest of, social reality it is gravely defective. The current emphasis on the Bible as literature does not suffer from this defectiveness because the scrutinising of the text constitutes the totality of the hermeneutic activity. There is of course a social dimension to this kind of interpretation and it is becoming widely recognised in modern literary theory that all literature and its interpretation involve political and social activities (cf. Jameson: 1981, 17–102). But the treatment of the text *as* text escapes from the problematics of reconstructing the background to the text in order to do social analysis of the historical reality imagined to be behind the text. As an approach to the understanding of the Bible it has the advantage of encountering the text in its fundamental literariness without recourse to reconstruction or hypothesised social contexts. What it gains by this concentration on the text as structure for analysis it may well squander by the use of alien theories, but that is a different topic and belongs to another collection of essays!

3. Problems of definition

The problem of defining the term 'prophet' and thereby 'prophecy' dogs biblical scholarship and undermines much of what passes for it. The biblical traditions themselves are equally unsure of, and indefinite about, *what* a prophet is, *who* is a prophet, and *whether* prophets are or are not a good thing. That is, the Hebrew Bible presents so many different, ambiguous and ambivalent stories and treatments of prophets that the modern reader has to admit that ancient Israelite writers had no clear image of what a prophet is or should be. This lack of clarity or definition can be seen in the way the book of 1 Samuel handles the notion of who or what a prophet is (esp. 1 Sam. 9–10; cf. Miscall: 1986, 51–62). Throughout the Hebrew Bible there is a strange tension between good reports about prophets and trenchant dismissals of them as deceivers and idolaters (contrast Num. 11.26–30; 12.6; Deut. 18.15–19; 2 Kings 17.13, 23; Amos 3.7; Jer. 25.4; 26.5; Joel 2.28 with Deut. 18.20–2; 1 Kings 22.13–23; Isa. 9.15; Jer. 23.9–40; 27.12–18; Ezek. 13.1–14.9; Zech. 13.2–5). Such an excess of contrary views about prophets in the Bible combined with the lack of a clear definition of 'prophet' should warn the modern exegete against too confident a reading of the data and should make for uncertainty and ambiguity in the interpretation of the text. The exegete should approach the text exhibiting the negative capabilities so loved by Keats – 'being in uncertainties, Mysteries, doubts, without any irritable reaching after fact & reason'!

The Bible offers no definition of what a prophet is (1 Sam. 9.9 is a most curious statement!) nor does the biblical word *nābî'* have any definite meaning in Hebrew that we can discern. The word 'prophet' is derived from the Greek translation of *nābî'* where the translators have opted to translate it by the word *prophētēs* meaning 'a public speaker' or 'one who speaks in the name of a god' or 'an interpreter of the will of a god', rather than by the word *mantis* 'a diviner', 'soothsayer', 'seer, prophet' (cf. Latin *vātes*). So already the word 'prophet' is an interpreted one and *distanced* from the Hebrew text. Modern analyses of biblical prophets prefer to treat the question of definition in terms of role models and view them as messengers or intermediaries or people possessed by spirits or by means of careful delineations of the various roles specified by different terms in the Hebrew Bible (cf. Petersen: 1981; 1987; Rendtorff: 1962; Westermann: 1967; Wilson: 1980). Each treatment is necessarily an approximation, a matching up of an ancient role with an identifiable modern activity, and the fit between the two is always open to question. If sometimes the gap between the biblical data and the modern analysis is too great to be tolerated then that is part of the overall problem of investigating the relationship between prophecy and society in ancient Israel.

Apart from the intrinsic problem of the meaning of the word *nābî'* and the classification of the roles of intermediary figures in the Hebrew Bible, there are numerous other definitional problems relating to prophecy. In Deut. 18.9–14, 15–22 divination and prophets are juxtaposed in such a way that prophecy looks like ancient Israel's equivalent of witchcraft and magical practitioners (cf. Lust: 1974). Confirmatory hints of this equivalence may be detected in 1 Sam. 28.3–19; Isa. 8.16–23; Mic. 3.5–8. Lack of sufficient data makes it difficult to pursue this line of enquiry, but the connections should not be ignored. Comparative materials on intermediaries in Mari and Assyria have raised questions about the relationship of such figures to the prophets of ancient Israel (eg Malamat: 1980, 62–82, 83–97; Moran: 1969; Wilson: 1980, 89–134), but not all scholars are convinced of the closeness of similarity between Mari and Israel (cf. Noort: 1977, 93–110). Differences of period and cultural values as well as ideological factors should be allowed for in any comparative study of the available data. All this comparative material underlines the difference between the material remains of ancient cultures and the ideologically controlled documents which represent the propaganda of a small religious elite constituted by the Hebrew Bible (cf. Smith: 1987). With regard to the biblical text we can never be sure how much is propaganda and the manipulation of information and how much reflects genuine social practices untainted by editorial control.

Prophecy and cult. The main focus of the enquiry into the social location of prophecy by most biblical scholars has been on the cultus and the relation of prophets to it (cf. Johnson: 1962; Tucker: 1985, 348–50). Like all evidence from the Hebrew Bible the data are ambiguous and inchoate, but there is sufficient material scattered throughout the prophetic traditions to make a connection between cultus and prophecy in terms of cult prophets (cf. Berger: 1963). To designate prophets as cultic personnel is to give them a specific social setting and a professional role in ancient Israelite society, which facilitates the social analysis of prophecy. Yet again we know very little about how the cultus functioned or how its functionaries were trained. Thus we know nothing about how cult prophets were produced, though various scholars have read 1 Sam. 3 as evidence for the training of a young prophet and Reventlow has argued at length for seeing in the book of Jeremiah the activities of a man ordained as a cult prophet (1963; cf. Reventlow: 1961; 1962). Collections such as Joel, Nahum and Habakkuk have been recognised as cultic prophecy and as affording an alternative mode of prophetic activity to that often associated with more 'individual' prophets (cf. Coggins: 1982). If the argument of part 2 above be followed it should be clear that we probably know no more about the so-called non-cultic prophets either, so the isolation of a cult prophet type among the traditions should place that kind of functionary on the same footing as other types of prophet. The editing of various prophetic traditions has associated them with the temple: cf. Jer. 1.1 which places Jeremiah in a priestly family and the Targum to it which makes him a priest; and the many statements in the book of Jeremiah which locate his activity in the temple (e.g. Jer. 7.2; 19.1–2, 14; 24.1; 26.2–7; 28.1, 5; 29.25–8; 35.2–4; cf. 36.5). However, such editorial framework references may not have any reliable historical basis but may represent a later interpretive treatment of the material in the tradition, so too much should not be based on the presentation of individual prophets as having had some functional location in the temple. At the same time it should be recognised that prophets are often associated with sacrifice (e.g. Num. 23.1–4; 1 Sam. 9.11–14; 10.8; 1 Kings 18.20–40) and within the prophetic traditions there is considerable liturgical material (e.g. Isa. 33; cf. Murray: 1982) which suggests a connection between prophecy and cult, if only at the editorial level of the growth of the traditions.

The contrast implicit in differentiating between prophets as cult functionaries and prophets independent of the cult centres is a distinction between individual and communal prophets. That is, individual figures regarded by the edited texts as prophets and those prophets who are collectivised in groups associated with the cultus, have as one mark of difference the differentiation between individual and group consciousness. Social analysis may deal with groups but finds individuals extremely difficult to relate to stereotypes and conventional roles. Unless specific information is provided for individuals then little or nothing can be said about them by way of social comment and there is very little reliable information available for those individuals associated with the prophetic traditions. Defining the prophet as a cult figure gives some specification of social activity and location in ways that viewing prophets as solitary individuals cannot, however defective the biblical information may be about prophetic groups.

A cultic location for all prophets, including the so-called 'canonical' or 'writing' (written *about*?) individual prophets, has been rejected by many scholars (typified by Williams: 1969) partly on the grounds of the anti-cultus bias and polemic contained in some of the traditions (eg Isa. 1.10–17; 66.1–6; Jer. 6.20; 7.1–15; Hos. 6.6; Amos 5.21–4, 25; Mic. 6.6–8). These attacks on sacrifices in the cultus or on the temple (cf. Mic. 3.12) need not be read as dismissals of cultic activity *per se* or may be understood as the prioritising of values whereby temple rituals were expected to be less primary than social justice. On the other hand, few of these references can be attributed with certitude to named prophets but tend to appear in the editorial framework of a book (e.g. Isaiah), particular editions of a tradition (e.g. the Deuteronomistic edition of Jeremiah), or in the additions to, and adjustment of, anthologies (e.g. Mic. 6.6–8). Thus the original speaker imagined to be behind the tradition need not be excluded from being a cult prophet on the grounds that such would *never* (a dubious proposition in itself!) criticise the cultus because it cannot be demonstrated that the criticism necessarily comes from such a person. Once again difficulties with the interpretation of the traditions prevent the establishment of *one* clear line of reference for any statement found within the anthologies. Hence defining a prophet as a cult figure cannot be challenged effectively by pointing to an anti-sacrifice or temple polemic in the collected statements appearing under the colophons of 1.1 in the prophetic books. More work, especially of a theoretical nature, needs to be done on these anthologies in relation to other traditional material in the Hebrew Bible and in conjunction with discussions of innovative and conservative elements, insofar as they can be discerned at all, in the traditions in order to work out what may be said about the relationship between prophecy and the social institutions of ancient Israel (cf. Clements: 1975).

In recent study the title of 'prophet' has been challenged as an accurate historical and social description of the named individuals identified with such collections as Isaiah, Jeremiah, Ezekiel, Hosea, Amos, Micah etc. and attributed to the editorial processes of a later period which created the traditions in the first place (Auld: 1983; 1984; Carroll: 1983; 1986, 50–64; cf. Vawter: 1985). We know from the Hebrew Bible that there developed a tendency to refer to all significant figures as 'prophets' (e.g. Gen. 20.7; Deut. 34.10–12; cf. Barton: 1986). Attempting to find a descriptive term less loaded than 'prophet' to categorise the figures associated with these anthologies is difficult and still operates with the notion that there was such a definite figure behind any one of these traditions. Alternative terms, such as 'poet' or 'intellectual', are themselves loaded down with prior assumptions and tend to be socially problematic if applied to ancient Israelite society. Furthermore, the status of poetry in the Hebrew Bible has recently been questioned (cf. Kugel: 1981) and others have insisted that poetry and prophecy are diametrically opposed (Geller: 1983). No satisfactory alternative title to 'prophet' is likely to emerge from this discussion because we do not have access to the society which produced these writings and must make do with the highly edited ideological documents produced by whatever circles created the traditions. Yet it should be recognised that the texts themselves draw sharp distinctions between the speakers within the traditions and prophets: Num. 12.6–8 contrasts Moses with prophets in terms of divine communications; the speaker of Mic. 3.8 differentiates himself categorically from 'the prophets' condemned in Mic. 3.5–7; the cumulative condemnation of 'the prophets' in Jer. 23: 10–40 is prefaced by a statement contrasting the state of the speaker with the evil ways of the prophets. So often there is no *prima facie* evidence for regarding any of these speakers as 'prophets' except for the secondary editing of the traditions and later traditional readings of the Bible. Thus defining the social location and activity of prophets from the paucity of evidence in the books Isaiah to Malachi may be a case of looking in the wrong direction altogether!

If biographical-historical elements in the anthologies are picked up as socially accurate details it may be possible to regard the social criticism features of some of the traditions (e.g. Isa. 3.1–15 [grossly expanded by additional material]; 5.8–23; Amos 5.10–12; 8.4–6; Mic. 1–3) as representing political activity by various individuals or groups. Such politically motivated criticisms of society may reflect special interest groups in ancient Israel who were determined to try to influence the shaping of society by programmes of reform (cf. Silver: 1983, 139–251). This is a highly interpretive reading of such texts scattered throughout discrete material and, apart from Mic. 1–3, may be an anachronistic (though very popular) understanding of statements which have been edited in such a way that specific social conditions have become generalised into virtually 'timeless' values applicable in any situation. The political dimensions of prophecy are not easy to delineate and the Deuteronomistic History's paralleling of the institutions of monarchy and prophecy may represent an ideological reading of history and society rather than an accurate reflection of past reality. Nothing which may be interpreted as political in the anthologies can evade the difficulties involved in the hermeneutical enterprise of understanding the political in biblical prophecy (cf. Jenni: 1956; a much simpler treatment is Albrektson: 1972). Also some very complex and complicated issues are involved in determining the political significance of prophetic material such as 'the oracles against the nations' (OAN). Too often the interpretation of the political dimension in prophecy has been overly simplistic and has ignored the cluster of interpretative problems facing the reader of such texts. At the same time, it must be recognised that there were probably larger political issues at work in the editing and transmission of the texts. That is, these collections of material *now* in written form may have been weapons in ideological conflicts within society and between communities and were therefore profoundly political in nature, intent, and publication. However, we know as little about these matters as we do about the circumstances of anything else in the production of the Hebrew Bible. So it is only possible to register an awareness of the political dimension in all literature and to make allowance for it in every interpretation of the text (cf. Jameson: 1981).

If the political definition of prophecy yields a further batch of problems the resolution of which will satisfy few scholars, there is one definition of the prophetic role which seems to attract a number of analysts and make for agreement between them. It is the notion of the prophet as the speaker of the divine word with reference to the future: 'Fundamental to the prophetic role in Israel was the utterance of God's word for the future' (Tucker: 1978, 45); 'The genre that is proper to prophecy must be considered the announcement of the future' (Schmidt: 1984, 184). The extent to which this definition usefully distinguishes the prophet from the priest who gave future-oriented *tōrōt* or announced the acceptance of specific sacrifices may be left aside as raising too many secondary issues, but like all definitions it does have its limitations. In relation to the social analysis of prophecy it posits a role in Israelite society of 'one who speaks for and about the future' and may make biblical prophecy equivalent to diviners, magicians, witches, soothsayers and other mantic roles found in most societies. It also puts the emphasis on the spoken utterance in the role of prophet and thereby ignores the actor-visionary aspects included in the biblical traditions. But it has the advantage of settling for the lowest common denominator with which virtually no scholar can disagree. Clearly prophecy is about speaking and generally there is a future reference somewhere in the utterance which justifies the definition, though exceptions (which prove the rule?) are easily found in the traditions (e.g. Isa. 9.8–21; Hab. 3).

The definitional approach to prophecy resolves no problems but introduces a number of different levels of varied interpretation of the sources which illustrates the complexities of seeking understanding by definition. Each defining process changes the significance of the data and the shifting around of the data along axis of definition cannot take us much further along the path of discovering the social location of prophecy. What each shift does achieve is the bringing into play of different bits of textual information and every shift contributes to the making of a kaleidoscope through which may be viewed the permanently changing surface-view of prophecy. To grasp the phenomenon itself is beyond the power of definitions!

4. Problems of analysis

The history of the analysis of prophecy is beyond the scope of this paper (cf. Blenkinsopp: 1983–4 for a useful survey of it), but a few specific analyses will be considered here because they belong to the most recent attempts to trace the social location of prophecy. Two in particular will be isolated because they demonstrate the problems of data and interpretation. Every analyst depends upon a definition of prophecy in order to launch the analysis and the above caveats about definitions will apply invariably to the analyses cited here. Yet as a starting-point a definition of prophecy may be a wise move because it allows for grouping together all phenomena which appear to correspond to the definition. It is a tool of convenience which in a perfect world would be adequate to the task but because the Bible is not a perfect world it tends to raise more problems than it resolves. The sprawling mass of data provided by the Bible and the ideological organisation of them by editorial controls make the social analyst's task incapable of satisfactory resolution. Defining the prophet is one way of trying to overcome such problematic data and working with comparative ethnographical material is another way of escaping the impasse created by recalcitrant biblical data. General agreement about the social nature of prophetic activity (cf. Emmet: 1956; Rigby: 1975; also Culley and

Overholt: 1982) may warrant the use of social theory to create a common pattern of analysis within which biblical prophecy may find its niche.

Central and peripheral prophets. Robert Wilson's *Prophecy and Society in Ancient Israel* (1980) is the most comprehensive analysis to date of ancient prophecy and its biblical counterparts. In a most useful discussion of the data and theories of various analysts Wilson settles for the neutral term 'intermediary' to describe the activities covered by such terms as prophet, shaman, medium and diviner (1980: 27–8). This allows him to consider a wide range of comparative data (ancient and modern) as well as much modern sociological and anthropological theory before providing a lengthy treatment of all the biblical material on prophets (1980: 135–308). Two social models stand out in his analysis: the notion of two fundamentally different traditions of prophecy in ancient Israel (Ephraimite and Judean) and the separation of prophecy into central and peripheral prophets. He replaces older views of prophetic behaviour as being ecstatic in nature with a preference for language about possession (1980: 32–42; cf. Wilson: 1979; Parker: 1978) which allows him to draw parallels between ancient Israelite practices and social phenomena from other cultures. The distinction between central and peripheral intermediaries relates to position and power within society and describes those who have power within a given structure (central) and those who, on the peripheries of society, only have power within their own small groups (peripheral; cf. Wilson: 1980, 69–88; Lewis: 1971). In a thoroughgoing analysis of all the relevant data Wilson differentiates between Ephraimite and Judean prophets and between the central and peripheral prophets in both ancient cultures. He concludes his survey with a short twelve-page sketch of the history of prophecy in ancient Israel which leaves the biblical order of things unchanged.

While there can be no doubting the valuable comparative material Wilson has assembled in his book there is a remarkably sanguine attitude to the biblical data surveyed in it and a curious lack of coherence and cogency to the arguments with which he analyses the texts into evidence for central and peripheral prophets, as well as for Ephraimite and Judean traditions. A lopsidedness appears in his treatment of the so-called Ephraimite material at almost three times the length of his analysis of Judean material (118 pages to 43 pages!). With the exception of the book of Hosea (and conceivably the book of Amos?) all the anthologies collected in the volume Isaiah–Malachi are believed to be Judean in origin and focus, yet Wilson concentrates most of his survey on materials outside this volume! This means the prophetic narratives in the Deuteronomistic History receive the lion's share of attention and that without due allowance for the difficulties of dating and analyzing that History. Accepting the prophetic data embedded in the History at face value allows Wilson to proceed uncritically as if, just because there appear to be no traces of Deuteronomistic editing in some of the narratives (e.g. the Elijah–Elisha material; 1980: 192), the conventional critical view of accepting such data as earlier deposits were unproblematic. Dating a hypothesised prophetic document embodied in the History (e.g. 1 Sam. 1–2 Kings 10 to the late ninth century as in Campbell: 1986) to a specific date really is to go well beyond any evidence available for such certitude and, in fact, draws its evidence from the editorial placement of the stories. The arguments for this move, if scrutinised, are circular (and not of the hermeneutic circle either!) and fail to make allowance for the well known lack of fit between the stories and the Deuteronomistic dating schema. The point is well made by Gottwald: '. . . there is a sense in which the excerpted chronicles of the two kingdoms and the prophetic narratives *move on two different levels of narration and interpretation which often fail to meet at a point of common discourse*' (1985: 341 emphasis added). The legends of the prophets in the History may come from any period of Israelite history, postexilic or otherwise, and therefore may only be used with great caution, if at all, for any reconstruction of the history, structure or nature of biblical prophecy. Wilson's failure to treat his sources with an appropriate epistemological caution renders his account much less sociologically accurate or valuable than he appears to imagine.

Similar defects are to be found in his central and peripheral distinctions between biblical prophets. The data are hardly of the nature which would allow such confident differentiations and his oscillating presentation of Isaiah as central, then peripheral, prophet illustrates this point (e.g. 1980: 270–4). Recognising the paucity of data for determining Micah's status Wilson still perseveres with reading him as a peripheral prophet (1980: 274 6). Perhaps a distinction between urban and rural prophets might have been more sustainable for the data given in the colophons to the prophetic traditions, though even that distinction does not take us very far. It could, however, help to develop an analysis of variations between city (*polis*) and country (*chōra*) which might yield some tentative results in conjunction with the material remains unearthed by archaeologists (cf. Lemche: 1985, 164–201; de Sainte Croix: 1981, 7–19). Such an approach would still have profound problems of inchoate data and the inevitable multiplicity of interpretations available for every text adduced in support of it. For Wilson to have demonstrated the coherence and cogency of his analysis would have required a much longer treatment of the Judean material and a much closer fit between the theory of central and peripheral intermediaries and his use of it for biblical figures. For example, if central prophets are solitary and peripheral ones appear in groups which are the groups condemned in the book of Jeremiah? Are they (e.g. Jer. 4.9; 5.31; 6.13; 14.13; 23.9; 27.16) peripheral groups functioning in the city, be it at court or in the temple, or are they rural prophets who, like Jeremiah, have come to the great city to overthrow the central institutions or gain power? If groups of prophets have support from the central power institutions (e.g. king, temple, court or army) how can they be peripheral and if they are in groups how can they be central? The questions multiply and all that I can say in Wilson's defence is that the data available in the Bible are part of the problem as well as his theoretical reading of them.

At a more fundamental level serious criticisms can be levelled at Wilson's handling of biblical prophecy. In order to do a serious work along the lines of the central–peripheral distinction in intermediation he needs first to show where real power lay in ancient Israelite society. What or who in that area generated the social values of the group? Did a Micah represent the social values of the people of the land directed against an alternative religious and social ideology centred on the cities? If he did (the if is admittedly a big one!) then who was central and who peripheral? What support groups did he have and what support did his opponents have? Because without support systems nobody could be a prophet in any society (cf. Long: 1977; 1982); but the matter becomes much more complicated when there are conflicting societies involved (i.e. rural and urban). Furthermore, the work of Lewis and other social anthropologists on central–peripheral shamans and other intermediaries relates to oral cultures rather than literate systems within large-scale civilisations and important adjustments may be required for the theory to be applied *simpliciter* from one set of cultures to another set. The question of appropriateness of fit between spirit possession cults and biblical prophecy also must be raised. Spirit possession seems to be a minor element in the prophetic texts (e.g. 1 Kings 22.21–4; 2 Kings 2.9–18; 5.26; Hos. 9.7; Isa. 61.1; Mic. 3.8; Zech. 4.6; 7.12), whatever the status granted to these statements. Given all these questions it would appear to be the case that Wilson's sociological analysis of prophecy in ancient Israel is gravely defective in a number of respects. This judgement is hardly surprising in the light of the difficulties of matching theory with data and the inevitable problems of cross-disciplinary studies. Wilson has assembled an invaluable collection of comparative data and then demonstrated how profoundly flawed is an application of such data to the Bible. In themselves those are two fine achievements and scholars will learn much from Wilson's failures in the art of attempting a sociological analysis of Hebrew prophecy.

The Handsome Lake parallel. Space only permits the briefest of mentions of a parallel which crops up frequently in the comparative anthropological data on intermediaries and prophets. A minor chief of the Iroquois Indians of New York State in the late eighteenth and early nineteenth centuries of the common era named Handsome Lake (real name Ganiodaiio), an alcoholic by middle age due to the devastations of Indian culture by the onslaught of Western 'civilisation' (French and early American), started to have trances which resulted in one hundred and thirty oracles which, after his death, were handed down in writing as 'The Code of Handsome Lake' (cf. Helms: 1971; Overholt: 1986, 321–31; Wallace: 1972). This 'Code' helped to transform the Iroquois culture in the nineteenth century by arresting cultural disintegration and redirecting the energies and activities of the Indians. Anthropologists call this organised attempt to produce a better culture a 'revitalisation movement' (Wallace: 1956). It is a fascinating story which shows how a culture can turn itself around by means of one man's visions transformed into ritualised readings and activities and enacted long after his death. Such a well documented revitalisation movement example has inspired some biblical scholars to enrol Handsome Lake in the cross-disciplinary study of biblical prophets (e.g. Overholt: 1982, 62–70; 1986, 338). Overholt chooses Jeremiah as his biblical model of a revitalisation movement and finds 'significant similarities' (1982, 73) beginning to emerge in his analysis of these two prophets, Jeremiah and Handsome Lake. I find it very difficult reading the available data on both figures to see even superficial similarities between them, except for a common background in a disintegrating culture being destroyed by a more powerful foreign empire (i.e. Babylon and transposed European culture). A good deal of wishful thinking (in my opinion) and a great lack of close reading of the text facilitate Overholt's handling of the two cases. If it could be shown that the book of Jeremiah functioned ritually and culturally in the postexilic period to revitalise Judean culture then there might be some sort of case to be made out for using the Handsome Lake parallel, but there seem to be better candidates in the Bible than Jeremiah (book or man!) for that attempt (e.g. the book of Deuteronomy or the creation of such figures as Abraham, Moses and, perhaps even Ezra?). The biblical data are again the problem because they do not permit us to see any coherent picture of social reality against which we might read the texts. It is also too easy to patch together bits of texts from all over a book in order to make a pattern which matches the model derived from comparative anthropological data and then shouting 'eureka!'. A case of too much theory chasing too little data, but it may well be the case that we must, in the words of a much better anthropologist than me, 'be satisfied with explications rather than explanations' (Burridge: 1982, 101) and settle for this stimulating kind of reading two disparate sets of data.

Social role models. A much more modest approach is followed by Petersen's analysis of the different terms used in the Hebrew Bible in terms of role enactment theory (1981). Although frustrated by lack of clear biblical data his approach has the virtue of starting from the text and analysing each different term used to describe prophetic material. He does tend to rely too heavily on the central–peripheral intermediary thesis and to follow the conventional analyses of biblical prophecy (i.e. the uncritical acceptance at face value of statements in the text), but the modesty of his project reflects the closeness with which he sticks to the text. Roles and expectations constitute social norms and complex role phenomena allow for more sophisticated treatments of the data. There is, however, a strictly limited range of information to be gained from Petersen's low-key approach and when he attempts to theorise further he has to make use of theoretical positions which the biblical data cannot sustain. This problem he shares with all the sociological analyses of the Bible examined in this essay and it is hardly to be expected that theoretical models can make good the lack of clear biblical data or override the ideological controls on those data. Such models fill in the gaps in the texts but they also, by producing a pattern of behaviour, ruin the particularity of the data under scrutiny and thereby fail to do justice to the texts (cf. Burridge: 1982, 101).

The dark glass: concluding remarks

The essentially negative tone of this essay contrasts with the confidence shown in many of the books on sociological analyses of the Bible and, in particular, on prophecy and society. It is intended to be a salutary reminder that the reading of biblical texts from a sociological vantage point is not as simple or as straightforward as is often imagined to be the case. The Bible is like a dark glass in which we see our own reflections more often than the social reality which produced the text. Our theories are also more frequently reflected than we allow for. Biblical texts are well-known for the disproportionate amount of background to foreground in them and this ration makes for lively literary readings of various texts. It does not, however, increase the likelihood of detecting social reality in and behind the text. The manipulation of the data by social theories does not produce the kind of comprehensive knowledge which is required for a coherent, cogent account of biblical society. What is absent in the texts is unlikely to be produced by modern theory! Reading into the Bible so much social theory in order to be able to construct a hypothesised account of the social reality behind the book cannot be regarded as a satisfactory enterprise. In this respect the literary approach which treats the text as literature and accepts the constraints of theory, whether reader-response or some version of structuralism/deconstructionism, is better placed than the sociological one. Both approaches have to be very sensitive to the amount of ideological editing involved in the creation of the text, editing which regularly distorts the historical-social roots of the text (cf. Garbini: 1988; Smith: 1987). From this viewpoint the Bible might even be regarded as a broken glass producing a confusion of reflections.

Putting forward the case for epistemological scepticism in these matters as well as emphasising how deep is our ignorance of the social realities behind the texts does not mean that absolutely nothing may be said about prophecy and society. On the contrary, many things can be said and much argument generated by the application of social theory to ancient texts. Many scholars have analysed the issues inherent in this approach and have outlined the important questions involved in scrutinising the texts sociologically. They have contributed to the creation of a considerable literature on the subject and have specified the limits of what may be said about these matters (cf. the useful critical remarks of Gottwald: 1982). A huge agenda of work remains to be done and many topics need to be reassessed. For example, the relationship between individual prophet and social institution still remains to be clarified (cf. McKane: 1982), the nature of the urban–rural divisions detectable in the prophetic traditions needs clarification, the extent to which the editorial construction of the traditions has transformed non-prophets into prophets, and the significant changes produced by the movement from oral utterance to written document (cf. Gunneweg: 1959). These are only a few of the aspects of prophecy which bear on a social analysis of the prophets and whose investigation will assist in the building up of a better picture of prophecy as a social phenomenon. At the same time, scholars must take more seriously our nescience on so many things and make due allowance for the darkness of the glass into which we peer when reading the Bible. No virtue is acquired by imagining that we know more than we do or can about ancient texts or societies. The beginning of wisdom is the admission of ignorance!

Bibliography

Albrektson, B., 1972. 'Prophecy and Politics in the Old Testament', in Biezais, H. (ed.), *The Myth of the State*, Scripta Instituti Donneriani Aboensis VI (Stockholm), 45–56.

Auld, A. G., 1983. 'Prophets Through the Looking Glass: Between Writings and Moses', *JSOT* 27, 3–23.

1984. 'Prophets and Prophecy in Jeremiah and Kings', *ZAW* 96, 66–82.

Barr, J., 1961. *The Semantics of Biblical Language* (Oxford).

Barton, J., 1986. *Oracles of God: Perception of Ancient Prophecy in Israel after the Exile* (London).

Baumann, G. (ed.), 1986. *The Written Word: Literacy in Transition*, Wolfson College Lectures 1985 (Oxford).

Berger, P. L., 1963. 'Charisma and religious innovation: the social location of Israelite Prophecy', *American Sociological Review* 28, 940–50.

Blenkinsopp, J., 1983–4. *A History of Prophecy in Israel: From the Settlement in the Land to the Hellenistic Period* (Philadelphia, 1983; London, 1984).

Burridge, K. O. L., 1982. 'Reflections on Prophecy and Prophetic Groups' in R. C. Culley, Burridge, K. O. L. and Overholt. T. W. (eds.), *Anthropological Perspectives on Old Testament Prophecy*, Semeia 21 1981 (Chico), 99–102.

Campbell, A. F., 1986. *Of Prophets and Kings: A Late Ninth-Century Document (1 Samuel 1–2 Kings 10)*, CBQ Monograph series 17 (Washington).

Carroll, R. P., 1979. *When Prophecy Failed: Reactions and Responses to Failure in the Old Testament Prophetic Traditions* (London).

1983. 'Poets Not Prophets: A response to "Prophets through the Looking-Glass"', *JSOT* 27, 25–31.

1986. *Jeremiah: A Commentary*, OTL (London).

1988. 'Inventing the prophets', *Irish Biblical Studies* 10, 24–36.

Clements, R. E., 1975. *Prophecy and Tradition*, Growing Points in Theology (Oxford).

1986. 'Prophecy as Literature: a Re-Appraisal', in D. G. Miller (ed.), *The Hermeneutical Quest: Essays in Honor of James Luther Mays on his Sixty-Fifth Birthday* (Pennsylvania), 59–76.

Coggins, R., 1982. 'An alternative prophetic tradition?', in R. Coggins, A. Phillips & M. Knibb (eds.), *Israel's Prophetic Tradition: Essays in Honour of Peter R. Ackroyd* (Cambridge), 77–94

de Sainte Croix, G. E. M., 1981. *The Class Struggle in the Ancient Greek World from the Archaic Age to the Arab Conquests* (London).

Culley, R. C. and Overholt, T. W. (eds.), 1982. *Anthropological Perspectives on Old Testament Prophecy* (*Semeia 21 1981*) (Chico).

Emmet, D., 1956. 'Prophets and Their Societies', The Henry Myers Lecture, 1956, *Journal of the Royal Anthropological Society* 86, 13–23.

Garbini, G., 1986. *History and Ideology in Ancient Israel* (London, 1988; Eng. Tr. of *Storia e Ideologia nell'Israel Antico*, Brescia).

Geller, S. A., 1983. 'Were the Prophets Poets?', *Proof Texts* 3, 211–21.

Gevaryahu, H. M. I., 1975. 'Biblical Colophons: A source for the "biography" of authors, texts and books', *Congress Volume: Edinburgh 1974*, SVT 28, 42–59.

Goody, J., 1986. *The Logic of Writing and the Organization of Society*, Studies in Literacy, Family, Culture and the State (Cambridge).

Gottwald, N. K., 1982. 'Problems and Promises in the Comparative Analysis of Religious Phenomena', in *Anthropological Perspectives on Old Testament Prophecy*, 103–12.

1983. 'Sociological Method in Biblical Research and Contemporary Peace Studies', *American Baptist Quarterly* 2, 142–56.
1983. 'Bibliography on the Social Scientific Study of the Old Testament', *American Baptist Quarterly* 2, 168–84.
1985. *The Hebrew Bible: A Socio-Literary Introduction* (Philadelphia).
Gunneweg, A. H. J., 1959. *Mündliche und schriftliche Tradition der vorexilischen Prophetenbücher als Problem der neueren Prophetenforschung*, FRLANT 73 (Göttingen).
Hahn, H. F., 1956. *The Old Testament in Modern Research* (London).
Helms, R., 1971. '"The Code of Handsome Lake": A Literary Study of Prophecy', *Genre* 4, 18–38.
Hodder, I., 1986. *Reading the past: Current approaches to interpretation in archaeology* (Cambridge).
Jameson, F., 1981. *The Political Unconscious: Narrative as a Socially Symbolic Act* (London).
Jenni, E., 1956. *Die politischen Voraussagen der Propheten*, ATANT 29 (Zürich).
Johnson, A. R., 1962. *The Cultic Prophet in Ancient Israel* (Cardiff, 1962²).
Kselman, J. S., 1985. 'The Social World of the Israelite Prophets: A Review Article', *Religious Studies Review* 11/2, 120–9.
Kugel, J. L., 1981. *The Idea of Biblical Poetry: Paralellism and its History* (Yale).
Laslett, P., 1976. 'The wrong way through the telescope: a note on literary evidence in sociology and in historical sociology', *British Journal of Sociology* 27, 319–42.
Lemche, N. P., 1985. *Early Israel: Anthropological and Historical Studies on the Israelite Society Before the Monarchy*, SVT 37 (Leiden).
Lewis, I. M., 1971. *Ecstatic Religion: An Anthropological Study of Spirit Possession and Shamanism* (London).
Lindblom, J., 1962. *Prophecy in Ancient Israel* (Oxford).
Long, B. O., 1977. 'Prophetic Authority as Social Reality', in Coats, G. W. and Long B. O. (eds.), *Canon and Authority: Essays in Old Testament Religion and Theology* (Philadelphia): 3–20.
1982. 'Social Dimensions of Prophetic Conflict', in *Anthropological Perspectives on Old Testament Prophecy*, 31–53.
Long, T. E., 1986. 'Prophecy, Charisma and Politics: Reinterpreting the Weberian Thesis', in Hadden, J. K. and Shupe, A. (eds.), *Prophetic Religions and Politics: Religion and the Political Order*, New York, 3–17.
Lust, J., 1974. 'On wizards and prophets', in *Studies on Prophecy: A Collection of Twelve Papers*, SVT 26 (Leiden), 133–42.
McKane, W., 1979. 'Prophecy and the Prophetic Literature', in Anderson, G. W. (ed.), *Tradition and Interpretation: Essays by Members of the Society for Old Testament Study* (Oxford), 163–88.
1982. 'Prophet and Institution, *ZAW* 94, 251–66.
Malamat, A., 1980. *Mari and the Bible: A Collection of Studies* (Jerusalem, 1980²).
Mays, J. L. and Achtemeier, P. J. (eds.), 1987. *Interpreting the Prophets* (Philadelphia).
Miscall, P. D., 1986. *1 Samuel: A Literary Reading*, Indiana Studies in Biblical Literature (Bloomington).
Moran, W. L., 1969. 'New Evidence from Mari on the History of Prophecy', *Biblica* 50, 15–56.

Murray, R., 1982. 'Prophecy and the cult', in *Israel's Prophetic Tradition*, 200–16.

Noort, E., 1977. *Untersuchungen zum Gottesbescheid in Mari: Die "Mariprophetie" in der alttestamentlichen Forschung*, AOAT 202 (Neukirchen-Vluyn).

Ong, W. J., 1982. *Orality and Literacy: The Technologizing of the Word* (London).

1986. 'Writing is a Technology that Restructures Thought', in Baumann, G. (ed.), *The Written Word*, 23–50.

Overholt, T. W., 1982. 'Prophecy: The Problem of Cross-Cultural Comparison', in *Anthropological Perspectives on Old Testament Prophecy*, 55–78.

1986. *Prophecy in Cross-Cultural Perspective: A Sourcebook for Biblical Researchers*, SBL Sources for Biblical Study 17 (Atlanta).

Parker, S. B., 1978. 'Possession Trance and Prophecy in Pre-Exilic Israel', *VT* 28, 271–85.

Petersen, D. L., 1981. *The Roles of Israel's Prophets*, JSOTS 17 (Sheffield).

(ed.), 1987. *Prophecy in Israel: Search for an Identity*, Issues in Religion & Theology 10 (London).

Rendtorff, R., 1962. 'Botenformel und Botenspruch', *ZAW* 74, 165–77.

Reventlow, H. G., 1961. 'Prophetenamt und Mittleramt', *ZTK* 58, 269–84.

1962. *Das Amt des Propheten bei Amos*, FRLANT 80 (Göttingen).

1963. *Liturgie und prophetisches Ich bei Jeremia* (Gütersloh).

Rigby, P., 1975. 'Prophets, Diviners, and Prophetism: The Recent History of Kiganda Religion', *Journal of Anthropological Research* 31, 116–48.

Rodd, C. S., 1979. 'Max Weber and Ancient Judaism', *SJT* 32, 457–69.

1981. 'On Applying a Sociological Theory to Biblical Studies', *JSOT* 19, 95–106.

Rogerson, J. W., 1985. 'The use of sociology in Old Testament studies', *Congress Volume: Salamanca 1983* (ed.), J. A. Emerton, SVT 36, 245–56.

Sawyer, J. F. A., *Prophecy and the Prophets of the Old Testament*, The Oxford Bible Series (Oxford).

Schmidt, W. H., 1965. 'Die deuteronomistische Redaktion des Amosbuches: zu den theologischen Unterschieden zwischen dem Prophetenwort und seinem Sammler', *ZAW* 77, 168–93.

1984. 'The Form of Prophecy', *Introduction to the Old Testament* (London), 173–93 (Eng. Tr. of *Einführung in das Alte Testament*, Berlin, 1982²).

Seeligmann, I. L., 'Die Auffassung von der Prophetie in der deuteronomistischen und chronistischen Geschichtsschreibung (mit einem Exkurs über das Buch Jeremia)', *Congress Volume; Göttingen 1977*, ed. J. A. Emerton, SVT 29, 254–84.

Silver, M., 1983. *Prophets and Markets: The Political Economy of Ancient Israel*, Social Dimensions of Economics (Boston/The Hague/London).

Smith, J. Z., 1982. 'In Comparison a Magic Dwells', pp. 19–35 of his *Imagining Religion: From Babylon to Jonestown*, Chicago Studies in the History of Judaism (Chicago & London).

Smith, M., 1987. *Palestinian Parties and Politics that Shaped the Old Testament* (London, 1987; orig, ed., New York, 1971).

van der Toorn, K., 1987. 'From Patriarchs to Prophets: A Reappraisal of Charismatic Leadership in Ancient Israel', *Journal of Northwest Semitic Languages* 13, 191–218.

Tucker, G. M., 1978. 'Prophetic Speech', *Interpretation* 32, 31–45.

1985. 'Prophecy and the Prophetic Literature', in Knight, D. A. and Tucker, G. M.

(eds.), *The Hebrew Bible and its Modern Interpreters*, SBL Centennial Publications 1 (Chico), 325–68.

Vawter, B., 1985. 'Were the Prophets *nabi's*?', *Biblica* 66, 206–20.

Wallace, A. F. C., 1956. 'Revitalization Movements', *American Anthropologist* 58, 264–81.

1972. *The Death and Rebirth of the Seneca* (New York, 1972; orig. ed., 1969).

Weber, M., 1952. *Ancient Judaism* (New York, 1952 Eng. Tr. of *Das antike Judentum*: vol. 3 of *Gesammelte Aufsätze zur Religionssoziologie*, Tübingen, 1921.

1966. *The Sociology of Religion* (London, 1966; Eng. Tr. of *Religionssoziologie*, Tübingen, 1956[4]).

Westermann, C., 1960. *Basic Forms of Prophetic Speech* (London, 1967; Eng. Tr. of *Grundformen prophetischer Rede*, Munich, 1960).

Williams, J. G., 1969. 'The Social Location of Israelite Prophecy', *JAAR* 37, 153–65.

Wilson, R. R., 1979. 'Prophecy and Ecstasy: A Reexamination', *JBL* 98, 321–37.

1980. *Prophecy and Society in Ancient Israel* (Philadelphia).

1984. *Sociological Approaaches to the Old Testament*, Guides to Biblical Scholarship (Philadelphia).

CHAPTER ELEVEN

The social world of the wisdom writers

R. N. WHYBRAY

A. Definitions and problems

The term 'the wisdom writers', when applied to ancient Israel, may be taken for practical purposes to refer to the authors of Proverbs, Job and Ecclesiastes, together with certain psalms and some books of the Apocrypha, notably Ecclesiasticus and the Wisdom of Solomon. These books probably originally formed part of a more extensive literature. Some other Old Testament books have been deemed by various scholars to have been written to a greater or lesser extent under the influence of a supposed continuing 'wisdom tradition', but no consensus of opinion exists on this question (see Whybray, 1974 and Morgan, 1981). The present survey, which is necessarily of a summary nature, will be confined to Proverbs, Job and Ecclesiastes and the so-called 'wisdom psalms'.

A discussion of the 'social world' of the authors of these works is beset by immense problems. Of these not the least is the difficulty of defining the notion of 'wisdom' which these writers are presumed to have had in common. This question has been endlessly debated in recent years, and a variety of definitions has been offered. This is not the place to attempt yet another definition (but see especially von Rad, 1970, Crenshaw, 1976, 22, Murphy, 1978). For the present purpose it must be sufficient to give a broad description of the themes discussed in the wisdom books which may help to explain why modern scholarship has placed them in a separate category from the other Old Testament books.

The wisdom books are distinctive in that they are primarily concerned with man and his world, and in particular with the potentiality and limitations of the individual. 'Wisdom' as a human attribute is the ability to discern the best way to achieve the best things in life: success, prosperity, happiness, longevity. But since this ability can come only as a gift from God who must himself be supremely wise, the treatment of wisdom in these books also extends to a wide range of theological and moral topics including the necessity of obedience to the will of God as a prerequisite for the attainment of wisdom, the limitations of human capability to attain what is essentially a divine prerogative, the folly of assuming that one can attain wisdom through one's own efforts, the manifestation of God's wisdom in the creation and maintenance of the world, and finally the moral and theological problems raised by the perception of the discrepancy between the actual state of the world and belief in a God who is both supremely wise and supremely righteous.

There is, then, some justification – apart from the fact that they use the terms 'wise' and 'wisdom' more frequently than all the other Old Testament writers put together – for referring to the authors of these books as 'the wisdom writers'. But the task of describing the 'social world' to which they belonged is complicated by the fact that their books were written at very different times and by the great diversity of their literary and intellectual character.

The dating of the wisdom books is itself a difficult problem. Nevertheless it is generally agreed on the one hand that the earliest material in Proverbs originated in the period of the monarchy, if not earlier; and, on the other, that Ecclesiastes was written in the Hellenistic age. (Ecclesiasticus and the Wisdom of Solomon were written even later than Ecclesiastes.) It is obvious that the social systems and circumstances of the pre-exilic period were completely different from those prevailing in the third century BC or later. The dates of Job, the later parts of Proverbs, and the wisdom psalms are less clear. But it cannot be assumed that any two of these compositions have the same 'social world' as their background. Each must be examined separately if the circumstances in which it was written are to be discovered. Unfortunately this obvious methodological principle has not always been observed. For example, scholars frustrated by lack of evidence in the earlier texts have sometimes tended anachronistically to use Ben Sira, the second-century author of Ecclesiasticus, as a model in order to fill out an otherwise meagre account of the Israelite 'wise man' of earlier periods.

It has been widely assumed by scholars that all these writers, of whatever period, represented a *continuous and unbroken* 'wisdom tradition' transmitted by a class of 'wise men' to which they all belonged. For this assumption there is no direct evidence at all (see Whybray, 1974 and Crenshaw, 1976, 22). Between the destruction of the Judaean monarchy in the early sixth century BC and the Hellenistic period when Ecclesiastes was written there is a complete gap in our sources of information. If there was indeed a class of 'wise men' who served in various capacities in the royal Judaean court before the Exile, some of whom were the authors of wisdom books, we do not know what happened to this class when its ostensible *raison d'être* and *locus standi* disappeared. Much later we hear of the existence of 'scribes' such as Ezra in the post-exilic period; and we find the 'wise man' Qoheleth who 'taught the people', and later still Ben Sira with his 'school'. Again in the New Testament we encounter 'scribes of the law', a class which, it has been suggested, may already have existed in embryo in the time of Jeremiah. But there is no evidence to connect these various 'scribes' and 'wise men' of later times with the pre-exilic wisdom writers which might justify the view that the former were the inheritors, through some mode of transmission now hidden from us, of an unbroken institutional 'wisdom tradition'. Nor is there any hint in the Book of Job of its author's having belonged to such an institution. To say that there were schools both in the pre-exilic and post-exilic periods in Israel (Lemaire, 1981) is no proof of an unbroken tradition.

As will be demonstrated below, the obvious differences between these works in various ways strengthens the impression that, despite some important similarities of theme, they do not belong to any continuing 'tradition' except in a very general sense. For example, although in both Job and Ecclesiastes we find aphorisms similar to those which are characteristic of much of Proverbs, the literary characteristics of these two books are quite different in every major respect not only from Proverbs but from one another. Moreover, the spirit in which they approach their subjects is quite different. The passionate outpourings of Job – not to mention the narrative framework of that book – are as different from the cold dissection of intellectual problems in Ecclesiastes as are both from the tiny pearls of wisdom which constitute the bulk of the Book of Proverbs.

In the wisdom writers, then, we encounter a series of quite different styles and approaches which reflect widely different intellectual and social worlds. Each of these will be given separate treatment in what follows.

B. The origin of literary wisdom in Israel

The history of scholarly discussion of this question during the past century is a complicated one. Here it is possible only to give a brief and somewhat impressionistic account of it, drawing attention to the most significant developments. Each of the hypotheses outlined below has had an influential following and is still supported, with some modifications, at the present time.

1. Early views: wisdom literature as a post-exilic phenomenon

Until comparatively recent times there was little perception of the existence of an Israelite wisdom tradition as a distinct element in Israel's religious thought. Meinhold's *Die Weisheit Israels*, 1908, seems to have been the first comprehensive account of it and its historical development. Previously Proverbs, Job and Ecclesiastes had generally been treated independently, and with not even approximate agreement about their periods of composition. However, by the end of the century there was an increasing tendency to see the post-exilic period as the matrix of the wisdom literature. In particular, Proverbs was regarded as the work of post-exilic scribes who interpreted the Law and the prophetical books, drawing out their implications for daily conduct (so, e.g., Wildeboer, 1897, Toy, 1899). Volz suggested in 1921 that there might be a connection between the aphoristic style of the individual, self-contained short sayings which constitute the bulk of Proverbs and the popular saying (*Spruchdichtung*) generally characteristic of earlier stages of culture throughout the world, but this approach to the origin of Israelite literary wisdom remained for a long time virtually unexplored.

2. The hypothesis of foreign literary models: court and school

The publication of the Egyptian *Wisdom of Amen-em-ope* in 1923 brought about a complete change of direction in the study of the Old Testament wisdom books. The view expressed by Erman (1924) and Gressmann (1924) that Prov. 22.17–24.22 was directly modelled on this Egyptian work quickly met with general scholarly acceptance (cf. Oesterley, 1927). The possibility – already suggested, but only very tentatively – that the literary phenomenon of Proverbs was not the product of the Israelite genius but was inspired in its themes and ideas as well as in its forms by foreign models now seemed to have been transformed into certainty. The whole range of known Egyptian and Mesopotamian literature was now brought into the discussion, and parallels were sought for every aspect of Proverbs and indeed of Ecclesiastes as well (e.g. Humbert, 1929). Some of the most surprising discoveries were made in the realm of religious ideas and of morals: various items of religious and ethical teaching in the Old Testament wisdom books were now seen to be remarkably similar to what had been taught in the Egyptian and Mesopotamian wisdom books at a much earlier date than anything to be found there. With regard to literary form, it was further observed that the individual sayings in Prov. 10–29, though they have few parallels in Egyptian literature, bear a strong resemblance to similar collections from Babylonia and to the *Wisdom of Ahikar* (Oesterley, 1929).

These discoveries were seen to have important sociological implications. Whereas the social background of the authors of the biblical wisdom books is virtually never directly alluded to either in these books themselves or elsewhere in the Old Testament (with the exception of the dubious attributions of parts of Proverbs and Ecclesiastes to Solomon and the references to Solomon's literary activity in 1 Kings 4.32–4 [*Heb*. 5.12–14]), some of the Egyptian and Mesopotamian works in question provide the most precise indications of their provenance and purpose. The Egyptian works in particular originated in the royal court or in schools closely connected with the court, where they served as textbooks. Their purpose was didactic: they were written for the instruction of kings, or, more frequently, for the education of young men of the upper class destined to occupy high places in the administration of the country.

It was accordingly concluded by Old Testament scholars that at least part of Proverbs must have originated in a similar milieu: in the royal courts of Israel, and in 'wisdom schools' closely associated with them (so, e.g., Baumgartner, 1933; Duesberg, 1938). The theory of the borrowing – as in the case of Prov. 22.17ff. – and imitation of foreign models thus also radically affected the dating of this material: it could not be post-exilic but must come from the period of the monarchy.

The theory also appeared to account for a characteristic of the biblical wisdom books which had hitherto been difficult to explain: their failure – which was unaccountable if their authors derived their teaching from scripture – to refer in any way to Israel or its history. It now appeared that the literary wisdom tradition of the Old Testament, although it made concessions to Israelite religious traditions – for example, in the use of the name Yahweh in Proverbs – was essentially an alien one (Fichtner, 1933). And to some extent, it was believed, it remained so: even the authors of the poem of Job and of Ecclesiastes in the post-exilic period made no reference to Israel and its history and even – unlike the authors of Proverbs – refrained from using the divine name Yahweh.

This understanding of the origin and nature of Israel's literary wisdom tradition received further strong support from von Rad's hypothesis (1944, 1957) of a 'spiritual enlightenment' which supposedly occurred in Israel in the reign of Solomon. He argued that the royal court in Solomon's reign modelled itself on that of Egypt so completely that there occurred a sudden and unusually rapid cultural development which brought Israel into the main stream of Near Eastern civilisation, a development which was clearly manifested in the literature of the period. This hypothesis was extremely influential during the decades which followed, and still finds support in scholarly circles, although it has increasingly been modified or challenged.

3. The 'nationalisation' of the wisdom literature

The theory of a foreign-dominated royal court as the matrix of the Israelite wisdom literature, and of 'wisdom schools' as the locus of its specific manifestations, did not, however, offer a complete explanation of the phenomenon. It was generally recognised that in its present form the Book of Proverbs, despite its lack of specific references to Israel, has its own Israelite flavour. It was held that it has undergone a gradual process of 'nationalisation' (Fichtner's expression), a process which extended well into the post-exilic period. The view was also put forward (e.g. by Fichtner and Baumgartner) that in its present form it is addressed not just to a narrow readership of courtiers and upper-class school pupils, but to a wider audience with different interests: it became a handbook of morals and religion for non-professional educated people belonging to a much wider stratum of society (so Skladny, 1962; Whybray, 1974; for a contrary view see Gordis, 1944).

It is of interest to note that the discovery of new Egyptian texts of the late period has shown that a comparable 'democratisation' of wisdom literature took place also in Egypt (Gemser, 1960; Lichtheim, 1983). This in turn has strengthened the likelihood, already pointed out many years ago by Humbert, that Egyptian influence on Israelite wisdom literature was not restricted to the period of the Israelite monarchy but affected the later books as well – a not surprising conclusion in view of the fact that there were close contacts between the two countries at all periods. This picture of an Israelite wisdom literature which constantly received fresh influence from Egypt – and from elsewhere – is not, however, incompatible with that of a steadily increasing 'nationalisation'. Israel was never totally isolated from the main stream of ancient Near Eastern culture.

4. 'Tribal wisdom' and the wisdom literature

The existence of a 'folk wisdom' in Israel comparable with that of other peoples and preceding the composition of wisdom books was recognised at an early stage in the history of modern study of the wisdom literature (e.g. Volz, 1921; Oesterley, 1929). But opinions differed widely on the question whether, and to what extent, this popular wisdom had played a part in the origin of the Book of Proverbs. Hermisson (1968) made an important contribution to this discussion. On the basis of a detailed study of popular sayings embedded in the historical and prophetical books of the Old Testament he demonstrated that the aphorisms in Proverbs are entirely different in form from these, and concluded that the one type cannot have developed from the other. However, the question continues to be debated (see von Rad, 1970; Thompson, 1974; Fontaine, 1982; Nel, 1982).

Meanwhile Audet (1960), Gerstenberger (1965) and Richter (1966) had put forward a somewhat different type of theory of an oral prehistory of some of the material in Proverbs. They attempted to show by means of form-critical arguments that the *Mahnspruch* or admonition which occurs frequently in the book was derived not from 'popular proverbs' in the usual sense but from specific codes of behaviour used in Israel's pre-monarchical tribal society (*Sippenweisheit*). Thus wisdom and law had to some extent a common origin (see Blenkinsopp, 1983, for a somewhat similar view). Wolff (1964) also argued that traces of such 'tribal wisdom' are to be found in Amos. This hypothesis also continues to be debated. The principal difficulty in assessing hypotheses of this kind is that our knowledge of the organisation and norms of premonarchical society in Israel is extremely limited (see Wilson, 1984 on the problems involved).

5. Analogies with 'oral literature' in the modern world

Recently attempts have been made to approach the problem of possible preliterate origins of the material in Proverbs by comparing the short sayings in the book with the aphoristic 'literature' of modern non-literate peoples which has been collected by folklorists and anthropologists. Westermann (1971),Barucq (1972) and Golka (1986) have carried out such investigations, mainly with respect to examples from tribal Africa. Many of these show remarkable similarities not only in theme but also in form to individual sayings in Proverbs. It appears that these African sayings served a variety of purposes, including those postulated by Audet and Gerstenberger for the Proverbs material. But there is a need for much more research into this matter and for an assessment of the enterprise by anthropologists before any firm conclusions can be drawn from such comparisons.

It is also not clear how the findings of the above scholars can be reconciled with the conclusions of Hermisson. It may be that the 'popular' sayings studied by the latter are on an entirely different level from the supposed tribal codes of conduct postulated by them; but it remains the case that Israelite tribal wisdom is a somewhat shadowy postulate. Whatever may be the truth of the matter, the question of the validity of the comparison of biblical material with that gleaned from modern peoples of a quite different culture from that of the ancient Semitic peoples is likely to be seriously questioned in the future.

6. Wisdom literature and institutional education

Lemaire (1981, 1984) has recently turned attention once more to the question of the part played by the school – now the 'scribal school' – in the composition of the wisdom books. He totally ignores the possible existence of popular or tribal wisdom as a background. For him, all literature – as distinct from mere ephemera – in the ancient Near East was copied and transmitted in scribal schools, and all wisdom literature was composed as textbooks in schools. It is therefore indisputable that the early wisdom literature of Israel was composed in the royal schools. After the Exile schools in Israel proliferated and were to be found not only in Jerusalem and the other cities but even in the villages; and it was in such institutions (that is, in those institutions of higher learning with a special interest in the subject) that the composition of wisdom books took place.

Lemaire's particular contribution to the discussion is that he has adduced a quantity of epigraphical material to prove the existence of schools in Israel, not only after but also before the Exile. The interpretation of this evidence is to some extent a matter of dispute, and much of it still remains to be evaluated. It is, however, legitimate to question whether his picture of an almost universal education in post-exilic Israel does not to some extent invalidate his own argument that the school was the only locus of composition, since there seems to be no reason why, from such a widely educated population, such books as – for example – Job could not have been written by persons engaged in occupations other than that of scribe, who had been educated in schools but were no longer connected with them (on schools in Israel see also Whybray, 1974; Lang, 1979, 1986; Golka, 1983; Crenshaw, 1985).

7. Wider notions of authorship

Clearly there is at present no consensus of scholarly opinion about the social world of the wisdom writers before the second century BC. But there is now a tendency among recent scholars (e.g. Murphy) to believe that *none* of the proposals made so far is sufficient by itself to account for the rather scattered pieces of evidence which we possess.

On the one hand it is *a priori* difficult to believe that royal scribes, even though writing under the influence of foreign culture, should have been so isolated from the general culture of their own pople that they totally ignored the folk wisdom which surrounded them and which, whatever may have been its outward forms, must have been to a large extent concerned with the same problems of daily life and behaviour as were the models which they imitated. On the other hand, the literary quality of most of the aphorisms in Proverbs and the clear dependence of some parts of that book on foreign works cannot be denied; and these presuppose a high degree of education and literary training, whether parental or institutional, which is associated with the professional scribe. To these two facts may be added the third consideration mentioned above: if education in Israel became more and more widespread, even extending, perhaps, at least in its lower forms, to quite ordinary people, there appears to be no reason why educated persons outside the scribal profession should not have contributed to the authorship of some of the wisdom books of the Old Testament.

C. The Book of Proverbs

A variety of different backgrounds and interests appears to be reflected in this book. Skladny (1962) attempted to determine the social milieux of chapters 10.1–22.16 and 25–9 by means of a statistical analysis of the frequency of recurrence of particular themes in the numerous short sayings of which these chapters consist. On this basis he distinguished four separate collections (10–15; 16.1–22.16; 25–7; 28–9), each of which, he claimed, comes from a different social class: 16.1–22.16, for example, is an instruction composed for the education of the sons of royal officials, while 25–7, with its frequent references to agriculture and to private domestic situations, is addressed to a less elevated and more countrified social stratum. Both Skladny's methods and the way in which he applied them are open to some criticism. In fact the differences between the activities and concerns manifested in these four sections of the book are far from absolute: there is a considerable overlap. Moreover Skladny probably overstates the rigidity of class distinctions in the early period to which he assigns these collections.

However, Skladny's conclusion that at least one section of Proverbs covers a range of interests considerably wider than those generally associated with a small class of royal officials is an important one. In general all these chapters seem to be addressed to a fairly wide readership, and, mainly at least, to an adult one. There is little here – despite the distinctions made by Skladny – to suggest a school or any kind of educational setting. These findings suppose a rather high standard of literacy, a supposition which can be defended from epigraphical material, and which has also – though not with universal agreement – been defended on the grounds that the alphabetic script in use in Israel was far more readily learned than Egyptian hieroglyphs or Mesopotamian cuneiform and without the necessity for a rigorous scribal training (see Lang, 1986, chapter 1).

On the other hand it has been widely believed that the references to the king, of which some occur in *each* of Skladny's collections, point to a setting in the royal court and so support the view that this material is indeed heavily dependent on Egyptian models. But these references are in fact few in number (about twelve in all), and constitute a very minor element in every section. Some of them (14.35; 16.14–15; 19.12; 22.11; 25.6–7, 15) can reasonably be interpreted as presupposing direct access to the king, and a few others have been thought to reflect the life of a courtier. But this interpretation has been disputed (most recently by Golka, 1986).

Some kind of connection with the court is, however, specifically claimed by 25.1, which states that the 'men of Hezekiah' – presumably his royal scribes – copied (or edited) the section which follows (a section, incidentally, which Skladny considers *not* to be connected with the court!). But this verse does not state, or even necessarily imply, that this section of the book was *composed* at the court. (It is, moreover, just possible that the verse may simply be an example of a tendency to attribute literary activity to appropriate outstanding figures of the past.) More probably it refers to a particular stage in the development of this collection (and probably of others as well): material predating the monarchy was added to and first formed into collections in a variety of social situations, and then edited or further developed at the royal court, which was undoubtedly an important cultural centre, before being eventually incorporated into the Book of Proverbs as it exists now.

A somewhat different theory of the development of these chapters is concerned with their religious content. McKane (1965, 1970) gave new currency to an older view, partly derived from the interpretation of Egyptian and other foreign wisdom as 'secular', that the 'religious' sayings in Prov. 10–29 (specifically, those which mention Yahweh by name) are embellishments added to earlier collections of what he called 'old wisdom'. In other words, an originally empirical 'wisdom' practised by statesmen who did not 'permit themselves the luxury of religious or ethical assumptions' (1965, 48) was transformed, under the influence of the prophets, in such a way as to make it conform to the tenets of the Yahwistic faith. This idea of a secular 'old wisdom', however, runs counter to the now generally agreed understanding of ancient Near Eastern wisdom in general as having been permeated with a religious spirit from the beginning (this was already perceived with regard to Egyptian wisdom by de Buck, 1932). In fact, far from standing out in these chapters of Proverbs as a religious intrusion, the 'Yahweh' here depicted functions to a large extent exactly in the same way as the 'god' or gods of Egyptian wisdom literature. This is not to say that the material in these chapters is uniform in character and all comes from the same social background; but up to the present no attempt to discover the way in which the chapters have developed, and so to discern distinct 'social worlds' which they may reflect, has commanded general assent. (Finkelstein's attempt to distinguish between 'patrician' and 'plebeian' individual sayings [1962, 203–11] is very arbitrary and indeed simplistic).

Prov. 22.17–24.22 and chapters 1–9 are altogether different from the chapters discussed above (McKane, 1970, identifies them as belonging, with 31.1–9, to an 'instruction genre' as distinct from the 'sentence literature' of the rest of the book). 22.17–24.22, with its clear dependence on an Egyptian handbook, certainly belongs to the sphere of education, and this is equally true of chapters 1–9. In the latter the frequent use of the phrase 'my son', the references to the father (and the mother) as teachers, and the contents of the teaching itself mark these chapters out as instruction for the young.

Apart from the portrayal of a personified 'Wisdom' in 1.20–33 and chapters 8 and 9, Prov. 1–9 consists of a series of short instructions remarkably similar to those which form a large part of Egyptian wisdom literature (Whybray, 1965; cf. Scott, 1965; Kayatz, 1966). Whether this instruction was institutional, as in Egypt, or parental is still debated (see the discussion on schools above). Unfortunately, apart from the fact that the setting is clearly an urban one, they provide little information about either their date or about the social class of the pupils. They have a certain 'timeless' quality like the Egyptian instructions, which continued to be copied for centuries because they never lost their relevance. On the personification of wisdom in these chapters, a feature which has no equivalent in their Egyptian counterparts (though see Kayatz on this point), see below.

It has been argued (e.g. by Whybray, 1965) that these 'instructions' in their present form have been developed from earlier, shorter pieces with a less developed 'wisdom theology'. Such a theological development does not, however, help us to determine their social background.

But Lang has recently (1986) proposed a quite new interpretation of these chapters, especially the poems in 1.20–33 and chapters 8 and 9, in which a personified Wisdom offers her gifts to those who desire them. Lang regards these poems as relatively early texts in which the features of an Israelite *goddess* of wisdom, the patroness of learning, are still clearly discernible despite later editing. Moreover, in the language of 1.20 ff., where Wisdom is portrayed as a teacher who appeals for pupils while standing 'in the street' and 'at the entrance of the city gates' (1.20–1) he claims that it is possible to discern the actual circumstances of the teaching practices of the pre-exilic 'school'.

There is, then, very little unanimity among scholars at the present time about the 'social worlds' of the authors of Proverbs. Only one aspect of the question commands general assent, and that a negative one: no part of

Proverbs identifies wisdom with the Law (unlike some of the 'wisdom psalms'). The 'law' or 'teaching' (*tōrāh*) referred to frequently in chapters 1–9 is not the law of Moses but the teaching of the human instructor (or of 'Wisdom', who stands behind him). Proverbs was certainly neither written nor influenced by the 'law-scribes'.

D. The Book of Job

Although it is frequently taken for granted that Job is to be counted among the 'wisdom books' of the Old Testament, many of those who have made a special study of it, including Volz (1921), Fichtner (1950), Weiser (1956), Gese (1958) and Westermann (1956), have opposed this classification, while others have accepted it only with reservations or have regarded the question as irrelevant. Gese's view that the theology of the book is 'fundamentally opposed to wisdom thought' (p. 77) is not untypical of modern opinion on the subject.

This opinion is not due to the fact that the author of Job questions the simple optimistic view of the world which is characteristic of the Book of Proverbs: that is equally true of Ecclesiastes, yet Ecclesiastes is universally classified as a wisdom book. It is due rather to the fact that Job, though dealing to a large extent with the same themes as Proverbs and Ecclesiastes, sets them in a much broader religious context: a context of personal faith and a struggle for personal integrity. These great themes are approached in a spirit of unfettered discussion which nevertheless betrays the intensity of the author's own involvement. The 'crucifixion' of Job (see Robinson's 'The Cross of Job', 1955) is too realistically portrayed for the 'dialogue' to be dismissed as an academic discussion in the 'wisdom schools', as has often been suggested. But equally there is no attempt to put forth a particular 'message' or dogma. Although some of the speeches in the book are strongly didactic, each is challenged by others. The contrast with the picture of the 'wise man' (*ḥāḵām*) Qoheleth who 'taught the people knowledge' (Eccles. 12.9) is striking. The aim of the book seems to be to promote serious thought rather than to teach a doctrine.

On any narrow institutional definition of 'wisdom', therefore, the book of Job does not qualify as a 'wisdom book'. If it is to be so considered, this can only be on the basis of a purely thematic description of 'wisdom' such as that proposed at the beginning of this chapter.

Very few attempts have been made, despite the immense quantity of literature on the Book of Job, to study its social setting. As late as 1978 H.-P. Müller, in a survey of this literature, commented that 'a thorough investigation of the socio-cultural background of the Book of Job belongs to the tasks of the future'. The problem lies above all in its uniqueness. That it is a work of genius is universally recognised. Because it is not didactic, it does not offer easily recognisable clues to the circumstances which led the author to contemplate the case of an innocent sufferer whose misfortunes, it should be noted, are attributed not to social injustice but to the hand of God. The theme of the 'righteous sufferer' is of course a traditional one well exemplified especially in Mesopotamian literature; but it cannot be assumed that Job was composed in circumstances similar to those which inspired those foreign compositions: the situation of the man who experiences exceptional misfortune for which he can discover no justification is an universal one.

A peculiar feature of the book is that it makes use of a number of literary genres and motifs culled from elsewhere: the prose narrative, which constitutes the framework of the poem, the lamentation, the motif of the law-court, the aphorism, and many others. But these have been woven into a literary whole which makes it impossible to determine its *Sitz im Leben* by means of form-critical analysis. The most distinctive formal feature of the book – the so-called 'dialogue' between Job and his friends – is, on the other hand, equally resistant to such analysis because there is nothing in the Old Testament which can be compared with it.

There is equal uncertainty about the date of the book, and even about the nationality of the author. A date in the Persian period (fifth or fourth century BC) is at present the most favoured one, but such estimates are almost always made with hesitation. The chief reasons usually given for a post-exilic date are the speculative nature of the book's theology, especially when compared with the older parts of the Book of Proverbs, and the supposed acquaintance of the author with other Old Testament writings such as Isa. 40–55. However, speculative theology was already being written in other parts of the ancient Near East before the first millennium BC; and the arguments for literary allusions to earlier Hebrew texts seem to the present writer to fall short of proof. Nevertheless it is clear that the author was a man of great erudition. The book could not have been written without a wide knowledge of the literary world of the ancient Near East outside Israel. This fact, together with the unexplained peculiarities of the language of the poetical part of the book, has led some scholars to suppose that the author was either a Jew living outside Palestine, or even a non-Jew.

The prose narrative (1–2; 42.7–17) which forms the framework to the poetical portions of the book places the protagonist, Job, in a definite though somewhat peculiar setting: he is a non-Israelite living in the unidentified though certainly non-Palestinian land of Uz, yet he is a worshipper of Yahweh. But there is no reason to suppose that this provides any information about the author's background: whether the narrative is his own composition or, as some scholars have supposed, a traditional folk-tale which he has adapted to his own purpose, it is deliberately set in a timeless past somewhat reminiscent of the period of the patriarchs of the Book of Genesis. One feature, however – the figure of the 'Satan' as a member of Yahweh's heavenly court – is usually taken to be an indication that at least in its present form the story is post-exilic, since the only other references to that figure in the Old Testament (Zech. 3.1 and 1 Chron. 21.1) are certainly post-exilic.

In the poem itself the two features most likely to provide an indication of the social background of the author are the figures of Job's three 'friends', Eliphaz the Temanite, Bildad the Shuhite and Zophar the Naamathite, and Job's own references in his speeches to his former status (especially in chapters 29–31). Since the arguments put forward by the three friends – who, like Job himself, are represented as non-Jews – tend to echo much of the teaching of Proverbs, especially the dogma that God rewards men according to their deeds, it has often been maintained that the author intended to portray them – perhaps in caricature – as 'orthodox' wise men whose traditional wisdom it was his concern, as a member of their guild, to confute, or at least to question, by the portrayal of Job as one whose experiences ran counter to their teaching. However, the views which they express were not in fact confined to the 'wise' but were held generally in pre-exilic Israel. In the passage in which they are introduced (2.11–13), the 'friends' are represented not as especially wise men but simply as acquaintances of Job who have come from distant places to visit him. The most natural interpretation of this passage is that, like Job himself, they are well-to-do pastoralists. If the Book of Job were an academic disputation composed in connection with some kind of wisdom school or academy – and we have no evidence that such disputations took place – it would be necessary to explain why they are depicted in this 'non-professional' guise.

To penetrate behind the ostensible social world of the 'story' to discover what was the real social world of the author is a task which few have seriously attempted. Virtually the only hope of doing this in the case of a book which is clearly a personal rather than a social document is to begin by assuming that the different groups of person referred to in the book correspond in some way – whether the author was conscious of this or not – with the social classes of the author's own time. Three such groups are alluded to: that to which Job himself belonged, who might be described as the 'pious wealthy' (see especially chapters 29 and 31), the 'wicked wealthy' (e.g. those described in chapter 20) and the poor and defenceless (referred to *passim*). Unfortunately this cast of characters is hardly restricted to any particular period or society. However, the relationships between these groups and their attitudes towards one another have been used as evidence of the social position and stance of the author.

Crüsemann (1980) saw in the plight of Job a reflection of the reduced economic and social circumstances of the former wealthy Israelite aristocratic class in the Persian period caused by the successive catastrophes of the collapse of the Jewish state, the Exile, and the ensuing social and economic upheavals and harsh conditions of Persian rule (cf. Neh. 5.1–5). He argued that Job's chief complaint was not so much about his physical afflictions as about his loss of social status; and that his appeal to God was made on a legal basis: he was demanding his rights rather than appealing for mercy. He had been reduced to the same miserable condition as that of the lowest class. Yet his attitude towards that class is typical of the aristocrat: while believing that it is the duty of the upper class to show kindness and generosity towards the less fortunate, he does not question the rightness of such social and economic differentiation within the social order (cf. also Smith, 1971, 157–9).

Albertz (1981) further identified the 'wicked' in the book, whose prosperity is so often contrasted with Job's present misery, with a class of unscrupulous magnates who exploited the poor, while Job represents the old-fashioned god-fearing aristocrats, now a dwindling minority, who were themselves being thrust out of their former positions of authority because of their refusal to indulge in such unscrupulous and extortionate behaviour. The author of the book, according to Albertz, belonged to this latter group; but his main purpose was not so much to defend his own class as to speak for the small farmer who was being forced into debt and slavery (Neh. 5.1–5 again). He was, in other words, a man of the same stamp and social standing as Nehemiah.

It is interesting to compare these views with the earlier work of Finkelstein (1962, 230–5), who regarded the book as having been, in its original form, the work of a disillusioned 'plebeian' writer with a sense of injustice who ranted against both God and the rich and powerful, the book having been later changed by major additions into a 'pious novel'. He found in the speeches of Job and of the friends assertions of the equality of all classes before God which could not have been uttered by a man of wealth: e.g. 'Did not he that made me in the womb make him?' (31.13) and the praise of the grave as the place where 'the servant is free from his master' (3.19). Finkelstein found similar 'plebeian' elements in Proverbs.

These few attempts which have so far been made to identify the social world of the Book of Job serve to show the difficulty of the problem. It is clearly important to be on one's guard against the temptation to allow one's own interests – for example, a view of history as a struggle between the classes – to dictate one's interpretation of an ancient text. A further difficulty which cannot be dealt with in detail here is that, as Finkelstein perceived, since the book is unlikely to have been written by a single author, each edition and each addition needs to be investigated separately to discover its particular social background. The fact that there is no scholarly consensus about the redactional history of the book renders this task particularly difficult. The social background of the Book of Job continues to be an enigma.

E. Ecclesiastes

In general terms there is substantial agreement about the social background of this book. That it is one of the latest, if not the latest, of the books of the Old Testament is indicated above all by the language in which it is written, which, though unique in various ways, has close affinities with post-biblical Hebrew (see Gordis, 1951). Further, its author, Qoheleth, is unique among the Old Testament writers in that he wrote in his own *persona*, presenting his thoughts as personal reflections in a manner characteristic of the Greek rather than the older Near Eastern literary tradition (see Hengel 1969, 214–17; ET, vol. 1, 116–17). It is also now agreed by most scholars that the book is essentially the work of one author and has not passed through a succession of editions, as was once believed.

That Qoheleth – and his readers – belonged to the upper ranks of society is evident. He took for granted the possession of wealth and the possibility of a leisured existence, even apparently assuming that his readers would have domestic slaves at their disposal (7.21). Only the well-to-do would have been in a position to follow his recommendation to enjoy the good things of life in the manner described in 9.7–8. It is also probable that he was a resident of Jerusalem. In 12.9 his editor states that he 'taught the people knowledge', and there is no reason to doubt that this was the case.

Some areas of uncertainty remain, however, with regard both to his precise role as a teacher and to his attitude towards the society of his time.

1. *Qoheleth's role as teacher*. It has been widely assumed that Qoheleth was a teacher in a 'traditional' wisdom school. He was evidently familiar with earlier wisdom teaching: although his own style of argument was peculiar to himself and owed virtually nothing to tradition, he not infrequently quoted or imitated aphorisms reminiscent of those in the Book of Proverbs. But to these he often gave a new twist, putting them into new contexts which either relativised their truth or gave them new

meanings (see Gordis, 1939/40, Fox, 1980, Whybray, 1981). The society in which he lived – that of the Ptolemaic era – was to some extent influenced by Hellenism, yet attempts to trace the sources of his thought in Greek or Hellenistic philosophy (see most recently Braun, 1973) have not been successful. Radical though he was in his criticism of received ideas, it was Jewish and not Greek notions that he took as his point of departure (Loretz, 1964, Gordis, 1951, Whybray, 1979). The Greek educational system had not yet been introduced into Jerusalem (Hengel, 130–40; ET, vol. 1, 70–6).

There is no direct evidence that Qoheleth was connected with an institution of learning, though this may have been the case. It has sometimes been assumed, on the grounds that the title 'Qoheleth' is related to *qāhāl*, 'assembly', that he was a member or convener of a learned academy; but this is pure speculation. The meaning of the word remains obscure. We know from Ben Sira (Ecclesiasticus) that by the early second century BC there were schools or academies in Jerusalem; but Qoheleth's teaching is so completely different from the *torah*-oriented teaching of Ben Sira with its interest in the national traditions and in the priesthood that no common setting for the two books seems possible.

Although 12.9–10 shows that Qoheleth had a personal following in his own day, his seems to have been a lone voice. As Bickerman (1967) put it, he 'has no known adherents or spiritual posterity in Jewish thought'. Von Rad also averred that 'his work is not the expression of any school', and that he was 'an outsider completely free of tradition' (1970, 303–4; ET, 235; cf. Gese, 1963).

2. *Qoheleth and his world.* Whether Qoheleth made any discernible impact on the society of his day or not, the characteristics of that society are nevertheless clearly reflected in his book. It was a society obsessed with the acquisition of wealth: with the making of commercial profits. Wealth – that is, its power, temptations, precarious nature and corrupting influence – had been a favourite theme of the earlier wisdom literature, but Qoheleth's remark that 'bread is made for laughter, and wine gladdens life; but money makes everything possible' (10.19) sums up the new scale of values. Profit (*yiṯrōn*) was the chief motivation of Qoheleth's world. The Ptolemaic era was a time when the incorporation of Palestine into the cosmopolitan Hellenistic world had introduced new methods of production and stimulated international trade and commerce (Hengel, 67–105; ET, 35–55). Profits could be made and just as quickly lost (5.13–17 [Heb. 12–16]). Many of Qoheleth's reflections are concerned with the effects of this new preoccupation with money. His book also reflects the disintegrating effect which it had on traditional Jewish values.

Qoheleth's attitude towards this society and its values has been variously assessed. But there is general agreement that although he was aware of political corruption (3.16; 8.10) and of the injustices and oppressions inflicted on the labouring and peasant classes by the wealthy and powerful and by a harsh government (4.1–2), he took these things for granted as symptomatic of human existence in general, and, far from seeing it as his duty to campaign against them, acquiesced in the political *status quo* which encouraged them (5.8–9 [Heb. 7–8]; 8.2–5). Bickerman (1967) saw him as a disillusioned man who nevertheless wished to give practical advice to his own class about the best – that is, the most sensible – use of their wealth: he was 'a sage who in an age of investment teaches not dissipation, but the enjoyment of wealth' (p. 165).

Crüsemann (1979) took a much harsher view of Qoheleth, seeing him as cynical and contemptuous of the underprivileged: for example, on the basis of 7.21–2 he depicted him as a callous slave-owner quite indifferent to the reason for his slave's covert hostility towards him. This reading of the book corresponds to Crüsemann's understanding of history: thus he interpreted the later Maccabaean Revolt rather simplistically as a rebellion of the underprivileged against the aristocrats who held views like those of Qoheleth.

There is a danger of over-interpretation here. It may be questioned whether such texts provide a sufficient basis for the sociological judgement which is derived from them. Most of those few writers who have attempted a sociological analysis of the book (e.g. Gese, Gordis, Hengel), while placing Qoheleth firmly in the ranks of the upper class, see him somewhat differently as a rather detached observer who neither defended nor condemned the structure of contemporary society.

F. The 'wisdom psalms'

Gunkel in his pioneering study of the Psalms (1933, 381–97) recognised the existence in the Psalter of a category of 'wisdom poems' (*Weisheitsgedichten*), although he did not use the expression 'wisdom psalms'. Since then most scholars (Engnell, 1970 and Luyten, 1979 are exceptions) have agreed that a certain number of the Psalms may appropriately be called 'wisdom psalms': that is, psalms which do not merely display affinities with the wisdom books, but are essentially wisdom compositions in intention.

But the consensus of opinion ends there. Firstly, there is no agreement at all about the psalms which ought to be included in this category. A comparison by the present writer of the lists of 'wisdom psalms' in the Psalter drawn up by fourteen scholars who have specialised in the subject shows that, although no less than thirty-three psalms have been so identified by one or more of these scholars, only one psalm (37) appears in all the lists, with three others (1, 49, 112) included in all but one. Next, Psalm 73 appears in eight of these lists, while the remainder are found in seven or less, and at the other end of the scale twelve psalms occur only once. The fact that no two of the lists are identical is significant.

This divergence of opinion is partly due, not surprisingly, to different definitions of 'wisdom' favoured by these various scholars. But this is not the only aspect of the problem. Even those scholars who are in general agreement on that question differ to a considerable extent in their assessments of different psalms. There is evidently a great deal of room for subjectivism here.

Since the literary context – that is, the collection of texts known as the Psalter or the Book of Psalms – offers no hint of the existence of a distinct category of wisdom psalms, the only criteria available for their classification are the internal ones of form (and language) and content.

With regard to *form*, it is generally admitted that there is no distinct *Gattung* of 'wisdom psalm' which may be compared with the other types identified by Gunkel and largely accepted, with modifications, by later scholars. In fact, several psalms which are often termed wisdom psalms can reasonably be ascribed to other *Gattungen* (see Luyten). There is in fact no recognisable structure characteristic of a wisdom psalm. On the other hand, some of the psalms in question undoubtedly contain formal features characteristic of other wisdom books: for example, Ps. 37 consists of a series of short independent sayings – now arranged in alphabetical order according to their initial letter – strongly reminiscent of sayings in the book of Proverbs; Ps. 49 begins, in a style which recalls that of the wisdom teacher in Prov. 1–9, with a formal statement of an intention to give instruction in wisdom; Ps. 34 includes an address to 'sons' who are admonished to heed their teacher; while other psalms (1, 73, 112, 127) are not cast in the form of prayers like the other psalms in the Psalter but are rather lengthy reflective or didactic poems comparable with some of the longer wisdom poems in Prov. 1–9 or Job.

The *themes* treated in some of these psalms are themes which occur in other wisdom books (for example, the contrast between the fates of the righteous and the wicked); but they adopt widely different attitudes towards these questions. Thus Ps. 37 is reminiscent of much of Proverbs and of the speeches of the friends of Job, while Ps. 90 has strong affinities with Ecclesiastes (see von Rad, 1962, pp. 453–4). In Pss. 49 and 73 we find the 'righteous sufferer', as in Job, struggling to reconcile his experiences of injustice with his faith. In other psalms (notably 1; 19.7 ff.; 119) the Law has assumed the place previously occupied by wisdom or the wisdom teacher, a development which is not found elsewhere in the Old Testament wisdom books but is close to the teaching of Ben Sira.

That such different points of view should be found in psalms which have some claim to be counted as 'wisdom psalms' is not surprising. As Gunkel already perceived, these psalms reflect changes in the understanding of wisdom which correspond to what we find in the other wisdom books. In one sense this fact might appear to solve the question of the social setting of the wisdom psalms: each of these psalms, it might be supposed, was composed in a setting similar to, or identical with, that of the wisdom book which it most resembles in form, or content, or both. But this is no real answer to the problem. An explanation is required for the fact that these poems now appear not in the setting of a wisdom book but in a collection of psalms which are now generally recognised as composed for use in worship.

Gunkel had attempted to show that the wisdom psalms were in fact composed for public worship, although he admitted that their precise liturgical functions are obscure. He pointed to the reference to singing to an instrument in Ps. 49.4 [Heb. 5], the divine oracle at the end of Ps. 91, and the titles given to many of these psalms, which he took to indicate that they had already belonged to the collections of liturgical poetry which preceded the final edition of the Psalter. He suggested that it was the popularity of wisdom literature among the laity which had led the priests and singers at the temple to compose psalms in that style (p. 394).

Jansen (1937) doubted the ability of priests or temple singers to compose wisdom literature. He consequently postulated the existence of a wisdom school attached to the temple at which professional 'wise men' composed psalms for both devotional and instructional purposes. But Mowinckel (1955, 1962) decisively rejected any connection at all between the wisdom psalms and the temple: pointing out that in the post-exilic period 'piety was . . . to a certain degree detached from the temple cultus, and found much of its nourishment in the synagogue and in the lecture room [school] or the learned men' (1955, 209). He argued that it was these 'learned men' and not the priests who were the final editors of the Psalter. They were the 'learned psalmographers' who both composed the wisdom psalms and included them in the final edition (cf. Kuntz, 1974; Perdue, 1977). Murphy (1963), on the other hand, attempted to defend the possibility of a cultic usage for the wisdom psalms by suggesting that the temple cult itself underwent a change in post-exilic times, allowing greater room than before for the expression of personal piety.

In fact all these theories presuppose a greater knowledge both of the post-exilic temple cult and of the wise men and their schools than we actually possess. Despite recent attempts to solve the problem of the milieu in which the wisdom psalms may have been composed, no fundamentally new theses have been put forward since the time of Mowinckel. Murphy's comment that 'It must be admitted that the precise life-setting of these poems eludes us' must be taken as accurately summing up the present state of scholarly research on this subject.

Bibliography

Albertz, R., 1981. 'Der sozialgeschichtliche Hintergrund des Hiobbuches und der "Babylonischen Theodizee"', *Die Botschaft und die Boten* (Wolff Festschrift), Neukirchen, pp. 349–72.

Audet, J.-P., 1960. 'Origines comparées de la double tradition de la loi et de la sagesse dans le prôche-orient ancien', *International Congress of Orientalists*, Moscow, vol. 1, pp.352–7.

Barucq, A., 1972. 'Proverbes (Livre des)', *Supplément au Dictionnaire de la Bible*, tome VIII, cols 1395–1476.

Baumgartner, W., 1933. *Israelitische und altorientalische Weisheit*, Sammlung gemeinverständliche Vorträge aus dem Gebiet der Theologie und Religionsgeschichte, 166, Tübingen.

Bickerman, E., 1967. *Four Strange Books of the Bible. Jonah/Daniel/Koheleth/Esther*, New York.

Blenkinsopp, J., 1983. *Wisdom and Law in the Old Testament. The Ordering of Life in Israel and Early Judaism*, Oxford Bible Series, Oxford.

Braun, R., 1973. *Kohelet und die frühhellenistische Popularphilosophie*, BZAW 130, Berlin.

De Buck, A., 1932. 'Het religieus karakter der oudste egyptische wijsheid', *Nieuw Theologisch Tijdschrift* 21, pp. 322–49.

Crenshaw, J. L., 1985. 'Education in Ancient Israel', *JBL* 104, pp. 601–15.

1976. 'Studies in Ancient Israelite Wisdom: Prolegomena', *Studies in Ancient Israelite Wisdom*, New York, pp. 1–60.

Crüsemann, F., 1980. 'Hiob und Kohelet. Ein Beitrag zum Verständnis des Hiobbuches', *Werden und Wirken des Alten Testaments*, Westermann Festschrift, Göttingen and Neukirchen, pp. 373–93.

1979. 'Die unveränderbare Welt. Überlegungen zur "Krisis der Weisheit" beim Prediger (Kohelet)', *Der Gott der kleinen Leute. Sozialgeschichtliche Bibelauslegungen*, ed. by W. Schottroff and W. Stegemann, Band 1, *Altes Testament*, Gelnhausen, pp. 80–104.

Duesberg, H., 1966. *Les scribes inspirés. Introduction aux livres sapientiaux de la Bible*, 2 vols. Paris, 1938; 2nd edn (with I. Fransen), Maredsous.

Engnell, I., 1970. 'The Book of Psalms', *Critical Essays on the Old Testament*, London, pp. 68–122 (Eng. Tr. of *Svenskt Biblikst Uppslagsverk*, 1962² II, cols (618–56).

Fichtner, J., 1933. *Die altorientalische Weisheit in ihrer israelitisch-jüdischen Ausprägung. Eine Studie zur Nationalisierung der Weisheit in Israel*, BZAW 62, Giessen.

1950. 'Hiob in der Verkündigung unserer Zeit', *Wort und Dienst*, N.F. 2, pp. 71–89 = *Gottes Weisheit. Gesammelte Studien zum Alten Testament*, Arbeiten zur Theologie II/3, Stuttgart, 1965, pp. 52–66.

Finkelstein, L., 1962[3]. *The Pharisees: the Sociological Background of their Faith*, 2 vols, Philadelphia.

Fontaine, C. R., 1982. *Traditional Sayings in the Old Testament. A Contextual Study*, Bible and Literature Series, 5, Sheffield.

Fox, M. V., 1980. 'The Identification of Quotations in Biblical Literature', *ZAW* 92, pp. 416–31.

Galling, K., 1952. *Die Krise der Aufklärung in Israel*, Mainzer Universitäts-Reden 19.

Gemser, B., 1960. 'The Instructions of 'Onchsheshonqy and Biblical Wisdom Literature', SVT 7, pp. 102–28 = Crenshaw, J. L. (ed.), *Studies in Ancient Israelite Wisdom*, New York, 1976, pp. 134–60.

Gerstenberger, E., 1965. *Wesen und Herkunft des 'apodiktischen Rechts'*, WMANT 20, Neukirchen.

Gese, H., 1963. 'Die Krisis der Weisheit bei Koheleth', *Les Sagesses du Prôche-Orient Ancien*, Paris, pp. 139–51 = *Vom Sinai zum Zion. Alttestamentliche Beiträge zur biblischen Theologie*, Beiträge zur evangelischen Theologie 64, Munich, 1974, pp. 168–79.

1958. *Lehre und Wirklichkeit in der alten Weisheit. Studien zu den Sprüchen Salomos und zu dem Buche Hiob*, Tübingen.

Golka, F. W., 1983. 'Die israelitische Weisheitsschule oder "des Kaisers neue Kleider"', *VT* 33, pp. 257–71.

1986. 'Die Königs- und Hofssprüche und der Ursprung der israelitischen Weisheit', *VT* 36, pp. 13–36.

Gordis, R., 1965. *The Book of God and Man. A Study of Job*, Chicago and London.

1951. *Koheleth – The Man and his World. A Study of Ecclesiastes*, Texts and Studies of the Jewish Theological Seminary of America 19, New York, 3rd edn 1968.

1939/40. 'Quotations in Wisdom Literature', *JQR* 30, pp. 124–47.

1944. 'The Social Background of Wisdom Literature', *HUCA* 18, pp. 77–118 = *Poets, Prophets and Sages. Essays in Biblical Interpretation*, Bloomington and London, 1971, pp. 160–97.

Gressmann, H., 1924. 'Die neugefundene Lehre des Amen-em-ope und die vorexilische Spruchdichtung Israels', *ZAW* 42, pp. 272–96.

Gunkel, H. (with Begrich, J.), 1933. *Einleitung in die Psalmen. Die Gattungen der Religiösen Lyrik Israels*, Göttingen.

Hengel, M., 1969. *Judentum und Hellenismus. Studien zu ihrer Begegnung unter besonderer Berücksichtigung Palästinas bis zur Mitte des 2.Jh. v. Chr.*, Tübingen (Eng. Tr. *Judaism and Hellenism. Studies in their Encounter in Palestine during the Early Hellenistic Period*, 2 vols., London, 1974).

Hermisson, H.-J., 1968. *Studien zur israelitischen Spruchweisheit*, WMANT 28, Neukirchen.

Humbert, P., 1929. *Recherches sur les sources égyptiennes de la littérature sapientiale d'Israël*, Neuchâtel.

Jansen, H. L., 1937. *Die spätjüdische Psalmdichtung*, SNVAO II, 3, Oslo, 1937.

Kayatz, C., 1966. *Studien zu Proverbien 1–9*, WMANT 22, Neukirchen.

Kuntz, J. K., 1974. 'The Canonical Wisdom Psalms of Ancient Israel', *Rhetorical Criticism: Essays in Honor of James Muilenburg*, Pittsburgh Theological Monograph Series 1, Pittsburgh, pp. 186–222.

Lang, B., 1979. 'Schule und Unterricht im alten Israel', *La Sagesse de l'Ancien Testament*, ed. M. Gilbert, ETL 51, Louvain, pp. 186–201.

1986. *Wisdom and the Book of Proverbs. An Israelite Goddess Redefined*, New York.

Lemaire, A., 1981. *Les écoles et la formation de la Bible dans l'ancien Israël*, OBO 39, Fribourg, Switzerland and Göttingen.

1984. 'Sagesse et écoles', *VT* 34, pp. 270–81.

Lichtheim, M., 1983. *Late Egyptian Wisdom Literature in the International Context. A Study of Demotic Instructions*, OBO 52, Fribourg, Switzerland and Göttingen.

Loretz, O., 1964. *Qohelet und der alte Orient. Untersuchungen zu Stil und theologischer Thematik des Buches Qohelet*, Freiburg im Breisgau.

Luyten, J., 1979. 'Psalm 73 and Wisdom', *La Sagesse de l'Ancien Testament*, ed. M. Gilbert, ETL 51, Louvain, pp. 59–81.

McKane, W., 1965. *Prophets and Wise Men*, SBT 44, London. Reprinted 1983.

1970. *Proverbs. A New Approach*, OTL, London.

Meinhold, J., 1908. *Die Weisheit Israels in Spruch, Sage und Dichtung*, Leipzig.

Morgan, D. F., 1981. *Wisdom in the Old Testament Traditions*, Atlanta.

Mowinckel, S., 1955. 'Psalms and Wisdom', *Wisdom in Israel and the Ancient Near East Presented to H. H. Rowley*, SVT 3, Leiden, pp. 205–24.

1962. *The Psalms in Israel's Worship*, vol. 2, Oxford.

Müller, H.-P., 1978. *Das Hiobproblem, seine Stellung und Entstehung im Alten Orient und im Alten Testament*, Erträge der Forschung 84, Darmstadt.

Murphy, R. E., 1963. 'A Consideration of the Classification, "Wisdom Psalms"', *VT* Suppl 9 (Congress Volume, Bonn, 1962), Leiden, pp. 156–67.

1978. 'Wisdom – Theses and Hypotheses', *Israelite Wisdom. Theological and Literary Essays in Honor of Samuel Terrien*, Missoula, pp. 35–42.

Nel, P. J., 1982. *The Structure and Ethos of the Wisdom Admonitions in Proverbs*, BZAW 158, Berlin.

Oesterley, W. O. E., 1929. *The Book of Proverbs with Introduction and Notes*, Westminster Commentaries, London.

1927. *The Wisdom of Egypt and the Old Testament in the Light of the Newly Discovered 'Teaching of Amen-em-ope'*, London.

Perdue, L. G., 1977. *Wisdom and Cult. A Critical Analysis of the Views of Cult in the Wisdom Literatures of Israel and the Ancient Near East*, SBL Dissertation Series 30, Missoula.

Rad, G. von, 1944. 'Der Anfang der Geschichtsschreibung im alten Israel', Archiv für Kulturgeschichte 32, pp.1–42. = *Gesammelte Studien zum Alten Testament*, TLB 8, Munich, 1958, pp. 148–88. (Eng. Tr. *The Problem of the Hexateuch and Other Essays*, Edinburgh and London, 1966, pp. 166–204.

1962. *Old Testament Theology*, vol. I, Edinburgh and London (Eng. Tr. of *Theologie des Alten Testaments*, Band I, Munich, 1957).

1970. *Weisheit in Israel*, Neukirchen (Eng. Tr. *Wisdom in Israel*, London, 1972).

Richter, W., 1966. *Recht und Ethos. Versuch einer Ortung des weisheitlichen Mahnspruches*, Studien zum Alten und Neuen Testament 15, Munich.

Robinson, H. W., 1955. 'The Cross of Job', *The Cross in the Old Testament*, London, pp. 9–54.

Scott, R. B. Y., 1965. *Proverbs, Ecclesiastes*, Anchor Bible 18, Garden City, N.Y.

Skladny, U., 1962. *Die ältesten Spruchsammlungen in Israel*, Göttingen.

Smith, M., 1971. *Palestinian Parties and Politics that Shaped the Old Testament*, New York.

Thompson, J. M., 1974. *The Form and Function of Proverbs in Ancient Israel*, The Hague and Paris.

Toy, C. H., 1899. *A Critical and Exegetical Commentary on the Book of Proverbs*, ICC, Edinburgh.

Volz, P., 1921². *Hiob und Weisheit (Das Buch Hiob, Sprüche und Jesus Sirach, Prediger)*, Die Schriften des Alten Testaments 3/2, Göttingen.

Weiser, A., 1956². *Das Buch Hiob*, ATD 13, Göttingen.

Westermann, C., 1956. *Der Aufbau des Buches Hiob*, Beiträge zur historischen Theologie 23, Tübingen, 2nd edn 1977.

1971. 'Weisheit im Sprichwort', *Schalom. Studien zur Glaube und Geschichte Israels, Alfred Jepsen zum 70. Geburtstag*, Stuttgart, pp. 73–85 = *Forschung zum Alten Testament. Gesammelte Studien*, Band II, ThB 55, Munich, 1974, pp.149–61.

Whybray, R. N., 1979. 'Conservatisme et radicalisme dans Qohelet', *Sagesse et religion, Colloque de Strasbourg, octobre 1976*, Bibliothèque des Centres d'Études Supérieures Spécialisés, Paris, pp. 65–81.

1981. 'The Identification and Use of Quotations in Ecclesiastes', SVT 32 (*Congress Volume, Vienna, 1980*), Leiden, pp. 435–51.

1974. *The Intellectual Tradition in the Old Testament*, BZAW 135, Berlin.

1965. *Wisdom in Proverbs. The Concept of Wisdom in Proverbs 1–9*, SBT 45, London.

Wildeboer, G., 1897. *Die Sprüche*, KHC 15, Freiburg i. B.

Wilson, R. R., 1984. *Sociological Approaches to the Old Testament*, Guides to Biblical Scholarship, Philadelphia.

Wolffe, H. W., 1964. *Amos' geistige Heimat*, WMANT 18, Neukirchen.

CHAPTER TWELVE

The social world of apocalyptic writings

PHILIP R. DAVIES

Defining the question

It is difficult in the present climate of scholarship to use 'apocalyptic', even as an adjective, unselfconsciously. The whole field of study is dominated by the question of definition, which either occupies the centre of the discussion or looms in the immediate background. What exactly are 'apocalyptic writings' and in what way, if at all, do they relate to a particular 'social world'? Both these questions are sometimes treated as if the answers were self-evident, but any account of recent work on this topic will have to recognise that answers, where given, can vary considerably.

Two general observations will be helpful at the outset. The first is that a study of the society from which biblical and intertestamental literature arose cannot simply be read off from that literature. Biblical criticism in the last 200 years has been predominantly a literary-historical enterprise. The history of Israel has been constructed largely from the biblical literature, more or less critically evaluated. But new archaeological methods and social-scientific research are challenging the traditional dominance of *literary*-historical criticism in reconstructing the world of ancient Israel (just as new literary methods challenge literary-*historical* criticism). Not only do these newer methods use different kinds of data (e.g. ecological) or different methods of formulating hypotheses (e.g. models), but, even where applied to well-trodden areas of history they have sometimes thrown up conclusions strongly at variance with the testimony of the literature. The biblical critic, when told that the Israelites are migrants from Canaanite cities, whose social organisation is a function of their subsistence economy or that the emergence of kingship in Israel is due to the natural evolution of social structures (e.g. Hopkins: 1986; Coote & Whitelam: 1987; Gottwald: 1979; Ahlström: 1986; Frick: 1986) will protest that these conclusions are not supported by the biblical evidence – indeed, that the biblical story runs quite differently. This new phase of conflict between biblical story and non-biblical data will not be resolved, however, by taking up sides in a new kind of Bibel–Babel controversy, but in enquiring more thoughtfully into the relationship between history, society and literature. In the case of apocalyptic writings, the dominance of traditional literary-historical methods, allied to the equally traditional theological-dogmatic approach, has led to the construction of a social entity called the 'apocalyptic community'. Certainly, apocalypses have social contexts, but the existence of a literary genre does not imply a correspondingly discrete social 'genre'. The anatomy of literature and the anatomy of society are not equivalent, and one cannot infer one from the other. The manner in which literature and society interact is without question a highly complex function to which we do not as yet have a satisfactory answer. So we have to begin our survey by defining 'apocalyptic literature' and enquiring *whether*, rather than assuming *that*, it has its own distinctive social context.

The noun 'apocalypse', from which the adjective derives, is essentially a literary designation. Although the Greek word *apokalypsis* means 'revelation', it acquired even in antiquity a secondary usage as the name of a writing containing the contents of a 'revelation' – more precisely, of a certain kind of revelation which the New Testament book typifies (Smith: 1983). In the last two centuries, however, (and especially in the last century) a wider usage has emerged: 'apocalyptic' designates a set of ideas, expressed either as individual dogmas or a vaguer 'world-view' which merit the name because the apocalypses are felt to reflect corporately and individually such ideology. It is only one step from this reconstructed ideology towards the social-historical phenomenon of 'apocalyptic' communities. These can only be understood as groups defined and/or sustained by the ideology derived from the apocalypses. Thus, the validity of the term 'apocalyptic' in a social sense depends on an ideological sense which in turn depends on its (proper) literary sense. Many scholars who have written recently on the problem recognise these different dimensions of 'apocalyptic' and the difficulties of interrelating all three. Some have wished to adhere as strictly as possible to a literary definition without wishing to extend the use of the term further (Rowland). Some regard as primary the genre 'apocalypse' while maintaining that implied in its use is a certain 'apocalyptic' world-view (Collins). Hanson has distinguished between 'apocalypse' (genre), 'apocalyptic eschatology' (religious perspective) and 'apocalypticism' (religio-social movement) (Hanson: 1976). But simply to acknowledge these distinctions is inadequate. The real problem is that the same word is being used for phenomena belonging to three different categories, and the use of the word inevitably implies that an intrinsic connection between the three phenomena exists. Yet this has only ever been assumed, and never demonstrated. Indeed, the opposite has been suggested. Collins has acknowledged that of the two 'apocalyptic' communities he identifies in Greco-Roman Palestine – the Qumran community and the early Christians – neither was characterised by the production of apocalypses. Indeed, the former wrote none, the latter only one (Collins: 1983, 140–1, 206). This means that most apocalypses were written by 'apocalyptic' individuals or non-apocalyptic communities: Collins presumably means the former. Who or what is an apocalyptic individual? We shall not address the question here, but to ponder it evokes some critical thoughts about the current use of the word in a non-literary sense. At all events, the transfer of a literary classification into the arena of social classification is potentially muddling. But if we were to employ social categories for social constructs, ideological categories for ideological constructs and literary categories for literary constructs, Collins' conclusion would be helpful instead of perplexing. If we spoke instead – for example – of 'millenarian communities', we should not only free ourselves from the need to assume some intrinsic connection between a literary form and a social form of the same name, but we should also be using a recognisable social-scientific category already in use (as does Isenberg). Collins (1983, 205f.) quite rightly comments that 'there is only limited overlap between the Jewish apocalyptic literature and anthropological descriptions of millenarian movements'; moreover, that 'the Jewish apocalypses were not produced by a single "apocalyptic movement" but constituted a genre that could be utilized by different groups in different situations'. Both these statements are entirely apt; what remains puzzling, even contradictory, is that Collins can nevertheless speak of an 'apocalyptic community'. He denotes, no doubt, a social group whose identity is defined by adherence to the sort of ideology found in the apocalypses. But apocalypses themselves are no proof that such communities ever existed, any more than 'prophetic communities or 'myth communities' or 'court-tale communities' are inferred by the respective genres.

The second of our preliminary observations concerns the extent and definition of the literary phenomenon of apocalypses. Any purely literary classification – which must be the proper procedure – will seek not only the fully-developed genre but also its components (if it is a mixed or composite genre) and its antecedents (as emphasised by Koch). Depending upon the narrowness or breadth of the definition, one may, for example, include among apocalypses Isaiah 24–27 and Zechariah 9–14 or nearly all of the contents of 1 Enoch. If the net be cast, as it should, beyond the Jewish world, one will find excellent examples in Egypt (the Demotic Chronicle) and Babylonia (there is a range of 'Akkadian apocalypses'), to say nothing of Greece and Rome. The genre was common in the Hellenistic period. The huge volume on *Apocalypticism in the Mediterranean World and the Near East* (ed. Hellholm) illustrates that the literary as well as social background of apocalyptic literature cannot be confined to Judaism (as all scholars would now agree, though many ignore), nor to a single social setting. Moreover, it is also clear (as Rowland has vigorously argued) that one cannot bind apocalypses to eschatology. *Pace* much of New Testament scholarship, it has proved impossible, once the field is expanded even to Jewish apocalypses as a whole, to exclude the past (G. Davies: 1978) or even to insist on a temporal concern, for there is enormous interest in the classification and interpretation of natural phenomena, for example, the movements of the heavenly bodies, the origins of the winds – even the succession of empires as in Daniel. (On classification, see Stone: 1976.)

The following discussion must necessarily be confined to Jewish apocalypses, but awareness of the very wide and varied context will help to dispel the notion that Jewish apocalypses can be explained in isolation – although it is fair to expect that the Jewish literature has characteristics of its own (Sanders: 1983). Let us define the genre of 'apocalypse' as follows: it is a literary communication of esoteric knowledge, purportedly mediated by a heavenly figure to (usually) a renowned figure of the past. This definition represents more or less the position adopted by Rowland, but is slightly broader than that of Stone or of Collins (1979); it nevertheless permits further sub-classification (political, eschatological, astronomical, halakhic, *listenwissenschaftlich*, etc.) and the flexibility necessary to avoid many (not all!) of the notorious borderline cases. Moreover, it is broad enough to contain the non-Jewish apocalypses which are otherwise an embarrassing problem. The possibility of defining a distinctive 'Jewish apocalyptic' (sub-) genre remains; but this particular specimen cannot be the yardstick for the entire phenomenon. The basic function of the apocalypse, then, is the transmission of esoteric knowledge acquired (as it is claimed) not by human observation or reason but by revelation; the heavenly origin of the revelation and the pseudonymous attribution of the literary report to a venerable figure of the past imply to the recipient that the knowledge is both irrefutable and powerful. The purpose and background of a particular apocalypse can sometimes also be inferred from non-essential ingredients; for example, many Jewish apocalypses contain exhortation and consolation. The purpose of the revealed knowledge in this case is to give assurance in the face of the desolation which man's own observation and experience invoke (e.g. Daniel, 4 Ezra). If the content of the apocalypse is legal (e.g. Jubilees, despite its historiographical guise), we may suppose that it represents a critique of alternative halakhic practice.

Apocalypses, then, are an identifiable literary genre, although sub-genres can and should be specified. This being established, it remains to be argued, rather than assumed, that apocalypses share a particular 'world-view' which can be dubbed 'apocalyptic'. It is, however, true that the *conventions of the genre itself* imply at least the belief in the existence and accessibility of heavenly secrets which enable one to understand, even predict, earthly phenomena. But it is doubtful how distinctive this belief is. It may be important to discover rather whether certain individuals or groups made a living from the application of this belief in practice.

Historical summary of recent research

a. Blind alley

In view of the considerable number of reviews already in print (Nicholson, Hanson: 1985, Nickelsburg: 1983) the following discussion can be fairly brief and will concentrate on the question of social background.

Most discussions of recent work take as their starting point Koch's *Rediscovery of Apocalyptic* (Koch: 1972), a work which possibly caused more confusion than clarity. An earlier and more influential (partly through the later work of Russell) work is Rowley's *The Relevance of Apocalyptic*, first published in 1944 (Rowley: 1963). Rowley represents a widespread set of assumptions, which makes his book a useful starting point, since many of these are still prevalent. First, he is concerned only with Jewish apocalyptic; whether he recognises any external parallels is doubtful: his account requires none, being couched essentially in terms of Jewish history, religion and literature, alone. Secondly (Jewish) 'apocalyptic' is apparently somewhere between a literary and a religious phenomenon. Nowhere is 'apocalypse' defined formally, for Rowley is concerned mostly with the ideas expressed by the literature, although he remarks occasionally on literary features, such as pseudonymity (40ff.). Thirdly, Rowley takes for granted that apocalyptic is a 'child of prophecy', (which adds to the confusion, since by 'prophecy' he might mean either a social or religious institution or a literary corpus). Fourthly, Rowley takes it that 'apocalyptic' arises in the second century BCE, when it is 'the re-adaptation of the ideas and aspirations of earlier days to a new situation' (15), that situation being the 'crisis' under Antiochus IV, Fifthly, the first and definitive apocalyptic writing is the book of Daniel.

At every level, the phenomenon of 'apocalyptic' is explained by Rowley in quite simple terms. The prophets addressed their contemporaries in times of historical crisis, or at least when a divine message was needed. The 'apocalyptists' did the same, their crisis being one of persecution, and their emphasis being on prediction of an imminent salvation. The historical matrix of 'apocalyptic' is persecution and distress. But Rowley does not attempt any more precise identification of those responsible for Daniel, or for the other works he discusses. In its uncritical use of concepts like 'prophecy', its simplification of historical situations and processes ('persecution'), its lack of literary classification and its lack of interest in the social process, Rowley is highly typical of the approach of biblical scholars of his period, and not deserving of the role of scapegoat. But the question more typical of our generation is unasked and unanswered: what accounts for the use (or appearance) of *this* particular literary form on *this* (or any) occasion? To say that apocalyptists are heirs of prophets is to explain neither apocalyptic literature nor prophecy; it is merely playing with theological picture-cards.

Rowley has some sins of his own to bear, however. The revised edition of his book (first published 1944), already acknowledges one major objection to its thesis: the dating of certain parts of Enoch, namely 6–36 and 'Apocalypse of Weeks' earlier than Daniel (Charles: 1913, 170f.). This view, if correct, left much of Rowley's explanation (as he admitted [93]) 'without basis'. Rowley's refutation of that objection was robust, but it is now almost universally accepted that parts of Enoch are older than the later chapters of Daniel. (Rowley's view that all of Daniel was composed in the Maccabean period is also obsolete: chapters 1–6 are widely accepted as not only earlier, but reflecting a different social setting from the visions of 7–12). The chronological primacy of Daniel among the apocalypses and hence its claim to be the 'typical' apocalypse has also waned. More problematic still, 1 Enoch and Daniel are rather different in character. Little of Enoch reflects either the influence of prophecy or a situation of persecution. The same objection arose regarding Jubilees (for the response, see Rowley, 99ff.): Jubilees is as different from Enoch as it is from Daniel.

Apart from the problems just referred to, the position adopted by Rowley contained two gaps: the historical, as opposed to doctrinal, connection between 'prophecy' and 'apocalyptic', and (as already noted) the identity of the producers of his first apocalypse, the book of Daniel. An attemp to fill these gaps was made by O. Plöger, whose solution entails the same assumptions as Rowley's. In turn, Plöger's thesis, in more sophisticated and differing forms, may be discerned in the later proposals of M. Hengel and P. D. Hanson. *Theocracy and Eschatology* (Plöger: 1964) attempts to account for the origins of 'apocalyptic' (meaning the distinctive ideas of the book of Daniel) and, like Rowley, begins its quest with the history of the Maccabean era and the book of Daniel. To the question 'who wrote the book of Daniel?' Plöger gives an answer already quite well established, but not loudly articulated: a group of Jews mentioned in 1 and 2 Maccabees by the name of *Hasidim* or 'Pious', loyal to the law and temporarily allies of the Maccabees (1 Macc. 2.42, 7.12f.). Two important features of these *Hasidim* which Plöger presents are their organisation into 'conventicles' or small groups, and their embrace of eschatological hopes. The first feature is drawn from the mention of a 'company' (*synagōgē*) of *Hasidim* in 1 Macc. 2.42f., 7.13f. and the second from Daniel itself, which is assumed to be their product. The passive, loyal and eschatological attitude of Plöger's *Hasidim* is contrasted with the attitude of the Maccabees themselves, which was non-eschatological and more political. Where, then, do the *Hasidim* and their beliefs derive from? Plöger accepts that eschatology points to prophecy, but he also sees differences between prophetic and apocalyptic eschatology which he seeks to explain by developments in the religion and society of post-exilic Judaism. First, the nation had become a religious community rather than a political entity – i.e. a theocracy. This theocracy was regarded by the religious establishment, represented in the Old Testament by P and the Chronicler, as an end in itself; the goal of life and history was the cult of divine worship of the one God in the one true Temple. In such an ethos of cult and law, there was no place for future hope. It was in conventicles – small, closed communities – which preserved, augmented and applied the older prophecies that eschatological traditions were sustained. On the one hand stood the monolithic Temple establishment, on the other the small 'anti-establishment' groups. This sharp duality of social and ideological character corresponds to what Plöger finds in the Maccabean period. To confirm his suggestion of a continuity throughout the post-exilic period, Plöger examines parts of the prophetic corpus which he regards as the products of such conventicles (Is. 24–7, Zech. 12–14 and Joel). Thus was furnished not only a historical link between prophecy and apocalyptic literature but an explanation of that literature in terms of a social and religious movement (or movements).

Different parts of this theory – which is untenable, as we shall see – were elaborated by Hanson (1975) and Hengel, though only the latter provides acknowledgement. Additionally, the notion that apocalyptic writings were the product of conventicles was restated by Vielhauer (1965). Hanson is, first of all, more careful to define his use of 'apocalyptic'. Recognising the differences between 'apocalypse', 'apocalypticism' and 'apocalyptic eschatology', he sets out to explain the origin and development of the last of these only, and this from 'prophetic eschatology', a derivation which, like Plöger, he seems to have assumed from the outset. According to Hanson the evolution from the one to the other came about through the existence of a deutero-prophetic visionary tradition beginning early in the Second Temple period. Whereas prophetic eschatology had kept a balance between the heavenly and the earthly sphere, permitting human action some scope in the unfolding of history, the apocalyptic visionaries placed their trust in heavenly action, despairing of the redemption of human affairs by human activity. The eschaton could, in their view, only occur through a heavenly act. 'Vision' and 'reality', wedded in prophetic eschatology, were divorced in its apocalyptic successor. Like Plöger, Hanson divides Second Temple Jewish society into two elements, and, like Plöger, he focusses on an analysis of deutero-prophetic writings, but he differs (a) in using a linguistic rather than a doctrinal analysis of the materials – though the exegesis is hardly more persuasive; (b) in recognising that the apocalyptic eschatology might have been carried by different groups at different times; and (c) in laying stress on the use of ancient mythical themes which spoke of direct divine action in the world of human affairs, including the motifs of Israel's 'divine warrior' and the 'heavenly court'. Significantly, Hanson does not deal with Daniel – an aspect of his work for which he has been criticised, particularly by reviewers brought up on Rowley or Plöger! But what emerges as strongly from Hanson's as from Plöger's work is that apocalyptic ideas belong to the counter-establishment, to those deprived of their aspirations, those on the fringes of political and religious power. Now, this is generally what sociologists also say of millenarian groups. But it is hard, as we shall see, to find very many apocalypses which clearly point to such authors. Quite the opposite, in fact. The assumption that the political establishment, being in favour of the status quo is therefore anti-'apocalyptic' or anti-visionary is rather simplistic. Appeal to esoteric knowledge, heavenly revelation and the use of myth are all equally, if not more, characteristic of the methods by which ruling cliques justify their status and exercise ideological control. Both Daniel and the Qumran community deny the dichotomy of Plöger and Hanson: they seem to have combined quite harmoniously a reverence for the 'established' priesthood and cult with a strong belief in an imminent eschaton; a reverence equally for prophecy and cultic legalism. Both more probably arise from *inner-'establishment' disputes*. There is absolutely no hint that Daniel is the product of a fringe; its opposition is only to the Seleucid monarchy; its writers are most probably aristocratic, even priestly, scribes. There are further substantial criticisms of Plöger's hypothesis in particular, to which we shall return presently.

In his classic *Judaism and Hellenism*, Hengel (1974) developed Plöger's thesis in a different direction. He minimised the link between prophecy and apocalyptic and emphasised the plurality of influences which were at work.

On the other hand, he tried to build a good deal on Plöger's shaky foundations by identifying the *Hasidim* with the ancestors of the Essene movement which, in his view, are the same as the Qumran community. These views were not widely disputed at the time, although they have since aroused considerable doubt. The attraction of Hengel's basic equations and the explanation which he built upon them was that he could identify as the 'bearers of apocalyptic' a community that could be socially identified and described. The way was open, at any rate, for a detailed description of the 'First Climax of Jewish Apocalyptic' (I, 175). For Hengel, as for Rowley, the impact of the 'Hellenistic reform' was paramount, though the analysis was this time rather more profound. Persecution led to a new interpretation of history, a calculation of the time of the end, a concentration on the decision of the individual. Sociologically, the 'apocalyptic' groups were characterised by strict adherence to the law (in the face of the Hellenisers' laxity) and a stress on penitence. Rejection of the entire post-exilic establishment took the form of denial that any restoration had taken place. Hengel's contribution is perhaps greatest in his appreciation of the wider connections of this earliest Jewish 'apocalyptic climax': he accepts the influence of Israelite prophecy but also of Iranian and Babylonian mythology and Greek Orphic ideas. In particular, he recognises very clearly the stress on revealed wisdom and instruction in the earliest Jewish apocalyptic literature, and correctly observes that in this literature 'the wise men acquired prophetic features, and the prophets became inspired wise men'. What he did not declare unequivocally (though he may have assented to the view) was that the mixture of prophecy and wisdom was characteristic of the Second Temple period generally, from the time that the Chronicler 'levitised' prophets until Ben Sira claimed the gift of prophecy and the wise man Daniel became a prophet to his interpreters.

Hengel gives a marvellously detailed and nuanced description of the multifaceted character of Jewish apocalyptic writing in the Maccabean era. But because of his rather narrow view of the social context, he has to allow 'new developments and alien influences in Essene teaching' (228) such as the intellectualisation of piety, dualism (from Iran), the idea of the 'plans of God' (i.e. determinism), angelology, interest in the stars and sun as indicators of a rational cosmic order, astrology, and manticism/magic. These characteristics are indeed foremost in apocalyptic literature; moreover, Hengel can illustrate them all from the Qumran literature. But that by itself does not suggest that the Essenes were the sole, or even the main, carrier of all these traditions. Rather, the traditions may well have formed part of the common Jewish repertoire. The sophistication of Hengel's description contrasts oddly with the naivety of his 'Hasidim–Essene' thesis. Let us therefore dispose now of some of the building blocks, including Plöger's (for detailed argumentation, see P. Davies: 1977). Examination of all of the brief references to *Hasidim* fails (a) to demonstrate that they were a clearly-defined group, and (b) to reconstruct any distinctive ideology, for according to 1 Macc. they participated in armed resistance (and were remembered for their prowess), and were 'devoted to the law'. Like Judas Maccabee they also sought peace with Alcimus. The rest of Plöger's characterisation (of which there is much) is pure invention. Nothing about these reports suggests any connection with the book of Daniel or with the Essenes. Finally, (c) although the Qumran community read and copied apocalypses like Enoch and Daniel, they do not seem to have composed them, (we could add that to equate all Essenes with the Qumran community looks increasingly unlikely: see below). We must face the fact that Rowley, Plöger, Hanson and Hengel took us a long way, but up the wrong road. Let us retrace our steps and follow another avenue.

b. Manticism

The derivation of 'apocalyptic' from 'prophecy' which was almost universally accepted twenty years ago was challenged (not for the first time; see Hölscher: 1919) by G. von Rad (1965). Well-directed as the assault was, it shared one failing of its target: it used the language of theological categories rather than of literary genres or social institutions. Von Rad's proposal to link 'apocalyptic' with 'wisdom' failed to convince not only because of the inertia of prejudice but because his definition of 'wisdom' created almost as many problems as had prophecy: the accepted setting of 'wisdom' was the court-based worldly instruction of Proverbs, based on observation and deduction, and promoting social order. But there is another sort of 'wisdom' represented in the Old Testament – that of the Egyptian and Babylonian 'wise men' and their Israelite counterparts Joseph and Daniel. This 'wisdom', widely attested in the ancient Near East but especially Mesopotamian literature, comprised knowledge derived from omens which had to be deciphered by those proficient in the esoteric rules of interpretation, the most common being the examination of animal entrails. To this art/science H.-P. Müller (1971) gave the name 'mantic wisdom' and demonstrated that it provided the key element in the background of Daniel. The recent resurgence of interest in the books of Enoch – touched off by the discoveries of fragments at Qumran published by Milik – has confirmed that the Enoch tradition must be traced back to Babylonian manticism; indeed, the placing of Enoch in the Genesis genealogy made him the counterpart of the ancestor of Babylonian mantic wisdom, Enmeduranki (see now VanderKam: 1984). Thus emerges a common cultural-social denominator for both Enoch and Daniel, suggesting that in the general *Weltenschauung* of the Babylonian mantics a firmer basis for understanding the rationale of apocalypses might be available. Although no formal account of the theory behind Mesopotamian manticism was ever left by its practitioners, we can enumerate the following elements (Wilson: 1980, 91; see also VanderKam: 1984). (1) Perception (perhaps 'conception'?) of all human experience as forming an 'interlocking totality', which made the associations of phenomena significant and potentially predictive. By cataloguing all instances of associations (such as a comet or an abnormal birth with a subsequent plague, assassination, military defeat) the recurrence of the omen could be interpreted as predictive of the subsequent event. Nothing that happens, then, is independent; the future is in principle discoverable through the application of the diviner's knowledge to the reading of signs. (2) Natural and supernatural reality are interrelated; the gods are implicated in human history. Natural events are the outcome of divine decisions, and concomitantly a clue to deciphering these intentions. Putting both these principles together, Wilson observes that since in principle any natural occurrence could be an omen, the accumulation of knowledge of 'natural science' is necessary for understanding all reality, including supernatural. This mantic lore is based on observation and the main difference between it and the court wisdom is that its knowledge includes the doings and decisions of the gods which can be deduced through the interpretation of the natural phenomena.

Here we had better meet an obvious objection. Mantic activity is surely cultic, not scribal; are not its practitioners priests rather than scribes or 'wise men'? The reply is as follows. (1) The interpreters of omens are depicted in Jewish apocalyptic literature (and the Joseph story) as 'wise men', not priests. (2) The two groups were not entirely mutually exclusive, and in any case their concerns overlapped considerably in Second Temple Judaism, embracing legal interpretation and cultic behaviour. (3) While mantic practice is a cultic activity, the recording of mantic lore and the pursuit of knowledge fundamental to it is scribal. It is from the study of mantic *lore*, not from its *practice*, that apocalyptic literature develops. This last point will be elaborated shortly.

If the connection of scribes with apocalypses is not yet clear, consider the feats of interpretation in Daniel: dreams and wall-writing are signs with a meaning from the god(s) which the wise man can decipher. The Babylonian 'wise men' (to use a convenient rendering) were expected to have the ability too, but not by divine inspiration, rather by the training which Daniel himself underwent (ch. 1). Thus, Dan. 2 puts the hero among a particular class of mantic. The biblical 'prophecy' in Dan. 9 is 'interpreted' like an omen. It is an earthly phenomenon, a written text, but has a meaning about the supernaturally determined course of history, the true meaning being given not to the prophet (who merely supplies the omen) but the mantic sage, whose inspired wisdom provides the decipherment. But did the Babylonian mantics (or their scribes) write apocalypses? Scholars do call certain texts 'Akkadian apocalypses' (Ringgren: 1983). They are not generically apocalypses, however, despite the name given to them, and some scholars prefer the term 'Akkadian prophecies' (e.g. Grayson and Lambert). Some of these are *vaticinia ex eventu*, 'predicting' the quality and length of the reigns of 'future' kings. They offer a parallel to Daniel 11, which also provides a sequence of political events in the form of a prediction. There is a text (Grayson and Lambert) in which a king speaks in the first person, as in Dan. 4 (though the editors overlook the similarity). The parallels with Enoch material, referred to earlier, are thoroughly discussed by VanderKam (1984). In short, there is a broad range of literary and conceptual parallels between Babylonian mantic literature and the books of Daniel and Enoch. The parallels are not only more striking than any offered from Old Testament prophecy, but they also imply a particular and identifiable social group as authors of the literature and transmitters of its contents.

However, while the eponyms of both Enoch and Daniel are mantic scribes (recipients of secrets but also authors), the authors and transmitters of the contents of the books are not 'mantic' in the sense of practitioners or writers of omen lists. Their literature, however, reflects a *world-view determined by the premisses and devices of manticism*. How is this? J. Z. Smith (1975) draws attention to the Babylonian priest Berossus, who wrote his *Babyloniaka* during the Seleucid period. According to Smith, Berossus was a member of the Babylonian intellectual elite whose interests were (103) 'astronomy, astrology, mathematics, historiography and the recovery of archaic ritual lore . . . These Babylonian intellectuals . . . stood in continuity with ancient Babylonian scribalism, and unbroken tradition from the Sumerian period to the sages of the Babylonian Talmud.' In this milieu Smith sees the link between scribalism and apocalyptic literature. Both, Smith argues (115) 'depend on the relentless quest for paradigms, the problematics of applying these paradigms to new situations and the *Listenwissenschaft* which are the characteristic activities of the Near Eastern scribe'. Smith also notes, as have others, that Egyptian scribalism too produces apocalypses, such as the Potter's Oracle and the Demotic Chronicle.

The social background of apocalyptic writing thus furnished is more fully described and precisely documented by the activity of politically 'establishment' and culturally cosmopolitan *scribes* than of visionary 'counter-establishment' *conventicles*. To paraphrase a well-known dictum, 'manticism is the mother of Jewish "apocalyptic"'; what determines the production of apocalyptic literature is not a millenarian posture nor a predicament of persecution, though these may be contributory factors. It is scribal convention.

Scholarship has offered, then, two matrices for the origin and development of apocalyptic writing in Jewish Palestine (or in the Jewish Diaspora, for that matter). These have sometimes been labelled as 'prophecy' and 'wisdom', but such terms are simplistic as well as inappropriate for social description. The real argument is about peripheral versus central, conventicle versus open, parochial versus cosmopolitan. Our discussion has no doubt indicated the balance of probability as we see it. We should, of course, remember (1) that manticism and prophecy are by no means mutually exclusive, even in the period of 'classical prophecy' (see VanderKam 1986); (2) the character of much exilic and post-exilic 'prophecy' makes the term 'prophet' problematic insofar as it implies a continuity of the pre-exilic institution (if there were such an institution, that is); (3) the preservation and augmentation of prophetic literature in the Second Temple period lay, of course, within the orbit of scribal activity; (4) there may be discernible a plausible development from the prophetic vision to the apocalyptic vision, from, say, Amos to Daniel via Zechariah (Niditch) – but is this development not explicable as a result of the influence of manticism upon earlier prophetic forms? It remains dubious that 'prophetic' explains 'apocalyptic'.

But does the mantic 'culture' explain our Jewish apocalypses? And what social or ideological profile do we have of the Jewish scribe of the Hellenistic period when Jewish apocalypses first appear? To answer, or begin to answer these questions we had better turn to Ben Sira. He is universally accepted as having been typical of the Jerusalem scribal establishment, moderate, conventionally pious, well-off (for the social profile, see Hengel I, 131–53). We shall concentrate on the 'apocalyptic' element in his profile, which has almost universally been overlooked, even denied. (Indeed, Ben Sira was often cited *against* von Rad's connection of 'wisdom' with 'apocalyptic'). This element, however, is clearly enough documented in the book (see Orton: 1987). First is the prominence he accords to Enoch in the famous catalogue of famous men: Enoch is mentioned twice (44.16; 49.14). One may also observe the 'oddly cryptic' (Orton, 74) mentions of Joseph, and especially Shem, Seth and Adam, 'suggestive of some esoteric *sous-entendre* that may have been intelligible to certain scribes'. The almost equally famous description of the model scribe (39.1–11) includes not merely study of the law and the preservation of the discourse of ancient men, nor even appearing before rulers and travelling abroad, but also 'seeking out the wisdom of the ancients' and the 'hidden meanings of proverbs', the 'obscurities of parables'. Ben Sira concludes with the following sentiment:

> If the great Lord is willing
> he will be filled with the spirit of understanding;
> he will pour forth words of wisdom
> and give thanks to the Lord in prayer
> He will direct his counsel and knowledge aright,
> and meditate on his secrets,

The preoccupation with understanding hidden things, secrets, often preserved by the ancients, by means of a 'spirit of understanding' does not confine Ben Sira to teaching the law or tutoring in etiquette. The range of the ideal scribe's interests coincides reasonably well with those of the Seleucid scribal schools described by Smith. The centrality of Jewish law in Ben Sira nevertheless indicates that for the Jewish scribe the law revealed by God to Moses took the place of the catalogues of omens which formed the canon of the Babylonian scribe. The comparison is not fanciful: the notion of the scriptures containing hidden truth which inspired study could unlock is not found only in Daniel, Qumran and the New Testament but provides the basic rationale of rabbinic exegesis (Tigay). But this line of investigation takes us further than necessary. Only if eschatology is made a *sine qua non* of apocalyptic literature can Ben Sira be excluded from the circles whose interests appear reflected in apocalypses.

To look more closely at social context of actual apocalypses, one has to examine them individually; apocalypses cannot be assumed to have any definitive purpose or audience. In the case of Daniel, eschatology – absent from Ben Sira's concerns – may seem to be a decisive characteristic. But only the hint of an eschatological resurrection and judgement separates this book from its obviously scribal ancestry. The four apocalypses of Daniel, appended to a cycle of court-tales which extol the virtues of the adopted Jewish mantic, draw most of their inspiration either from the tales or from mantic-scribal conventions and interests, such as the 'plot' of history in the sequence of world-kingdoms (ch. 7), the hidden meaning of ancient books (ch. 9), the pseudo-predictions of political events (chs. 10–12), and ancient mythical motifs. More dramatically, the influence in Daniel's symbolism of the Babylonian mantic catalogues such as the *šumma izbu* series has been demonstrated by P. A. Porter (1983). All these features merely confirm what the book itself says about its authors: they are *maskilim*, undoubtedly scribal leaders and teachers. Nothing suggests they form a split-off group, nor that they are hostile to the 'establishment' – the Temple or its cult, whose defilement so dominates the apocalyptic chapters. In a time of unprecedented and incomprehensible events, these scribal leaders of the people – the intellectual and religious elite – offered an explanation of the times using the techniques of their own scribal traditions, plus traditional tales of a mantic hero which they themselves re-interpreted. They adopted or adapted the apocalyptic genre not only because it blended well with the milieu created by the tales of chs. 1–6, but because it was a scribal form. Its application to the teaching and consolation of the people rather than as an inner-scribal game, which it may originally have been, can also be seen in the literature collected in the corpus known as 1 Enoch.

Adopted or adapted? Created or developed? 1 Enoch contains material older than Daniel. The most ancient section is now generally held to be the Astronomical Book, 72–80. It is an attempt to explain the workings of the cosmos through the medium of a narrative in which Enoch is guided through heaven by an angel – perhaps our earliest extant Jewish apocalypse; but its purpose is probably the same as much of Old Testament wisdom: to demonstrate the order with which the universe has been created. Some of the demonstration is based on correct observation, some on an *a priori* scheme. One important demonstration is the lack of symmetry between sun and moon. Since God made these two as 'signs' (Genesis 1), their independence from each other is a problem. The moon governs the months, the sun the days – and the seasons. Therefore the moon is in error, moving contrary to the divine plan. The year which this treatise describes is not one of twelve lunar months (which would distort the seasons) but 364 days, a solar year (more or less). The plausible *Sitz im Leben* for this erudite yet speculative discourse is an intellectual one: the scribal profession, whose interest in astronomical observation (cf. Matthew's magi) is well-attested, and whose interest in the natural world (including heavenly objects) is evident throughout the ancient Near East. In a Jewish context, however, since heavens dictate calendar and calendar dictates cult, astronomical observation can be easily connected with religious schism – as the later parts of 1 Enoch reveal.

Interest in the heavenly phenomena in this text is not wholly dispassionate. The lack of complete order in creation cannot be simply accepted. Men must in the meantime ignore the moon, but God must, in time, restore his original system. The present anomaly will obtain only 'until the new creation' (72.1). This hint at the eschaton has been considerably developed at the close, where further disruption in the heavens is predicted, with effects like the shortening of the day. Wickedness in the earth will also increase. We noted earlier the mantic correlation between human and divine worlds, so that disorders in one created, or attested, events in the other. Here too heavenly and human disorder are connected, but the connection is now ethical, while in Daniel 10–12 it is political (angels representing nations fight in heaven for world supremacy).

The Apocalypse of Weeks (93.1–10+91.11–17), originally an independent composition, is also represented as the content of a revelation given to Enoch and passed on to his children. The interest moves from astronomy to history, classification takes the form of periodisation and interest in calendrical matters is extended to the formation of a world-calendar: time is segmented into ten 'weeks' – discrete units displaying an individual and collective structure. The author appears to be situated in the seventh, in a time of maximum wickedness but at the dawn of progressive improvement leading to a reconstruction of creation. Daniel's periodisation of history is slightly different – seventy weeks of years – but this is inspired by a biblical prophecy, which also obliges it to commence with the Babylonian captivity. The Melchizedek fragments from Qumran have a calendrical system which gives ten jubilees, probably the same total as Daniel's 490 years. The calculations do not always agree on the starting point (creation or exile) or the total time. But such a calendar implies an end of history.

Another concern of 1 Enoch is answered by heavenly revelation: the origin and nature of sin. This theme further illustrates the fact that Jewish scribes in the second century BCE (and Ben Sira can be included) were grappling increasingly with a religious crisis as they saw it: an increasing lack of moral order in their society. Was this provoked by Israel? Or Gentiles? One scribal answer was that it was ultimately preordained and brought about by disorder in heaven – though this view was not unanimous even in 1 Enoch, and Ben Sira resisted it, although giving more than one answer himself.

Some variations between 1 Enoch, Daniel and 11QMelch are sociologically significant. In the 'Apocalypse of Weeks' the preservation of a righteous group, the true 'Israel' (a definition which *might* characterise a sect) is foreseen – it is presumably already in existence. In Daniel the *maskilim* form a distinct group, but not a sect. In 11 QMelch the picture is not clear: the redemption of all Israel may be implied, though some dualistic language (Melchizedek has a *goral*, a 'lot', 'party') may suggest a sectarian mentality – perhaps the fragments represent a Qumranic revision of an earlier composition. Clearly, however, from the early second century

BCE at least we have indications of sectarianism within the apocalyptic literature. The issues involved are calendrical, as we have seen, but also halakhic, as Jubilees and other non-apocalyptic but related works (the Temple Scroll, the Damascus Document) show. Much of the halakhah concerns Temple cult. Priestly concerns are evident in these issues: priestly does not necessarily mean non-scribal! As yet we cannot draw a sketch, let alone paint a picture, of the development of Second Temple sectarianism, but, while the apocalyptic literature affords us some access to the process, it only reveals the extent to which the scribal profession was involved. While other professions or groups might have been involved, such involvement remains to be demonstrated and the bulk of *literary* evidence relates to scribes – which is, of course, rather to be expected!

Our next question is: to what *extent* does the extant Jewish apocalyptic literature reflect social/religious schism? It seems that the authors did not belong to exclusive groups, but regarded themselves as responsible to the nation as a whole (this is apparently also the view of Collins 1977, 191–224). But in the second century BCE apocalypses nonetheless reflect social-religious divisions, no doubt because these divisions became threatening of national unity. Reid (1983) has sought to identify the 'apocalypse of Weeks' and the 'Animal Apocalypse' with 'a community of a rising élite which often offers material gain as a reward for membership' and which he defines as a 'utopian community' (156). The analysis of Reid is suggestive but perhaps suffers from importing too much sociological theory into too little text. The social background of the 'Epistle of Enoch' has been investigated more cautiously by Nickelsburg (1982; 1983). His conclusion is that the Epistle highlights a tension between two groups (e.g. 'sinners' and 'righteous'), the former powerful and oppressing the latter. The former are also accused of religious apostasy. Nickelsburg notes parallels with some of the Qumran literature (especially CD), but also differences. He regards Enoch 92–105, the 'Animal Apocalypse' and CD as products of a 'common religious movement, probably proliferated in its sociology' (1983, 645). He also suggests that the Epistle might be called 'pre-Essene' (1982, 347).

This last suggestion reminds us of the conclusions of Hengel, for whom, as we saw, the Essenes were the 'bearers of apocalyptic'. Like Nickelsburg, he identifies the Essenes with the Qumran community and identifies a 'pre-Essene'' 'movement' – which, as we have seen, he identifies as *Hasidim*. Since the *Hasidim* theory (which was also accepted by Stegemann) is now discredited, we ought to mention the theory of Murphy-O'Connor that the Essenes originate with immigrants from Babylon in the third or second century BCE. The Babylonian origin of the Astronomical Book of Enoch has been proposed by VanderKam (1984, ch. 4), and significant agreements between the Epistle of Enoch, Jubilees and the Damascus Document have been drawn up (Davies: 1987, 107ff). Is it possible, as Murphy-O'Connor argues, that a group from the diaspora immigrated to Palestine, and that their ideological and halakhic differences led to proselytising and then to opposition and finally withdrawal into separate communities? Since much (not necessarily most) of the apocalyptic literature is connected in some way with Essenes, the origin and history of this movement is presumably a major element in the social context. However, it must be repeated that the apocalypses we have been reviewing are not the product of clearly schismatic groups; they do, on the other hand, give us insight into scribal disputes which, no doubt, led to the formation of Pharisees and Sadducees – and no doubt others.

Nevertheless, although apocalypses predate the period, the effects of the so-called 'Hellenistic reform' and the ensuing warfare can be seen in the apocalyptic literature. Not only the history and laws of the Jewish people were under threat, but, in the view of the scribes (or some scribes) the order of creation which the Jewish God sustained. Recognising their role as the (acknowledged) divinely-appointed teachers of the people, these scribes applied their traditional skills (literary in particular) to articulating an explanation of the chaos of their own society (and the world at large), and this they did by, among other things, predicting a radical change in the future course of history. Such changes in history had long been the bread-and-butter of mantic prediction or pseudo-prediction, but in the apocalypses written in the 'Hellenistic crisis' we find the articulation of a once-for-all reversal of the decline of creation. By means of the authority of ancient figures bearing divine revelations they consoled their flock with the assurance that God was in control of both history and nature; that evil had a rational explanation and an imminent end. Among these explanations we find some with a basically identical analysis and vocabulary, and others which adopt different perspectives (e.g. the 'Apocalypse of Weeks' is militant, Daniel pacific). There is no one 'apocalyptic group', though a *literary* 'apocalyptic movement' at this time might be imagined. But we must recognise that the *genre* of apocalypse was not created *by* a situation but adapted *for* a situation.

Thus far we have discussed only the origins and background of apocalypses in the third–second century BCE. It is interesting that few apocalypses appear again until after 70 CE (the 'Similitudes of Enoch' is only possibly from this era), though we do get testaments, e.g. the Testament of Moses) – when again Ezra and Baruch, both scribes, are the eponyms. Much of what has been said already applies here too: these works are not from or for a sectarian group, not millenarian; they are, again, provoked by questions to which the traditional answerer of questions, the scribe, must respond. The re-use of the apocalypse genre was perhaps prompted by the precedent of Daniel (as in the book of Revelation). And here, moreover, the readers were not being addressed in the heat of persecution but some time afterwards. The tone of 4 Ezra in particular can be described as *academic*; not only has it a 'question-and-answer routine', but it addresses an 'academic question' in the colloquial sense: all is lost – can anything be retrieved? The author was apparently too much of an academic even to give an unambiguous answer! But the need for some intellectual consolation is clearly addressed. The book is quite obviously a scribal *tour de force* (or *tour de faiblesse*, depending on one's judgement). Both it and 2 Baruch are apparently from within 'mainstream' Judaism (Collins: 1984, 169 n. 45).

On the other hand, the book of Revelation speaks from a different perspective; persecution there seems to be, and in response the hope of imminent and glorious vindication. Gager (1975, 49–57) has no hesitation in treating it as a 'millenarian' text. There is, of course, no reason why an apocalypse should not be written for a millenarian group or groups. But if this is the case with Revelation, the book is an exception to the norm. And, from the generic point of view, the 'Apocalypse' is not a pure example of the genre. It represents itself as a 'revelation' (*apokalypsis*) but its nature as prophetic ('predictive'? Or 'like Old Testament prophecy'?). That its *Sitz im Leben* is persecution seems a reasonable conclusion, but we can infer little else from this idiosyncratic product of an individualistic writer.

Finally, we should note non-Palestinian Jewish apocalypses. The background of the Sibylline Oracles is, of course, also mantic, though not Mesopotamian but Egyptian. According to Collins (1984, 94) 'there was a tradition of prophecy in Egypt which looked for the restoration of native Egyptian rule and the demise of the Greeks'. He refers to the Demotic Chronicle and the Potter's Oracle. The circumstances were not dissimilar in Palestine, where we also find establishment reaction to political oppression, using mantic scribal traditions. Taking our investigations further into the Mediterranean and Near Eastern world we should find the same: 'apocalyptic' is a literary function with an immediate *cultural* context (mantic-scribal), often a *political* (anti-Hellenistic, nationalistic), and a number of *social* contexts – inner-scribal *Listenwissenschaft*, polemics (Jubilees, Epistle of Enoch), social-religious encouragement to the populace (Daniel) consolation (4 Ezra), enthusiastic moral fortification of a millenarian group (Revelation). To rescue the term both from theological dogmatics and amateur sociology is a long overdue task, but the omens are favourable that research presently underway, especially into the society of Second Temple Palestine, will greatly elaborate the necessarily very sketchy portrait given here.

Bibliography

Ahlström, G. W., 1986. *Who were the Israelites?*, Winona Lake: Eisenbrauns.

Blenkinsopp, J., 1981. 'Interpretation and the Tendency to Sectarianism: An Aspect of Second Temple History', in E. P. Sanders and A. Mendelsohn (eds), *Jewish and Christian Self-Definition*, London: SCM/Philadelphia: Fortress, 1–26, 299–309.

Charles, R. H., 1913. 'Book of Enoch', in Charles (ed), *Apocrypha and Pseudepigrapha of the Old Testament* II, Oxford: Clarendon Press, 163–277.

Collins, J. J., 1977. *The Apocalyptic Vision of the Book of Daniel*, Missoula: Scholars Press.

1979. (ed.), *Apocalypse: The Morphology of a Genre*. (*Semeia* 14), Missoula: Scholars Press.

1984. *The Apocalyptic Imagination*, New York: Crossroad.

1986. 'Apocalyptic Literature', in Kraft and Nickelsburg (eds), 345–70.

Coote, R. B. and Whitelam, K. W., 1987. *The Emergence of Early Israel in Historical Perspective*, Sheffield: Almond Press.

Davies, G. I., 1978. 'Apocalyptic and Historiography', *JSOT* 5, 15–28.

Davies, P. R., 1977. 'Hasidim in the Maccabean Period', *JJS* 28, 127–40.

1987. *Behind the Essenes*. Atlanta: Scholars Press.

Frick, F. S., 1986. 'Social Science Methods and Theories of Significance for the Study of the Israelite Monarchy: A Critical Review Essay', *Semeia* 37, 9–52.

Gager, J. G., 1975. *Kingdom and Community: The Social World of Early Christianity*, Englewood Cliffs, NJ: Prentice-Hall.

Gottwald, N. K., 1979. *The Tribes of Yahweh*. Maryknoll: Orbis/London: SCM.

Grayson, A. K. and Lambert, W. G., 1964. 'Akkadian Prophecies', *JCS* 18, 7–30.

Hanson, P. D., 1975. *The Dawn of Apocalyptic*, Philadelphia: Fortress.

Hanson, P. D., 1976. 'Apocalypticism' in *Interpreter's Dictionary of the Bible, Supplementary Volume*. Nashville: Abingdon, 30–31.

1983. (ed.), *Visionaries and their Apocalypses*, London: SPCK/Philadelphia: Fortress.

1985. 'Apocalyptic Literature', in D. A. Knight and G. M. Tucker (eds.), *The Hebrew Bible and its Modern Interpreters*, Philadelphia: Fortress/Chico: Scholars Press, 465–88.

Hellholm, D., 1983. (ed.), *Apocalypticism in the Mediterranean World and the Near East*, Tübingen: Mohr-Siebeck.

Hengel, M., 1974. *Judaism and Hellenism*, London: SCM.

Hölscher, G., 1919. 'Die Entstehung des Buches Daniel', *TSK* 92, 113–39.

Hopkins, D., 1986. *The Highlands of Canaan*, Sheffield: Almond Press.

Isenberg, S. R., 1974. 'Millenarianism in Greco-Roman Palestine', *Religion* 4, 26–46.

Kee, H. C., 1977. *Community of the New Age*, Philadelphia: Fortress.

Koch, K., 1972. *The Rediscovery of Apocalyptic*, London: SCM.

Kraft, R. A. and Nickelsburg, G. W. E., 1986. (eds.), *Early Judaism and its Modern Interpreters*, Philadelphia: Fortress/Atlanta: Scholars Press.

Kvanvig, H. 1988. *Roots of Apocalyptic: The Mesopotamian Background of the Enoch Figure and of the Son of Man* (Wissenschaftliche Monographien zum Alten und Neuen Testament, 61), Neukirchen: Neukirchener Verlag.

Milik, J. T., 1976. *The Books of Enoch*, Oxford: Clarendon.

Müller, H.-P., 1972. 'Mantische Weisheit und Apokalyptik', *VT Supp 22*, Leiden: Brill, 268–93.

Murphy-O'Connor, J., 1974. 'The Essenes and their History', *RB* 81, 215–44.

Nicholson, E. W., 1979. 'Apocalyptic', in G. W. Anderson (ed.), *Tradition and Interpretation, Essays by Members of the Society for Old Testament Study*, Oxford: Clarendon, 189–213.

Nickelsburg, G. W. E., 1982. 'The Epistle of Enoch and the Qumran Literature', *JJS* 33, 333–48.

1983. 'Social Aspects of Palestinian Jewish Apocalypticism', in Hellholm (ed.), 1983.

Niditch, S., 1983. *The Symbolic Vision in Biblical Tradition*, Chico: Scholars Press.

Orton, D., 1987. *The Scribes and Matthew: A Comparative Study of Perception of the Scribe in the First Gospel in the Light of Intertestamental and Early Jewish Literature*, Ph.D. Dissertation, University of Sheffield.

Plöger, O., 1968. *Theocracy and Eschatology*, Oxford: Blackwell.

Porter, P. A., 1983. *Metaphors and Monsters*, Lund: CWK Gleerup.

Rad, G. von, 1965. *Old Testament Theology*, Edinburgh: Oliver & Boyd.

Reid, S. B., 1983. '1 Enoch: The Rising Elite of the Apocalyptic Movement', *SBL Seminar Papers 1983*, 147–56.

Ringgren, H., 1983. 'Akkadian Apoacalypses' in Hellholm (ed), 379–86.

Rowland, C., 1982. *The Open Heaven: A Study of Apocalyptic in Judaism and Christianity*, London, SPCK/New York: Crossroad.

Rowley, H. H., 1963. *The Relevance of Apocalyptic*, London: Lutterworth, (rev. edition).

Russell, D. S., 1964. *The Method and Message of Jewish Apocalyptic*, London: SCM.

Sanders, E. P., 1983. 'The Genre of Palestinian Jewish Apocalypses', in Hellholm (ed.), 447–60.

Smith, J. Z., 1975. 'Wisdom and Apocalyptic', in B. A. Pearson (ed.), *Religious Syncretism in Antiquity*, Missoula: Scholars Press.

Smith, M., 1983. 'On the History of APOKALYPTO and APOKALYPSIS' in Hellholm (ed.), 9–20.

1961. 'The Dead Sea Sect in Relation to Ancient Judaism', *NTS* 7, 347–60.

Stegemann, H., 1971. *Die Entstehung der Qumrangemeinde*, Bonn: privately published.

Stone, M. E., 1982. *Scriptures, Sects and Visions*, Oxford: Blackwell.

1976. Lists of Revealed Things in the Apocalyptic Literature', Cross, F. M. & Lemche, W. E. (ed.), *Magnalia Dei: The Mighty Acts of God*, 414–52.

1978. 'The Book of Enoch and Judaism in the Third Century BCE', *CBQ* 40, 479–92.

Tigay, J., 1983. 'An Early Technique of Aggadic Exegesis', in Tadmor, H. and Weinfeld, M. (ed), *History, Historiography and Interpretation: Studies in Biblical and Cuneiform Literatures*, Jerusalem: Magnes Press, 169–89.

VanderKam, J. C., 1984. *Enoch and the Growth of an Apocalyptic Tradition*, Washington: CBA.

1986. 'The Prophetic- Sapiential Origins of Apocalyptic Thought', in Martin, J. D. and Davies, P. R. (eds.), *A Word in Season, Essays in Honour of William McKane*, Sheffield: JSOT Press, 163–76.

Vielhauer, P., 1965. 'Apocalypses and Related Subjects', Hennecke and Schneemelcher (eds.), *New Testament Apocrypha*, London: SCM/Philadelphia: Westminster, II, 581–607.

Wilson, B., 1973. *Magic and Millennium*, London: Harper & Row.

Wilson, R. R., 1980. *Prophecy and Society in Ancient Israel*, Philadelphia: Fortress.

Fuller bibliographies in Collins 1984; 1986, Hanson 1985.

PART IV

Ideas and ideals

CHAPTER THIRTEEN

Holiness and cult

PHILIP J. BUDD

1. Early trends

The laws on holiness and cult in the Old Testament have long posed problems for interpreters. In the pre-critical period it was common for allegorical, confessional, and homiletic interests to dominate – see, for example, the suggestions cited in Matthew Henry's commentary (Henry: 1708/1960, 124) on Lev. 11.1–8:

> We must not be filthy nor wallow in the mire as swine, nor be timorous and faint-hearted as hares, nor dwell in the earth as rabbits; let not man that is in honour make himself like these beasts that perish.

The development of critical and historical study in the nineteenth century seemed to offer the possibility of new, more consistent, and better informed insight into the meaning of the biblical texts. In particular an increasing awareness of cultic procedures in other ancient cultures provided a wider context within which more detached and academically serious study could proceed. The developing disciplines of social anthropology were an essential tool for the task.

W. Robertson Smith was by no means the founding father of modern middle-eastern anthropology, but he has probably been one of its most influential exponents, particularly in matters relating to holiness and cult, and the interpretation of these phenomena in the Old Testament (cf. Smith: 1889). At the heart of his research was the identification of 'survivals' – religious phenomena which persist in later sources, and which provide the key clues to discovering the beginnings of religious observance. He maintained that the rules governing conduct at sanctuaries were survivals of primitive ideas of holiness, in effect of *taboos*. This concept of holiness does not denote an inherent purity, ethical or otherwise, nor does it have an exclusive reference to relationships with deities. It denotes rather a natural life possessed by holy things which men interfere with at their peril. As applied to gods and sanctuaries the point is not so much that holy things are the property of the god, set apart for his use, but that they are charged with a divine and dangerous energy for which electricity provides a useful metaphor (Smith: 1889, 151).

The same interest in the original ideas from which more sophisticated understandings grow and develop is evident in Robertson Smith's interpretation of sacrifice. He maintained that the earliest evidence about sacrifice suggests, not a gift or tribute offered to the god as E. B. Tylor had previously argued (Tylor: 1871), but a communion meal in which both parties, the god and the worshippers, participate. The sacramental language should not obscure the primitive *totemistic* procedures that Robertson Smith envisaged here – 'the conveyance of the living blood to the godhead, and the absorption of the living flesh and blood into the flesh and blood of the worshippers' (Smith: 1889, 339). An atoning power, which does away with any alienation or estrangement between the god and the community, is also recognised (Smith: 1889, 320). Thus this theory of sacrifice fits in well with Robertson Smith's fundamental beliefs about gods as fully integrated members of primitive societies, and about the importance of religion in such contexts as an expression of kinship and social cohesion.

There is much in Robertson Smith's work, both substantially and methodologically, which modern anthropologists would wish to reject. Few would deny that there are some historical processes which may reasonably be described as evolutionary, but Robertson Smith's overall interpretative framework, involving a progress from 'savage religion' through 'the higher heathenism' to the 'positive religions' (Judaism, Christianity, and Islam), is too simple and too rigid to account adequately for all the data. There is a serious risk that the presuppositional framework controls the data with respect both to their selection and interpretation. It may well influence the process by which phenomena are identified as 'survivals', while the assumptions about 'primitive' and 'sophisticated' mentalities introduce value judgements which would widely be considered inappropriate. In the comparative studies there is also a tendency to lift material from its distinctive social context, and to ignore the peculiarities of *independent* cultural progress in different societies (cf. Rogerson: 1978, 22–45 for a review of influence and criticisms).

Yet for several reasons Robertson Smith's studies constitute a major development of continuing importance. As well as insisting that Israelite views of holiness and cult cannot be understood in isolation from the wider religious world, he had also a perceptive awareness of the socially cohesive function of ancient ritual, which led him at the outset to make that, rather than myth, the priority for study. The first concern must be to study institutions and how they shaped lives, not beliefs in isolation. There are also striking insights of a politico-economic nature, tracing key religious developments to the appearance of monarchy (Smith, 1889: p. 74), and identifying the emergence of property relations as a crucial factor in the development of new ideas about holiness and of the gift theory of sacrifice (Smith: 1889, pp. 391–92). What he failed to recognise was that these same or similar material influences need to be considered in relation to the so-called 'positive' or 'spiritual' religions.

The earliest critical approaches to social anthropology, of which Robertson Smith's work is a good example, opened up possibilities in various directions.

(1) In the first place the comparative studies could be extended, and the evolutionistic perspective consolidated. It was J. G. Frazer who engaged in this task, amassing a much greater range of comparative material, from well beyond the Semitic world (Frazer: 1922). In relation to holiness (1922: 223–4) and sacrifice (1922: 447–94) the material was handled somewhat unsystematically, but the evidence gathered was generally interpreted in a manner consonant with the conclusions of Robertson Smith. M. F. C. Bourdillon (1980) finds in Frazer a theory of sacrifice involving the ritual control of death; most sacrifices arise from a concern to find a substitute for the killing of the divine king. Frazer's work on the Old Testament exhibits the same interest in identifying survivals as the clue to understanding the beginnings and subsequent development of Israel's religious practice and belief (Frazer: 1919).

Frazer's prodigious efforts in assembling material and identifying analogies deserve respect, but they lack theoretical rigour (however illuminating they may seem analogies are not enough), and in terms of anthropological assumptions and method were outdated even in their own day (note the criticisms of Hahn: 1956, pp. 53–9, and Rogerson: 1978, pp. 46–51). S. Talmon describes them as comparative method on the grand scale, with a strong generalising trend that ignores the distinctive and particular, and which is essentially random in its failure to relate to the overall social system of which the phenomena under discussion are part (Talmon: 1978). Frazer's concluding distinctions between magic, religion, and science, and his attempts to trace a development in human history through these three phases betray the basic underlying assumptions (Frazer: 1922, 711–14); in the late twentieth century these distinctions would be questioned on all counts. Most problematic perhaps is the effect such a perspective has on the criteria by which phenomena are identified as primitive; earliest elements may be both falsely identified and falsely interpreted.

(2) A second set of possibilities were more strongly sociological, and potentially more fruitful. Durkheim himself acknowledged a debt to

Robertson Smith (Durkheim: 1912, 45 n. 2; cf. also Pickering: 1975, 281), and his own influential insights about religion in society build on the notion, affirmed by Robertson Smith, that in primitive societies gods are integral members of the community. Religion from Durkheim's perspective consists in the idea of the sacred, itself of social origin, and entails a belief in the power or forces resident in the social group (cf. Pickering: 1975, 98). Social organisations are therefore the key to understanding religious feeling and practice. Holiness is in effect the sacredness that is the essence of religion. An object or being considered holy has this character not by virtue of intrinsic attributes; its holiness derives rather from 'impressions of comfort and dependence which the action of the society provokes in the mind'. The contagion of holiness is not a secondary process of propagation; it is the very process by which holiness is acquired (Durkheim: 1912, 323–5). Cult gives expression to the mutual interdependence of gods and human beings. It has the effect of renewing men because 'forces which were languishing are now reawakened in the consciousness'. Similarly it renews the gods who 'can live only in the human consciousness', and who would otherwise die if cult were not rendered. In recognising that the gods are a symbolic expression of society we touch 'the solid rock upon which all the cults are built . . .' (Durkheim: 1912, 346–7).

It is true that in some ways Durkheim seems dated. His attempts to establish a line of demarcation between religion and magic are questionable, though even here he has to be credited with recognising that the line is blurred and that there are overlapping interests and concerns (Durkheim: 1912, 42–7, 361–2). As H. F. Hahn argues it is among followers of Durkheim, in particular H. Hubert and M. Mauss, that the idea emerges that both religion and magic draw on the same forces, the former in the interests of the social group and the latter by the individual for purely personal ends (Hahn: 1956, 62–3).

Hubert and Mauss also provide an alternative to the gift theory of sacrifice as well as to Robertson Smith's sacramental suggestions (Hubert & Mauss: 1898). These theories, in their view, seek to bring the multiplicity of sacrificial forms into a single principle in an inevitably arbitrary way. The unifying element in sacrifice is not an idea, but a mechanism, one that establishes contact between the sacred and profane worlds. The death of the victim, rendering it sacred, can therefore have many effects and many beliefs about its purpose may be associated with it; its essential function always is to allow the two worlds to interpenetrate yet remain distinct. In the tradition of Durkheim, Hubert and Mauss also stress the social character of religious belief. In their view sacrifice, with its combination of

disinterestedness and denial on the one hand and self-interest on the other, exhibits the social character of religion very effectively.
(3) A third possibility was to detach comparative studies from the evolutionistic framework, and to look for alternative systems of interpretation. For some time the so-called pan-Babylonian school had advocated the view that human culture spreads by a process of diffusion from one or more developed centres (for analysis and comment cf. Cook: 1925, 58–64; Rogerson: 1978, 28–33). This theory could be expressed as simplistically as evolutionistic theories, but it deserves consideration as a factor in processes that were evidently complicated. The work of S. H. Hooke and others arose from an awareness of new comparative data, from a new association of myth with ritual, and from a special interest in cult, not simply prophecy, as a creative and influential factor in Israelite religion (Hooke: 1933, 1935, 1958; cf. Rogerson: 1974, 66–84). It did not preclude evolutionary developments, but it was critical of evolutionism as a general theory, and was diffusionist in its overall tendency (cf. Brandon: 1958, 264–5; Leach: 1983, 7–32 who trace anthropological influences from Elliott Smith, Perry, and Hocart). Hooke himself was critical of anthropology's preoccupation with the 'savage mind', and in seeking to re-establish the claims of historical anthropology, envisaged three concentric circles, the innermost and most influential of which was the culture of the ancient near east (Hooke: 1956, 9–25). He was clearly convinced that the concept of Darwinian evolution as applied to history needed modification (Hooke: 1956, 14), and argued that in the case of Canaan we are concerned with what he called 'processes of culture mixture and degradation, rather than with a process of evolution . . .' (Hooke: 1956, 254). He saw his work as in large measure a conscious revolt against non-historical comparative approaches, and particularly against Frazer (Hooke: 1958, 4–5). The concept of diffused culture 'patterns' was widely used to account for similar phenomena; in the ancient near east Hooke called this 'a natural and convenient term to describe an observed group of ritual practices exhibiting a certain order, and bound together by the Akkadian kingship ideology' (Hooker: 1958, 7).

It is appropriate to mention here the work of E. O. James who shared a similar background to Hooke's and who contributed to the myth and ritual movement. He explored the relationship between magic and religion, concluding that they represented different psychological approaches to the sacred, while his enquiries into the origins of sacrifice led him to the view that the death of the victim, the shedding of blood, was the fundamental element by which it must be understood (James: 1933). The death of the victim, he claimed, has a 'liberating vitality'. This life set free has various beneficial effects. It augments the power of the god to act beneficently, it confronts the forces of death and destruction with a new potency, and it opens up lines of communication between the natural and supernatural orders. Some affinities with the views of Hubert and Mauss are evident here, and some awareness too of the social significance of sacrifice.

Assumptions about the ubiquity of 'patterns' laid the myth and ritual approach open to criticism (cf. e.g. Frankfort; 1951: Brandon; 1958). In points of detail it became increasingly easy to challenge the notion that superficially similar phenomena could be explained in terms of a single controlling ideology. S. Talmon sees in the myth and ritual method clear 'Frazerian underpinnings', in other words a a more sophisticated retention of the comparative approach (Talmon: 1977). What is required, as he sees it, is a holistic approach which refuses to isolate aspects of society and cult from the wider social framework, and which makes interpretation within that framework, with all its peculiarities and distinctiveness, the primary task. According to Leach, despite the criticisms of Frazer's method in these writers, the content continues to be heavily dependent upon him (Leach: 1983). Leach also criticises the tendency to fill gaps with ancient near eastern material, the assumption that rituals can be inferred from myths, and the belief that kingship was a unified institution. These critical observations would be widely accepted today, but the myth and ritual approach has some lasting merits. The influence of commerce, conquest, and colonisation does demand attention as a factor in the spread and development of human culture. Moreover in establishing kingship as a key religious institution, and in insisting that it be taken seriously as such in relation to Israel, Hooke and his colleagues had a major influence on thinking about the nature of the pre-exilic cult at Jerusalem.

In this same connection it is essential to mention independent work with the same general direction and effects being undertaken by a variety of Scandinavian scholars (e.g. S. Mowinckel, J. Pedersen, G. Widengren, I. Engnell). Their work interacted at times with the British movement represented by Hooke, but according to Widengren was based less on anthropological considerations, and more on the study of Semitic language and culture in the context of the history of religions (Hooke: 1958, pp. 154–55). It owed much to the work of the Danish philologist and historian Grønbech, who interpreted cult as ritual drama. Though it would be wrong to press the work of the Scandinavians into a single mould it did much to extend an awareness of the pervasiveness of common themes and motifs in the religion of the ancient near east, of the importance of myth in cultic practice, and to establish solid connections between kingship and cult.

It will be apparent that during the first part of the twentieth century there was a common interest among social anthropologists in 'primitive mentalities', evident in all the trends we have considered. Even Hooke's queries seem to be more concerned with excessive preoccupation with the idea and the failure to handle it historically than with the concept itself. The writings of the anthropologist L. Lévy-Bruhl tended to consolidate this interest, and to accentuate the differences between ancient worlds and ours (cf. Hahn: 1956, 61; Rogerson: 1978, 53–9). He took the view that primitive societies have 'pre-logical' and 'mystical' modes of thought which see the occult everywhere, and which are immune to modern experimental proofs and the laws of contradiction. One positive effect was to break down further the distinctions between magic and religion (Hahn: 1956, 62–3); within the scope of primitive mentality both are means of constraint intended to influence the invisible powers.

The influence on biblical study of this search for primitive mentality cannot be measured in detail here (for suggestions see Rogerson: 1978, 46–65). It is interesting to note in H. H. Rowley's article on sacrifice how three attempts to establish such a mentality are described as 'theories of the primary meaning of sacrifice' (Rowley: 1950/1).

A good example of an attempt to identify and describe Israel's primitive thought processes and psychology, as found in the Old Testament is provided by J. Pedersen's *Israel* (1926). Pedersen paid full attention to Israel's social system, and maintained that the individual is integral to the social group; Israelite psychology is therefore in all essentials corporate. A distinctive feature of his presentation is the notion that 'holiness has its root in the soul' (Pedersen: 1926, II, 12), and that it is to be identified with deep strong forces, extending through men and things, and traceable ultimately to the divine powers. Holiness is the additional strength needed by all life, and which for the community is acquired in religious observance at those places where there are special concentrations, namely the sanctuaries (Pedersen: 1926, II, 32). Its distinctive psychological dimensions are evident in the fact that among human beings holiness is manifest in various ways 'according to their nature' (Pedersen: 1926, II, 264). On this view the key function of cult is to turn on or renew the flow of holiness, to make effective the resources of spiritual strength that are available. 'But it is in man's power to contribute to the renewal of holiness . . . This life-sustaining activity is exercised through the cult in the holy places' (Pedersen: 1926, II, 299).

Pedersen's theories are open to criticism on a number of counts (Hahn: 1956, 71–3), among them his tendency to press diverse biblical data into a single, possibly dubious mould. There is a recognition that the transition to city life led to adjustments in the way holiness was understood (Pedersen: 1926, II, 295), but in essence the univocal interpretation prevails, and many would criticise his work for a lack of sustained historical depth. Anthropology was increasingly recognising the need for the sort of fieldwork that does justice to the distinctive features of particular social contexts, and to avoid blanket generalisations about things primitive which may be seriously distorting. Pedersen's concern to see Israel as a social whole and her cult as an expression of that totality are points of continuing importance in his work.

While it is doubtless true that attempts to locate and describe a single 'primitive mentality' are inherently hazardous, progress had been made in establishing the importance of historical study in relation to holiness and cult. It remains likely that there are indeed earlier and distinctive ways of thinking in both these areas which are worth identifying, albeit with a proper awareness of the problems and complexities involved, and a readiness to allow careful biblical exegesis to influence the conclusions drawn with regard to Israel. Equally important was the recognition, among some at least, of the reality of social forces in religious observance and in understandings of the sacred, which in turn provide and strengthen social cohesion; a persuasive and sustained application of this perception to the relevant biblical texts was lacking.

2. Structural anthropology and holiness

In the first half of the twentieth century major developments in anthropology were taking place with important consequences for biblical study. In particular functionalist interpretations sought to show how beliefs and customs contribute to the maintenance and cohesion of particular societies (see Rogerson: 1978, 1–21 for an overall survey). To the extent that they are successful these interpretations show how such beliefs and customs are entirely logical and sensible; notions of 'the primitive' from this perspective seem either simplistic or inappropriate. An increasing emphasis on the peculiarity and distinctiveness of particular societies and on the importance of fieldwork, along with a resistance to generalising theory, began to raise doubts about the suitability of ancient texts, such as those contained in the Old Testament, for anthropological enquiry. It was the structuralist approach of Claude Lévi-Strauss that was to revive an interest in general theory, and to provide opportunities for a distinctive interpretation of biblical texts relating to holiness.

Mary Douglas was the first to seize this opportunity, and to apply structuralist theory to the holiness laws in Leviticus (Douglas: 1966), though there are grounds for doubting whether her work as a whole should be categorised as structuralist (S. R. Isenberg and D. E. Owen: 1977). At the heart of the theory is the conviction that human minds have an inherent and general tendency to organise experience into opposites (the binary principle). Such forms of *classification* are bound to leave *anomalies* unaccounted for, and these, the classification systems and the anomalies, are the fundamental phenomena which provide the clues to understanding why human beings find some things acceptable and others abhorrent. Furthermore her analysis of the concept of 'dirt' has the important effect of showing that pollution rules are not primarily concerned with hygiene, nor are they narrowly religious.

In her Old Testament investigations Douglas identifies blessing as the source of all good things, and its withdrawal (the curse) as the basis of all negative life experiences. For the priestly writers blessing may be expected when people conform to the holiness of God, and disaster and death when they deviate from it. Holiness may be understood in terms of *separateness*, but equally if not more important is the notion of *wholeness*, a point emphasised by the priestly preoccupation in a wide range of laws with physical perfection. This principle is also perceived by Douglas in laws that focus on incomplete enterprises or half-hearted attitudes (e.g. Deut. 20.5–8), and in those that abhor a confusion of categories (e.g. Lev. 18.23; 19.19). It is precisely for this reason that clarity about categories within the created order, proper definition and discrimination, are crucial to the priestly perspective. The unethical behaviour proscribed in Lev. 19 can also be seen in this light. Theft, lying, false witness and so on entail dissimulation and a contradiction therefore between what seems and what is, a denial of wholeness.

This idea of *wholeness* provides Douglas with the key to an understanding of the food laws. Creatures are considered unclean because in one way or another they are perceived to be anomalies. Domesticated animals are clean because they, like the land itself, are part of the divine blessing, and live within the covenant. This makes cloven hoofed and cud-chewing creatures the model by which the acceptability of wild animals as food is to be decided. The priestly laws on this matter deal with borderline cases where one or other of these requirements is lacking. The uncleanness of hare, rock badger, camel and pig is based on criteria of classification and category, and has nothing to do with their behaviour or habits; on physical grounds they cannot be classified with domesticated animals, and therefore lack the wholeness which characterises the order of divine blessing and covenant.

There is another principle that determines category, with a particular application to creatures of air and water. This principle relates to environment and locomotion; those creatures whose movement in any of the three basic environments (air, earth, water) fails to conform to certain norms are considered anomalies and therefore unclean. They are imperfect members of their class, or constitute a class which is thought to confound the divine order in the world. Douglas draws attention to the threefold distinction in Genesis between earth, waters, and firmament. A creature can be considered whole, and therefore clean, if it is equipped with the means of locomotion considered appropriate to its environment. Water creatures without fins and scales are therefore unclean. Flying insects with more than two feet are unclean. Earth creatures which have 'hands' which they use as front feet (such as weasels, mice, lizards, and crocodiles) are also unclean. Swarming or crawling creatures (eels, worms, reptiles, some insects) exhibit what Douglas calls 'an indeterminate form of movement' in the sense that it is not proper to any particular element; they therefore infringe the basic classification. They are not fish, flesh or fowl. Douglas finds support for her emphasis on the means of locomotion in the case of the locust. If it crawled it would be unclean, but its capacity to hop renders it acceptable (Lev. 11.21). The birds remain something of a problem, in part because translation is difficult, but Douglas suspects that those defined as unclean exhibit some anomaly, perhaps in their capacity to swim and dive. The essential point Douglas wishes to make throughout is that *physical characteristics* rather than patterns of behaviour or other factors and associations determine whether a creature is anomalous; furthermore the classification system itself derives from fundamental features of the human mind.

It is important to read *Purity and Danger* in association with further articles by Mary Douglas, particularly those contained in *Implicit Meanings* (Douglas: 1975). The tendency of the individual mind to classify phenomena is here given a larger social context, and linked explicitly with Durkheim's theories about the socially determined nature of knowledge. The two points at which she differs from Durkheim are clearly indicated. First there is his assumption that primitives are radically different from us. For Douglas 'we can only approach primitive mentality through introspection and understanding of our own mentality' (Douglas: 1975, 50). Second there is his belief in objective scientific truth with its attendant distinction between the religious and the secular. These dubious presuppositions, as Douglas sees them, inhibit the natural development of Durkheim's approach. His fundamental perception is that symbolism and ritual, whether strictly religious or not, expresses 'society's awareness of its own configuration and necessities'. This approach she believes is strengthened if all pollution rules, including those not narrowly religious, are included in one overall picture (Douglas: 1975, 54–5). Douglas also provides some further clarification of what she sees as the function of pollution beliefs; they protect a society's 'most vulnerable domains, where ambiguity would most weaken the fragile structure' (Douglas: 1975, 58). It follows that the world views which are most tightly constructed and ordered are those that most require pollution controls. She recognises that primitive cultures do possess an urge to unify experience and create order, and that to the extent that we moderns are able and willing to allow our guiding concepts to be constantly subject to review and criticism we exhibit a different tendency increasingly immune from cosmological pollutions. Thus while pollution ideas draw their power from the human intellectual constitution they have an important role in protecting a social system from unpalatable knowledge (Douglas: 1975, 245).

In a further article Mary Douglas considers criticisms to the effect that her analysis of the biblical laws affecting diet need to take account of the larger and wider dimensions of Israel's life and thought (Douglas: 1975, 249–75). In response she points out that her approach to the question of what is fit for the table (and what is not) is consonant with the way issues relating to what is fit for sacrifice are handled. Analogies are evident in the structuring of the Temple and in the way Israelites relate to non-Israelites; they are to other humans as their livestock are to other quadrupeds. The clearly bounded physical specimens mirror the perfectly bounded Temple which in turn, as Douglas sees it, mirrors the bounded territory of the land. In this way Israel's laws on pollution are related specifically to her historical experiences in winning and defending the promised land. The emphasis on physical perfection creates new problems arising from biological needs (eating and procreation) which damage completeness, and these are resolved in a range of other laws by means of avoidance or consecration. Douglas recognises that there are complicating factors of multiple pollution, as for example in the case of the pig, but maintains her fundamental contention that the various boundaries delineated by pollution laws mark off areas of structured social relations – in short '. . . the ordered system which is a meal represents all the ordered systems associated with it' (Douglas: 1975, 273).

Some of the distinctive features of Israel's classification system are stressed in another article (Douglas: 1975, 276–318). The abhorrence of anomaly, as found in Israel, is by no means universal – some cultures respect or venerate it – and Douglas links Israel's liking for boundaries and tendency to regard anomaly as hostile intrusion to her political experience as 'a people surrounded by powerful, rapacious enemies' (Douglas: 1975, 304–5). Half eligibility, whether in the case of the pig which parts the hoof but fails to chew the cud or in the case of marriage with a half-blooded Israelite attracts a special odium.

Mary Douglas's approach has attracted support from various quarters. The social dimensions her later writing identifies are taken up, for example, by B. J. Malina (1981). He suggests that 'human meaning-building is a process of socially contriving lines in the shapeless stuff of the human environment, thus producing definition, socially shared meaning' (Malina: 1981, 124–5). The set of social lines we learn provides us with a map that helps and compels us to order persons, things, places, and events. The clearer the line drawing, the sharper the definitions, and the less ambiguous the meanings we embrace. The concept of *purity* is specifically concerned with arrangement within social time and space, and about the boundaries separating inside and outside. The unclean is that which blurs the boundaries or which does not fit in the defined space in which it is found. Every culture is confronted to a greater or lesser degree with anomalies – realities which do not fit the socially determined patterns and norms, and if these are ignored then confidence in the culture and its norms will be undermined.

Malina maintains that crucial cultural lines in first century CE Judaism concerned inherited position in society, and shows how marriage rules effectively draw the lines. Persons are classified in terms of their proximity to the Temple, their membership of the covenant community, and their capacity to transmit their status within the covenant community.

Malina also finds that this categorisation of persons closely corresponds with the distinctions between clean and unclean animals. The parallel between Israel and its livestock is evident in the fact that the first to open the womb – of animals as well as human beings – belongs to Yahweh (Exod. 13.2; 22.29b–30; Lev. 27.26–7; Num. 3.13; 8.17–18; 18.15), that only domestic animals qualify as sacrifices (Lev. 1.2), that they too are to observe the sabbath (Exod. 20.8–11; Deut. 5.12–15; Lev. 25.6–7), and that crossbreeding is forbidden (Lev. 19.19).

In dealing with the clean/unclean distinction Malina follows Mary Douglas fairly closely. The three habitats are crucial, and creatures that live in more than one are immediately rejected as anomalies. Proper land animals are those that part the hoof and chew the cud (Lev. 11.3). Proper water creatures are those that have fins and scales (Lev. 11.9). Proper air creatures are those that can fly or hop with their wings and two legs, and that are not carrion (Lev. 11.13–22). The introduction by Malina here of a *behavioural* characteristic (flesh eating) should be noted. Other anomalies are those creatures that seem to have the defining physical characteristics of other categories. Land animals that 'swarm' like fish or insects are rejected (Lev. 11.29–37), and so too are winged creatures that go on all fours like land animals (Lev. 11.20). The fact that 'swarming' creatures occur in all three environments means that they lack physical criteria by which they can be allocated to one class; they must therefore be rejected (Lev. 11.41–2).

Malina also follows Douglas in relating the purity scale to Temple and sacrifice. In this context it is easy to see how animals replicate persons, and fit into their allotted places in the scheme of things. Persons with skin disorders, blemishes, or abnormal emissions, or who have had contact with corpses correspond with blemished animals. They lack wholeness and fail to replicate the envisaged ideal.

Michael Carroll acknowledges the new perspectives Douglas's work fosters, but is critical of certain aspects of her argument, in particular the premise that unclean animals are anomalous (Carroll, 1978).

He argues that in Genesis we should focus our attention not on the three environments, but on the *five* types of creature identified there – fish (Gen. 1.26, 28), birds (Gen. 1.20, 21, 22, 26, 28), cattle (Gen. 1.24, 25, 26), beasts of the earth (Gen. 1.24, 25, 30), and creeping things (Gen. 1.24, 25, 26, 30). From this point of view the hare and rock badger can readily be seen as 'beasts of the earth', and are thus *not* anomalous. The same applies to the flying insects which belong to the category established in Gen. 1.26. In the same vein six of the eight 'swarming' creatures in Lev. 11.29–30 are identified as land-based reptiles, which must certainly belong to the 'creeping things' in Genesis, and which would therefore not be anomalies. He also seeks to exploit Douglas's somewhat speculative treatment of the birds in Lev. 11.13–19, and of the word in Lev. 11.27, where she proposes evidence of an anomalous form of locomotion.

Carroll accepts Douglas's general theory, but considers it misapplied in the case of Leviticus. Instead he makes use of a distinction drawn from Lévi-Strauss between *nature* and *culture*. The 'swarming' creatures of Lev. 11.29–30 (nature) appear to be those that might be encountered in the home (culture), judging by the further discussion in vv. 32–5. It is their invasion of the culture realm, and their blurring of the distinction between nature and culture that renders them unclean.

Carroll then applies this principle to the birds listed in Lev. 11.13–19, and suggests that whatever problems of translation there may be there is sufficient clarity to argue that these are carnivorous birds. He then suggests that within the framework established by Genesis (1.30; 9.3) meat eating is only appropriate within the human realm. These flesh-eating birds blur the distinction between nature and culture and are therefore unclean. Turning to the insects, and having identified the seven most widely mentioned in the Old Testament, he suggests that many of these do indeed invade the realm of culture by eating garments (moths) or by bite or sting (flies, bees, gnats, hornets). Those that are clean (locusts, grasshoppers) lack precisely these characteristics; they stick to the realm of nature.

In considering land animals those that go upon 'their paws' (Lev. 11.27) are evidently wild, and Carroll cites carnivores such as the lion, the bear, and the wolf as the most frequently mentioned in the Old Testament. The creatures that meet the criterion – cloven footed and cud chewing – are grass-eating ungulates; the omnivorous pig is unclean.

Carroll recognises that his theory is less persuasive in relation to water creatures – the point perhaps where Douglas seems strongest. It is not obvious how eels or shellfish blur the nature/culture distinction, yet they lack the fins and scales that mark out the clean water creatures. Carroll thinks nevertheless that the theory may shed light on the otherwise redundant 'and scales'. The carnivorous shark is a creature that has fins but lacks scales; it must therefore be excluded.

Like Douglas, Carroll is anxious to apply these ideas about diet to the wider concern with holiness. Discharge may likewise be thought to threaten the distinction between nature and culture, but also, following Leach, the distinction between self and outside world. Childbirth may also be thought to blur this latter distinction.

The 'leprosy' laws fit in well with Carroll's perspective. The mould or mildew that affects garments and buildings (Lev. 13.47–59; 14.33–53) is an obvious invasion of culture by nature, the equivalent to the vermin defined in Lev. 11.29–38. With regard to human skin diseases the distorted appearance may be held to blur the nature/culture distinction; the torn clothes and loose hair demanded in Lev. 14.45 reflect a disassociation from culture.

This kind of approach could be extended to other areas. It is easy to see why creatures which die naturally or which are killed by other animals are also unclean (Exod. 22.31 (22.30 Heb.); Deut. 14.21; Lev. 7.24; 17.15). Such deaths belong to the realm of nature, that world outside human control. To make use of them for consumption or religious purposes would be fatally to confuse the crucial distinction. Other areas of interest which fit the general picture are contact with corpses (Lev. 21.11), and the matter of blemishes (Lev. 21.17). It is easy to see death as beyond human control, and therefore as an intrusion from the other world of nature. Blemishes likewise may be thought to be an intrusion from the unstructured chaotic world beyond the familiar human world of culture; they are phenomena which humans cannot determine or control.

As Carroll himself appreciates, what he has done is not to dismantle but to reapply Douglas's general theory. He has replaced her emphasis on wholeness and on anomaly in locomotion and environment with the nature/culture distinction. Anything that threatens that distinction is dangerous and unclean. This has some persuasive force. The realm of culture is that which human beings create, order, and control. The realm of nature, by contrast, is outside human control, and therefore inherently dangerous; where it intrudes steps must be taken to control it or otherwise exclude it. Such a perspective is in fact not far removed from Douglas's observations about the difference between the domesticated creatures which are within the realm of divine 'blessing', and the wild creatures that are not.

There are however some aspects of Carroll's discussion that need further consideration. It should be noted that Lev. 11, independently of Gen. 1, has its own way of classifying creatures, in this case into *four* primary types (v46); the anomaly issue should be addressed first to this system of categories. It may also be the case that the essential point in Gen. 9.1–7 is not that flesh-eating is the sole right of human beings (thereby marking out carnivorous creatures as intruders in the realm of culture), but that such creatures will consume blood as well as flesh (v4). While the unclean water birds may indeed be flesh eaters they cannot be depicted as consumers of blood. The water creatures remain a problem. It is possible that some of the unclean fish familiar to Israelites (see F. S. Bodenheimer: 1962, 272) could be considered intruders from the 'chaotic' world of the sea, with its mythological overtones of menace and disorder, but it is not clear that carnivorous or other behavioural factors are important. It may well be the case that Lev. 11.22 is concerned to limit the types of locust that may be considered clean, but difficulties in identifying the types specified mean that we cannot be sure that the destructive types are excluded; in short clean locusts may constitute a substantial threat to agriculture. Douglas' suggestions about the fish and also the land and flying creatures that 'swarm' (exhibiting locomotion features inappropriate to their environment) continue to be as persuasive as any.

Nevertheless Carroll's basic proposal has attractions as one factor in a process that was probably complex. The distinction between worlds which we control and those we do not, with all their potential dangers, may well be relevant. It seems that Mary Douglas herself is not unaware of this dimension in the discussion. She cites Hab. 1.14 with its reference to the 'crawling things that have no ruler', and refers to swarming things, such as the worm, which 'belong in the realm of the grave, with death and chaos' (Douglas: 1966, 71). Gen. 1.20) seems to suggest that the proper environment of 'swarming' creatures is the waters, but it may also be the case that their mode of locomotion is suggestive of things haphazard, anarchic, and therefore dangerous. The need to allow for a 'cognitive anthropology' is well made by E. Hunn (1979); in other words it is neither necessary nor desirable to look for comprehensive symbol systems. His study of the birds in Lev. 11.13–19 allows for empirical and creative human reactions to perceived correlations in the natural environment. Douglas would presumably accept this, since it helps to explain how the undomesticated creatures listed in Deut. 14.4–5 are considered clean. Her basic point about the fundamental importance of physical anomaly remains firm.

3. Structural anthropology and sacrifice

An interest in the sociological aspects of ritual, and in the role of sacrifice as a marker of boundaries is evident in the work of E. Leach (Leach: 1976). He identifies two complementary models which provide a basis for a structuralist interpretation, both entailing the perception that there are two worlds – this world of mortal impotent human beings, and the other world of immortal omnipotent gods, the source of life, health and fertility. Adopting the spatial model religious performance provides a connecting bridge through which the power of the other world becomes available to human beings. From the perspective of the temporal model religious performance effects the transitions at the beginning and end of a period of sacred non-time, or the time of the other world, which is experienced in the procedures of the cult as a whole.

Turning to the key question of the significance of death Leach finds that gift/tribute theory is often supported by the language. He suggests that the death of the gift is necessary so that its metaphysical essence can be separated from the material body, and function effectively as the bridge between the two worlds. From the temporal perspective mortuary rituals provide the paradigm. These are above all rituals of transition, and the death of the sacrificial victim is therefore an appropriate event as the worshippers move between the 'times' of the two worlds.

Leach also offers some comment about the three-zone stage on which ritual takes place, and applies it to the Tabernacle laws in Exod. 25–7. The three categories of cosmological space – this world, the other world, and the intermediate zone – can all be linked with textual categories in the biblical text. Representing this world is the bulk of the space inside and outside the camp. Representing the other world are the ark, the mercy seat, and the holy of holies. The intermediate zones are to be found within the Tabernacle and its court, with phenomena such as the altar and the permanent fire marking the threshold between the two worlds. Leach also considers the rituals in Leviticus, and maintains in particular that Lev. 8.4–21 exhibits the temporal transitions already identified, with the priest returning, at the termination of the rite, to this world with a new social status. A transition in the opposite direction is perceived in the scapegoat ritual in Lev. 16. Aaron is progressively separated from the contaminations of this world and ends the process at the centre of the camp. The goat is progressively loaded with these contaminations and ends the process in the wilderness, far removed from the ritual stage, but still alive, loaded with the impurity from which death would separate it. Animal sacrifice therefore, as Leach sees it, has a key role in marking temporal transitions in various rites of passage involving the two worlds.

J. W. Rogerson (1980) finds that this approach would also work well in Lev. 14 with the rehabilitation of lepers, but thinks it inappropriate in relation to Lev. 16. In that situation the period of social timelessness required by the model seems to be absent.

D. Davies has sought to provide a more comprehensive theory of sacrifice, with special reference to sin and guilt offerings, based on a broad structuralist approach (Davies: 1977). This he considers offers a more secure alternative to gift theory, with its outmoded evolutionism, and to psychological theories which stress devotion. From this perspective it is possible to interpret sacrifice without searching for obscure and probably irrecoverable historical origins, and without doubtful assumptions about cross cultural borrowing.

Davies' main conclusion is that sacrifice is essentially a social institution by which the life of the nation in all its aspects (religious, social and moral) is conceived and ordered. It is precisely the life of the nation, and the continuance of the covenant, that is threatened by sin in all its forms. Davies identifies five categories of interaction (God–Nation: God–Priesthood: God–Israelite: Israelite–Israelite: Israelite–Nation) within which there is risk to the well-being of the social whole.

By way of illustration Davies pays special attention to the God–Nation category of interaction evident in atonement ritual. In identifying two basic realms – the sacred and the profane with various transitional phenomena – his approach has much in common with that of Leach. The sacred signifies not only God and Temple but also Life, Being, and Order. By contrast the profane is represented by Gentiles, the Wilderness, Death, Nothingness, and Chaos. Between these poles is Israel, its camp and priesthood, and the world of transient existence. In essence the sacred/profane polarity is also the order/chaos polarity; the essential function of ritual is to avert the threat of chaos, and where necessary restore the desired condition of wholeness and order.

In atonement ritual the priests are seen initially to be located at the profane pole, along with Israel and all her sin; the sacrifice of the one goat and the despatch of the other to the wilderness are the key events that bring this chaotic danger to an end. The scapegoat has been sent not to Azazel, as in some traditional theory, but to the disordered nothingness that lies beyond the people of God. The two goats move in different directions within the continuum, one through its destruction entering the realm of the sacred, and the other in its despatch entering the chaotic realm of the wilderness. Changes of status occur in the process for those who lay their hands on the victims. The importance of the blood as agent in establishing normal relationships is evident, though a symbol such as this operates on several different levels of meaning, and answers to some of the questions about its significance are likely to remain elusive. It is important to realise too that in some rituals the priests are located at the sacred pole, mediating the holy to the people who remain in the profane sector. At their ordination the priests occupy a transitional position, neither sacred nor profane. These observations help to explain various detailed features in the laws of Leviticus – why for example the priest may eat from sacrifices which are offered for the sins of others (on these occasions the priests represent God at the sacred pole), but not from the sacrifices for sin with which they are in some way identified. The effects of the death of the high priest (Num. 35.28), whereby the refugee homicide may return to his home, suggests to Davies that the death of the sacred (as in sacrifices) has the effect of restoring confused categories.

The same function is evident in relation to sacrifices which concern the individual Israelite and the community. At the heart of the rites that readmit healed lepers to the full life of the community are two sacrifices. One is offered outside the camp, because at that point the individual is outside structured society, and he is duly anointed with the blood. The second sacrifice takes place at the altar, the outcome of which is the individual's recovery of full status as a social person. The two pigeons in these rites are performing the same role as the goats in the atonement ritual. That very similar rites are applied to houses is important for Davies's argument. Notions of moral guilt are absent here. The point is that whatever disrupts the social life of Israel, for example houses that cannot be inhabited, require ritual actions in which sacrifice is essential and central – cf. also the woman's sacrifice after childbirth. Where moral guilt is connected with sacrifice it must be understood as something disruptive to social life. Indeed a key merit of Davies's suggestions is their capacity to see the range of material in Leviticus – holiness, ethics, ritual – in an holistic way. All pertain to the social ordering and well-being of the community.

B. J. Malina also makes some suggestions with respect to offerings and sacrifice, by linking the difference between the sacred and the profane with the process by which objects, experiences, or states and conditions become ours (Malina, 1981). This is normally a three phase process. Initially the object, experience or condition is separate from us, and therefore profane, but we may move into a marginal phase in which it becomes potentially ours. If we move on from there and appropriate it, the object, experience, or condition becomes fully ours, and therefore sacred. The process can also be viewed spatially. The sacred is that area that belongs to us, the profane that which does not.

Malina applies these ideas to Israel's thinking about God. His space is the Temple, which itself replicates within it the land and the whole world. While the purity rules mark out those persons and animals fit to interact with God, and also special times within the year (the feasts and other calendrical observances), the process of interaction itself is sacrifice. Malina suggests that this interaction takes place in a special zone of transition between the area which is God's alone, and that in which properly prepared persons can assemble. In terms of the wilderness arrangements portrayed in the priestly code the latter area is the court of the tent, and the former the holy of holies (the tent with the ark). In the transition zone is the altar and laver, the table with the seven-branched candlestick, and the curtain before the sanctuary, and this essentially is the place where interaction between God and people takes place.

In considering the purpose of sacrifice Malina associates it with social status, particularly that perceived by dyadic personalities, and suggests that sacrifices offered to God are analogous to gifts given to higher-class patrons. The dyadic personality is taken by Malina to be characteristic of people in the biblical world, and consists essentially in a tendency to understand self in and through the expectations and stereotypical characteristics of the group to which the individual belongs. The offerer as member and representative of his group seeks the benefits of God's patronage. The offered object must be prescribed and clean, and as such represents the offerer himself. It is taken into the transitional zone, where the interaction takes place, and the benefits of patronage are passed to the donor. Those elements of the sacrifice that are burned symbolise the passage of the donor to God; those elements that are consumed by the offerer and the Temple personnel symbolise the fellowship that exists between a benign and sympathetic patron and his clients. The offerer thus pays proper respect to God his patron, and God accepts the offerer as his client. Though he does not demonstrate it in a sustained and detailed way Malina is evidently of the opinion that this hypothesis can be helpfully applied to the rituals of Lev. 1–4. It should be stressed that Malina is primarily concerned to understand the situation in first century Judaism, and to explain developments among the early Christians, but there is no reason for thinking his ideas inapplicable to earlier periods. While his view of the function and purpose of sacrifice would be open to debate from other structuralist perspectives, there is in his approach the same interest in the polarities between sacred and profane, and in the intermediate space between them where the crucial ritual interactions and transactions take place.

There are other areas in relation to sacrifice which could be explored. J. H. M. Beattie (1980) provides a useful outline of the interests and ideas current in this area among anthropologists. It may be that his interest in sacrifice as a manipulation of and release from different kinds of power could be usefully probed in relation to Israel's system. The same could be said about Mary Douglas's explorations of the social functions of ritual (1970). These are sympathetically analysed by S. R. Isenberg and D. E. Owen (1977), who find there a useful method of coming to grips with ritual.

4. Concluding Observations

A number of general questions about the approach of the structural anthropologists may legitimately be raised. On occasions they may be tempted to over generalise, and to overlook specific and distinctive features (cf. e.g. the criticism of Douglas offered by Leach: 1983, 20–1). R. Alter (1979), who is otherwise sympathetic, comments critically on a tendency to tidy up uneven data in the interests of preserving the neatness of the system, suspecting that any cultural system is likely to exhibit inconsistencies and haphazard elements. J. W. Rogerson cites criticism to the effect that in the last analysis the theories of Lévi-Strauss are impervious to proof or disproof, and that a method which applies procedures drawn from linguistics to the analysis of social data may be suspect (Rogerson: 1978, 110). Is there not a danger that too much is being traced ultimately to the functioning of the human mind? Rogerson also points to problems arising from the nature of the Old Testament texts (1980). Uncertainty about the liturgical material accompanying sacrificial rites in Israel makes interpretation from an anthropological perspective difficult. There is also the fact that the texts are not the data that the field working anthropologist would observe and collect. A similar point about the nature of P texts in the Pentateuch is made by J. Neusner (1973, pp. 119–30). On the other hand Rogerson is appreciative of the lasting influence of Lévi-Strauss on social anthropology, and is sympathetic to Douglas's achievement in developing and extending his approach (Rogerson: 1978, 112–14).

B. Lang considers briefly the criticism that structural models may in fact distort the evidence rather than illuminate it (Lang: 1985). This will depend very much on the attitude taken to the models and the way they are used. Are such models definitive, or are they allowed to be subject to revision and amendment? It is hard to avoid the conclusion that models and structures are essential, particularly, as is usually the case, where evidence is limited, ambiguous or untidy. If we adopt Leach's view, cited by Lang, that the structures are patterns of aesthetic perception, offering insights and not full understandings, the dangers of distortion can be minimised.

More serious questions about structural anthropology and its functionalist method concern its readiness and ability to admit diachronic approaches, those concerned with the specifics and peculiarities of historical development (Gottwald: 1979, 721–2). Without such a dimension its explanatory power is greatly diminished. Aspects of a necessary dialogue between history (Neusner) and anthropology (Douglas) emerge in J. Neusner's study of purity (1973), and despite certain problems of communication, the outcome is promising.

It seems clear that there is a challenge from the social sciences which biblical study cannot permanently evade, a challenge succinctly presented by Gottwald in Part X of his major work on Israel's beginnings (Gottwald: 1979). If his conclusions are rejected then what he calls 'idealism' will have to be rehabilitated as a persuasive theoretical model, or else the explanatory adequacy of structural anthropology will have to be critically affirmed. It will be apparent that much of the work under consideration has been essentially functionalist, in Gottwald's terms, and it is reasonable to suppose, as he argues, that diachronic questions do need to be raised in a more fundamental way.

This is not to deny that there is scope for a thorough and sustained consideration of the priestly literature as a whole from the perspective of structural anthropology, gathering, evaluating, and extending the work done hitherto. On the other hand the role of holiness and cult within the socio-political/economic development of Israel also deserves sustained attention. It is true that scholars have been generally aware of the importance, for example, of the pre-exilic Jerusalem cult in providing ideological support for the Davidic order; what has often been lacking is a thorough and theoretically rigorous investigation of the theme, and a readiness to apply such interpretative models to Israel's history as a whole. Much ink has been spilt in attempting to give an 'idealistic' and essentially conceptual meaning to sacrifice; relatively little by contrast on the social operation of the system, its costs to the various strata in society, and its relationship to the exercise of power and the maintenance of status in the community.

It is also important to try to see Israel's history, not merely as the activity of individuals or discrete groups, but with an eye to the dynamics of cultures, seeking to discern how societies are transformed as they interact with their total environments, physical as well as social. F. S. Frick has made some suggestions about transitions in early Israel from segmentary society, through chiefdom, to nation state (Frick: 1985). Whether or not 'segmentary' was ever an appropriate description of Israelite society his comments in relation to ritual and the practice of religion, though brief, are suggestive. Its important role in bringing people into a larger community that transcends the minimal segment (Frick: 1985, 66), and in helping to legitimate chiefdom deserves further consideration (pp. 80–1). Here he cites Netting to the effect that religious modes of focussing power are often primary in overcoming the critical structural weaknesses in stateless societies.

In theory the social sciences should be integral to biblical critical methodology, along with the better established literary and historical modes of analysis and enquiry; with respect to holiness and cult there is more to be done if the potential is to be realised.

Bibliography

Alter, R., 1979. 'A New Theory of Kashrut', *Commentary* 68, 46–52.

Beattie, J. H. M., 1980. 'On Understanding Sacrifice', *Sacrifice* (ed. M. F. C. Bourdillon and M. Fortes) (London: Academic Press), 29–44.

Bodenheimer, F. S., 1962. 'Fish', *Interpreters Dictionary of the Bible*, vol. 2 (Nashville/New York: Abingdon), 272–3.

Bourdillon, M. F. C., 1980. 'Introduction', *Sacrifice* (ed. M. F. C. Bourdillon and M. Fortes) (London: Academic Press), 1–27.

Brandon, S. G. F., 1958. 'The Myth and Ritual Position Critically Considered', *Myth, Ritual, and Kingship* (ed. S. H. Hooke), (Oxford: Clarendon), 261–91.

Carroll, M. P., 1978. 'One More Time: Leviticus Revisited' *AES* 99, 339–46. Reprinted in B. Lang (ed.), *Anthropological Approaches to the Old Testament* (London/Philadelphia: SPCK/Fortress, 1985), 117–26.

Cook, S. A., 1925. 'The Religious Environment of Israel', *The People and the Book* (ed. A. S. Peake), (Oxford: Clarendon), 41–72.

Davies, D., 1977. 'An Interpretation of Sacrifice in Leviticus', *ZAW* 89, 388–98. Reprinted in B. Lang (ed.), *Anthropological Approaches to the Old Testament* (London/Philadelphia: SPCK/Fortress, 1985), 151–62.

Douglas, M., 1966. *Purity and Danger. An Analysis of Concepts of Pollution and Taboo* (London: Routledge & Kegan Paul). Page numbers from Penguin edition (Harmondsworth, Penguin Books, 1970).

Douglas, M., 1970. *Natural Symbols. Explorations in Cosmology* (London: Barrie & Rockliff).

Douglas, M. 1975. *Implicit Meanings* (London: Routledge & Kegan Paul).

Durkheim, E., 1912. *Les Formes élémentaires de la vie religieuse. Le système totémique en Australie* (Paris). Page numbers from English translation, *The Elementary Forms of the Religious Life* (London: Allen & Unwin, 1975 (2nd edition)).

Frankfort, H., 1951. *The Problem of Similarity in Ancient Near Eastern Religions* (Oxford: Clarendon).

Frazer, J. G., 1919. *Folklore in the Old Testament*, (London: Macmillan).

Frazer, J. G., 1922. *The Golden Bough. A Study in Magic and Religion* (London: Macmillan, (abridged edition). This work was first published in two volumes in 1890.

Frick, F. S., 1985. *The Formation of the State in Ancient Israel. A Survey of Models and Theories* (Sheffield: Almond).

Gottwald, N., 1979. *The Tribes of Yahweh. A Sociology of the Religion of Liberated Israel 1250–1050 BCE* (Maryknoll/London: Orbis Books/SCM, 1979/1980).

Hahn, H. F., 1956. *The Old Testament in Modern Research*, (London: SCM).

Henry, M., 1960. *Commentary on the Whole Bible in One Volume* (ed. L. F. Church), (London: Marshall, Morgan & Scott). The complete commentary first appeared 1708–1710.

Hooke, S. H. (ed.), 1933. *Myth and Ritual* (London: OUP).

Hooke, S. H. (ed.), 1935. *The Labyrinth* (London/New York: SPCK/Macmillan).

Hooke, S. H., 1956. *The Seige Perilous, Essays in Biblical Anthropology* (London: SCM).

Hooke, S. H. (ed.), 1958. *Myth, Ritual, and Kingship* (Oxford: Clarendon).

Hubert, H. and Mauss, M., 1898. 'Essai sur la Nature et la Fonction du Sacrifice', *L'Année Sociologique* (Paris). Page numbers from English translation *Sacrifice: its Nature and Function* (London: Cohen & West, 1964).

Hunn, E., 1979. 'The Abominations of Leviticus Revisited', *Classifications in their Social Context* (ed. R. F. Ellen and D. Reason) (London: Academic Press), 103–16.

Isenberg, S. R. and Owen, D. E., 1977. 'Bodies Natural and Contrived: The Work of Mary Douglas', *Religious Studies Review* 3, 1–17.

James, E. O., 1933. *Origins of Sacrifice* (London: Murray).

Lang, B., 1985. 'Anthropology as a New Model for Biblical Studies', *Anthropological Approaches to the Old Testament* (London/Philadelphia: SPCK/Fortress), 1–20.

Leach, E., 1976. 'The Logic of Sacrifice', *Culture and Communication* (Cambridge: CUP), 81–93. Reprinted in B. Lang (ed.), *Anthropological Approaches to the Old Testament* (London/Philadelphia: SPCK/Fortress, 1985), 136–50.

Leach, E., 1983. 'Anthropological Approaches to the Study of the Bible during the Twentieth Century', *Structuralist Interpretations of Biblical Myth*, Leach, E. and Aycock, D. A.), (Cambridge: CUP), 7–32.

Malina, B. J., 1981/1983. *The New Testament World. Insights from Cultural Anthropology* (Atlanta/London: John Knox/SCM).

Neusner, J., 1973. *The Idea of Purity in Ancient Judaism with a Critique and a Commentary by Mary Douglas* (Leiden: Brill).

Pedersen, J., 1926. 1940 *Israel. Its Life and Culture* (London/Copenhagen: Cumberlege OUP/Branner OG Korch).

Pickering, W. S. F. (ed.), 1975. *Durkheim on Religion* (London: Routledge & Kegan Paul).

Rogerson, J. W., 1974. *Myth in Old Testament Interpretation, BZAW* 134 (Berlin/New York: de Gruyter).

Rogerson, J. W., 1978. *Anthropology and the Old Testament* (Oxford: Blackwell).

Rogerson, J. W., 1980. 'Sacrifice in the Old Testament', *Sacrifice* (ed. M. F. C. Bourdillon & M. Fortes) (London: Academic Press), 45–59.

Rowley, H. H., 1950–1. 'The Meaning of Sacrifice in the Old Testament', *BJRL* 33, 74–110. Reprinted in H. H. Rowley *From Moses to Qumran* (London: Lutterworth, 1963), 67–107.

Smith, Robertson, W., 1889. *Lectures on the Religion of the Semites* (London: Black). Page numbers from 2nd edition 1907.

Talmon, S., 1978. 'The "comparative method" in biblical interpretation – principles and problems', *Congress Volume Göttingen 1977* (Leiden: Brill), 320–56.

Tylor, E. B., 1871. *Primitive Culture: Researches into the Development of Mythology, Philosophy, Religion, Art and Custom* (London: Murray), vol. 2, 328–400.

CHAPTER FOURTEEN

The concept of holy war

GWILYM H. JONES

'Israel means *El fights*, and Yahweh was the fighting El after whom the people named itself. The war camp was the cradle of the nation, it was also the oldest sanctuary.' It was with these words that Julius Wellhausen emphasised the importance for Israelite faith and history of the concept that Yahweh was a warrior who engaged in battle on behalf of his people (Wellhausen: 1884, 10; 1965, 18. cf. Smend: 1970, 27). The Old Testament refers to these battles as 'the wars of Yahweh' (*milḥ^{a}môṯ* Yhwh, Num. 21.14; 1 Sam. 18.17; 25.28, cf. also Exod. 17.16; 1 Sam. 17.47), which must be regarded as a technical term giving an adequate description of the Old Testament phenomenon (Smend: 1970, 38; Weippert: 1970, 396). Israelite traditions (cf. Deut. 11.30; Jos. 10.14) confirm what is succinctly expressed in Exod. 15.3:

> The LORD is a man of war;
> the LORD is his name.

In attempting to bring together the Old Testament material depicting God as leader of an army and as an individual fighter, H. Fredriksson gave attention to the armies led by Yahweh, his various functions, his weapons and the technical terms that are used in these connections (Fredriksson: 1945). The mythological background of the imagery in Near Eastern literature became the subject of further investigation undertaken by P. D. Miller (Miller: 1973), and it was correctly observed that holy war was not confined to Israel.[1] However, since the beginning of this century the term 'holy war' has been used to describe these wars in which Yahweh fought as warrior (cf. Schwally: 1901; Caspari: 1912, 110–58; Weber: 1922, 99ff.).

With the publication of historical records and other documents relating to the ancient Near East it has become obvious that the main groups of people in the area interpreted national warfare as holy or religious wars, which 'from start to finish . . . were waged in an atmosphere of religion, as though the battlefields were temples' (Fish: 1939, 399; de Vaux: 161, 253). Comparative material is available from an extensive geographical area and from a wide temporal span; that belonging to the same area and roughly to the same time as Israel, and found in texts from Ugarit and Mari and from the Hittite and Neo-Assyrian kingdoms (Fish: 1939, 387–402; Labat: 1939, 253–74; Saggs: 1963, 145–8; von Soden: 1963: 137–44; Glock: 1968; Heintz: 1969, 112–38; Weippert: 1972, 460–93; Miller: 1973, 8–63), can be supplemented by parallels from other areas, such as Egypt (Breasted: 1906–7; Morenz: 1973) and the Arabian desert (Musil: 1908; 1928) and from periods falling before (Labat: 1939, 253–74) and after (Moser: 1963, 133f.; A. Noth: 1966) the Israelite era.

Accepting the general presupposition that the affairs of a nation were controlled by its deities, territorial conquests and military successes were attributed to effective surveillance by the national gods. In an account of Sargon's rule it is asserted that 'Enlil did not let anyone oppose Sargon' (*ANET*, 267*b*), and in similar vein Mesha, king of Moab, extolled the god Chemosh 'because he saved me from all the kings and caused me to triumph over all my adversaries' (*ANET*, 320*b*). Although Assyrian records list an impressive number of gods who could be called upon to assist a king against his enemies, some have special responsibilities in this area. Nergal is called 'the king of battle' (Luckenbill: I, 174) and is described by Sargon as 'the all-powerful among the gods, who goes at my side, guarding my camp'. (Luckenbill: II, 99). Ishtar too is called 'lady of conflict and battle, whose delight is warfare' (Luckenbill: I, 195, 212), and it was she who prompted 'to the waging of war and battle' (Luckenbill: I, 141). But activity in warfare was in no way restricted to these deities, for the Assyrians invoked all their gods, including the supreme god Assur, to help them in a time of crisis. Similarly in Syria–Palestine, Baal is depicted as warrior-god, who does battle with the sons of Aṯirat, and in Southern Canaan El was depicted as a warrior leading his armies to battle (Miller: 1973, 38, 62). National enemies were regarded as enemies of the gods, and reprisals had to be taken against them because they had broken 'the oath sworn by the great gods' (*ANET*, 285*b*).

The religious nature of warfare is well illustrated in pre-battle preparations. The king visited a shrine, where he prostrated himself in prayer before the deity and implored him for help. Prayers were accompanied by signs of grief and lamentation (*ANET*, 268*a*; 285*b*), as well as by the use of audible means of calling his attention, such as clapping hands (*ANET*, 289*b*). Naturally such prayers invoked the deity to execute punishment on the enemy because of his arrogance, and made a request for destruction in unmistakable terms: 'rip him open in the fight, as one rips open a bundle; let loose upon him a tempest, an evil wind' (Luckenbill: II, 331–2). The elaborate Hittite *Ritual before Battle* (*ANET*, 354*b*–355*a*) indicates that sacrifices were offered to the gods on the frontiers of enemy country.

Another aspect of these preparations was the consultation of omens before engaging in battle. Indications of the divine will were extracted from observing the moon and stars (Labat: 1939, 255), and obviously some days and months were regarded as favourable for battle. Hepatoscopy was also practised, for careful observation of the movement of an animal's entrails brought a message from the gods (Labat: 1939, 256; Fish: 1939, 395). It was only after receiving a favourable divine oracle that the king could be certain of victory in battle (*ANET*, 277; 294*b*). After taking preliminary steps, which included offering prayer and sacrifice, pronouncing curses, consulting omens and seeking an oracle, the kings were satisfied that everything had been done to ensure divine participation in the war. An oracle assuring the king of divine support was usually a sign to proceed to battle.

Further steps were taken during battle to make sure that the deities were present on the field. Emblems representing the gods were carried in front of the troops; an emblem of reddish gold was made by Hammurabi and a disc carried on a chariot represented Assur (see figures in Labat: 1939, 260; *ANET*, 270*a*). The records also suggest that there was a special connection between the deity and the king's weapons. It was the god who made powerful the king's weapons (Luckenbill: II, 116, 234) and who stood by his side to make bitter his arms (Luckenbill II, 139). In many instances it is implied that the very weapons used by the king had been placed in his hand by god; such powerful, unsparing and merciless weapons were gifts from the deity. But divine support meant more, for the gods were actually present with the armies. For instance, in granting Esarhaddon an oracle encouraging him to proceed to battle, the gods promised 'We will march with you' (*ANET*, 289*b*). Whichever position was taken by the deity, before the king and his armies or beside him, he was there to participate fully in the battle. It was the gods who fought furiously at the king's side, assailed the opponents, made their weapons ineffective and finally overran them. The gods' actions are variously described as 'butting my enemies with her mighty horns . . . cutting the throats of my enemies with his sharp point' (*ANET*, 300*a*), raining flames on the foes, making terrible battle and spying out the evil designs of the enemy (Luckenbill: I, 72). The king's own efforts were but a pale reflection of the activities in which the deity was engaged. Thus victory in battle is always attributed to the terrifying power of the gods (*ANET*, 281*b*); this had a paralysing effect upon the opponents, leaving them in confusion and weakness 'like an owl fleeing before an eagle' (Luckenbill: II, 83) and turning them into madmen (*ANET*, 289*b*).

Post-battle celebrations duly acknowledged the key role of the gods in achieving success. After victory the kings took it to be their duty to give thanks, which was usually accompanied by offering sacrifices. Sheep-offerings are mentioned several times in Babylonian and Assyrian historical texts (*ANET*, 276*b*; 278*a*), and 'sacrificial dues' to the patron deity of the conqueror were imposed upon the conquered (*ANET*, 293*a*). An elaborate 'Festival of the Warrior-God' was observed by the Hittites (*ANET*, 358 ff.). Stelae bearing the conqueror's name and image were erected in conquered lands, and on these were suitable inscriptions praising the might of the god responsible for the king's victory (*ANET*, 293*a*). Temples were also built to commemorate victories, and the first fruits of spoil taken in battle were offered to the gods (Fish: 1939, 398). Also featuring prominently in the celebrations were hymns of victory (*ANET*, 376 ff.; 373 ff.; on the place of victory songs, see Craigie: 1968, 121 ff.).

Even this brief selection from the sources available confirms that in the ancient Near East war was regarded as a religious enterprise. When preparing for battle every means possible was used to ensure divine participation; in describing the campaign signs of divine activity were recognised, and in celebrating victory there was always due acknowledgement of the divine conqueror. However it is difficult to establish satisfactorily which factors, if any, distinguished the Israelite holy war concept from what was found in the Near East in general. On the one hand, it is suggested that all features of holy war belonged to Eastern and Mediterranean states in general.[2] On the other hand, attempts have been made to show that, within the general recognition that the gods participated in war, there were peculiar Israelite characteristics, such as making it unnecessary for the warriors to fight[3] or noting the Israelite emphasis on surprise attack.[4] Such definitions are all the more difficult to achieve because of the need to establish first what happened in Israelite practice and what was imposed on that tradition by later theological reflection.[5]

II

A major study of the holy war concept in Israel was published by G. von Rad in 1951. Surprisingly perhaps no attempt was made to set the Old Testament concept in the context of Near Eastern thought. Von Rad's study concentrated entirely on the evidence which he found in the Old Testament itself, and, in analysing the relevant texts, he found in them constant formal elements; it was these elements that constituted a holy war, which he was thus able to describe and place in its correct *Sitz im Leben*.[6] The constant and stylised elements can be briefly summarised as follows (von Rad: 1951, 6–14). Holy War began with the sounding of a trumpet as a sign for the troops to assemble (Jud. 6.34f.); another particularly solemn method for summoning troops was to send pieces of animal flesh among the people in the hands of messengers (1 Sam. 11.7). These assembled forces formed the 'militia of Yahweh' (*ʿam yhwh*, Jud. 5.11) and were duly consecrated (Jos. 3.5). Before setting out to battle, sacrifices were offered and an oracle from Yahweh was sought (Jud. 20.23, 26). God's favourable reply was usually pronounced in the perfect tense: 'Yahweh has given the enemy into your hand' (Jos. 2.24); the declaration of victory with such certainty was an important factor in Holy War. Then Yahweh went out before them to battle (Jud. 4.14). This kind of war was Yahweh's war, the enemies were Yahweh's enemies (Jud. 5.31), and the campaign was completely in his hands. It was Yahweh too who caused panic to seize the enemies, for his fear fell upon them (Jos. 2.8), so that they became faint-hearted (Jos. 2.24). The battle itself opened with a loud battle-cry (*tᵉrûʿa*, Jud. 7.20), and all through the fighting God was active creating panic and terror among the enemies (Jos. 10.10; Jud. 4.15). The war was brought to a conclusion with the ban (*ḥerem*); men and animals were put to death, but silver, gold and other possessions were declared 'sacred' to Yahweh (Jos. 6.18–19). After this the army disbanded and the men returned to their tents (Jud. 20.8). All these formal elements are not preserved together in any single account of a battle, but they become clear in a synopsis of various campaigns.

Because of the rites associated with it, from the opening blast of the trumpet to the final devoting of the conquered to the ban, holy war obviously had a cultic character. In seeking to define its *Sitz im Leben* more specifically, von Rad placed Israel's holy war, both its theory and its practice, in the period of the amphictyony (von Rad: 1951, 14–33). He accepted as a working basis Martin Noth's theory that a sacral confederacy of tribes played an important part in Israelite life in pre-monarchic times (Noth: 1928, 39–121), and so took Israel's holy war to be an institution belonging to that period and specifically to that confederacy of tribes. The emphasis on holy war as an activity of the Israelite tribes and their levies under the leadership of Yahweh means that it belonged to a period before Israel became a state, i.e. between the settlement and the foundation of the monarchy. The campaigns belonging to this period are defined as 'defensive' wars in the sense that their aim was to secure for Israel the territory guaranteed to them by Yahweh; they were not the same as the wars of imperialistic expansion fought by David after the foundation of the monarchy. It is for this reason that the victories gained in these wars were called 'the righteous acts of Yahweh' (*sidᵉqôt yhwh*) (Zimmerli: 1978, 60).

Von Rad's thesis was very influential during the decade following its publication. Further investigation demonstrated that the concept could be traced in a number of areas other than the restricted period between the settlement and the monarchy.[7] As noted by M. Weippert, it became acceptable to different schools of thought in Old Testament studies and was further explored and developed (Weippert: 1972, 463, with a list of authors who later worked on the concept). Nevertheless, von Rad did not escape criticism, and with the passing of the years a number of weaknesses in his thesis were exposed.

The definition of holy war as an amphictyonic exercise has been challenged (especially by Smend: 1970; see further Jones: 1975, 464ff.). Our study is not directly concerned with Noth's amphictyonic theory, and with rehearsing the reasons for and against his proposals,[8] but rather with the narrower issue of the proposed connection between holy war and the amphictyony. R. Smend has argued convincingly for separating holy war, a political-military institution, from the amphictyony, a sacral-cultic institution (Smend: 1970, 13–25). Some tribes did not participate in the wars of the Judges, notably Judah and Simeon who took no part in the campaign described in the Song of Deborah; this is not an indication of an early ten-tribe alliance, as is sometimes argued, but is one instance among several of alliances that were not constituted of twelve tribes and thus demonstrates that the tribal confederacy was not engaged in these wars. A concerted action by all Israel only appears in response to the Philistine threat at a later period, but it was superimposed on the material relating to the period of the Judges because this was the concept accepted by the Deuteronomistic historians. Smend found the home of Israel's war traditions among the Rachel tribes occupying central Palestine, which is confirmed by the connection between the ark and the tribes of Joseph and Benjamin and by the presence of Ephraim in all these early wars. Whereas the Rachel tribes represented the war element, the Leah tribes represented the amphictyonic element in Israel's traditions (Smend, 1970: 107, accepting the suggestion that there was at one stage a six-tribe amphictyony, Noth: 1928, 75). The war element represented by these tribes originated with the Exodus, for Moses was a man of Yahweh's war. Thus a strong case has been made for the eminence of the Rachel tribes. Nevertheless, Smend tends to underestimate the activities of other tribal groups, as for instance the group of northern tribes, particularly Zebulun and Naphtali, in the battle described in Jud. 4–5 (especially in 4.6, 10 and 5.14, 15, 18), and a tribal group in the south that was also independent of the mid-Palestinian Rachel group (cf. Exod. 17.8–16; for a further discussion of the northern and southern groups, see Jones: 1975, 646–8). Although Smend's position may need some modification, his main argument that the wars in which these tribal groups were involved was not an amphictyonic exercise stands. It was clearly a case of various tribal groups in northern, southern and central Palestine, in the period before they had become the people of Israel, acting independently.

Another aspect of von Rad's treatment that has been questioned is his narrow definition of the period and character of holy war. To think of it as belonging to the period before the monarchy is questionable, for wars bearing exactly the same characteristics were waged in the time of Saul and David; those two kings were charismatic leaders engaged in Yahweh's wars in exactly the same way as the judges of the pre-monarchic period (Weippert: 1972, 464). Further challenge to von Rad's definition of holy war comes from the comparisons outlined above with the concept of war in the Near East in general. The concept associated with the Israelite tribes during a fairly brief period was in no way confined to the Israelite community, but was widely known among other peoples. As has already been noted, one of M. Weippert's conclusions, after comparing von Rad's definition with texts from the same region and belonging roughly to the same time, was that the concept and custom as reconstructed from the Old Testament was not a specifically Israelite, but a common oriental institution (Weippert: 1972, 483ff.). It would be as correct to refer to an 'Ištar-war' or a 'Ninurta-war' as it is to refer to a 'Yahweh-war'. Again Weippert could find no justification for the distinction between a defensive and offensive war in the royal texts of the neo-Assyrian Empire nor in the Old Testament (Weippert: 1972, 491). Furthermore, he raised the more fundamental issue of distinguishing between 'holy war' and 'profane war', a distinction he was unable to demonstrate from either the Old Testament or ancient oriental texts (Weippert: 1972, 490). Although warfare practices in the ancient world were accompanied by cultic practices, that does not mean that war was a cultic celebration (Smend: 1970, 36). As part and parcel of life it was not holy or sacred in a sense that birth, weaning, marriage, death and sheep-shearing were not (Fohrer: 1973, 118).

Whereas von Rad linked holy war with amphictyony, Smend argued that the war of Yahweh existed in some form or other prior to the conquest and he traced its roots back to the event of the Exodus (Smend: 1970, 109ff.). However, the American scholars F. M. Cross and P. D. Miller have maintained that consideration must also be given to the conceptions of divine warfare in other parts of the Near East, and especially to their mythological motifs, for these too influenced the concept of Yahweh as divine warrior. F. M. Cross' main criticism of von Rad was that he had failed to deal with mythological elements in holy war as practised in Israel (Cross: 1966, 11–30); he further claimed that the figure of Yahweh appearing in the earliest strata of Israelite tradition was constituted of two elements, the Divine Kinsman or 'God of the fathers' and the Canaanite El, who was the leader of cosmic armies, and also that cosmic elements were prominent in the holy war ideology of pre-Israelite and early Israelite times. Similarly P. D. Miller in his study (Miller: 1973) explored the mythological-theological conceptions associated with Israel's early wars. Yahweh fought for Israel as commander of the armies of heaven and earth, with the general, but not too rigid, distinction that the historical practice of holy war is described in prose, and the cosmic, mythopoetic aspects in poetry. Both these works have introduced an aspect of holy war that had not been investigated by von Rad.

Penetrating and basic questions about both the theory and practice of holy war were raised for further investigation by F. Stolz (Stolz: 1972). After discussing the question whether holy war was an exclusively Israelite institution or was similarly practised by other nations, Stolz proceeded to find the particular moment at which holy war began in Israel. Possible periods of origin, such as nomadic times, the exodus, possession of the land and the establishment of the monarchy, were explored, but Stolz realised that he had first of all to distinguish between ancient tradition and the use made of it by its bearers, between the original practice and the form in which it has been preserved. For example, in discussing the Deuteronomistic war regulations, he conceded that ancient material derived from nomadic culture had been included, but that it had been incorporated within a Deuteronomistic mode of thought. Thus an issue of supreme importance has been raised, viz. the exact relationship between practice and theory in holy war. In the discussion that followed an attempt was made to reverse the relationship between them that had been suggested by von Rad; instead of accepting that there was initially an ideology or theory that had then come to dominate Israel's later practices, it was suggested that practice had preceded the theory. 'Yahweh War' became a technical term for the practice and 'Holy War' for the theory (Jones: 1975, 655–8).

III

One possible reaction to von Rad's admission that not all the elements constituting a holy war were present in any single battle (von Rad: 1951, 14) is to ask if holy war really existed, and, if it existed, was it practised in the way described. This involves a very close scrutiny of the biblical material. Some of the poetic pieces, which are very old and have been taken from a book of ancient war poetry (see Caspari: 1912, 110ff.; Tur-Sinai: 1959–60, 146ff.) provide evidence of primary importance for reconstructing Israel's early wars. The war traditions in the books of Joshua are introduced in a Deuteronomistic setting, but with the help of traditio-historical investigations earlier stages in the development of the material can be traced and an original core uncovered.[9] An examination of such texts as Exod. 15.21; Exod. 17.8–16 and Jud. 5[10] demonstrates the early emergence of the concept that in Yahweh's wars it was he who conquered his and his people's enemies. According to many exegetes Exod. 15.21 is a victory celebration song that arose directly from the Exodus event (Smend: 1970, 110); although it provides no details of the event itself, it clearly attributes victory to Yahweh. A prose account of the same event in Exod. 14 gives a fuller picture of the course of events (especially in vv. 21–3) and at the same time underlines Yahweh's responsibility for the victory (vv. 14, 18, 25); it has elaborated upon the interpretation found in the ancient song.[11] Similarly the much later Song of the Sea in Ex. 15.1–18 describes in more detail the opening of the sea (vv. 4–10), but adheres to the initial interpretation that victory was gained by Yahweh who was a 'man of war' (v. 3). Although these two later elaborations provide more details of the event, they repeat the interpretation of the event as Yahweh's victory that belonged to the earliest of the traditions. The second passage, Exod. 17.8–16, has grown from an ancient kernel in vv. 8–13, which originated from a clash between an early tribal group in the south and Amalek (Grønbaek: 1964, 26–45). Victory is attributed to Yahweh, for the outcome of the battle was determined by Moses' action in stretching out his hand holding 'the rod of God' in the direction of the enemy. The later addition in vv. 14–16, which may have originated from Davidic times, possibly depended on two older traditions, namely the old oath formula 'A hand upon the banner of Yahweh' (Gradwohl: 1962, 491–4), which was intended to seek God's aid in war, and the war-cry 'Yahweh has a war with Amalek.' Nevertheless, the addition merely repeats the presupposition of the original, that Yahweh was responsible for victory. Undoubtedly the Song of Deborah (Jud. 5), if not in its entirety, at least in parts, must be regarded as an early celebration song composed soon after the event (cf. Craigie: 1968, 131–52, although he took it as a unit that is not to be divided into parts). It may well be that an original profane hero-song to Jael in vv. 24–30, and coming from the period of nomadic epic or hero poetry, has been attached to a song of praise to Yahweh (vv. 6–8, 11–13, 19–23), which attributes victory to Yahweh (for an analysis, see Müller: 1966, 446–59). In the same tradition as Exod. 15.21 it portrays Yahweh using the forces of nature to achieve victory over the enemies. These three ancient passages, therefore, support the conclusion that Yahweh's activity in war was recognised in the period between the exodus and the settlement in Canaan.

Early traditions of Yahweh war do not indicate any particular characteristics of practice that distinguish it from ordinary profane warfare. The set of regulations governing exemptions from war service in Deut. 20.1–9 provides a good example. After extracting the Deuteronomistic introduction in vv. 1–4 and the stereotyped formula for presenting the exemptions in vv. 5–9, there remains a list of four categories granted exemption: men who have built a new house, recently planted a vineyard, betrothed a wife or who are fainthearted. There is nothing specifically Israelite about the list, but it rather reflects the generally accepted practice in warfare;[12] the custom in secular warfare became acceptable, and it is only its setting within a holy war formula that gives it a religious significance. This similarity of practice is confirmed by the notable example of profane war preserved in Num. 21.21–32, which records the swift defeat of Sihon the Amorite after he had refused to let Israel pass through his land. No mention is made of Yahweh in the narrative nor in the victory song of vv. 27–30, and this is particularly strange in view of the narrative's similarity in content and in phraseology to later accounts of Yahweh's wars. It seems that in outward practice (defeating the enemy 'with the edge of the sword' and 'taking possession of the land') there was no marked distinction between the so designated Yahweh wars and profane warfare; nor was there a sufficient distinction of terminology in a profane victory song[13] to exclude it from usage in a context which assumes that Yahweh gave victory.

If the present holy war framework in which the campaigns of the Judges have been set is ignored, some of those wars too appear as no more than ordinary acts of warfare. All profane narratives about heroes, without any direct reference to Yahweh, form the basis of the Ehud narrative (Jud. 3.15–30), one strand in the Gideon complex (Jud. 8.4ff.) and the beginning of the Jephthah narrative (Jud. 11.1–11) (the three narratives discussed by Stolz: 1972, 127 and following the analysis of Richter: 1963, 339ff.). The core of the Ehud narrative in 3.15*b*–26 has no religious content whatsoever, and makes no reference to Yahweh or his activity; it is in fact an example of a political assassination, which, by being set in a holy war framework (vv. 15*b*, 27–30), has been transformed into a typical example of holy war. Again, one strand in the Gideon narrative (8.4–21) portrays a profane, non-Yahweh event, in which Gideon appears as the sole hero. Its central theme is the execution of blood revenge, and the war described is simply a background for pronouncing an oath and then executing it; but by setting it within the Gideon complex, the narrative has been transformed into another example of holy war. There is again no indication in the opening account of Jephthah's war against the Ammonites that it was a Yahweh war (Jud. 10.17–11.11); Jephthah himself was the warrior, and the few references to Yahweh (vv. 10, 11) do not imply that it was an ancient tradition of Yahweh War. These narratives, therefore, describe profane warfare, but in the course of time the heroes became saviour figures and their wars were considered as examples of holy war. This transformation was only possible because there was no distinction in practice between profane and holy war; the latter was a matter of faith, but in practice there seems to have been no difference between them.

It is also difficult to determine which rituals were connected with Yahweh wars in their three consecutive stages of making preparations, campaigning and final celebration. If Israel did use practices known elsewhere, then how is the constitutive essence of Yahweh war to be described? An examination of early material does not suggest an elaborate war ritual in Israel, and the evidence is not sufficient to establish a set pattern according to which every Yahweh war had to be waged. However, it is probable that Israel's wars had attracted a number of commonly known practices. There is evidence that sympathetic magic was used in order to obtain the help of Yahweh, as was the case when Moses held up a rod in the battle against Amalek (Exod. 17.8–16),[14] or when Joshua stretched a javelin in the direction of Ai to secure its defeat (Jos. 8.18, 26).[15] Possibly too there was some consultation with endowed persons in the early stages of a Yahweh war; a partnership between military leader and inspired person in some of the early narratives may contain a hint of this, as was the case when Joshua's success in Ex. 17 depended on the efficacy of Moses' ritual and when Barak, a commander of the army, acted upon the initiative and continued inspiration of Deborah, 'the prophetess' (Jud. 4–5). Although the significance of such collaboration must not be exaggerated, it seems right to understand it in the context of consulting an inspired person prior to battle (1 Sam. 15) and specific requests for an oracle prior to battle (1 Sam. 28.6; 30.7–9). The occasional trace of a war-cry at the commencement of a campaign suggests that it was in this way dedicated to Yahweh. 'For Yahweh and for Gideon' in Jud. 7.18 opened the battle, and at the same time indicated its nature and purpose. Possibly too Exod. 17.16, after referring to the name of the altar 'A hand upon the banner of Yahweh', contains what was originally an ancient war cry 'Yahweh's war against Amalek' (Noth: 1962, 112–15). It is, however, impossible to list a number of these practices and to state categorically that without their presence a campaign could not be called a 'Yahweh war'; in other words, a given formula for Yahweh war cannot be established.

This conclusion is confirmed by examining the use of the ban (*ḥerem*) in Israel's early wars. Texts proving the antiquity of the ban are rare; some of them, such as the accounts of wars against Amalek (1 Sam. 15) and against Syria (1 Kgs. 20), introduce religious motives, bear the marks of theological tension between prophet and king, and are of uncertain historicity

(Brekelmans: 1959, 153ff.), whilst others, such as Jos. 6–7, are distinctly Deuteronomistic. Num. 21.1–3 provides an ancient piece of evidence that the ban was known among the Israelites of the south; nevertheless it appears to have been an exceptional rather than a regular war practice, and so falls short of proving that the ban was a necessary part of Yahweh war. There is a close parallel to Num. 21.1–3 in the Meša inscription (*ANET*, 320*b*) and a similar consecration of the enemy to the godhead in Mari under the technical term *asakhu*.[16] But it may well be that this generally known custom had been modified by the Israelites, as is perhaps indicated by the almost total absence of offering a life to the godhead in gratitude for success in battle (the only example being in Jud. 11.30ff.). The issue is further complicated by examples in the Old Testament itself of a total annihilation of the enemy as an act of political expediency rather than action arising from religious motives. After taking all these factors into consideration, it is impossible to affirm that practising the ban was one of the necessities of a Yahweh war.

Another difficult problem arises in connection with the Ark, which plays a prominent part in Israel's war traditions, sometimes being directly involved and being carried out into battle (Num. 14.44; 1 Sam. 11.11), but at other times appearing in a war context without a specific war function (Jos. 7.6; 8.33). Although it has been described as a war palladium (Ger. *Kriegsheiligtum*), the reliability of the tradition connecting the Ark in its pre-Jerusalemite period with Israel's war tradition is debatable.[17] Both narratives referring to the Ark in the book of Joshua (Jos. 6; 3f.) are treated as complex compositions in which the ark element is taken to belong to the latest recension of these chapters (Maier: 1965, 37–9, 21–5). The Ark strand, it has been claimed, depended on the Ark narratives in 1 Samuel, belonged to the Jerusalem priestly tradition and clearly reflects its place in the theology of the Jerusalem Temple. The connection between the Ark and the Philistine wars in the ancient tradition behind 1 Sam. 4.1–7.1 is not as significant as it seems. The Ark, which had not been taken out to the first battle, was brought in desperation to the second, and this can be interpreted as evidence that it was not at that time used as a war palladium (Smend: 1970, 77; Maier: 1965, 47–8). Sayings about the Ark in Num. 10.35–6 are taken to be independent liturgical phrases which have been connected with the Ark and the period of Israel's desert wanderings by means of the two introductions supplied by an interpolator (Maier: 1965, 5–12). This short survey of some key passages, without attempting to trace the history of the Ark or the use of transportable shrines among other peoples, confirms the general picture of the early period; there was no fixed procedure for engaging in a Yahweh war, and because the Ark may have been used on some occasions but probably not on others it can hardly be regarded as a war palladium.

Not only was there no fixed procedure, but it appears too that the whole concept of a Yahweh war was not clearly expressed in the early period. Yahweh's participation in Israel's wars was understood rather loosely and perhaps vaguely. Although his participation was taken for granted (Ex. 15.21), no attempt was made to define more precisely the manner of his intervention; it was assumed that he was working through the miraculous co-operation of natural phenomena, or else through the activities of leaders and heroes (cf. Jud. 7.18). The only firm evidence is that it was immediately *post eventu* that a war became recognised as a Yahweh war.

IV

Whilst both the practice and concept of Yahweh war in early Israel were indistinct, the holy war theory of later tradition is unmistakably clear. A brief examination of some key texts will reveal its essential features and the way in which the theory has been superimposed on earlier traditional material. For instance, an analysis of the narrative in Jud. 4 shows that it consists of three sections (cf. Richter: 1963, 32ff.): (i) an old section about Jael in vv. 17–22, originating probably from the tribes connected with Mount Tabor and belonging to the time of the oppression described; (ii) the Deuteronomistic formulae in vv. 1–3, 23–4; (iii) an account of Barak and Deborah's war against Sisera (vv. 4–16), which displays the main characteristics of Holy War – the handing over formula (*Übergabeformel*), 'I will give him into your hand' (vv. 6–7, 14), summoning volunteers to battle (v. 10), attributing victory to Yahweh (vv. 14–15) and the unquestionable defeat of the enemy 'by the edge of the sword' (vv. 15–16), a form of executing the ban, so that not a man was left. This latter section presents a highly formalised account in traditional language; because of the domination of the form of presentation, the account lacks the vividness of the narrative in the older section. Again two complete versions of the holy war schema appear in Jud. 6–8 (Richter: 1963, 238ff.). In the first (6.33–7.22), which contains a summoning of troops (6.33f.), rallying for battle (7.1) and notice of victory (7.22), the tradition about Gideon's visit to the camp (7.11*b*, 13–21) has been included. The use of the handing over formula and of the 'do not fear' theme bring vv. 9–11*a* also into the scheme. Obviously an old tradition about Gideon's participation in a Yahweh war has by now been made part of the holy war scheme. The second version in 7.23–8.21 does not build upon an earlier war tradition; it has transformed an account of Gideon's revenge on the men of Succoth (8.5–9, 14–21) into a holy war tradition by including a summoning of the troops (7.23f.), a rallying for battle (8.4) and a notice of victory (8.10–13). As in Jud. 4, so also in Jud. 6–8, the holy war scheme has come to dominate the presentation of the material.

Another significant example of the holy war scheme appears in the Ammonite war account in 1 Sam. 11.[18] The main elements in the narrative are: a reference to oppression (v. 1), possession by the spirit (v. 6), conscription of forces (in a very unusual fashion in v. 7), an account of the battle culminating in a notice of victory and the total annihilation of the enemy (v. 11). Some of the features observed in the previous examples are not as clear in this version, and their distinctly religious tones are absent. Because of this W. Richter has suggested that there were two different holy war schemes. Firstly, the one in the narrative in 1 Sam. 11 and in constructed reports in Jud. 3; 6f. has five elements: description of the situation and denunciation of the enemy, the coming of the spirit, conscription of fighters, victory and total annihilation. Because of the prominence given to the part played by the coming of the spirit, this scheme is connected with prophetic circles. Secondly, such texts as Exod. 14; Jos. 10; Jud. 4 and 1 Sam. 7 contain a scheme which concentrates on these elements: God's exhortation and instructions, Yahweh's own activity causing confusion and a statement affirming that the enemies had been utterly destroyed. This second scheme is connected with priestly circles, most notably the house of Eli; it is therefore older than the first.

W. Richter's studies have brought out one important aspect of the holy war theory, namely that it could be presented in a variety of forms and was not as uniform as had been maintained by G. von Rad. It is difficult, however, to justify his conclusion that the presence of divergence in the narrative points to two distinct holy war schemes. What emerges is that the presentation of holy war exhibits a number of constant elements, but with room for flexibility and variety in the presentation. In outline the holy war theory moved logically from one phase to another: a situation of oppression and distress, the rise of a leader, calling followers and their response, engagement in battle and reaching a climax with total victory over the enemies. An element that is brought out very clearly in the formulaic presentation of holy war is Yahweh's participation. Whilst this was always recognised by Israel's ancient tradition, it was frequently assumed without being specifically expressed; but as the presentation became stylised, this element stands out prominently in the general outline as well as in formulaic details. Whatever its past history, the handing over formula,[19] 'I have given . . . into your hand', appears consistently in schematic presentations. It does so in a constant form constituted of three elements: the divine subject, a verb in the perfect tense and the enemy as object (cf. Jud. 4.7; 7.9; 3.28; 4.14). The formula was intended to declare beforehand that Yahweh was participating in the battle. The same emphasis is achieved in the accounts of the war leaders in the book of Judges by referring to their possession by the divine spirit (cf. Othniel, 3.10; Gideon, 6.34; Jephthah, 11.29 and Samson, 13.25; 14.6, 19; 15.24). It was after their possession by the spirit that the leaders summoned troops (6.34), took up their position (11.29, 32) and went out to battle (3.10). On analysing the narratives it would appear that references to the spirit belong to the holy war scheme rather than to the traditional material incorporated in it; this is especially clear in the case of Jud. 6.33f. and 11.29–33. It is obviously therefore another way of emphasising Yahweh's participation in the war.

Key phrases in the holy war regulations in Deut. 20 (especially vv. 1–4) and in the Deuteronomistic edition of the book of Joshua make the same point. In the regulations the Israelites are encouraged not to be afraid, for God was with them, and was ready to go with them to battle and fight for them. It was indeed God that caused fear and confusion in the enemy camp (Jos. 10.10) and drove them out of the land; realising that victory was given by Yahweh, Israel was to avoid self-congratulation (Deut. 9.4ff.; 8.17). In the account of Israel's defeat of the Adonizedek coalition in Jos. 10.6–11, three of the these Deuteronomistic elements stand out very clearly: the introduction contains a combination of 'do not fear' and the handing over formula (v. 8), panic among the enemies is attributed to Yahweh (v. 10) and there is an unmistakable concluding affirmation that victory belonged to Yahweh (v. 11*b*). With such an emphasis on Yahweh's participation, Israel's part is transformed into a secondary one which is sandwiched between Yahweh's activity in v. 10*a* and his complete devastation of the enemy in v. 11*b*. Although the scheme concentrates on Yahweh's intervention at the expense of the exploits of the war leaders, there is always an undefined synergism of Yahweh and the Israelite warriors (von Rad: 1951, 62; Lind: 1980, 2f.).

The Holy War schema can thus be defined by resorting to the biblical texts: but, was there a holy war? The issue to be settled is: was holy war ever practised according to the pattern outlined and constituted therefore a cultic institution, or is the pattern due entirely to the fact that the redactors have superimposed their own projection on the material they used? Despite his admission that he could not point to a single example of the holy war pattern in its entirety, von Rad maintained that the schema was but a reflection of what was practised historically and that its original *Sitz im*

Leben was cultic (von Rad: 1951, 29ff.). Similarly W. Richter, although his solution is more intricate than what von Rad had proposed, admitted that leaders like Ehud and Gideon were holy war figures (Richter: 1963, 178–9). An entirely different view, claiming that holy war was not cultic and was never practised historically, has been taken by R. Smend (Smend: 1970, 36ff.). The most reasonable solution to this problem is to accept that the holy war scheme has been founded on the earlier tradition of the ancient Yahweh wars, and has sought to grasp and to emphasise what was considered to be fundamental to that tradition (Jones: 1965, 656). Although those ancient battles had cultic preliminaries, they were basically non-cultic events; but the fundamental conviction behind them was that because of Yahweh's activity they could be called Yahweh's wars. The holy war schema, by adopting a pattern of cultic and formulaic sequences, made Yahweh's activity more dominant. Original historical events were presented within the formula set by later interpreters, and the whole account is then regarded as a true record of what had happened; in this way the dichotomy of event and formula is avoided. Furthermore, it seems that, after it had become standardised, the theory in turn influenced the practice; in some instances, such as the Aramean wars of 1 Kgs. 20 and possibly the later Maccabean battles, the sequence of events has been determined by the theory.

Although the holy war formula appears in its classical form in the book of Deuteronomy, and plays a significant part in books whose present form is clearly Deuteronomistic, especially in the account of the conquest of Canaan in Joshua and in the narratives of Judges, the formation of the holy war theory is not exclusively the work of the Deuteronomists. Some standardisation of the holy war concept had occurred in the pre-Deuteronomistic stages of the tradition. W. Richter's attempt (Richter: 1963, 319f.; 1964, *passim*) to establish a pre-Deuteronomistic *Retterbuch* as a basis for the book of Judges is significant, for the original book, before its two Deuteronomistic redactions and its final redaction at the hand of the Deuteronomistic historians, had two main themes – the call of the judges and holy war. Furthermore, the suggestion that one of the main characteristics of the *Retterbuch* was antipathy to the kingship may give some indication of the circumstances in which the holy war theory was formulated. Charismatic spontaneity was soon lost in the more formal business of waging war professionally in the time of the monarchy. By the time of Solomon the responsibility for war seems to have passed over entirely into the hands of professional soldiers (von Rad: 1951, 36). This shift of emphasis provided the occasion and the impetus for underlining the essentials of the old Yahweh war tradition, especially the character of those wars as being Yahweh-centred. The old traditions were formalised to draw attention to this feature, and it was from this that the holy war ideal was born.

Another valuable suggestion is that criticism of the monarchy was especially prominent among the prophetic circles of the northern kingdom (Richter: 1963, 339). As has been already noted, Israel's war traditions recognised the place of an inspired person; but it was also noted that references to the spirit belonged to the holy war scheme rather than to the ancient material incorporated in the schema (Richter: 1963, 61–63, with comments on Jud. 4.4*a*). The inspiration of charismatic war leaders would be of interest to the prophetic movement, which was particularly concerned with the devaluation of the role of such leaders after the establishment of the monarchy. The point is clearly made in 1 Sam. 14.1–46, which demonstrates that Yahweh's participation was found, not in the regular, orderly, institutionalised war led by Saul, but in the spontaneous action of Jonathan (Stolz: 1972, 132ff.). The old custom of consulting an inspired person seems to have been directed especially towards the priesthood in the time of David (1 Sam. 23.1, 9ff.; 30.7ff.), but after his time the prophets seem to have taken over the role of pre-war consultants. It can be suggested that the prophets regarded themselves as the true inheritors of the tradition associated with the early charismatic war leaders, and that in this role they became active in three areas: (i) they assumed the role of the inspired persons to be consulted before engaging in battle; (ii) they criticised the move to make warfare the responsibility of the reigning monarch; (iii) they revived the ancient war tradition with its emphasis on inspired leadership and gave the concept a formalised expression.

The holy war concept, therefore, seems to have developed in three stages. Firstly, the Yahweh war tradition in its simplest form asserted that Yahweh was active in granting Israel success against its enemies. Secondly, in circles critical of the monarchy it became necessary to emphasise once again that Yahweh wars were God centred; tradition was now given a formula in order to make this point, and the theory emerged. Thirdly, this tradition was most acceptable to the Deuteronomistic redactors; it suited their emphasis on the possession of Canaan as a gift from Yahweh and on their overall scheme for interpreting history. Yet another stage can be traced by comparing the Chronicler's account of some of the wars covered in the Deuteronomistic History (e.g. 2 Chron. 14.9–14; 20.1–30) (von Rad: 1951, 80–1). As a result of further theological reflection holy war has become a cultic undertaking that was accompanied by prayers, singing and processions; cultic personnel, especially the Levites, have been given prominence. The miraculous element has also been heightened, and it appears frequently as if Israel's role is cultic rather than military, with victory being entirely God's achievement.

V

The holy war concept is by no means confined to Israel's war traditions, but is claimed to have influenced several other areas of Israel's life and thinking as reflected in Old Testament literature. An example of its impact on Israel's literary forms has been found in the use of the 'do not fear' (*'al tîrā'*)formula. It is a phrase that appears prominently in the holy war regulations (Deut. 20.11ff.), as it also does in the accounts of warfare (Jos. 11.6), and is often attached to the statement that Yahweh had given Israel's enemies into her hands. The later use of the formula in prophetic literature and in Psalms may be a case of borrowing from Israel's war traditions,[20] and not from the priestly salvation-oracle as had been previously claimed (as by Begrich: 1934, 81–92).

A more significant influence is observed when pursuing the later use of the ancient war oracles and its subsequent modification in Israelite tradition (see especially Christensen: 1975). Attention is focused in this connection on the corpora of prophetic oracles against Foreign Nations. The similarities between the oracles and Israel's war traditions in phraseology and motifs have been explored (Margulis: 1966; Jones: 1970) and it has been claimed that two particular forms of prophetic speech, the summons to battle and the summons to flight, owe their origin to Israel's institution of holy war (Bach: 1962). Undoubtedly the oracles against foreign nations have their roots in Israel's early wars, but their usage was not limited to this one particular area; they also played an important part in Israel's royal and political life (Hayes: 1964, 93–172; 1968, 81–92; Christensen: 1975, 87–8). During the period of the monarchy there was some change in the usage of oracles against nations, a change that becomes obvious in the shift of emphasis towards a judgement speech. A further change may be seen in the transformation of the oracle in early apocalyptic writing where the traces of historical existence have become fainter. How the ancient war oracle was transformed into a judgement speech in prophetic preaching may be seen in the earliest collection of oracles against the nations in Amos. 1–2 (Christensen: 1975, 16ff.). The speech against foreign nations in the form of a war oracle has now become a judgement speech in which Israel itself has been included. D. L. Christensen found another significant transformation in the time of Jeremiah, when the oracle concentrated on the Divine Warrior's preservation of his people in exile (Christensen: 1975, 183ff.). In whichever way the various changes in the tradition are described, there seems to be a general consensus that this particular form of prophetic speech has its origin in Israel's war oracle tradition and is an extension of it.

The concept was also important in Israel's cult and made a significant contribution to its development. According to F. M. Cross (Cross: 1966, 11–30), the development of Israel's cultic themes and institutions was a complex one in which historical and mythic features were combined. On the one hand was a historical memory of the Exodus, Covenant and Conquest; on the other hand was the concept of the Divine King, creator and leader of the armies. Although mythological themes stood in tension with historical themes, there was in Israel a joining of the conquest theme with kingship in the royal cult, and in Cross' view the link was provided by the holy war ideology. Holy war made possible the transition from the cult of the tribal league to the cult of the kingdom; because cosmic elements were present even in early tradition (cf. Jud. 5.20, 23; Jos. 10.12–13), it was possible for the theme of conquest to be mythologised after the institution of kingship and the inauguration of a temple in Jerusalem. It was the holy war concept too that helped the later transition to apocalyptic ideology and the battle of the sons of light against the sons of darkness and the leadership of the Divine Warrior. The conclusions drawn by P. D. Miller in his study of the Divine Warrior theme were similar (Miller: 1973, 166–75). Behind Israel's epic tradition, according to Miller, stood the ancient songs of Yahweh's and Israel's wars; Yahweh as warrior was not only an early part of Israel's understanding of God, but also played a dominant part through its faith. Myth and history had become combined in the central theme of Yahweh as the Divine Warrior and the commander of the armies of heaven and earth.

The inclusion of an oracle against Israel in Amos' collection of oracles against the nations points to another usage of the holy war concept. There has been a reversal of the concept in its use in passages describing God's judgement upon Israel; this is seen especially in the biblical interpretation of the fall of Samaria in 722 BC and the fall of Jerusalem in 587 BC that is evident in the Deuteronomistic History and in pre-exilic prophecy (Lind: 1980, 161ff.). In some instances the term 'war' has been used technically for Yahweh's war, and that not simply for a war in which Israel was engaged against other nations (Jer. 51.27; Joel 4.9), but also for Yahweh's war against his own people (Mic. 3.5; Jer. 6.1–6; 22.7) (Soggin: 1960, 79–83). Holy war is completely turned back against Jerusalem itself, and it was envisaged that Yahweh himself would fight against the city. There has been an interchange of roles and Israel has now passed over into the position previously occupied by the attacked enemy nations (Reventlow: 1959, 37).

Of particular interest in this connection is Jer. 21.1–7 (as analysed by Weippert: 1970, 396–409), where Yahweh himself declares that, after turning back the weapons of war that were used by Israel, 'I myself will fight *against you* with outstretched hand and strong arm.' Admittedly other elements, such as the curse associated with breaking the covenant, cannot be ignored in attempting to understand the text; but combined with such elements, and underlying the whole section, is the tradition of holy war in its reversed form. The concept was so familiar in Israelite thinking that the judgement implied by its total reversal could not be missed.

Notes

1 The ἱερος πόλεμος appears in Greek writers for a war undertaken as punishment for sacrilege or as a crusade, cf. Thucydides I, 112; Aristophanes *Av*. 556.

2 According to M. Weippert: 1972, 485 all but two of the thirteen features of Israelite holy war were practised by Eastern and Mediterranean states.

3 According to F. Schwally: 1901, 27f., divine participation outside Israel was a stimulation for the warriors to fight harder; in Israel it made it unnecessary for the warriors to fight. See further M. C. Lind: 1980, 24.

4 According to A. Glock: 1968, 191–2, Israel emphasised surprise attack and there was no real siege of a city before the time of David.

5 On the interpretations of holy war that derive the miraculous element from later theological reflection rather than from historical events, see M. C. Lind: 1980, 24–31.

6 cf. G. von Rad: 1951, 5f. where the method is described. For short analyses of his thesis see further H.-J. Kraus, 'Krieg II', *RGG*[4] IV, 64; W. Zimmerli: 1978, 60; J. H. Grønbaek: 1964, 26–45; M. Weippert: 1972, 460ff.

7 One of these developments was von Rad's own thesis that the 'Day of the Lord' concept in prophetic literature originated from the holy war tradition, see von Rad: 1959, 97–108.

8 A discussion of the main objections to the theory and a list of dissenters is given by G. Fohrer: 1966, 801–16, 893–904. For a further discussion see G. W. Anderson: 1970, 135–51 and A. D. H. Mayes: 1974. Others, whilst admitting that the amphictyony was given an exaggerated importance in discussions of Israel's early period, do not challenge its existence, cf. R. Smend: 1971, 626–30.

9 F. Stolz: 1972, 15 defined the aim of his study as the analysis of the earlier formation (practice) and the later developments (theory) of Israel's wars. On examining each war passage in detail he found a core of traditional material within the given ideological presentation.

10 This selection of texts is not arbitrary; these are the sources of primary importance, according to recent researches, the first two being noted by F. Stolz: 1972, 90f., 97ff., and the latter by R. Smend: 1970, 13ff., 101f.

11 To take the prose account as an elaboration of an original poetic account is a more satisfactory explanation than what was proposed by L. Hey: 1964, 397–403, where it is maintained that the holy war tradition presupposed an earlier straightforward narrative of a military encounter between the Hebrews and their enemies.

12 The same practice is found in the Ugaritic Krt-epic (W. Herrmann: 1958, 215ff.), in the Bablyonian Gilgamesh epic (*ANET* 50ff.) and among bedouin tribes (A. Musil: 1928, 508).

13 vv. 27–30 are taken to have been originally a profane song which was later understood as a celebration of Yahweh's victory, cf. F. Stolz: 1972, 74.

14 On the possibility that the rod was mistakenly introduced in v. 8 and that power lay in the outstretched hand of Moses (v.12), see J. H. Grønbaek: 1964, 31–9.

15 The javelin ritual is thought to have belonged to the older traditional material incorporated in the present Deuteronomistic version. See further F. Stolz: 1972, 81–4.

16 A. Malamat: 1966, 49f. On the custom of undertaking strict purity laws, which was by no means confined to the Orient, see F. Schwally: 1901, 35, 59ff.; F. Stolz: 1972, 194–5; A. Goetz: 1963, 129.

17 This is but one of the many problems associated with the Ark. See further G. H. Davies: 1966–7, 30–47; J. Maier: 1965; E. Nielsen: 1960, 6–74.

18 R. Smend: 1970, 20f. and W. Richter: 1963, 177ff. both consider 1 Sam. 11 to be an important passage, but F. Stolz: 1972, 129, does not think that it is a characteristic holy war narrative.

19 Whereas F. Stolz: 1972, 21–2 has the term *Übergabeformel* for this phrase, W. Richter: 1963, 21ff. uses the term *Übereignungsformel*.

20 cf. F. Stolz: 1972, 184ff., and especially J.-G. Heintz: 1969, 112–38, where similar phraseology is found in letters from Mari and the case for connecting it with the holy war tradition is argued. E. W. Conrad: 1965, arguing from a *Sitze im Text* rather than a *Sitz im Leben* study, claims that it is a phrase used for comforting a warrior. A case against Heintz has been argued by P.-E. Dion: 1970, 565ff.

Bibliography

Anderson, G. W., 1970. 'Israel: Amphictyony; 'AM; KĀHĀL, 'EDÂH', *Translating and Understanding the Old Testament*, Essays in Honor of H. G. May, ed. H. T. Frank and W. L. Reed (Nashville, Tenn.), 135–51.

Bach, R., 1962. *Die Aufforderungen zur Flucht und zum Kampf in alttestamentlichen Prophetenspruch*, WMANT 9 (Neukirchen: Neukirchener Verlag).

Begrich, J., 1934. 'Das priesterliche Heilsorakel', *ZAW* 52, 81–92.

Breasted, J. H., 1906–7. *Ancient Records of Egypt*, 1–5 (Chicago).

Brekelmans, C. H. W., 1959. *De Herem in het Oude Testament* (Nijmegen).

Caspari, W., 1912. 'Was stand im Buche der Kriege Jahwes?' *ZwTh* 54, 110–58.

Christensen, D. L., 1975. *Transformations of the War Oracle in Old Testament Prophecy. Studies in the Oracles against the Nations*, Harvard Dissertations in Religion (Missoula: Scholars Press).

Conrad, E. W., 1985. *Fear Not Warrior. A Study of 'al tîrā' Pericopes in the Hebrew Scriptures* Brown Judaic Studies 75 (Chico: Scholars Press).

Craigie, P. C., 1968. *Ancient Semitic War Poetry*, Unpublished Dissertation (University of Aberdeen).

Cross, F. M., 1966. 'The Divine Warrior in Israel's Early Cult', *Biblical Motifs, Origins and Transformations*, ed. A. Altmann (Cambridge Mass.), 11–30.

Davies, G. Henton, 1967. 'The Ark of the Covenant', *ASTI* 5, 30–47.

Dion, P.-E., 1970. 'The "Fear Not" Formula and Holy War', *CBQ* 32, 565–70.

Fish, T., 1939. 'War and Religion in Egypt and Mesopotamia', *BJRL*, 387–402.

Fohrer, G., 1966. 'Altes Testament – "Amphiktyonie" und "Bund"?', *ThLZ* 111, 801–16, 893–904.

1973. *History of Israelite Religion* (London: SPCK), Eng. Tr. of *Geschichte der israelitischen Religion* (Berlin: de Gruyter, 1968).

Fredriksson, H., 1945. *Jahwe als Krieger; studien zum alttestamentlichen Gottesbild* (Lund: Gleerup).

Glock, A., 1968. *Warfare in Mari and Early Israel*, Unpublished Dissertation (University of Michigan).

Goetz, A., 1963. 'Warfare in Asia Minor', *Iraq* 25, 124–30.

Gradwohl, R., 1962. 'Zum Verständnis von Ex. 17.15f.', *VT* 12, 491–4.

Grønbaek, J. H., 1964. 'Juda und Amalek. Überlieferungsgeschichtliche Erwägungen zu Exodus 17.8–16', *StTh* 18, 26–45.

Hay, L. S., 1964. 'What really happened at the Sea of Reeds?', *JBL* 83, 397–403.

Hayes, J. H., 1964. *The Oracles against the Nations in the Old Testament. Their Usage and Theological Importance*, Unpublished Dissertation (Princeton Seminary).

1968. 'The Usage of Oracles against Foreign Nations in Ancient Israel', *JBL* 87, 81–92.

Jones, G. H., 1970. *An Examination of Some Leading Motifs in the Prophetic Oracles against Foreign Nations*, Unpublished Dissertation (University of Wales).

1975. '"Holy War" or "Yahweh War"?', *VT* 25, 642–58.

Kraus, H.-J., 'Krieg II', *RGG*[4] IV, 64.

Labat, R., 1939. *Le Caractère Religieux de la Royauté Assyro-Babylonienne*, Études d'Assyriologie (Paris).

Lind, M. C., 1980. *Yahweh is a Warrior. A Theology of Warfare in Ancient Israel* (Pennsylvania).

Luckenbill, D. D., 1926–7. *Ancient Records of Assyria and Babylonia*, 2 vols. (Chicago: Univ. of Chicago).

Maier, J., 1965. *Das Altisraelitische Ladeheiligtum*, *BZAW* 93 (Berlin; de Gruyter).

Malamat, A., 1966. 'The Ban in Mari and the Bible', *Biblical Essays 1966*. Proceedings of the 9th meeting 'Die Ou-testamentiese Werkgemeenskap in Suid-Afrika' (Potchefstroom), 40–9.

Mayes, A. D. H., 1974. *Israel in the Period of the Judges*, *SBT* 29 (London: SCM).

Margulis, B., 1966. *Studies in the Oracles against the Nations*, Unpublished Dissertation (Brandeis University).

Miller, P. D., 1973. *The Divine Warrior in Early Israel*, Harvard Semitic Monographs 5 (Cambridge Mass.).

Morenz, S., 1973. *Egyptian Religion* (London), Eng. Tr. of *Ägyptische Religion* (Stuttgart, 1960).

Moser, A., 1963. 'Griechisches zur Institution des Heiligen Krieges', *ThZ* 16, 133–4.

Müller, H.-P., 1966. 'Der Aufbau des Deboraliees', *VT* 16, 446–59.

Musil, A., 1908. *Arabaia Petraea* III (Vienna).

1928. *The Manners and Customs of the Rwala Bedouins* (New York).

Nielsen, E., 1960. 'Some reflections on the history of the ark', *SVT*. 7, 6–74.
1961. 'La Guerre considérée comme une religion et la Religion comme une guerre. Du chant de Débora au Rouleau de la Guerre de Qoumran', *StTh* 15, 93–112.
Noth, A., 1966. *Heiliger Krieg und Heiliger Kampf in Islam und Christentum*, Bonner historische Forschung 28 (Bonn).
Noth, M., 1928. *Das System der zwölf Stämmes Israels*, BWANT (Stuttgart: Kohlhammer).
1962. *Exodus*, *OTL* (London: SCM), Eng. Tr. of *Das zweite Buch Mose, Exodus*; übersetzt und erklärt, *ATD* 5 (Göttingen: Vandenhoeck and Rupprecht, 1964²).
Rad G. von, 1951. *Der Heilige Krieg im alten Israel* (Zurich), 4th edition (Göttingen, 1965).
1959. 'The Origin of the Concept of the Day of Yahweh', *JSS* 4, 97–108.
Reventlow, H. Graf, 1959. 'Die Völker als Jahwes Zeugen bei Ezechiel', *ZAW* 71, 33–43.
Richter, W., 1963. *Traditionsgeschichtsliche Untersuchungen zum Richterbuch*, BBB 18 (Bonn).
1964. *Die Bearbeitungen des 'Retterbuches' in der deuteronomischen Epoche*, BBB 21 (Bonn).
Saggs, H. W. F., 1963. 'Assyrian Warfare in the Sargonid Period', *Iraq* 25, 145–8.
Schwally, F., 1901. *Semitische Kriegsaltertümer*. I *Der Heilige Krieg im alten Israel* (Liepzig).
Smend, R., 1970. *Yahweh War and Tribal Confederation* (Nashville, Tenn., Eng. tr. of *Jahwekrieg und Stammebund* (Göttingen, 1963).
1971. 'Zur Frage der altisraelitischen Amphiktyonie', *EvTh* 11–12, 623–30.
Soden, W. von, 1963. 'Die Assyrier und der Krieg', *Iraq* 25, 131–44.
Soggin, J. A., 1960. 'Der prophetische Gedanke über den Heiligen Krieg, als Gericht gegen Israel', *VT* 10, 79–83.
Stolz, F., 1972. *Jahwe und Israels Kriege. Kriegstheorien und Kriegserfahrungen im Glauben des alten Israels*, ATANT 60 (Zürich).
Tur-Sinai, N. H., 1959–60. 'Was there an Ancient Book of the Wars of the Lord?', *BIES* 24, 146ff.
Vaux, R. de, 1961. *Ancient Israel. Its Life and Institutions* (London: Darton, Longman & Todd), Eng. Tr. of *Les Institutions de l'Ancien Testament* (Paris, 1958, 1960).
Weber, M., 1922. *Gesammelte Aufsätze zur Religionssoziologie*. III *Das antike Judentum* (Tübingen).
Weippert, H., 1970. 'Jahwekrieg und Bundesfluch in Jer. 21.1–7', *ZAW* 82, 364–409.
Weippert, M., 1972. '"Heiliger Krieg" in Israel und Assyrien. Kritische Anmerkungen zu Gerhard von Rads Konzept des "Heiligen Krieges im alten Israel"', *ZAW* 84, 460–93.
Wellhausen, J., 1884. *Skizzen und Vorarbeiten* I (Berlin).
1965. *Grundrisse zum Alten Testament*, ed. R. Smend, ThB 27 (Munich).
Zimmerli, W., 1978. *Old Testament Theology in Outline* (Edinburgh: T. & T. Clark), Eng. Tr. of *Grundriss der alttestamentlichen Theologie* (Stuttgart: Kohlhammer, 1972).

CHAPTER FIFTEEN

Covenant ideology in ancient Israel

ROBERT DAVIDSON

'. . . the real importance of the Decalogue-Covenant is not its form but its social and religious function in the formation of the community and the foundations of convictions which determined the entire subsequent history of the biblical religious tradition. Much as it was modified, changed, rejected, and readapted in the centuries following Moses the covenant tradition nevertheless was what underlay the community's self-understanding until the radical changes that took place during the Hellenistic and Roman Empires made the disintegration of the old tradition in favour of radically new adaptations inevitable.' This verdict of Mendenhall in 1973 represented a synthesis of historical, sociological, literary and religious approaches to Old Testament traditions which, by way of agreement and disagreement, have ensured that covenant ideology has played a lively role in recent Old Testament study. But what are we to understand by 'covenant ideology' and how do we detect its presence? Is it to be found in and confined solely to passages in which the word *b^e^rît* occurs or is there a wider semantic field which in certain circumstances may be taken to imply the ideas of covenant even when the word *b^e^rît* itself does not occur? What kind of relationship – or relationships – is implied by the word *b^e^rît* when it occurs in the context of ancient Israel's political life, institutions and social experience, and how, in particular, is the word used in the context of Israel's religious and theological vocabulary? When we turn to the religious use of *b^e^rît* is there such a thing as a uniform covenant ideology, or are we faced with a complex of traditions which coexist as much in tension as in harmony with each other? What, for example, is the relationship between the covenant traditions associated with Mt. Sinai (Exod. 19–24) and those of a covenant with Abraham (Gen. 15; 17) and with David (Ps. 89; Jer. 33.19–23), and with the hope of a new covenant (Jer. 31.31–4)? When and why did these different covenant traditions enter the life and thought of ancient Israel? Complex historical, literary and traditio-historical questions arise whenever we attempt to answer such questions.

1. Linguistic factors

The word *b^erît* itself is of very uncertain etymology. It has been linked

(a) As a feminine noun with the root *brh* to eat, thus eating together as one form of symbolising a relationship e.g. Gen. 31.54; Exod. 24.11.

(b) with the homonym *brh* to see, to look for, to determine, to decide, hence that which has been decided.

(c) with an original biconsonantal stem *br* to separate, hence something special, a special privilege or advantage.

(d) with the Akkadian noun *birtu* meaning clasp or fetter.

(e) A prepositional origin has also been claimed on the analogy of the Akkadian preposition *birit* between.

Convenient summaries and analyses of the etymological arguments are to be found in Weinfeld: 1972/73, Barr: 1977, and Nicholson: 1986. None of the etymologies suggested carry total conviction, nor do they account satisfactorily for the linguistic peculiarities of *b^erît* in the Old Testament (see Barr op. cit.), nor for the wide range of usages of the word in the Old Testament. Detailed linguistic studies have attempted to show that *b^erît* does not primarily mean *Bund*, covenant, but *Eid*, oath, or *Verpflichtung*, duty or obligation, whether self-obligation or obligation imposed upon another party, with the meaning *Bund* a late development. There remains, however, widespread agreement that *b^erît* in the Old Testament cannot be separated from the concept of relationships or the acts that lead to such relationships, and relationships of very varied types. Thus it can be used of a relationship which a superior attempts forcibly to impose upon a weaker party (1 Sam. 11.1–2) or an agreement in terms of which a superior makes promises to those under his control (Jer. 34.8); a relationship between equals involving mutual obligations (Gen. 21.27; 31.44) or a solemn pledge of friendship (1 Sam. 20.8). It can denote a political deal (2 Sam. 3.13), a treaty between states (1 Kings 5.12) or the marriage relationship (Mal. 2.16). Such covenants and covenant making were a matter of everyday life in ancient Israel. Thus relationships beyond the normal ties of kinship were established, confirmed or renewed. They could be entered into in different ways, for example by a pledged word or oath, by a rite such as a shared meal, or by both (Gen. 21.22–32); and all of this merely reflects customary usage found elsewhere in the Ancient Near East. It is when we come to the specifically religious use of the word *b^erît* to describe the relationship between Yahweh and Israel or Yahweh and particular individuals, e.g.

Abraham and David, that questions concerning the nature of such relationships and their provenance and function within the life of ancient Israel become crucial and highly debatable.

2. Treaty and covenant

A new phase in the debate on covenant ideology was inaugurated by G. E. Mendenhall in 1955 when, drawing upon Hittite treaty documents, previously published by V. Korošec in 1931, he proposed the thesis that law, with its associated sanctions, and covenant were in Israel essentially religious in origin and that the closest analogy to the Decalogue and the Sinai covenant tradition was to be found in such Hittite suzerainty treaty texts dating from circa 1400 to 1100 BCE. Such treaty texts had a distinctive genre with six principal parts:

(1) Preamble – identifying the inaugurator of the treaty, the great king of the Hittite Empire.
(2) A Historical Prologue – outlining the events relevant to the parties.
(3) Stipulations – prominent among them the vassals' exclusive loyalty to his imperial overlord.
(4) Provision for the depositing of the treaty document, often in a temple, and for the periodic public reading of it.
(5) A List of the divine witnesses to the treaty, beginning with the gods of the overlord and leading into the gods of the vassal.
(6) Curses and Blessing – with the curses aimed at the total destruction of those who violate the provisions of the treaty.

The analogy with the Decalogue was enticing. The parallel to the Preamble was 'I am the LORD your God' (Exod. 20.2); the parallel to the Historical Prologue 'who brought you out of the land of Egypt, out of the house of bondage'. There follow the stipulations, prominent among them the demand for the people's exclusive loyalty 'You shall have no other gods before me' (Exod. 20.3). As far as the other elements in the treaty documents were concerned, a) a list of divine witnesses to the covenant would obviously have been wholly out of place in the non-polytheistic setting of the Decalogue. b) what is missing in the Decalogue is to be found elsewhere in the Pentateuch, notably in the book of Deuteronomy with its injunction to deposit the book of the law 'by the side of the ark of the covenant of the LORD' (Deut. 31.26) and the provision for the periodic reading of the law by the Levites to 'all Israel' (Deut. 31.9–13). In particular it is Deuteronomy which develops the theme of the curses and the blessings falling upon the entire community as the result of its obeying, or failing to obey, the divine stipulations, though it is argued that this is already hinted at in the emphasis in the Decalogue upon Yahweh as a 'jealous God' punishing, yet holding out rewards for obedience (Exod. 20.5–6).

Mendenhall's work sparked off a growth industry in the study of Ancient Near Eastern treaty texts. Not only were Hittite treaty documents of the second millenium studied in depth, and distinctions drawn between *vassal treaties* designed functionally to regulate relationships between the great king and his subject peoples, and *parity treaties* between those who regarded themselves as political equals, but increasing attention was focussed upon the treaties in terms of which the Assyrian Empire regulated relations with its subject peoples from the thirteenth to the eighth century BCE. These Assyrian documents came to be regarded as of particular significance since some of them developed at length the curse element in a way which seemed to be reflected in Deuteronomy 28. Not only were such treaties, spanning many centuries, regarded as constituting a genre which functioned sociologically in regulating and protecting imperial structures within a framework of divine sanctions, but the particular language used in such treaties was thought to provide clues as to the distinctive use of certain Hebrew words in covenant contexts in the Old Testament. Thus the command to love imposed by the Assyrian overlord upon his vassal people provided, so it was argued, the background to the command to love which is so prominent in Deuteronomy (e.g. Deut. 6.4–5). Likewise certain usages of the verb 'to know' in contexts which imply a covenant relationship (e.g. Amos 3.2) found their rationale in the parallel use of the verb 'to know' in treaty texts. Attention has also been directed not only to the treaty texts and their distinctive language, but to statements, oral and otherwise, which announce various types of union between different groups or individuals. P. Kaluveetil (Kaluveetil: 1982) has examined in detail such declaratory formulae in a wide range of secular covenants in the Old Testament in the light of other Ancient Near Eastern documents, and has argued that since covenants throughout the ancient world are always concerned with relationships and are designed to create unity or community in one form or another, words referring to such relationships may in certain contexts signify a covenant union, even when the word covenant itself does not occur. The net has been widely spread, but we must question whether the mesh has not at times been so fine that what has been caught remains highly heterogeous. In fact it is so heterogenous that to gather it together and provide it with a covenant label, particularly a treaty-covenant label, raises more questions than it answers.

3. The influence of the treaty-covenant model

With the treaty-covenant model affirmed as part of Israel's experience from Mosaic times, a new impetus was given to the understanding of Israel's religious and sociological history in terms of the development and adaptation of covenant ideology. It was widely assumed that the final nail had been driven into the coffin of the Wellhausen view that the Old Testament concept of covenant was a late post-prophetic, post-exilic theological idea replacing the earlier natural bond model of Yahweh's relationship with Israel (Wellhausen: 1885). Theologically the concept of covenant as early and definitive for Israel's understanding of God, man and the world, had already been the basis of W. Eichrodt's *Theology of the Old Testament*, (first volume originally published in 1933) and he continued vigorously to defend this position against criticism from many quarters. Thus, in the preface to the fifth edition of his Theology, he declares, 'The word covenant . . . is so to speak a convenient symbol for an assurance much wider in scope and controlling the formation of the national faith at its deepest level, without which Israel would not be Israel. As an epitome of the dealings of God in history, the covenant is not a doctrinal concept . . . but the characteristic *description of a living process* which was begun at a particular time and at a particular place' (Eichrodt: 1961, 14). And for Eichrodt that time was, and remained, the age of Moses and the place Mt Sinai. The treaty-covenant model, following Mendenhall, seemed to place this view upon a firmer foundation. There is room here only to mention two of the many studies which worked on this assumption. D. R. Hillers (1969, 64; cf. Baltzer: 1971; Unterman: 1985, 190–2) argued that 'Israel took a suzerainty treaty as a model for God's treaty with her.' Only such a treaty-covenant bond could have held the Israelite tribes together before the advent of the monarchy. He then traced the history of this basic covenant idea in Israel through the changes and development it underwent right up to New Testament times. John Bright likewise presupposes the post-Mendenhall synthesis. 'We may with some confidence believe that Israel did in fact come into being as a sacral confederation formed in covenant with Yahweh and that this covenant followed broadly the pattern of the international suzerainty treaties that are known to us from texts of the second millenium BC' (Bright: 1977, 42). On this basis he argued that the Sinai suzerainty covenant taken together with the Abraham covenant tradition – different in origin but likewise having its roots in pre-monarchical Israel (cf. Clements: 1967) – provided that balance between grace and obligation, promise and obedience, which is constitutive of the biblical witness to God and of the life of the church.

An early date for the covenant concept, however, has been equally congenial to many whose approach to the Old Testament has been primarily historical and sociological, and indeed it is consistent with a view which is deeply suspicious of any interpretation of the Old Testament depending upon a religious idealism which seeks to defend the uniqueness of Israel's faith. Covenant as a functional concept has been a useful tool in the hands of sociologists. A sociological approach to elements in the religion of Israel is hardly novel. It was already expressed by W. Robertson Smith in 1889 in noting the public and social function of religion in fostering and preserving the welfare of society (Smith: 1889). The God of early Israel is described as the god of a confederation of tribes, and religion in this context, is characterised rightly as 'covenant religion' (Smith: 1889, 319 n. 2).

Until comparatively recently the most comprehensive attempt to understand ancient Israel in sociological terms was that presented by Max Weber (Weber: 1952, 135). He argued that in pre-monarchical Israel the covenant *functioned* as a means of uniting the disparate elements of Israel and uniting them under Yahweh who was not only Israel's war god 'but also the contractual partner of its law established by *b^erît*, above all of its socio-legal orders' (Weber: 1952, 135). It was this tradition of the *b^erît*-law of the old confederacy which formed the basis of the ethical teaching of the later prophets. Into this context Martin Noth's thesis of pre-monarchical Israel being constituted as a twelve tribe amphictyony fitted neatly (Noth: 1930). Joshua 24 preserved the memory of the central role played by the covenant in instituting this amphictyony, its only misleading feature being the assumption that all the groups which coalesced to form the Israelite amphictyony had experienced the Exodus and Sinai events.

The most thorough and radical attempt to provide a sociological analysis and explanation of early Israel has been presented by Norman Gottwald (Gottwald: 1979). Working on, and refining, the internal revolt model of the settlement in Canaan propounded by Mendenhall (Mendenhall: 1973), Gottwald, while rejecting the suzerainty-treaty covenant model, Noth's amphictyonic model and Mendenhall's religious idealism, nevertheless still argues for the importance of the covenant mode of thought as fulfilling an essential socio-egalitarian function. 'The novelty and threat of early Israel was not the introduction of new religious ideas and practices as such, but the conjunction of previously and contradictory social groups in a united and mutually supportive network of relationships' (Gottwald: 1979, 645). Amid the social tensions and struggles in Canaan in the fourteenth and early thirteenth centuries BC, when various groups such as the *Apiru*, transhumant pastorals and peasants were struggling for survival with cohesion against ruling-class enemies, covenant functioned as 'the bonding of decentralised social groups in a larger society of equals committed to cooperation without authoritarian leadership, and a way of symbolising the locus of sovereignty in such a society of equals' (*ibid.*, 692). Thus stripped of what is claimed to be all false religious idealism the covenant plays an important role in the emergence of Israel from the womb of Canaanite feudalism.

There is therefore a world of difference between the theological understanding of covenant in Bright's *Promise and Covenant* and Gottwald's sociological approach, even though both join in affirming that covenant had an important role to play in the life of Israel prior to the emergence of the monarchy.

4. Prophecy and covenant

One of the major puzzles in the study of covenant in the Old Testament has been the surprising absence of the word *b^erît* in the writings of the prophets of the eighth century BC, even in contexts where the word *b^erît* would seem to have been the natural word to use. The exceptions are Hos. 6.7 and 8.1. Attempts have been made to explain this silence by drawing attention to the particular religious situation in which the prophetic word was spoken. W. Eichrodt, noting that in secular usage *b^erît* always implies an essentially bilateral relationship, argues that, since the prophets were struggling 'to eradicate all thought of an *opus operatum*, the covenant could not help them for . . . the weakness inherent in it, which made it a potential danger to religious life, was precisely its legal character, because of which it was liable to become the seed bed of a parasitic "*do ut des*" religion' (Eichrodt: 1961, 52; cf. Zimmerli: 1978, 55).

This has never been an entirely satisfactory explanation since it is not obvious that the best way to deal with a potentially misleading idea is to ignore it, particularly if that idea already has wide-spread religious currency. It has also been urged that the prophets' reticence in using the word *b^erît* stems from the fact that the word had been hijacked by royal ideology, the covenant with the Davidic dynasty, an ideology to which many of the prophets were strenuously opposed. Jerusalem, therefore, dominated by the monarchy, proved uncongenial soil for the continuing nurture of the Sinai covenant tradition, though it remained alive in rural Judah and in northern prophetic and levitical circles (cf. Bright: 1977, 79).

But protest against such a hijacking, in the context of attacks on the monarchy, would surely have been a much more effective attack.

The treaty-covenant model was to provide a new context within which the debate could develop. Against this background it could be claimed that, although the word 'covenant' was absent, the complex of ideas associated with such a covenant tradition was present as 'an invisible framework' (Hillers: 1969, 140). It followed that 'without the prior fact of the covenant the prophets' words would be unintelligible to us, whilst at the same time it is doubtful as to whether we should today know anything of what the covenant once meant were it not for the preaching of such men as Amos and Hosea' (Clements: 1965, 126). Increasingly it was affirmed that it was the *b*ᵉ*rît*-law of the old tribal confederacy which was the basis of the ethical teaching of the later prophets in Israel.

This case was to be argued, however, not merely in general terms of religious plausibility, but by appeal to key features in prophetic literature. Particular attention was directed to the *rîb*-form in terms of which Yahweh brings charges against his people; e.g. Deut. 32; Isa. 1.1–2; Jer. 2.4–13; Mic. 6.1–8. Such passages frequently feature an appeal to heaven and earth or to the mountains to act as witnesses in the case. Outside the Old Testament such appeals are characteristic of, and virtually confined to, treaty documents. Thus the label 'covenant lawsuit' was commonly attached to such passages, with the God of the covenant bringing charges against his rebellious people on the analogy of the imperial overlord bringing charges against his rebelling vassal-states (Huffmon: 1959, 285ff.; Wright: 1962, 26–67). Likewise in the varied pattern of prophetic threats against Israel and Judah parallels were found to the treaty curses, with stress being laid, not only upon the linguistic parallels, but upon the functional parallel, the treaty curses being invoked as a consequence of the vassal's rebellion. The prophetic doom was then pronounced upon a people in rebellion against their divine overlord (Hillers: 1964, 43–79). Prophetic texts also provided examples of what was taken to be a distinctive use of the Hebrew verb *yada*ʾ – to know, with parallels to be found in the twofold use of its semantic equivalent in treaty documents either to refer to the suzerain recognising his vassal, and vice versa, or to refer to the binding nature of the treaty stipulations (Huffmon: 1966, 31–7). The logic in the prophet's message, therefore, was traceable to the fact that God and Israel recognised that they were bound together by covenant, and that the stipulations of such a covenant were binding upon Israel and that any attempt to ignore, or violate, them led to curse.

In terms of this approach, the prophets were to be thought of as not merely remembering or interpreting the treaty-covenant tradition, but as the heirs of a cultic tradition, or traditions, in which the covenant had played an important role. Much of this material took its impetus from S. Mowinckel's studies on the Psalms (cf. Mowinckel: 1962) in which he argued that many of the psalms had their setting in the autumnal Feast of Tabernacles which focussed upon the ritual re-enthronement of Yahweh as king in a great religious drama enacted in Jerusalem and the temple. Among the many facets of salvation re-experienced in this annual religious drama were the deliverance of Israel from Egypt and the making of the covenant between Yahweh and Israel at Sinai. This covenant was the very essence of Israel's life and blessing came to the individual, insofar as he was a member of this covenant community and was prepared to live in the light of its demands. Such demands are to be found expressed in psalms such as Pss. 50, 81 and 95. G. von Rad's traditio-historical work on the Hexateuch seemed to point in basically the same direction. He separated two originally independent traditions, the Exodus-Settlement tradition and the Sinai-Covenant tradition. The latter he located in the autumnal Feast of Tabernacles, as originally celebrated at Shechem, with the Sinai narrative reflecting a cultic occasion in which 'God declares himself and communicates his demands, sacrifice is offered and the covenant is sealed' (von Rad: 1966, 21; cf. Alt: 1966 [1934], 79ff.).[1]

This Shechem covenant tradition is preserved in Joshua 24 and finds its fullest expression in Deuteronomy. It remained for the Yahwist to bind together the hitherto separate Exodus and Sinai traditions and thus blend what were to be the two indispensable elements in the biblical tradition – Law and Gospel. The importance of the covenant for this autumnal festival was taken a stage further by A. Weiser in his work on the Psalms. The covenant, instead of being one element in the cultic setting of many of the psalms, now became the central element, with the autumnal festival being primarily a festival of covenant renewal (Weiser: 1962, *passim*). Against this background the prophets were seen as fulfilling an important cultic function. Just as Moses mediated the covenant to Israel at Mt Sinai, so the later prophets fulfilled a continuing Mosaic role in the covenant renewing ceremony. They acted as covenant mediators, proclaiming the demands of the covenant to the people which are reflected in the oracular words in such passages as Ps. 50, 7–15 and 81.6–14. They further brought the covenant lawsuit against a rebellious people and pronounced a threatening curse upon the disobedient. Thus J. Muilenburg could say that the prophets were 'sent from the divine King (Yahweh), the suzerain of the treaties, to reprove and to pronounce judgement upon Israel for breach of the covenant . . . We no longer speak of Moses or the prophets, or of the law or prophecy, but rather of Moses *and* the prophets' (Muilenburg: 1965, 97).

H. Graf Reventlow, in studies on Amos and Jeremiah, asserted that these prophets, in condemning the people for failing to observe the commands of Yahweh, were acting in an official capacity as covenant mediators of the cult (Reventlow: 1961, 269ff.). Even when, as in the case of von Rad, the prophets are regarded not primarily as preachers of repentance but as proclaiming an eschatological message, their eschatology arises from the fact that the old religious traditions, among which the covenant was prominent, had become null and void: 'The prophetic teaching is only eschatological when the prophets expelled Israel from the safety of the old saving actions and suddenly shifted the basis of salvation to a future action of God' (von Rad: 1965, 118). If the old had not contained covenant ideology, and a covenant spelled out in terms of the Sinai tradition, this future action of God could never have been expressed in terms of the new covenant in Jer. 31.31–4.

5. Reaction

Can the thesis be sustained that covenant, modelled on the treaty form, played an important, and perhaps decisive, role in the formation of Israel, whether in religious or sociological terms? Or must we agree with the recently expressed verdict that 'though for a time research into the possible influence of suzerainty treaties upon O.T. covenantal texts seemed to offer striking results, in reality it has yielded little of permanent value' (Nicholson: 1986, 8)? The first detailed critique of Mendenhall's dependence upon the Hittite treaty model for the Sinai covenant tradition appeared in a study by D. J. McCarthy (McCarthy: 1963; 2nd ed. 1978; cf. also 1972, *passim*). He did not deny that aspects of the Sinai tradition were old, nor that they contained covenant ideology. Nevertheless he emphasised the extremely complex literary and traditio-historical problems involved in any analysis of Exodus 19–24 and argued that the Hittite treaty model was neither necessary nor illuminating for our understanding of the tradition. In essence the core of the Sinai covenant was an affair of ritual: 'The rites constituted it and gave it a special meaning. More than a matter of agreement it is a question of adoptive kinship. Israel is not only the subject of Yahweh, but is his adopted family. And so the laws are not the terms of a treaty, but the conditions covering continued action in the family' (McCarthy: 1978, 295). Furthermore, suzerainty treaties continued in existence in the ancient Near East for centuries after the end of the second millennium BC, so nothing could be proved about the date and provenance of the Sinai tradition by invoking Hittite treaty parallels. Indeed for a variety of reasons McCarthy came to a conclusion which was to play a large part in subsequent discussion, namely that the closest parallels to the treaty form are to be found in the book of Deuteronomy. This is the product of the theological reflection of circles who were politically aware of the language of international treaties, particularly Assyrian treaty documents, and which flourished under the Hebrew monarchy. The covenantal formulation, though transposed into a testamentary discourse, is to be seen at its clearest in the central section of Deuteronomy, with 4.44–11.32 providing the historical and parenetic introduction, 12.1–26.15 contain the stipulations, with 26.16–19 and 28.1–68 constituting the concluding oath and rite, blessing and curse. The strong links between Deuteronomy and the treaty form were further developed, especially by M. Weinfeld (Weinfeld: 1977; 1973, 781ff.). Deuteronomy for Weinfeld emanates from the wisdom tradition, from those who held public office under the Hebrew monarchy and who were thus familiar with the political treaties of the day. They also had at their disposal a corpus of Deuteronomic religio-literary material which had already conjoined covenant and law. This material they enriched 'by introducing all the elements of the vassal treaties' (Weinfeld: 1977, 157). This had the effect of blurring the covenantal pattern by putting it into a homiletic setting. In particular, the lengthy list of curses in Deuteronomy 28 is claimed to have an exact parallel in the treaty which Esarhaddon made with his eastern vassals regarding the coronation of his son Ashurbanipal in 672 BC. By imitating such Assyrian treaty documents Deuteronomy was emphasising that the pledge of loyalty to the Assyrian emperor had been replaced by the pledge of loyalty to the divine king, Yahweh, a move particularly relevant against the background of Josiah's bid for liberation from Assyrian domination in the seventh century BC. Thus Weinfeld sought to delineate a historical and political milieu in which the appeal to the language of the treaty texts would be understandable, to identify the wisdom and court circles which might reasonably make such an appeal, and to stress the theological underpinning of such an appeal.

However, just as McCarthy questioned whether the appeal to Hittite treaty texts was either necessary or illuminating in the study of the earliest form of the Sinai covenant tradition, so the same questions have been increasingly asked concerning the link between Deuteronomy and the Assyrian treaty texts. Here we inevitably enter the highly disputed area of the provenance of the book of Deuteronomy in its present form and its relationship to the Deuteronomistic history or the successive editions of it (Noth: 1981 [1943]). Is Deuteronomy best explained in terms of a covenantal pattern, following the treaty model, which has been blurred by being put into a homiletic framework, or is it rather an extended oration in homiletic style which sometimes alludes to, and makes use of, treaty language (cf. Mayes: 1979, 37)? Certainly many of the arguments used to stress the link between Deuteronomy and treaty texts are far from convincing. The supposed formal relationship between Deut. 28 and the Esarhaddon treaty curses has been subjected to a detailed and sharply critical analysis by E. W. Nicholson (Nicholson: 1986). It has been pointed out that in the framework to the legislation in Deut. 4.25–31 and 30.1–10, curse and blessing do not stand side by side as alternatives, as in the treaty documents, but occur in historical succession, with curse a present reality to be followed by blessing on condition of repentance; which suggests that 'the curse of the law is that which Israel in exile is now experiencing, but there is blessing to follow. Israel in exile is encouraged with the promise of renewal and restoration' (Mayes: 1979, 33). Nor is the appeal to distinctive Deuteronomic language, such as the command to love, necessarily, or indeed plausibly, a sign of the influence of treaty terminology. 'The reality is surely that terms such as these and others, supposedly derived by the biblical writers from their knowledge of treaties, belonged in the first instance to familiar settings of everyday life, and needed no treaties to mediate them or give them a special nuance . . . why should it be strange, as Moran and McCarthy contend, that love is "commanded"? The Israelite is commanded to love his neighbour (Lev. 19.18, 34) and the stranger (Deut. 10.19); Hosea is commanded to love a woman (Hos. 3.1) . . .' (Nicholson: 1986, 79).

This comment applies with equal force to some of the linguistic arguments adduced by P. Kaluveettil (1982). That Deuteronomic theology is covenant theology, and covenant theology set within a Mosaic Sinaitic mould, can scarcely be doubted, but the precise provenance of this theology, its relationship to contemporary events and the extent to which it feeds upon earlier covenant traditions, are still matters of lively debate.

6. Prophecy and covenant reconsidered

A similar caveat concerning the appeal to linguistic features applies with equal force in the question of the relationship between prophecy and covenant. It is hard to see why, for example, the use of the verb *yd*ʿ, to know, in passages such as Amos 3.2 should derive from a treaty background when the verb is so widely used across the Old Testament to refer to a rich variety of human relationships and experiences. Nor is it obvious that the *rîb*-form need have any other background than formal civil and courtroom proceedings in ancient Israel or other occasions, such as a courtroom ceremony, in which oaths of fidelity were demanded from the people and the consequences of failing to maintain such pledged loyalty spelled out (McCarthy: 1978, 40). The picture of the prophet functioning as a covenant mediator closely linked to earlier cultic traditions has also been subject to a good deal of critical analysis. In *Prophecy and Tradition* (1975) R. E. Clements significantly modified the views he had expressed ten years earlier in *Prophecy and Covenant* (1965). It was now accepted that covenant theology only gradually emerged within the life of ancient Israel to receive its classic formulation in the Deuteronomic literature. Many of the features which posit the prophet as the covenant mediator are no more than the result of the Deuteronomic redaction of prophetic literature. Prophetic preaching may have contributed elements to the full expression of covenant theology in Deuteronomic circles, but their preaching hardly presupposes an already extant covenant theology (Phillips: 1982, 217–32; McKane: 1979, 163–88). A wider theological framework must be sought for prophetic preaching. Features in the ethical stance of the prophets which tended to be attributed to a covenant background have been traced to other roots, e.g. in family or clan wisdom (Wolff: 1973, 88ff.; Terrien: 1962, 108–15), or to widely accepted concepts of natural or international law (Barton: 1979, 1–14). That the prophets are reflecting an ethical tradition in Israel rather than acting as the protagonists of a new morality is hardly to be doubted, but it is an open question as to what extent this ethical stance was inevitably bound up with covenant, and in particular with a covenant relationship which had its roots in the Mosaic Sinaitic traditions. It can be rightly claimed that in the present text of the Old Testament 'every series and code preserved in the Pentateuch is anchored in a covenant-making account, and these narratives prepare for the proclamation of the divine will to Israel or put it into force. Each legal corpus evinces the covenant setting in the speaker and in the addressee and in the provisions of the law and their homiletical amplification' (Patrick: 1985, 26). To what extent, however, does this merely reflect a redactional process, and if so when did the redaction – or redactions – take place?[2] When the prophets appeal to earlier legal or ethical provisions this does not mean that they knew them in a covenant setting. Certainly prophetic preaching makes no sense except on the assumption of a particular relationship between Yahweh and Israel, and there are still those who would, therefore, confidently affirm that covenant ideology is an important element in the message of the prophets. Nevertheless they tend no longer to appeal to treaty forms or language, nor to covenant law books, nor covenant renewal festivals, nor to the prophets as covenant mediators, but rather to an 'amalgam of traditions and influences which the prophet borrowed consciously or unconsciously from the total culture in which he lived' (van der Woude: 1982, 38f.).

7. The impact of literary criticism

The question as to when the concept of *b^erît* became part of that total culture has been given added sharpness by literary-critical studies. Prominent among such studies, and continuingly influential, is that of L. Perlitt (Perlitt: 1969). He begins by directing attention to the undeniable fact that the word *b^erît* is most intensively used in the book of Deuteronomy and in the Deuteronomistic literature of the seventh and sixth centuries BC. This corpus of literature reflects a time of ever increasing crises in the life of ancient Israel. In this setting the word *b^erît* and its associated word *torah* take on a new theological significance to point to that distinctive relationship and codified law which bring necessary and inevitable judgement upon God's people. The one reference to Yahweh's covenant with Israel in the eighth-century prophets, Hos. 8.1, is regarded by Perlitt as a secondary Deuteronomic addition, as are the references to covenant in Exod. 24.3b–8; 34.10–16 and Jos. 24. Perlitt's literary analysis was essentially confirmed by E. Kutsch (Kutsch: 1973) who traced *b^erît* back to an original meaning of duty, or obligation, and denied that there was ever any theological use of the word earlier than the seventh century. On this analysis Jos. 24 neither describes an ancient historical event, nor does it preserve the memory of an early festival tradition. A somewhat similar, though modified, judgement is to be found in E. W. Nicholson's study (Nicholson: 1986, 151).[3] After tracing the history of the approach to covenant in the Old Testament from the time of Wellhausen onwards, Nicholson rejects entirely the significance of treaty texts for our understanding of either the Exodus, or the Deuteronomic, covenant traditions. He then proceeds to subject the texts to a detailed analysis.

The earliest Sinaitic strand in Exod. 24.1–2, 9–11 has no covenant connection but is concerned solely with a remarkable *visio dei*. Exod. 34.10–28 is relatively late and provides no testimony to more ancient tradition, while Jos. 24 is of exilic provenance. It is a Deuteronomistic narrative 'concerned with the judgement that has deservedly fallen on Israel because of its faithlessness to the covenant' (Nicholson: 1986, 161). Exod. 19.3b–8 is an amalgam of Deuteronomic, priestly and prophetic elements which point either to the late exilic, or early post-exilic, periods. Only Exod. 24.3–8 is pre-Deuteronomic, and, when taken in conjunction with Hos. 8.1, is evidence for the fact that 'the notion of the covenant is already known in Israel in the mid-eighth century, but there is nothing to suggest a much earlier provenance'. It follows therefore that 'the thesis that the covenant as a full blown theological concept was a late arrival in Israel is substantially vindicated and that in this regard we seem to have been brought back, like Perlitt and some others recently, to almost the view of Wellhausen a century or so ago' (*ibid.*, 88).

Nicholson, however, offers us a richer and more broadly based theology of covenant than that of Wellhausen. Drawing upon insights from the sociology of religion, with its insistence that religion is part of society's endeavour to come to terms with, and to impose meaning upon, its experience of the world, Nicholson proposes a revised theology of covenant, linking it closely with Israel's demythologised world-view, or theology of creation. Such a view arose not 'in one creative founding period in the beginning, rather . . . it was wrought out of controversy within Israel which centred upon the nature of God and his relationship to the world and to Israel' (*ibid.*, 201). Although there were antecedents, the decisive step came with the prophets who, as Wellhausen rightly saw, broke the natural bond between God and Israel and transformed it onto the plain of moral response and commitment. The theological understanding of the covenant between God and Israel was the result of this decisive change. In terms of cash value it affirms 'that religion is based not on natural or ontological equivalence between the divine order and the human but on *choice*: God's choice of his people and their "choice" of him, that is their free decision to be obedient and faithful to him' (*ibid.*, 215).

Covenant theology is therefore much more radical than Wellhausen imagined. From an early period Israel's God was not merely a tribal god, but Creator and it is into this cosmic context that covenant theology introduces the note of choice and the need for a freely given faith. It is not, however, clear why this note of choice should be so closely tied to covenant theology and there is a real danger that the term Deuteronomistic can be used to close the door too quickly on legitimate questions raised by the traditio-historical approach to Old Testament material. W. Zimmerli's verdict on Perlitt's approach may be applied with equal validity to Nicholson's: 'it is a critical warning to the traditio-historical method of operation that it should not evade by means of traditio-historical surmises questions posed by literary criticism. Yet on the other hand its pan-Deuteronomic attitude . . . fails to carry conviction in the analysis of important passages like Gen. 15; Exod. 24; 34 and Jos. 24' (Zimmerli: 1979, 379). As the reference to Gen. 15 indicates this is an unresolved issue which becomes central to the debate when we turn from the Sinai covenant tradition to the Abraham-covenant traditions.

Before turning to the Abraham traditions, however, we should take a brief look at Jer. 31.31–4, a passage which stands firmly within the Sinai covenant tradition, but projects it by way of continuity and contrast into an unspecified future, there to find fulfilment. The passage has provoked an extensive literature with the most varied responses as to its authorship and its theological significance. On the one hand we find the view represented by J. Bright who asserts: 'As regards its authenticity, it ought never to have been questioned. Although the passage may not represent the prophet's *ipsissima verba* it represents what might well be considered the high point of his theology. It is certainly one of the profoundest and most moving passages in the Bible' (Bright: 1965, 287). Bright has then sought to show elsewhere how the passage drives us to the Gospel (Bright: 1966, 188–210; cf. Hillers: 1969, 168). On the other hand there are those who advocate a post-exilic date and who question the theological profundity of the passage. It has been regarded as a post-Deuteronomic hope, transforming the Deuteronomic use of *b^erît* which always involves obligations between two parties, which may be kept or broken, into a metaphor for a Utopian society which does not, and cannot, exist, but which provides fertile ground for new movements which far transcend anything envisaged in the Jeremianic tradition (cf. Carroll: 1986, 609–14).

8. The covenants with Abraham and David

It has long been recognised that the tradition of a covenant with Abraham has developed independently of, and reflects a different ethos from, that of the Sinaitic tradition. The two narrative accounts of a covenant with Abraham, the one in Genesis 15 in documentary terms usually assigned to the 'J' source, and the other in Genesis 17 assigned to the 'P' source, agree that this is not a covenant involving bilateral obligations on the two contracting parties. It is in essence rather 'a binding promise –or better a promissory oath – on the part of God' (Bright: 1977, 25). Not only in this fundamental respect, but also in the characteristic language used, which is that of 'establishing (*hēqîm*) the covenant', the description of the covenant as 'everlasting' and the promise that 'kings shall spring from you' (Gen. 17.4), the Abrahamic covenant tradition has clear links with the tradition of the covenant between God and the Davidic royal family (cf. e.g. 2 Sam. 7.8–16; Ps. 89). This is most notably the case in the 'P' tradition. However we must ask which comes first? Is the Abraham covenant tradition merely a reading back into what were thought to be the origins of Israel's life of an ideology which developed around the royal family in Jerusalem, or is the influence the other way round, so that the Davidic covenant ideology had its roots in pre-monarchic traditions? In *Abraham and David* (1967) R. E. Clements argued that there was a two way relationship between the Abraham and Davidic covenant traditions. The Davidic covenant, which arose no later than the Solomonic era as a piece of 'covenant theology which proved to be eminently successful in establishing the claim of the Davidic house over Israel' (Clements: 1967, 32), had its roots in the recollection in Jerusalem of an ancient tradition of a covenant with Abraham. The nucleus of this tradition, which is to be found in Gen. 15.7–21, minus a few later additions, is the promise of land to Abram, and is linked to a local cult-legend attached to Mamre-Hebron. This was one of a series of such legends linking the patriarchs with important cult-centres in Canaan.

The original deity involved was probably the El of Memre, and the covenant would initially have involved obligations on Abram's part. However: 'The Yahwist in his literary presentation of the Abraham covenant was concerned for reasons of his own to heighten the emphasis upon divine promise, so that it is understandable that any reference to this obligation should have dropped out' (Clements: 1967, 34). While Genesis 15, therefore, reflects the Yahwist's theology, its picture of the covenant between Yahweh and Abram is influenced by covenant ideology already existing in Canaan and we may compare the reference to the temple of El-B^{e}rît at Shechem (Ju. 8.46). This pre-monarchic Abram covenant tradition was part of the Caleb-Judah traditions and, given David's links with Judah and Hebron, it was natural enough that it became part of royal Davidic ideology. The Yahwist intended the Abram tradition to point forward to such an ideology. Being subsumed under the Davidic covenant, the Abraham tradition is not mentioned by the pre-exilic prophets, but comes into its own again when the future of the Davidic dynasty is in doubt (e.g. Isa. 51.1–2). There are, *per contra*, elements in the tradition, particularly in the 'P' tradition in Genesis 17 such as the emphasis upon the covenant being everlasting, which first came to prominence in the Davidic tradition. Thus the Abraham and Davidic covenant traditions interacted upon one another.

It should be obvious that if the Davidic covenant was Solomonic in origin, it would hardly be given much credence in Northern Israel in the era of the post-Solomonic divided kingdom. If the Davidic covenant played a dominant role in Jerusalemite thinking, it is arguable that the Sinai covenant tradition would find a more natural home in the north. An interesting, though at points highly subjective, attempt to distinguish between northern and southern covenant traditions from an early period is made by M. Newman (Newman: 1962).[4] Deuteronomy can then be seen as an attempt to effect a compromise between the rival traditions during the seventh century BC when the northern kingdom had been swallowed up by the Assyrians and Judah alone was left as heir to the traditions of the people of Yahweh.

The date and provenance of the Abraham covenant tradition have been widely discussed and the arguments have largely followed the pattern already seen in our discussion of the Sinai traditions. On the one hand there are those who argue, like W. Zimmerli (Zimmerli: 1978, 57; Alt: 1966 [1929], 1–77; Hillers: 1969, 103; Bright: 1977, 21) that the 'J' tradition in Genesis 15 preserves a ritual originally belonging to the secular realm which has been adapted to refer to a covenant between God and Abraham, and that this religious adaptation is certainly pre-Deuteronomic. On the other hand Perlitt regards the covenant with Abraham as being no more than a proto-Deuteronomic formula emanating from early in the seventh century BC at the earliest. It was designed to intensify, in the light of the destruction of the northern kingdom, what had previously been no more than an expression of promise, as in Gen. 12.2. Similarly E. Blum (Blum: 1984), claiming to work not on literary-critical, but on traditio-historical premises, argues that we can know nothing of any traditions earlier than the existence of Israel as a nation-state, since there is no knowledge of historical circumstances or events from such a period to which the traditions could be attached. Such a view is implicitly accepted in several recent histories of ancient Israel (Soggin: 1984; cf. Hayes and Miller: 1986, 54–79).

It is within the context of recent *literary* studies of the problem of the Pentateuch, however, that there has arisen the most serious questioning of the date and provenance of the Abraham covenant traditions. The appeal to archaeological evidence and to extra-biblical texts to vindicate the early date and the essential historicity of the patriarchal traditions has proved as fragile as the appeal to Hittite treaty-texts to vindicate the Mosaic link with the Sinai covenant tradition. With the documentary hypothesis increasingly under attack, or the date of its sources radically revised, with the increasing emphasis being placed upon a holistic approach to the Pentateuch as literature, or as a prime example of ancient historiography, there has been a marked tendency to place the origins of the Abraham traditions in the exilic period. J. van Seters, for example, places the earliest Yahwist in the sixth century BC and regards the pre-Yahwistic material as meagre (van Seters: 1975; cf. also van Seters: 1983 and Thompson: 1987 which significantly changes his attitude towards the Abraham traditions from that he expressed in: 1974).

Developing the new literary approach to the Pentateuch, and expressing scepticism towards the results attainable by a traditio-historical approach,

R. N. Whybray has gone one step further and argued that 'There appears to be no reason why (allowing for the possibility of a few additions) the first edition of the Pentateuch as a comprehensive work should not have been the final edition, a work composed by a single historian' (Whybray: 1987, 232f.). As for the sources used by this historian there is no assured way of differentiating between written and oral sources, and no way of discovering their antiquity. Much of the material in the narrative sections of the Pentateuch is probably a mixture of folklore and fiction, the only tradition which can safely be regarded as ancient being that of the exodus, the nucleus of which is to be found in the Song of Miriam in Exod. 15.21.

This historian of the sixth century BC had at his disposal a mass of material 'most of which may have been of quite recent origin and had not necessarily formed part of any ancient Israelite tradition. Following the canons of the historicity of his time he radically reworks this material, probably with substantial additions of his own invention, making no attempt to produce a smooth narrative free of inconsistencies, contradictions and unevennesses. Judged by the standards of ancient historiography, his work stands out as a literary masterpiece' (Whybray: 1987, 247). If this approach is accepted then any attempt to prove that the Abraham covenant tradition is part of ancient Israelite tradition, or earlier than the sixth century BC, runs into insuperable difficulties. A literary approach, however, can lead to very different conclusions. It has been argued, on the basis of an analysis of the redactional structuring of Genesis, that the whole of the book of Genesis is 'brilliantly constructed, the accomplishment of an ancient Israelite genius who formed the book into a literary whole' (Rendsburg: 1986). This genius is then claimed to have flourished in the period of the early monarchy. This would support the view that the Abraham covenant traditions were part of Israel's religious heritage by the time the monarchy came into existence.

The question of the antiquity of the Abraham covenant traditions cannot, however, be decided solely on the basis of the Pentateuchal narratives. The question of the silence of the pre-exilic prophets concerning Abraham must be faced. Does their silence mean that they knew nothing of any such traditions? Alternatively, it may be argued that precisely because theologically the Abraham traditions placed such heavy emphasis upon God's grace and his unconditional promises, they would have been out of place in a situation where the true prophetic word had to be one of judgement upon a sinful people. There is also reference to God's covenant with Abraham in Ps. 105.9. The fact that this passage is quoted in 1 Chron. 16.16 is hardly proof that Psalm 105 is post-exilic, nor is there anything else in the psalm which necessitates a post-exilic date (cf. Dahood: 1970, 51). The burden of proof must still lie with those who argue that the covenant with Abraham cannot be traced back into the life of pre-exilic Israel. There is a real danger of the exilic period becoming a convenient catchment area for much of what is regarded as theologically significant in the Old Testament with too little concern to trace back to their source the varied rivulets which flow into this catchment area.

Whatever conclusions may be reached concerning the antiquity of the Abraham-covenant traditions, there can be no denying that there was a place for the covenant with David within the context of royal Judean ideology. The extent to which the Psalms reflect such a royal ideology and the precise nature of this ideology are still matters of considerable dispute, but Psalm 89 clearly witnesses to Yahweh's covenant with David (vv. 3, 28, 34, 39), and that in a situation where events, either historical or cultic, seem to be calling into question the continuing validity of the promises made to the Davidic king in terms of this covenant. Other references to this Davidic covenant, with stress upon its everlasting nature, are to be found in 2 Sam 23.5; Ps. 132.11–12; Jer. 33.21, and its presuppositions are clearly indicated in the oracle of Nathan in the Succession Narrative in 2 Sam. 7.8ff. But what is the precise function of this Davidic covenant? It has been argued that it represents a move to legitimise the dynastic principle over against the old charismatic leadership (Alt: 1966 [1951]). It is noticeable elsewhere in the Old Testament that where alternative institutions are envisaged the idea of the covenant is attached only to the institution which has some recognised permanency in the social or religious structure. Thus it is used of Yahweh's relationship with priests and Levites (Num. 25.13; Mal. 2.4), but not of a charismatic figure such as a prophet. Equally the covenant with David could find its natural context in the struggle to legitimise the house of David over against the Saulides, or to assert the validity of the house of David over against what, from the Jerusalem point of view, was regarded as the schismatic northern regime. Such a validity received added momentum through events when the northern kingdom collapsed before the imperialism of Assyria (cf. Ps. 78 which, using the election rather than the covenant theme, strongly affirms this ideology). With the collapse of the Judean state before neo-Babylonian imperialism questions inevitably arose concerning the covenant with the Davidic dynasty, not least because of its unqualified assertion that this was a covenant which must last for ever. In Isa. 55.3 there seems to be an attempt to democratise this everlasting Davidic covenant and to transfer its privileges and responsibilities to the community as a whole and thus to ensure that its continuing validity was not permanently tied to the continuance of the Davidic dynasty (Eissfeldt: 1962, 196–207). Unless we are prepared to see nationalism and particularism as the key to second Isaiah's thinking, the description of the purpose of this covenant in Isa. 55.4–5 may be interpreted in a universalistic sense. This is also the case with the occurrence of covenant in Isa. 42.6 where Servant-Israel is summoned to be 'a covenant of the people, and a light to the nations'. Yet this promise of a Davidic covenant for ever could also find a new and rich future within the hope of a Davidic king still to come, who would renew the old royal covenant temporarily annulled by events.

9. The covenant with Noah

A brief reference must be made to the covenant with Noah in Genesis 9.8–17. Linguistically it shares many features with the Abraham-covenant tradition in Genesis 17. Unlike any other of the covenant traditions we have examined, however, it has no immediate historical or political reference. It moves rather within the orbit of a theology of creation, with its 'never again' (v. 15) affirmed over against the cosmic destruction of the flood. Our preoccupation with political and historical covenant models may well, as a recent essay has urged (Murray: 1982, 200–16), have blinded us to the fact that such a cosmic covenant model is much more central to Old Testament thinking than had previously been recognised. This would also fit in well with the emphasis placed by Nicholson upon the demythologising of nature in the development of covenant theology. Not that the linking of covenant with the stability of the created order is entirely divorced from covenant in its political aspects, since such a covenant has strong links with royal covenant ideology (so Jer. 33.20–4; Ps. 89, 28–9 and Isa. 11.5–9). This link may well have been most clearly enunciated in the New Year Festival. Likewise this covenant tradition is used in Isa. 54.9–10 as a model for the unchangeable love of God which will guarantee that the future of God's people will be marked by a covenant of *šālôm* that shall never be broken.

There can be little doubt that covenant ideology had an important part to play in the shaping of Israel's religious traditions. Emerging from a varied secular background, the concept appears in the traditions of Israel's origins, in the promises of land and progeny (Abraham); it is used to define the relationship between Yahweh and Israel (Sinai tradition); it provides justification for one of the most important political institutions in Israel's life (the Davidic tradition); it has links with a theology of creation (Noah) and it enshrines one strand in Israel's hopes for the future (the new covenant). The key questions around which debate continues, involving the use of extra-biblical material and the relationship between traditio-historical methodology and the new literary approaches to the Old

Testament, concern the provenance of these different covenant traditions and their inter-relatedness. It is doubtful whether the pan-Deuteronomic thesis, or theories of exilic redaction, which have characterised much recent study, can have the last word to say on these issues.

Notes

1 A critique of von Rad's thesis and a reiteration of an original connection between the Exodus and Sinai traditions, combined with a marked emphasis upon the centrality of the covenant idea in early Israel is presented by W. Beyerlin: 1961.

2 For a negative view on the relationship between law and covenant see W. M. Clark, 'Law' in Old Testament Form Criticism, 99–139; J. D. Levenson, *HTR* 73, 1980, 17–33. *Per contra* Dale Patrick: 1985 and W. Zimmerli: 1965.

3 This marks a significant change from Nicholson's remarks in *Deuteronomy and Tradition*: 1967, when he found the link between the Sinai tradition and the treaty texts convincing.

4 For a somewhat different view of the relationship between the Sinai and the Davidic covenant traditions see Clements: 1965, 56ff.

Bibliography

Alt, A., 1966 [1929]. 'The God of the Fathers', *Essays on Old Testament History and Religion*, Eng. Tr. R. A. Wilson. Oxford: Blackwell, 1–77. Originally published as *Der Gott der Väter*, Stuttgart: Kohlhammer, 1929.

1966 [1934]. 'The origins of Israelite Law', *ibid.*, 79–132, originally published Leipzig: Hirzel, 1934.

1966 [1951]. 'The Monarchy in the Kingdoms of Israel and Judah', *ibid.*, 329–59. Originally published *VT* 1, 1951. 2–22.

Alter, R., 1981. *The Art of Biblical Narrative*, London: Collins.

Baltzer, K., 1971 [1964]. *The Covenant Formulary*, Oxford: Blackwell. Eng. Tr. by D. E. Green of *Das Bundesformular*, WMANT 4, Neukirchen: Neukirchener Verlag.

Barr, J., 1977. 'Some Semantic Notes on the Covenant', *Beiträge zur alttestamentlichen Theologie. FS W. Zimmerli 70. Geburtstag.* eds. H. Donner, R. Hanhart, R. Smend, Göttingen: Vandenhoeck & Rupprecht, 23–33.

Barton, J., 1979. 'Natural Law and Poetic Justice in the Old Testament', *JTS*. NS 30, 1–14.

1980. *Amos' Oracles Against the Nations: A Study of Amos 1.3–2.5*, Cambridge: CUP.

Beyerlin, W., 1965. *Origins and History of the Oldest Sinaitic Traditions*, Oxford: Blackwell. Eng, Tr. by S. Rudman of *Herkunft und Geschichte der ältesten Sinaitraditionen*, Tübingen: Mohr, 1961.

Blum, E., 1984. *Die Komposition der Vätergeschichte*, WMANT 57, Neukirchen: Neukirchener Verlag.

Bright, J., 1965. *Jeremiah: A New Translation with Introduction and Commentary*, Anchor Bible 21, Garden City: Doubleday.

1966. 'An Experiment in Hermeneutics: Jeremiah 31: 31–34', *Int*, 20: 188–210.
1977. *Covenant and Promise. The Future in the Preaching of the Pre-exilic Prophets*, London: SCM.
Carroll, R. P., 1981. *From Chaos to Covenant*, London: SCM.
1986. *Jeremiah*, Old Testament Library, London: SCM.
Clark, W. M., 'Law', *Old Testament Form Criticism*, ed. J. H. Hayes, San Antonio: 99–139.
Clements, R. E., 1965. *Prophecy and Covenant*, SBT 43, London: SCM.
1967. *Abraham and David. Genesis 15 and its Meaning for Israelite Tradition*, SBT, Second Series 5, London: SCM.
1976. 'Covenant and Canon in the Old Testament', *Creation, Christ and Culture*, ed. R. W. A. McKinney, Edinburgh: T. & T. Clark, 1–12.
Dahood, M. 1970. *Psalms III*, New York: Doubleday.
Eichrodt, W., 1961 [1959]. *Theology of the Old Testament*, vols. 1 and 2 (1967 [1964]). Eng. Tr. by J. A. Baker of *Theologie des Alten Testaments*, Bds. 1 (6th ed.) and 2 (5th ed.), Stuttgart: Klotz & Vandenhoeck & Rupprecht.
Eissfeldt, O., 1962. 'The promises of Grace to David in Isaiah 55.1–5', in *Israel's Prophetic Heritage*, eds. B. W. Anderson and W. Harrelson, London: SCM, 196–207.
Frankena, R., 'The Vassal-Treaties of Esarhaddon and the Dating of Deuteronomy', *OTS* 14, 123–54.
Gerstenberger, E., 1965. 'Covenant and Commandment', *JBL* 84, 1965, 38–51.
Gottwald, N. K., 1979. *The Tribes of Yahweh. A Sociology of the Religion of Liberated Israel 1250–1050 BCE*, London: SCM.
Hayes, J. H. and Miller, J. Maxwell (eds.), 1977. *Israelite and Judean History*, London: SCM.
Hillers, D. R., 1964. *Treaty Curses and the Old Testament Prophets*, Biblica et Orientalia 16, Rome: Biblical Institute.
1969. *Covenant. The History of a Biblical Idea*, Baltimore: John Hopkins Univ.
Huffmon, H. B., 1959. 'The Covenant Lawsuit in the Prophets', *JBL* 78, 1959, 285–295.
1966. 'The Treaty Background of Hebrew YADA'', *BASOR* 181, 31–37.
Jepsen, A., 1961. 'Berith. Ein Beitrag zur Theologie der Exilzeit', *Verbannung und Heimkehr. Beitrage zur Geschichte und Theologie Israels im 6. und 5. Jahrhundert v. Chr. FS. W. Rudolph*, ed. A. Kuschke, Tübingen: Mohr, 161–79.
Kaluveetil, P., 1982. *Declaration and Covenant*, Analecta Biblica 88, Rome: Biblical Institute.
Kutsch, E., 1973. *Verheissung und Gesetz. Untersuchungen zum sogenannten "Bund" im Alten Testament*, BZAW 131, Berlin: de Gruyter.
1980. 'Bund', *Realenzyklopädie*, Bd. 8, Berlin, 397–410.
Lohfink, N., 1967. *Die Landverheissung als Eid. Eine Studie zu Genesis 15*, SBS 28, Stuttgart: Katholisches Biblewerk.
Mayes, A. D. H., 1974. *Israel in the Period of the Judges*, SBT, Second Series 29, London: SCM.
Mayes, A. D. H., 1979, *Deuteronomy*, London: Marshall-Pickering.
McCarthy, D. J., 1963. *Treaty and Covenant*, Analecta Biblica 21, Rome: Biblical Institute; 2nd ed. 1978.
1965. 'Notes on the Love of God in Deuteronomy and the Father-Son Relationship between Yahweh and Israel', *CBQ* 27, 144–7.
1972. *Old Testament Covenant. A Survey of Current Opinions*, Oxford: Blackwell.

McKane, W., 1979. 'Prophecy and the Prophetic Literature', *Tradition and Interpretation*, ed. G. W. Anderson, Oxford: Clarendon, 163–88.

Mendenhall, G. E., 1955. *Law and Covenant in Israel and the Ancient Near East*, Pittsburgh.

1962. 'Covenant', *IDB*, vol. 1, 714–23.

1973. *The Tenth Generation*, Baltimore: John Hopkins Univ.

Mowinckel, S., *The Psalms in Israel's Worship*, Eng. Tr. D. R. Ap-Thomas, 2 vols., Oxford: Blackwell.

Muilenburg, J., 1959. 'The Form and Structure of the Covenantal Formulations', *VT* 9: 345–65.

1965. 'The Office of the Prophet in Ancient Israel', *The Bible in Modern Scholarship*, ed. J. P. Hyatt, Nashville: Abingdon, 74–97.

Murray, R., 1982. 'Prophecy and Cult', *Israel's Prophetic Tradition*, R. J. Coggins, A. Phillips and M. A. Knibb (eds.), Cambridge: Cambridge Univ. Press, 200–14.

Newman, M. L., 1962. *The People of the Covenant. A Study of Israel from Moses to the Monarchy*, Nashville: Abingdon Press.

Nicholson, E. W., 1967. *Deuteronomy and Tradition*, Oxford: B. H. Blackwell.

1986. *God and His People. Covenant and Theology in the Old Testament*, Oxford: Oxford UP.

Noth, M. 1972 [1948]. *A History of Pentateuchal Traditions*. Eng. Tr. B. W. Anderson, Englewood Cliffs: Prentice Hall. Translated from *Überlieferungsgeschichte des Pentateuch*, Stuttgart: Kohlhammer, 1948.

1981 [1943] *The Deuteronomistic History*. JSOTSS 15. Eng. Tr. J. Doull et. al. Sheffield: JSOT Press. Translated from *Überlieferungsgeschichtliche Studien* I, Tübingen: Niemeyer, 1943.

Oden, R. A. Jr., 1987. 'The Place of Covenant in the Religion of Israel', *Ancient Israelite Religion*, eds. P. D. Miller, P. D. Hanson and S. D. McBride, Philadelphia: Fortress, 429–47.

Patrick, D., 1985. *Old Testament Law*, Atlanta: John KNox.

Perlitt, L., 1969. *Bundestheologie im Alten Testament*, WMANT 36, Neukirchen: Neukirchener Verlag.

Phillips, A., 1982. 'Prophecy and Law', *Israel's Prophetic Tradition*, R. J. Coggins, A. Phillips and M. A. Knibb (eds.), Cambridge: CUP, 217–32.

Rad, G. von, 1966 [1938]. 'The Form-Critical Problem of the Hexateuch', *The Problem of the Hexateuch and Other Essays*, Eng. Tr. by E. W. T. Dicken, Edinburgh: Oliver & Boyd, 1–78. Translated from *Das formgeschichtliche Problem des Hexateuchs*, BWANT IV, 26, Stuttgart: Kohlhammer, 1938.

1965 [1960] *Old Testament Theology*, Vol. II, Edinburgh: Oliver and Boyd. Translated from *Theologie des Alten Testaments*, Bd II, Munich: Kaiser Verlag, 1960.

Rendsburg, G. A., 1986. *The Redaction of Genesis*, Winona: Eisenbrauns.

Reventlow, H. Graf, 1962. *Das Amt des Propheten bei Amos*, FRLANT 80, Göttingen: Vandenhoeck & Rupprecht.

1963. *Liturgie und prophetisches Ich bei Jeremia*, Gütersloh: Gütersloher Verlagshaus.

Smith, W. R., 1889. *The Religion of the Semites*, London: A. & C. Black.

Soggin, J. A., 1984. *A History of Israel*, Eng. Tr. J. S. Bowden, London: SCM.

Terrien, S. L. 1962. 'Amos and Wisdom', *Israel's Prophetic Heritage*, eds. B. W. Anderson and W. Harrelson, London, SCM, 108–15.

Thompson, T. L., 1974. *The Historicity of the Patriarchal Narratives. The Quest for the Historical Abraham*, BZAW 133, Berlin: de Gruyter.

1987. *The Origin Traditions of Genesis and Exodus* 1–23, JSOTSS, Sheffield: Sheffield Academic Press.

Unterman, J., 1985. 'Covenant', *Harpers Dictionary of the Bible*, ed. P. J. Achtemeier, New York: Harper & Row, 190–2.

Van Der Woude, A. S., 1982. 'Three Classical Prophets', R. J. Coggins, A. Phillips and M. A. Knibb (eds.), *Israel's Prophetic Tradition*, Cambridge, Cambridge U.P., 32–57.

Van Seters, J., 1975. *Abraham in History and Tradition*, New Haven: Yale U.P.

1983. *In Search of History. Historiography in the Ancient World and the Origins of Biblical History*, New Haven: Yale U.P.

1984. 'Joshua 24 and the Problem of Tradition in the Old Testament', *Essays on Ancient Palestinian Life and Literature in Honor of G. W. Ahlström*, JSOT Supp 31, Sheffield Academic Press, 139–58.

Weber, M., 1952 [1921]. *Ancient Judaism*, London. Translated from *Gesammelte Aufsätze zur Religionssoziologie* III, Tübingen, 1921.

Weinfeld, M., 1972. *Deuteronomy and the Deuteronomic School*, Oxford: Oxford UP.

1977 [1973]. 'Covenant', *TDOT*, II, 253–79; Translated from 'berith', *ThWAT*, I, 1973, 781–808.

Weiser, A., 1962. *Die Psalmen*, Göttingen, 5th ed. 1959, Eng. tr. *The Psalms: A Commentary*, London, SCM.

Wellhausen, J., 1885 [1883]. *Prolegomena to the History of Israel*, Eng. Tr. J. S. Black, Edinburgh: A. & C. Black, Translated from *Prolegomena zur Geschichte Israels*, Berlin, 1883.

Whybray, R. N. JSOTSS 53, Sheffield: Sheffield Academic Press.

Wilson, R. R., 1984. *Sociological Approaches to the Old Testament*, Philadelphia: Fortress.

Wiseman, D. J., 1958. *The Vassal Treaties of Esarhaddon*, London.

Wolff, H. W., 1973 [1964]. *Amos the Prophet. The Man and His Background*, Philadelphia: Fortress. Eng. Tr. by F. R. McCurley from *Amos geistige Heimat*, WMANT 18, Neukirchen: Neukirchener Verlag, 1964.

Wright, G. Ernest, 1962. 'The Lawsuit of God. A Form-Critical Study of Deuteronomy 32', *Israel's Prophetic Heritage*, eds. B. W. Anderson & W. Harrelson, London: SCM, 26–67.

Wurthwein, E., 1949–50. 'Amos Studien', *ZAW* 62, 10–52.

Zimmerli, W., 1965. *The Law and the Prophets*, Eng. Tr. R. E. Clements, Oxford: Blackwell.

1978. *Old Testament Theology in Outline*, Eng. Tr. D. E. Green, Atlanta: John Knox. Translated from *Grundriss der alttestamentliche Theologie*, Stuttgart: Kohlhammer, 1972.

1979. 'The History of Israelite Religion', *Tradition and Interpretation*, ed. G. W. Anderson, Oxford: Clarendon, 351–84.

CHAPTER SIXTEEN

Land: its rights and privileges

ERYL W. DAVIES

There can be little doubt that land, with its concomitant rights and privileges, was a factor of great historical and theological significance for the life and faith of Israel. On the one hand, it was the primary source of economic wealth, and provided the basis for the prosperity of individual families and of the nation as a whole. On the other hand, it was imbued with a profound theological significance, and became a visible sign of the abiding relationship which existed between Yahweh and his people. It is not surprising, therefore, that the theme of land occupies a place of some importance in the Old Testament. However, while some important studies have been published in recent years on land and its significance for Israel's faith,[1] the subject has remained a much neglected area of Old Testament research; indeed, it has been appropriately described by one scholar as the 'Cinderella of both Christian and Jewish scholarship' (Davies: 1982, xiii). One reason for this neglect may be that the Old Testament does not provide a single doctrine of the land which is clearly defined and articulated; rather, it offers a bewildering variety of ideas and concepts which are not formulated in any coherent or systematic way. Thus any adequate discussion of the theme of land in the Old Testament would have to take into account the different interpretations of its significance found in the various traditions, and due allowance would have to be made for the fact that changes in Israel's fortunes inevitably entailed corresponding changes in the manner in which the land was perceived. Such a discussion would, of course, involve the writing of a full-scale study, and would clearly be beyond the scope of this essay. Consequently, this chapter will be limited to an appraisal of a few important aspects relating to the theme of land in the Old Testament, and no attempt will be made to offer a comprehensive analysis of the subject under discussion.

1. Land as gift

The story of Abraham begins with a divine promise of the gift of land. At first, this promise is articulated in rather vague terms as the patriarch sets out from his homeland (Gen. 12.1–3),[2] but it is later made more specific (Gen. 12.7), and is repeatedly affirmed, with varying formulations, both to Abraham himself (Gen. 13.14–17; 15.18–21; 17.8) and to his descendants (Gen. 26.3f.; 28.13–15; 35.11f.).[3] The promise of land, although sometimes appearing in isolation, is frequently interlaced with other promises, which have been variously analysed and categorised, viz., the promise of a son/descendants/progeny (Gen. 13.16; 15.1–6; 16.10–12; 26.4), the promise of God's presence/blessing (Gen. 26.24; 28.13–15), and the promise of a new relationship with God (Gen. 17.4–8).[4] Of all the promises, however, it was the promise of land that was to prove the most important and decisive for Israel, for this promise was reiterated and reinterpreted from one generation to the next in such a way that it became a living power and a seminal force in the life of the people.

From the viewpoint of Old Testament faith, the promise was significant for two reasons. First, it emphasised the fact that the people did not dwell in a land to which the changes and chances of history just happened to have brought them, but in a land which had been destined for them by Yahweh before Israel even became a nation. Israel's occupation of Canaan was therefore not to be regarded as an historical coincidence, but as part of God's purposive action in history. Secondly, the promise served to remind Israel that it was not native to the land of Canaan, but had been granted it by the will of God. Thus the land that was to become Israel's possession was not one which Abraham had inherited by natural right from his ancestors, but one which had been freely granted as Yahweh's gracious gift (Zimmerli: 1976, 67f.).

The concept of the land as a gift is further developed in Deuteronomy (Miller: 1969; Plöger: 1967, 79ff.). Here, the land is described in the most extravagant terms, and extolled as a place filled in abundance with all the necessary provisions of life (Deut. 8.7–10). Indeed, in its richness and desirability, it is compared with the land of Egypt, to which it is far superior (Deut. 11.10–12), and its fertility is expressed by the recurring formula 'a land flowing with milk and honey' (Deut. 6.3; 11.9; 26.9, 15; 27.3; 31.20).[5] According to Deuteronomy, this land was the supreme gift which Yahweh was to bestow upon his people, and it was a gift which patently transcended all human expectation. In addition to the gift of land itself, Israel's life therein was to be characterised by freedom from war and conflict, and the ideal envisaged in Deuteronomy appears to have been that of the chosen people dwelling in a pleasant land at peace with all its enemies (von Rad: 1933, 95).

Deuteronomy recognised, however, that life in the promised land was not without its inherent dangers. Israel might be tempted to become arrogant and self-confident once it had settled in Canaan, and attribute to its own power and ability that which it owed to Yahweh's blessing and providence (Deut. 7.7f.). In order to counter such presumption, Deuteronomy emphasised that Israel had not come into possession of the 'good land' by its own unaided effort or military prowess (Deut. 8.17; cf. 7.22–4); rather, the people had received the land, and all the benefits that derived from it, as a free and undeserved gift by the grace of God (Deut. 6.10–12). Moreover, while it was true that Yahweh had expelled the previous inhabitants from the land because of their wickedness and depravity, it was not due to any corresponding virtue on its part that Israel had been given possession of it. The gift of land was by no means a reward for Israel's righteousness (Deut. 9.4f.); rather, it was a token of the fact that God was acting to fulfil his promise to the patriarchs (Deut. 6.23; 9.5; 10.11).[6] The initiative was therefore entirely Yahweh's, and arose out of his deep and abiding love for his people (Deut. 4.37f.; 7.8). Thus any claim that Israel had a natural or intrinsic right to possess the land is immediately discounted in Deuteronomy, and it is repeatedly affirmed that Israel was given the land, and all the benefits and privileges that were associated with it, solely by the grace of God (Brueggemann: 1977, 47ff.).

Further, Deuteronomy emphasises that the land was a gift which was imparted to all the people of Israel. Indeed, Deuteronomy seldom refers to the hereditary land (*naḥalāh*) of the individual clan or tribe (cf. Deut. 10.9; 29.7f.); its emphasis is rather upon the inheritance of Israel as a whole – a notion which is seldom found in the pre-Deuteronomic writings and which, according to von Rad, finds adequate expression only in Deuteronomy (1943, 81, 91f.; cf. also McConville: 1984, 19; Clements: 1968, 30f.; Diepold: 1972, 79f.). One consequence of Deuteronomy's view of Israel as a single, unified whole was its insistence that no member of the community was to be denied the privilege of enjoying the benefits of the land and its produce. Deuteronomy recognised, of course, that certain members of the community might benefit more than others from Yahweh's gift, and that there would always be some in the land who would be poor and impoverished; nevertheless, it maintained that those who were privileged to receive Yahweh's gift were obliged to ensure that its benefits were shared with all those unfortunate enough not to possess any land of their own. In this regard, special provisions were made for the Levite, for 'he has no portion or inheritance with you' (Deut. 14.27), and also for the sojourner, the widow and the orphan, who similarly had no landed property of their own (Deut. 26.12f.). Among the provisions legislating for their support, Deuteronomy commands that at the time of the harvest some of the produce should be left behind in the fields for the benefit of the weakest members of the community (Deut. 24.19–21), and that every third year a tithe of the crops was to be set aside so that the needy may 'come and eat and be filled' (Deut. 14.28f.). Such generosity was enjoined because Deuteronomy recognised that every member of the community had a basic right to enjoy some of the benefits which derived from possession of one's own property.

It is clear from such provisions that a particular form of conduct was regarded as appropriate for Israel's life in the land. The land offered many benefits and opportunities, but at the same time it placed significant demands upon the individual and corporate life of the people. Thus, corresponding to the notion of the land as divine gift, there was a human dimension which was to manifest itself in Israel's response. Yahweh's gift to Israel implied a requirement on his part, and throughout Deuteronomy there is a continued demand for Israel's obedience, and an emphasis on the obligations which the people owed to God. Various statutes were promulgated for observance at the time of entry into the land (Deut. 5.31; 11.31f.; 12.1), and it was made clear that continued occupation of the land was contingent upon Israel's compliance with Yahweh's commands. Indeed, Israel's relation to the land, as depicted in Deuteronomy, seems to be highly dialectical, for the privilege of dwelling in the land is constantly counterbalanced by a recognition of the fact that the people could always, by their disobedience, lose possession of it.

It has frequently been observed by commentators that the precise nature of the relation between the law and the land in Deuteronomy is somewhat ambivalent: on the one hand, the commandments seem to be regarded as regulatory, i.e., they are intended to provide guidance for the behaviour of the people in the land (cf. Deut. 12.1ff.; 18.9ff.; 19.1ff.; 26.1ff.); on the other hand, they appear to be conditional, i.e., only if they are obeyed can the land be received and possessed (cf. Deut. 6.18f.; 8.1; 11.8f.; 16.20). The law was thus viewed both as the norm of Israel's life in the land and as the primary condition of its occupation. This view of the nature of the law, however, inevitably resulted in a certain tension between the concept of gift and that of commandment, for it is implied that without obedience to the law, there could be no land-gift, and consequently the gift itself appears to be made conditional (cf. Perlitt: 1983, 54). Indeed, it has been suggested that the conditional nature of the promise of the land in Deuteronomy tends to distract from its overall theology of the land as an unmerited gift, and von Rad has raised the question whether this does not 'pave the way for a declension from grace into law' (1943, 91).

Not all scholars, however, would agree that the notions of gift and commandment in Deuteronomy must necessarily be viewed in terms of conflict. P. Diepold, in particular, has argued that these concepts should be regarded as complementary rather than contradictory, and he maintains that the tension between them is resolved by Deuteronomy's theology of the covenant (1972, 88ff.). Diepold argues that Deuteronomy's emphasis is always on the prior action of Yahweh in Israel's affairs, and that consequently its entire theology is predicated on Israel's grateful response to Yahweh's initiative. It was because Yahweh had taken steps to establish a covenant that Israel was able to enter into it, and it was because he had granted the gift of land that the people were able to possess it (cf. McConville: 1984, 12f.). Yahweh's sovereign action in history always demanded a reciprocal action from Israel, and it is in this light, according to Diepold, that Deuteronomy's pronouncements regarding the law should be viewed. The commandments were given prior to Israel's entry into the promised land, but their observance became meaningful only after the conquest and settlement. Here again, therefore, the indicative is made the basis for the imperative, and observance of the law – far from being regarded as a burden upon the people – is presented as their thankful response to the privileges granted to them by Yahweh. Once viewed in this light, the law becomes not so much a qualification for entry into the land as its necessary accompaniment; it is not so much a counterpart of divine grace as an important expression of it (cf. Clements: 1968, 59f.). Thus Deuteronomy can be absolved from the charge of legalism, for its covenant theology 'prevents the indicative from being reduced to cheap grace, and prevents the imperative from degenerating into works of righteousness' (Diepold: 1972, 100). Israel cannot earn its salvation by obedience to the law; yet, it is only when Israel hears and obeys God's commands that it can fully realise its existence as the chosen people in the promised land.

2. The prophets and the land

Many passages in the prophetic writings are imbued with an awareness of the significance of the land for Israel's faith (Zimmerli: 1985). The prophets emphasised that Israel had no perpetual, inalienable right to the land, and that the people could, by their unfaithfulness and disloyalty to Yahweh, lose possession of it. Amos, in particular, stressed that Israel was not indigenous to the land (Am. 2.10) and had no inviolable right to dwell in it; indeed, he warned that the nation, because of its iniquity, would suffer a calamitous military defeat and would be taken into exile 'away from its land' (Am. 7.17; cf. 2.13–16; 3.11; 5.3, 27; 7.7–9). Hosea also spoke of a deportation from the land, although he envisaged it not as an exile but as a return to the wilderness period, when Israel would be transported back to the beginning of its history and would be led again into the promised land (Hos. 2.14f.). Micah, like Amos, condemned those who were intent upon exploiting the poor, and he warned that the wealthy landowners would be dispossessed, and that those who had brought ruin on others would themselves be subjected to the same fate (Mic. 2.1–5). The threat of devastation of the land also features in Isaiah (5.8–10; 6.11–13), although his main concern appears to have been the destruction of the once faithful city and its surrounding territory, rather than the annihilation of the entire land brought about by the unfaithfulness of its inhabitants (cf. Is. 1.21ff.; 29.1ff.).

Jeremiah's pronouncements concerning the land call for special attention, since it is undoubtedly he who gives the fullest expression to its abiding significance for the life of the people. These pronouncements have recently been the subject of a detailed examination by P. Diepold, who concludes that many of the statements regarding the land in Jeremiah bear an unmistakable Deuteronomistic stamp in both language and ideology (1972, 155ff.; cf. Nicholson: 1970; Thiel: 1973, 1981). He argues, however, that the prophet's original message can be distinguished from the later Deuteronomistic expansions and revisions. One of the most notable features of Jeremiah's original proclamation, according to Diepold (1972, 106ff.), was his personification of the land (cf. Jer. 6.19; 8.16; 22.29); indeed, the land occasionally appears to be identified with the people of Israel, and both are similarly designated as Yahweh's 'inheritance' (*naḥalāh*; cf. Jer. 12.7–13). The land of Israel was Yahweh's land, and the people of Israel were Yahweh's people, and so close was the association between the people and the land that the destinies of both were inextricably connected. Thus Yahweh's judgement involved devastation of the land and exile of the people; by the same token, the restoration of the relationship between Yahweh and Israel could only be sealed conclusively by the restoration of the people to their land.

Land, therefore, played a crucial role in both the judgement and salvation of the people. Jeremiah emphasised that Israel had been brought into a fertile land (Jer. 2.7), which was the most beautiful inheritance of any nation (Jer. 3.19), but the people had proved unworthy of the gift; consequently, the land would be made desolate, Jerusalem would become uninhabited, and the people themselves would be driven into exile (cf. Jer. 4.5ff.; 6.1ff.). Yahweh's judgement, however, did not mean the irrevocable surrender of the divine gift of land, for Jeremiah believed that there would be a return from exile, although his letter to the deportees in Babylon suggests that such a return was not to be regarded as an imminent prospect (cf. Jer. 29.5f.).[7] That a return to the land was, indeed, part of God's ultimate plan for his people is well illustrated in the narrative recounting Jeremiah's purchase of a portion of family inheritance from his kinsman at a time when Jerusalem was already besieged by the enemy (Jer. 32.6ff.). The prophet's action, concluded legally with the necessary deeds of purchase (*v.* 11), was a visible demonstration of his faith in Yahweh's promise that, after the period of judgement and exile, 'houses and fields and vineyards shall again be bought in the land' (Jer. 32.15). Such hope for the future restoration of Israel is, however, seldom found in the authentic passages of Jeremiah, and it was left for the Deuteronomistic editors of the book to affirm clearly that Israel's future in the land was assured and unconditional (Diepold: 1972, 155ff.).

In accord with Jeremiah's own conviction, the Deuteronomistic editors insisted that Israel's sin was the cause of the disaster of 587 BC (cf. Jer. 44.22); the judgement had come because the people had abandoned Yahweh (Jer. 5.19) and his law (Jer. 9.13), and had worshipped other gods (Jer. 9.14; 16.11). Nevertheless, the Deuteronomistic editors affirmed that Yahweh's faithfulness did not cease on account of Israel's unfaithfulness, and consequently the people could look forward to a new exodus which would be followed by a new conquest and a new gift of land (Jer. 24.6f.; 27.22; 32.37–41). The old affirmation ('As the Lord lives who brought up the people of Israel out of the land of Egypt') would be replaced by a new one ('As the Lord lives who brought up and led the descendants of the house of Israel out of the north country and out of all the countries where he [LXX] had driven them'; Jer. 23.7f.). The Deuteronomistic editors recognised, however, that a mere return to the land would not, in itself, be enough, for the history of apostasy would simply be repeated; therefore, Yahweh had to create something new in the land, and this he did by establishing a new and eternal covenant with his people (Jer. 31.31–4). The old covenant had preceded the conquest and settlement, i.e., there was a demand to be obeyed before the promise of land could be fulfilled; the new covenant, on the other hand, was not the condition of entry into the land, but its consequence (Diepold: 1972, 174–6). That which had previously been given by Yahweh conditionally was now promised unconditionally, and Yahweh's gift would not henceforth be dependent upon Israel's obedience to the requirements of the law. The people would therefore be able to return to the land, purged of all uncleanliness, and rebuild within it a new community that would truly reflect the chosen Israel of God (Jer. 30.1–3, 18–21).

3. Land in the Deuteronomistic History

The importance of land for the existence of Israel as a nation is a central theme in the Deuteronomistic History (=DtrH). This work, which comprises Deuteronomy – 2 Kings, was essentially composed during the period of the Babylonian exile, and it presents a theological reflection upon the historical events which led to the destruction of Jerusalem, the devastation of the land, and the deportation of the people in 587 BC. How could Yahweh have allowed such a catastrophe to happen, and how could it have been possible for him to reject his people in such a decisive fashion? DtrH seeks to answer such questions by indicating that the tragic fate which befell the people was not due to an arbitrary decision on Yahweh's part, but was rather the inevitable consequence of Israel's long history of disobedience and apostasy. For DtrH, observance of the law was the *conditio sine qua non* for Israel's original occupation of the land and for its continued existence therein; by implication, therefore, Israel's failure to observe the stipulations of the law would inevitably result in forfeiture of the land (cf. Josh. 23.15f.). It is on the basis of this principle that DtrH seeks to explain the loss of territory which the people suffered as a result of the defeats inflicted in 722 and 587 BC (cf. 2 Kgs. 17.1ff.; 18.11f.; 21.10ff.). These disasters were not due to Yahweh's weakness or helplessness; rather, they were the fully justified and unavoidable consequence of the people's rejection of God. Indeed, DtrH shows that from the very beginning of Israel's life in the land, the people had transgressed against the covenant and had failed to live in obedience to Yahweh's will, and the entire subsequent history of Israel was marked by the people's continued sinfulness and infidelity (2 Kgs. 21.14f.).[8] It is clear from the interpretative passages in Judges (cf. 2.11–15; 3.7–11; 10.6–16) that the primary sin of Israel was the worship of other gods, and it is frequently the case in DtrH that the punishment prescribed for such apostasy entailed the forfeiture of land (cf. 1 Kgs. 9.1ff.; 14.15). Thus DtrH, in effect, constructs a history of land given and land lost, and indicates that obedience to the law would be rewarded by possession of land, but that disobedience would inevitably result in its loss. The exile which the people now suffered was therefore not due to any fault or neglect on God's part; rather, the people had themselves wilfully forfeited the land as a result of their own misconduct.

According to Noth, DtrH interpreted Yahweh's judgement upon the people in 587 BC as something final and definitive, and consequently the work was entirely devoid of any hope or promise for the future (1981, 97ff.). Its outlook was basically one of unrelieved pessimism, for it merely sought to explain the past, and was not even remotely concerned with the possibility as to whether the catastrophe which had befallen the people might inaugurate a new era of salvation. The devastation of the land and the exile of the people were already, from the point of view of DtrH, a grim reality, and the history of Israel and Judah seemed all but at an end; logically, therefore, there appeared to be no hope or future left for the people of God.

Noth's assessment of the purpose and outlook of DtrH, however, has not won widespread support among Old Testament scholars, for it is thought that there would have been little point in addressing such a negative message to a generation which had already, to all intents and purposes, been written off by Yahweh (Wolff: 1975, 83ff.; von Rad: 1962, 346; Nicholson: 1970, 75). Thus, despite its general aura of gloom, it is argued that the ultimate aim of DtrH was more positive, constructive and edifying than Noth's analysis would seem to suggest. Yahweh had indeed punished Israel for its sins, but that judgement did not necessarily mean the end of God's people, for it was still his wish that they should turn (*šûḇ*) to him again and repent for their past misdeeds (cf. 1 Sam. 7.3; 1 Kgs. 8.33, 35f.). Such repentance had been urged by every prophet in Israel, but their words had always fallen on deaf ears (2 Kgs. 17.13f.); now, however, the people were being given another chance to repent, and nothing but their blatant refusal to turn would constitute the end of the people of God (Wolff: 1975). Consequently, it is not surprising that occasional references are found in DtrH to the possibility of forgiveness and renewal (cf. Deut. 4.29–31; 1 Kgs. 8.46–53), and it is sometimes implied that a return of the people to God would bring them even richer blessings than those which they had hitherto received (cf. Deut. 30.1–6). Of course, DtrH could no longer appeal to the gift of land as a motivation for repentance, since that had already been forfeited; nevertheless, appeal could be made to Yahweh's 'good word' to the house of David (2 Sam. 7), for this was something which endured in every crisis and could be relied upon even when the land had been lost (Brueggemann: 1968). That the promise of Yahweh to David's house still remained valid is affirmed, according to some scholars, by the concluding statement of DtrH concerning the release of Jehoiachin from prison (2 Kgs. 25.27–30), for it is supposed that this event would have led the exiles in Babylon to look forward to a restoration of the nation's fortunes, and would have confirmed their belief in the survival of the Davidic dynasty.[9]

It is probable, therefore, that, *contra* Noth, the outlook of DtrH was not entirely pessimistic, negative and backward-looking; rather, it addressed the dispirited exiles with a message of hope and promise for the future. The positive stance of DtrH must not, of course, be exaggerated, for it occupies only a comparatively small portion of what is, after all, a lengthy historical work (cf. Klein: 1979, 43); nevertheless, it must not be entirely overlooked, for behind the pronouncement of judgement, a note of hope and promise can be discerned: if those in exile were prepared to repent and trust in Yahweh's promise to the house of David, then the way would be clear for them to realise once again their existence as God's people in God's land.

4. Individual property rights

The notion of individual property rights in Israel can be traced to the traditions concerning the division of land between the tribes. After the occupation of Canaan, the Israelite tribes were each allotted their territorial areas, and it is clear from Josh. 13–19 that the land was allocated in such a way that every tribe received a portion corresponding to its need (cf. Rendtorff: 1970, 160). The land was apportioned by casting lots 'before the Lord' (Josh. 18.10), and thus it was made clear that it was Yahweh himself who was ultimately responsible for allocating to each tribe the portion of land which it was to possess. The traditions concerning the distribution of land between the tribes were important for two reasons. First, they served to emphasise the fact that the right of each tribe to the land it possessed was guaranteed by Yahweh, since he alone was responsible for its original allocation. Secondly, the traditions reflected Israel's belief that land was to be divided on a broadly equitable basis, so that each clan and each individual household had a right to a share in the inheritance of God's people (cf. Wright: 1983, 54). The ideal cherished in Israel, therefore, was that of a kinship structure based on a large number of landowning households, and many of Israel's laws and institutions were designed to keep this kinship structure intact.

With the establishment of the monarchy, however, this ideal was soon eroded as the traditional pattern of land-tenure was undermined. The king himself engaged in various commercial enterprises, and his demand for property would have been a necessary prerequisite for the effective continuance of the institution of the monarchy. Indeed, even before the appearance of the first king, Samuel had warned of the costly burden of the monarchy, and had mentioned among the constitutional rights of the king the possibility that he would confiscate private lands and give them to his own servants (1 Sam. 8.14).[10] It is not surprising, therefore, to find that the kings of Israel and Judah were owners of vast estates (cf. 2 Chron. 26.6ff.), and some of the revenue from this land was no doubt used for the upkeep of the royal household. Evidence for the existence of crown-property in Israel may also be found in the allusions in the Old Testament to the *corvée* or forced labour (2 Sam. 12.31; 20.24; 1 Kgs. 11.28; cf. Mendelsohn: 1962), and it is probable that the kings made use of such a system as a means of securing unpaid assistance for their building activities and for work on the royal estates (1 Chron. 27.25–31; 2 Chron. 26.10; 32.27–9).

But how did the kings of Israel and Judah come to possess so much property? Opportunities no doubt occasionally arose for the king to purchase land, and evidence of such transactions may be found in 2 Sam. 24.24 and 1 Kgs. 16.24 (cf. Alt: 1959, 361–3). Moreover, it is possible that dynastic changes contributed to the enlargement of the royal estates, for each king would have taken over his predecessor's property (cf. 2 Sam. 9.7; 12.8), and much land may have accumulated in this way, especially if – as was the case in the early period of the northern kingdom – there was a rapid succession of kings upon the throne (cf. Noth: 1927, 212f.). Further, there is some evidence to suggest that new stipulations governing landed property were promulgated by the king's officials in their attempt to expand the royal estate (cf. Is. 10.1–4), and such stipulations would no doubt have ensured that the king had a means of acquiring land beyond that which was warranted by the normal customary procedure (Davies: 1981*a*, 78–83). Naturally, such developments were a direct threat to the economic freedom of the rural peasantry, for the rights of the individual to his land were being continually undermined as the king and his officials made ever-increasing incursions into the traditional Israelite system of land-tenure.

The establishment of the monarchy in Israel had, of course, made the country an important political factor in the ancient Near East, and had succeeded in creating the necessary conditions for considerable economic progress (Neufeld: 1960). However, the rising monetary economy inevitably led to a serious crisis among many of the small landowners (Donner: 1963; Bardtke: 1971). Their needs were often supplied by loans obtained from their wealthier neighbours, and it was no doubt frequently the case that the poor farmers, owing to unforeseen circumstances (e.g., crop-failure), found it almost impossible to return the goods which they had borrowed (Lang: 1983, 114ff.). Clearly, therefore, a considerable risk was involved in lending to those in need, and in order to provide the creditor with some incentive to lend, the law permitted him to take from the borrower, at the time the loan was made, some guarantee of security in the form of a pledge (cf. Ex. 22.26; Deut. 24.6, 10–13, 17). The retaining of such a pledge may, indeed, have proved profitable, especially if it consisted of the debtor's land or a member of his family. While it is true that the creditor could never realise the value of the pledge by sale or exchange for the purpose of satisfying his claim, there is nothing to suggest that he could not use it to his own advantage (Neufeld: 1962; de Vaux: 1961, 171f.). That such a commodity as land may occasionally have been taken for this purpose is suggested by the incident recorded in Neh. 5.1ff., for this narrative depicts a situation where sons and daughters who were in bondage could not be redeemed by their parents because their fields and vineyards had been forfeited. When, as in this case, property was taken in pledge, the creditor would have been able to make full use of the land, and its usufruct would have provided interest on the loan and contributed to the gradual amortisation of the debt. It is quite possible that this custom, whereby the creditor could never become the actual owner of the pledge but could nevertheless use it for his own benefit, was adopted in Israel as a means of circumventing the law regarding the inalienability of land (Lev. 25.23). The basic principle underlying this law was that all property belonged to Yahweh and could not, therefore, be bought or sold at will. However, property given as a pledge could not be regarded as having been 'alienated' in the strict sense of the term, since the creditor could never become its possessor, and the pledge always remained redeemable. By means of such casuistry, land may often have been appropriated without necessarily transgressing the legal provisions safeguarding the rights of the individual to his patrimony.

It must be noted, however, that Hebrew legislation did provide various means by which an impoverished farmer, who had been compelled to surrender his land, might be able to regain his inheritance. The provisions regarding redemption of land by the kinsman (Lev. 25.25) and the Jubilee (Lev. 25.8ff.) must be mentioned here, for both were concerned to relieve those whom misfortune had reduced to poverty, and to prevent the accumulation of immoderate wealth in the hands of the few. The law relating to redemption of land decreed that if a person had been forced through poverty to part with his patrimony, the next-of-kin had the right – and indeed the duty – to redeem that which his relative had sold, thus keeping the family property intact.[11] However, it is doubtful whether this provision would always have provided an effective means of alleviating the situation of the impoverished farmer. In the first place, it is clear that the land could only be redeemed if the kinsman was a person of some financial means and was willing to fulfil his social obligation; in those cases where the farmer belonged to a family who possessed neither wealth nor influence, it is probable that the duty of redeeming the land would not have been performed (Neufeld: 1961, 34f.). Moreover, the law did not force a reluctant kinsman to redeem his relative's property, and consequently it could not have been difficult for him to evade his obligation (cf. Ruth 3.13). It is significant, in this regard, that Lev. 25.26f. envisaged a situation where an impoverished farmer had no kinsman to act on his behalf, and in such cases the owner himself was encouraged to repurchase his land if he later acquired the means of doing so. However, this would seldom have taken place, for once a debtor had been ruined to such an extent that he had to surrender his land and forgo his liberty, the chances of his recovering on his own must have been very slender.

The law of the Jubilee year (Lev. 25.8ff.) represented a further measure designed to preserve the independence of the smaller family unit, for its aim was to hinder the development of an extensive latifundism by providing that all property, after a period of seven weeks of years, was to be returned to its original owner or to his descendants.[12] Since most people in Israel would have had a certain measure of economic independence if they owned a piece of land, the enactment of the Jubilee simply sought to ensure the preservation of the economic basis upon which the social order rested. However, as was the case with the law of redemption, there are grounds here, too, for scepticism regarding the effectiveness of this provision to relieve the plight of the impoverished in the community. In the first place, the reversion of land to its original owner in the Jubilee year would inevitably have involved a great upheaval, since vast tracts of land would have changed hands at the same time, and this would have caused serious repercussions in practically every sphere of human life. Further, if the Jubilee occurred in the fiftieth year, as opposed to the seventh Sabbath year, this would have entailed two successive fallows (cf. Lev. 25.18–22), which would almost certainly have proved economically disastrous. Moreover, even if families had been given an opportunity to re-establish their position in the community, it is doubtful if many would have succeeded, for such a prolonged period of servitude would have constituted a disaster from which most people could never have expected to recover.[13]

It is clear, therefore, that although certain laws were designed to keep land within the family, and to facilitate its recovery when lost, such provisions did not always achieve their objective. Consequently, many people would no doubt have found themselves permanently deprived of their ancestral inheritance. It cannot be too strongly emphasised that such a loss would have had far-reaching implications for the social structure of Israel, since it would have involved not only severe economic hardship but also, in all probability, a loss of representation in the local assembly. Those who were entitled to participate in the assembly were the elders, i.e., the full citizens of the community, and while it is not entirely certain how such citizenship was defined, it is probable that possession of house and property was a determinative factor (Frick: 1977, 120f.; Davies: 1981*a*, 100–2). Thus while the people remained free, land-owning householders, the general affairs of the community would be administered on a truly democratic basis, since each family would be fairly represented in its deliberations; dispossession of land, on the other hand, meant that many would have been deprived of their rights in the community and would have ceased to enjoy the advantages of full citizenship (Köhler: 1956, 152f.; Wright: 1983, 169f.).

It is in this light that the prophetic concern for the plight of the widow and orphan in Israel should be viewed, for it is clear from the pronouncements of the prophets that their position was particularly vulnerable in the local judicial proceedings (cf. Is. 1.17, 23; 10.1f.). While the *paterfamilias* was alive, the rights of his wife and children would have been protected, since he, in his position as an elder in the community, would have been able to plead their cause before the legal assembly. However, when the husband died, the widow and her children would often have been quite defenceless, and would have remained at the mercy of the community at large. The position of the widow in Israel was no doubt exacerbated by the fact that no provision was made for her to inherit the property of her deceased husband;[14] consequently, she would have been deprived of a commodity which would not only have provided her with some measure of security, but which would also have ensured her position in the life of the community. It is not surprising, therefore, that consideration for the widow and orphan is constantly enjoined in the Old Testament, and, as has already been noted, the law sought to legislate for their support by awarding them the privilege of gleaning the fields after the harvest (Deut. 24.19–22; cf. Lev. 19.9f.; 23.22), and by ensuring that a triennial tithe was distributed among them to relieve their need (Deut. 14.28f.; 26.12–15).[15] But it is doubtful whether such enactments were in themselves adequate to relieve their unenviable position in society, for no amount of provisions enabling them to glean the fields and vineyards of others could ever make up for the loss of civil rights which befell those who possessed no land of their own.

Hebrew legislation did, however, make one provision which might have enabled a childless widow to benefit from the property of her deceased husband. This was the law known as the levirate marriage (Deut. 25.5–10), which stipulated that if a man had died without leaving progeny, the brothers of the deceased had the responsibility of providing the widow with male heirs (Burrows: 1940; Leggett: 1974). As long as the levirate obligation was dutifully performed, the plight of the widow would have been, to some extent, alleviated, for her brother-in-law would have ensured her protection and support, and would have provided her with male offspring who would inherit her husband's estate. However, it is probable that the levirate custom would, in practice, have been rather limited in its effect. In the first place, the provision was not clothed with any legal sanction; rather, it was a rule which derived its only force from the general disapprobation falling upon those who transgressed it. Secondly, the disadvantages of performing the duty may often have outweighed the advantages, for the brother-in-law would probably have forfeited to the son born of the levirate union the inheritance which he himself might otherwise have possessed. Further, by stipulating that performance of the duty could only be carried out while brothers lived together on the unpartitioned family estate (Deut. 25.5), the law must have imposed a severe restriction on the practice of the custom in Israel. Consequently, it is probable that the levirate duty was not often performed, and the widow would, as a result, have remained propertyless and at the mercy of the community at large (Davies: 1981*b*).

5. Conclusion

It is clear from the above discussion that the right of possession of land and the privilege of dwelling within its boundaries were regarded as central concepts for the life and faith of Israel. The land had been granted to the people solely by the grace of God, and thereby it acquired a special significance as the visible manifestation of Israel's elect status. However, possession of the land carried with it various duties and responsibilities, and it is clear in Deuteronomy that Israel's continued existence therein was contingent upon the people's willingness to comply with Yahweh's commands. The eighth-century prophets also emphasised that Israel had no inviolable right to dwell in the land, and that God's action in history allowed not only for the gift of land but also for Israel's expulsion from it. The prophetic warnings were vindicated in the catastrophes which befell Israel and Judah in 722 and 587 BC, and it was left for the editors of the Deuteronomistic History to explain that these disasters were the inevitable consequence of the people's rejection of Yahweh. However, the message of DtrH was not entirely devoid of hope for the future, for it promised that God would have compassion upon his people and restore them to their land if they were prepared to repent and return to him.

The land was clearly important not only for Israel's existence as a nation, but also for the existence and economic viability of each individual household within Israel. While the people remained free, landowning householders, their position in the life of the community was relatively secure; dispossession of land, however, would have entailed not only severe economic hardship but also, in all probability, a loss of representation in the local assembly. It is not surprising, therefore, that various laws were promulgated which were designed to keep the land within the family and to facilitate its recovery if lost. The provisions concerning the redemption of land by the kinsman and the Jubilee year were particularly important in this regard, for both were designed to provide the impoverished farmer with an opportunity to regain his land and to re-establish his position in the life of the community. However, it was suggested that such provisions would not always have proved an effective means of alleviating the situation of those who had been forced, by adverse circumstances, to part with their patrimony. Finally, it was observed that the unenviable position of the widow in Israel was primarily due to the fact that no provisions were made to enable her to inherit the property of her deceased husband, and although the custom known as the levirate marriage was designed to ease her situation, it is probable that this provision would also, in practice, have been very limited in its effect.

There can be little doubt, therefore, that land was a factor of paramount importance in Israel, whether viewed from a sociological or a theological perspective. Clearly, much research remains to be done on various aspects of the subject under consideration, but it may be suggested, in conclusion, that any adequate treatment of the theology of the Old Testament must take seriously its understanding of the land, and give due recognition to its profound significance for Israel's faith. Indeed, the concept of land may provide a suitable focus around which a theology of the Old Testament can be constructed, for it is arguable that no other theme encompasses in such a fashion so many aspects of Israel's life and thought. On the theological level, it was clearly an integral part of the relationship established between Yahweh and his people; on the sociological level, it served to symbolise the ideal of equality which was supposed to exist between each man and his neighbour. As such, the land represented a challenge for all members of the covenant community to reassess their relationship to one another and to Yahweh, for the gift had been granted to each individual within Israel so that, together, they might fulfil their destiny as the chosen people of God.

Notes

1 Cf. the studies by Brueggemann: 1977; Davies: 1974, 1982; Diepold: 1972; Gnuse: 1985; Ohler: 1979; von Rad: 1943; Rendtorff: 1970; Strecker (ed.): 1983; von Waldow: 1974; Wildberger: 1956; Wright: 1983; Zimmerli: 1976, 1985. For a discussion of some of the terms used in connection with land and inheritance in the Old Testament, cf. Horst: 1961; Rost: 1934.

2 Wolff (1966, 140) argues that the promise of land recedes completely into the background in Gen. 12.1–3, and appears 'in an almost unrecognizable form'. However, von Rad (1943, 84) suggests that by being deliberately kept apart from the great pronouncement in which Yahweh declares his purpose (Gen. 12.1–3), the distinctive nature of the promise of land is actually highlighted.

3 To attempt to assess the different theories which have been proposed regarding the historical origins of the promise of land would clearly transgress the limits of this essay, but reference should be made to the important studies by Alt: 1966; Clements: 1967; Hoftijzer: 1956; von Rad: 1938; van Seters: 1975; Westermann: 1980.

4 The distinction between the promise of a son and the promise of many descendants is emphasised by Westermann (1980, 11ff.), and the promise of a new relationship with God as an independent category is advocated by von Rad (1943, 79f., 84).

5 Herrmann (1965, 65ff.) argues that this expression represents an independent complex of tradition, and did not originate in the same life-setting as the traditions connected with the patriarchs.

6 Miller (1969, 454) notes that there are eighteen explicit references in Deuteronomy to Yahweh's promise of land to the patriarchs. Von Rad (1943, 80) maintains that in Deuteronomy the promise to the patriarchs is understood only in terms of land (cf. also Plöger: 1967, 66ff.); however, while it is true that the promise of land is dominant in Deuteronomy, other elements of the patriarchal promise are occasionally mentioned (Deut. 1.10; 10.22; 28.62). Cf. Clines: 1978, 58–60.

7 The letter, in its present form, has been considerably expanded by the Deuteronomistic editors of Jeremiah (cf. Nicholson: 1970, 97ff.); however, it is probable that *vv*. 4–7 were a part of the original letter (so, e.g., Diepold).

8 Cf. von Rad: 1962, 337, who claims that the work of the Deuteronomist is to be understood 'as a comprehensive confession of Israel's guilt'.

9 Cf. von Rad: 1953, 90f.; 1962, 343; Ackroyd: 1968, 78–81; Zenger: 1968, 16–30; Nicholson: 1970, 78–80. For a different interpretation of this passage, however, see Noth: 1981, 97f.

10 Whether 1 Sam. 8.10ff. is to be regarded as an authentic description of semi-feudal Canaanite society as it existed during the time of Samuel himself (cf. Mendelsohn: 1956, 17–22), or whether it represents a later reflection upon the actual experience of the ways of the kings in Israel and Judah (cf. Clements: 1974, 398–410), need not detain us here, but it may be taken for granted that the monarchial administration of David and Solomon did include many features such as those listed in this passage.

11 The institution of redemption of land by a kinsman is presupposed in Lev. 25.25; Jer. 32.6ff. and Ruth 4. The situation in Ruth 4, however, is complicated by the combination of two separate customs, namely, levirate marriage and land-redemption; cf. Davies: 1983, 231–4.

12 It is not certain whether the Jubilee was intended to be observed on the forty-ninth year or on the fiftieth. On the one hand, Lev. 25.8f. stipulates that the Jubilee was to be held on the seventh Sabbath year, but on the other hand, Lev. 25.10f. designates the Jubilee as the fiftieth year. For a detailed discussion of the problem, see North: 1954, 109ff.

13 On the basis of such considerations, some scholars have argued that the institution of the Jubilee was no more than an idealistic proposal which was never actually enforced in Israel (so, e.g., de Vaux: 1961, 175–7). However, this seems unlikely, and the existence of similar institutions elsewhere in the ancient Near East (cf. Alexander: 1938; Lewy: 1958) suggests that the Jubilee law was not simply an Utopian concept which was never realised (Neufeld: 1958, 122). It is true that there is no evidence to indicate that the law was ever applied in Israel on a regular basis, but this may merely suggest that the custom fell into desuetude at a comparatively early stage.

14 The narrative recorded in Num. 27.1ff. is important in this regard, for it indicates that if the widow had children of her own, her husband's estate would have passed to them, but if she had no children, the nearest kinsman of the husband would have succeeded to the property. The possibility thus seems to be precluded for the widow to inherit the estate of her deceased husband. Cf. Epsztein: 1986, 113f.

15 Concern for the protection and support of the widow and orphan was a common phenomenon in the ancient Near East, and it is reflected in some of the oldest law codes. Cf. Fensham: 1962, 129–39.

Bibliography

Ackroyd, P. R., 1968. *Exile and Restoration* (London: SCM Press).

Alexander, J. B., 1938. 'A Babylonian Year of Jubilee?', *JBL* 57, 75–9.

Alt, A., 1959. 'Der Anteil des Königtums an der sozialen Entwicklung in den Reichen Israel und Juda', in *Kleine Schriften zur Geschichte des Volkes Israel*, vol. III (Munich: C. H. Beck), 348–72.

1966. 'The God of the Fathers', in *Essays on Old Testament History and Religion* (Oxford: B. H. Blackwell, 1966), 1–77 (English translation of *Der Gott der Väter*, BWANT 12 (Stuttgart, 1929); reprinted in *Kleine Schriften zur Geschichte des Volkes Israel*, vol. I (Munich: C. H. Beck, 1953), 1–78.

Bardtke, H., 1971. 'Die Latifundien in Juda während der zweiten Hälfte des achten Jahrhunderts v. Chr.', in A. Caquot and M. Philonenko (eds.), *Hommages à André Dupont-Sommer* (Paris: Adrien-Maisonneuve), 235–54.

Brueggemann, W., 1968. 'The Kerygma of the Deuteronomistic Historian', *Interpretation* 22, 387–402.

1977. *The Land* (Philadelphia: Fortress).

Burrows, M., 1940. 'Levirate Marriage in Israel', *JBL* 59, 23–33.

Clements, R. E., 1967. *Abraham and David*, SBT, Second Series 5 (London: SCM Press).

1968. *God's Chosen People* (London: SCM Press).

1974. 'The Deuteronomistic Interpretation of the Founding of the Monarchy in 1 Sam. VIII', *VT* 24, 398–410.

Clines, D. J. A., 1978. *The Theme of the Pentateuch*, JSOT Supplement Series 10 (Sheffield: JSOT Press).

Davies, E. W., 1981. *Prophecy and Ethics: Isaiah and the Ethical Traditions of Israel*, JSOT Supplement Series 16 (Sheffield: JSOT Press, 1981) (=1981*a*).

1981. 'Inheritance Rights and the Hebrew Levirate Marriage', *VT* 31, 138–44, 257–68 (=1981*b*).

1983. 'Ruth IV 5 and the Duties of the Gō'ēl', *VT* 33, 231–4.

Davies, W. D., 1974. *The Gospel and the Land* (Berkeley, Los Angeles and London: Univ. of California).

1982. *The Territorial Dimension of Judaism* (Berkeley, Los Angeles and London: Univ. of California).

Diepold, P., 1972. *Israels Land*, BWANT 95 (Stuttgart: Kohlhammer).

Donner, H., 1963. 'Die soziale Botschaft der Propheten im Lichte der Gesellschaftsordnung in Israel', *OrAnt* 2, 229–45.

Epsztein, L., 1986. *Social Justice in the Ancient Near East and the People of the Bible* (London,

1986) (English translation of *La Justice Sociale dans le Proche-Orient ancien et le Peuple de la Bible* (Paris, 1983)).

Fensham, F. C., 1962. 'Widow, Orphan, and the Poor in Ancient Near Eastern Legal and Wisdom Literature', *JNES* 21, 129–39.

Frick, F. S., 1977. *The City in Ancient Israel*, SBL Dissertation Series 36 (Missoula, Montana: Scholars Press).

Gnuse, R., 1985. *You shall not Steal: Community and Property in the Biblical Tradition* (New York).

Herrmann, S., 1965. *Die prophetischen Heilserwartungen im Alten Testament*, BWANT 85 (Stuttgart: Kohlhammer).

Hoftijzer, J., 1956. *Die Verheissungen an die drei Erzväter* (Leiden: E. J. Brill).

Horst, F., 1961. 'Zwei Begriffe für Eigentum (Besitz): *naḥalāh* und *'ḥuzāh*, in A. Kuschke (ed.), *Verbannung und Heimkehr* (Tübingen: J. C. B. Mohr), 135–56.

Klein, R. W., 1979. *Israel in Exile* (Philadelphia: Fortress Press).

Köhler, L., 1956. *Hebrew Man* (London: SCM Press, 1956) (English translation of *Der hebräische Mensch* (Tübingen: J. C. B. Mohr, 1953)).

Lang, B., 1983. *Monotheism and the Prophetic Minority* (Sheffield: Almond Press).

Leggett, D. A., 1974. *The Levirate and Goel Institutions in the Old Testament* (Cherry Hill, New Jersey: Mack Publishing Co.).

Lewy, J., 1958. 'The Biblical Institution of *Deᵉrôr* in the Light of Akkadian Documents', *Eretz-Israel* 5, 21–31.

McConville, J. G., 1984. *Law and Theology in Deuteronomy*, JSOT Supplement Series 33 (Sheffield: JSOT Press).

Mendelsohn, I., 1956. 'Samuel's Denunciation of Kingship in the Light of the Akkadian Documents from Ugarit', *BASOR* 143, 17–22.

1962. 'On Corvée Labor in Ancient Canaan and Israel', *BASOR* 167, 31–5.

Miller, P. D., 1969. 'The Gift of God', *Interpretation* 23, 451–65.

Neufeld, E., 1958. 'Socio-Economic Background of *Yōbēl* and *Sᵉmiṭṭā*', *Rivista degli Studi Orientali* 33, 53–124.

1960. 'The Emergence of a Royal-Urban Society in Ancient Israel', *HUCA* 31, 31–53.

1961. '*Ius Redemptionis* in Ancient Hebrew Law', *RIDA*[3] 8, 29–40.

1962. 'Inalienability of Mobile and Immobile Pledges in the Laws of the Bible' *RIDA*[3] 9, 33–44.

Nicholson, E. W., 1970. *Preaching to the Exiles* (Oxford: B. H. Blackwell).

North, R., 1954. *Sociology of the Biblical Jubilee*, Analecta Biblica 4 (Rome: Biblical Institute).

Noth, M., 1927. 'Das Krongut der israelitischen Könige und seine Verwaltung', *ZDPV* 50, 211–44.

1981. *The Deuteronomistic History*, JSOTSS 15 (Sheffield: JSOT Press, 1981) (English translation of *Überlieferungsgeschichtliche Studien* (2nd edition, Tübingen: J. C. B. Mohr, 1957).

Ohler, A., 1979. *Israel, Volk und Land. Zur Geschichte der wechselseitigen Beziehungen zwischen Israel und seinem Land in alttestamentlicher Zeit* (Stuttgart: Kohlhammer).

Perlitt, L., 1983. 'Motive und Schichten der Landtheologie im Deuteronomium', in G. Strecker (ed.), *Das Land Israel in biblischer Zeit* (Göttingen: Vandenhoeck & Rupprecht), 46–58.

Plöger, J. G., 1967. *Literarkritische, formgeschichtliche und stilkritische Untersuchungen zum Deuteronomium*, BBB 26 (Bonn: Peter Hanstein).

Rad, G. von, 1933. 'There Remains Still a Rest for the People of God', in *The Problem of the Hexateuch and Other Essays* (Edinburgh: Nelson, 1966), 94–102 (English translation of 'Es ist noch eine Ruhe vorhanden dem Volke Gottes', in *Zwischen den Zeiten* 11, 104–11; reprinted in *Gesammelte Studien zum Alten Testament* ThB 8 (Munich: Chr. Kaiser, 1958), 101–8) (=1933).

1938. 'The Form-Critical Problem of the Hexateuch', in *The Problem of the Hexateuch and Other Essays*, 1–78 (English translation of *Das formgeschichtliche Problem des Hexateuch*, BWANT 26 (Stuttgart: Kohlhammer, 1938); reprinted in *Gesammelte Studien zum Alten Testament* ThB 8 (Munich: Chr. Kaiser, 1958), 9–86) (=1938).

1943. 'The Promised Land and Yahweh's Land in the Hexateuch', in *The Problem of the Hexateuch and Other Essays*, 79–93 (English translation of 'Verheissenes Land und Jahwes Land im Hexateuch', *ZDPV* 66 (1943), 191–204; reprinted in *Gesammelte Studien zum Alten Testament* ThB 8 (Munich: Chr. Kaiser, 1958), 87–100) (=1943).

1953. *Studies in Deuteronomy*, SBT, First Series 9 (London, 1953) (English translation of *Deuteronomium-Studien*, FRLANT 58 (revised edition, Göttingen: Vandenhoeck & Rupprecht, 1948) (=1953).

1962. *Old Testament Theology*, vol. I (Edinburgh and London: Nelson, 1962) (English translation of *Theologie des Alten Testaments*: vol. I, 'Die Theologie der historischen Überlieferungen Israels' (Munich: Chr. Kaiser, 1957) (=1962).

Rendtorff, R., 1970. 'Das Land Israel im Wandel der alttestamentlichen Geschichte', in W. Eckert, N. P. Levinson and M. Stöhr (eds.), *Jüdisches Volk-gelobtes Land* (Munich: Chr. Kaiser), 153–68.

Rost, L., 1934. 'Die Bezeichnungen für Land und Volk im Alten Testament', in *Festschrift Otto Procksch* (Leipzig: A. Deichertische – J. C. Hinrichs, 124–48.

Van Seters, J., 1975. *Abraham in History and Tradition* (New Haven and London: Yale Univ. Press).

Strecker, G. (ed.), 1983. *Das Land Israel in biblischer Zeit: Jerusalem-Symposium 1981 der Hebräischen Universität und der Georg-August-Universität* (Göttingen: Vandenhoeck & Rupprecht).

Thiel, W., 1973. *Die deuteronomistische Redaktion von Jeremia 1–25*, WMANT 41 (Neukirchen-Vluyn: Neukirchener Verlag).

1981. *Die deuteronomistische Redaktion von Jeremia 26–45*, WMANT 52 (Neukirchen-Vluyn: Neukirchener Verlag).

de Vaux, R., 1961. *Ancient Israel: Its Life and Institutions* (London: Darton, Longman & Todd, 1961) (English translation of *Les Institutions de l'Ancien Testament* I–II (Paris: Editions du Cerf, 1958, 1960)).

Waldow, H. E. von, 1974. 'Israel and her Land: Some Theological Considerations', in H. N. Bream, R. D. Heim and C. A. Moore (eds.), *A Light unto my Path: Old Testament Studies in Honor of Jacob M. Myers* (Philadelphia: Temple Univ. Press), 493–508.

Westermann, C., 1980. *The Promises to the Fathers* (Philadelphia, 1980) (English translation of *Die Verheissungen an die Väter*, FRLANT 116 (Göttingen: Vandenhoeck & Rupprecht, 1976)).

Wildberger, H., 1956. 'Israel und sein Land', *EvTh* 16, 404–22.

Wolff, H. W., 1966. 'The Kerygma of the Yahwist', *Interpretation* 20, 131–58 (English translation of 'Das Kerygma des Jahwisten', *EvTh* 24 (1964), 73–97; reprinted in *Gesammelte Studien zum Alten Testament*, ThB 22 (Munich: Chr. Kaiser, 1964), 345–73).

1975. 'The Kerygma of the Deuteronomic Historical Work', in W. Brueggemann and H. W. Wolff (eds.), *The Vitality of Old Testament Traditions* (Atlanta: John Knox, 1975), 83–100 (English translation of 'Das Kerygma des deuteronomistischen Geschichtswerks', *ZAW* 73, (1961), 171–85; reprinted in *Gesammelte Studien zum Alten Testament,* ThB 22 (Munich, 1964), 308–24).

Wright, C. J. H., 1983. *Living as the People of God* (Leicester: IVP Press).

Zenger, E., 1968. 'Die deuteronomistische Interpretation der Rehabilitierung Jojachins', *BZ* 12, 16–30.

Zimmerli, W., 1976. 'Land and Possession', in *The Old Testament and the World* (London: SPCK, 1976), 67–79 (English translation of 'Land und Besitz', in *Die Weltlichkeit des alten Testaments* (Göttingen: Vandenhoeck & Rupprecht, 1971)).

1985. 'The "Land" in the Pre-Exilic and Early Post-Exilic Prophets', in Butler, J. T., Conrad, E. W., and Ollenburger, B. C. (eds.), *Understanding the Word* JSOTSS 37 (Sheffield: JSOT Press, 1985), 247–62 (English translation of 'Das "Land" bei den vorexilischen und frühexilischen Schriftprophten', in G. Strecker (ed.), *Das Land Israel in biblischer Zeit* (Göttingen: Vandenhoeck & Rupprecht, 1983), 33–45.

CHAPTER SEVENTEEN

Women in ancient Israel

GRACE I. EMMERSON

The upsurge of feminism in recent years and the current interest in feminist hermeneutics (cf. Tolbert: 1983, 113–26) have stimulated fresh, sometimes impassioned, discussion of the biblical view of women. As an aspect of this, the status and role of women in ancient Israel have assumed new relevance in the light of contemporary issues. We have moved a long way from the attitude exemplified in the work of Köhler (1953) on Hebrew man which was content to devote scarcely two pages to Hebrew woman!

The Old Testament, born out of the patriarchal society of ancient Israel, has sometimes been accused of contributing to the subordination of women over the centuries. We must question whether this negative view is inherent in the Old Testament, or is consequent upon misinterpreting it. Again, we must ask whether there are conflicting attitudes within the Old Testament, and signs that within the patriarchal culture there was a 'depatriarchalising principle' (Trible: 1973, 48) at work, challenging the structures of society.

In approaching the material we face problems on two fronts: first, regarding the nature of the material itself, and second over the difficulty of interpreting such ancient texts. The limited material available to us has been transmitted mainly, if not entirely, by men. Inevitably it has a male perspective. Does it give a balanced view of Israelite society as it was in reality? Was female leadership, for example, as rare as the Old Testament implies? Is this impression, in part at least, due to the silence of the documents?

If perspective is significant, so also is literary genre. Legal texts and narrative cannot be treated alike as evidence. McKeating (1979, 65) warns that 'we cannot simply read off our assessment of a society's ethical values from the laws which it produced (or rather, from the laws which happen to have been preserved for us).' We need to know to what extent the law was rigidly applied. Narrative literature, he notes, offers examples of actual behaviour, and the acceptability or otherwise of that behaviour is shown by the reaction of characters in the story and by the comments of the narrator.

But here caution is needed for stories tend to be told about the extraordinary rather than the typical, and it is dangerous to generalise on the basis of individual narratives. It is at this point that conflicting assessments arise. Uncertainty as to the date of some material further compounds the problem. Sakenfeld warns that we need to avoid 'generalizations about one thousand years of culture that are based on fragments of indeterminate origin' (Sakenfeld: 1982, 14).

Not all the difficulties encountered in attempting to reach a balanced assessment of the subject are, however, inherent in the material. Hermeneutical theory has made us increasingly aware of the influence on interpretation of our own preconceptions (cf. Tolbert: 1983, 114). There are undoubtedly some who, for one reason or another, have overemphasised the subordination of women in the Old Testament. Others, in attempting to restore the balance and to rehabilitate the Old Testament, have minimised the unequivocal evidence of inequality between the sexes (as Otwell: 1977, 151 and 193f.).

1. Women in leadership roles

Without doubt women of distinction influenced the course of Israel's history by their role in the community. Few of them appear in the Old Testament, but, when they do, the fact that their female sex is apparently considered unremarkable suggests that their contribution, even in leadership roles, was not infrequent. The reference in Neh. 3.8 to women engaged in rebuilding the wall of Jerusalem may seem to us noteworthy.[1] The fact that it passes without comment suggests that this was not uncommon. At an even more momentous crisis in Israel's history we find women contributing significantly to the turn of events. Israel's liberation from Egypt began with the refusal of a few women to cooperate with oppression. Trible comments whimsically that 'if Pharaoh had realized the power of these women, he might have reversed his decree (Exod. 1.16, 22) and had females killed rather than males' (Trible: 1973, 34). Not only so, but as the exodus account continues 'Moses, as well as the deity, takes on female attributes, providing for the people on their journey from Egypt to Canaan (see especially Num. 11.11–14 for explicit feminine metaphors) (Exum: 1983, 82). Reassessment of our traditional assumptions about women's roles in the biblical story is in order', she comments. This, however, would take us far beyond the scope of the present essay. Nevertheless, it is for this reason that we may begin, not with women in the domestic sphere, but with the role of women in the community in relation to monarchy, prophecy and wisdom, even though the evidence is sparse. It is, however, unwise to assume that only those few women whose stories are preserved in the Old Testament rose to leadership in ancient Israel. This is unlikely to be true either for women or for men.

2. Women and monarchy

For women to rule is seen as a symptom of a disordered society. (Isa. 3.12).[2] It is perhaps significant that, in contrast to the many occurrences of the word 'king', the title of queen is nowhere used of any female member of the royal house of either Israel or Judah, not even of Athaliah, a reigning monarch (2 Kings 11.1–16; 2 Chron. 22.10–23.15). Apart from a poetic reference in the plural to Solomon's many wives (Song. 6.8f.), the title relates only to the royal ladies at foreign courts, such as the Queen of Sheba (1 Kings 10.1; 2 Chron. 9.1), and Vashti and Esther (Est. 1.11f.; 2.18). In three instances, however, the queen mother is called *g^eb̲îrāh*.[3] Of these, Maacah (1 Kings 15.13; 2 Chron. 15.16) and Jezebel (2 Kings 10.13) belonged to the court of Israel, and Nehushtah, Jehoiachin's mother (Jer. 13.18; 29.2), to Judah. That this is a title signifying an official position is evident from the fact that Asa was able to remove his mother 'from being queen mother (*g^ebîrāh*) because she had an abominable image made for Asherah' (1 Kings 15.13; 2 chron. 15.16). In investigating the precise significance of the title we have to face the question whether these rare occurrences reflect the reality of the situation, or whether its omission elsewhere is merely fortuitous.

In an attempt to uncover the existence of specifically female institutions which were later forgotten or suppressed through the long transmission of ancient Hebrew literature within a patriarchal society, Brenner (1985, 9) starts from the premiss that the title was as rare as the Old Testament indicates. She then attempts to isolate as the clue to its use a factor common to the three instances cited. She concludes that the title *g^eb̲îrāh* was conferred when an interruption occurred in the normal transfer of power from a monarch to his heir and the queen mother acted as regent (1985). Her argument rests on the view that Asa and Jehoiachin, who both came to the throne after an elder brother's death, were minors at the time, thus requiring a regency.[4] In Jezebel's case the sudden death of her son Jehoram created a break in the succession (2 Kings 9.24). Brenner notes, however, that the title *g^eb̲îrāh* is not given to Athaliah, though she assumed power after the death of her son Ahaziah in much the same circumstances as Jezebel (2 Kings 11.1; 2 Chron. 22.10). For Athaliah this was not a temporary measure, and Brenner argues that in this instance the title has been suppressed out of hostility to a woman who established herself as monarch. The argument from silence is somewhat dangerous, for if we conjecture that the title was omitted in Athaliah's case, we cannot be sure that this was not so elsewhere. Its meaning would then have to be sought on broader evidence.

The title apart, when we question what role or influence belonged to the mother of a reigning king, the evidence is scanty. Bathsheba, personally treated with great courtesy by her son Solomon, is devoid of any authority, as his stern rejection of her request testifies (1 Kings 2.19–25). Maacah's position as *g^eb̲îrāh* is dependent on her son's goodwill (1 Kings 15.13). Athaliah, undoubtedly a woman of personal influence, is described as Ahaziah's counsellor, yet, since this is qualified by 'in doing wickedness' (*l^eharšîaʿ*) (2 Chron. 22.3), it may not refer to an official position.[5]

One royal consort, however, stands out, not merely as a power behind the throne, but as a woman of public authority and of considerable personal wealth (1 Kings 18.19). Jezebel, a foreign princess, alone seems to have achieved so powerful a position. Brenner describes her as 'a real queen, assistant and partner in government to her husband Ahab' (1985, 20). She it was, not Ahab, who persecuted the prophets of Yahweh (1 Kings 18.4), and whose threat led Elijah to flee for his life (1 Kings 19.2f.). In the Naboth story she is represented as writing letters in Ahab's name and sealing them with his seal (v. 8). Yet when Naboth is dead the messengers return not to Ahab but to Jezebel (v. 14). On these grounds Brenner surmises that here, too, out of opposition to a woman ruler the Old Testament has distorted the evidence. Jezebel, she argues, acted on her own authority, using her own seal, 'the symbol of the permanent institutional authority Ahab delegated to her' (1985, 27). She notes with due reservation the discovery of a seal inscribed *yzbl* belonging broadly to this period.[6]

The Old Testament's refusal to recognise Jezebel's position as co-ruler with her husband is reflected also, Brenner suggests, in 2 Kings 9.34 where Jehu justifies her burial by reference, not to her status in Israel's royal house, but to her origin as a foreign princess. Was it by virtue of personality alone that Jezebel achieved such a uniquely powerful position? Brenner's hypothesis is that Jezebel was a Baal priestess, and on this basis her active fanaticism and special status at her husband's court are to be explained.

3. Women and prophecy

Of the many prophetic figures in the Old Testament only four are women, and these belong to widely different periods from the exodus to the fifth century BC. Each is named: Miriam, Deborah, Huldah and the false prophetess Noadiah. Apart from the last, who has only a passing mention (Neh. 6.14),[7] each is identified by reference to a male relative, despite her obvious importance in the community.[8]

Miriam's involvement with music and dancing led Noth (1962 [1959], 121) to categorise her as an ecstatic (Ex. 15.20). The imbalance between her song (15.21) and Moses' Song of the Sea (15.1–18) is striking. Is this perhaps an example of the instinctive relegation of a woman to a secondary role? The precise relation of the two songs remains a problem though their attribution of the songs to different sources has been largely abandoned. In discussing the redactional framework of the Song of the Sea, Childs (1974, 248) comments that 'the tendency to ascribe an ancient poem to Moses would have taken precedence over Miriam's authorship'. The dispute of Miriam and Aaron with Moses (Num. 12.1–15) results in a reaffirmation of Moses as uniquely bearer of the word of the Lord (vv. 6ff.), but this is clearly not a male versus female conflict (cf. Burns: 1985, 48–79). God's wrath is turned against Aaron as well as Miriam, and Aaron acknowledges joint sin (v. 11), though only Miriam suffers punishment. Yet there is no hint anywhere of anti-female motivation which judges Miriam for having stepped outside a woman's traditional role. A more likely explanation is that Miriam initiated the rebellion, since her name occurs first in v. 1. The story bespeaks both compassion (vv. 12f.) and respect for Miriam (v. 15). She is included on equal terms with Moses and Aaron as God's agent in Israel's deliverance (Mic. 6.4).

Deborah is both prophetess and judge in the community (Jud. 4.4), and possibly, though this is not capable of proof, author of the song preserved in Jud. 5.2–31.[9] There is no hint in the text that her authority is suspect because of her sex. Taking the initiative in a crisis, she summons Barak (v. 6). His response is immediate, his only reservation being his need for Deborah's personal support in the military engagement envisaged. Deborah's involvement, equally with Miriam's, is not related to traditional female roles, but is concerned with the survival of the tribes of Israel (5.7).[10]

Huldah's name bursts suddenly upon the scene (2 Kings 22.14) and as quickly disappears. Only one short oracle of hers is preserved in contrast to the sayings of Jeremiah and Zephaniah her contemporaries, yet her reputation is obviously already known, and her status high. Why else would Josiah's emissaries have sought her assistance at a time of such unease? Her involvement with matters of the utmost consequence for king and people is no different in essence from the prophetic activity of Amos or Isaiah, and her courage in delivering an unpalatable message is equal to theirs. Hers is genuine prediction, as is evident from v. 20. Why Huldah, not Jeremiah, is often asked. The Old Testament shows no prejudice against women in prophetic roles. They are not considered stop-gaps in the absence of prophets. The prophetess is as much respected as the prophet. C. J. Vos (1968, 184) suggests that the link which already existed with the temple through the occupation of Huldah's husband (2 Kings 22.14) may have been the reason.[11]

We conclude that the Old Testament affords no evidence that female sex was a disadvantage in the exercise of prophetic gifts, though it may have a bearing on the extent to which a woman's prophetic oracles were preserved. It is reasonable to suppose that the few mentioned by name are representative of others. Certainly their female sex seems to have occasioned no surprise. The future expectation of Joel 2.28f. includes both women and men. The only condemnatory note appears in Ezek. 13.17–23 against a group of women described as prophesying, though the nature of their activities suggests that they are engaged in magic. It is clear from the way they are addressed that they are Israelite women, but their magical arts, reminiscent of Babylonian practices, are carried out in exile, and fall outside the scope of this essay. It is evident, however, from the need to prohibit such activities by imposing the death penalty for both women and men (Lev. 20.27) that this was not unknown in Israel. The narrative of 1 Sam. 28.1–25 shows a witch in action. The king specifically requests a woman practitioner, having expelled the male representatives of the art (v. 3). She remains anonymous throughout, but is clearly a woman of repute, selected for the king, and visited by him at her home. Her pastoral care for her royal client in his consequent distress should be noted (vv. 21ff.). The narrative is unique in the Old Testament.

4. Women and wisdom

The Old Testament knows of other influential women, besides those with prophetic gifts, who were involved in matters of consequence for the state. Such are the women of Tekoa (2 Sam. 14.2) and of Abel (2 Sam. 20.16), both designated simply as 'a wise woman' *'iššāh ḥ*a*ḵāmāh*). 'The wise' in the Old Testament, unlike the prophets, are a rather nebulous group, rarely identified by name. So it is that these two women, unlike the women prophets, remain anonymous.

The epithet 'wise' is here not merely descriptive, as it is in Exod. 35.25; Jer. 9.17., but signifies a recognised role in the community in the time of judges and early monarchy, though there is no evidence for its existence later. Such is Camp's thesis (1981, 16) based on elements implicit in both 2 Sam. 14 and 20. She describes this role as 'a regularised set of functions rather than an official position'. The two women are identified only by the adjective 'wise' and by the name of their respective town. This by itself was evidently sufficient, Camp argues, to evoke 'features of a culturally stereotyped character' in the hearers' minds. Both speak with authority. The woman of Tekoa, assuming the part of a widow, naturally presents her story humbly to the king, but in her accusing rhetorical question (14.13) we see one 'accustomed to making and delivering such judgments' (1981, 17). Though 'Joab put the words in her mouth' (v. 3) she is not in any sense a passive figure and Camp compares Ex. 4.14f. where Yahweh instructs Moses to put his words in Aaron's mouth precisely because he has already shown himself to be eloquent. As for the woman of Abel, only a defined role in the community can account for the fact that she has sufficient authority not only to summon Joab but to ensure that he treats her advice with respect, though they have not previously met (20.17). Similarly, when she 'went to all the people in her wisdom' (v. 22), her words were put into effect immediately. The use of proverbial language by the women (2 Sam. 14.7; 20.18f.) Camp also finds significant, comparing it with a similar use of proverbs by the royal advisers, Ahithophel and Hushai (2 Sam. 17.3, 8, 10, 12).

The manner in which the wise woman of Tekoa approaches the king has certain similarities to the approach to Ahab by an anonymous prophet (1 Kings 20.35–43) and to Nathan's approach to David (2 Sam. 12.1ff.). There is, however, a significant difference in that the prophets are conscious of receiving direct communication from Yahweh, whereas the woman is commissioned by Joab. Hoftijzer (1970, 444) comments that the woman appears to proceed more humbly and circumspectly than the prophets, for as an 'ordinary person' she has 'to excuse her behaviour in order not to fall into disgrace' with the king, whereas a prophet has a status others do not have. He notes that, unlike the prophets mentioned, she prostrates herself before the king (v. 4), ensures that the king confirms his ruling by an oath (v. 11), and, before she confronts David with the consequences of his ruling, asks his permission to proceed (v.12). The first of these, at least, can be accounted for, however, by her assumed role of widow. The woman of Abel, in contrast, acts rather in the manner of a military leader. Camp (1981, 22) draws a comparison with the Rab-shakeh of the Assyrian army in his confrontation with Hezekiah's men (2 Kings 18.28ff.) and Abner's confrontation with Joab (2 Sam. 2.24–28.).

Camp suggests that this role of the wise woman was based on a mother's role in instructing her children. By extension the village wise woman was concerned not only with education but with political decisions. This she considers to be an example of the egalitarian attitude of early Yahwism in a functional, if not always explicit, sense.[12] She concludes her study with the suggestion that, although 'female images, either in the form of significant "historical" persons or of symbolic figures, are relatively rare in the Old Testament', the emphasis both here and in Proverbs on female imagery associated with wisdom 'reveals a latent tendency in Israel's theological reflection, underdeveloped because of the male-dominated priesthood and generally patriarchal milieu, but not insignificant in Israel's understanding of the relationships between persons in community and between the community and Yahweh' (1981, 29).

5. Women in the covenant community

It is commonplace to remark that male members only of the community were required to attend the three major annual festivals (Exod. 23.17; Deut. 16.16). But difference of obligation does not necessarily imply inequality, and in this case probably arose from practical considerations attendant on the birth and care of children. Certainly Deuteronomy makes it clear that women were present at the festivals, sharing in the rejoicing (Deut. 12.12), and participating in the sacrifices (Deut. 12.18).[13] The feasts of weeks and booths are specifically mentioned (Deut. 16.10f., 13f.) This may well represent an advance on earlier law in the direction of equality, a feature which seems to be characteristic of Deuteronomy. This book presents women as participants in the covenant ceremony (Deut. 29.10–13), and consequently under full obligation to observe Yahweh's law (Deut. 31.12).[14] Equally with men they could be held guilty of transgressing the covenant, for which the penalty was death (Deut. 13.6–11; 17.2–5). The evidence suggests that it was deuteronomic law which first explicitly brought them within the covenant. The view that women are fully accountable before Yahweh continues in the post-exilic period (2 Chron. 15.12f.; Neh. 8.2).

Was there discrimination against women within the covenant community? It seems not. Although in general the male head of the household represented the family in the offering of sacrifice, where an individual offering was stipulated a woman was expected personally to fulfil the requirement (Lev. 12.6; 1 Sam. 1.24) (cf. Vos: 1968, 130). The exceptional consecration entailed under the Nazirite vow was open to women (Num. 6.2–21). Indeed, this passage with its single feminine reference (v. 2) is a timely reminder that grammatically masculine forms may be intended in an inclusive sense, and the linguistic convention must not be misunderstood. We may compare also Deut. 29.18ff. where women are specified in v. 18, but masculine forms are used thereafter in vv. 19f.

The one role in worship from which women were certainly excluded was the priesthood, as also were the majority of men. The reasons behind the exclusion of women are probably complex, though 'since "physical wholeness" and ritual purity were the essential conditions for sacred service (Lev. 21.1ff.; Ezek. 44.15ff.), woman's periodic uncleanness as menstruant and mother must have played no small part in excluding her from priestly office' (Hayter: 1987, 70; cf. Vos: 1968, 194f.). Female members of priestly families were permitted, however, to eat of the 'holy things' set aside for the priests (Lev. 22.13). It is open to debate whether there were women who had an official place in worship. Exod. 38.8 speaks of 'women who ministered at the door of the tent of meeting'. Although the nature of their service is not clear, Childs comments that the verb *ṣbʾ* used here denotes an organised service like the professional Levites (Childs: 1974, 636; contra de Vaux, 1961, 383f.). Whether officially[15] or not, women shared in cultic worship, dancing, singing and playing musical instruments (Exod. 15.20; Jud. 21.21; Ps. 68.26).

The regular involvement of women in the cult is implied by the strict regulations concerning their ritual purity. An interesting aspect of this is the law relating to uncleanness after childbirth (Lev. 12). An identical offering was to be brought whether the newborn child was male or female (v. 6), but the period of uncleanness after the birth of a daughter was twice that after the birth of a son. The legal requirement is unambiguous; its motivation is not. Thus Noth (1962 [1959]) comments that 'the cultic inferiority of the female sex is expressed in giving the female birth a double "uncleanness" effect, shown also in the double period required in this case before the mother is once more clean'. In contrast, on the grounds that Israel believed that God was 'intimately active in all stages of birth from conception to delivery', Otwell (1977, 176f.) suggests that this uncleanness after childbirth was due to the woman's involvement with 'the work of deity', an idea of holiness as in the expression "books which defile the hands" used of the canonical scriptures. It is, Otwell argues, for this reason that the period of being 'de-energised' would need to be twice as long for the birth of a child which might become capable in its turn of bearing children as for a male child. He supports this argument by noting that when, in preparation for the theophany at Sinai (Exod. 19.15), and likewise as a condition for eating the holy bread (1 Sam. 21.4), the men are to keep from women, these are illustrations of the law of Lev. 15.18 concerning male uncleanness, not indications of the intrinsic uncleanness of women.

Though the examples are few, there are several instances in the Old Testament of women in encounter with God. The angel of the Lord addresses Hagar (Gen. 21.17) and the wife of Manoah (Jud. 13.3), in both instances concerning children. When Manoah requests a further theophany, it is to his wife that the angel again appears (13.9). Women independently approach the prophets to enquire of the Lord (1 Kings 14.1; 2 Kings 4.22ff.), and on their own account seek him in prayer (Gen. 25.22f.; 30.6), again for family reasons. Hannah's prayer, too, has this motivation (1 Sam. 1.10–17), and its answer elicits a psalm of praise (1 Sam. 2.1–10),[16] a reminder that a feminine perspective should not be overlooked in the psalms in general.

6. The position of women within the family

(i) Their legal status

As regards legal status, a woman was clearly at a disadvantage. Throughout her life she was regarded as under the authority first of her father, then of her husband. As head of the household he, not the courts, was responsible for all matters of family law (Phillips: 1973, 351). Phillips cites two illuminating instances in evidence of a woman's lack of independent legal status. In cases of the seduction of an unbetrothed girl, Exod. 22.16f. stipulates that the man who seduced her shall marry her, giving the customary marriage present. If her father should decide otherwise, an equal sum is to be paid as compensation to him, and he suffers no financial loss either way. The law belongs to the section on damage to property, and Phillips (Phillips: 1973, 350) does not hesitate to describe the girl as the personal property of her father. On the other hand, Childs comments that, although this appears to be a traditional sequence, 'the content of the Hebrew law shows remarkable transformation in respect to other ancient Near Eastern codes', for 'the seduction of an unengaged maiden was no longer simply viewed as property damage' (Childs: 1974, 476). The seducer has to take full responsibility for his action and marry the girl. Monetary compensation was not an option open to the seducer, but to the girl's father. What of the girl herself? In theory, v. 17*a* could be said to allow opportunity for the girl's wishes to be consulted, but this was not safeguarded in law and would depend on the quality of the individual relationship of father and daughter. As a second example Phillips adduces Exod. 21.22 where, if a man injures a pregnant wife and a miscarriage ensues, he is to compensate the husband.[17]

Widows and orphans, without normal family protection, were regarded as under Yahweh's special care (Deut. 10.18), though, as Sakenfeld comments, a widow was not better off, sociologically speaking, because the religion claims that God values and defends her (Sakenfeld: 1979, 423).[18] However, the community, if true to its obligations, would ensure the wellbeing of such (Exod. 22.22; Deut. 24.17ff.). There was also the possibility, if not the absolute right, of direct appeal to the king for justice, not only by the widowed (2 Sam. 14.1ff.; 2 Kings 8.3–6) but by others lacking family protection, such as the prostitutes of 1 Kings 3.16ff.

The idea of a man's legal responsibility for his household also lies behind the regulation that vows made by a woman must be ratified by father or husband as the case may be (Num. 30.3–16). That this was not due to doubts about a woman's inherent sense of responsibility is shown by the fact that the widowed and the divorced were entitled to make legally binding commitments (v. 9). Otwell considers that it 'reflects more the primacy of the family in ancient Israel than an inferior status of woman before the Lord' (Otwell: 1977, 170). Since 1 Sam. 1.11 shows Hannah making a vow of considerable consequence to the family independently of her husband, it may be that the law of Num. 30 is a later restriction. Undoubtedly the laws of inheritance put women at a disadvantage. A wife did not inherit her husband's property, nor daughters their father's, unless there was no male heir (Num. 27.6–11). Naomi's case seems to be somewhat exceptional (Ruth 4.3), though to be compared with Jud. 17.2ff.; Job. 42.15 (cf. Neufeld: 1944, 240ff.). Phillips (1973, 356) suggests that it may have been the abandonment of the practice of levirate marriage which led to this innovation by the priestly legislator whereby daughters could inherit property and so continue the name of their father.[19]

For the above reasons de Vaux compares adversely the social and legal position of an Israelite wife with the position of women in Egypt and Babylon. In the former the wife was often the head of the family; in the latter 'she could acquire property, take legal action, be a party to contracts, and she even had a certain share in her husband's inheritance' (de Vaux: 1961, 40).

The legal dependence of women, despite the restrictive inequalities it inevitably imposed, is not, however, to be confused with personal oppression. The Old Testament does not play down the initiative and resourcefulness of women. Abigail is consulted by a manservant in a dilemma (1 Sam. 25.17), and in response acts resourcefully (v. 18ff.). The implication of v. 25 is that, had she known of the arrival of David's men, it would have been quite within her power to deal with them without consulting her husband. The efficient wife of Prov. 31.10–31 is no downtrodden creature, but self-confident and outgoing, and this not merely an individual but an ideal to be followed. M. B. Crook describes the passage as 'instruction for a marriageable maiden on a par with that given to young men as a part of their preparation' (Crook, 1954, 139). She contrasts it with the marriage preparation a girl might expect to receive from her mother, describing this poem as 'a memorandum from a school answering to the needs of young women who will shortly be assuming positions of wealth and importance in their communities'.

(ii) The marriage relationship

How appropriate is it to describe a wife in ancient Israel as her husband's possession? Two factors in particular seem to have contributed to this impression: the use of the word *baʿal* for 'husband', and the practice of giving *môhār*, commonly translated as 'brideprice'. It is not infrequently pointed out that, when applied to a house (Exod. 22.8) or a domestic animal (Exod. 21.28), *baʿal* means 'owner'. It is however the word in its context which determines meaning, and the transfer of crude ideas of ownership from one context to another is inadmissible. The word *ʾîš* is also frequently used to mean 'husband'.[20] Still more significantly, the imagery of marriage is considered appropriate to describe both Yahweh's love relationship with Israel (Hos. 1–3; Jer. 2.2), and Israel's joy when redeemed by the Lord (Isa. 62.4f.). Here is the Israelite ideal of marriage, from which in practice many no doubt fell short. The crude idea of ownership is entirely inappropriate here, as it is also in Jer. 31.32. To suggest that a wife was little better than a slave is certainly incorrect. Slaves, and in extreme necessity even a daughter (Exod. 21.7), might be sold. We may note the distinction drawn by Phillips (1981, 7) between a wife's position as 'an "extension" of the husband himself (Gen. 2.24)' and a daughter's. Sons, too, could be sold (Neh. 5.5). Not so a wife, even a slave wife (Exod. 21.8–11) or one captured in battle (Deut. 21.14). The instructions of wisdom literature concerning obedience are addressed to children, not to wives.[21] Indeed, in the law concerning the rebellious son, the mother equally with the father is to see him brought to justice (Deut. 21.18–21).

Concerning the practice of giving *môhār*, the translation 'marriage present' represents it more adequately than does 'brideprice' (de Vaux: 1961, 26f.; Neufeld, 1944, 95ff.). The term occurs only three times in the Old Testament: in Gen. 34.12 in conjunction with *mattān* 'gift'; in Exod. 22.17, with the cognate verb in v. 16, and in 1 Sam. 18.25 where Saul makes a bizarre request in place of the normal marriage present. The only instances where the language of buying and selling is used in connection with marriage are the requirement that the seducer should pay money (*šāqal kesep*) equivalent to the marriage present if he is *not* permitted to marry the girl (Exod. 22.17), the angry words of Leah and Rachel who accuse their father of having sold them and 'used up our money' (Gen. 31.15), and Boaz' statement that he has bought (*qānîṯî*) Ruth as his wife (Ruth 4.10), although Ruth was clearly no unwilling, passive partner in the arrangement, but had largely taken the initiative. What is in fact purchased is the inheritance on which Ruth has a claim for a potential heir. Thereby the inheritance and the marriage are linked together. Hos. 3.2 is a different matter for the woman in this case was bought from prostitution or slavery. She, too, is anything but a chattel; she is to be loved 'as the Lord loves'.

The marriage-present was given by the bridegroom to the bride's father, probably as compensation for the work which otherwise the daughter would have continued to contribute to her parents' household (Meyers: 1978, 98). Women 'looked after the flocks, worked in the fields, cooked the food, did the spinning' (de Vaux: 1961, 39). The amount paid may have been regulated according to the status of the bride's family (1 Sam. 18.23ff.), though the implication of Shechem's open offer (Gen. 34.12) is that this was exceptional to meet unusual circumstances. Deut. 22.29 stipulates fifty shekels of silver, but if this is taken as a penalty for rape of a virgin, the usual amount may have been less (de Vaux, *ibid*., 26; but cf. Phillips: 1981, 12) R. de Vaux considers that, although the marriage present was given to the bride's father, it probably belonged to the girl in fact, hence Leah's and Rachel's description of it as 'our money' (Gen. 31.15). The bride's father would be entitled to interest accruing from it, but the capital would revert to the girl when her father died, or earlier if her husband died, as provision against penury. He finds support for this view in Assyrian and Babylonian custom, and in the marriage contracts from Elephantine. The giving of a dowry by the bride's father was not practised in Israel, the only exception being Pharaoh's gift (*šillūḥîm*) on the occasion of his daughter's marriage to Solomon (1 Kings 9.16). Meyers (1978, 98; but cf. Mace: 1953, 175) considers this an indication of the relative shortage of women, in that fathers had no need to entice husbands for their daughters.

Certainly marriage was the norm, and for a woman to have to remain unmarried was considered a disgrace (Isa. 4.1; Prov. 30.23[22]). Although practice varied at different periods in Israel's history, monogamy was far more common than polygamy. Apart from the patriarchal narratives and the stories of Gideon and Samson, there is little reference to anything other than monogamy. With the exception of royal harems, Samuel's father Elkanah alone in the books of Samuel and Kings is the husband of more than one wife. The law of Deut. 21.15ff., however, regards bigamy as lawful, and the implication is that it was not altogether uncommon. The problems to which bigamy could give rise in a household are evident in the

Old Testament. The cause of jealousy on the part of a childless wife (Gen. 30.1) and of provocation by her rival (1 Sam. 1.6) was often the question of children. Such was the prestige of motherhood, particularly when sons were born, that even a slave wife might begin to lord it over her mistress (Gen. 16.4f.). But if Gen. 30.15f. indicates the humiliating rivalry for a husband's favours which could develop, it also shows women taking the initiative in sexual relationships. The quaint blessing with which Rebekah's family bid her farewell (Gen. 24.60), and the celebration of children in Ps. 127 and 128, highlight their importance as guarantee for the future. It was, to some extent, for practical reasons that sons were valued above daughters,[23] for a daughter upon marriage would join her husband's family, thus relatively weakening her own. Female relatives, however, were respected, and a priest was permitted to defile himself for the burial of female relatives as well as male (Lev. 21.2).

It is a misrepresentation of marriage in ancient Israel to speak as if a wife was valued only for the sons she bore. The wife who gave birth to sons was not necessarily the favourite (Gen. 29.32, 34; 1 Sam. 1.4), and Elkanah's sentiments (1 Sam. 1.8) need not have been unique. It is interesting to note that here, as in Gen. 30.1, it is the wife rather than the husband who frets at the lack of sons. The value set on sons was not absolute. For a widow, however, bereft of the support of male relatives, a grandson seemed nothing short of 'a restorer of life' (*l^emēšîḇ nep̄eš*, Ruth 4.15). This passage is instructive for what it reveals of the close and satisfying relationships which could exist between women.

What freedom did a woman have to marry the man of her choice? Phillips comments that, since matters of family law were solely under the control of the head of the household, 'a man had an unfettered right to dispose of the women under his protection as he liked, whether as a father making a marriage for his daughter, or as a husband divorcing his wife. Neither the daughter nor the wife had any ultimate say in the matter, nor could they appeal to the courts' (Phillips: 1981, 351. He notes, however, that the story of Jephthah's daughter is not so much an illustration of a father's authority, as of the power of an oath). The full extent of a father's authority is seen in Caleb's offer to give his daughter as a reward for military success (Jos. 15.16; Jud. 1.12), and in Tamar's attempt to avoid rape by her brother Amnon (2 Sam. 13.13). Rebekah was not consulted about her marriage, only about the time of her departure from home (Gen. 24.57f.). Nor was Isaac, yet the narrative shows that a love relationship developed. Ruth (Ruth 3.7ff.) and Abigail (1 Sam. 15.40ff.), both widows, made their own choice. On occasion the mother as well as the father took responsibility in arranging a marriage. In Rebekah's case, her mother acted in conjunction with her brother Laban, the implication being that her father was dead.[24] It is interesting to note that the only point at which Laban acts independently of his mother is in his care of the servant's camels (Gen. 24.29–31)![25] Samson's mother was equally involved with her husband in their son's marriage plans (Jud. 14.2ff.). R. de Vaux considers that 'young people had ample opportunity for falling in love, and for expressing their feelings, for they were very free' (de Vaux: 1961, 30). Michal's love for David was both known and taken account of, though primarily, it seems, because it suited Saul's schemes (1 Sam. 18.20f.).

Certainly for some women there seems to have been rather less freedom or dignity. Particularly was this true of the women of the royal harem. David's treatment of his concubines (2 Sam. 20.3) illustrates the total lack of control some unfortunate women had over their own lives. It is in such situations that they do seem to be regarded as little better than chattels. Solomon's harem may have been for him a sign of wealth and status; for the women concerned it was demeaning. In the early days of the monarchy a king's harem seems to have passed to his successor (2 Sam. 12.8). Absalom is depicted as publicly approaching his father's concubines for political reasons, apparently in this way asserting his right to the throne.

In marked contrast can be set the respect which was accorded the mother in the family. A mother's instruction was to be observed by her son (Prov. 1.8f.; 6.20), and in one instance was considered sufficiently important to be passed on (Prov. 31.1).[26] Both parents are spoken of with like affection (2 Sam. 19.37). Indeed the obligation to treat mother and father with equal respect is emphasised frequently, from the Decalogue to the many instances in Proverbs (Prov. 15.20; 19.26; 23.22, 25; 28.24).[27] One particularly dramatic expression of this obligation deserves to be noted:

> The eye that mocks a father and scorns to obey a mother will be picked out by the ravens of the valley and eaten by the vultures.
>
> (Prov. 30.17 RSV, but cf. McKane: 1970, 657)

(iii) Divorce

Nowhere do the inequality of the sexes and the limitations on a woman's freedom appear more starkly than in the matter of divorce. There was no circumstance in which a wife might divorce her husband, whereas a husband's right to divorce his wife at any time and for any reason was absolute. How much this freedom was exercised in practice it is impossible to tell, but the strong opposition to divorce expressed in Mal. 2.14–16, and the praise of marriage in Prov. 5.15–19 and Eccles. 9.9 must be set against it.

The law of Deut. 24.1 has sometimes been regarded as an attempt to restrict a husband's absolute right to divorce his wife, making adultery the sole ground for such action. Phillips (1981, 355) takes issue with this view on the grounds that the Deuteronomic law stipulates in Deut. 22.22 that execution not divorce is the penalty for adultery. He argues that the expression *ʿerwaṯ dāḇār* has no moral connotation (cf. Deut. 23.14) but applies to anything a husband found objectionable in his wife, other than adultery. It should be translated as 'something distasteful' rather than 'indecent' (cf. Neufeld: 1946, 176, who sees this as an advance in the position of women in that divorce cannot take place gratuitously. In Deuteronomic legislation, however, a husband's right to divorce is withdrawn in two circumstances, namely as the penalty for false accusation concerning his bride's virginity[28] at the time of marriage (22.19), and in a compulsory marriage consequent upon the rape of an unbetrothed girl (22.28).

In earlier law the punishment for a woman's adultery was divorce, not execution (Hos. 2.4; Jer. 3.8), for the man concerned was held the more accountable. Phillips (1973, 353) notes that Abimelech not Sarah, and David rather than Bathsheba, are held to be accountable. Deuteronomic legislation in contrast, as noted above, imposed the death penalty on both offenders alike where collusion might reasonably be presumed (Deut. 22.22–7). In spite of this move towards equality women continued to be regarded as under the authority of a male relative, as is evident from the fact that in cases of rape compensation was still paid to the girl's father (Deut. 22.29).

The significant contrast in legal procedure between cases of divorce and of adultery is discussed by Phillips. The former, since it was unlikely to be the cause of disorder in the community, was regarded as a private matter and belonged to family law (1973, 350). The husband had the right to act independently of the community and the ceremony to terminate a marriage took place privately in the home (Hos. 2.4f.) not in court, as is often supposed. It was effected by the husband's pronouncement of the divorce formula. The divorced wife would normally return to her father's house. Where adultery was the ground for divorce, a ritual of stripping may have preceded expulsion from the home, as a sign not merely that the husband's responsibilities for her maintenance were withdrawn but chiefly of her shamelessness (Hos. 2.12; Jer. 13.26f.; Ezek. 16.37f.; 23.10.29). (cf. Neufeld, 1944, 166; Gordon, 1936, 277ff.). As proof that the marriage had been terminated a document of divorce (*sēp̄er kᵉrîṯûṯ*) was given so that the woman might remarry without incurring the charge of adultery (Deut. 24.1, 3; Jer. 3.8; Isa. 50.1).

In contrast to divorce procedure, adultery was regarded as a crime and not a private matter. Its prosecution was undertaken by the state, not by the injured husband. Phillips argues that the latter was not entitled to take matters into his own hands either for vengeance, for settlement, or for forgiveness. In this respect, he maintains, Israel differed from other countries of the ancient Near East where adultery was considered simply an injury to the husband, who could, therefore, determine the punishment of the offenders, or if he wished forgive them (Phillips: 1973, 353f.; 1981, 3f.).

On this point McKeating (1979, 58) is in disagreement. Noting that there is no instance in the Old Testament (apart from Susanna in the Greek version of Daniel) where the biblical law of adultery is put into effect, he raises the question, 'Are the laws, taken by themselves, a sufficient indication of how adultery was dealt with?' He argues that in Proverbs damage to reputation, and the risk of the injured husband's anger figure prominently as sanctions against adultery (Prov. 6.27–35). This would hardly be so if the death penalty were the normal consequence. References to death in the condemnations of adultery (Prov. 7.22f.; 9.18; Eccles. 9.9) appear to be metaphorical. He concludes that 'adultery was not infrequently dealt with outside the framework of the law'. He also raises the question of how far proceedings in cases of adultery can safely be reconstructed from prophetic language. Certainly in the reference to mutilation in Ezek. 23.25 the metaphor of adultery has receded behind the reality of conquest.

Since adultery is not included among the ancient curses of Deut. 27, or mentioned in the book of the Covenant, McKeating contends that it was the lawmakers of Deuteronomy and of the Holiness Code who attempted, albeit unsuccessfully, to make the death penalty mandatory for adultery (1979, 64)[29] thus removing the matter from the sphere of family law where the husband had discretion.

7. Prostitution

Whereas adultery was a crime, prostitution was tolerated in Israelite society. The warnings against seductive women in Proverbs concern adultery rather than prostitution (Prov. 6.26; 7.19). The picture emerges of prostitutes touting for business in public places (Gen. 38.14; Ezek. 16.25), recognisable by their dress (Gen. 38.15; Prov. 7.10), and negotiating terms with their clients (Gen. 38.16; Ezek. 16.31). In certain circumstances some embarrassment attached to the practice (Gen. 38.23), and strong disapproval is expressed in the laws of Lev. 19.29 and 21.9.

In discussing ancient Israelite society a distinction is generally made between common or secular prostitution and cultic prostitution, to which, broadly speaking, the terms *zônāh and qᵉḏēšāh*, with the corresponding masculine *qāḏēš*, are held respectively to correspond. Secular prostitution, provided that the woman was unmarried, was not an offence but 'a recognised social institution with few moral inhibitions attached to it despite its being looked upon with mixed feelings'.[30] Cultic prostitution, on the other hand, involving persons of both sexes, was forbidden absolutely (Deut. 23.18), though not uncommonly practised, to judge from the prophetic polemic against it. In fact, the distinction in usage of *zônāh* and *qᵉḏēšāh* is by no means absolute. Both terms are used of Tamar (Gen. 38.15, 21f.), and appear to be synonymous in Hos. 4.14 and Deut. 23.18f.

This distinction between secular and religious prostitution has long been taken as axiomatic. The evidence ought, however, to be reviewed. Barstad (1984, 22ff.) has queried the existence of cultic prostitution as a widespread phenomenon in the ancient Near East, since explicit references occur only in late texts. Its existence in Israel must, therefore, be re-examined. From a survey of the textual evidence Barstad argues that *qdšh/qdš* is a designation for female and male members of the non-Yahwistic or syncretistic priesthood. The references to *qᵉḏēšāh* and *zônāh* in Deut. 23.18f. and Hos. 4.14 are not intended as synonyms, but represent two separate prohibitions and accusations respectively (1984, 29). He notes that Deut. 23.18 does not speak against the occupation of the *qḏšh* and *qḏš* in general, but prohibits Israelites from holding these positions. The weakest point in Barstad's argument, as he himself recognises, is the Tamar story with its unexplained shift from *zônāh* to *qᵉḏēšāh*. Nevertheless it is significant that the story is without any cultic context which would suggest reference to ritual prostitution (contra, G. von Rad: 1961, 359f.).

8. Women and slavery

There are in the Old Testament two categories of female slave to which the terms *šipḥāh* and *ʾāmāh* broadly relate, though the distinction in usage is not always maintained. The former applies, generally speaking, to the virgin bondmaid whose task it was to serve the mistress of the house (Gen. 29.24, 29; Isa. 24.2; Ps. 123.2; Prov. 30.23), the latter to the maidservant who belonged to her master,[31] sometimes as a concubine (Jud. 9.18; 19.19; Ezek. 23.12). Thus in Gen. 16 Hagar is described as Sarah's maid (*šipḥāh*: vv. 1, 2, 6) whom she gives to Abraham to bear children.[32] In Gen. 21, as his slave wife, she is described as *ʾāmāh* (vv. 10, 12, 13). In the first instance Sarah has the authority to expel Hagar (Gen. 16.6), in the second it is Abraham's responsibility (21.10). Of the two, the *šipḥāh* seems to have undertaken the more menial tasks (1 Sam. 25.41).

In general, male and female slaves were treated alike in law (Exod. 21.20, 26f.), with one major exception. In the Book of the Covenant no provision is made for the release of a female slave after six years along with her male counterpart (Exod. 21.7–11), for as an *ʾāmāh* she was her master's concubine and continued as part of the larger family. It should not, however, be assumed that this was due to the inferior status of the female slave, or to the fact that she, in particular, was regarded as her master's personal property, but rather, as Wolff comments, that 'the man and wife relationship is thought of primarily as a lasting one, even with the slave' (Wolff: 1974, 201).[33] Her rights were protected by law. In the event of her master's tiring of her, she was not to be resold (Exod. 21.8). Her family was entitled to buy her freedom. If designated for her master's son, she was to be treated as a daughter (v. 9). If her master took another wife, her marital rights were not to be diminished (v. 10). Otherwise she must go free. 'If the relationship comes to an end, then it always ends in freedom. The regulations which govern the exceptions all have the interests of the slave in mind, not those of her master' (Wolff: 1974, 201). For this reason Wolff feels justified in describing the relationship between master and female slave as 'by no means a loveless relationship'. Indeed he characterises it as 'full of solicitous concern'. The corresponding law of Deut. 15.12–18 does not differentiate between male and female slaves, but gives them equal rights of release after six years. On the grounds that Jer. 34.9–11 similarly makes no distinction between male and female slaves (Heb. *šipḥāh*). de Vaux (1961, 86) concludes that by this period there were no longer slave-concubines. The later law of Lev. 25 makes no mention of female slaves.

Wolff (1974, 202) sees in Job 31.13 the possibility that slaves, male and female, might bring a lawsuit against their master. *Rîḇ* may, however, be intended in a less formal sense of 'complaint' (cf. NEB). However the reason for a slave's right to justice is unambiguous:

> Did not he who made me in the womb make him?
> and did not one fashion us in the womb? (v. 15)[34]

9. The ideal of equality

It is appropriate that discussion of women and slavery should be followed by the counterbalance to all that was oppressive of women in ancient Israelite society, in what has been described as 'a latent potentiality for liberation'.[35] This is to be found in the creation narratives of Genesis without which our assessment of the material would be incomplete. In contrast to the prevailing patriarchal culture of ancient Israel, there is in the Old Testament evidence of what Trible terms a counter culture, a 'depatriarchalising principle' at work. This, she affirms, 'is not an operation which the exegete performs on the text. It is a hermeneutic operating within Scripture itself' (1973, 48).

Man and woman are created in God's image (Gen. 1.27). Both share the commission to subdue the earth and have dominion. There is no hint here of subordination. Man and woman, created together and blessed together, are named Adam (Gen. 5.2). It is in Gen. 2–3 that justification for woman's subservience has traditionally been found. Several misconceptions need to be corrected. Woman, equally with man, is created solely by God. Man is not participant, not even onlooker at the divine activity which builds[36] a rib into woman. Her creation is no afterthought. The structure of Gen. 2 is an example of *inclusio*. 'The creation of man first and of woman last constitutes a ring composition whereby the two creatures are parallel. In no way does the order disparage woman' (Trible, 1973, 36). She is designed by God to be man's helper (*ʿēzer*), a helper appropriate, equal and adequate for him (*kᵉnegdô*). The word *ʿēzer* is, as Trible notes, a relational term and does not specify position within the relationship. Overwhelmingly the word relates to Yahweh as helper of his people (Exod. 18.4; Deut. 33.20, 26; Ps. 33.20; 70.6; 115.9ff.; 146.5).[37] 'God is the helper superior to man; the animals are helpers inferior to man; woman is the helper equal to man' (Trible: 1973, 36).[38]

Why is the woman tempted by the serpent? Not because of some inherent weakness. The narrative gives no hint of this. The man is portrayed as passive, following his wife without question, though God's prohibition came direct to him (2.17). But the woman is 'intelligent, independent and decisive, fully aware as theologian when she takes the fruit and eats', writes Trible (1976, 965). In writing thus, her aim is 'not to promote female chauvinism but to undercut patriarchal interpretations alien to the text' (1973, 40).

Lastly, Gen. 3.16 is not a licence for male supremacy. It is a symptom of the disorder of creation, of the rupture of the relationship with God which brings in its train a rupture of the human relationship. Along with pain and oppressive toil the subservience of women is to be overcome, and the ideal restored (Evans: 1983, 19f.).

A similar ideal of equality appears in the Song of Songs, which Trible describes as a midrash on Gen. 1–3. Discerning in the woman's joyful confidence, 'I am my beloved's and his desire is for me' (Song. 7.10), a reversal of Gen. 3.16, she sees here that description of sin transformed into an affirmation of mutuality and delight (1973, 46). In the Song there is no subservience of woman. With her the Song begins as she initiates the love-making (1.2), and with her it ends as she calls to her beloved (8.13). May it be that a woman was its author? (cf. Brenner: 1985, 46ff.).

Sadly there is another strand in the Old Testament, a deterioration in the view of women which becomes evident in the post-exilic period (cf. Terrien: 1985, 85f.). Trible contrasts the female imagery used by Deutero-Isaiah to depict God's love for his people in exile (Isa. 49.15; 66.13) with Ezekiel's use of sexual metaphors demeaning to women. In this, and in the striving for racial purity in the time of Ezra (Ezra 10.2f., 44), she traces the development of misogyny which sees woman as inferior and impure. 'Nevertheless, that view did not replace altogether the dynamic thrust of OT faith . . . that thrust challenged, corrected, and transcended the culture. Accordingly, OT faith undercuts all manmade structures and ideas to place both man and woman *sub specie aeternitatis*' (Trible: 1976, 966).

Notes

1 For a woman's authority to commission building works see 1 Chron. 7.24.

2 So RSV. Whether the revocalisation as *nōšîm* ('usurers' cf. LXX) is more appropriate is not our concern here. The MT *nāšîm* indicates that traditionally it was understood to refer to women.

3 The only other occurrence of the word in the OT refers to the Egyptian queen Tahpenes (1 Kings 11.19) which lies outside the scope of this essay.

4 There is some confusion about the relationship of Asa to Abijam; cf. 1 Kings 15.2, 10 with 15.8. In Asa's case the evidence is circumstantial, namely that Abijam had reigned for only three years (1 Kings 15.2). The evidence about Jehoiachin varies; 2 Chron. 36.9 puts his age at eight years, whereas 2 Kings 24.8 has eighteen.

5 P. A. H. de Boer, *Fatherhood and Motherhood*, 1974, 4 considers it to have been an official position.

6 cf. N. Avigad, *IEJ* 14, 1964, 274ff.

7 The mention of Noadiah by name may reflect her status, or possibly the fact that as time went on women in leadership roles became less common and she was consequently the more noteworthy.

8 The unnamed woman of Isa. 8.3, generally presumed to be the prophet's wife, is also called *n^e^bîāh*, but there is no evidence of any independent prophetic activity.

9 See especially v. 7, 'until I, Deborah, arose' (*ʿad šaqqamtî*), unless this is to be taken as an archaic 2nd-person ending (GK 44h).

10 P. A. H. de Boer, *Fatherhood and Motherhood*, 1974, 31, associates the description of Deborah as 'a mother in Israel' with the idea of a mother-goddess: 'there is nothing of a motherly character in the picture of Deborah. In the song she is the bellicose leader of the united tribes'.

11 Contrast J. Gray, *Kings*, 1964, 660. His suggestion that Huldah was likely to cause less embarrassment than a male prophet reflects the writer's view of women rather than the Old Testament's!

12 cf. Meyers, *BA* 41, 1978, 101, for reasons why women's importance to society gradually diminished.

13 The omission of 'wife' is due to the fact that both men and women are addressed here. cf. Exod. 20.8; Deut. 5.14.

14 In this connection see Evans, *Woman*, 1983, 27, who notes that in Gen. 17, when circumcision is introduced as a covenant sign, reference to Sarah's special blessing (vv. 15–19) is incorporated into it.

15 cf. also Ezra 2.65, and especially 1 Chron. 25.5f. which may imply that Heman's daughters held an official position as temple musicians alongside his sons.

16 The sudden intrusion of the masculine singular 'and he worshipped' (v. 28b) is strange, and perhaps significant of attitudes.

17 Note in contrast the ruthless treatment of the wife in Deut. 25.11f., which constitutes the only instance of mutilation in Israelite legislation.

18 On the definition of 'widow', see Fensham, *JNES* 21, 1962, 136f.

19 For levirate marriage, cf. Neufeld, *Marriage*, 1944, 23ff.; T. and D. Thompson, *VT* 18, 1968, 79ff.

20 The two are used in parallel with no significant difference of meaning in 2 Sam. 11.26. The contrast between them in Hos. 2.16 is due to the particular theological context.

21 Contrast the late saying of Ecclus. 25.26. It is tempting to note that in one instance Abraham is instructed to 'obey' (*šāmaʿ bᵉqol*) Sarah (Gen. 21.12)!

22 The meaning is uncertain. McKane, *Proverbs*, 1970, *ad loc.*

23 The valuation of shekel (Lev. 27.1–8) need not be understood to refer to the intrinsic worth of persons, but to their contribution to the family, as in present day compensation settlements: cf. Wolff, *Anthropology*, 1974, 121.

24 The reference to Bethuel in Gen. 24.50 may be secondary. Against this see Selman, 'Patriarchal Age', 1980, 116.

25 cf. T. L. Thompson, *Historicity*, 1974, 249, who comments that none the less this is not evidence of matriarchy.

26 Wolff, *Anthropology*, 1974, 178, notes that the same verb (*ysr* in Piel) is used of both mother's (Prov. 21.1) and father's (Deut. 8.5) training of children. A mother also often named the child, though de Boer, *Fatherhood and Motherhood*, 7, notes that this is not so in late texts assigned to priestly writers.

27 cf. also Ex. 21.15, 17; Lev. 20.9; Deut. 27.16. On the unusual precedence of mother over father in Lev. 20.9, Noth, *Leviticus*, 1965, 140, asks whether some loosening of kinship and family arrangements in connection with the end of pre-exilic Israel gave special prominence to respect for parents, particularly the mother.

28 For the view that *bᵉtûlîm* refers 'to the age and marks of adolescence and not to virginity' see Wenham, *VT* 22, 1972, 330ff., followed by Phillips, *JSOT* 20, 1981, 6f. A full discussion of the passage is given in Locher, *Die Ehre*, 1986.

29 For criticism of this view, see Phillips, *JSOT* 20, 1981, 6–15 and *JSOT* 22, 1982, 142f., and for McKeating's response, *JSOT* 20, 1981, 25f.

30 Barstad, *Religious Polemics*, 1984, 19, who points out that the seriousness of the offence in Hos. 2; Ezek. 16.32; 23.5, lies in the fact that it is adultery. Mace, *Marriage*, 1944, 241, notes that one can speak of a man's adultery only in so far as this interferes with another's marriage; cf. also Phillips, *JSOT* 20, 1981, 7.

31 cf. Wolff, *Anthropology*, 1974, 199. The terms seem to be used interchangeably, however, in Gen. 30.3; 31.33; 2 Sam. 14.15f. In an Egyptian context Pharaoh's daughter's attendant is called *ʾāmāh* (Ex. 2.5), whereas Ex. 11.5 refers to the firstborn of the *šipḥāh*

working at the mill. Jepsen, *VT* 8, 1958, 425, has demonstrated that the difference in terminology is 'für eine Quellenscheidunng unbrauchbar'.

32 cf. van Seters, *JBL* 87, 1968, 403, who notes that this is primarily for the wife's sake, not the husband's. See also Selman, 'Patriarchal Age', 1980, 127.

33 We may compare the Silwan tomb inscription where the relationship continues in death; Gibson, *Inscriptions*, 1971, 24.

34 cf. the sense of fundamental equality in Deut. 5.14f.

35 P. D. Hanson, *Ecumenical Review*, 27, 1975, 318.

36 For a delightful play on the verb *bānāh* associating it with *bînāh* 'understanding, discernment', see Bab. Talmud, *Niddah*, 45.2.

37 cf. also Vos, *Woman*, 1968, 16, who notes that out of nineteen occurrences of the word, fifteen are used of God's activity in bringing help to his people.

38 cf. Terrien, *Heart Sings*, 1985, 10f., who describes woman as man's saviour who 'brings out of the man and to the man the totality of existence. She comes as if he had cried out, "Help! Help!"'

Bibliography

Avigad, N., 1964. The Seal of Jezebel, *IEJ* 14, 274–6.

Barstad, H. M., 1984. *The Religious Polemics of Amos*, VT Supp 34 (Leiden: Brill, 1984).

Bird, P., 'The Place of Women in the Israelite Cultus', *Ancient Israelite Religion: Essays in Honor of Frank Moore Cross*, Miller, P.D., Jr., Hanson, P. D. and McBride, S. D. (eds.) (Philadelphia: Fortress, 1987).

de Boer, P. A. H., 1974. *Fatherhood and Motherhood in Israelite and Judean Piety* (Leiden: Brill, 1974).

Brenner, A., 1985. *The Israelite Woman: Social Role and Literary Type in Biblical Narrative* (Sheffield: JSOT Press, 1985).

Burns, R. J., 1985. *Has the Lord Indeed Spoken Only Through Moses* (Atlanta, GA; Scholars Press, 1985).

Camp, C. V., 1981. 'The Wise Women of 2 Samuel: A Role Model for Women in Early Israel', *CBQ* 43, 1981, 14–29.

Childs, B. S., 1974. *Exodus* (London: SCM, 1974).

Crook, M. B., 1954. 'The Marriageable Maiden of Prov. 31.10–31' *JNES* 13, 1954, 137 40.

Evans, M., 1983. *Woman in the Bible* (Exeter: Paternoster, 1983).

Exum, J. C., 1983. '"You shall let every daughter live": A Study of Exodus 1: 8–2: 10', *The Bible and Feminist Hermeneutics*, Semeia 28, 1983.

Fensham, F. C., 1962. 'Widow, Orphan and the Poor in Ancient Near Eastern Legal and Wisdom Literature', *JNES* 21, 1962, 129–39.

Gibson, J. C. L., 1971. *Syrian Semitic Inscriptions*, I (Oxford: OUP, 1971).

Gordon, C. H., 'Hos. 2: 4–5 in the Light of New Semitic Inscriptions', *ZAW* 54, 1936, 277–80.

Hanson, P. D., 1975. 'Masculine Metaphors for God and Sex-Discrimination in the Old Testament', *Ecumenical Review*, 27, 1975, 316–24.

Hayter, M., 1987. *The New Eve in Christ* (London SPCK: 1987).

Hoftijzer, J., 1970. 'David and the Tekoite Woman', *VT* 20, 1970, 419–44.

Jepsen, A., 1958. 'Ama^{h} und Schiphcha^{h}', *VT* 8, 1958, 293–7, 425.

Köhler, L., *Hebrew Man* (London: SCM, 1956) tr. from *Der Hebräische Mensch* (Tübingen, 1953).

Locher, C., 1986. *Die Ehre einer Frau in Israel: exegetische und rechtsvergleichende Studien zu Deuteronomium 22, 13–21* (Göttingen, 1986).

Mace, D. R., 1953. *Hebrew Marriage* (London: Epworth, 1953).

McKane, W., 1970. *Proverbs* (London: SCM, 1970).

McKeating, H., 1979. 'Sanctions against Adultery in Ancient Israelite Society, with some Reflections on Methodology in the Study of Old Testament Ethics', *JSOT* 11, 1979, 57–72.

1981. 'A Response to Dr Phillips', *JSOT* 20, 1981, 25–6.

Meyers, C., 1978. 'The Roots of Restriction: Women in Early Israel', *BA* 41, 1978, 91–103.

Neufeld, E., 1944. *Ancient Hebrew Marriage Laws* (London, 1944).

Noth, M., 1962. *Exodus* (London: SCM, 1962) Transl. from *Das zweite Buch Mose, Exodus* (Göttingen, Vandenhoeck & Rupprecht, 1959).

1965. *Leviticus* (London: SCM, 1965) trans. from *Das dritte Buch Mose, Leviticus* (Göttingen, 1962).

Otwell, J. H., 1977. *And Sarah Laughed. The Status of Women in the Old Testament* (Philadelphia: Westminster, 1977).

Phillips, A. C. J., 1973. 'Some Aspects of Family Law in Pre-exilic Israel', *VT* 23, 1973, 349–61.

1981. 'Another Look at Adultery', *JSOT* 20, 1981, 3–25.

1982. 'A Response to Dr McKeating', *JSOT* 22, 1982, 142–3.

von Rad, G., *Genesis* (3rd rev. ed., London: SCM, 1972) tr. from *Das erste Buch Mose, Genesis* (9th ed., Göttingen, 1972).

Sakenfeld, K. D., 1979. Review of Otwell, J. H., *And Sarah Laughed*, *JBL* 98, 1979, 423–4.

1982. 'Old Testament Perspectives: Methodological Issues', *JSOT* 22, 1982, 13–20.

Selman, M. J., 1980. 'Comparative Customs and the Patriarchal Age', *Essays on the Patriarchal Narratives*, Millard, A. R. and Wiseman, D. J. (eds.), (Leicester: IVP, 1980).

Seters, J. van, 1968. 'The Problem of Childlessness in Near Eastern Law and the Patriarchs of Israel', *JBL* 87, 1968, 401–8.

Terrien, S., 1985. *Till the Heart Sings: A Biblical Theology of Manhood and Womanhood* (Philadelphia: Westminster, 1985).

Thompson, T. and D., 1968. 'Some Legal Problems in the Book of Ruth', *VT* 18, 1968, 79–99.

Thompson, T. L., 1974. *The Historicity of the Patriarchal Narratives*, BZAW 133 (Berlin: de Gruyter, 1974).

Tolbert, M. A., 1983. 'Defining the Problem: The Bible and Feminist Hermeneutics', *The Bible and Feminist Hermeneutics* (Semeia 28, 1983).

Trible, P., 1973. 'Depatriarchalising in Biblical Interpretation', *JAAR* 41, 1973, 30–48.

Trible, P., 1976, 'Woman in the OT', *IDBS* (Nashville, 1976).

de Vaux, R., 1961. *Ancient Israel: its Life and Institutions* (London: Darton, Longman & Todd, 1961) (Transl. from *Les Institutions de l'Ancien Testament* I and II, Paris, 1958 and 1960).

Vos, C. J., 1968. *Woman in Old Testament Worship* (Amsterdam, 1968).

Wenham, G. J., 1972. 'Bᶜṯûlāh, a girl of marriageable age', *VT* 22, 1972, 326–48.

Wolff, H. W., 1974. *Anthropology of the Old Testament* (London: SCM, 1974), transl. from *Anthropologie des Alten Testaments* (Munich: Beck, 1973).

CHAPTER EIGHTEEN

Life and death in the Old Testament

MICHAEL A. KNIBB

Beliefs about life and death, whether consciously articulated or not, form part of the make-up of all human beings, and the people of the Old Testament provide no exception in this respect. There are approximately eight hundred occurrences of the root *ḥāyāh* ('to live') in the Old Testament and one thousand occurrences of the root *mûṯ* ('to die'; for the statistics see Gerleman, 1971*a*, 1971*b*), and in addition there are numerous references to one or other aspect of the themes of life and death that do not make use of either of these roots; the sheer wealth of the material is an indication of the importance of these themes within the Old Testament. The occurrences of the roots *ḥāyāh* and *mûṯ* are discussed by Ringgren (1980 [1977]) and by Ringgren, Illmann and Fabry (1984), in both cases with some consideration of relevant material from the ancient Near East, while a comprehensive treatment of life and, particularly, of death and resurrection in the Old Testament was provided by Martin-Achard (1960 [1956]) in a work which contains very full references both to the relevant biblical material and to the older secondary literature.

1. Basic beliefs about life

Basic to the Old Testament is the belief that Yahweh has power over both life and death (cf. e.g. Deut. 32.39; 1 Sam. 2.6), and it is in accordance with this belief that life is frequently depicted in the Old Testament as the gift of God. This is of course the view of the creation narratives (Gen. 1.1–2.4*a*; 2.4*b*–3.24), as is expressed above all in Gen. 2.7: 'then the LORD God formed man of dust from the ground, and breathed into his nostrils the breath of life; and man became a living being'. But this idea is also reflected in a number of passages in which God is mentioned as the subject, and 'life' as the object, and God is said, for example, to 'make' (Job 10.12), or 'give' (Mal. 2.5), or 'command' (Ps. 133.3) life (cf. Gerleman: 1971*a*, 554–5). It is also reflected in the thought that God is the 'fountain of life' (Ps. 36.9 (Hebr. 10)) and is implied in the description of Yahweh as the 'living God' (cf. Johnson: 1964, 106–7).

The belief that Yahweh is the living God finds expression both in those passages in which he is described as such (e.g. Deut. 5.26 (23); 2 Kings 19.4; Josh. 3.10) and in passages which use the common oath formula 'by the life of Yahweh' (e.g. Judges 8.19, and for the translation cf. Greenberg: 1957). In a study entitled 'Der lebendige Gott' (1967, reprint 1972) Kraus has argued that the theological ideas associated with the oath formula are indicated in the relative clauses that are in some cases attached to them (e.g. 2 Sam. 4.9; in 1 Sam. 14.39 a participle is used), and that the emphasis in these passages is on Yahweh's active intervention on behalf of his people (e.g. Jer. 16.14–15; 23.7–8). Similar ideas occur in those passages which refer to Yahweh as the 'living God' in that the term is used in contexts which refer to Yahweh's presence among (e.g. Josh. 3.10) or intervention on behalf of (Hos. 1.10 (Hebr. 2.1)) his people, sometimes in polemical contexts in which Yahweh has been insulted (2 Kings 19.4, 16), or a contrast is drawn with powerless idols (Jer. 10.10). It is significant, however, that in Jer. 38.16 the oath formula is used in association with the thought of the creation of man: 'By the life of the LORD who made our souls' (cf. NEB, 'By the life of the LORD who gave us our lives'); this passage indicates that one of the ideas associated with the belief that Yahweh is the living God is that he is the giver of life (cf. Kraus: 1972, 5–30; but note his conclusion that the thought of Yahweh as the 'fountain of life' did not remain confined to the natural sphere, but was shaped by Israel's trust in his saving activity).

The belief that life is the gift of Yahweh is also reflected in the idea that he is the one who sustains and preserves life. Thus the Pi ʿel of the verb *ḥāyāh* is used in Neh. 9.6 with reference to Yahweh's 'preserving' the whole of creation and in Ps. 33.19 with reference to his 'keeping alive' in a time of famine those who fear him (cf. the use of the Hiph ʿil in Josh. 14.10). The Pi ʿel of *ḥāyāh* is also employed in psalms of lament and thanksgiving to refer to Yahweh's 'preserving the life' of the psalmist, that is delivering him from danger or distress caused by enemies or curing him of sickness (cf. Johnson: 1964, 99–100). This usage is illustrated in Ps. 143.11:

> 'For thy name's sake, O LORD, preserve my life!
> In thy righteousness bring me out of trouble!'

or Ps. 30.3 (Hebr. 4):

> 'O LORD, thou hast brought up my soul from Sheol,
> restored me to life from among those gone down to the Pit.'

Cf. also such passages as Ps. 41.2 (Hebr. 3); 71.20, and, with reference to the nation, 85.5–6 (Hebr. 6–7); 80.18 (Hebr. 19). The fact that in some of these psalms (e.g. 30.3 (Hebr. 4)) the sickness or distress is seen to bring the psalmist into the power of death and the underworld will need to be considered below.

The passage quoted above about the creation of man (Gen. 2.7) deserves further attention because of the light it casts on Israelite beliefs about the nature of man, i.e. about the way in which he was thought to be a 'living being'. By way of background to an examination of this passage reference should first be made to the important study by Johnson (1964) on the Old Testament conception of man (cf. also Wolff: 1974 [1973]). Johnson's main concern was to urge 'that in Israelite thought man is conceived not so much in dual fashion as "body" and "soul", but synthetically as a unit of vital power or (in current terminology) a psycho-physical organism' (1964, 87). He took as the starting point of his argument the idea that Israelite thinking, like that of so-called 'primitive' peoples, was predominantly synthetic and was 'characterized in large measure by what has been called the grasping of a totality', according to which phenomena were 'perceived as being in some kind of relationship.' This approach conditioned Israel's conception of man inasmuch as 'in Israelite thought psychical functions have close physical associations' (1964, 1, 4). Johnson sought to demonstrate his view that man was seen as a psycho-physical organism by a careful examination of the wide range of meanings that attach themselves to the terms used for the constitution of man, namely *nep̱eš* ('conventionally 'soul'), *rûaḥ* (often 'wind', but with reference to both God and man conventionally 'spirit'), and the various parts of the body, including, as the most important, *lēḇ* or *lēḇāḇ* (conventionally 'heart'). He pointed to the fact that these terms are used, at one end of the spectrum, in a purely physical sense and, at the other, with reference to the whole range of man's emotional, volitional, and intellectual activity. With regard to the parts of the body he pointed out that 'besides being referred to in a simple straightforward way as mere instruments of the *ego* . . ., they are sometimes spoken of as themselves actively engaged in some form of personal behaviour, or as characterised by some personal quality' (1964, 37), and that they are in consequence in some cases subject to a moral judgement (cf. e.g. 1964, 45, 82–87).

The various terms used to refer to the constitution of man have also been examined in detail by Wolff, who, in the first part of his study, offers what he describes as an 'anthropological language primer' (1974: 5–80 [1973, 19–124]). His approach and conclusions in many ways overlap with those of Johnson. However, it is not intended to pursue here the question of the Old Testament conception of man except insofar as it relates to the way in which man was conceived to be a 'living being'.

The account of the creation of man in the 'Yahwistic' narrative of the creation and fall (Gen. 2.4*b*–3.24) epitomises the Old Testament view of the constitution of man: 'Yahweh God formed man out of dust from the ground and breathed into his nostrils the breath of life (*nišmat ḥayyîm*); and the man became a living being (*nepeš ḥayyāh*)' (Gen. 2.7). It is widely recognised that there is no suggestion here of a dichotomy between body and soul; the 'breath of life' is not conceived of as having an existence somehow separate from the body, and it is man as an entity who becomes a 'living being'. Thus, for example, Westermann comments: 'a human being does not consist of a number of parts (like body and soul and so on), but rather is "something" that comes into being as a human person by a quickening into life . . . a person is created as a *nepeš ḥayyāh*; a "living soul" is not put into one's body' (1984: 206–7 [1974: 282–3]).

The idea that man's life depends on the breath breathed into him by God is expressed in the Old Testament in a variety of ways. Gen. 2.7 uses the expression 'the breath of life' (*nišmat ḥayyîm*), but in Job 33.4 (cf. 32.8) this is explicitly identified as 'the breath of the Almighty':

> 'The spirit of God has made me,
> and the breath of the Almighty gives me life.'

Here 'spirit' (*rûaḥ*) and 'breath' (*nešāmāh*) are used virtually synonymously, as they are also in Isa. 42.5; and in some later passages *rûaḥ* is used with the meaning 'breath' simply as a synonym of *nešāmāh*: cf. Gen. 6.17; 7.15 (both 'breath of life'); Zech. 12.1. Gen. 7.22, in a redactional passage, employs the composite expression 'breath of the spirit of life'. Again, just as the life of man is dependent on the gift by Yahweh of the 'breath' or 'spirit', so the withdrawal of this by Yahweh means the death of man: cf. e.g. Ps. 104.29–30,

> 'When you take away their breath [*rûaḥ*], they die
> and return to their dust.
> When you send forth your breath [*rûaḥ*],they are created,
> and you renew the face of the earth.'

Cf. Ps. 146.4; Job 34.14–15; Eccl. 12.7. Correspondingly, in Ezekiel's vision of the renewal of the nation (Ezek. 37), sinews, flesh and skin first come upon the bones, but life only returns to them after the 'breath' (*rûaḥ*) comes into them at Yahweh's command.

According to what has just been said, the principle of life within man lies in the 'breath', but sometimes in the Old Testament it is the *nepeš* (conventionally 'soul') that represents the vital element within him. (There is an overlap in the Old Testament between such concepts as *rûaḥ* and *nepeš*, for which Wolff uses the idea of 'stereometric thinking'; cf. e.g. 1974: 7–8, 33 [1973: 22, 59], and his reference to Landsberger: 1965, 17.) As mentioned earlier, the term *nepeš* has a wide range of meanings: at the physical level it can signify 'throat', 'neck', 'breath', but it is also used with the meaning 'life', and then as something like 'soul' in contexts where it is seen as the seat of feelings and emotions, and hence it can mean 'desire'; it can also mean 'person' (as in Gen. 2.7), or even 'corpse', and it is sometimes used with pronominal suffixes as a substitute for the personal or reflexive pronoun (see e.g. Johnson: 1964, 3–22; Wolff: 1974, 10–25 [1973: 25–48]). Our concern here is only with the use of *nepeš* to refer to the life force, the vital principle within men and animals, and hence as meaning 'life' (cf. e.g. Prov. 7.23). This meaning is reflected most clearly in the idea that 'life' is, or is contained in, the blood; cf. Deut. 12.23, 'the blood is the life [*nepeš*]'; Gen. 9.4; Lev. 17.10–14. Because it is the life force within man, the loss of the *nepeš*, like the loss of the 'breath' (see above), means the death of the individual. Thus at death the *nepeš* is said to be 'breathed out' (Job 11.20; 31.39), or 'poured out' (Ps. 141.8; Lam. 2.12; cf. 2 Sam. 14.14), or to 'depart' (Gen. 35.18), while in the case of the recovery of the son of the woman of Zarephath the *nepeš* is said to 'return' (1 Kings 17.21–2). However, inasmuch as there is, from one point of view, no clear-cut distinction in the Old Testament between life and death, fainting can also be described in terms of the 'breathing out' (Jer. 15.9) and despair in terms of the 'pouring out' (Job 30.16) of the *nepeš*, i.e. in terms of the loss of vitality, while the recovery of strength or spirit can be described in terms of the restoration of the *nepeš* (e.g. Lam. 1.11; Ps. 23.3), i.e. in terms of the regaining of vitality. There is an overlap here with the many instances in the Old Testament in which the *nepeš* is the seat of the feelings or emotions and thus can be said, for example, to 'faint' from hunger (Ps. 107.5).

The nature and characteristics of life in the Old Testament (and in ancient Near Eastern writings) were considered by C. Barth in an influential monograph (1947: 21–36; cf. Martin-Achard: 1960, 3–15 [1956, 11–20]). Here it is important to observe that although 'life' in the Old Testament can be thought of in terms of mere physical existence – the verb *ḥāyāh* can, for example, be used of survival (Gen. 20.7; 43.8), or of existence at a place (Gen. 47.28) or over a period of time (Gen. 5 *passim*), just as the noun *ḥayyîm* can be used of the length of an individual's life (Gen. 23.1; 25.7), or of life in contrast to death (Jonah 4.3, 8) – the concept often carries with it the notions of prosperity, blessing, health, strength, etc., that is of life in its fullness (cf. Barth: 1947, 27–33; Johnson: 1964, 95–106). This follows, first of all, from the fact that *ḥayyîm* is sometimes used in combination with such notions as 'long life' (Deut. 30.20; Ps. 34.12 (Hebr.

13); Prov. 3.2), 'good' (i.e. 'prosperity' (*ṭôb*), Deut. 30.15), 'blessing' (*b^e^rāḵāh*, Deut. 30.16, 19; Ps. 133.3), and 'peace' (i.e. 'well-being, prosperity' (*šālôm*), Mal. 2.5; Prov. 3.16–18). It is also implied in the idea that an individual in trouble, whether caused by sickness (e.g. Ps. 88), or the attacks of enemies (e.g. Ps. 86, see vs. 13), or some unspecified cause (e.g. Ps. 40, see vs. 2 (Hebr. 3)), is already within the realm of death, i.e. in Sheol, and that deliverance from such a situation involves being 'brought up' from Sheol (e.g. Ps. 30.3 (Hebr. 4)). Furthermore, the Piʿel of *ḥāyāh* is sometimes used in psalms of lament and thanksgiving to refer to Yahweh's 'preserving the life' of the psalmist, i.e. rescuing him from the assaults of enemies or healing him of sickness, as we have seen (above, pp. 396–7). In a similar way the Qal of *ḥāyāh* can be used with the meaning 'be healed, recover' (e.g. Num. 21.8–9; Josh. 5.8), or 'revive' (Gen. 45.27 (from a state of despair); Judges 15.19 (from faintness); 1 Kings 17.22 (from apparent death)), just as the Hiphʿil can have the meaning 'cure' (someone of sickness, Isa. 38.16) or 'restore to life' (someone apparently dead, 2 Kings 8.15). The clear implication of all this is that any impairment of, or threat to, life is a form of death, and that by contrast 'real' life is life that is not in any way impaired or threatened, but is life in its fulness.

It is against the background of such an understanding of life that the frequent references to life in Deuteronomy and in Proverbs should be seen. In Deuteronomy the attainment of life is dependent on obedience to the commandments (cf. also Lev. 18.5; Neh. 9.29), and life itself is usually associated with possession of the land and with such concepts as well-being and long life: cf. e.g. 5.33, 'You shall walk in all the way which the LORD your God has commanded you, that you may live, and that it may go well with you, and that you may live long in the land which you shall possess'; cf. also, for example, 4.1; 8.1; and especially 30.15–20.

The approach in the book of Proverbs is not dissimilar. Here the attainment of life is frequently depicted as the consequence of obedience to the teachings of the wisdom teacher (e.g. 3.1–2; 4.10), or is linked with the acquisition of wisdom (e.g. 3.13–18; 8.35), the receiving of instruction (4.13), or the like. Occasionally other concepts, such as well-being or riches, are associated with life (e.g. 3.2, 16–18; 4.22), and this indicates that life is understood to mean a full, happy and prosperous life (cf. 15.27).

So far as the prophets are concerned, it is noticeable that it is only in Ezekiel that references to life occur at all frequently (cf. Zimmerli: 1963 [1957], 178). In Ezekiel the unconditional promise of the renewal of the life of the nation and of the return to the land (37.1–14; cf. 47.9) has to be held in balance with the two disputations (18; 33.10–20) in which the promise of life is dependent on the observance of the 'statutes of life' (33.15; cf. 18.9,

17; 20.11, 13, 21; and see Zimmerli; 1963)). These two disputations take up the complaints of the exiles that they are being treated unjustly (18.2, 25, 29; 33.10, 17, 20), and despite the appearance created by the mode of argument, which makes use of individual case histories, the concern is primarily with the fate of the exilic generation as a group, rather than with that of individuals. The prophet argues that each generation is responsible for its own fate. There is an inescapable link between sin and death on the one hand, and righteousness and life on the other. The righteous man who turns from his righteousness must inevitably die; the sinner who turns from his sin will live. The exiles are urged to repent in order to obtain life (cf. 18.23, 30–2; 33.11).

Zimmerli (1963; cf. 1979 [1969*a*]) has made a particular study of the background of the literary form of the disputations. He argued with reference to 18.5–9 that the combination of the recapitulation of a series of legal pronouncements, the declaratory formula 'he is righteous', and the promise of life 'he shall live', reflected the procedure of a ceremony of admission to the temple in which the worshipper had read to him the rules of the temple, to which he affirmed his adherence – or himself recited a list of rules as a form of confession of innocence – and was then declared 'righteous' and was admitted to the temple (Zimmerli: 1963, 182–4; 1979, 375–6 [1969*a*, 397–9]); cf. Gunkel-Begrich: 1933, 408–9; von Rad: 1966, 244–5, 254; 1958 [1950], 226–7, 235–6). Zimmerli further maintained that 'the third element of Ezek. 18.5–9, the promise of life, also points to an event in the sanctuary. 'Life' is especially the gift given in the sphere of the sanctuary as the place of God's presence' (1979, 376 [1969*a*, 399]). A similar point had earlier been made by von Rad. In comment on Deut. 30.15, 19 he pointed out that the promise of life was intimately linked to the proclamation of the commandments, such as occurred on certain great cultic occasions (e.g. the feast of booths, cf. 31.10–13). He argued that it was within the cultus that the individual received the assurance that he would have life, and that this assurance was given not just on great cultic occasions when the commandments were recited, but also in more 'private' circumstances, when the individual in distress came to the temple (von Rad: 1966, 253–4 [1958, 234–6]). Zimmerli found indirect support for his view inter alia in the words of Amos 5.4–5, 'Seek me and live; but do not seek Bethel . . .', behind which has been seen to lie the viewpoint of the priests of Bethel, 'Seek Bethel and live'. The priests of Bethel sought to encourage pilgrimage to the sanctuary at Bethel by the promise of life, but Amos (cf. 5.4–5, 6, 14), like Ezekiel after him, was concerned to stress the conditional character of this promise of life. Recognition of the cultic background of Ezek. 18.5–9, and in particular the promise of life (vs. 9), is important for understanding what is meant by 'life' in Ezek. 18 (and in 33.10–20). Whereas 37.1–14 specifically mentions return from exile (see vs. 14), the promise of life is left undefined in 18 and 33.10–20. Zimmerli drew attention to the way in which the salvation promised in the cult 'was not primarily the promise of a specific, and materially defined, gift, but more broadly a promise "God will be with you"', as indeed life is defined in Amos 5.14. He argued that in a similar way the promise of life in Ezek. 18 was left open and deliberately not restricted to a return from exile. 'That God promises his "Yes", and therewith his assurance of "life", to the man who confesses obedience to him and his commandments is here also the important factor' (1979, 381–2; [1969*a*, 406–9]).

2. Death in the Old Testament

Relatively more attention appears to have been paid in recent studies to the theme of death in the Old Testament than to the theme of life. Mention has already been made of the article by Ringgren, Illmann and Fabry (1984) and of the volume by Martin-Achard (1960 [1956]). Other general studies include those by Kaiser (Kaiser and Lohse, 1977; Eng. Tr., 1981), Ringgren (1963, 218–26, 293–5; Eng. Tr., 1966, pp. 239–47, 322–3), Maag (1964, reprint 1980), Fohrer (1968), Wolff (1973, 150–76 (Eng. Tr., 1974, 99–118), and Plöger (1978). Studies that are concerned more with the theological understanding of death in the Old Testament include von Rad (I, [2]1958, 274–6, 385–9 (Eng. Tr., 1962, 275–7, 387–91); II, [2]1961, pp.361–2 (Eng. Tr., 1965, 349–50)), Zimmerli (1971), Brueggemann (1976), and Bailey (1979, especially, 23–74). Funeral rites are discussed by de Vaux (I, 1958, 93–100; Eng. Tr., 1961, 56–61). Other works will be mentioned in the course of what follows.

Despite such passages as Rom. 5.12; 6.23; Wisd. Sol. 2.23–4; 2 Esdras 3.7, there is no suggestion in the narratives of the creation and fall, nor indeed in the Old Testament as a whole, that man was created immortal and lost his immortality as a result of disobedience. In Gen. 2.17 death is certainly prescribed as the penalty for eating the tree of the knowledge of good and evil, but there is no hint that man had originally possessed immortality, and in any case the actual punishment was different (cf. Gen. 3.17–19). In Gen. 3.19 death is mentioned as marking the end of man's toil on the earth, not as a punishment, while the implication of 3.22, 24, which refer to the tree of life which might have given man immortality, is that man did not at that time possess it (cf. e.g. Martin-Achard: 1960, 19–20 [1956, 23–4]); Wächter; 1967, 198–203; and on Gen. 3.19 see Westermann: 1974, 362–3 (Eng. Tr. 1984, 266–7), with references to other views). There is thus no idea in the narrative of the creation and fall that man had once been immortal. In contrast Gen. 3.19*c*, 'you are dust, and to dust you shall return', reflects the view that death is the inevitable fate of all men, a view that, under a variety of images, occurs throughout the Old Testament: cf. e.g. 1 Kings 2.2; 2 Sam. 14.14; Job 14.1–2.

Attitudes towards death in the Old Testament are, however, much more varied than mere acknowledgement of death as the common lot of mankind, as Wächter (1967) has shown (cf. also Bailey: 1979, 47–61, 71–4). Wächter distinguished between instinctive attitudes towards death and the theological evaluation of death in the Old Testament. Under the former he regarded aversion to, or fear of, death as the most common reaction, expressed at its simplest in the flight of an individual in the face of the threat of death (e.g. 1 Sam. 19.11–12) or the panic of a group in the face of an enemy attack (e.g. 2 Kings 7.6–7; Josh. 2.9), and at a deeper level in terror at the prospect of meeting God (e.g. Num. 16.34; Judg. 13.22). But he also noted other attitudes, including both acceptance of death (e.g. Job 5.26; 2 Sam. 19.34–7 (Hebr. 35–8)), particularly when it occurs in 'good old age' (e.g. Gen. 25.8), but also sometimes a common human longing for death (e.g. Exod. 14.11–12; 1 Kings 19.4), and in Ecclesiastes a weariness with life (2.15–18; 6.2–6). The Old Testament also speaks of death as the inevitable fate of all men (see above), and Wächter drew attention to the variety of contexts in which this notion occurs and the variety of purposes to which it is put (e.g. as the basis of an appeal to God's forbearance (Job 14.1–3), or as the means of emphasising the eternal love and righteousness of God (Ps. 103.13ff.)). So far as the theological evaluation of death is concerned, Wächter noted that death is predominantly seen as divine punishment, whether of communities (e.g. Deut. 28; Lev. 26) or of individuals (e.g. Amos 7.9, 11). But whereas sudden or premature death is clearly seen as a divine punishment in the Old Testament, mortality as such is not so regarded (Ps. 90 forms a partial exception (cf. Kellermann: 1976, 264–6); for Gen. 2–3, see above). Throughout Wächter drew on ancient Near Eastern as well as Old Testament sources. He surveyed – and carefully evaluated – an enormously wide range of material, and it is in this that the usefulness of his study lies.

At death the individual was placed in the grave, but he was at the same time thought to go down to the realm of the dead, i.e. to Sheol, as that realm is most commonly named in the Old Testament (cf. e.g. Gen. 37.35). Maag (1980, 184ff.) draws a sharp distinction between the grave and Sheol, but it seems clear that the two concepts frequently overlap, as is shown particularly by Ezek. 32.17–32. Pedersen's comments in relation to this passage are still apposite: 'Sheol is the entirety into which all graves are merged . . . The "Ur"-grave we might call Sheol; it belongs deep down under the earth, but it manifests itself in every single grave . . . Where there is grave, there is Sheol, and where there is Sheol, there is grave' (Pedersen, I–II, 1959, 462, quoted by Tromp: 1969, 133, cf. 139; and also Barth: 1947, 83–5).

The studies of the two scholars just mentioned, Tromp and Barth, have considerably increased our understanding of the Old Testament conception of the realm of the dead. Tromp (1969) devoted the first part of his monograph to the listing and discussion of the many names and epithets used for the nether world in the Old Testament. For the sake of convenience he divided the names into three groups: those in which the local aspect is the predominant common element, such as Sheol, *ʾereṣ* ('nether world', e.g. Exod. 15.12), or *bôr* ('pit', e.g. Isa. 38.18); those which reflect something of the character of the realm of the dead, such as Abaddon ('place of destruction') or *ʿāpār* ('dust', e.g. Job 17.16); and those which refer to death as a personal reality, such as *môṯ* ('Sir Death', e.g. Isa. 28.15) or *melek ballāhôṯ* ('king of terrors', Job 18.14). In the second part of his study Tromp attempted to draw out the implications of the material he had assembled in Part I in relation to other biblical descriptions of the realm of the dead. Here he treats such topics as the nether world as a city, or a prison, death as a personal force and the demons associated with him, and the inhabitants and conditions of the nether world. The distinctive feature of Tromp's study is the extent to which he makes use of the evidence of the Ugaritic texts in his elucidation of the Old Testament material. Whether or not one agrees with all the details of his interpretation of the Old Testament texts, there is no question that his monograph marked an important advance in the study of the subject. Not the least point of interest is his demonstration of how widespread was the concern with death and the realm of the dead in the Old Testament.

An equally important advance was marked by Barth's somewhat older study (1947), which has remained very influential. Barth (76–91), who made extensive use of parallels drawn from Mesopotamian and Egyptian sources, treated a good deal of the same Old Testament material as Tromp in the context of a study whose particular purpose will be discussed later. Here attention should be drawn to Barth's views on the location of Sheol, which is conventionally regarded as being under the earth. Barth, who was strongly influenced by the ideas of Pedersen (cf. I–II, 1959, 460–70), argued that the various locations and names of Sheol expressed something of the character of Sheol and were not to be understood as providing precise geographical information. Thus the common idea that Sheol lies in the depths of the earth reflects the separation of Sheol from the world of life.

The conception of Sheol as being in the depths is derived from the grave, which itself is to be regarded as a manifestation of Sheol. But Sheol also manifests itself in other phenomena, particularly the ocean (cf. e.g. Ps. 69.2, 14–15 (Hebr. 3, 15–16); 71: 20), which was perceived as the embodiment of death and destruction, and the desert. Barth concludes: 'The realm of death is present wherever death exercises its rule. The location of the realm of death cannot be defined more precisely or more comprehensively' (*ibid.*, 88; see particularly 80–9).

There is undoubtedly an element of truth in Barth's view of the descriptive character of what is said of the realm of the dead and its location in the Old Testament, but to some extent his argument represents an overstatement. Tromp (1969, 129–40), while paying tribute to the importance of Barth's study, nonetheless offered a number of qualifications to his views. So far as the location of Sheol is concerned it must suffice here to quote the following comment: 'It seems imperative to distinguish between death's province comprising both local realities as ocean and desert, and other realities as prison, illness, and wild beasts – and the abode of the dead proper, which is seated deep in the earth. Sheol then is the complete reign of Death, the abode of the dead from which nobody returns; it is partially identical with the grave and with the primeval ocean also' (*ibid.*, 133).

The Old Testament conception of the realm of the dead as a place of darkness, in which the dead lead a shadowy existence, cut off from men and God, unable to praise God and indeed unable to do anything, is well-known and has often been discussed by scholars (see e.g. Martin-Achard: 1960, 36–46 [1956, 36–43]); Wächter, 1967, 181–93). The Old Testament gives vivid descriptions of this realm in such passages as Isa. 14.9–20*a*; Ezek. 32.17–32; Ps. 88; Job 3.13–19; 10.21–2; 14.12; Eccl. 9.5, 10. It is not intended to discuss the nature of this realm here, except to note that the dead were believed to continue in existence in Sheol, albeit in a very weak and reduced state. 'Death is to be explained in terms of life. It is a weak and indeed, insofar as it marks the final disintegration of one's *nep̱eš*, the weakest form of life' (Johnson: 1964, 88, and see 88–95). The idea that the dead survive in a much reduced form of life is presupposed by the practice of offering food and drink to the dead (cf. Deut. 26.14; Sir. 30.18), which may well have been intended to strengthen the dead (cf. Wächter: 1967, 186–93). But it is also reflected in 1 Sam. 28, the account of the conjuring up of the ghost of Samuel by the woman of En-dor (cf. vs. 13, 'I see a ghost [*ʾᵉlōhîm*] coming up from the nether world'), in which Samuel complains at being disturbed (vs. 15); and above all in the taunt-song against the king of Babylon (Isa. 14.3–23), in which the 'shades' (*rᵉp̱āʾîm*, here a term referring to former rulers) are roused from their thrones to greet the arrival of the dead tyrant in Sheol:

> 'Sheol beneath is stirred up
> to meet you when you come,
> it rouses the shades to greet you,
> all who were leaders of the earth;
> it raises from their thrones
> all who were kings of the nations.
> All of them will speak
> and say to you:
> "You too have become as weak as we!
> You have become like us!"'
> (vss. 9–10, cf. vss. 16–17)

(For the *r^e pā'îm* and their relationship to Ugaritic *rp'um*, see Healey: 1978*a* and *b*; Spronk: 1986, 161–96.)

The conception of death as a very weak form of life forms the counterpart to the belief that any impairment of, or threat to, life represents a form of death (cf. Johnson: 1964, 95). It is against the background of this conception of life and death, and against the background of the perception that the realm of death cannot simply be defined in terms of Sheol as a place deep in the earth, that those passages in the individual laments and thanksgivings which speak of the individual in distress as being already in the realm of death have to be interpreted. Barth's discussion of the Old Testament understanding of life (1947, 20–51) and death (*ibid.*, 52–91) was intended to provide the necessary basis for the interpretation of just these psalm passages (91–122). Barth, who built on the work of Pedersen (I–II, 1959, 153ff., 460–70) and Baumgartner (1959 [1933], 125), noted that in an earlier period passages which referred to the individual who was sick or otherwise in distress as being in Sheol were understood as metaphor, or exaggeration, or poetic fantasy. The character of the language used in the individual laments might at first appear to support this view. The laments, which in any case tend to avoid the ominous overtones of the name 'Sheol', and to use synonyms instead, speak of the individual being 'like' those who go down to the pit, etc., or 'near' to death, the gates of death, etc. (cf. e.g. Ps. 28.1; 31.12 (Hebr. 13); 88.3–5 (Hebr. 4–6); 107.18); the individual in distress never directly identifies himself with the dead. It is only in the thanksgivings that the individual is said in retrospect to have been completely within the power of death and so can be said, for example, to have been 'brought up' (Ps. 30.3 (Hebr. 4)) or 'delivered' (Ps. 86.13) from Sheol. (The difference in approach is illustrated by the difference in language in verses 22 and 28–30 of Job 33). It would, however, be a mistake to interpret the language of the laments as metaphorical, and the language of the thanksgivings as exaggeration, for this would fail to do justice to Old Testament ways of thinking. We have already seen that from one point of view there is no clear cut distinction in the Old Testament between life and death, and that the realm of death cannot simply be defined in local terms. Further, similarity implies real identity. Thus Barth argues that the experience of death of the individual in distress is real, but only partial. The difference between the individual in distress in the realm of death and the dead man is that for the former there is still the possibility of a change in his situation, of a deliverance by God; the latter is completely cut off from God and without any hope of deliverance (cf. Ps. 88.10–12 (Hebr. 11–13)).

Wächter (1967, 48–50) has criticised Barth's approach as being too 'philosophical' and has argued that the references to the underworld were intended metaphorically. But on the whole Barth's views have been accepted and have been widely influential (cf. e.g. Maag: 1980, 187–9; or the psalm commentaries of Kraus and Anderson). Reference should, however, be made here to the careful qualifications of Tromp (1969, 129–40, particularly 135–9). Two points may be mentioned here. Barth spoke of the individual being in 'the domain of the dead' (*Totenreich*), but Tromp, while accepting the main thrust of Barth's arguments, prefers rightly to speak of 'the domain of death'. Further, Tromp takes up the question of the character of the spatial language used of residence in, and deliverance from, the realm of death, and the extent to which this retained its force. He concludes: 'The use of nether-world terminology, though implying a real experience of death and consequently being more than mere poetic ornamentation, must, as far as the peculiar use in the individual laments and thanksgivings is concerned, be considered as secondary and technical.' The extent to which such language is 'secondary and technical' (*ibid.*, 139) or 'figurative' (*ibid.*, 138) requires further consideration.

3. Life after death

One of the characteristics of Sheol is that it is 'the land of no return' (cf. e.g. 2 Sam. 12.23; Job 7.9–10; 10.21–2; 16.22; Barth, 1947, pp. 77–8; Tromp, 1969, pp. 189–90), and this raises the question of how far there is present in the Old Testament a belief in resurrection or in life after death. Dan. 12.2–3 clearly expresses the belief in the resurrection of some, or all, Jews (cf. Plöger: 1965, 171), and there would probably be fairly general agreement that Ezek. 37.1–14 refers to the restoration of the nation in exile (cf. Zimmerli: 1983, 264–5 [1969*b*, 900]). Beyond this there is a very considerable difference of opinion about the interpretation of the relevant Old Testament evidence. Thus, for example, in recent studies Isa. 26.19 has been understood to refer metaphorically to the restoration of Israel (Wildberger: 1978, 995; cf. Fohrer: 1968, 260; Clements: 1980, 216), to refer explicitly to the resurrection of the dead, but to be a later interpolation (Kaiser: 1973, 169, 173–7; Eng. Tr., 1974, 210, 215–20), and to refer to the physical resurrection of the faithful as the climax of the 'heart' of the Isaiah Apocalypse (Hasel: 1980, 275). Again, several passages in the psalms have been thought to refer in some way to life after death. Thus Ps. 49.15 (Hebr. 16) and 73.24, to mention two of the most important, have frequently been interpreted as referring to a future life, as expressing, for example, a belief, however, tentative, in life after death (cf. e.g. von Rad: I, [2]1958, 403–5 (Eng. Tr. 1962, 405–7); Kraus: 1961, 367–8, 509–10; Anderson: 1972, I, 379–80, II, 535–36), as referring to the translation of the soul (Maag: 1980, 190–93), or as expressing the conviction that the communion of the faithful with Yahweh would not be broken by death (Kellermann: 1976, especially 275–7; cf. Martin-Archard: 1981*a*, 309–10). In contrast, Barth (1947, 152–66, particularly 158–63) argued that Ps. 49.15 (Hebr. 16) refers to deliverance from distress in this life, not to a future life, and that Ps. 73.23ff. refers to life this side of death; and Wächter (1967, 195–8) believes that only Ps. 73 may express the hope of communion with God continuing after death. To take one final example, Isa. 53.10*b*–12 has been traditionally understood to refer to the resurrection of the servant, or at least – even though it is impossible to define it precisely – to 'an act done upon him after his death and on the far side of the grave' (Westermann: 1969, 267 [1966, 215]); but Whybray (1975, 171–83; 1978, 79–106) has argued that there is no idea of resurrection, or indeed of the death of the servant, in Isa. 53.

The diversity of views in the three cases just mentioned illustrate the difficulties that beset any attempt to trace the development in the Old Testament of a belief in resurrection or life after death, difficulties that are compounded by the uncertainties concerning the date of many of the relevant passages (e.g. Isa. 26.19). It is unlikely that the belief in resurrection only emerged at the time when Dan. 12.2–3 was composed, i.e. at the time of the persecution by Antiochus Epiphanes, and indeed Eccl. 3.19–21; 9.2–6 show that the question of the fate of man after death was in the air in the Hellenistic period; but we cannot be at all sure how far back the idea of resurrection is to be carried. Isa. 26.19 *may* provide evidence of a belief in resurrection, but if so, it is hard to say whether this would be evidence of what was believed at a time not much earlier than that of Dan. 12.2–3, or of what was believed at a much earlier time, i.e. in the exilic or early post-exilic period. Psalm passages such as 49.15 (Hebr. 16) and 79.24 *may* hint at, if not actually express, a belief in some form of life after death, but this is by no means clear, and in view of what has been said earlier in this article, it seems more likely that Barth's approach is correct, and that the passages refer to deliverance from distress and from the power of death in this life. In any case, there is again the problem of the date of the material.

It is not possible to pursue this question here. For a detailed discussion of all the relevant Old Testament material, reference may be had to the studies of Martin-Achard (1960: 49–181 [1956, 45–144], supplemented by his two articles of 1981) and of Spronk (1986). Here it is only possible to refer briefly to attempts to use new materials and new methods in tackling this subject.

In his three-volume commentary on the Psalms Dahood (1965, 1968, 1970) has argued that the belief in resurrection and immortality is widely reflected in the psalter – he speaks of it occurring in some forty texts – and hence that the belief existed in Israel at a much earlier stage than is commonly assumed: 'the opinion of Sigmund Mowinckel that "neither Israel nor early Judaism knew of a faith in any resurrection nor is such a faith represented in the psalms" will not survive serious scrutiny' (1965, xxxvi; see further particularly 1970, xli–lii). Dahood based his argument on his interpretation of the Ugaritic texts, notably KTU 1. 17. VI, 25–38, and maintained, for example, that *ḥayyîm* can have the meaning 'life eternal' and *ʾaḥ^a^rîṯ* the meaning 'the future' or 'future life'. Thus, to mention only two instances, he translates Ps. 16.11*a*, 'You will make me know the path of life eternal', and Ps. 109.13, 'May his future life be cut off, from the age to come his name erased.' (For a similar treatment of material in Proverbs, see Dahood, 1963 (e.g. 28–9, 48–9).)

Dahood's views have not on the whole been accepted, but here it must suffice to mention only two of the criticisms that have been made (cf. Martin-Achard: 1981*a*, 307–8). Vawter (1972) rightly pointed out that Dahood had too one-sidedly read the material in the light of what was philologically possible and had taken insufficient account of what was theologically probable (161–2), i.e. he had not taken account of the whole context of the book of Psalms, and of the Old Testament in general, in which death is usually presented as the inevitable end of all men. Further, Loretz (1979, 462–8) has shown that Dahood's reliance on the evidence of KTU 1. 17. VI, 25–38 was based on a misinterpretation of the passage. He concluded that the Ugaritic texts confirmed anew that ancient Canaan and pre-exilic Israel were convinced of man's mortality and his unenviable fate after death, and that it was only after the breakup of the old Semitic culture in the exilic and post-exilic period that the way was open for new speculation about the life and the fate of man after death.

Dahood was not of course the only person who has attempted to make use of the Ugaritic texts in relation to the emergence in Israel of a belief in resurrection, or life after death. As representative of the work of other scholars in this area reference may be made here to the recent study by Spronk (1986). Spronk places his treatment of the Old Testament material in the context of a discussion of ancient Near Eastern conceptions of a beatific afterlife, and makes particular use of the evidence of the Ugaritic texts. He argues that the Israelites were clearly familiar with, even if Yahwism did not adopt, 'the Canaanite belief in Baal rising from the netherworld every year and taking the deified spirits of the royal dead with him' (p. 324), and that although Israelite belief in a life after death was clearly distinguished from Canaanite belief – particularly because it was not tied to the cycle of nature, but depended totally on Yahweh himself – the way in which the belief was formulated was influenced by the Ancient Canaanite conception of a beatific afterlife. He maintains that Canaanite traditions survived for a long time in the folk religion of Israel (not in the official Yahwistic religion) and were thus able to be influential as late as the second century BC, and he believes that some elements in Jewish and Christian conceptions of life after death can be traced back to this influence. It remains to be seen how far all the details of Spronk's study will be accepted, but this work represents an important contribution to the subject, not least because of its comprehensive treatment of all the relevant Ugaritic and Old Testament evidence.

Sawyer (1973) has used linguistic techniques in his treatment of the theme of resurrection. He noted the value both of studying a word, not only in its immediate linguistic environment, but also in 'its situational or non-verbal context, that is to say, the "universe of discourse" in which it was used', and of studying a word's 'associative field'. He discussed the associative field of the Hebrew term *tᵉḥiyyaṯ hammēṯîm*, 'resurrection of the dead', and observed that most of the examples come from Hebrew of the Middle Period, the period that covers the later parts of the Hebrew Bible, the Dead Sea Scrolls, and mishnaic and mediaeval Hebrew. It was just in the early part of this period that belief in resurrection began to be a live issue, and Sawyer notes that whereas Ben Sira rejects this belief, there is no indication that all the late psalms were orthodox in this sense. It was also in the early part of this Middle Period that the Prophets and the Writings received their final form. Against the background of these considerations he suggests that a belief in the resurrection is reflected in the final form, but not necessarily the original context, of some twenty passages, mostly passages in which the belief has traditionally been sought, and he endeavours to illustrate this by a discussion of Ps. 1.5; Job 19.25–7, and Isa. 53.11.

The linguistic techniques to which Sawyer has drawn attention clearly have their value for the study of the 'resurrection' passages, but there remains a considerable degree of uncertainty about the interpretation of these passages – even in the context of the final form of the text. Thus it is, for example, by no means clear that Job 19.25–7 was already understood in the context of the final form of the book as referring to the resurrection of Job from the dead (Sawyer: 1973, 232–33). What applies in the context of the final form of the text applies even more in the original context, and the difficulties in tracing the emergence of the belief in resurrection and life after death remain.

4. Distinctive formulas relating to death

The themes of life and death in the Old Testament raise many other issues which it is not possible to consider here. But by way of conclusion reference may be made to two studies which are concerned – in quite different ways – with the language used of death.

Illmann (1979) examined the Old Testament formulas used about death, and his approach in this monograph underlies his treatment of the root *mûṯ* in the *Theologisches Wörterbuch zum Alten Testament* (Ringgren, Illmann and Fabry, 1984, cols. 768–86). (Treatment of formulas relating to death is not in itself new, and mention may be made here of Alfrink's discussion of the expressions 'he slept with his fathers' and 'he was gathered to his people' (1943, 1948; cf. Driver, 1962, 137–43); what is distinctive of Illmann's study is his comprehensive treatment of one particular root and his concern about methodology). Illmann noted that his purpose in his 1979 volume was twofold: 'to describe the characteristics of the Hebrew formula from the horizon of the stem *mûṯ*', and 'to find out whether the formulaic use of this stem is an essential feature to be borne in mind in interpreting its meaning' (1979, 178). He defines a 'formula' as 'a repeated word group or repeated word combination', but also as one which has 'a distinct function within the larger context' (*ibid.*, 18), and he attempts, both in his introduction and throughout the book, to distinguish a 'formula' from an 'idiom' (where the criterion of function is lacking, and the word group is the natural Hebrew way of expression), a 'repetition' (where the word group is repeated within a limited context and generally by the same author), and a 'coined phrase' (where the word group is borrowed by another author). The formulas are grouped under such rubrics as 'Recognizing Death', 'Death and Burial', etc., and the study is restricted almost entirely to the occurrences of the root *mûṯ*. Illmann notes that he is primarily concerned with the mode of expression, with *how* the Old Testament speaks about death, and although the approach has its limitations, the arrangement and discussion of the material in terms of the formulas used often cast an interesting light on the interpretation of particular passages.

One of the formulas studied by Illmann is *môṯ yûmaṯ* ('he shall be put to death'), and the sentences that conclude with this formula (e.g. Exod. 21.12, 'Whoever strikes a man so that he dies shall be put to death') were investigated by Schulz (1969) in an important form-critical study (cf. Wagner: 1972, 16–31). A series of these *môṯ yûmaṯ* sentences, in which the first part consists of a participial phrase, occurs in Exod. 21.12, 15, 16, 17, and a further series, in which the participle is replaced by a relative clause, occurs in Lev. 20. Schulz began his inquiry by referring to the uncertainty that exists as to whether the *môt yûmat* sentences of the type represented by Exod. 21.12 are to be categorised as apodictic law, as Alt argued (1966, 109–14 [1953, 307–13]; cf. Boecker: 1980, 191–7 [1976, 166–72]), or as a form of casuistic law (cf. e.g. Gese: 1960, 147–50). Schulz maintained that the *môṯ yûmaṯ* sentences represented a transformation of the prohibitive law of the clan (thus, e.g., Exod. 21.12 was based on the prohibition of Exod. 20.13, 'You shall not kill') and constituted a distinct legal form. He placed this transformation at the time of the occupation of the land and argued on the basis of a study of Gen. 26.1–11 that the *Sitz-im-Leben* of this legal form belonged in the tribal community, in the proclamation of law by the tribal leader. After the settlement the responsibility of pronouncing the death sentence was taken over by the local community, which for this purpose – so it is argued on the basis of 1 Kings 21, Jer. 26.7ff., and Jer. 7 – was constituted as a cultic community in order that the community might thereby avoid any risk of blood guilt. An analysis of Lev. 18–20, in which it is striking that there are close links between the *môṯ yûmaṯ* sentences of chapter 20 and the prohibitions of chapter 18, indicates that the influence of cultic institutions in such proceedings continued in the post-exilic period. It is argued that underlying Lev. 18–20 the various stages of a cultic procedure can be traced, by which the cultic community pronounced the sentence of death. Schulz also suggests that the influence of this legal tradition can be discerned in material in Ezekiel which he regards as secondary.

Schulz has not been the only one to study the *môṯ yûmaṯ* sentences (see the discussion, with bibliography, by Boecker), but to pursue this further would take us beyond the limits of this article. Schulz's monograph offers much of interest, but the soundness of his overall thesis stands or falls on the soundness of his interpretation of a large number of individual passages in the Old Testament, and there must inevitably be a question about his treatment of some of the material, not least the use that he makes of Gen. 26.1–11; 1 Kings 21; Jer. 7 and 26. However, it must suffice to refer to the detailed and careful review by Zimmerli (1970). What may be said here is that the form-critical study by Schulz and the treatment of formulas by Illmann both point to areas where there is yet room for further work in relation to the themes of life and death in the Old Testament.

Bibliography

Alfrink, B., 1943. 'L'expression *šāḵaḇ ʾīm ʾᵃḇôṯāw*', *OTS* 2: 106–18.

1948. 'L'expression *neʾᵉsap bel-ʿammāw*', *OTS* 5: 118–31.

Alt, A., 1966 [1953]. 'Die Ursprünge des Israelitischen Rechts', Leipzig, 1934 (=*Kleine Schriften zur Geschichte des Volkes Israel*, Band 1, Munich, 1953, 278–332; Eng. Tr., *Essays on Old Testament History and Religion*, Oxford: Blackwell, 1966, 79–132).

Anderson, A. A., 1972. *The Book of Psalms*, NCB, 2 vols., Grand Rapids and London: Eerdmans.

Bailey, L. R., SR., 1979. *Biblical Perspectives on Death*, Overtures to Biblical Theology, Philadelphia: Westminster.

Barth, C., 1947. *Die Errettung vom Tode in den individuellen Klage- und Dankliedern des Alten Testamentes*, Zollikon.

Baumgartner, W., 1959 [1933]. 'Der Auferstehungsglaube im Alten Orient', *ZMR* 48 (1933), 193–214 = *Zum Alten Testament und seiner Umwelt*, Leiden: Brill, 124–46.

Boecker, H. J., 1980 [1976]. *Recht und Gesetz im Alten Testament und im Alten Orient*, Neukirchener Studienbücher 10, Neukirchen-Vluyn, 1976; Eng. Tr. *Law and the Administration of Justice in the Old Testament and Ancient East*, London, SPCK, 1980.

Brueggemann, W., 1976. 'Death, Theology of', *IDBS*: 219–22.

Clements, R. E., 1980. *Isaiah 1–39*, NCB, Grand Rapids and London: Eerdmans.

Dahood, M., 1963. *Proverbs and Northwest Semitic Philology*, Scripta Pontificii Instituti Biblici 113, Rome: Biblical Institute.

1965, 1968, 1970. *Psalms: Introduction, Translation, and Notes*, 3 vols., Anchor Bible, 16, (1965), 17 (1968), 17A (1970), Garden City: Doubleday.

Driver, G. R., 1962. 'Plurima mortis imago', in M. Ben-Horin, B. D. Weinryb, and S. Zeitlin, eds., *Studies and Essays in Honor of Abraham A. Neuman*, Leiden: Brill, 1962, 128–43.

Fohrer, G., 1968. 'Das Geschick des Menschen nach dem Tode im Alten Testament', *KuD* 14; 249–62.

Gerleman, G., 1971*a*. '*ḥjh* leben', *THAT* 1: 549–57.

1971*b*. '*mūt* sterben', *THAT* 1: 893–7.

Gese, H., 1960. 'Beobachtungen zum Stil alttestamentlicher Rechtssätze', *ThLZ* 85: 147–50.

Greenberg, M., 1957. 'The Hebrew Oath Particle *ḤAY*/*ḤĒ*', *JBL* 76: 34–9.

Gunkel, H., and Begrich, J., 1933. *Einleitung in die Psalmen*, Göttingen: Vandenhoeck & Rupprecht.

Hasel, G. F., 1980. 'Resurrection in the Theology of Old Testament Apocalyptic', *ZAW* 92: 267–84.

Healey, J. F., 1978*a*, 'Ritual Text KTU 1.161 – Translation and Notes', *UF* 10: 83–8.

1978*b*. '*MLKM*/*RPʾUM* and the *KISPUM*', *UF* 10: 89–91 = 1978*b*).

Illmann, K.-J., 1979. *Old Testament Formulas about Death*, Meddelanden från Stiftelsens för Åbo Akademi Forskningsinstitut 48, Åbo.

Johnson, A. R., 1964. *The Vitality of the Individual in the Thought of Ancient Israel*, 2nd ed. Cardiff: Univ. of Wales.

Kaiser, O., 1974 [1973]. *Der Prophet Jesaja. Kapitel 13–39*, ATD 18, Göttingen. Vandenhoeck & Rupprecht, 1973; Eng. Tr., *Isaiah 13–39: A Commentary*, OTL, London: SCM.

Kaiser, O. and Lohse, E., 1981 [1977]. *Tod und Leben*, Biblische Konfrontationen, Stuttgart, 1977; Eng. Tr., *Death and Life*, Biblical Encounters Series, Nashville: Abingdon, 1981.

Kellermann, U., 1976. 'Überwindung des Todesgeschicks in der alttestamentlichen Frömmigkeit vor und neben dem Auferstehungsglauben', *ZThK* 73: 259–82.

Kraus, H.-J., 1961. *Psalmen*. 1. Teilband, BKAT, XV/1, Neukirchen: Neukirchener Verlag.

1972 [1967]. 'Der lebendige Gott: Ein Kapitel biblischer Theologie', *EvTh* 27 (1967), 169–200 = *Biblisch-theologische Aufsätze*, Neukirchen-Vluyn: Neukirchener Verlag, 1972, 1–36.

Landsberger, B., 1965. *Die Eigenbegrifflichkeit der Babylonsischen Welt*. von Soden, W., *Leistung und Grenze sumerischer und babylonischer Wissenschaft*, Darmstadt.

Loretz, O., *Die Psalmen. Teil II*, AOAT, 207/2, Kevelaer and Neukirchen-Vluyn: Neukirchener Verlag.

Maag. V., 1980 [1964]. 'Tod und Jenseits nach dem Alten Testament', *SThU* 34, 17–37; = *Kultur, Kulturkontakt und Religion: Gesammelte Studien zur allgemeinen und alttestamentlichen Religionsgeschichte*. Zum 70. Geburtstag herausgegeben von H. H. Schmid und O. H. Steck, Göttingen, 1980, 181–202.

Martin-Achard, R., 1960 [1956]. *De la mort à la résurrection d'après l'Ancien Testament*, Bibliothèque théologique, Neuchâtel and Paris, 1956; Eng. Tr., *From Death to Life: A Study of the Development of the Doctrine of the Resurrection in the Old Testament*, (Edinburgh and London, 1960).

1981*a*. 'Trois remarques sur la résurrection des morts dans l'Ancien Testament', in A. Caquot and M. Delcor, eds., *Mélanges bibliques et orientaux en l'honneur de M. Henri Cazelles*, AOAT, 212 (Kevelaer and Neukirchen-Vluyn, 1981), pp. 301–7.

1981*b*. 'Résurrection dans l'Ancien Testament et le Judaïsme,' *DBS* X/55: 437–87.

Pedersen, J., 1959. *Israel: Its Life and Culture*, 2 vols. (I–II, III–IV) 2nd edition, London and Copenhagen).

Plöger, O., 1965. *Das Buch Daniel*, KAT, XVIII, Gütersloh: Gerd Mohn.

1978. 'Tod und Jenseits im Alten Testament', in H.-J. Klimkeit, ed., *Tod und Jenseits im Glauben der Völker*, Sammlung Harrassowitz, Wiesbaden, 1978, 77–85.

von Rad, G. 1966 [1958]. '"Gerechtigkeit" und "Leben" in der Kultsprache der Psalmen', Festschrift für Alfred Bertholet, Tübingen: Mohr, 1950, 418–37 = *Gesammelte Studien zum Alten Testament*, ThB8, Munich, 1958, 225–47; Eng. Tr. *The Problem of the Hexateuch* and Other Essays, Edinburgh and London, 1966), 243–66.

1962 [1958] 1965 [1962]. *Theologie des Alten Testaments*, Munich, Band I, 2. Auflage, 1958, Band II, 2. Auflage, 1961; Eng. Tr., *Old Testament Theology*, Edinburgh and London, vol. I, 1962, vol. II, 1965.

Ringgren, H., 1966 [1963]. *Israelitische Religion*, Die Religionen der Menschheit 26, Stuttgart, 1963; Eng. Tr., *Israelite Religion*, London: SPCK.

1980 [1977]. '*ḥājāh, ḥaj, ḥajjîm, miḥjāh*', *ThWAT* 2 1977, 874–98; Eng. Tr., '*chāyāh; chai; chaiyîm; chaiyāh; michyāh*', *TDOT* 4, 1980, 324–44.

Ringgren, H. Illmann, K.-J. and Fabry, H.-J., 1984. '*mûṯ, māw œṯ, tᵉmûṯāh, mᵉmôṯîm*, *ThWAT* 4, 763–87.

Sawyer, J. F. A., 1973. 'Hebrew Words for the Resurrection of the Dead', *VT* 23: 218–34.
Schulz, H., 1969. *Das Todesrecht im Alten Testament: Studien zur Rechtsform der Mot-Jumat-Sätze*, BZAW 114 Berlin.
Spronk, K., 1986. *Beatific Afterlife in Ancient Israel and in the Ancient Near East*, AOAT 219 Kevelaer and Neukirchen-Vluyn.
Tromp, N. J., 1969. *Primitive Conceptions of Death and the Nether World in the Old Testament*, Biblica et Orientalia, 21, Rome: Biblical Institute.
De Vaux, R., 1961 [1958, 1960]. *Les Institutions de l'Ancien Testament*, 2 vols., Paris, 1958, 1960; Eng. Tr., *Ancient Israel: Its Life and Institutions*, London: Darton, Longman & Todd.
Vawter, B., 1972. 'Intimations of Immortality and the Old Testament', *JBL* 91: 158–71.
Wächter, L., 1967. *Der Tod im Alten Testament*, Arbeiten zur Theologie II/8, Stuttgart.
Wagner, V., 1972. *Rechtssätze in gebundener Sprache und Rechtssatzreihen im israelitischen Recht: Ein Beitrag zur Gattungsforschung*, BZAW 127, Berlin: de Gruyter.
Westerman, C., 1969 [1966]. *Das Buch Jesaja. Kapitel 40–66*, ATD 19, Göttingen, 1966; Eng. Tr., 1969, *Isaiah 40–66: A commentary*, OTL, London: SCM.
Westermann, C., 1984 [1974]. *Genesis*. 1. Teilband: *Genesis 1–11*, BKAT I/1, Neukirchen-Vluyn, 1974); Eng. Tr. 1984, *Genesis 1–11: A Commentary*, London: SPCK.
Whybray, R. N., 1975. *Isaiah 40–66*, NCB London: Marshall-Pickering.
Whybray, R. N., 1978. *Thanksgiving for a Liberated Prophet: An Interpretation of Isaiah Chapter 53*, *JSOT* Supp 4, Sheffield: JSOT Press.
Wildberger, H., 1978. *Jesaja*. 2. Teilband: *Jesaja 13–27*, BKAT x/2, Neukirchen-Vluyn: Neukirchener Verlag.
Wolff, H. W., 1974 [1973]. *Anthropologie des Alten Testaments*, Munich: Beck; Eng. Tr. 1974, *Anthropology of the Old Testament*, London: SCM.
Zimmerli, W., 1963 [1957]. '"Leben" und "Tod" im Buche des Propheten Ezechiel', *ThZ* 13, 494–508 = *Gottes Offenbarung: Gesammelte Aufsätze zum Alten Testament*, ThB 19, Munich, 1963, 178–91.
Zimmerli, W., 1970. Review of H. Schulz, *Das Todesrecht im Alten Testament*, *ThLZ* 95, 891–7.
Zimmerli, W., 1971. *Die Weltlichkeit des Alten Testaments*, Göttingen.
Zimmerli, W., 1979 [1969*a*]. *Ezechiel*. 1. Teilband: *Ezechiel 1–24*, BKAT XIII/1, 1969, Neukirchen-Vluyn: Neukirchener Verlag; Eng. Tr. 1979, *Ezekiel 1: A Commentary on the Book of the Prophet Ezekiel, Chapters 1–24*, Hermeneia, Philadelphia: Fortress.
1983 [1969*b*]. *Ezechiel*. 2. Teilband: *Ezekiel 25–48*, BKAT, XIII/2, 1969, Neukirchen-Vluyn: Neukirchener Verlag; Eng. Tr. 1983, *Ezekiel 2: A Commentary on the Book of the Prophet Ezekiel, Chapters 25–48*, Hermeneia, Philadelphia: Fortress.

Index – Authors

Index – Biblical References

Genesis

Exodus

Leviticus

Numbers

Deuteronomy

Joshua

Judges

Ruth

I Samuel

2 Samuel

1 Kings

2 Kings

1 Chronicles

2 Chronicles

Ezra

Nehemiah

Esther

Job

Psalms

Proverbs

Ecclesiastes

Song of Songs

Isaiah

Jeremiah

Lamentations

Ezekiel

Daniel

Hosea

Joel

Amos

Jonah